WORKING AMERICANS
1810–2015

Volume VI: Women At Work

WORKING AMERICANS
1810–2015

Volume VI: Women At Work
Second Edition

by Scott Derks

A UNIVERSAL REFERENCE BOOK

Grey House Publishing

PUBLISHER: Leslie Mackenzie
EDITORIAL DIRECTOR: Laura Mars
PRODUCTION MANAGER: Kristen Thatcher
MARKETING DIRECTOR: Jessica Moody
COMPOSITION: David Garoogian

Grey House Publishing, Inc.
4919 Route 22
Amenia, NY 12501
518.789.8700
FAX 845.373.6390
www.greyhouse.com
e-mail: books @greyhouse.com

Publisher's Cataloging-In-Publication Data
(Prepared by The Donohue Group, Inc.)

Derks, Scott.
    Working Americans ... / by Scott Derks. — 2nd edition.

        volumes : illustrations ; cm

    Date range in the title varies.
    1st ed. published in 2000.
    "A Universal Reference Book."
    Includes bibliographical references and indexes.
    Contents: v. I. The working class — v. VI. Women at work.
    ISBN: 978-1-59237-564-6 (v.1)
    ISBN: 978-1-68217-077-9 (v.6)

    1. Working class—United States—History. 2. Labor—United States—History. 3. Occupations—United States—History. 4. Social classes—United States—History. 5. Immigrants—Employment—United States—History. 6. United States—Economic conditions. I. Title.

HD8066 .D47 2015
305.5/0973/0904

Table of Contents

1800-1899

1980-1989

1990-1999

2000-2009

Introduction

This second edition of *Working Americans: Women At Work* updates the sixth volume in the 13-volume *Working Americans* series. It includes 42 profiles of working women, from 1810 to 2015. Like the other titles in the *Working Americans* series, this work observes the lives of working Americans—American women in this case—decade by decade. It covers women young and old, from a wide range of geographical and social backgrounds, and from a vast variety of professions. Some careers focus on fortune, some on fame, some on a regular paycheck, and some on no paycheck at all. But all profiles demonstrate the continuous challenge faced by working women in America, whether they push papers, pitch a baseball, play the piano, change public opinion, or join the Navy.

Arrangement

Each profile averages 12 pages. The fist page includes a summary sentence and photograph of the subject. Three sections of bulleted text follow: **Life at Home** includes details about what life was like in the woman's home, whether with her parents, husband, or children. It might include what her house looked like, what kind of food she ate, what her daily routine was, and how she dressed. **Life at Work** details what life was like during her workday, whether in an office, at school, or in the military. You will learn about specific tasks, co-workers, and accomplishments. **Life in the Community** is designed to offer insight into the community, or neighborhood, that the profiled woman lives and/or works in. This section often includes some historical background, and a sense of the area's economy and recreational opportunities.

An **Historical Snapshot** follows these sections, which is an interesting collection of firsts and significant events that happened in the year profiled. Then, **Selected Prices** offers a number of everyday items, from violin to hotel room, and what they cost. This is followed by **Primary Sources**, which includes magazine and newspaper articles, speeches, letters and diary entries. These original pieces offer the reader the chance to put the life of the profiled individual into historical context. **Further Reading** and **Index** end the volume.

Content

Like the other volumes in this series, *Women At Work* is a compilation of original research—personal diaries, school files, family histories—combined with government statistics, commercial advertisements and news features. The text is presented in bulleted format, and supported by hundreds of graphics—from personal photographs to national campaign advertisements.

This volume celebrates the contributions of women, chronicling both the progress they have made and the roadblocks they have faced. In a detailed fashion, the profiles and primary source materials help the reader reflect on the transformation of female independence and their transition into the workplace. It's a fact: In the early 1970s, when *Ms.* magazine was in its infancy, women received approximately 10 percent of the nation's graduate degrees in medicine, law and veterinary medicine. Today, women represent half of all law and medical students and more than half of all veterinary and pharmacy students.

As in previous volumes, each story is unique, as each of us is unique, from an unchallenged matron of a Southern estate whose husband's reversal of fortune in 1810 forced her to start a new, much reduced life in rural Kentucky, to a successful, contemporary Boston artist in 2015, who struggled to break free of the restraints placed on her by growing up in a traditional Italian family.

The study of history offers all of us the opportunity to view change over time. The actions and contributions of one generation are rarely lost on the next. *Working Americans 1810-2015: Women At Work* presents an engaging way to study the progress of working women's transformation into today's workforce.

1810: Estate Matron

Fifty-seven year-old Lucy Childress, left with nothing but debts in Virginia, decided to travel with her family to western Kentucky to start a new life.

Life at Home

- Lucy Childress was grateful to have a house to live in, and proud to have helped build it herself.
- But she missed the comforts of her former life and the home she left behind in Virginia.
- Once the unchallenged matron of a Southern estate, Lucy, along with her husband and younger daughter, had been reduced to living in a rustic log dwelling in the wilderness of western Kentucky, on a small parcel of land belonging to her son, Randolph.
- She missed her eldest daughter, Elizabeth, and her son-in-law, Mr. Peyton, who had always been so generous and helpful; they stayed in Virginia when she moved west to escape years of accumulated debt.
- Without Mr. Peyton to lean on, Lucy could only turn to her husband and sons, who were preoccupied with problems of their own.
- Her husband, Col. Charles L. Childress, of Albemarle County, Virginia, had lost everything, and had nothing but debts to pass along to his sons.
- Formerly a wealthy landowner, slave holder and militia officer during the Revolutionary War, Col. Childress had accumulated so many debts in Virginia that he was forced to sell his land, slaves and most of his other property.
- The Colonel's reversal of fortune affected every member of the household and extended family; instead of having wealth and prestige to pass along to his sons and daughters, he had become a burden and an embarrassment.
- He was not alone.

Lucy Childress traveled to Kentucky with her family to start over.

1

Colonel Childress had always counted on others to manage his property and business.

- Decades of bad farming practices in Virginia had led to depletion of the soil and poor crop yields; years of war and political turmoil had disrupted the traditional European markets, leaving thousands of planters' finances in a shambles.
- In the fall of 1807, two of the Childress boys, Randolph and Lilburne, decided to make a new start and move their families to western Kentucky.
- They persuaded their parents to join them in making the arduous journey that started with a long, overland trip by wagon to Pittsburgh and culminated in a frightening sail aboard a flat boat down the Ohio River to western Kentucky.
- It was customary and cost effective for families to make long-distance moves in one big caravan; in all, the Childress party consisted of 21 family members and about 20 slaves.
- The two brothers purchased parcels of undeveloped land in Livingston County, Kentucky, and now were responsible not only for their wives and children, but for their parents and younger sisters, who came to Kentucky to keep the family together.
- But starting over was difficult.
- Col. Childress and Lucy were so destitute they were only able to bring four elderly slaves and a few meager possessions.
- The Colonel had never expected to be in this situation, and was ill-equipped to take responsibility for clearing land, planting crops, and building a new homestead in the wilderness.
- He had always depended on overseers to run his large holdings, and had never taken much interest in agriculture or the practical skills necessary for farming, such as plowing, animal husbandry, seed planting and carpentry.
- A year after the move, Randolph, Lucy's oldest son, was struggling with debts and the consequences of poor financial planning.
- He had virtually no cash to spare for any of their household needs.
- He charged $18.25 at a store in Salem, Kentucky in 1809; in 1810 he was summoned to court to pay up his overdue account.
- Lilburne, too, was short of cash, and had limited means of earning a living.
- He rented out some of his slaves on an extended basis for some income, but that left him with fewer workers in his own fields.
- When malaria and other serious illnesses struck his family, Lilburne ran up a large bill with the local doctor for house calls and medicine.
- Eventually, the doctor took him to court to force him to pay his debt.
- The youngest son, Isham, had stayed behind in Virginia; he didn't write letters very often, and Lucy wasn't sure when and if he might ever show up for a visit.
- Lucy worried about her three young daughters, wondering how they would attract eligible suitors without money for fine fabrics, shoes, handkerchiefs, books, dance lessons, or piano—all important for acquiring social skills and refinements.
- Since Lucy and her daughters no longer had servants, it was necessary for them to handle chores formerly beneath their station, such as cooking, laundry, gardening and weaving.
- Lucy could not expect much physical help from the old, frail slaves who accompanied them to Kentucky.
- Fortunately, though, the older slaves did know how the chores should be done, and they adapted well to the Spartan conditions, so they were a calming and steady influence for Lucy and her daughters.
- Among the seven slaves who came with Randolph, two were grown men, two were rented out, two were elderly, and one, Matilda, was 10 years old.
- Matilda, often called "yellow Matilda," was fathered by Col. Childress' son, Charles, and her mother was a slave in the Childress' family.

Lucy's daughters were now forced to help the servants with daily chores.

- Matilda's mother and other relatives were sold off in 1806, but Matilda stayed with the family—her master and uncle, Randolph Childress, and Lucy, her grandmother.
- Lucy often wondered how things would turn out for her grandchildren, who were forced to grow up with so little money for education and the finer things in life.
- She worried about Lilburne, too, who began associating with the wrong crowd and spending too much time in taverns, drinking too much whiskey.
- As for the Colonel, he seemed rather lost and angry.
- He wanted good meals served at his table, he wanted the neighbors to show him respect, and he often mumbled about the way things used to be.
- Each day he would walk out to the field and find fault with one thing or another, and then come back to sit idly on the porch and stare out toward the Ohio River.
- Lucy tried to soothe him and keep him cheerful, but it wasn't easy.

Life at Work

- Lucy Childress could barely remember how to perform the chores she had learned when a child, but now she had to perform those chores and many others.
- She remembered as a little girl watching one of her family's slaves warp the old loom, a process that would take many hours, and how another slave would start weaving.
- Lucy never did learn how to weave any of the complicated patterns, but she enjoyed watching the shuttle fly back and forth as sheets of cloth magically appeared.
- One of her neighbors in Kentucky offered to help Lucy and her daughters build a loom, since they had not brought one from Virginia, to make plain fabric.
- Lucy remembered how to spin, but she wasn't sure about all the steps involved in preparing flax, hemp or cotton.
- Unless something changed, Lucy realized that if the family was to have clothes and other household furnishings, she would have to relearn many of these domestic arts.
- She knew how to knit stockings, crochet coverlets, piece a quilt, and sew a dress or shirt, but weaving and flax hackling, were unfamiliar to her.
- Lucy was distraught to look down at her hands.
- They were once soft and white, with perfectly manicured nails—a sure sign of her privileged status.
- Now her fingers were puffy and red, with hard and calloused pads on her thumbs.
- Her rings had become so tight she often had to force them off.
- Lucy tried to keep her head and arms covered when she was in the fields to help with planting or harvesting, but she noticed freckles on her arms and ankles, and, alas, horrible welts caused by insect bites.
- She never imagined having hundreds of mosquitoes swarming through the air, eager to bite in every place imaginable.
- The unending drudgery of repetitive household chores, too, was more overwhelming than she had ever considered.
- The Colonel kept commenting on the fertility of the soil and the abundance of game and fish, but was oblivious to the work required to support the family's daily needs.
- He was brought up to expect a life of gentlemanly leisure, and always kept a safe distance from "women's work."

Relearning domestic arts, such as stitching and weaving, were necessary for Lucy and her daughters.

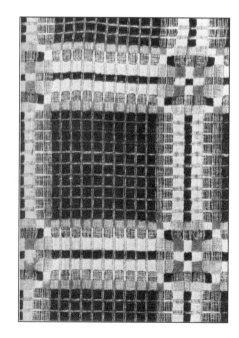

The Childress cabin in Kentucky was a far cry from their fine home in Virginia.

- And what a chore it was to prepare meals in that cramped little log house!
- Instead of a broad stone hearth equipped with cast iron trivets, gratings, and hinged hangars, the cabin had a modest fireplace with room for a few skillets and pans—not much better than the cooking arrangement in slave quarters back home.
- Lucy longed for the varieties of herbs and vegetables grown in the garden back home, too, and wondered how they would survive much longer in this place without a better food supply.
- Since there was no money to purchase sugar, tea and spices—"luxury" items that were now nearly unattainable—Lucy had to produce things they could barter with.
- In addition to teaching her daughters to spin and weave, they developed other skills with market value, such as raising chickens, hogs or sheep.
- Lilburne and Randolph always enjoyed hunting, but now, didn't have time for it.

Lucy's sons enjoyed hunting, but now had little time to for it.

- Lucy wished they could find time to hunt for fresh game—it would have been a welcome relief from the steady diet of chicken and ham.
- Lucy had never felt so tired, and at 57, the constant work load and worry began to sap her strength, leaving her vulnerable to illness that often surrounded her.
- And the Colonel did not have money to pay the local doctor for house calls.

Life in the Community: Western Kentucky

- Despite the relative isolation of their farm, Lucy Childress and her daughters had frequent opportunities to meet neighbors, make friends and participate in community-wide activities.
- There was a large gathering of families who helped Randolph and Lilburne construct their houses and barns.
- The population of Kentucky was growing dramatically, and many of the newcomers were old friends the family had known in Virginia.
- Since the Childress family had been prominent landowners in Virginia, they were initially greeted with respect by the local Kentucky families.
- Lucy was embarrassed to be living in a dwelling so much less spacious and elegant than her Virginia home, and avoided entertaining.
- She was alarmed to learn about the violence and lawlessness in Kentucky.
- She heard from her sons about cases of drunkenness, robbery and murder that were brought before the justices.
- Four towns had been erected in Livingston County: Eddyville, Centreville, Kirksville and Smithland.
- Eddyville was the largest town in the county and boasted a grist mill, paper mill, distillery and saw mill and, in 1805, an impressive shipyard, building ships up to 150 tons.
- Centreville became the new county seat of government in 1804 and by 1808 its population was about 40 whites and six slaves, with a log courthouse, a jail, two taverns, and a Presbyterian church.

Lucy was alarmed to learn of the violence and lawlessness in Kentucky.

- Kirksville was smaller, with fewer than 25 people, but located only about five miles from Cave-in-Rock, a cave made famous by visits from riverboat pirates.
- The men who lived in Cave-in-Rock preyed on unsuspecting boatloads of settlers coming down the Ohio.
- These men would pretend to be trained guides but then steer the boats into the worst and most dangerous section of the shoals, causing them to capsize.
- The pirates would let the folks drown, while accomplices waited to collect their property.
- Lucy also heard tales of taverns that allowed so much drinking that unruly customers sometimes bit off ears and gouged out their opponents' eyeballs.
- Smithland, the little town located about four miles from Lilburne's farm, at the mouth of the Cumberland, had a population of about 100 people, with two ferries and no churches.
- James McCawley, who became a good friend to Lilburne, operated a tavern in Smithland with the county's first billiard table.
- The shops in Smithland were designed to attract the business of rivermen, and business was good along a river that averaged about 15 craft a day.
- McCawley had a reputation for violence and was frequently brought before the court on charges of brutality, often in connection with his participation in a four-man gang that terrorized slaves and Indians.
- Court records revealed that John Gray was indicted for saying "God damn your fool soul," to his bay horse at Harkins stable.
- Joseph Woods, who ran a warehouse and inspection station, was charged with the failure to deliver 2,000 pounds of lead for a customer in Ohio, and in another case, found guilty of replacing tobacco with cotton in a large shipment of hogsheads.

HISTORICAL SNAPSHOT
1810

- The U.S. Census recorded the United States population of 7,239,881, 19 percent of whom were black
- The Maryland legislature authorized a lottery to build a memorial to George Washington
- The first United States fire insurance joint-stock company was organized in Philadelphia
- Spanish artist Francisco Goya began his series of etchings *The Disasters of War* depicting the Peninsular War
- Illinois passed the first state vaccination legislation in the U.S.
- Goats were introduced to St. Helena Island and began the devastation that eventually caused extinction of 22 of the 33 endemic plants
- An electrochemical telegraph was constructed in Germany
- The French Catholic Church annulled the marriage of Napoleon I and Josephine
- The first Irish magazine in America, *The Shamrock*, was published
- The British Bullion Committee condemned the practice of governments printing too much money and causing inflation
- King Kamehameha conquered and united all the Hawaiian Islands
- The first billiard rooms were established in London, England
- The sale of tobacco in France was made a government monopoly
- The Cumberland Presbyterian Church of Kentucky was excluded from the Presbyterian Church
- Napoleon ordered the sale of seized U.S. ships
- Tom Cribb of Great Britain defeated American negro boxer Tom Molineaus in 40 rounds in the first interracial boxing championship
- Simon Bolivar joined the group of patriots that seized Caracas in Venezuela and proclaimed independence from Spain
- Australian Frederick Hasselborough discovered Macquarie Island while searching for new sealing grounds

Selected Prices

Chamber Pot $0.37
Coffee Roaster $0.50
Men's Knee Buckles $2.00
Mule $80.00
Pitchfork $0.50
Scissors . . . . .12½ cents
Surgical Instruments $8.00
Toll, Horse Crossing Dan River $0.08
Wagon Whip $2.50
Watch, Gold $50.00

Letters from the South, New York, 1817:

In almost every part of the United States where I have chanced to be, except among the Dutch, the Germans, and the Quakers, people seem to build everything ex tempore and pro tempore, as if they looked forward to a speedy removal, or did not expect to want it long. Nowhere else, it seems to me, do people work more for the present, less for the future, or live so commonly up to the extent of their means. If we build houses, they are generally of wood, and hardly calculated to outlast the builder. If we plant trees, they are generally Lombardy poplars that spring up of a sudden, give no more shade than a broomstick stuck on end, and grow old with their planters. Still, however, I believe all this has a salutary and quickening influence on the character of the people, because it offers another spur to activity, stimulating it not only by the hope of gain, but the necessity to exertion to remedy past inconveniences.

Rural taste in silver, letter from William Pelham in Zanesville, Ohio, to Sidney Gardiner, Philadelphia silversmith, April 23, 1815:

In his letter to me Mr. Fletcher mentions that you will probably have many articles which I might find it advantageous to deal in. I should think you would not have many such, as your assortments will be calculated for the refined taste of an opulent city, whereas my trade must be necessarily limited to articles and necessity suitable to the first stages of civilized life.

Letter from Lucy Childress to her brother upon leaving Virginia for West Kentucky, 1807:

Dear Brothar,

I now take up my pen to bid you a dieu supposing I never shall have the pleasure of again seeing you tomorrow we shall be on our way to the Mouth of the Cumberland River, you may think it strange that Ould people take so great a Journey. Nearly all my children remove to that place and their desire for their parents to go appears very great. . . . I feal much hurt at leaving two Brothers, for evar, and not seeing eather. I wish you all the happiness that can possibly be expressed by an affectionate Sister.

Letter, former President John Adams, 1813:

Science had liberated the ideas of those who read and reflect, and the American example kindled feelings of right in the people. An insurrection has consequently begun, of science, talents and courage against ranking birth, which have fallen into contempt. . . . Science is progressive, and talents and enterprise on the alert.

Cooking fish, *The Old Farmer's Almanac,* 1800:

Take the fish while still alive and scour and run him clean with water and salt, but do not scale him. Open him and put him with his blood and liver in a small kettle. Add a handful each of Sweet Marjoram, Thyme, and Parsley, and a sprig each of Rosemary and Savory. Bind the herbs in two or three small bundles and put them into the fish with four or five whole onions, twenty pickled oysters, and three anchovies. Pour on your fish as much Claret Wine as will cover him and season well with salt, cloves, mace, and orange and lemon rind. Cover the pot and put on a quick fire till it be sufficiently boiled. Then take out the fish and lay it with the broth in a dish. Pour upon him a quarter of a pound of fresh melted butter beaten with six spoonfuls of the broth, the yolks of two or three eggs, and some of the herbs, shredded. Garnish with lemons and serve it up.

1826: Schoolteacher

Female Academy founder Sarah Goodwin challenged her young female students in Litchfield, Connecticut, with expectations driven by her strong religious convictions.

Life at Home

- Sarah Goodwin had been active as a schoolteacher for over 30 years in Litchfield, Connecticut.
- She focused her energies on improving the minds of the young ladies attending her school.
- Sarah started her quest in 1792 with only one pupil under her instruction in her dining room.
- Over time her reputation spread and the number of students grew; parents sent their daughters to be molded with a rounded education focused on history, English and the arts.
- As her instruction and number of pupils grew, teaching in her home proved troublesome; by 1798 Sarah managed to convince Litchfield's prominent men to construct a school building.
- A number of subscribers agreed to contribute funding for the building; in all a total of $385 was raised.
- The one-room schoolhouse was roughly 30 feet by 70 feet with most of the space used to hold plain pine desks for the students, who sat on long plank benches.
- Sarah kept her materials on a small desk beside her elevated teacher's chair.
- These items represented all the building's furniture, excluding a small movable piano in one of the building's two closets.
- The second closet was used to house bonnets and other garments the students brought to class.
- With a permanent building for instruction, the school was called the Female Academy, attracting national recognition.

Sarah Goodwin was a schoolteacher in Litchfield, Connecticut.

- Over time, girls began to arrive from as far as Boston, New York and Savannah, Georgia, to receive instruction.
- When the summer term started in late May, most of the young ladies arrived in Litchfield by stagecoach.
- For some it was the first time away from home, and Sarah often assisted in placing them in respectable homes for boarding near the academy.
- The boarding expense was $1.75 to $2 per week, exclusive of washings, collected by the school, which reimbursed the families with whom the students resided.
- A number of girls were forced to share a room and expressed frustration over sleeping arrangements and sharing a bed.
- Sarah disliked the petty arguments the girls voiced and developed an extensive set of rules of conduct.
- Each young lady was expected to memorize the rules, most of which focused upon daily prayer, conduct within a family's home, personal behavior and academic excellence.
- One of the rules required that two hours must be "faithfully devoted" to close study each day while out of school.
- The ladies with whom the girls boarded were expected to report any student who failed to study the two hours required.
- Over the years Sarah heard a number of complaints; for new students it usually pertained to homesickness and not receiving letters from home.
- One young lady visited the post office too often, even on Fridays, knowing fully well that the mail from New York City did not arrive on that day.
- Sarah removed 30 credit marks from her grades for the homesickness.
- With over 30 years of instructing students, Sarah spent her time teaching her students history and geography.
- Sitting at their desks, students would write their lessons from her lectures within their books.
- One of the books each student was required to use was Sarah's *Universal History*.
- After years of trying to locate an adequate history book for the ladies to study, she gathered sufficient historical information from several texts into one book.
- After a week's instruction, she tested the ladies on their knowledge and memorization of materials.
- Each was called in turn to answer questions when addressed; a correct answer would earn the student credits.
- Sarah was disappointed with one student who grew up along the Delaware River but could not recall the source of the river.
- It was a simple answer for the child, who rapidly lost any appearance of thought.
- One student made a great error when called to parse, or break down a sentence into parts of speech.
- In her haste she placed a verb in the infinitive mode in the imperfect tense.
- She failed to catch the error in time and only earned five credits that day.
- With so many ladies to teach, Sarah was grateful for the assistance of those she hired.
- She was especially pleased with her nephew John Brace, who provided instruction in the areas of botany and natural history.
- Sarah thought it important to have a broad knowledge of the world, including the world of science.
- John would collect plant and insect specimens and present them in class.
- He had an extensive collection of bugs, including two from China that were in excellent condition.
- The remainder of the bugs were of Litchfield descent and John was capable of tracing the pedigree back to when Noah first entered the ark.

Sarah's nephew, John Brace, taught the students botany and natural history.

- Aside from insects, many of the girls enjoyed the botany lessons Sarah's nephew provided.
- Inspired by his lectures, the ladies acquired numerous wild plants, such as white braneberry, carrion flower, violets and Solomon's seal, to transplant them around the school.
- Most were placed in the beds by the school's door-yard.
- The sight pleased Sarah and reinforced the students' interest to apply their learning to the real world.
- Aside from learning about the world, its language and history, Sarah made Christian study an imperative for each student.
- Saving the student's immortal soul was of more importance than all the education she could provide.
- Each student was expected to read a portion of Scripture both morning and evening with meditation and prayer.
- Aside from the prayer and reflection, she expected her students to keep holy the Sabbath by attending church.
- Sarah even incorporated Scripture studies on Saturday after the ladies recited the school's rules.
- Often they read various passages from the Bible and Sarah would explain what they had read.
- During the weekly testing, she would provide credit marks for those who memorized the assigned Scripture verses and answered religious questions.
- One of Sarah's students, Eliza Sheldon, answered correctly to the question, "What is sin?"
- Eliza responded that "Sin is any want of conformity unto or transgression of the law of God."
- Sarah clearly understood that not all her students were responsive to learning about Christianity.
- When one student openly laughed during morning prayer, Sarah exclaimed that the student would possibly be cast into darkness where there is gnashing of teeth.

- The laughing young lady replied, "Then I suppose those who have no teeth will have to gum it!" which was followed by a chorus of giggles.
- Sarah Goodwin removed five of her credit marks for her poor behavior.
- With all the credits accrued by the students in all topics taught at school, Sarah recognized their accomplishments halfway in the term.
- Sarah permitted the girls to select their seats based upon the number of credit marks earned.
- Those with the most credit marks had the right to select their seat of choice, often a location near the window to get as much of the summer breeze as possible.
- Students with the lowest number of marks often had fewer options: those away from the window or next to girls they disliked.
- Girls who applied their talents also received invitations for tea with Sarah on Wednesday afternoons.
- During these periods, a circle of girls would gather around her tea table and engage in conversations that challenged their reasoning of what they had learned.
- On one occasion, while the girls ate shaved, smoked beef and some cakes with preserves, they discussed the opening of the Erie Canal, recited poetry they had written and sang songs they had memorized from their music lessons.
- Only years later would the young ladies realize that such gatherings were another lesson Sarah was providing: the ability to entertain and conduct oneself as a lady in a social setting was important, especially in acquiring a future spouse.
- A real treat occurred at one tea party when Edward Clarke, an older English gentleman visiting the area, brought his perspective glass for the girls to view.
- The device, also known as a zograscope, enabled them to look at hand-colored lithographic scenes through a reflecting glass and magnifying lens.

How to conduct oneself as a lady in social settings was an important lesson at the Female Academy.

Students learned to care for small animals and took music lessons.

- The scenes viewed through the perspective glass provided depth to the flat images and fascinated the young ladies greatly.
- Sarah was disappointed that Mr. Clarke had no images of American scenery.
- Nonetheless, she was pleased to allow the Englishman to show his country in a favorable light.

Life at Work

- Sarah Goodwin's life as headmistress of the Female Academy included the receipt of distressing news regarding the death of one of her students.
- It was common through the year to receive four such letters, which always upset her.
- She also hated to see a young lady leave the school upset over trivial differences and encouraged the parties to forgive one another before parting.
- It was also a part of preservation of one's soul to reconcile so that they all could meet in heaven.
- Recently, the school received a heartrending account of the *Albion*, a packet-ship that left New York for Liverpool.
- The ship was lost just off the coast and all on board were assumed lost as well.
- The entire academy was horrified because the news devastated one of the teachers, Miss Beecher.
- Her fiancé was on board the ship.
- After a week of waiting for any possible news of hope for survivors, a memorial service was held at the Congregational church next to the school.
- Most of the students conducted themselves well in church, knowing fully well it was offensive to God if they failed to do so, but they would receive deductions in their credit marks also.
- Bad behavior was rarely a problem, but issues did occur within the community.
- One problem arose outside of the Congregational church itself between the academy students and the girls of the Litchfield community.
- The battlefield was a set of two benches fenced in with conventional high lattice work and away from the adult church members.
- Each week one group of girls would arrive and monopolize both benches, preventing the other group from using the space.
- It was not uncommon for one of the groups to arrive early to "pack the seats" before church and prevent the other group from using the space; pin pricking, pinching and punches through the lattice also occurred.
- Within the town was an ale house by an animal pound, and it was frequently visited by the students from the Litchfield Law School.
- It was a common occurrence for students to write over the door "Ale by the pound."
- The act infuriated the ale keeper, who constantly complained to both Sarah and the proctor of the law school.

- Sarah would have nothing to do with the ale keeper because she viewed him as an impudent villain.
- She asked the law school's vice chancellor to handle the matter because it was not the place for a lady to converse with this character, especially a lady who has strong opinions on intemperance.
- Sarah viewed this as a community issue; years before, she helped form Litchfield's Temperance Society and wrote numerous articles in the local paper on the subject.
- In one article she wrote that married women should "make the house of your husband the most interesting place on earth."
- Sarah informed her readers that men typically are led into the habit of intemperance by the poor behavior of their wives at home.
- A home that is welcoming to the husband would not lead him to the evil habit.
- Watching the behavior of men was common in Sarah's world, especially boys studying at the law school who sought every opportunity to pass part of the day with the ladies from her school.
- During her afternoon walks she would encounter small groups of students walking together on Prospect Hill towards Echo Rock.
- Other times she heard of ladies taking boat rides on Lake Bantan during the summer days.
- These acts did not bother Sarah in the slightest, and it pleased her to know her ladies were behaving well.
- What infuriated her was when young men failed to heed her rules when visiting the young ladies boarding in her home on prescribed days and times.
- One method she employed to control the conduct of young men was providing access to the monthly balls for the young students.
- Only young men in good graces with Miss Goodwin received invitations.
- She often heard, to her pleasure, that the invitations were prized at the law school.
- This was primarily due to the fact that the number of ladies attending was traditionally double that of the men present.
- Many would arrive in their best party attire to enjoy an evening of dancing and conversation.
- Three or four musicians came to the school on a Saturday evening around 6 o'clock after all the invitees had arrived and played until 9 o'clock.
- Besides the traditional dances, the academy hosted a two-day public exhibition at the end of each term for the Litchfield community.

Creative penmanship was practiced.

- At this venue the ladies could display their talents, which included theater, art, poetry and music.
- In addition, Sarah expected each girl to bring home to her parents evidence of her studies.
- Those talented in watercolor drawings or embroidering could proudly display their work on the walls in family parlors.
- The less gifted were advised to paint their family coat of arms, which they could acquire with the assistance of the local Looking Glass & Picture Store.
- In exchange for the research assistance, there was a promise that the store would be employed to frame the students' works.
- Every year prominent members of the Litchfield community were asked to judge the students' best work.
- Their role was to evaluate each piece of artwork in the various categories and award the winners the Prize of Merit.
- The opinion of community leaders kept the judging without bias from those involved in the school, thus strengthening the significance of the award.
- Even with numerous works on display during the exhibition, the highlight was often the theater performance.
- The school's ladies invited young men to see them perform acts they had practiced diligently during their free time.
- Some of the plays were classics, but it was not uncommon to see performances written by Miss Sarah Goodwin herself.
- Those productions commonly involved events in history.
- At the end of the exhibition, Sarah presented her address to the students, thus concluding the summer term in late October.
- Afterwards, the students departed to visit family members for the month or travel with one of their classmates home.
- After several decades of teaching, Sarah appreciated the month-long respite the young ladies' absences offered.
- Nonetheless, she had to prepare for the start of the winter term and did not believe in being idle.

Life in the Community: Litchfield, Connecticut

- Litchfield, Connecticut, was a primary city in the western part of the state where significant commerce passed.

- Its location on a high road made it part of a great inland route from Boston to New York City as well as from West Point to Connecticut's capital, Hartford.
- The initial travel that occurred was postage coaches that rode daily through the town delivering mail along the way.
- Because of the strength of the roads into and out of Litchfield, daily mail routes were established between the city and Hartford, New Haven, Norwalk, Poughkeepsie and Albany.
- It was not uncommon to see the large, red, four-horse coaches roll through town making great noise with the drivers cracking their whips and blowing horns at a great pace.

- One could acquire fare at Deming's Tavern and leave Litchfield on a stage at 5 o'clock in the afternoon for New York or Albany and arrive by 1 o'clock the next day.
- Being a large city along a major roadway and with a population of over 4,600 people in 1810, Litchfield witnessed a great deal of commercial and industrial activity develop.
- Iron was the primary manufacturing activity in Litchfield, which boasted four iron forges, a slitting mill and one nail factory.
- It also had 18 saw mills, five grain mills, a paper mill, an oil mill and a cotton factory, to name only a few other industries.
- Other smaller tradesmen were located in the area to take advantage of the city's opportunities.
- One example of an entrepreneurial endeavor concerned the numerous carriages rolling into town.
- The city's central location between primary travel destinations encouraged two carriage makers to locate operations within the community.
- By 1820 Litchfield ranked fourth in the state's population, following only New Haven, Hartford and Middletown.
- The city boasted numerous natural resources, most prominently the mineral spring containing chalybeate and sulfurous waters only a half mile from the court house.
- Many visitors made a point to spend time there to enjoy the water's effectiveness in curing disease.
- One popular location was Prospect Hill where many walked for exercise and pleasure.
- Also present in this location was Echo Rock, where visitors would cast their voices and hear them call back to them.
- By 1827, the growth of the city's population and number of visitors encouraged an inventor to propose locating a machine that would raise individuals in one of four two-person carriages to a height of 50 feet into the air.
- He indicated that: "recommended by the most eminent physicians in the United States, the recreational device planned to help take an airing."

Litchfield residents enjoyed the countryside.

HISTORICAL SNAPSHOT
1826

- The American Temperance Society was formed in Boston

- Beethoven's String Quartet #13 in B flat major (Opus 130) premiered in Vienna

- Samuel Mory patented the internal combustion engine

- Weber's opera *Oberon* premiered in London

- The USS *Vincennes* left New York to become the first warship to circumnavigate the globe

- Russia and Norway established a border that superseded the arrangement made 500 years earlier in the Treaty of Novgorod

- Simón Bolívar helped the new South American republic of Bolivia gain independence and recognition from Peru

- Former U.S. presidents Thomas Jefferson and John Adams both died on July 4, the fiftieth anniversary of the signing of the Declaration of Independence

- A Pennsylvania law made kidnapping a felony, effectively nullifying the Fugitive Slave Act of 1793

- Explorer Gordon Laing became the first European to reach Timbuktu

- Lord & Taylor opened in New York at 47 Catherine Street

- Connecticut's six-mile Windsor Locks Canal opened to provide safe passage around the Enfield Falls and rapids in the Connecticut River 12 miles upstream from Hartford

- The first horse-powered railroad in America opened in Quincy, Massachusetts, at a granite quarry with three miles of track

- Gideon B. Smith planted the first of the new quick-growing Chinese mulberry trees in the United States and spurred development of the silk industry

- French chemist Antoine-Jérôme Balard discovered the element bromine

- After Pope Leo XII ordered that Rome's Jews be confined to the city's ghetto, thousands of Jews fled Rome and the Papal States

- Sing Sing Prison opened its first cell block some 30 miles north of New York City on the Hudson River

- The Zoological Gardens in Regent's Park were founded by the Zoological Society of London

Selected Prices

Bonnet, Silk $15.00
Candlesticks, Plated $11.00
Dictionary $3.50
Fabric, Velvet, Yard $5.50
Mirror $22.00
Pencil $0.22
Piano $2,000.00
Tea Kettle $18.00
Tea, Pound $15.50
Thimbles, Box $11.00

Terms of Tuition at Female Academy

1826
Litchfield Female Academy
Conducted by Miss Goodwin and Mr. Brace

Terms of Tuition

Writing, History, Geography, Grammar, Arithmetic, Rhetoric, and Composition, with plain
Needlework, per quarter $5

The above, with Natural and Moral Philosophy, Logic, Chemistry, Mathematics,
the Principals of Taste and Criticism, with the Latin and
Greek Languages, per quarter $6

French Language $5

Drawing $3

Music 12

Board in respectable families near the Academy, from $1.75 to $2 per week, exclusive of
washing.

The Summer Term, commences May 16.

The Winter, November 29.

Wood etchings.

Recipe for a toothache, Diary of George Youngglove Cutter, 1820:

1 Tablespoonful of spirits
1 Tablespoonful of vinegar
1 Teaspoonful of common salt

"An Address to the Moon," Ann M. Richards, New York:

Sweet Moon if like Cretona's sage
By any spell my hand should dare
To make thy disk my ample page
And write my thoughts my wishes there

How many a friend whose careless eye
Now wanders o'er that starry sky
Would smile upon that orb to meet
The recollection fond and sweet

The reveries of fond regret
The promise never to forget
And all my heart and soul would send
To many a dear lov'd distant friend

Stage Coach Advertisement, *Litchfield Monitor,* November 10, 1829:

Litchfield, New Milford, Danbury and Norwalk Mail Stage.

This stage leaves Josiah Park's Hotel, Litchfield, on Tuesdays, Thursdays and Saturdays at 3 in the morning, passing thro' New Preston, New Milford and Brookfield and arrives at Danbury to lodge: leaves Danbury next morning for Norwalk and arrives in time for passengers to take the steam boat for New York. No Night Travelling.

Fare through to New York 3.25

Returning Takes the Norwalk passengers at Danbury on Monday, Wednesday and Friday morning, and arrives in Litchfield the same day.

For seats apply at the Bar at Parks Hotel, Litchfield, H. Barnes, Proprietor

Boat Excursion Advertisement, *Litchfield Monitor*, June 27, 1826:

The new and elegant Horse boat, *Bantam*, having been recently built for the express purpose of accommodating pleasure parties on the Bantam Lake, is now completely prepared to accommodate ladies and gentlemen who may wish to take advantage of this safe and neat mode of taking a trip upon our pleasant waters. Parties wishing to engage the boat for a trip must give two days' notice to the subscriber residing at the north end of the Lake.

—Harmon Stone

"Partial list of Rules at Litchfield Ladies Academy," *Chronicles of a Pioneer School,* Emily Vanderpool:

1st—You are expected to rise early, be dressed neatly and to exercise before breakfast. . . . You must consider it a breach of politeness to be requested a second time to rise in the morning or retire of the evening. . . .

8th—Every hour during the week must be fully occupied either in useful employments, or necessary recreation. Two hours must be faithfully devoted to close study each day, while out of school: and every hour in school must be fully occupied. . . .

12th—The truth must be spoken at all times though it might seem more advantageous to tell a falsehood. . . .

14th—Tale bearing and scandal are odious vices and must be avoided: neither must you flatter your companion by any remarks on their beauty, dress or any accomplishment, in order to increase their vanity, and let everyone thus flattered remember that such compliments are an insult offered to the understanding. . . .

17th—No young lady is allowed to attend any public ball, or sleigh party till they are more than 16 years old. . . .

19th—You must write a letter to be corrected and sent home to your friends once in four weeks—excepted excused. You must not write a careless note or any careless writing. . . .

23rd—You must not walk for pleasure after 9 o'clock in the evening. . . .

1858: Plantation Wife

At nineteen years old, Emily Jameson left her wealthy family in Philadelphia, married a plantation owner's son, and moved to Charleston, South Carolina.

Life at Home

- Emily Jameson's father was a celebrated lawyer and her grandmother was a noted author of novels; Emily had been raised in an urban world of plenty.
- She was fluent in both French and Italian and fully capable of reading Goethe in German.
- The busy ports of Philadelphia regularly brought exquisite exotic imports from France, Italy and Britain, while local silversmiths, furniture makers and carriage shops turned out some of America's finest quality products.
- Between the 1820 and 1840 Philadelphia and its immediate suburbs had grown from 100,000 residents to well over 200,000; New York, America's major metropolis, went from 123,000 to over 312,000 in the same 20 years.
- In 1842 she married a naval officer from the low country plantations of South Carolina and moved 800 miles, where she lived with her new extended family for six years before building a home of her own.
- William's father owned four plantations on the Santee River, worked by 103 slaves.
- The primary crop was cotton, but they enjoyed homegrown corn, rice, flour, poultry, mutton and vegetables; sugar, coffee, salt, fruits, and candy were available only in Charleston.
- When Emily could obtain raisins from Philadelphia, they were saved for special occasions, along with the chocolate bon-bons created in the shape of fresh strawberries.

Emily Jameson married a plantation owner's son when she was 19 years old.

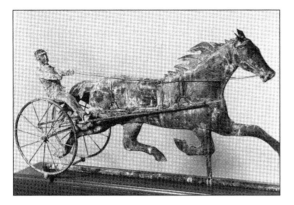

Horseracing was very popular on the plantation.

- Emily often missed the excitement of Philadelphia: "I have had quite enough green trees and roosters and am panting for brick walls and noise. I have been engaged in making preserves and jelly for next winter which I hope will turn out well. The strawberry seems so nice that I must bring on a jar with me."
- In South Carolina Emily quickly discovered that her new family was steeped with rabid hunters, expert farmers and devoted horsemen; a racetrack with regular races sponsored by the upper St. Johns Jockey Club had been constructed on the property.
- "It is ridiculous the care they take of them. The horses eat the most dainty things and have to be rubbed with whiskey and actually drink it too. Every day before they take exercise they eat twenty eggs," she wrote in letters home.
- Fascinated by botany, Emily maintained a regular correspondence concerning flower seeds, cuttings and root clippings.
- "I enclose 12 cents in this letter and wish you would buy me a paper of the best mignonette seed and also a paper of Heart's Ease seed of the large dark purple sort."
- Emily made regular trips away from the plantation, including an annual excursion to Philadelphia aboard a fast sailing regular packet schooner christened *Emma*.
- Trips overland to Virginia with friends included carriage rides across vanishing roads that reappeared as mud swamps and wet adventures aboard slow moving flat-bottom boats.
- "When we were about a quarter of a mile from the carriage a regular mountain storm came up and we were forced to get in again. . . . All four curtained in and the carriage would bump first one side and then the other and the horses would rear and slip and Miss Hannah shrieked and Miss Sally shuddered. Miss Hannah would insist on peeking through the curtains. I told her not to. She would call out, the horse fell then and now my side of the carriage is touching the ground. I could not help laughing but I was very glad to get home safe with only soreness from the jolt."
- Everyone's lives were dictated by the weather, making it a topic for discussion and humor.
- "The weather is quite warm enough to satisfy any reasonable person, planters and farmers not included of course. For those worthy individuals incorporate themselves so thoroughly in the feelings of their crops that instead of enjoying the cool nights and mornings and a blanket at night they're thinking of the shivering cotton which tho it warms others unfortunately cannot warm itself."

Life at Work

- Emily Jameson's home was a large frame four-bedroom house with big central rooms, a front hall, large piazzas and big double chimneys.
- Typical of plantation houses built near a river, it was constructed high off the ground on six substantial brick arches.

Emily Jameson's home.

- It was heated by fireplaces; the occasional Southern wintertime cold spell accompanied by snow could be miserable.
- "The ice was so thick in my room that we could not break it and even in Eliza Manning's room where she kept a fire burning all night, the water froze hard. I assure you it was entirely too cold to be pleasant."
- Meals were plentiful, leisurely and served three times daily.
- Even after a decade of living in the South, Emily continued her Philadelphia custom of eating wheat toast for breakfast and was always amazed at her husband's regular breakfast of hot-cakes, waffles, biscuits and hominy.
- A typical dinner party might include vermicelli soup, boiled turkey, celery sauce, bouilli ham, wild duck, omelette soufflé, charlotte polonaise and plum pudding—much of which she helped prepare.
- Emily's passion was for desserts; she generally served three different kinds as a finale to her dinner parties.
- These included puddings made from blackberries and plums served with wine, or sugar-based sauce custards made from sugar, cream and eggs produced on the plantation.
- She was especially proud of her recipe for charlotte Russe, accented by napkins folded in a fan shape and finger glasses with a slice of lemon.
- To prepare these dishes, sugar was an essential ingredient and was kept—along with other staples—under lock and key.
- Therefore, Emily learned to use liberal amounts of molasses, boiled down from homegrown sorfhum.
- Life also centered around children, planting, housekeeping, reading and singing.

Plantation chickens produced eggs for Emily's fancy desserts.

Two of Emily's and William's five children.

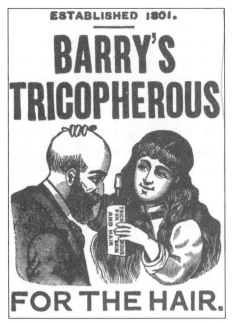

- Emily and William had five children, one of whom had died as a baby; Emily took an active role in teaching the children to read and play the piano.
- William taught them all how to ride at an early age.
- She also carefully recorded effective ways to fashion lard candles, window glass cleaner (pulverized indigo mixed with vinegar wine), and three types of soap: soap with concentrated lye, potash soap and cosmetic soap.
- Her formula for homemade hair wash included lac sulphur and sugar of lead with instructions to wash the whole head twice a week.
- To expel ants, Emily explained how a sugared sponge loaded with ants could be dropped in boiling water.
- During the summer months, when malaria was a constant threat, Emily and the children would rent a house on Sullivan's Island where the sea breezes brought relief from the heat.
- "Very nice fish can be bought at the Break water, nearly in front of our house. A remarkably nice fish called the Whiting and Sheep's-Heads are the most caught. Crabs and shrimps in any quantity tho I have refrained from getting any. Every inch of ground near Charleston is now taken up with English and Northern truck farmers. White potatoes are really splendid and I am provoked that there is no steamer running to Philadelphia for I want so much to send you a barrel."
- A particular pleasure during the summertime trips was reading serialized romance novels, for which Emily drew criticism from her highbrow sister.
- "I would have you to know that I am rather more cultivated and enlightened in my tastes than you think."
- Both William and Emily loved to read; their personal library numbered nearly 600 books including *Jane Eyre*, *The Poetical Works of Robert Southey*, and *Domby and Son* by Charles Dickens—which she found tiresome.
- Charleston had one of the first subscription libraries in the country, and Emily was one of its most loyal members.
  - "I can get as many books out as I want," she wrote her parents.
  - In addition, William subscribed to several periodicals, including *The Cultivator* at a cost of $10 a year to stay abreast of modern farming techniques.
  - Newspapers and magazines such as the *London News* were also favorites and every copy was well circulated to all the other plantations by request.
  - Emily especially enjoyed reading copies of the Saturday editions of the Philadelphia papers that described who was getting married and other social details concerning her friends.
  - And to stay abreast of Northern fashion, she regularly read *Leslie's Fashion Monthly* which emphasized the Second Empire mode since Napoleon III had revived the French court.
  - Long, leisurely days were spent with books and music; family singing, in German and Italian, was accompanied by a mother-of-pearl inlaid guitar from Spain and a Steinway piano imported from Hamburg Germany costing $500.
  - To entertain guests, Emily and her sister-in-law would be asked to sing duets, often relying upon Jenny Lind's most popular songs such as "Coming Through the Rye," and "The Last Rose of Summer."

William Jameson taught his children how to ride at an early age.

- Christmas, too, was an important time of celebration for the entire family, attracting more than 40 relatives to her father-in-law's house.
- "This season of Christmas is here. In the first place, staying at Eutaw for nearly a week with a house there full of company involves a good deal of brushing up of the children's wardrobe, then there is to be the grandest Christmas tree ever known which is to be hung with wax lights and all manner of gilt things beside presents for the children. . . . And the servants' Christmas. Not only do I get them all rice, sugar and coffee and William kills a ox for them but there is no end to the business of exchanging. They come to me with eggs and chickens for which they wish me to give them sugar, coffee, wheat flour, tobacco etc. etc. Of course I never refuse, and the consequence is I am at a loss to know what to do with all I have. I have now upwards of 100 chickens straggling about and an immense box of salt filled eggs."

Life in the Community: Charleston, South Carolina

- Charleston, South Carolina, one of America's largest cities with a population of 40,000, was 40 miles away by railroad, plus a 10-mile carriage ride from the plantation.
- There Emily Jameson adored taking part in the gaiety of the teas, carriage rides, shopping on Kings Street and walking the Battery, where land met water, and going to dances.
- In February the entire family descended upon Charleston for the horse races, "by far the best time to see Charleston to advantage."
- The construction of a 120-mile railroad into the interior South Carolina 25 years before had dramatically altered plantation commerce.
- When Andrew Jackson was first elected to the presidency in 1828, only a few miles for a road track had been laid across the nation.

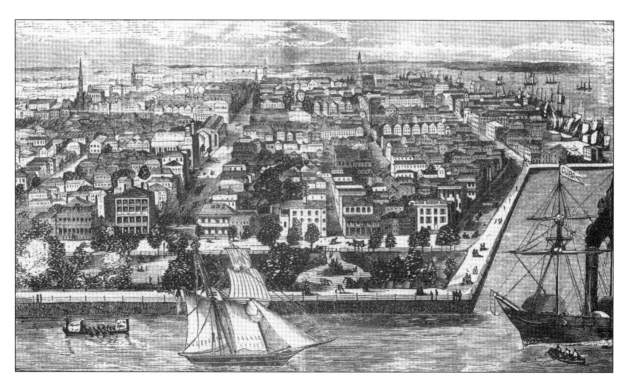

Charleston, South Carolina.

Creation of a railroad line attracted new businesses.

- By 1840 trains were running on more than 3,000 miles of track.
- Historically, cotton and rice had been hauled to the port of Charleston by flat-bottom boat through the Santee Canal, a sometimes risky mode for moving a year's worth of product to market.
- The creation of a railroad line attracted significant new business; the number of cotton bales arriving by train more than doubled from 187,000 bales in 1844 to 393,000 bales in 1859.
- The train also shipped large quantities of flour, grain, barrels of naval stores and livestock.
- By 1858 Charleston was also operating 11 schools with nearly 3,000 students as part of an effort to reduce illiteracy among white workers.
- It was a classless system in which children of the elite went to school with the working poor.
- At the same time, South Carolina maintained the country's strictest laws prohibiting the teaching of blacks, slave or free.
- Although well known as a city of commerce, Charleston was also in the center of the national debate over slavery.
- During the late 1850s, the debate was raging whether the northern Democratic Party could represent them or whether a southern party should be created to represent Southern issues.
- A third party faction known as the American party or "Know nothings" had placed its focus on nationalism, Protestantism, native Americanism, and was best known for its opposition to immigration, especially Catholic immigration.
- The United States Supreme Court's ruling in the Dred Scott decision in 1857 strengthened the hand of stay-the-course Southern conservatives and cut the legs of those eager to carry the South out of the Union immediately.
- But Southern plantation owners were eagerly searching for ways to protect their way of life.
- Newspapers, particular the *Charleston Standard*, were leading a campaign to reopen the African slave trade, a movement branded the "Congo Party" and rejected by the establishment.
- The discussion did popularize the concept that slavery would be best secured for all time by making practically every white man the owner of at least one slave.

HISTORICAL SNAPSHOT
1858

- RH Macy & Company opened its first store at 6th Avenue in New York City

- Italian chemist Stanislao Cannizzaro differentiated between atomic and molecular weights

- The Butterfield Overland Mail Company began delivering mail from St. Louis to San Francisco

- Charles R. Darwin and Alfred Wallace independently proposed natural selection theories of evolution

- The invention of the Mason jar stimulated use of large quantities of white sugar for preserves

- U.S. Senate candidate Abraham Lincoln first used the phrase "A house divided against itself cannot stand"

- Minnesota became the thirty-second state

- A pencil with an eraser attached to one end was patented by Hyman L. Lipman of Philadelphia

- An admission price of $0.50 was charged at the All Star baseball game between New York and Brooklyn

- Hamilton Smith patented a rotary washing machine

- The New York Symphony Orchestra held its first performance

- The first edition of Gray's *Anatomy of the Human Body* was published

- Mary Ann Evans published her first collection of tales, *Scenes of Clerical Life*, under the pseudonym George Eliot

- The first transatlantic cable was completed and then failed after less than one month in operation

- Mendelssohn's *Wedding March* was first played at the wedding of Queen Victoria's daughter Princess Victoria to the crown prince of Prussia

Selected Prices

Harness $84.00
Ladder $10.50
Pain Reliever $3.36
Pig $10.50
Pillowcases, Muslin, Pair $5.25
Pistol $367.50
Saddle Wallets $10.50
Saddle $126.00
Slave, 30-Year-Old Male $5,250.00
Tea Kettle $36.75

Letter from Emily Wharton Sinkler to her parents in Philadelphia, 1842:

Perhaps you would like to know how we spend our days. Breakfast is from half past eight to quarter to nine. I get up at seven. Mr. Sinkler five mornings out of seven gets up at four or five and mounts a horse and goes off to shoot English wild ducks or deer or foxes. All the family assemble at nine thirty for family prayers. There is a great variety of hot cakes, waffles, biscuits. I don't take to all these vanities, however, always eat toast for breakfast and supper. They make excellent wheat bread and toast it very nicely by the coals. Hominy is a very favorite dish. They eat it at all their meals. It is what is called grits in Philadelphia. We take breakfast in the hall and sit there all the morning. Soon after breakfast our little carriage comes to the door and we set off to take a drive. . . . The carriage is perfectly plain just holding two persons. The horses are very dark brown with plain black harness. When we set out the dogs come running up so we have a cortege of two greyhounds and two terriers generally. We are always preceded by Sampson on horseback to open gates. We are home at twelve or one and I then read and sew until dinner time. We dine between three and four. Eliza is an excellent housekeeper, and the ice cream here is really the best I ever tasted. We have supper at half past eight which is very much like breakfast except we have cold meat and after the cloth is removed wine and cordials. In the evening we have music, both piano and guitar.

Letter from Emily Sinkler to her parents in Philadelphia, February 11, 1843:

Housekeeping is very different at the South and the North though I think one thing is, people here give themselves to much trouble about it and have a great many servants about the house which of course causes great confusion. For instance there is but four bedrooms to be attended to in the house and there are five chambermaids to attend them so of course that makes five times as much confusion as necessary.

Journey through the Seaboard Slave States, Frederick Olmsted, 1856:

The plows at work, both with single and double mule teams, were generally held by women, and very well held, too. I watched with some interest for any indication that their sex unfitted them for the occupation. Twenty of them were plowing together, with double teams and heavy plows. They were superintended by a Negro man who carried a whip, which he frequently cracked at them, permitting no dawdling or delay at the turning; and they twitched their plows around on the head-land, jerking their reins, and yelling to their mules, with apparent ease, energy, and rapidity.

Throughout the Southwest the Negroes, as a rule, appeared to be worked much harder than in the Eastern and Northern Slave States. . . . They are constantly and steadily driven up to their work, and the stupid, plodding, machine-like manner in which they labor, is painful to witness. This was especially the case with the hoe-gangs. One of them numbered nearly two hundred hands (for the force of two plantations was working together), moving across the field in parallel lines, with a considerable degree of precision. I repeatedly rode through the lines at a canter, without producing the smallest change or interruption in the dogged action of the laborers, or causing one of them, so far as I could see, to lift an eye from the ground. . . . I think it told a more painful story than any I had ever heard, of the cruelty of slavery. It was emphasized by a tall and powerful Negro who walked to and fro in the rear of the line, frequently cracking his whip, and calling out in the surliest manner, to one and another, "Shove your hoe, there! Shove your hoe!" But I never saw him strike anyone with the whip.

Life on the Old Plantation in Ante-Bellum Days, or, A Story Based on Facts, by Irving E. Lowey, 1911:

That smoke-house was never without meat and lard, and that store-room contained barrels of flour, barrels of sugar, barrels of molasses and sacks of coffee from one year to another. And the corn, oh, there was no end to that. There were several barns, some big and some little, but when the corn was gathered and the "corn-shucking" was over and the crop was housed, the barns were full to overflowing. They would remind one of Pharaoh's barns in Egypt at the end of the seven years of plenty. There was very little cotton raised on that plantation in those days. Four or six bales were considered a good crop. But the corn, peas, potatoes, hogs, cattle, sheep and goats, there was no end to these. It was a rare thing to buy anything to eat on that plantation save sugar and coffee. Shoes were bought, but the clothing for the white folks and the slaves was made at home. It was the good old "home-spun." On rainy days, when it was too wet to do outdoor work, the men and boys got out corn, as they said in plantation language, for the mill, while the women and girls carded and spun cotton and wool. A task of so many hanks of yarn was given them for a day's work, which was a reasonable task, and when it was finished they carded and spun for themselves. They more or less completed their tasks before night, and by working after night they were enabled to do almost as much for themselves as they did for the white folks during the day. The weaving was almost invariably done by the young white ladies, or by some one of the servant girls who was taught especially to do it. Thus everybody on the place was kept well clothed, both the white folks and the slaves. That which the slave women carded and spun at night was their own, and they usually hired their young missus, or some other white woman of the neighborhood, to weave it into cloth for them, and thus they always had good, clean clothing for Sunday wear, so that they could go to "meetin'" without embarrassment.

On the east side of the white folks' house was the orchard. It occupied a space of about five or six acres and contained a large number of fruit trees of every description. There could be found the apple in variety, the peach, the pear, the apricot and the plum. On the west side was a large vegetable garden, which contained, in addition to the supply of vegetables for the table, several varieties of grapes. The arbors built for these grapes were large, strong and well cared for. And the slaves got their portion of all these delicious fruits. Of course, they were not allowed to steal them (but this does not signify that they never resorted to this method of obtaining fruit), but they could, and did, get fruit by asking for it.

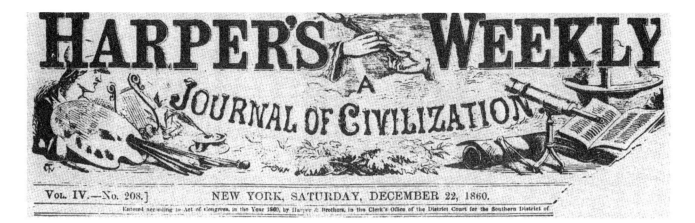

HARPER'S WEEKLY
A JOURNAL OF CIVILIZATION

VOL. IV.—No. 208.]   NEW YORK, SATURDAY, DECEMBER 22, 1860.

Entered according to Act of Congress, in the Year 1860, by Harper & Brothers, in the Clerk's Office of the District Court for the Southern District of

---

"Monthly Record of Current Events," *Harper's New Monthly Magazine*, September 1851:

In South Carolina a large meeting was held in Charleston, on the 29th of July, for those who are in favor of co-operation for the purpose of resistance, and opposed to separate state action, under present circumstances. John Rutledge, Esq., was chosen chairman. A letter was read from the Honorable Langdon Cheve, approving the object of the meeting, asserting the right of secession, but affirming it would not be "a moral or social one on the part of one Southern state in reference to sister states of the South." He thought South Carolina to secede, but not alone; and that a union in favor of secession would take place. . . . A series of resolutions was passed, declaring that the measures of The Federal Government, taken in conjunction manifestation of feelings up north, showed a subtle purpose to deprive the southern states of their rank as equals in the Confederacy; and tended to do the abolition of slavery and the establishment of a consolidated government; and the time it therefore come when the Union ought to be dissolved, and a Southern Confederacy formed; but they would still willingly give trial to any scheme proposed by the South, short of dissolution, for reinstating them in their rights. That, as the subject of controversy concerned all the Southern states as much as South Carolina, the true policy to be observed was concert of action; and that separate state action must be deprecated as tending to alienate the other states and thus "prevent the formation of the Southern Confederacy," delay would insure the co-operation of other states; while separate action would place South Carolina in the position of a foreign country; in which case the laws preventing the introduction of slaves in the United States would subject her "practically to the Wilmot Proviso in its worst form."

CHARLESTON MERCURY

EXTRA:

Passed unanimously at 1.15 o'clock, P. M., December 20th, 1860.

AN ORDINANCE

To dissolve the Union between the State of South Carolina and other States united with her under the compact entitled "The Constitution of the United States of America."

We, the People of the State of South Carolina, in Convention assembled, do declare and ordain, and it is hereby declared and ordained,

That the Ordinance adopted by us in Convention, on the twenty-third day of May, in the year of our Lord one thousand seven hundred and eighty-eight, whereby the Constitution of the United States of America was ratified, and also, all Acts and parts of Acts of the General Assembly of this State, ratifying amendments of the said Constitution, are hereby repealed; and that the union now subsisting between South Carolina and other States, under the name of "The United States of America," is hereby dissolved.

THE

UNION

IS

DISSOLVED!

1881: Educational Reformer

Teacher Mary Greene, after two years of college and two years of teaching in rural Michigan, was ready to embrace the educational reform sweeping the country.

Life at Home

- When Mary Greene entered her tiny, one-room school in Wisconsin in 1881 for the first time, she was well aware of the educational reforms sweeping the prairielands.
- Industrialist Horace Mann—building off the ideas of Thomas Jefferson—had seen to that.
- A modern education required a standard curriculum, universal attendance and graduated steps to completion; Mary was proud to be at the center of the transformation.
- In 1778, Thomas Jefferson, while still a member of the Virginia Assembly, proposed that all children be guaranteed three years of public schooling.
- It was a radical concept that he believed was essential to the perpetuation of democracy.
- "General education will enable every man to judge for himself what will secure or endanger his freedom," Jefferson said.
- "But was it necessary?" asked his fellow landowners, who already paid a fee to send their children to private "dame schools"; besides, no one was sure that field hands needed the capacity to read William Shakespeare.

Teacher Mary Greene was ready for educational reform.

Horace Mann was at the center of education reform.

- The debate raged for decades.
- Despite a professed belief that free, universal education was essential to the perpetuity of democracy, by 1840 America still offered few educational opportunities to the children of its agrarian workers and industrial workforce.
- With no state supervision, inconsistent local budgets and a tepid commitment to instructing the masses, America's schools languished.
- Most of the schools offered an education linked to the Protestant Bible; the most common schoolbook was the New England Primer—used to teach reading and the fundamentals of Protestant catechism.
- The few older boys who went beyond the grammar school years studied mathematics, Latin and philosophy.
- Mary Greene was fully aware of the role Horace Mann played in changing attitudes for her sake.
- His personal inspection of 1,000 Massachusetts schools over a six-year period had demonstrated that most lacked adequate light, heat and ventilation.
- With no standardized textbooks, pupils spent hours memorizing or reciting passages from books they brought from home, no matter how dated or irrelevant they might have been.
- Mann supported a new system called "common schools" that would serve all boys and girls and teach a common body of knowledge that would give each student an equal chance at life.
- "It is a free school system, it knows no distinction of rich and poor…education, then, beyond all other devices of human origin, is the equalizer of the conditions of men, the great balance wheel of the social machinery."
- Mann proposed that the state establish both a taxation system adequate to meet the needs of the school and create standards or expectations on a statewide basis.
- Additional innovations included the introduction of school desk chairs with backs, standardized textbooks, a bell to signal the time and the visibility of a blackboard.
- Convinced that an educated citizenry benefited the entire community, he was also a major proponent of teacher education and universal taxation.
- Fearing any statewide control, local school boards attacked the plans vociferously, but the debate fully exposed the concept that everyone in society should pay for universal education.
- In 1879, a uniform grading program was instituted in Wisconsin.
- In 1881, for the first time, students would be formally charted on their progress.
- Mary had grown up in Wisconsin schools that mirrored the educational process that Mann criticized.
- During Mary's schooling, the role of the teacher was largely to oversee and monitor pupil behavior; there was no clear curriculum and no graduated steps to higher grades.
- Raised on a farm as one of nine children, Mary's father loved school so much that his parents agreed to extend his education to the sixth grade, whereas most of his classmates and siblings left school after three years.
- Her mother had had no formal education beyond Bible reading at home, and desperately wanted one of her children to acquire enough education to become a preacher, a teacher, or an undertaker, since all three guaranteed paying jobs.
- Growing up, Mary was taught to commit to memory words for public recitation; the person who possessed the best word memory was the most satisfactory pupil.
- Education experts speculated that since the object of education was to strengthen the innate properties of the mind, recitations served as the rigorous, muscle-building exercise children needed.

- Mary also experienced the custom of "boarding 'round," in which her teachers moved from house to house every two weeks, spending time in the home of each child who attended her school.
- Mary was thrilled when the teacher came to stay at her house; only years later did she realize that the custom was necessary because of the low wages paid to female teachers, and that few adults would wish to change their location every two weeks.

Life at Work

- Mary Greene's first challenge as a newly hired teacher was to figure out when the school year started.
- Every year the school board set the dates for the start of the school year based upon the amount of school taxes that had been collected; the funds covered teacher wages and contingency.
- Only after the numbers were in could the local school board establish the calendar for the winter and summer terms—each running about four months.
- Generally, school attendance in the country was an erratic, seasonal activity based on the farming needs of the family, the opening day of hunting season, or the unexpected illness of a prized animal.
- In Otsego, Wisconsin, the summer term traditionally began after the spring planting of the potato crop, and the winter term started after the harvest.
- Some boys only attended school in the summer session.
- In years past, men were hired as schoolteachers in the winter term when boys were considered more obstreperous and difficult to teach; women were hired for the summer term.
- From 1867 to 1880, the one-room school in Otsego was served by 25 different teachers.
- It made for very poor continuity, and the skills of the students lagged.
- At the same time, women were beginning to dominate teaching.
- Women were considered more temperamentally suited to the teaching profession and would work for less.
- For the first time in years, the school board had contracted with Mary to cover the entire year, and told her they wished to break the cycle of frequently changing teachers.
- But unlike her predecessors, Mary was experienced in teaching and in the ways of politics.
- Before the school year had begun, she visited the most influential families in the area to demonstrate why an education should take precedence over potato farming; as important, she talked about the future as a time of change when their children would need the ability to read and write effectively.
- The community listened and threw its support behind education; they even embraced the statewide curriculum that established graded steps toward graduation using statewide standards, including an expectation that a child's education should last eight years.
- Using the plans distributed by the Wisconsin State Superintendent's Office, pupils were to be graded or grouped based on their abilities into one of three levels: primary form, middle form, and upper form.
- Movement from one grade to the next was to be determined based on a system of examinations.
- The year Mary arrived, the school was transitioning from the New England Primer to the McGuffey Reader.
- McGuffey Readers, including a primer, a speller, and five readers, had been around since 1836; nearly 100 million copies had been sold in the prior 34 years.
- The Readers were designed to become progressively more challenging with each volume; word repetition in the text was featured as a learning tool, helping to develop reading skills.
- Sounding out, enunciation and accents were emphasized, gradually introducing new words and carefully repeating the old.

Outdoor recess for Wisconsin school children.

- McGuffey also listed questions after each story to aid the teacher and assist in the statewide plan to establish grades.
- While Mary's youngest students, eager to catch up with their older brothers and sisters, loved the energy and focus of the new curriculum, the older students fought the changes.
- A year earlier, they knew exactly what was required to obtain high grades; now, everything was unfamiliar.
- So on the last day of the first week, the older students staged a strike by refusing to re-enter the classroom after recess.
- Mary simply ignored them while she taught the first graders and left the protest alone.
- One by one her charges, looking very sheepish, reappeared in her classroom.
- They all expected to be paddled—a punishment Mary avoided.
- "I don't plan to tell your parents what you have done," she proclaimed at the end of the school day, and "I expect no more student strikes—leave that to the unions that are fighting for workers' rights."
- The next day, Mary devoted the first hour of the day to explaining why change was taking place.
- She told her 28 charges that "what was good enough for pa is good enough for me" was no longer true.
- "The world is getting more competitive; hundreds of thousands of people arrive in America searching for work. They want jobs—your jobs—to raise their families."
- With that out of the way, she got out a map of Europe to show everyone where the immigrants were coming from, and then helped everyone with their arithmetic by demonstrating how many zeros were in 100,000—as in 100,000 new immigrants.
- She then used a horseshoe to demonstrate how to measure in inches—then she asked one of the boys to throw the horseshoe and showed how to measure in feet.
- Then a student brought in a plot of his family's property, and the next class was devoted to acres, divisions and calculating triangles.
- But when one of her quietest students brought in figures showing the shoulder height of her cows compared to their weight and asked how math could be used to determine the weight of cows in the field, Mary knew it was going to be a good year.

Life in the Community: Otsego, Wisconsin

- Otsego, Wisconsin, got its start as a transportation center and functioned as a station on the Chicago, Milwaukee & St. Paul Railroad.
- Situated in the prairie region north of Madison, it served as the center of agricultural and dairy; potatoes dominated the agricultural crops throughout the county.

Mary Greene outside her one-room school.

- By 1881, amenities included a graded school, and Lutheran and Catholic churches, while the Modern Woodmen of America and the Catholic Order of Foresters added to the sociability of the area.
- The first settler to the area, Wayne B. Dyer, arrived in 1844 and erected a log house in which to live and entertain weary travelers.
- Being on the direct route between Milwaukee and Stevens Point, Dyer prevailed upon quite a number of travelers to settle around his hostelry, and by December 1847, the Post Office of Otsego was established.
- As other hotels were built, the village attained a fair degree of prosperity.
- In January 1849, the growing community was organized into a town to which was given the name of Otsego.
- The two largest cities nearby were Milwaukee and Madison.
- Madison was created in 1836 when former federal judge James Duane Doty, planning to build a city on the site, purchased over a thousand acres of swamp and forest land on the isthmus between Lakes Mendota and Monona.
- The Wisconsin Territory had been created earlier that year and was tasked with choosing a permanent location for its capital.
- Doty lobbied aggressively for the legislature to select Madison as the new capital, offering buffalo robes to the freezing legislators and promising choice Madison lots at discount prices to undecided voters.
- Doty named the city Madison for James Madison, the fourth president of the U.S., who had died on June 28, 1836, and he named the streets for the other 38 signers of the U.S. Constitution.
- Even though Madison was still only a city on paper, the territorial legislature voted on November 28 in favor of Madison as the capital, largely because of its location halfway between the new and growing cities around Milwaukee in the east and the long-established strategic post of Prairie du Chien in the west.
- When Wisconsin became a state in 1848, Madison remained the capital, and the following year it became home to the University of Wisconsin-Madison.

HISTORICAL SNAPSHOT
1881

- Thomas Edison and Alexander Graham Bell formed the Oriental Telephone Company
- The city of Phoenix, Arizona, was incorporated
- Kansas became the first state to prohibit all alcoholic beverages
- Black colleges Spelman College in Georgia and the Tuskegee Institute in Alabama opened

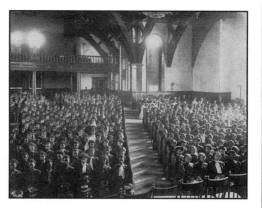

- The Four Dead in Five Seconds Gunfight erupted in El Paso, Texas
- The University of Connecticut was founded as the Storrs Agricultural School
- Clara Barton established the American Red Cross
- The USS *Jeannette* was crushed in an Arctic Ocean ice pack
- President James Garfield was shot by Charles Julius Guiteau and died 11 weeks later; Vice President Chester Arthur became the nation's twenty-first president
- Sheriff Pat Garrett shot and killed outlaw William Henry McCarty, Jr.—widely known as Billy the Kid—outside Fort Sumner, New Mexico

- Sioux Chief Sitting Bull led the last of his fugitive people in surrender to U.S. troops at Fort Buford in Montana
- The fifth hurricane of the Atlantic season hit Florida and the Carolinas, killing about 700
- Francis Howell High School in St. Charles, Missouri, and Stephen F. Austin High School in Austin, Texas, opened on the same day, September 12, putting them in a tie for the title of the oldest public high school west of the Mississippi River
- Atlanta, Georgia hosted the International Cotton Exposition
- In London, Richard D'Oyly Carte opened the Savoy Theatre, the world's first public building to be fully lit by electricity, using Joseph Swan's incandescent light bulbs
- The Gunfight at the O.K. Corral in Tombstone, Arizona, captured nationwide media attention
- The magazine *Judge* was first published
- New York City's oldest independent school for girls, the Convent of the Sacred Heart, was founded
- The United States National Lawn Tennis Association and The United States Tennis Association were established, and the first U.S. Tennis Championships were played
- The Vatican's archives were opened to scholars for the first time

Selected Prices

Carriage, Wire or Wooden Wheels……….........................$12.35

China, 130-Piece Dinner Set……………..........................$30.00

Fruit, Wine, and Jelly Press……….................................$3.00

Hotel Room, New York……………….............................$1.00

Music Box..$2.50

Pocket Watch………………..$10.00

Suspenders………………...$0.05

Violin…………………..$5.00

Whisk Broom Holder………………..................................$0.20

Woman's Storm Cape…………………..............................$8.25

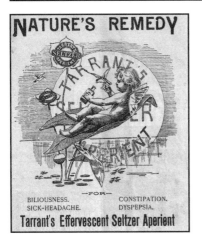

"The Macnicol Case," *The Fitchburg Sentinel* (Massachusetts), January 1883:

The approaching trial of a Kentucky school teacher for various offenses of dress will decide the important question whether there is any particular style of dress which a schoolteacher must adopt, and whether certain peculiarities of dress are in themselves sufficiently immoral to justify the offenders removal from all connection with the great work of educating Kentucky's small boys.

It appears that Mr. Macnicol, of the Norville School District, has been charged by the ladies of his district with "official misconduct." The specifications are four in number. It is alleged that he does not wear a coat; that his trousers are so ragged as to expose portions of his body; that he wears only one suspender, and that he never puts on a pair of stockings. The charge and specifications are to be investigated by a School Commissioner, and the results of the investigation are awaited with intense anxiety.

There seems a strong possibility that the four specifications above cited will be sustained by sufficient evidence. It is said that witnesses without number may be made to testify to the condition of Mr. Macnicol's trousers and suspenders, and to his habitual rejection of coat and stockings. It does not follow, however, that the charge of official misconduct will be sustained. Whether a schoolteacher who is guilty of ragged trousers, of one suspender, and a dislike of coat and a dislike of wearing stockings is also necessarily guilty of "official misconduct" is a question of law rather than of fact.

There are many pleas which Mr. Macnicol can urge in defence of his conduct. He may insist that the so-called ragged condition of his trousers is due to an excessive love of neatness. What his indiscriminating accusers regarded as rents may be simply holes made by cutting out pieces of cloth that have become accidentally stained with ink. Or he may take the broad general ground that his trousers have been worn out in the cause of education and that the alleged rags are the glorious scars sustained while endeavoring to instill the multiplication table into the system of a boy peculiarly impervious to clubs and reason. There is no particular pattern of trousers prescribed by any school regulation which has yet been brought to his knowledge, and he can claim the same right to wear openwork trousers that his fair accusers claim for themselves in connection with open work stockings.

As to Mr. Macnicol's failure to wear a coat, it is merely an evidence of his zeal in the cause of education. How can a Kentucky schoolteacher hope to teach half-grown Kentucky boys with his coat on? If he "means business," and proposes to accomplish any real good, he must take off his coat. Does not the Kentucky preacher take off not merely his coat, but his collar, whenever he means to preach a really eloquent sermon? And did anyone ever hear of a Kentucky political orator or barroom debater who either spoke or argued with his coat on? Mr. Macnicol, if he is wise, will confess to teaching without a coat and glory in it. The ladies of the Norville School District are doubtless admirable women, but they know very little about teaching Kentucky boys if they fancy it can be done with a coat on. No coat ever yet made would last a Kentucky teacher for a single week if he did not take it off before grasping his cane and summoning a boy to come to him and acquire the first principles of arithmetic....

Continued

"The Macnicol Case," ... *(Continued)*

It is to be hoped that Mr. Macnicol will be triumphantly acquitted. If he is found guilty of official misconduct, no schoolteacher will be safe who does not obtain written instructions from the ladies of the district as to which articles of clothing he must wear and who does not habitually dress in the presence of witnesses. And if women can dictate how the male schoolteacher shall clothe himself, men will have the right to say what clothes a female teacher must wear. From such a state of things, the acquittal of Mr. Macnicol alone can save us.

Editorial, *The Cambridge City Tribune* (Indiana), May 29, 1879:

"The editor of the *Newcastle Mercury* is exasperated over the fact that the superintendent of the Cambridge City Schools receives $1,500 a year for his services, while "four lady teachers, each of whom performs her part well," receive "about the same amount in the aggregate." He will, no doubt, be shocked to learn that the superintendent of the Car Works at this place receives as much per year as three or four of the daily laborers in his employ, each of whom performs his part well. If Bro. Parker will direct his attention to the elevation of his own cheap school instead of meddling with what he acknowledges to be "none of his business," he will find full employment for his talents. We already pay our lady teachers more than they receive in most places, and give employment to two or three more of them than we should do if we did not have a superintendent who understands his business. It takes brains to secure attendance at school of 81 percent of all the persons in the district between six and 21 years of age; and for that kind of brains we are ready to pay at least fair market price.

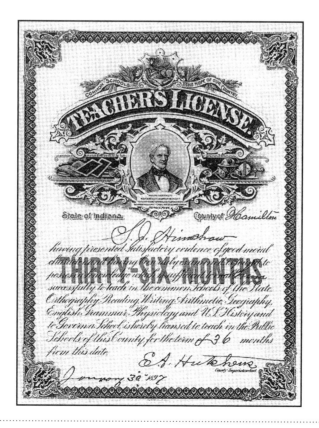

There is a snail-paced gait for the advance of new ideas…. People have more feeling for canals and roads than education."

—Thomas Jefferson, 1817

You crowd from 40 to 60 children into that ill-constructed shell of a building, there to sit in the most uncomfortable seats that could be contrived, expecting that with the occasional application of the birch they will then come out educated for manhood or womanhood.

—Horace Mann

"Pay of School Teachers," *The Cambridge City Tribune* (Indiana), May 29, 1879:

On Friday our Public Schools completed their tenth year—eight of which have been under the supervision of the present superintendent. Eight pupils, having completed the full course of study prescribed in this school, received diplomas which will enable them to enter the freshman class in the State University without further examination—a similar privilege having been accorded them by Hanover and other Colleges. The number of graduates is greater than any former occasion; and the records of the school show a larger attendance than in any previous year—a larger one, we believe, than can be shown by any town of the same size in the state. Out of 726 persons entitled to the benefit of the Common School Fund, 588, or more than 81 percent have been enrolled—while few other towns show as high as 75, and some of them fall as low as 30 percent.... In the absence of a law making education compulsory, we doubt if our own town, or any other, will ever show a larger enrollment than during the past year….

In regard to teachers, also, our schools have made an advance upon all former years. During the past year, two teachers admirably qualified in every other way were compelled to resign on account of ill health; but their places were promptly supplied, and at the close of the term, there was not a single exception to the mental, moral and physical qualifications of the teachers employed, all of whom were emphatically first-class.

It is cheering to know that, notwithstanding these facts, our people have been subjected to no additional tax for educational purposes. From the year 1869 down to 1876, the school trustees found it necessary to levy a tax for "Special School Revenue," of $0.60 on each $100 worth of taxable property, in addition to the annual tuition tax of $0.25 levied by the Town Board. This made a total tax for school purposes of $0.75 on each $100. Last year, each board made a levy of only $0.20, and we believe they have done the same this year, so that our people can pay a total school tax of only $0.40, or a little more than half what they paid for the first half dozen years after the establishment of the schools. Yet we are told that the education of our children is costing too much, and that some of our teachers are receiving extravagant pay for their services. There is no doubt that we pay higher salaries in some schools we could name, and it is equally true that we could procure teachers of some sort for less money. Prof. Hall now has applications from 30 persons desiring to teach, many of whom would, no doubt, accept situations for $25 per month. But if experience in education matters has demonstrated any one thing beyond peradventure, it is this: that it don't pay to employ low-priced teachers and cheap superintendents.

The Authentic Life of Billy the Kid, Pat Garrett, 1882:

(On the night of July 14, 1881, Sheriff Pat Garrett and his two deputies were hunting for the outlaw Billy the Kid. The residents of that section of New Mexico were sympathetic to the Kid and the lawmen could extract little information. Garrett decided to seek out an old friend, Peter Maxwell, who might tell him the Kid's whereabouts. As chance would have it, the Kid stumbled right into the Sheriff's hands. Garrett published his account of the incident a year after it happened.)

I then concluded to go and have a talk with Peter Maxwell, Esq., in whom I felt sure I could rely. We had ridden to within a short distance of Maxwell's grounds when we found a man in camp and stopped. To Poe's great surprise, he recognized in the camper an old friend and former partner, in Texas, named Jacobs. We unsaddled here, got some coffee, and, on foot, entered an orchard which runs from this point down to a row of old buildings, some of them occupied by Mexicans, not more than 60 yards from Maxwell's house. We approached these houses cautiously, and when within earshot, heard the sound of voices conversing in Spanish. We concealed ourselves quickly and listened; but the distance was too great to hear words, or even distinguish voices. Soon a man arose from the ground, in full view, but too far away to recognize. He wore a broad-brimmed hat, a dark vest and pants, and was in his shirtsleeves. With a few words, which fell like a murmur on our ears, he went to the fence, jumped it, and walked down towards Maxwell's house.

Little as we then suspected it, this man was the Kid. We learned, subsequently, that, when he left his companions that night, he went to the house of a Mexican friend, pulled off his hat and boots, threw himself on a bed, and commenced reading a newspaper. He soon, however, hailed his friend, who was sleeping in the room, told him to get up and make some coffee, adding: "Give me a butcher knife and I will go over to Pete's and get some beef; I'm hungry." The Mexican arose, handed him the knife, and the Kid, hatless and in his stocking-feet, started to Maxwell's, which was but a few steps distant.

When the Kid, by me unrecognized, left the orchard, I motioned to my companions, and we cautiously retreated a short distance, and, to avoid the persons whom we had heard at the houses, took another route, approaching Maxwell's house from the opposite direction. When we reached the porch in front of the building, I left Poe and McKinney at the end of the porch, about 20 feet from the door of Pete's room, and went in. It was near midnight and Pete was in bed. I walked to the head of the bed and sat down on it, beside him, near the pillow. I asked him as to the whereabouts of the Kid. He said that the Kid had certainly been about, but he did not know whether he had left or not. At that moment a man sprang quickly into the door, looking back, and called twice in Spanish, "Who comes there?" No one replied and he came on in. He was bareheaded. From his step I could perceive he was either barefooted or in his stocking-feet, and held a revolver in his right hand and a butcher knife in his left.

He came directly towards me. Before he reached the bed, I whispered: "Who is it, Pete?" but received no reply for a moment. It struck me that it might be Pete's brother-in-law, Manuel Abreu, who had seen Poe and McKinney, and wanted to know their business. The intruder

Continued

> ### *The Authentic Life of Billy the Kid . . . (Continued)*
>
> came close to me, leaned both hands on the bed, his right hand almost touching my knee, and asked, in a low tone: "Who are they, Pete?" at the same instant Maxwell whispered to me, "That's him!" Simultaneously, the Kid must have seen, or felt, the presence of a third person at the head of the bed. He raised quickly his pistol, a self-cocker, within a foot of my breast. Retreating rapidly across the room he cried: "Quien es? Quien es?" ("Who's that? Who's that?") All this occurred in a moment. Quickly as possible I drew my revolver and fired, threw my body aside, and fired again. The second shot was useless; the Kid fell dead. He never spoke. A struggle or two, a little strangling sound as he gasped for breath, and the Kid was with his many victims.

1896: Anti-Corset Advocate

Wife of a Connecticut doctor and mother of three daughters, Cora Gaillard was convinced that corsets were detrimental to women's health and well-being.

Life at Home

- Cora Gaillard had heard about the attacks for years on the wearing of corsets.
- At times it seemed that every bellicose speaker who could spell "M.D." had a reason to condemn the sturdy undergarment, revered for its ability to fashion an hourglass figure.
- Some doctors blamed tightly-laced corsets for weak stomach muscles in girls, fainting spells, numbness of the legs, and even infertility.
- Others emphasized the impact on the respiratory system of women, which was widely understood to be different from that of men.
- And cartoonists and stereographic card manufacturers loved to show sisters pulling the lacing so tight on one another that a foot braced on the back was often required.
- The conversion of Cora Gaillard began with her three teenage daughters and was supported by her husband, a medical doctor in Bridgeport, Connecticut.
- After several years of hearing complaints from her husband's patients, Cora was convinced the corset made the marriage bed uncomfortable and generally led to reduced sexual relations between husband and wife.

Cora Gaillard suspected that corsets were damaging to women's health.

- Fashion dictated, and vanity decided, that corsets must create continuous and severe constriction.
- Even waists that naturally measured 25 inches could be cinched back to 19 inches when a French-designed back-fastening corset with a long steel busk down the front was worn.
- As a teenager, Cora remembered well the sacrifices she had made to achieve a waist smaller than her age using a modern steam-moulded, spoon busk corset with enough boning and cording to create a perfect hourglass shape.

- But whenever she rebelled against the confining garment, her mother invariably reminded her that wearing a corset was "the hallmark of virtue" and that "an uncorseted woman reeked of license."
- But Cora now had another motivation: healthy teenage children, nearing a marriageable age, and the production of numerous healthy grandchildren.
- She was also concerned that fainting, poor circulation, and lethargy in women were all a result of tightly laced corsets.
- Cora began dressing her girls in corsets when each reached the age of nine.
- The two oldest, Florence and Lucca, willingly accepted the confining strictures as a symbol of growing up.
- The youngest, Carolina the tomboy, hated corsets and more than once abandoned the undergarment behind the rose bush hedge.
- Maybe it was a sign: The two oldest girls had been named for the Italian hometowns of their great-grandparents, Florence and Lucca, to honor the first Proiettis to come to America.
- They were conservative, hardworking, and religious.

- Carolina had been named for the home state of her paternal grandmother, who was from the undisciplined city of Charleston, South Carolina, where liquor drinking, horse races, and cock fights were practiced openly, even on Sundays.
- Despite her tussles with the untamed spirit of Carolina, Cora was convinced that tight corsets deformed young women, restricted their movement, and limited their ability to produce healthy children.
- Although Cora believed it was prudent for herself to continue wearing a corset, she bought bust girdles for her daughters so they could make full use of their lungs, and maybe avoid the many complaints so common to corset-wearing women.

The Gaillard's three daughters wore modified corsets to avoid common ailments brought on by the garment.

Life at Work

- For most of her married life, Cora Gaillard had assisted in her husband's medical practice; she was nurse, office manager, counselor, and substitute doctor.
- Despite her husband's fancy diplomas and advanced education, Cora was convinced that she knew as much about medicine as he did, especially when it came to women's health.
- Day after day she cared for women who were in pain because of the clothing they wore, while men all agreed that women just liked to complain.
- That's why she wrote that letter to the editor that had stirred up so much trouble.
- She had not shown it to her husband first because she knew he would object and be no help at all.

- However, she hadn't expected this much of a reaction.
- Now, what was done was done, and she was going to accept the Bridgeport Women's Club's invitation to speak about corsets the following month.
- Besides, someone needed to speak out about how fashion, vanity, tradition, and the preferences of men affected women's health.
- Cora was riled up about long skirts that dragged the ground collecting all manner of filth, the tendency of women to faint because of excessive constriction, and the disgusting way that tight corsets rearranged vital organs and prevented women from doing normal house tasks because they could not bend over.
- And she hadn't even addressed the burden of multiple petticoats that hung off the waist or the tyranny of tight garters that cut off circulation to the legs.
- Cora had even read somewhere that Susan B. Anthony had said, "I can see no business avocation in which woman in her present dress can possibly earn equal wages with man."
- But Cora was in enough trouble with her husband without quoting the words of a feminist; that would court accusations that she supported both equality and free love like the radicals.
- Already she was being accused of trying to de-sex women now that she was older and had stopped having children.
- Cora even heard herself compared to Washington's Dr. Mary E. Walker, who had advocated that men and women were so similar in anatomy that the sexes should dress identically.

- All because of one letter to the editor.
- Cora encountered criticism from every corner—including her embarrassed daughters—that she wanted the sexes to be equal when all she wanted was good health for women.
- What was so radical about one-piece flannel underwear in place of a confining corset, and a skirt four inches off the floor so women could walk without stumbling?
- Besides, it was obvious that the freedom offered by the modern bicycle was going to propel changes in courting, dress, and women's health.
- Her girls were going to be part of the future no matter what anyone said, even if the oldest girls were not speaking to her and Carolina insisted on sitting separately at church.

Life in the Community: Bridgeport, Connecticut

- The city of Bridgeport, Connecticut, had long seen itself as a business town that was proud of its manufacturing tradition, including gun cartridges, brass goods, and corsets.
- Warnco, a renowned manufacturer of corsets, relocated to Bridgeport in 1876, and Cora's husband treated many of its workers.
- Many in the community were proud of the notoriety Warnco was receiving for its Redfern satin corset, designed in Paris.
- To many, Cora's corset protest was bad for the future of the community.
- Secretly, she believed that any town that would elect P. T. Barnum as its mayor should not take itself so seriously.
- Beginning in the 1830s, the invention of the metal eyelet and its use in corsets allowed greater force to be exerted when lacing tightly.
- About the same time, the medical attacks on corsets began, especially as more women attempted to attain the wasp-like figure then in vogue.
- Corsets were commonly worn 14 hours per day; some women also employed night-stays to ensure that the waist was retrained to the smaller size.
- Complaints associated with tight lacing included nervous disorders, hysterical fits of crying and insomnia, constipation, indigestion, headache, backache, curvature of the spine, respiratory problems and fainting, apoplexy, apathy, stupidity, soured temper, lack of appetite, starvation, displacement of the liver, effects on the secretion of bile, anemia, chlorosis, interposes, neurasthenia, hernia, imperfect circulation, dyspepsia, nausea, vomiting, pressure on the breast, inflamed nipples, displacement of the uterus, and lack of sexual desire.
- Elizabeth Stuart Phelps was unequivocal about the corset in 1874: "Make a bonfire of the cruel steels that have lorded over your thorax and abdomen for so many years and heave a sigh of relief, for your emancipation, I assure you, from this moment has begun."

- Doctors, too, railed that the contraption was harmful, documenting that corsets put up to 80 pounds of pressure on every square inch of a woman's torso, squeezing her rib cage in, while pressing on her internal organs.
- However, the medical community was far from united: While some said tight lacing reduced fertility, others claimed that the weaker sex needed corsets to support their frail bodies.
- According to outspoken feminist Frances Willard, "Niggardly waists and niggardly brains go together. A ligature around the vital organs at the smallest diameter of the womanly figure means an impoverished blood supply to the brain, and may explain why women scream when they see a mouse."
- Yet, a flood of advertisements pitched a corset for every activity, including leisure, sleeping, riding, bicycling, as well as pregnancy and nursing corsets.
- By the 1890s, more than 400 brands were being manufactured as they became more affordable and accessible to the working class women.

HISTORICAL SNAPSHOT
1896

- "Yellow journalism" was named after the color comic figure featuring the Yellow Kid that ran in the Hearst *New York Journal* and the Pulitzer *New York World*
- Theodore Herzl called for a Jewish homeland in Palestine
- Legendary lawman Wyatt Earp refereed a heavyweight title fight between Bob Fitzsimmons and Tom Sharkey
- F. W. Rueckheim & Brother of Chicago received a trademark for the candy treat "Cracker Jack"
- The United States Army took over the operation of Yellowstone National Park
- The Anchor Brewing Company was founded in San Francisco
- An advertisement appeared in *Horseless Age,* the first automotive trade journal, for the Duryea Motor Wagon Company
- Swedish chemist Svante Arrhennius explained the "greenhouse effect," predicting that the planet would gradually become warmer
- American physician Franz Pfaff discovered that the oily residue in poison oak was responsible for the painful rash
- Utah was admitted to the Union as the forty-fifth state
- Dr. Henry Louis Smith at Davidson, North Carolina, produced the first x-ray photo in the United States to reveal a bullet in a dead man's hand
- Civil War photographer Matthew B. Brady died in the charity ward of a New York hospital at age 73
- U.S. Marines landed in Nicaragua to protect U.S. citizens in the wake of a revolution
- The first modern Olympic Games, with eight nations participating, formally opened in Athens, Greece, after a lapse of 1,500 years
- The Vitascope system for projecting movies onto a screen was demonstrated in New York City
- The United States Supreme Court ruled 7 to 1 in *Plessy v. Ferguson* and endorsed the concept of "separate but equal" racial segregation
- The Dow Jones Industrial Average was first published by Charles H. Dow using an index of 12 industrial companies
- William Jennings Bryan propelled himself to presidential candidacy when he stood before the Democratic Convention and made his famous "Cross of Gold" speech
- Booker T. Washington became the first African American to receive an honorary degree from Howard University

Selected Prices, 1896

Corset	$1.25
Hair Remover	$1.00
Horse Muzzle	$2.50
House, Four-Room Cottage	$1,800.00
Rifle, Remmington	$30.00
Shirt, Man's	$1.50
Theater Ticket, *Comic Elephants*	$0.40
Tuition, Columbia Female College, Year	$200.00
Typewriter	$25.00
Writing Paper, Linen, 72 Sheets	$0.75

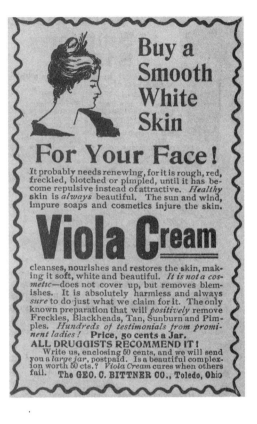
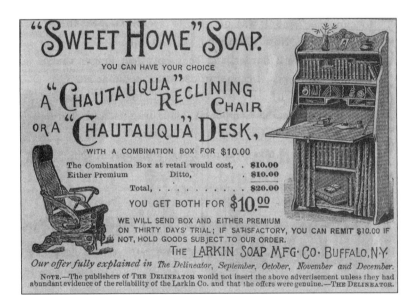
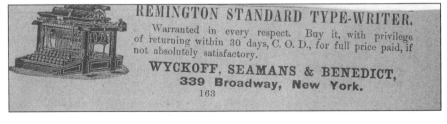

Timeline of Corsets and Ladies' Undergarments

Early 1700s

Corsets were a must for bourgeois and noble women in Europe, eager to separate themselves from the popular classes, who could not afford the specialized garment.

Working class women adopted a "little corset" which laced up the front, rather than the back, and was more affordable.

Mid-1700s

An anti-corset campaign raged across Europe by doctors concerned that corsets deformed women's bodies.

Frenchman Jacques Bonnaud wrote a pamphlet about the effect of corsets on women entitled, "The Degradation of the Human Race Through the Use of the Whalebone Corset: A Work in Which One Demonstrates That It Is to Go Against the Laws of Nature, To Increase Depopulation and Bastardize Man, So to Speak, When One Submits Him to Torture from the First Moments of His Existence, Under the Pretext of Forming Him."

Corset manufacturers asserted that corset-wearing city girls had better bodies than country girls because of the corset.

1795

Following the French revolution, the corset was exiled temporarily.

1804

The corset reappeared in France in support of the empire waist style that emphasized a high waist to accentuate a woman's breasts.

1830s

Swiss industrialist Jean Werly built the first corset factory to mass produce affordable corsets.

Corset advertisements began appearing in European magazines, while expensive American magazines such as *Godey's Lady's Book* would not show them for another 30 years.

continued

Timeline . . . *(continued)*

1840s

New-style corsets emerged, made from white twill cotton that used vertical rows of whalebone shaped to the natural body.

1850s

Major innovations in undergarment production included eyelet holes strengthened with metal rings, while India rubber and elastic were alternatives to whalebone.

Women corset-makers began to dominate in England, France, and Germany, all of which supplied the United States market.

1860

The number of corsetières working in Paris totaled 3,772, while stay manufacturing in London employed 10,000 workers.

1868

Britain produced three million corsets a year for its own use and imported two million more corsets from France and Germany.

1874

Mary J. Safford-Blake, M.D., lectured against the immovable bondage of the corset, while Carolina E. Hastings called the corset "an instrument of human torture" and blamed the deterioration of the thoracic muscles on its wearing.

1880

The popularity of ready-to-wear corsets encouraged manufacturers to expand the line of corsets using different varieties of materials, colors, sizes, and fits; brightly colored corsets also became more acceptable.

1881

The New York Times predicted that all women would be wearing trousers within two or three years.

1886

Bustles returned and in a more exaggerated form than before; they sometimes jutted out at right angles from the center back of the body.

Steel strips were attached to the insides of dresses to exaggerate the backward curve of the bustle.

1890s

To promote better health, Dr Gustave Jaeger marketed a range of woolen underwear including "Sanitary Woolen Corsets" for women.

Manufacturers interested in selling health-supporting corsets advertised the electric corset, to emphasize the metallic composition of the garment.

1896

The Sears, Roebuck catalogue featured 20 types of corsets; the most popular was Dr. Warner's Health Corset, which featured straps over the shoulders and light boning.

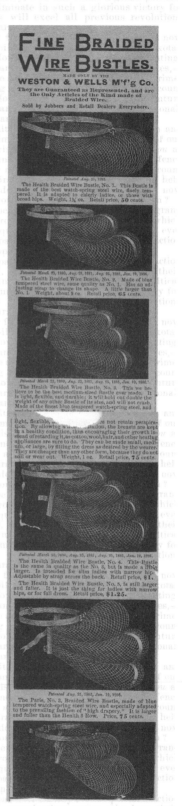

Stages of a Corset in the Life of a Woman, by French Corset Specialist Violette:

At 10 a girl puts on her first brassiere—a light underbodice reaching down to the waist.

At 18, for her debut in the world, she dons a batiste corset with supple stays.

When she marries, it is time for the nuptial corset with very firm stays.

"Fresh Censure of the Corset, Prominent Medical Testimony Against Any Use of Stays," *The New York Times*, February 12, 1893:

An Englishwoman's periodical is carrying on a crusade against tight lacing. In this evil, a serious obstacle is the Pharisaical element. As in temperance, it is the "moderate drinker" who is the most hard to reform, and in religion, the "moral man" most difficult to convert, so of corsets it is the woman who "does not lace" who perhaps is chiefly responsible for a failure to abolish entirely the use of stays. She wears them, oh, yes, but "so loose they cannot possibly do any harm." And her abhorrence of wasp waists equals that of the most active reformer. These lukewarm impediments will do well to read what an English medical expert says about any use of the corset:

"This apparatus is, per se, an unscientific appliance, and many women suffer from its use who do not in any way 'pull in.' Strip a man to the waist and you will see no markings of the skin; similarly examine the waist of a woman who has been wearing a corset however loosely applied, and the skin is found marked by pressure, pinched up, and corrugated. While the skirts are suspended from the waist, some protection from pressure in the way afforded by the corset, even if modified, is necessary, and it seems, therefore, that the fundamental error of dress in women is suspension from the waist, entailing pressure on important organs, instead of from the shoulders, as in men."

The corset should be discarded; but if it must be retained...it should be made without whalebone or steel springs, and should be held up by a band over the shoulder. . . . Nothing ought to interfere with the action of the abdominal muscles and the diaphragm.

—Lecture by Arvilla B. Haynes, M.D., 1874

"Narcotics and Improper Dress," *The New York Times;* October 14, 1897:

First in importance, because of its widespread character and of the profound mischief which it works in the human organism, must be mentioned the narcotic habit. Whatever may be the particular poison to which the individual may be addicted, whether alcohol, tobacco, opium, cocaine, tea or coffee, chloral, absinthe, or hasheesh, the vice is one and the same. The recent studies of Andriesen, Tuke, Hodge, and others have shown how these drugs destroy man, soul and body, by producing degeneration of the delicate fibres by means of which nerve cells communicate with one another, thus isolating the individual units of the cerebrum, and so destroying memory, coordination, will, and judgment, and wrecking the individual physically, mentally, and morally.

Next in the category of destructive forces, I must enumerate the slavery to conventional dress.

A careful study of this subject has convinced me that, aside from the liquor and tobacco habits, there is no deteriorating force which deals such destructive blows against the constitution of the race as the wrong, unphysiological customs in dress which prevail among civilized American women.

Scarcely a woman can be found who has reached the age of 25 or 30, and who has worn the conventional dress, who is not suffering from dislocation of the stomach, the kidneys, the bowels, or some other important internal organ. The present outlook is, however, somewhat hopeful. The bicycle has forever delivered women from the thralldom of long skirts, and gives encouragement that the necessity for breathing capacity may yet banish the corset and its accompanying tight bands.

74. Reveries.

"Bicycling and Its Attire," *The Delineator,* April 1896:

Bicycling is an evolution. For several years merely a branch of athletics, indulged in as a pastime by the ultra, it has developed into a serious factor in fin de siècle progress. Its merits are many and its pleasures incalculable. No other mode of travel, save, perhaps horseback riding, is capable of giving such thorough enjoyment as the wheel, so exhilarating is the ease and rapidity of its motion, and none is more conductive to health and symmetrical bodily development. Many for whom outdoor exercises have heretofore possessed no attraction and whose habits were sluggish for the lack of them, are fascinated by the wheel, claiming it is without rival, its influence being felt mentally as well as physically. Distances are rapidly and easily covered; varied prospects are successfully presented, and new ideas and trains of thought are engendered.

The hygienic value of wheeling appeals to every admirer of vigorous and healthy manhood and womanhood. While certain muscles are brought more into action than others, all are benefited by the exercise. The power of the respiratory organs is strengthened by the large quantities of pure air taken into the lungs, creating a more perfect oxygenation of the blood and invigorating the entire system, a tonic far pleasanter than any yet compounded by chemist. Physicians now generally concede the value of the wheel in the treatment of invalids and convalescents able to take a form of exercise requiring so much physical exertion. . . .

The best dress for wheeling is still a mooted question, opinion being divided between the short skirt and the bloomer costume. Whichever is adopted, it should be as light in weight as possible and so fashioned that it will in no wise hamper the movements of the rider. In long full skirts there lurks danger; they become easily entangled in the chain or pedals and thus bring about disaster. Wool sweaters with large sleeves are fashionable, but are objected to by some on the score of their snug fit, which sharply defines the figure. They absorb perspiration, however, and are for that reason particularly desirable for warm weather wear. Fashion provides numerous other waists as smart as they are convenient. If a corset is insisted upon (the rider will be far more comfortable without one), a short, lightly boned affair that ends above the hips and is made without steels in front, should be chosen.

"Her Point of View," *The New York Times*, February 25, 1894:

The dress reform symposiums which have been held at the Madison Square Garden through the week have evidently driven the wedge of sensible dress a little further in. It is still apparently a case of St. Anthony preaching to the fishes,

> "Much delighted were they,
> But preferred the old way."

But in point of fact there is a large class of women who are convinced that they are miserably clothed, and who are only waiting for custom to pave the way for a change in their garments.

It is a melancholy truth that men who rail at women's slavery to fashion and foolish notions of dress are among the chief obstacles in the way. They talk and inveigh, but when it comes to the women's—their women's—acting, they prove the stumbling blocks. When physicians who urge their patients to doff corsets, wear untrammeling gowns and broad-soled boots, are not able or willing to insist that their wives and daughters shall reap the benefits of this advice, it militates against its usefulness. And the lay husbands and fathers are no better. "You women are geese to dress as you do," is a kind of stock phrase with them, but they are tremendously tenacious that their womenkind shall be counted in with the flock.

"Nice woman, that Mrs. So-and-So," a man says, "but a little odd, you know. Affects thick waists, short skirts, and that sort of thing." And the same man will look over his wife's gown and comment, with a little mournful philosophy: "My dear, I'm afraid you're growing stout. Where is that slender sylph I married?"

Men have got a distinct office in this dress reform movement. They have got to accord their individual support as well as to indulge in abstract theorizing. A happy destiny has emancipated them in a great degree. But they did not achieve this greatness; it was thrust upon them. There is abundant evidence to prove that men are as devoted to dress and custom as women, have about as many vanities concerning their personal appearance, and are as willing, many of them, to sacrifice personal comfort to accomplish them.

Aside from the men, however, it is of course undeniable that woman is her own worst foe in the matter. She is learning though, slowly, but surely, and her emancipation is not far away.

Conservative women do not look for or desire the radical changes that are offered by many reformers. A skirt that clears the ankles is a sensible and convenient length, possessing for walking all the advantages that one of knee length does. Many women wear the former now and are unnoticed.

The chief points that should be insisted upon are the suspension of the garments from the shoulders, the doing away of stiff boning and heavy cumbersome trimmings and methods of cut. This Mrs. Jenness Miller and others have shown that it is possible to accomplish, and yet accommodate the gown in general features to the prevailing mode. Nor is a variety of fabric and design to be frowned upon. It must follow that different tastes and purses will dictate different choosings.

Any reform must come gradually. The physical culture movement is doing its work, even though the women lace themselves into corsets after their hour of exercise. Pretty soon the operation will be too difficult and the corset will be discarded. Many corset-wearing mothers are keeping them from their growing daughters. This is the way for the work to go on, slowly and without a startling innovation. It will not be done in a day or a month or a year, but 50 years from now women will study with amazement the fashion plates of today and wonder that their sisters could have lived in such clothing.

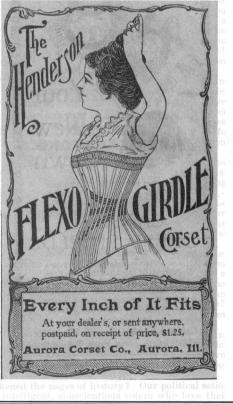

The Henderson FLEXO GIRDLE Corset

Every Inch of It Fits

At your dealer's, or sent anywhere, postpaid, on receipt of price, $1.25.

Aurora Corset Co., Aurora, Ill.

"What Women May Wear, Not Corsets, of All Things, Said Mrs. M. S. Lawrence,"
The New York Times; May 22, 1895:

A large and interested audience of girls was gathered in the Teachers College, at Morningside Heights, yesterday afternoon, when Mrs. Margaret Stanton Lawrence, the physical director of the college, gave a lecture upon dress, with all the necessary illustrative accompaniments.

A skeleton, revealed by the open door of a little portable closet, rattled his bones rather cheerfully than otherwise against the narrow walls of his abiding place. The Venus of Milo, hanging complacently by the side of an abnormally ugly specimen of the wasp-waisted woman, the interior of the human structure in various natural and unnatural conditions on charts, and the figure of the modern woman, as she appears occasionally in a comparatively healthy condition, were exhibited.

There was to be seen a bicycle gown, a part of a rainy day dress, and sundry mysterious packages which revealed in time the few hygienic garments the woman who considers herself properly clad wears beneath her gowns, bicycle or otherwise.

The lecture was particularly intended for the mothers of the college girls, but owing to the weather they did not appear. Mrs. Elizabeth Cady Stanton, Mrs. Lawrence's mother, was the guest of honor, and was heartily applauded by the girls as she came into the room with her daughter.

The corset is the bête noire against which Mrs. Lawrence contends with every principle of theory and practice, and it was the basis of all her remarks yesterday. The organs contained in the thorax were illustrated by a cheerful-looking artificial set of cheese cloths made to measurement by Dr. Eliza Mosher of Brooklyn, under whom Mrs. Lawrence studied. The heart was a dainty pincushion affair of red and blue, and other bodily organs were represented in a like manner. The lungs were such a commodious breathing apparatus that every girl present wondered if it could be possible that there was space enough in her chest to contain such an amount of delicate mechanism.

"I have been asked," said Mrs. Lawrence, "if the various organs were colored in this way, but they are not. The colors merely indicate the different organs.

"The development of women is most important, for it depends upon their condition whether those who come after will be well or ill able to stand the tremendous strain that comes upon the people of the nineteenth and twentieth centuries.

"It is because of the corset that one of the toasts at all medical dinners is, 'Woman, God's Best Gift to Man and the Support of the Doctors.' The corsets are pretty machines, often trimmed with gay ribbon and lace, but the loosest corset causes a pressure of 40 pounds on the most sensitive part of the body, and a tight corset a pressure equal to 70 or 80 pounds. 'Armorsides, warranted not to break,' I have seen on some of the corset advertisements, and it is a very good name, I think."

continued

"What Women May Wear, Not Corsets, of All Things . . ." *(continued)*

Then Mrs. Lawrence showed her pretty cheesecloth organs in their proper places and how they all suffered from pressure upon any one of them. It was about this time that a gentle ripple of laughter started at one side of the room, and gradually spread over it. It was only an innocent and unsuspecting young man, who with notebook in hand had mistakenly wandered into a woman's dress convocation.

"Has that man gone?" said Mrs. Lawrence, as she made her way back to the charts. He had gone very quickly, and every one laughed again.

"A man and a woman breathe exactly alike when properly dressed," went on Mrs. Lawrence. "It is necessary to have plenty of oxygen, and that is only obtained by deep breathing. Dr. Austin Flint says that after they are grown, women do not breathe as men do, but that is not so. He has experimented with fashionable women only. Dr. Mosher has made experiments with men. Without a corset, breathing is low down, and with a corset, merely in the chest.

No.
31R322
$11.50

No.31R321
$11.00

No.31R323
$10.50

No.
31R324
$13.50

LADIES' TAILOR MADE SUITS.

We furnish these in sizes from 32 to 42 inches around the bust and from 38 to 44 inches in skirt length; the average length of waist in back is 16 inches and the length of inside sleeve 18½ to 19 inches; these are regular measurements; sizes different than these must be made to order, in which case we charge 20 per cent above the regular price. **If for some reason** you have to return a suit to us, never return skirt or jacket alone; return both and we will be pleased to exchange the suit; parts of suits will not be accepted.

No. 31R321 LADIES' TAILOR MADE SUIT. Made of all wool Venetian cloth, coat shaped collar and lapels, fly front, yoke effect, finished with tailor made flaps of the same material; tailor made straps on the back seams; bell sleeves trimmed with straps; jacket lined throughout with romain lining; skirt tailor made with graduated flounce stitched several times, lined with black glazed lining and interlined at the bottom, bound with velvet. An exceptionally pretty suit. Colors, a new shade of gray, or castor.
Price... **$11.00**

No. 31R322 LADIES' TAILOR MADE SUIT. Consisting of a jacket and a rainy day skirt; coat collar and lapels on jacket faced with black peau de soie; double breasted dip front; back reaches only to the waist; velvet collar; bell sleeves; jacket is lined throughout with black satin; tailor made skirt, stitched twelve times around the bottom; silk band around the waist; inverted plait in the back. We can furnish in black or blue wool mixed melton cloth with narrow, invisible white stripes. Price.... **$11.50**

No. 31R323 LADIES' STYLISH BLOUSE SUIT. Consisting of blouse and skirt, made of all wool cheviot serge. The blouse is made with a rolling collar, large lapels and revers, as shown in illustration; trimmed with satin straps; bell sleeves trimmed like the jacket; satin strap trimming in back of jacket, which reaches to the waist only. The jacket is lined throughout with black satin. Tailor made skirt with graduated flounce, trimmed with two rows of satin strap trimmings above the flounce; glazed lining and interlining in the flounce, velvet binding. Colors, black, blue or brown. Price... **$10.50**

No. 31R324 LADIES' TAILOR MADE SUIT. Consisting of jacket and skirt, made of all wool Venetian cloth. Jacket has coat shaped collar and lapels, single breasted, can be worn as a blouse or buttoned; neatly trimmed with three satin straps reaching from the waist in front all around the shoulders to the waist in back; belt all around the blouse trimmed with satin straps; similar trimmings on the cuffs. The jacket is lined throughout with a good quality of satin lining. The skirt is strictly tailor made, has a graduated flounce, has four rows of satin strap trimmings; glazed lining, interlining at the bottom, velvet binding. Colors, black, royal blue or castor. Price... **$13.50**

No. 31R325 LADIES' TAILOR MADE SUIT. Consisting of jacket and skirt, made of all wool Venetian cloth. Eton effect jacket, which can be worn open as well; neatly trimmed with satin around the coat shaped collar and lapels and all around the waist; similar trimming on both sides of the front as well as on the back of the jacket, which reaches to the waist only; fancy cuffs, trimmed to match the suit. Jacket lined throughout with black silk lining. The skirt is tailor made, with graduated flounce, trimmed with satin straps stitched around the bottom; has a drop skirt made of black glazed lining. They are the newest things shown for the coming season. Colors, black, castor or blue. Price... **$13.75**

No. 31R326 LADIES' TAILOR MADE SUIT. Consisting of jacket and skirt. The jacket is made full moire, shaped collar, new shaped lapels, dipped front, yoke effect, stitched and finished with straps of same material from yoke to the bottom of the jacket; strap trimming on the back of the jacket, which reaches to the waist only; several rows of stitching all around the jacket; jacket lined all through with taffeta silk; cuffs made of black moire or watered silk. The skirt is well tailor made, has a graduated flounce, trimmed with strips made of the same material and stitched several times; finished with small, silk covered buttons; is lined throughout with black glazed lining and interlined around the bottom; velvet binding, and silk ribbon around the waist. Colors, black, blue or castor. Price... **$16.50**

1898: Child Prodigy Composer

Amy Beach embraced musical composition as a child, and wrote the first symphony by an American women performed by the Boston Symphony Orchestra.

Life at Home

- Amy Marcy Cheney Beach crushed the widely held belief that the female brain had not evolved enough to handle the complexity of a multipart symphony.
- Born in 1867 in West Henniker, New Hampshire, Amy began to make music before she could speak.
- At the age of one year, she could accurately hum 40 tunes, most of them in the key in which she first heard them.
- At age two, she could improvise a perfectly correct alto to her mother's soprano and demanded—often loudly—a steady flow of singing and songs from the adults around her.
- Amy's mother, determined that her daughter should grow up as a normal child, restricted Amy's use of the piano—she made practicing a special treat—a "top drawer event" always to be desired.
- At the same time, middle-class Victorian girls were consistently taught to be modest, not take undue pride in their accomplishments, and never be boastful.
- Amy was taught that her musical talent was a gift from God, preserving her modesty while suggesting the magnitude of the gift.
- Influenced by Horace Bushnell's child-rearing book *Christian Nature*, Amy's mother Clara believed indulgence of any kind corrupted a child, and that by withholding the sensuous medium of music, she was teaching discipline.

Child prodigy Amy Beach wrote, at 29 years old, the first symphony by an American woman to be performed by the country's leading orchestra – the Boston Symphony.

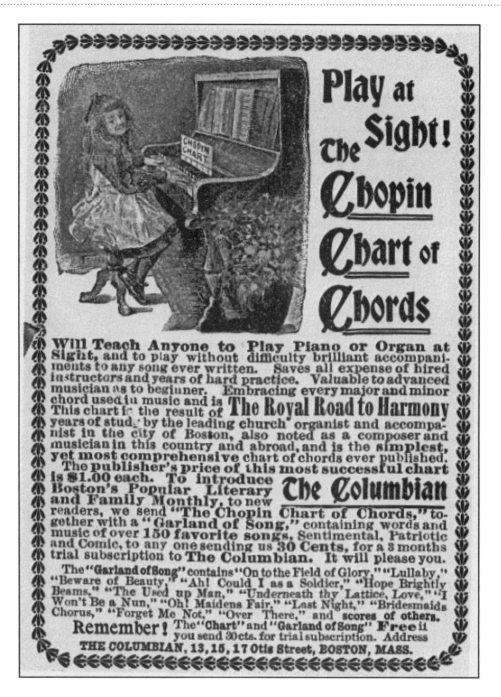

- The first piece Amy played on the piano at age four was a Strauss waltz she had learned simply by listening to her mother play.
- Later, to punish misbehavior, Amy's mother played the piano in minor keys, knowing it would make her sensitive daughter sad.
- Amy's first composition—a waltz—was created when she was four while visiting her grandfather in the country; because no piano was available, she wrote the music in her head.
- By the time she was five, she had devised a color association system for the major modes that designated the mood produced by the major keys: E was yellow, G was red.
- When she was six, her mother finally agreed to provide her formal piano lessons; by the time she was seven, she started giving public recitals, playing works by Handel, Beethoven, Chopin, and her own pieces.
- But Amy chafed under the restrictions customarily imposed on Victorian girls.

Amy resented that young boys were given trousers and groomed to become men of good character, while young girls were taught to be submissive.

- Until the age of five or six, most children, boys and girls alike, were treated with little gender differentiation; both sexes wore long dresses and were taught to be compliant and submissive.
- But when boys turned six they were "breeched" and given trousers with the expectation that strong wills as children would make boys manly men of good character.
- Girls continued to be dressed in restrictive clothing and taught to be submissive.
- The intense and emotional Amy resented the continuous restrictions.
- In 1875, the Beach family moved to Boston, where they were advised to enter their talented eight-year-old into a European conservatory.
- Some musical teachers even proposed that she be booked on a music performance tour across the Eastern seaboard.
- Her parents declined the opportunity but continued her education, despite the dangers espoused by nineteenth-century physicians that girls should not divert too much energy toward intellectual pursuits lest they harm their health and make them prone to disease.
- Boston, a city that considered itself the Athens of America, was filled with musical opportunities for a prodigy eager to fulfill her potential.
- Although most of Amy's lessons were taken in her home, she was permitted to attend concerts.
- Eventually, she moved on to private lessons by Carl Baermann, a pupil of Franz Liszt and a former professor of music at the Munich Conservatory.
- By 1883, at age 16, she made her piano debut; "No words can tell the pleasure I felt performing with the band instrumentalists.... I can only compare my sensations with that of the driver who holds in his hands the reins that perfectly control a glorious, spirited pair of horses. One must live through such an experience to properly appreciate it."
- Amy played Chopin's *Rondo in E-flat* and Moscheles's *G-minor Concerto*.
- Nine Boston newspapers and the *New York Tribune* covered the event; the *Boston Gazette* said "her natural gifts and her innate artistic intelligence were made apparent in the very first phrases she played."
- At her solo debut with the Boston Symphony Orchestra in 1885, she earned glowing reviews for her performance of Chopin's *F-minor Concerto*.
- During the next year, as she began to fully explore life as a music composer, she exhibited an extraordinary memory for musical sounds, and often composed without the aid of a piano or even a pencil and paper.
- Yet she was not eligible for serious study of composition.
- Most of the leading music conservatories still barred women from the composition classes because it was generally believed women's brains were less highly evolved than men's and less capable of responding to the intricate training.
- So Amy started a multiyear process of self-education focusing on the major composers in history while making a name for herself as a concert pianist.
- At 18, Amy married a man 24 years her senior—older than her father.

- At age 42, her husband was a surgeon at Massachusetts General Hospital and taught surgery at Harvard Medical School.
- Dr. Henry Beach was a man of his age: he believed that the man should support his wife.
- He demanded that Amy limit her concert performances to one or two a year and donate all the fees she earned giving concerts to charity.
- Dr. Beach wanted Amy to devote her time to composition, in which he believed she had an important gift, and even though she reveled in the intensity of live performances, she agreed.
- In addition, Amy halted her private piano lessons with Baermann and, at the urging of her husband, did not hire a composition teacher in an effort to keep her style pure: women were assumed to be too impressionable to retain control of their own creativity when coached.

Life at Work

- The marriage of Amy Beach changed her musical focus from performances to composition at the insistence of her new husband.
- The child prodigy, whose life had been dominated by her mother, now had to find her musical destiny as the bride of an influential doctor more than two decades her senior.
- Blessed with the good fortune to compose without a concern for money, Amy retreated to the solitude of her music room, where her discipline was self-imposed and well practiced.
- "Very few people would be willing to work so hard. It may be that it kept for me my individuality; at any rate, I enjoyed it immensely."
- To prepare properly for a career as a composer, she collected dozens and dozens of composition books and created a workbook that detailed the works of others.
- There, she copied and memorized whole scores of symphonies until she knew perfectly just how they were made.
- She described it as "...like a medical student's dissection. I began to know instrumentation on paper."
- She learned to recognize each voice in the orchestra as intimately as she knew the voices of her own family; once she learned a score, she would write it out from memory and then go to the concert hall in order to compare her work with that played by the orchestra.

- "I learned whole movements from symphonies by heart."
- She also improved her critical thinking by writing reviews of orchestral and chamber performances she attended.
- And she composed her own works.
- Her first major success was the *Mass in E-flat major*, which was performed in 1892 by the Handel and Haydn Society, a 75-minute work for solo quartet, chorus, organ, and orchestra.
- Since the Renaissance, composers had engaged the Mass as a way to demonstrate their skills through the production of a "masterpiece."
- As recently as 1865, John Knowles Paine of Boston had created his first large-scale work using the Mass.
- The well-received performance of the Mass moved Amy into the rank of America's foremost composers.
- It was a long, intricate process.
- Amy had written the vocal and choral parts as early as 1887 and completed the orchestral score in 1889.

- The Boston Commonwealth heralded the production as "one of the chief musical events of the season" and an important celebration of women's achievement in music.
- The public was intrigued by the novelty of such a large work by a woman, especially one as young as Amy, whose diminutive size made her look even younger.
- When Antonin Dvořák, the new director of the National Conservancy of Music in New York, stated that women's intellectual inferiority would prevent them from being trained as professional composers, Amy fought back.
- She wrote Dvořák a letter detailing the 153 works composed by women from 1675 to 1885, including 55 serious operas, six cantatas, and 53 comic operas.
- In her newly acquired status as America's leading woman composer, Amy went on to explain the reason for the small number of female composers: "Music is the superlative expression of life experience, and woman, by the very nature of her position, is denied many of the experiences that color life."

Amy composed the dedication for the Women's Building at the World's Columbian Exhibit in Chicago, which brought together female composers, performers and teachers.

- Her work and her words triggered several commissions, including a piece for the dedication the Women's Building at the World's Columbian Exposition to be held in Chicago in 1893.
- Theodore Thomas, head of the Exposition's Bureau of Music, promised to prove to an international crowd in the millions that art music had risen to the pinnacle of the Darwinian evolutionary ladder in America.
- The Columbian Exposition brought together for the first time female composers, performers, teachers and representatives of the emerging music club movement in a showcase of talent.
- The Exposition was also a celebration of America's coming of age as a world power and an opportunity to lay claim to the cultural achievements of a young nation so often dismissed by the European élite.
- Amy's commissioned work was entitled *Festival Jubilate* built on the theme of Psalm 100, "Oh, be joyful in the Lord, all ye lands"; it was completed in six weeks.
- Presented at the Exposition following a robust critique on the limitations currently placed on women, Amy's work opened her to a wider audience and attracted several newspaper features extolling her work and potential.
- Next came a symphony, despite the shadows cast by Beethoven.
- As in the past, she mastered composition problems including orchestration without assistance.
- In 1894, Amy began work on her *Gaelic Symphony in E-minor*; its premiere on October 30, 1896, was given by the Boston Symphony Orchestra.
- Headlines celebrated the work as the first symphony by an American woman, stressing her gender but ignoring any nationalist implications of her composition.
- Fixated on the gender of the composer, one critic commented that the work "has not the slightest trace of effeminacy, but is distinctly entirely masculine in every effect."
- Following the Boston Symphony's first performance of the piece in 1897, a reviewer from the *Brooklyn Eagle* praised its "strong writing" as "manful."
- A review in the suffragette publication *Women's Journal* stressed the intellectual and scientific aspects of the work, praising "technical skills in orchestration, and that rare inner sense of tone-color and picturesqueness belonging only to the sensitive musician."
- Finally, a woman had written a symphony and one of the country's leading orchestras had given its premiere—an American-trained woman at that.

- No critic declared it as an American piece even though it fit the contemporary definition of a nationalist work, as it drew on the music of an ethnic group in the United States—the Irish.
- Four of the symphony's themes are traditional Irish-Gaelic melodies, hence, the designation "Gaelic."
- In choosing Irish music, Amy tapped into a rich heritage that had been part of the American musical mainstream for at least a century, and by the 1890s, was assimilated into the new genre called popular music.
- Amy believed that the older the tunes, the more authentic, and found her source for the symphony in a collection published in 1841 by a folk-song collector in Dublin.
- A lively fiddle tune appeared as the closing theme of the first movement, orchestrated to recall the chanter and drone of the bagpipe.
- The first and second themes, however, were Amy's own, borrowed from her turbulent sea song, "Dark is the Night," op. 11 no. 1.
- The monothematic second movement had as its theme a Gaelic love song, first presented as an oboe solo, next by the full woodwind choir, and repeated by strings.
- As her talents grew, so did her wealth.
- With the royalties from the sale of her song "Ecstasy," Amy purchased five acres of country property in New Hampshire.
- But it was Boston that nurtured her career.
- During the city's long history, it had developed a legacy in literature, art and music.
- By 1898, Amy, who signed all her music "Mrs. H. H. A. Beach," had become the youngest member of the Boston composers' group, the "Second New England School" alongside composers John Knowles Paine, Arthur Foote, George Chadwick, Edward MacDowell, George Whiting, and Horatio Parker.
- When Second New England School composer George Chadwick wrote to congratulate Amy on her symphony, he remarked, "I always feel a thrill of pride myself whenever I hear a fine work by any of us, and as such you will have to be counted in, whether you will or not—one of the boys."

Life in The Community: Boston, Massachusetts

- Boston, the capital of and largest city in Massachusetts, was one of the oldest cities in the United States.
- The largest city in New England, Boston had long been regarded as the unofficial "Capital of New England" for its economic and cultural impact on the entire New England region.
- During the late eighteenth century, Boston was the location of several major events during the American Revolution, including the Boston Massacre and the Boston Tea Party.
- Through land reclamation and municipal annexation, Boston has expanded beyond the peninsula and, after American independence, became a major shipping port and manufacturing center, and claimed several firsts, including America's first public school, Boston Latin School (1635); America's first public park, the Boston Common (1634); and the first subway system in the United States (1897).

Faneuil Hall, "The Cradle of Liberty", Boston, Mass.

- With numerous colleges and universities within the city and surrounding area, Boston became a center of higher education and medicine.
- A dense network of railroads facilitated the region's industry and commerce, and from the mid- to late nineteenth century, Boston flourished culturally.
- It became renowned for its rarefied literary culture and lavish artistic patronage, as well as a center of the abolitionist movement.
- In the 1820s, the city's ethnic composition changed dramatically with the first wave of European immigrants, especially Irish immigrants.
- By 1850, about 35,000 Irish lived in Boston; during the latter half of the nineteenth century, the city saw increasing numbers of Irish, Germans, Lebanese, Syrians, French Canadians, and Russian and Polish Jews settle in the city.
- By the end of the nineteenth century, Boston's core neighborhoods had become enclaves of ethnically distinct immigrants—Italians inhabited the North End, Irish dominated South Boston and Charlestown, and Russian Jews lived in the West End.
- Irish and Italian immigrants brought with them Roman Catholicism.
- Following the Great Fire of 1872, Boston was rebuilt with more parks, grander roads, and elaborate plans for transforming the mud flats of the Back Bay with elegant homes.
- At the same time, Boston's musical community was expanding at Harvard, where John Knowles Paine was appointed the first professor of music.
- Boston also boasted a plethora of touring musicians including numerous women of accomplishment, both American and German trained.
- Meanwhile, construction was underway on Boston's Symphony Hall, an acoustical marvel that was regarded as one of the world's great concert halls.
- Unlike most American concert halls, which tended to favor a wider, fan-shaped configuration, Symphony Hall was built along European lines—deep, narrow and high.

HISTORICAL SNAPSHOT
1898

- New York City annexed land from surrounding counties, creating the City of Greater New York composed of five boroughs: Manhattan, Brooklyn, Queens, The Bronx, and Staten Island
- Emile Zola published *J'Accuse*, a letter accusing the French government of anti-Semitism
- The electric car belonging to Henry Lindfield of England hit a tree, becoming the world's first fatality from an automobile accident on a public highway
- The USS *Maine* exploded and sank in Havana Harbor, Cuba, killing 266 men—the event that led to the United States declaring war on Spain
- Robert Allison of Port Carbon, Pennsylvania, became the first person to buy an American-built automobile when he bought a Winton automobile that had been advertised in *Scientific American*
- Wild West Show entertainer Annie Oakley wrote President William McKinley offering the government "the services of a company of 50 'lady sharpshooters' who would provide their own arms and ammunition should war break out with Spain"
- Photographs of the Shroud of Turin revealed that the image appeared to be a photographic negative
- The 1898 Boston Beaneaters won their second straight National League baseball pennant—their eighth overall
- The Trans-Mississippi Exposition World's Fair opened in Omaha, Nebraska
- During the Spanish-American War, the United States captured Guam, making it the first U.S. overseas territory, and then annexed the Hawaiian Islands
- Joshua Slocum completed a three-year solo circumnavigation of the world
- Caleb Bradham named his soft drink "Pepsi-Cola"
- Ojibwe tribesmen defeated U.S. Government troops in northern Minnesota in the Battle of Sugar Point
- The Phi Mu Alpha Sinfonia Fraternity was founded at the New England Conservatory of Music in Boston
- A two-day blizzard known as the Portland Gale piled snow in Boston, Massachusetts, and severely impacted the Massachusetts fishing industry
- Marie and Pierre Curie announced the discovery of a substance they called radium
- As a result of the merger of several small oil companies, John D. Rockefeller's Standard Oil Company gained control of 84 percent of United States oil and most American pipelines

Selected Prices

Child's Suit	$2.00
China, 130 Pieces	$30.00
Flour, Half Barrel	$2.50
Folding Bed	$15.00
Fountain Pen	$3.50
Hair Curler	$1.00
Music Box	$2.50
Parasol, Satin	$3.90
Piano Lessons, 24	$8.00
Woman's Bicycle Costume	$7.50

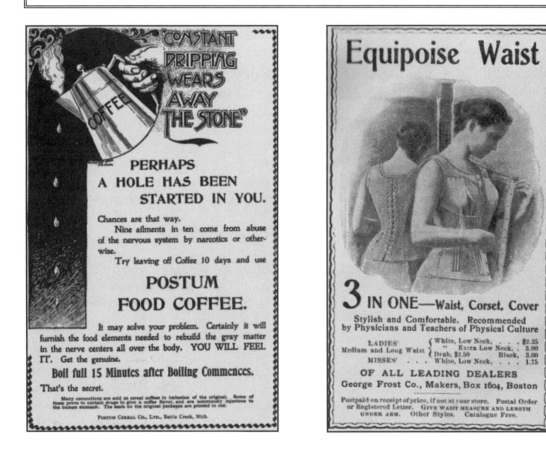

The Yorkville Enquirer (South Carolina), November 7, 1897:

A new disease, contagious and fatal, says a New York dispatch of Sunday, has reached that port, causing much alarm among the health authorities at quarantine. The disease is imported from Japan, where it is known as "Beri-Beri." The *H. P. Cann* arrived off quarantine yesterday, 170 days out of Iliola, and reported that two deaths from the disease had occurred en route. Both were buried at sea. When the ship arrived in Norfolk, Virginia, the first mate and seven men were stricken with Beri-Beri, were put ashore and sent to the hospital. The disease is unknown here. The authorities were at a loss how to handle it should other ships follow with the disease on board. *Cann* is laden with sugar and tea, and makes the third vessel which has reached this port in the last four weeks in which deaths from the disease have been reported. The disease is said to resemble the yellow fever somewhat, but it is more fatal. The *Cann* will be detained at quarantine and thoroughly disinfected, while stringent measures will be adopted to cope with the disease from other vessels arriving from fever-stricken Japanese ports.

"Women in the World of Music, Her Influence, Indirect Rather Than Active, Is Yet Appreciable," *The New York Times*, July 22, 1894:

Mr. L. C. Elson, in a recent lecture, discussed the influence of women on music. Why is there no George Eliot of music? Mr. Elson admitted that there were no great women composers, but he dwelt on the indirect influence of women upon music, illustrated by the fact that many compositions owe their origin to the power of woman exerted upon this or that composer. It was not until the Middle Ages that women achieved any prominence in music. Among the first and most notable women composers was Anne Boleyn, who, just before she was beheaded, composed the words and music to that pathetic dirge, "Oh Death, Rock Me to Sleep." In reviewing the history of music, it was noted that in the intellectual period of music, the influence of women was slight. The period of the emotional marks the dawn of the musical sense of woman. Bach, one of the pioneers of this school, owed much to his first wife's artistic inspiration. Mozart and Weber were greatly assisted in the vocal value of their works by their wives, who are vocalists….

Another, more striking example of the musical sense in woman is that of Wagner's first wife, Monica Planer, a most talented woman, who would doubtless have been famous had she never met Wagner. He rewarded her self-sacrifice by treating her shamefully. He worshiped (next to himself) his second wife, daughter of Franz Liszt, and upon the birth of their son, Siegfried, Wagner composed the exquisite Siegfried Idyll.

Among the women composers who have attained some reputation are Miss Chaminade of Paris; Miss Augusta Holmes, the Irish musician in Paris; Mrs. Beach (Miss Cheney), the head of the American list; Miss Lang; Miss Sparmann, the author of the very able philosophical treatise on music; and last of all Clara Schumann. None of these, however, would be classed as "great composers." In spite of the absence of feminine genius in musical composition, it is only just to acknowledge the influence of women upon our great composers and to recognize the fact that the old-fashioned notion that women should be slaves of men in at least one instance prevented a woman from becoming a great composer. Mr. Elson accounts for the lack of women composers by the fact that they are too anxious to please and are "too susceptible to influences…." The next century is likely to produce great musical composers among women as well as great novelists, teachers, and artists.

Recorded Popular Songs: 1898

- "At A Georgia Camp Meeting"
(words/music: Kerry Mills), Sousa's Band on Berliner Gramophone, Dan W. Quinn on Columbia Records

- "The Battle Cry Of Freedom"
(words/music: George Frederick Root), John Terrell on Berliner Gramophone

- "Believe Me, If All Those Endearing Young Charms"
(words: Thomas Moore, music: Trad.), J. W. Myers on Berliner Gramophone

- "Break The News To Mother"
(words/music: Charles K. Harris), George J. Gaskin on Edison Records

- "Chin, Chin, Chinaman"
(words: Harry Greenbank, music: Sidney Jones), James T. Powers on Berliner Gramophone

- "Happy Days In Dixie"
(music: Kerry Mills), Arthur Collins on Edison Records

- "A Hot Time In The Old Town"
(words: Joseph Hayden, music: Theodore A. Metz), Sousa's Band on Berliner Gramophone, Len Spencer with banjo, Vess L. Ossman on Columbia Records, Roger Harding on Edison Records

- "I'se Gwine Back To Dixie"
(words/music: C. A. White), Edison Male Quartette on Edison Records

- "Just Before The Battle, Mother"
(words/music: George Frederick Root), Frank C. Stanley on Edison Records

- "Mister Johnson Don't Get Gay"
(words/music: Dave Reed Jr.), Press Eldridge on Edison Records

- "My Old Kentucky Home, Good Night"
(words/music: Stephen Collins Foster), Diamond Four on Berliner Gramophone, Edison Male Quartette on Edison Records

- "Rocked In The Cradle Of The Deep"
(words: Mrs. Emma Hart Willard, music: Joseph Phillip Knight), William Hooley on Edison Records

- "She Was Bred In Old Kentucky"
(words: Harry Braisted, music: Stanley Carter), Albert C. Campbell on Edison Records

- "Stars And Stripes Forever"
(music: John Philip Sousa), Sousa's Band on Berliner Gramophone

- "Sweet Rosie O'Grady"
(words/music: Maude Nugent), Steve Porter on Berliner Gramophone

- "When Johnny Comes Marching Home"
(words/music: Louis Lambert), Frank C. Stanley on Edison Records

- "Yankee Doodle"
(Trad.), Frank C. Stanley on Edison Records

"Wonders of Patient Teaching, How Helen Keller, Without Sight or Hearing, Learned to Speak," *The New York Times*, December 29, 1891:

The Volta Bureau of Washington has prepared a souvenir of the first summer meeting of the American Association to Promote the Teaching of Speech to the Deaf. The book deals solely with the case of Helen Adams Keller, the wonderful child who at the age of 11 years has learned to speak and to write, although she is blind and deaf.

The child's progress was the subject of an essay at the last meeting of the Association by Sarah Fuller, Principal of the Horace Mann School for the Deaf of Boston. The child was possessed of all the faculties and senses of a healthy child, so far as was known, until after recovery from a serious illness at the age of 18 months she was found to have lost her hearing and sight. In 1887, she was placed under the supervision of Miss A. M. Sullivan, who had been educated at the Perkins Institute for the Blind in Boston. Under this instruction, Helen developed with astonishing rapidity the genius which has since commanded the admiration of those interested in instructing the deaf.

In 1888, Helen paid a visit to the Horace Mann School. The interest that she then manifested in the children and in the course of instruction suggested to Miss Fuller that she could be taught to speak. It was nearly two years later, however, before any effort was made in this direction. Learning at that time that a deaf and blind child had acquired speech, Helen became anxious to learn to speak, and Miss Fuller was quite ready to undertake to teach her.

Miss Fuller's essay describes how she gave the child her first lesson. It was evidently a task requiring much patience, for Helen was obliged to learn how to use her organs of speech by feeling her teacher's mouth and throat and determining by the same means the position of the tongue and teeth. She proved an apt pupil, and in a little while she was able to pronounce the vowels and give utterance also to some of the consonants.

Having gone through this preliminary drill, the teacher shaped her lips with a vowel "A" and, with the child's fingers as guides, she slowly closed her lips and pronounced the word "arm." Without hesitation, Miss Fuller says, the child arranged her tongue, repeated the sound, and was delighted to know that she had pronounced a word.

Her next attempt at pronunciation was with the words "Mama," and Papa," which she tried to speak before going to the teacher. The best she can do with these words was "mum-mum" and "pup-pup." The teacher commended her efforts, and in order to illustrate to her how the word should be correctly pronounced, she drew her finger along the back of the child's hand to show the relative height of the two syllables, the child's other hand in the meantime resting in the teacher's lips. After a few repetitions, the words "Mama" and "Papa" came with almost musical sweetness from her lips.

There were nine lessons after this in which the child proved an ideal pupil, following every correction with the utmost care, and seeming never to forget anything told her. At the close of her lessons, she used speech fluently.

1901: Anti-Cigarette Advocate

Wife and mother of two Ella Louise Scouras was convinced that cigarette smoking was ruining Chicago's youth, and fought to eliminate it.

Life at Home

- Ella Louise Scouras was determined to stop cigarette smoking in its tracks.
- With two children of her own, she knew how the devil "drink" and its sister "smoke" loved to lurk in the shadows, just waiting to slip into the back door of the unsuspecting or the weak.
- In the previous year alone, 4.4 billion cigarettes were consumed, but that number was falling, thanks to the work of the Anti-Cigaret League based in Chicago.
- If her husband would permit it, Ella Louise would make saving Chicago's youth from cigarettes her full-time work, although she admitted that she was freer to make her own decisions than were most women.
- Her American-thinking husband let her come and go pretty much as she pleased.
- When Illinois native Lucy Page Gaston launched a war on cigarette smoking, focused on the city's newsboys and shop boys, Ella Louise had both a champion and a cause.
- Thirty-six-year-old Ella Louise had enjoyed a comfortable life as the wife of a Chicago road commissioner who earned more than $2,400 a year in good times and bad.
- Unlike most factory workers, he was paid year 'round and was never laid off.
- According to a report on employment, the average Illinois family earned $756.63 annually, including wages of the husband, wife, working children, and income from boarders.

Ella Louise Scouras fought to eliminate smoking among Chicago's youth.

- In addition, the income of most factory workers suffered from periodic, unpaid lay-offs, allowing most of them to earn wages only 42 weeks a year.
- Without question, Ella Louise knew she was far better off than her Greek immigrant grandparents who brought the family to Chicago two decades earlier.
- Her grandfather, like most immigrants, spoke little English when he arrived, but was not afraid of hard work—even in the smelly, dangerous stockyards.
- He believed in loving his family, earning his wages, drinking his share, and dressing well—sometimes in that order.
- Mrs. Scouras, as her husband invariably called her, felt both fortunate for herself and desperate to help others, especially now that her children were in school most of the day and the Welsh nanny was available when they returned home.
- She also knew that as the wife of a road commissioner who carried enormous responsibility, she must not get her priorities confused.
- Home and her husband's well-being came first.
- That included watching out for her son, who told everyone that he was going to become a famous baseball player for the White Sox, and a daughter who loved to ride her new bicycle.
- But Ella Louise never let her husband's burden stray far from her thoughts.
- At the time, Chicago had 2,790 miles of streets, of which 1,206 miles were "improved."
- The paving materials used to improve roads varied: cedar block, 749 miles; macadam (crushed stone), 387 miles; asphalt, 100 miles; brick, 49 miles; and granite block, 29 miles.
- And no one could agree on what was best.
- Much of the wood block paving was prone to rotting and did not stand up well to heavy steel such as wheeled wagon traffic.
- Asphalt was smooth, but provided poor footing for horses in the winter.
- The legion of bicyclists hated macadam; motorists disliked brick.
- The other 1,500 miles, found predominately in the poorer and outlying areas, were unpaved and often turned muddy and impassable when it rained.
- Then, there was the question of whether the streets should be lighted at night.
- Although street lighting had long been in use in Chicago, some people still equated street lighting at night with immoral activity.
- Every day, Ella Louise's husband George had to make hundreds of tough decisions concerning which neighborhood got a road or sidewalk and which did not.
- When one community won, another lost; the loser always claimed the fix was in and a bribe was involved, a very insulting accusation, Ella Louise felt.
- Despite all the corruption she heard about in municipal Chicago, she was sure that none had walked through her door.
- George was wrestling mostly with the future of sidewalks.
- Alongside the 2,790 miles of streets were 5,889 miles of sidewalks.
- Most of Chicago's sidewalks were made of wood, 4,490 miles in all; concrete sidewalks comprised 1,076 miles, and stone, 286 miles.
- Changing from wood to concrete was expensive and often upset shopkeepers, but the maintenance of wood was astronomical.
- And because George and Ella Louise were members of a local cycling club that rode on Sunday afternoons, they received lots of advice.
- Riding together was one of their great pleasures; bike riding was adventurous and liberating.

George and Ella Louise Scouras were active members of a local cycling club.

- Her other passion was movie watching.
- Ella Louise simply could not abide the atmosphere created within the hundreds of nickel-shops where short movies were shown.
- They were noisy, smoky, and filled with the wrong sort of people.
- So to watch moving pictures—especially focused on exotic travel—Ella Louise talked George into ordering the Edison kinetoscope so they could watch movies such as *Around the World in Eighty Minutes.*

Life at Work
- Ella Louise Scouras first met Lucy Page Gaston when they both attended a Women's Christian Temperance Union rally in downtown Chicago four years earlier.
- As though it were her right and her place, Lucy spoke eloquently about the ruination brought about by alcohol; Ella Louise listened in rapt attention.
- Imagine the courage it must have taken to stand up and speak out, she thought, especially in front of a group of cigar-smoking men.
- Spinster and former schoolteacher Lucy Page Gaston was from the tee-totaling town of Harvey, Illinois, where the Gaston family had moved in 1893.
- At an early age, Lucy became active in temperance affairs, which then evolved into her special mission of saving boys from the evils of tobacco, especially cigarettes.
- Ella Louise fully understood that the fight to stop men from spending all the family money on drink had been a struggle for Christian-minded women for more than 60 years.
- Yet saloons in Chicago were both legal and numerous, numbering approximately 8,000.
- To Ella Louise's way of thinking, a city's issuing liquor licenses was the same as sanctioning drunkenness.
- Even worse, not one single restriction existed to stop Sunday drinking.

- When the two women met, the campaign to stop men from drinking had become an exhausting, uphill battle even with all the power of the nationwide Women's Christian Temperance Union and the Anti-Saloon League.
- But the nasty habit of cigarette smoking was new and seemingly everywhere in the streets of Chicago.
- According to Lucy Gaston, cigarette smoking was an evil that could be stopped if action was taken immediately, especially so if the focus was on the youth of Chicago.

- As a key aid and assistant to Lucy, Ella Louise was able to meet people, organize protests, and type recruitment letters.
- Ella Louise loved to help write (mostly edit) the articles used in the National Anti-Cigaret League's broadside, *The Boy.*
- The publication emphasized the perils of "smoker's face" caused by the chemical "furfural" ingested during the process of cigarette smoking.
- Furfural, Lucy had learned through scientific reading, was formed in the combustion process from glycerin, used as a moistening agent in tobacco products.
- Ella Louise's writing explained the science of smoking, but she especially enjoyed helping to write the stories that linked immoral and heinous criminal behavior to cigarette users ranging from incorrigible youths to adult murderers.
- Even her own children, good Greek Orthodox, churchgoing youths raised in a good home, were constantly clamoring for the giveaway cards in cigarette boxes: exotic animals, scantily clad actresses, flags of the world.
- There was always something more to collect.

- And the worst part was the willingness of her own brother—a pharmacist no less—to sell cigarettes and push the collector card books on anyone willing to buy.
- Anyone who put animal pictures in cigarette boxes was clearly attempting to lure more children into the filthy habit.
- Chewing tobacco was bad—her father carried plug tobacco in his pocket every day of his adult life—but smoking was worse.
- Luckily there was a way to recover from smoker's face.
- According to the research done by Miss Gaston, smoker's face and its related ailments could be healed with a weak solution of silver nitrite after every meal for three days running, especially when combined with eating a bland diet and taking plenty of warm baths.
- Ella Louise was amazed at Lucy's energy and willingness to stand up to businessmen and call their product "coffin nails" straight to their faces.
- Already the nation was paying attention.
- In 1898, Congress had pushed up taxes on the cigarette 200 percent as a way to pay for the Spanish-American War, a tax which boosted the cost of a ten-for-a-nickel pack of cigarettes by 20 percent.

- In 1899, the Anti-Cigaret League held its first convention in Chicago, attended by 100 boys.
- Some of the boys came from Sunday schools, but many were ragamuffins from the street, bolstered by Lucy's best supporters—newsboys who worked the streets and their friends the shop boys.
- Four Chicago businesses had totally banned their 1,100 employees from smoking.
- Giant retailer Montgomery Ward said it was convinced that the smell of nicotine was not only offensive to customers, but that cigarettes would "stunt growth, befog the memory, and prevent an alert intellect."
- Foremen at Montgomery Ward had even been assigned the task of spying on employees in their homes to make sure they didn't smoke on their off-duty hours.
- Ella Louise was proud to tell anyone who would listen that Iowa, Tennessee, and North Dakota had outlawed the sale of cigarettes, thanks to the work of Gastonites and their allies.

- In addition, a dozen states were considering legislation to ban the sale of cigarettes or their use in the workplace.
- Cigarette production was 4.9 billion units in 1897, but by 1901, fewer than 3.5 billion were produced.

Life in the Community: Chicago, Illinois

- Ella Louise Scouras was convinced that Chicago was the greatest city in America, due to the hard work of the mayor and the Chicago Road Commission.
- Often she marveled at the engineering know-how that allowed the City of Chicago to reverse the flow of the Chicago River as a way to dispose of city wastewater.
- At the turn of the new century, Chicago boasted 1.6 million pedestrians, approximately 50,000 horse-drawn vehicles, 377 registered automobiles, and dozens of riding horses.
- Chicago was the center of bicycle manufacturing, thanks to the Schwinn Bicycle Company, established in 1895.
- Schwinn made the modern safety bicycle that was replacing the high wheel or "ordinary" bicycle.
- Some bicycles were used for business and commuting, but an explosion of interest had been shown by middle- and upper-class young adults for exploring the countryside.

- The fast vehicles—electric streetcars, light carriages, and automobiles—had top speeds of about 20 miles per hour, but a pace of this sort was often impossible, illegal, and reckless.
- Chicago was served by a 500-mile network of streetcars that charged $0.05 per ride, but did not provide transfers; riders paid every time they boarded.
- The "L" or elevated railroad also charged $0.05, and the streetcars and "L" provided 260 million rides each year, or about 160 rides annually for each Chicago resident.
- The busiest streets were those with streetcar lines.
- In addition to the many pedestrians and streetcars, slow moving wagons would take advantage of the steel rails; a horse could pull a wagon much easier along the rails than over other pavements.
- Other problems such as a broken cable or an obstruction on the tracks could stop an entire streetcar line for a prolonged period of time.
- Only the wealthy could afford the expense and inconvenience of buggies and carriages, and the stabling, feeding, and care of horses.
- Most of the horse-drawn vehicles were wagons used to deliver freight from the railroads, docks, and warehouses.
- Urban working-class horses were often imported from farms toward the end of their lives and worked the same 60-hour weeks as their owners.
- Many horses returned to the same crowded tenement districts as their human counterparts and occupied crowded stables on the rear of the lots, or even in basements.
- Many of the 377 automobiles were basically wagons with an electric, gasoline, or steam motor, and a steering wheel or tiller attached.
- There were only 21 automobiles used for business purposes; most were owned by wealthy eccentrics and trendsetters.
- The private cars were hand-built, expensive, and usually required a chauffeur to drive and maintain them.
- According to the 1900 census, approximately one-third of Chicago's 1.7 million residents were foreign-born and recent immigrants.
- The city's 354,000 families mostly rented; only 86,000 families lived in homes they owned.
- The average rent paid in the poor districts was $8-$10 per month, bath and heat not included.
- Toilets were either shared indoor water closets, or two-hole outhouses underneath the sidewalk or stairs; a bath cost $0.25, although the city would provide a laborer a public bath for free.
- The lodging hotels favored by single men with steady employment charged between $0.25 and $0.50 a night and featured a bathroom down the hall and separate rooms for each lodger.
- The cheapest hotels provided floor space shared among hundreds of other men for $0.02.
- For $0.05, a mattress was provided.
- Older houses in the more fashionable neighborhoods rented for $25-$60 per month.
- Apartments for the upper class along the fashionable boulevards could be rented for $100-$300 per month.
- Select Lakeshore Drive palaces went for $1,000 per month, and featured conveniences such as bathtubs and flush toilets; a few even had new electric lights, telephones, and steam heat.

OUR ACME WONDER JUVENILES.

OUR $10.75 BICYCLE. NEW 1902 MODEL.

AT $10.75 we offer the highest grade Boys' Bicycle made, the equal of bicycles that others sell at double the price. Our $10.75 price is based on the actual cost of material and labor, with but our one small percentage of profit added, the lowest price ever quoted on a **Strictly High Grade Guaranteed Bicycle for Boys.**

$10.75

No. 19R69
Select Size and
Order by Number.

FOR BOYS FROM 7 TO 12 YEARS OF AGE.

EQUIPMENT. These bicycles, made especially for boys from 7 to 12 years of age, carry the highest grade equipment, including the same tire that we use on our highest grade adults' wheels, the celebrated Seroco single tube pneumatic tire, covered by the regular association 30 days' guarantee, a tire that with care will last many seasons.

TEN DAYS' TRIAL OFFER. While we require you to send cash with your order, we give you the privilege of a ten days' trial of the bicycle, during which time if you have any reason to feel dissatisfied with your purchase, simply return the bicycle to us and we will immediately return your money including transportation charges.

OUR GUARANTEE. Every bicycle is covered by our binding guarantee, covering every piece and part that enters into the wheel. We guarantee the material perfect, and if not so the wheel can be returned to us at once and your money will be cheerfully refunded.

DESCRIPTION.

TWO SIZES—Be careful in ordering. The small size, for boys from 7 to 9 years of age, has a 16-inch frame, the wheels being 24 inches; specify Catalogue No. 19R69. The large size, for boys 10 to 12 years old, has an 18-inch frame with 26-inch wheels, and should be ordered from Catalogue No. 19R71.

TIRES—The celebrated Seroco single tube.

PEDALS—Ball bearing rat trap.

CHAIN—High grade ⅜-inch chain.

HANDLE BAR—High grade raised steel handle bar, full nickel plated, full finished, complete with leather grips.

ENAMEL—Frames are enameled either maroon or black; elegantly finished. All usual bright parts are highly nickeled.

From the above illustration, engraved by our artist from a photograph, you can form a very good idea of the appearance of this handsome new 1902 Model $10.75 Bicycle for Boys.

NOTE—The 16-inch frame is for boys from 7 to 9 years of age. The 18-inch frame is for boys from 10 to 12 years of age.

SADDLE—Special high grade Juvenile saddle.
GEAR—Every wheel geared to 60 inches.
HANGER—We use the very latest 1902 style Juvenile hanger, the strongest, best finished and nicest hanger used on a boys' wheel.

SPROCKETS—We use handsome sprockets, latest 1902 style, both front and rear; highly finished, heavily nickel plated and polished; assorted designs. At our special $10.75 price, we include a fine leather tool bag, complete with wrench, oiler, pump and tire repair outfit.

No. 19R69 Boys' bicycle, 16-inch frame with 24-inch wheels, **$10.75**
for boys 7 to 9 years of age..........

No. 19R71 Boys' bicycle, 18-inch frame with 26-inch wheels, **$10.75**
for boys 10 to 12 years of age..........

OUR $10.75 NEW 1902 MODEL DROP FRAME GIRLS' BICYCLE FOR GIRLS FROM 7 TO 12 YEARS OF AGE.

THIS SPECIAL $10.75 BICYCLE is the highest grade bicycle made for girls. Made of the highest grade material, by skilled mechanics, equipped with the highest grade equipment, including the celebrated single tube guaranteed Seroco tire, and offered at our special $10.75 price, at a price based on the actual cost of material and labor, with but our one small percentage of profit added.

THIS IS THE EXACT SAME BICYCLE as our special $10.75 boys' wheel, with the exception of the girls' style of drop curved frame.

YOU WILL NOTE we furnish these wheels with 16-inch frame for girls from 7 to 9 years of age, 18-inch frame for girls from 10 to 12 years of age. The price is the same. In ordering be sure to note the different size frames to accommodate the different ages.

UNDERSTAND, every bicycle is covered by a binding guarantee as to quality of material and workmanship. Every pair of tires is covered by our regular guarantee.

..DESCRIPTION..

This bicycle is exactly the same as the boys' bicycle, with the exception of the drop curved frame. The frames are 16 or 18 inches high, made from highest grade tubing, nicely enameled, nicely finished, made extra strong in every part. The wheels are 24 or 26 inches in diameter, strictly high grade. We use high grade, full finished spokes, non-warpable hickory rims. Hubs are strictly high grade, drawn from bar steel, full finished, heavily nickel plated, ball bearing throughout, with ball retainers.

TIRES—Tires are the celebrated Seroco single tube pneumatic tires, fully guaranteed. Tires come complete with quick tire repair outfit.

SADDLE—We use a special high grade Juvenile saddle.

HANDLE BAR—We furnish a strictly high grade steel, raised handle bar, heavily nickel plated, highly finished, complete with leather grips.

BEARINGS—We use strictly high grade bearings, drawn from bar steel, full finished, accurately gauged and adjusted, tempered to a straw color, highly finished and fully guaranteed.

$10.75

No. 19R74
Select Size and
Order by Number.

TEN DAYS' TRIAL OFFER. While we require you to send cash with your order, we give you the privilege of a ten days' trial of the bicycle, during which time, if you have any reason to feel dissatisfied with your purchase, simply return the bicycle to us and we will immediately return your money, including transportation charges.

From the above illustration, engraved by our artist from a photograph, you can form some idea of the appearance of our handsome new model, $10.75 bicycle, the 1902 wheel, but you must see, examine and compare this bicycle with bicycles offered by other houses at greatly advanced prices to appreciate the extraordinary value we are offering.

CHAIN—We use a high grade ⅜-inch chain, the best chain used on any juvenile wheel.
PEDALS—We use high grade combination pedals, full ball bearing, heavily nickel plated and highly finished.
HANGER—We use the very latest 1902 hanger.
SPROCKETS—Sprockets are the latest style for 1902, made from the very best steel, highly polished, heavily nickel plated and beautifully finished, assorted designs.

GEAR—Geared to 60 inches.
EQUIPMENT—You get in this wheel the very highest grade equipment, the same high grade equipment that goes on our highest grade ladies' wheel, including the very best Seroco tires, finest nickel plated handle bars, ball bearing pedals, extra quality saddle, tool bag, quick repair outfit, wrench and oiler.
ENAMEL—Enameled in either black or maroon, as desired, handsomely finished, all usual parts heavily nickel plated on copper.

No. 19R74 Girls' 16-inch drop frame bicycles, with 24-inch **$10.75**
wheels, for girls 7 to 9 years of age..........

No. 19R78 Girls' 18-inch drop frame bicycle, with 26-inch **$10.75**
wheels, for girls 10 to 12 years of age..........

HISTORICAL SNAPSHOT
1901

- North Carolina proposed a literacy amendment for voting to diminish the role of the Black vote
- The Spindletop oil field produced 80,000 barrels a day, making the United States the world's premier supplier of petroleum
- When William McKinley became the third American president to be assassinated in 35 years, Vice President Theodore Roosevelt took office
- Jergens lotion, automobile licenses, Cadillac, Mercedes, motor-driven bicycles, instant coffee, Clicquot Club ginger ale, Quaker oats, and synthetic dye all made their first appearance
- In the art world, Mary Cassatt completed her painting, *The Oval Mirror,* Frederic Remington sculpted *The Cheyenne,* and the Chicago museums featured 49 works by John Twachtman
- Businessman Andrew Carnegie donated $5.2 million to the New York Public Library for its first branch offices
- South Dakota made school attendance mandatory for children aged 8 to 14
- Forty-two cereal makers were located in Battle Creek, Michigan
- Russian pogroms drove many Jews to emigrate to America
- The construction of freight tunnels in Chicago was begun to carry telephone and telegraph wires and cables
- Popular songs included "Ain't Dat a Shame?," "Way Down in Old Indiana" and "Rip Van Winkle Was a Lucky Man"
- *The Settlement Cookbook* including the words, "the way to a man's heart is through his stomach" was published by a Milwaukee woman working with immigrants
- The widows of four Revolutionary War soldiers were still alive and drawing pensions
- In *The World of Graft,* Josiah Flynt exposed bribe-taking in New York, Boston, and Chicago
- In baseball, new rules mandated that the catcher stand behind home plate at all times and not catch the first two strikes on a bounce
- For women, fashion demanded that hair was puffed, padded, and piled high under hats to emphasize the "S" curve of the mature bust and hips
- The giraffe was discovered in Africa by Europeans
- Popular movies included *A Trip Around the Pan-American Exposition, Execution of Czolgosz, New York in a Blizzard,* and *The Conquest of Air*
- Booker T. Washington wrote *Up from Slavery,* Mark Twain published *To a Person Sitting in Darkness* and John Muir wrote *Our National Parks*
- President Theodore Roosevelt was widely criticized for inviting Black educator Booker T. Washington to dine with him at the White House
- The "five civilized tribes," including the Cherokee, Creek, Choctaw, Chicasaw, and Seminole, were granted United States citizenship

Selected Prices, 1901

Adding Machine	$10.00
Alarm Clock	$2.50
Automobile, Two-Passenger	$1,900.00
Bedroom Suite, Hardwood	$21.00
Butter, Pound	$0.28
Camera, Delmar Folding	$3.75
Eyeglasses	$2.50
Motor Bicycle	$200.00
Rubber Teething Ring	$0.10
Whiskey, Gallon	$3.50

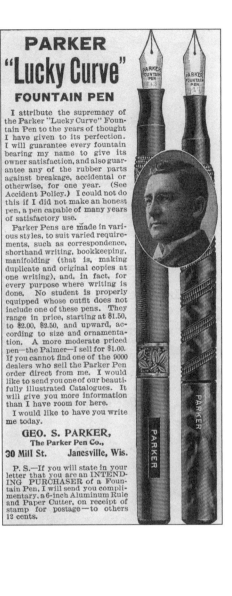
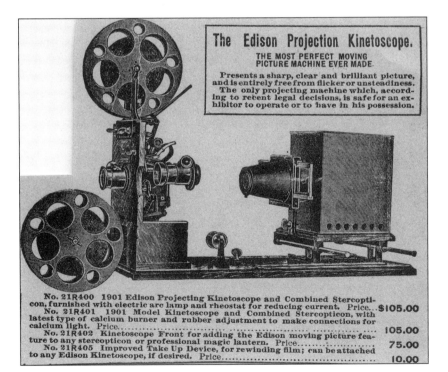

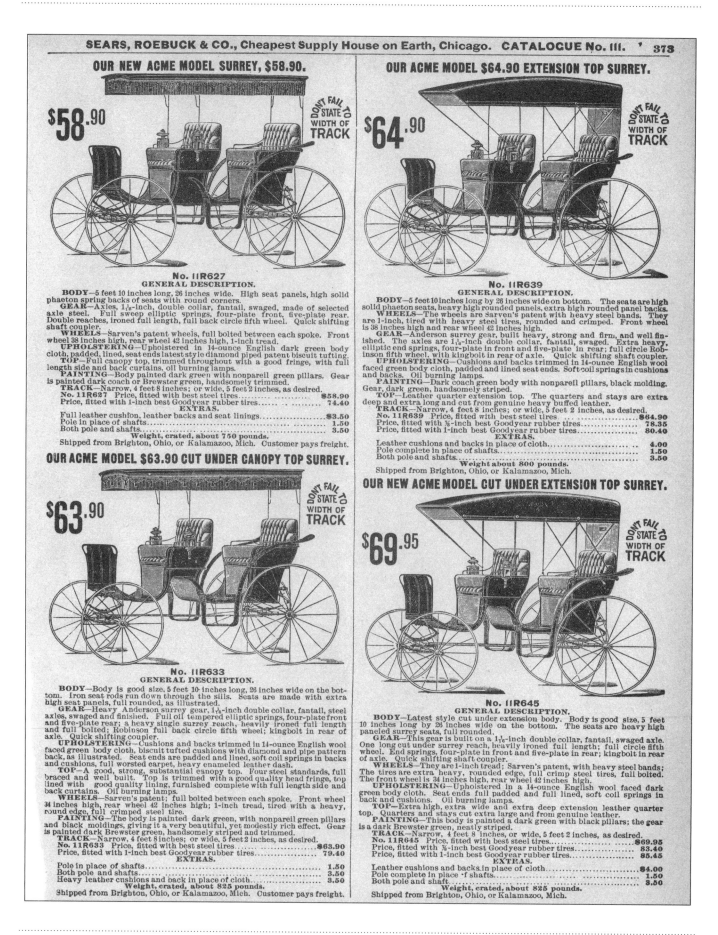

OUR NEW ACME MODEL SURREY, $58.90.

$58.90

DON'T FAIL TO STATE WIDTH OF TRACK

No. 11R627
GENERAL DESCRIPTION.

BODY—5 feet 10 inches long, 26 inches wide. High seat panels, high solid phaeton spring backs of seats with round corners.

GEAR—Axles, 1 1/16-inch, double collar, fantail, swaged, made of selected axle steel. Full sweep elliptic springs, four-plate front, five-plate rear. Double reaches, ironed full length, full back circle fifth wheel. Quick shifting shaft coupler.

WHEELS—Sarven's patent wheels, full bolted between each spoke. Front wheel 38 inches high, rear wheel 42 inches high, 1-inch tread.

UPHOLSTERING—Upholstered in 14-ounce English dark green body cloth, padded, lined, seat ends latest style diamond piped patent biscuit tufting.

TOP—Full canopy top, trimmed throughout with a good fringe, with full length side and back curtains, oil burning lamps.

PAINTING—Body painted dark green with nonpareil green pillars. Gear is painted dark coach or Brewster green, handsomely trimmed.

TRACK—Narrow, 4 feet 8 inches; or wide, 5 feet 2 inches, as desired.

No. 11R627 Price, fitted with best steel tires.................... $58.90
Price, fitted with 1-inch best Goodyear rubber tires............ 74.40

EXTRAS.

Full leather cushion, leather backs and seat linings................. $3.50
Pole in place of shafts... 1.50
Both pole and shafts... 3.50

Weight, crated, about 750 pounds.

Shipped from Brighton, Ohio, or Kalamazoo, Mich. Customer pays freight.

OUR ACME MODEL $63.90 CUT UNDER CANOPY TOP SURREY.

$63.90

DON'T FAIL TO STATE WIDTH OF TRACK

No. 11R633
GENERAL DESCRIPTION.

BODY—Body is good size, 5 feet 10 inches long, 26 inches wide on the bottom. Iron seat rods run down through the sills. Seats are made with extra high seat panels, full rounded, as illustrated.

GEAR—Heavy Anderson surrey gear, 1 1/8-inch double collar, fantail, steel axles, swaged and finished. Full oil tempered elliptic springs, four-plate front and five-plate rear; a heavy single surrey reach, heavily ironed full length and full bolted; Robinson full back circle fifth wheel; kingbolt in rear of axle. Quick shifting coupler.

UPHOLSTERING—Cushions and backs trimmed in 14-ounce English wool faced green body cloth, biscuit tufted cushions with diamond and pipe pattern back, as illustrated. Seat ends are padded and lined, soft coil springs in backs and cushions, full worsted carpet, heavy enameled leather dash.

TOP—A good, strong, substantial canopy top. Four steel standards, full braced and well built. Top is trimmed with a good quality head fringe, top lined with good quality lining, furnished complete with full length side and back curtains. Oil burning lamps.

WHEELS—Sarven's patent; full bolted between each spoke. Front wheel 34 inches high, rear wheel 42 inches high; 1-inch tread, tired with a heavy, round edge, full crimped steel tire.

PAINTING—The body is painted dark green, with nonpareil green pillars and black moldings, giving it a very beautiful, yet modestly rich effect. Gear is painted dark Brewster green, handsomely striped and trimmed.

TRACK—Narrow, 4 feet 8 inches; or wide, 5 feet 2 inches, as desired.

No. 11R633 Price, fitted with best steel tires...................... $63.90
Price, fitted with 1-inch best Goodyear rubber tires.............. 79.40

EXTRAS.

Pole in place of shafts... 1.50
Both pole and shafts... 3.50
Heavy leather cushions and back in place of cloth................. 3.50

Weight, crated, about 825 pounds.

Shipped from Brighton, Ohio, or Kalamazoo, Mich. Customer pays freight.

OUR ACME MODEL $64.90 EXTENSION TOP SURREY.

$64.90

DON'T FAIL TO STATE WIDTH OF TRACK

No. 11R639
GENERAL DESCRIPTION.

BODY—5 feet 10 inches long by 26 inches wide on bottom. The seats are high solid phaeton seats, heavy high rounded panels, extra high rounded panel backs.

WHEELS—The wheels are Sarven's patent with heavy steel bands. They are 1-inch, tired with heavy steel tires, rounded and crimped. Front wheel is 38 inches high and rear wheel 42 inches high.

GEAR—Anderson surrey gear, built heavy, strong and firm, and well finished. The axles are 1 1/8-inch double collar, fantail, swaged. Extra heavy, elliptic end springs, four-plate in front and five-plate in rear; full circle Robinson fifth wheel. with kingbolt in rear of axle. Quick shifting shaft coupler.

UPHOLSTERING—Cushions and backs trimmed in 14-ounce English wool faced green body cloth, padded and lined seat ends. Soft coil springs in cushions and backs. Oil burning lamps.

PAINTING—Dark coach green body with nonpareil pillars, black molding. Gear, dark green, handsomely striped.

TOP—Leather quarter extension top. The quarters and stays are extra deep and extra long and cut from genuine heavy buffed leather.

TRACK—Narrow, 4 feet 8 inches; or wide, 5 feet 2 inches, as desired.

No. 11R639 Price, fitted with best steel tires. $64.90
Price, fitted with 7/8-inch best Goodyear rubber tires............. 78.35
Price, fitted with 1-inch best Goodyear rubber tires.............. 80.40

EXTRAS.

Leather cushions and backs in place of cloth...................... 4.00
Pole complete in place of shafts.................................. 1.50
Both pole and shafts.. 3.50

Weight about 800 pounds.

Shipped from Brighton, Ohio, or Kalamazoo, Mich.

OUR NEW ACME MODEL CUT UNDER EXTENSION TOP SURREY.

$69.95

DON'T FAIL TO STATE WIDTH OF TRACK

No. 11R645
GENERAL DESCRIPTION.

BODY—Latest style cut under extension body. Body is good size, 5 feet 10 inches long by 26 inches wide on the bottom. The seats are heavy high paneled surrey seats, full rounded.

GEAR—This gear is built on a 1 1/8-inch double collar, fantail, swaged axle. One long cut under surrey reach, heavily ironed full length; full circle fifth wheel. End springs, four-plate in front and five-plate in rear; kingbolt in rear of axle. Quick shifting shaft coupler.

WHEELS—They are 1-inch tread; Sarven's patent, with heavy steel bands; The tires are extra heavy, rounded edge, full crimp steel tires, full bolted. The front wheel is 34 inches high, rear wheel 42 inches high.

UPHOLSTERING—Upholstered in a 14-ounce English wool faced dark green body cloth. Seat ends full padded and full lined, soft coil springs in back and cushions. Oil burning lamps.

TOP—Extra high, extra wide and extra deep extension leather quarter top. Quarters and stays cut extra large and from genuine leather.

PAINTING—This body is painted a dark green with black pillars; the gear is a dark Brewster green, neatly striped.

TRACK—Narrow, 4 feet 8 inches, or wide, 5 feet 2 inches, as desired.

No. 11R645 Price, fitted with best steel tires.................. $69.95
Price, fitted with 7/8-inch best Goodyear rubber tires............ 83.40
Price, fitted with 1-inch best Goodyear rubber tires.............. 85.45

EXTRAS.

Leather cushions and backs in place of cloth..................... $4.00
Pole complete in place of shafts................................. 1.50
Both pole and shaft.. 3.50

Weight, crated, about 825 pounds.

Shipped from Brighton, Ohio, or Kalamazoo, Mich.

Salaries in Chicago, 1900:

The Chicago Budget for 1900 listed the following public sector annual wages:

- Janitors (male), $720; (female), $540
- Coal passers, $720-$780
- Firefighters, $840-$1,134
- Patrolmen, $1,000; police matrons, $720
- Laborers, $600
- Stenographer (female), $900; male clerks, $900-$1200
- Mayor, $10,000
- Department heads, $3,000-$6,000

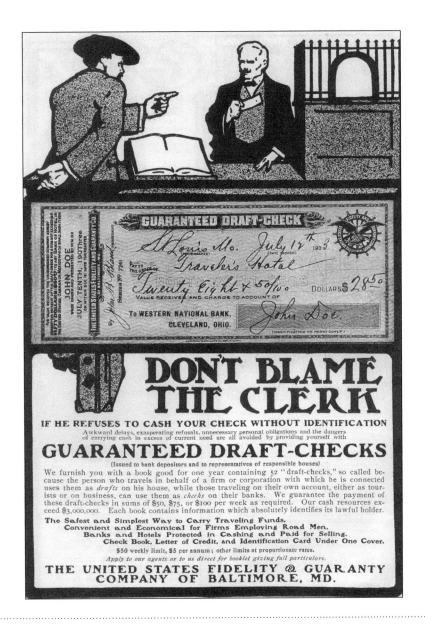

Smoking Timeline

1880

The first cigarette machine patent was issued.

1881

James Buchanan "Buck" Duke began manufacturing cigarettes in Durham, North Carolina.

1883

Congress eliminated the Civil War excise tax on cigars imposed in 1862.

1884

Buck Duke took his tobacco business national by forming a cartel that eventually became the American Tobacco Company.

Buck Duke began using cigarette manufacturing machines; his company alone produced 744 million cigarettes, more than the combined national total in 1883.

1886

A patent was issued for a machine to manufacture plug tobacco.

"Cameo" brand cigarettes were created to attract women smokers.

1887

Buck Duke slashed cigarette prices, sparking a price war.

1889

Buck Duke spent $800,000 in billboard and newspaper advertising.

The five leading cigarette firms were combined.

1890

The Women's Christian Temperance Movement published "Narcotics" that discussed the evils of numerous drugs including tobacco and cocaine.

Chewing tobacco consumption in the U.S. was three pounds per capita.

"Tobacco" appeared in the *US Pharmacopoeia*, an official government listing of drugs.

Twenty-six states and territories outlawed the sale of cigarettes to minors.

The American Tobacco Company was formed.

1892

Congress received a petition to prohibit the manufacture, importation, and sale of cigarettes.

Book matches were invented.

1893

Washington State's ban on the sale and use of cigarettes was overturned on constitutional grounds as a restraint of trade.

1895

Admiral cigarettes produced the first known motion picture commercial.

1896

Smoking was banned in the House of Representatives, but chewing was still allowed.

continued

Timeline . . . *(continued)*

1898

Congress raised taxes on cigarettes 200 percent at the start of the Spanish-American War.

The Tennessee Supreme Court upheld a total ban on cigarettes, ruling "their use is always harmful."

1899

Lucy Page Gaston founded the Chicago Anti-Cigaret League.

The U.S. Senate Finance Committee rolled back the wartime excise tax on cigarettes.

The Pall Mall brand was introduced by Butler & Butler Tobacco Co.

1900

Washington, Iowa, Tennessee, and North Dakota all outlawed the sale of cigarettes.

For the year, 4.4 billion cigarettes were sold.

Price competition and the anti-cigarette movement pushed many smaller companies out of business.

Buck Duke's companies controlled nine out of 10 cigarettes sold in America.

The U.S. Supreme Court upheld Tennessee's ban on cigarette sales.

R.J. Reynolds reluctantly merged his company into Duke's Tobacco Trust.

Approximately 300,000 cigar brands were on the market.

1901

Strong anti-cigarette activity was recorded in 43 of the 45 states, with only Wyoming and Louisiana having no organized campaign.

Duke combined his Continental Tobacco and American Tobacco companies into Consolidated Tobacco.

Duke's Consolidated bought the British Ogden tobacco firm in order to enter the British market.

Consumption topped 3.5 billion cigarettes and six billion cigars; four in five American men smoked at least one cigar a day.

The Sears, Roebuck and Company catalogue advertised a "Sure Cure for the Tobacco Habit."

"Anti-Cigaret War Commences, Convention Called by Miss Gaston Attended by about 100 Boys—Approved by Judge Burke," *Chicago Daily Tribune*, April 2, 1899:

Boys from the streets and boys from Sunday schools, newsboys, ragged youngsters, who soon departed, boys from business establishments and boys from children's homes, constituted the first anti-cigaret convention, which was held yesterday in Willard Hall, where Miss Lucy Page Gaston opened her anti-cigaret campaign. The number of boys, about 100, did not realize the best expectation of the promoters of the convention, but they announced that the meetings will be held each month, with hopes of larger audiences. The newsboys won the prize for the largest attendance, their presence augmented by the presence of the Daily News Band.

The principal speaker at the convention was to have been Judge Edmund Burke. He was unable to attend, but he sent his speech in a letter to Miss Gaston, and it was read to the boys by Miss Elizabeth Burdick. After approving the effort to check the spread of the cigarette habit among boys, Judge Burke's letter said:

"You act upon the theory adopted by all teachers of youth, if the early years are guarded and spent in purity, manhood is safe and liberty of choice will not be a curse but the highest blessing. There is no mother or father of whatever creed or race but will bid you Godspeed.

"Great is the danger. While presiding in the criminal court last year an unbroken procession of boys, from Monday to Saturday, week after week, month after month, passes before me. Almost every boy is found to be addicted to the cigaret habit. It seems to demoralize him, to take away his moral fiber, and to make him an easy prey to other vices. I cannot believe that our laws and times would tolerate for a single moment the cigaret evil if the desolation that it works could be fully realized."

"Pin-Swallowing Woman May Have Appendicitis," *Chicago Daily Tribune*, May 12, 1901:

As a result of swallowing pins while at work on the hats in the millinery department of Marshall Field & Co., Miss Winifred Voss was taken to her house in Austin yesterday, being too ill to continue her work. She suffered acute pains, and the opinion of the doctors who attended her is that the pins may have caused appendicitis.

This termination of Miss Voss' pin-eating days comes after several weeks' experience in swallowing the small bits of metal. It was during the stress of spring trimming that Miss Voss swallowed her first pin, but after that she began to swallow so many, not because she wanted to but because they would slip down, that her associates no longer marveled. Until yesterday they suggested fields of remarkable promise in the line of mysterious feats as being open to young women.

After a while the pins began to reappear, coming from her body and arms. One came out of the wrist, another out of the forearms, and several out of her back. The girl reined in health and strength, however, and never missed a day at her work until yesterday.

"Mayor Harrison Hints at Having Fourth Term," *Chicago Daily Tribune*, May 12, 1901:

Mayor Harrison hinted broadly at a meeting of old-time Chicago wheelmen last night that he might want to run for mayor a fourth time. At the meeting, which was held at the Chicago Athletic club, the Mayor said he had ridden into office on a bicycle.

"I think I have done a good deal for wheelmen in Chicago," said the Mayor, "and I am going to do more for them, because I may want to run for Mayor again. I am not one of the oldest cyclists in the city, but I am still in the ring. Some years ago, when I didn't dare ride a high wheel, I contented myself with spinning around on a tricycle. I am not one of those who are giving up the wheel for the automobile. In fact, I long prided myself that I never had ridden in one. A few days ago, however, when I was in Washington, I got into an automatic 'bus' without knowing what sort of vehicle it was, and I am now without my distinction."

The banquet was attended by many of the early bicyclists, who met to toast old bicycle clubs which long have been defunct. Edward F. Brown and Burley B. Ayers, said to be the first men in Chicago to ride the high wheel, were present.

"[It is] the rudest thing . . . a man throwing his smoke into the face of women and children as they pass up and down the street. Have you a right to throw in my mouth what you puff out of yours? That foul smoke and breath! And you would like to be called a gentleman."

—Letter to the Editor, *The Smasher's Mail*, March 23, 1901

1905: Irish Servant

Dierdre Mellane followed her brothers when they left the family in Ireland for a better life in America, and settled in Boston as a servant for a wealthy family.

Life at Home

- By the time Dee Mellane made her final decision to leave Ireland and journey to America, her community in County Mayo was depleted.
- So many young people had left Mayo for a better life, it was no longer a custom to stage an "American wake"—a farewell celebration to mark the passage of an Irish person to America.
- For more than 50 years, Irish men and women had been leaving the poverty of Ireland for the promise of America; most never returned.
- Dee was even forced to walk to the train station by herself since her brothers had already left for America and her sisters were angry that she was leaving, too.
- For the last decade, Irish women had been emigrating in such large numbers, more women than men were leaving Ireland, the only emigrant group in which this was the case.
- Irish women were in demand as servants, a better paying job than most men could find.
- In Ireland women had few opportunities for employment; even marriage held almost no prospects for women, since relatively few men possessed the dowry required for claiming a bride.
- Since the 1840s the Irish had been fleeing their homeland in large numbers, most with hopes of improving their condition, while retaining grateful recollections of the land they left.
- Ireland was still home to them, and held strong ties to their affection.
- Dee, at 19 years old, had come to her decision to emigrate late.
- For more than a year she had been engaged to a local farmer whose work habits and lack of luck prevented him from raising a dowry.
- Recently, against the advice of her mother and sisters, she called the wedding off and announced she was leaving for America.

Dierdre left Ireland to work for a wealthy family in Boston.

99

A large staff of servants was not uncommon for many upper class Boston families.

- When she was finally persuaded to stay, she received a letter from her cousin in Boston asking her emigrate and work in the home of a wealthy family.
- Then she decided to go.
- Under the proposal, her passage would be paid in advance by the family who was eager to hire another Irish girl to help tend their four children and serve meals.
- Irish servants knew their place, the letter said, and were easier to manage despite their Catholic upbringing.
- A slowing of the Irish immigration had created a tight labor market in Boston among the upper class, who typically needed half a dozen or more servants to maintain their homes.
- It wasn't the life Dee had anticipated, but she hoped to be luckier in love in America than she had been in Ireland.
- She was hired after three Welch women quit all at once and moved to New York City where salaries were higher.

Life at Work

- Dee's biggest surprise on her first day at work was not the size of the house or the sound of a water closet being flushed, but the presence of dogs inside the house.
- In Ireland dogs were used for herding, hunting and protection, and were expected to live outside.
- In America, even the dogs lived a life of luxury.
- The Vale family's three rambunctious terriers were allowed in every part of the house and were even taken for walks instead of simply being turned out when they became a nuisance.
- But that was not Dee's only surprise.
- Even the sunlight and smells of Boston seemed to be different from her native Ireland.
- At first she thought it was the burning of so much coal in the close area that created the difference, but slowly she came to realize that light, especially early morning light, was different in Boston.
- This realization was disquieting and sparked a serious case of homesickness within days of arrival.
- When she first arrived, she was provided with dresses for every occasion celebrated within the home, including toiletries in a linen handkerchief so fine she wept.
- As a live-in maid, the hours were long—17 hours—but at least she was warm and well fed.
- Her work day began at 5:30 a.m., when she cleaned the kitchen floors and heated the water.
- By 6:30 a.m., she woke the more senior staff and helped light the fires in the eight fireplaces located throughout the house.
- Next, she prepared the other servants' breakfast and delivered breakfast to the upstairs maid, who worked in the nursery.
- By 7:30 a.m., she was appropriately dressed in morning attire and assigned the responsibility of carrying jugs of water upstairs to the children; during the same trip she took away the chamber pots that had become full during the night.
- Chamber pots were emptied and replaced three or four times during the day; in addition, some of the senior servants had their own chamber pots, although most relieved themselves in an outhouse located behind the back kitchen.
- The servants' breakfast was at 7:45 a.m., followed by morning prayer services using a Protestant liturgy in the parlor with the lord and lady of the house and their four children.

Deirdre's workday began at 5:30 am when she cleaned the floors.

- The family breakfast then ensued, followed by cleanup, which could take up to an hour depending on the number of serving dishes used that day.
- Dee then took a short break to change her dress and then began to assist with the cleanup on the main floor of the house, which was covered from stem to stern with souvenirs from numerous trips along the East Coast and throughout Europe.
- In the library, a special display of seashells from around the world had been created, complete with labels that named the shells and gave their scientific designation, date of collection and location.
- Dee learned early that even commenting on a shell would evoke long, elaborate tales about where it came from and the circumstances under which it was discovered.
- At times the stories felt like extended lectures; at other times the wonderful tales of world travel made her feel like she was part of a wealthy and influential family.
- At 1 p.m., lunch was served; Dee and the other servants wore black dresses and white aprons which were always clean and well starched.
- After lunch ended at 2:30 p.m., Dee was free to nap or walk.
- Strolling through Boston listening to the sounds of a modern city excited her.
- And the prospect of romance occupied her thoughts.
- Her daydreams were often filled with a good, hard-working Irish boy picking her out of the crowd, courting her in a proper manner and proposing marriage, while her wealthy employers begged her to stay on.
- In her well-rehearsed daydream, her suitor was also handsome and articulate, with eyes that sparkled with a deep passion.
- Boston was a city endowed with many good-looking Irish boys; the question was, How would she properly entertain one when her mother and sisters were back in Ireland?
- After all, she could hardly expect to use her employer's fancy parlor for entertaining male suitors.
- Several days a week, normally when guests were in the house, the family celebrated high tea at 4:30 p.m.
- Otherwise, Dee was well occupied by 6 p.m., setting the long, custom-made mahogany table for dinner, which was normally served at 7 p.m.
- Dinner preparation included arranging the elaborately embroidered table linen, which required three servants to do properly.
- Dinner, of course, always required formal dress by the family and servants.
- During the first month she was in the home, changing clothes five times a day was exciting, but the ritual quickly lost its glitter.
- Unlike the chance to play with the children.
- In America, wealthy children were expected to play and were given dozens of toys toward that end.
- Dee was fascinated by the tiny carts, twirling tops and elaborate puzzles that the children owned, and by their willingness to share the joy of playing with them.
- Most evenings, dinner was over by 9 p.m., when she and the rest of the servants would eat their final meal of the day before retiring at 10 p.m.
- Her meals often mirrored those eaten by the family, and she was delighted to savor the sweetness of an orange on her first day at work.
- She discovered that the orange skins, when covered by a cloth, could retain their smell for weeks.
- After that, an orange symbolized all that was new and different about America, and why it might become her permanent home.

Dierdre was fascinated by the privilege enjoyed by children of wealthy families in America.

Many Irish immigrants were hardworking merchants.

Life in the Community: Boston, Massachusetts

- Anyone who knew anything about Boston told Dee that she was privileged to work on the South Side in one of its many fine homes.
- There, too, could be found the Cathedral of the Holy Cross, the largest church in New England.
- The interior was grand, she thought, divided by lines of bronzed pillars which upheld a lofty clerestory and an open timber roof.
- The chancel was very deep, and contained a rich and costly altar, and the great organ, at the other end of the church, was one of the best instruments in the country.
- The chancel's stained-glass windows depicted the Crucifixion, Nativity, and Ascension, and the transept windows, each of which covered 800 square feet, represented the Finding of the True Cross, and the Exaltation of the Cross by the Emperor Heraclius, after its recovery from the Persians.
- But Dee quickly discovered there was little in Boston of which Bostonians were more truly proud than the Common and the Public Garden.
- Other cities had larger and more elaborate public grounds, but none of them, she was repeatedly told, could boast a park of greater natural beauty.
- Everything, they said, was "of the plainest and homeliest character, the velvety greensward and the overarching foliage being the sufficient ornaments of the place."
- Dee especially enjoyed the Frog Pond with its fountain, where boys sailed their miniature ships.
- Also, on one of the little hills near the Frog Pond, was the elaborate soldiers' and sailors' monument.
- All the malls and paths were shaded by fine old trees, which formerly had their names conspicuously labeled upon them, giving an admirable opportunity for the study of grand botany.
- Near the Public Garden was the Boston Public Library, one of the most beneficent institutions that had been conceived by the public-spirited and liberal citizens of Boston.
- The immense collection constituting this library was valuable not only because of the variety and number of volumes it contained, but because of its accessibility.
- The library was open to all, and no one who made use of its offerings was charged.
- If a book not in the library was requested, it was ordered and the inquirer notified when it arrived.
- Generous donations by many wealthy and large-hearted men and women from time to time swelled the permanent fund of the institution to upwards of $100,000.
- Large additions to the general library were made yearly, and it numbered more than 450,000 volumes and over 200,000 pamphlets.
- The annual circulation amounted to about 1.3 million separate issues and thus was superior in number of volumes to the Library of Congress.

Bostonians were proud of their open space and many spent leisure time enjoying the outdoors.

HISTORICAL SNAPSHOT
1905

- Thirty-five state Audubon organizations incorporated as the National Association of Audubon Societies for the Protection of Wild Birds and Animals
- China initiated a boycott of American goods to protest the United States' treatment of upper-class Chinese tourists
- Russian Orthodox Father George Gapon was leading a procession in St. Petersburg of 200,000 when panicked troops fired into the crowd, igniting the Russian Revolution of 1905
- Elastic rubber began replacing whalebone in women's undergarments such as corsets
- Congress granted statehood to Oklahoma; New Mexico and Arizona remained territories
- The Rotary Club was founded in Chicago by lawyer Paul Percy Harris and several friends
- President Theodore Roosevelt threatened to abolish college football by executive order if rough play was not curtailed after 18 men died and 150 were seriously injured playing the game
- American auto production topped 25,000 cars
- Congress discontinued the coinage of gold dollars
- The average American farmer cultivated 12 acres of land
- Undertaker A. B. Stroenger invented the dial telephone
- Archeologists unearthed the royal tombs of Yua and Tua in Egypt
- Rebel battle flags captured during the Civil War were returned to the South
- Berlin and Paris were linked by telephone
- A Japanese baseball team from Waseda University in Tokyo toured the West Coast for three months, playing 26 games
- Japan and Russia agreed to peace talks brokered by President Theodore Roosevelt
- The world's first theater geared exclusively for motion pictures opened in Pittsburgh
- The International Workers of the World was formed by William Haywood of the Western Federation of Miners, Daniel De Leon of the Socialist Labor Party, and Eugene V. Debs of the Socialist Party
- Race riots in Atlanta, Georgia, killed 12
- Orville Wright piloted the first flight longer than 30 minutes
- Former President Grover Cleveland wrote an article for *The Ladies' Home Journal*, saying "sensible and responsible women do not want to vote"

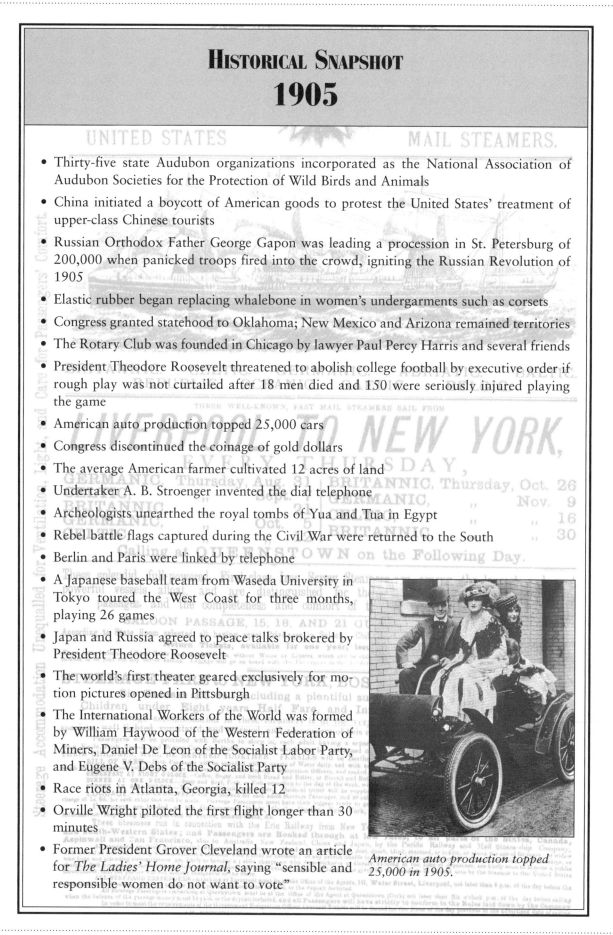

American auto production topped 25,000 in 1905.

Irish Immigration Timeline

1776

Men of Irish birth or descent formed between one-third to one-half of the American Revolutionary forces, including 1,492 officers and 26 generals.

1790

The first census of the United States recorded 44,000 Irish-born residents, more than half of whom lived south of Pennsylvania.

1791

Irishman James Hoban designed the White House, modeled upon Leinster House in Dublin.

1798

When a revolutionary uprising by the Society of United Irishmen was quelled by the British, many of the Society's members elected to emigrate to the United States.

1801

The Act of Union between Great Britain and Ireland abolished the Irish legislature and created the United Kingdom of Great Britain and Ireland.

1820-1830

Irish immigrants numbering 50,000 entered the United States.

1829

The Emancipation Act lifted penalties for Catholics and Presbyterians in Ireland.

1830-1840

Irish immigrants numbering 237,000 entered the United States.

1838

Poor Relief for Ireland was enacted.

1840-1850

The Great Famine forced more than one million Irish men and women to emigrate.

1840-1850

Irish immigrants numbering 800,000 entered the United States.

1846

All of Ireland was mapped for the first time.

1852

The Tenement Act provided for a uniform evaluation of property for tax purposes in Ireland.

1868

The Irish Reform Bill passed in British Parliament, which allowed a million more men the right to vote.

1870

The Irish Land Act provided protection for tenants.

Selected Prices

Adding Machine $10.00

Baking Powder, Pound $0.10

Drug, Worm Syrup, for Children $0.18

Handkerchief, Men's, White Linen $0.50

Iron Stove $19.50

Rocking Chair, Leather $9.75

Rolltop Desk $37.50

Saddle $19.90

Stockings, Women's $0.25

Tooth Cleanser, Tube $0.25

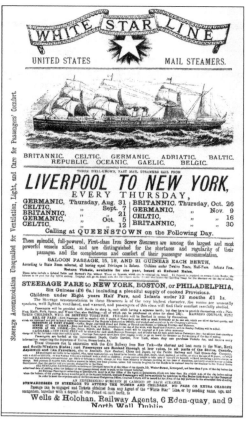

"Ireland in America," *The New York Times*, April 2, 1852:

On Sunday last, 3,000 immigrants arrived at this port. On Monday there were over 2,000. On Tuesday 5,000 arrived. On Wednesday the number was over 2,000. Thus in four days 12,000 persons were landed for the first time upon American shores. A population greater than that of some of the largest and most flourishing villages in the State, was thus added to the city of New York within 96 hours. Every setting sun has seen, thrown amongst us, men, women and children enough to constitute a town. And every year brings to our shores, from foreign lands, more than 300,000 souls. A city almost as large as Philadelphia is annually emptied from ships upon the New York docks. . . .

These are startling facts, and are well fitted to arrest attention, even in an age of startling events. The increase in American population by immigration, is now half as great as the natural increase. And everything indicates that this ratio will continue to advance, that the number of emigrants will be greater every year, for an indefinite time to come. . . .

There is no hope for Ireland, under the present state of things. Her prosperity has been sacrificed to the ambition of England. Her enforced Union to the British Empire prostrated all the barriers by which her own enterprise and industry had been encouraged, and reduced her to an unequal and ruinous competition with her conqueror. Provisions are even now as cheap in Ireland as they are with us. But there is no demand for labor at prices sufficient to pay for them. Emigration, desperate and hard as it is, seems to be the only resource of the Irish people. Transplantation to the United States is all the chance of growth that is left to them. They cannot here, of course, preserve for many generations their nationality. But they can do what is much more important for themselves and their children—they can take deep root in this soil, and grow up with the vigorous and fruitful American tree, which is soon to overshadow this portion, at least, of the planet of which we dwell. . . .

In 1847 alone, *300,000* of the Irish people perished from starvation, or from diseases incident to the lack of food. That same year, 73,000 cattle, 43,143 pigs, and 26,599 crates of eggs were sent into England from the very districts where the famine raged with most severity.

For although the Irishman had nothing for himself or his family to eat, though doomed to stand by and see his wife and children perish day by day from lack of food, he must pay his rent. The landlord must receive his due. And now, in every part of Ireland, men, women and children are turned into the open air, the roof is torn from above them, and the bare walls are leveled to the ground that they may no longer give them shelter, by the barons, or dukes, or earls, to whom the rent is due for their occupation. Is it surprising that men, when they see such inhumanities practiced in the name of order and vested rights, when they see the most heartless cruelties inflicted by grasping avarice, is it surprising that execrations against such laws should rise in the heart and to the lips of men compelled to see and to suffer such things?

The first time I saw the Statue of Liberty, all the people were rushing to the side of the boat. "Look at her, look at her," in all kinds of tongues. "There she is, there she is," like someone was greeting them.

—Elizabeth Phelps, 1920

The first man I saw on the New York pier was a black-skinned human being. He was out in front of the shed, waiting to catch a hawser from the Furnessia. The friendly sunlight dwelt on him; it was October 6, and 1901 as he stood by the bollard in his faded light blue overalls, gazing up at the rope that was being cast to him. America was his fate. It was going to be mine, so we would be having the country in common.

That was a big surprise to me, a colored man. I knew them, since one had come with a circus to Kilkenny. But here was this one, easy and free, giving a hand to us to land in his country. That was something new. It was all going to be new and different.

—Irish immigrant Francis Hackett, age 18, 1901

Make your bargain for your passage with the owner of the ship, or some well-known respectable broker ship-master. Avoid by all means those crimps that are generally found about the docks and quays where ships are taking in passengers. Be sure the ship is going to the port you contract for, as much deception has been practiced in this respect. It is important to select a well-known captain and a fast sailing ship, even at a higher rate.

—Guidebook for Irish immigrants

"Swelling Tide of Immigration Here, Irish the Only Nationality Showing a Falloff," *The New York Times*, October 19, 1902:

The annual report of Commissioner of Immigration Sargent was made public today. It [says] that of the 648,743 immigrants who arrived in the United States during the last fiscal year, 466,369 were males and 182,374 females. Of the entire number of arrivals, Italy supplied 178,373, an increase of 42,379 over the number for 1901; Austria-Hungary 171,989, an increase of 58,599; and Russia 107,347, an increase of 22,090. Most European countries showed an increase, but there was a falling off in arrivals from Ireland amounting to 1,423, the total from that country being 29,138. The figures concerning Asiatic immigration show a decrease from China of 810, the total being 1,649, and an increase from Japan of 9,001, the total being 14,270, or a 170 percent increase. Of the entire number arriving, 162,188 were unable to read or write, but 74,063 were under 14 years of age. Commenting upon this circumstance, Commissioner Sargent says:

"It can be roughly estimated from the foregoing figures how effective in excluding the aliens would be a reading test, such as that proposed during the recent session of Congress, which would not be applied to children under 15, adults over 50."

The total number of aliens who were refused permission to land was 4,974, or about two-thirds of 1 percent of the total arrivals. Of these, 3,944 were paupers, 709 had diseases, nine were convicts, and 275 were contract laborers.

"Immigration, a Fascinating Subject as It Is Discussed in Prescott F. Hall's Book on Its Effects in This Country," by Edward A. Bradford, *The New York Times*, March, 1906:

This current week a single immigrant ship debarked 2,000 wretched creatures, broken in spirit, weak in body, and just able to pass Inspection admitting them to our shores as not certain to become public charges. And this ship's company is no exception in either quality or number. Speaking first regarding numbers, there is an amazing contrast between the new and old volume of immigration. When single ships bring thousands, it is no wonder the single year's arrivals exceed a million, and that this year's total is at an unprecedented rate. New England's population was produced from 20,000 immigrants before 1640. Less than a generation before the Revolution, Franklin estimated the colonies at about one million descendents from an original immigration of 80,000. The first census after the Revolution, in 1790, gave a total population of four million. The records of immigration begin with 1820, and during the generation from the close of the Revolutionary War until then, immigrants numbered a quarter million, a single quarter year's arrivals now. Before this current year is so ended, the arrivals from 1820 will exceed 24 million.

There is nothing to equal it in history, and history is itself little more than a compendium of migration of races. The Tartar invasion of Europe, the Roman invasion of more than one continent, the invasion of America first by the Spaniards, later by the English, and lately all the tribes of the earth, each migrant people drifting or traveling to the west; these are the greatest facts in the development of peoples and nations. We are assisting and witnessing a racial development rivaling Burbank's experiments in plant life. Never was and never again can be such an opportunity for human stirpiculture. Yet immigration is thought dry and tedious even by those who marvel at Burbank's almost incredible results with plants, although we could if we would most powerfully mold and direct the sort of person a typical American should or will be. And indeed by merely failing to mold him for the better, we are molding him for the worse, and will yet be sorry for it.

It is bathetic to treat such a question as matter of dollars and cents, but this generation has ears for no other call. And the economic effects are stupendous. It cost $1,000 to rear a child to 14. The ages of the last million to arrive are unknown, but it is not exaggeration to say that the immigration of 1905 added a billion to the national wealth. But this is only the beginning. Millions have preceded them, and the product of their labor is authoritatively estimated $800 million annually. Paper and pencil will be needed to figure out what billions that makes her each generation. It's hardly worth mentioning that in 1904 immigrants showed at the Barge office $21 million in cash. There is an offset, of course. There are towns in Ireland and entire districts in Italy which are identifiable by the prosperity diffused by remittances from the United States. But this is rather fuel for flames than money lost to us, or

continued

"Immigration, a Fascinating Subject as It Is Discussed in Prescott F. Hall's Book on Its Effects in This Country" . . . *(continued)*

it stimulates further immigration as nothing else could do. At times it seemed that this flood of labor has created another offset nearer home, but of recent years there has been no unemployed problem except the strikers. Economically it must seem that the question whether immigration pays has been answered affirmatively. We would have developed more slowly in wealth and numbers except for foreign recruits. . . .

The high quality of early immigration needs no proof. It has proved his quality by its works. The Pilgrims, the Quakers, the Pennsylvania Dutch, German rebels, the refugees of later years, the Irish expelled by famine—these were stocks to produce a people to be proud of. Not all of them came among the earliest. They're not enough of them even so late as the Civil War, when native Americans were the stoutest in body and heart in the Army's north and south alike. In those days travel was so tedious and so costly that oceans were crossed only under the stimulus of the strongest motives. Weaklings who attempted that strenuous struggle for life succumbed and the survivors were men indeed, with women worthy of them. But those of this sort come in decreasing numbers and pitifully small totals nowadays. As travel became easier and cheaper, not love of liberty at any sacrifice, but mercenary motives animated later comers. It would have been bad enough if a worst quality of the same familiar stocks joined us as a result of state-aided immigration, meaning assisted departures of dependents, defectives and delinquents. It would be flattering to believe that recent arrivals were attracted by admiration of our institutions. The truth is to say they come by thousands for no better reason than the steamship companies advertise us like a show for the sake of earning passage money for dividends. Oceans are traversed as easily as the journey from New York to Albany was made contemporaneously with early immigration, and the cost is a tithe. Under these conditions, we no longer get the people to whom we are kin, who understand us and whom we understand. We get people of alien bloods and tongues and habits. We are developing race and class and social distinctions and hatreds such as were unknown when even Parsons worked with their hands and every man respected his neighbor. We have foreign colonies whose numbers are below the arrests of that nationality each year. We have in America crimes and criminals of outlandish names. We export as well as import anarchists. When the next depression strikes us, we shall have an unemployment problem to dwarf our Coxey Army, and perhaps to cause London to marvel even as we are marveling at London's misery.

The evils of immigration are largely temporary and local, while the benefits are permanent and national. The flow of immigration to our shores is not alone an index of our prosperity; it is also no insignificant element of the causes of that prosperity. Had an anti-foreign or Know Nothing spirit prevailed half a century ago, our great manufacturing and commercial development would have been driven to other lands.

—Oscar Straus, Secretary of the Department of Commerce and Labor, 1907

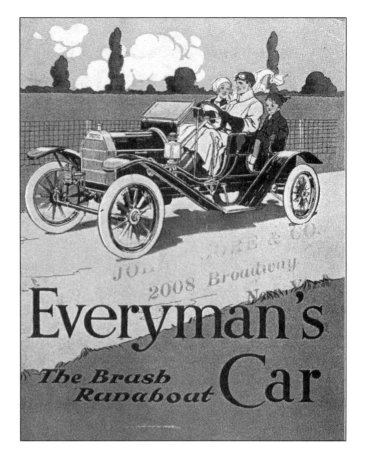

Everyman's Car
The Brush Runabout

There was a custom, which must have grown up in the famine of 1848, known as the "American wake." It occurred on the eve of an Irish emigrant's departure for the United States. In those days most emigrants never returned, hence the term "wake." My relatives and neighbors gathered in the house, stood around and encouraged me. They said such things as, "Well you're going to be with your brothers, so it will be just like home." I knew that was not true, but I smiled just the same. The older people were saddened, and I had mixed emotions. I feared going to America, but I knew there was nothing left for me in Mayo. . . .

The neighbors left about midnight. Each one pressed a coin into my hand. The sum came to seven dollars in all, a tremendous amount for the poor of our parish to part with. My mother had purchased a new suit for me, tightly fitted and in keeping with the latest Irish style. It was a blue serge suit and the bottom of the jacket barely came to my hips.

The next morning my mother and sisters accompanied me on the trip to the railroad station by pony and trap. There were periods of silence when we faltered in making the best of it. At the station my sisters cried, and my mother didn't. It wasn't manly to cry, so I didn't either until the train left the station. Then I did. I felt bereft and terrified.

—Paul O'Dwyer, 1925

"They Who Never Were Brides," *The Ladies' Home Journal,* June, 1898:

A woman, unless for extraordinary reasons, rarely reaches the years of maturity without having had a chance to marry. But the chances which come into our lives are not always the opportunities which we can embrace. Chances make heralded successes of some people, of others they make silent heroines. It is not always when we turn and grasp an opportunity that we show our greatest strength: the truest character is sometimes shown when the chance comes and we stand aside and resolutely let it pass us, when it might have been ours with the simple taking. That is a quality which is rare, and yet that is a quality which is possessed by so many women who are called "old maids." It is not that these women valued any less the power of a man's love. It was not that they did not believe in it. It was not that they did not know that love was joy, and to be loved great happiness. It is not that they wish the highest gift which can come to a woman should pass through their lives instead of becoming an abiding part of them.

The consciousness of seeing her own charms reflected in a man's eyes is something which appeals to every woman. Nothing else ever makes her so proud and so happy in exactly the same way. But that consciousness is not always for expression; sometimes it is a thing for one's inner self, to be enjoyed at the time he lived over in the years to come. No; women do not willfully turn away from their own happiness. But they do sometimes darken their own lives to make brighter the lives of others who may be closer or dependent upon them. Some higher fundamental duty sometimes calls, loftier motives sometimes quiet the deepest heart longings, a God-given task sometimes points women in the opposite direction of her own instincts. There is such a thing not known to the young, albeit years bring the knowledge as a woman turning away great happiness to insure the greater comfort and happiness of others, choosing their comfort as her life-work. Men do it now and then. But women oftener do it. Memories take the place of realities, and in those memories, sweet and tender, many women are living today. They have never been brides. But they might have been. At one time in their lives the necessity of choice came to them. Prayerfully and fearfully, and yet resolutely she made the choice. Today they are not wives simply because they are heroines. And who will say which is the greater?

1907: Teacher & Organizer

As leader of the Chicago Teachers Federation, Margaret Haley fought tirelessly for better pay and conditions, and against the restraints placed on teachers by bureaucracies.

Life at Home

- Margaret Haley spent most of her career on "hectic battlefronts of the unending war" to bring power to teachers when few thought they deserved respect.
- It was her lot to come into maturity just when women were struggling for political, economic and social independence.
- It was also in her nature to stand up to a challenge.
- Margaret was born in 1861 at the cusp of the Civil War in Juliet, Illinois, the home state of the War President, Abraham Lincoln.
- Juliet was also the locale of Elijah Lovejoy's murder by a pro-slavery mob determined to shut down his abolitionist printing press.
- Margaret was one of eight children born to immigrant parents of Irish descent; her mother came from Ireland and her father from Canada.
- He had moved his growing family to Illinois after he witnessed the anti-immigration, anti-Irish, anti-Catholic political party known as the Know Nothings burn a convent to the ground in the East.

Margaret Haley worked tirelessly on behalf of her fellow teachers.

- During her early years, Margaret attended a little school near the farm, primarily in the summer and fall; during the winter, impassable roads and heavy snows kept the school closed.
- Her mother taught the children to follow through on anything they started, and firmly believed in the value of education, an opportunity denied the Irish-Catholics in their homeland.

Financial hardship on her family's farm forced Margaret to start teaching at age 16.

- Margaret recalled that her mother "knew by experience the truth of the old Irish maxim, "Educate in order that your children may be free.""
- By the time Margaret turned 16, economic turmoil and her father's refusal to pay a bribe brought financial distress to the family and forced her to turn from student to teacher.
- Almost immediately, she began to experiment with new ways of teaching, including the emerging emphasis on phonics, a method of sounding out words that propelled a five-year-old boy into one of the best readers in the class.
- At home, she continued to listen to her politically active father talk about the economic impact of the Panic of '73, the personality of presidential candidate James G. Blaine, the work of the Molly Maguires, and the railroad strike of 1877.
- She also learned how to stand up for what she believed in.
- Teachers were badly paid and lacked pension benefits or job security.
- Moreover, they were spied upon in their community, and the women were expected to resign if they married.
- Teaching positions were dispensed through political patronage.
- Immigration, urbanization and westward expansion had both swelled and changed the face of the student population.
- Teachers in urban schools were asked to lift up children from impoverished families who spoke little English.
- They taught in overcrowded, dark and poorly ventilated classrooms; expectations were low, yet America was thirsting for an educated but pliable workforce.
- To become prepared for teaching, Margaret attended the Cook County Normal School and the Buffalo School of Pedagogy, where she received instruction from progressive educators Francis Wayland Parker and William James.
- Normal schools were created to train high school graduates to be teachers; a primary goal was to establish teaching standards, or "norms"—hence, their name.

- As a rural schoolmarm, Margaret was paid $35 per month in 1880, compared to $124 for men and $48 for women in city schools.
- She moved to Chicago in 1882 to teach in the Cook County school system; in 1884, she took a position as a sixth grade teacher.
- In cities such as Chicago, City Boards of Education, which were increasingly composed of business and professional men, promoted teacher reform as a way to ensure real student achievement—and better workers.
- In 1900, few students expected to attend school beyond the sixth grade; that year, elementary schoolteachers constituted 94 percent of Chicago's teachers.
- At the same time, the Boards of Education wanted to impose uniformity and efficiency on classrooms of restless children, so they discouraged individual initiative by teachers, whom they considered too limited to enact worthwhile change.
- Margaret's goals focused on teachers themselves.
- Teachers deserved respect for the task of educating the nation's citizens.
- But her entry into newspaper fame and court dramas was through the Women's Catholic Order of Foresters, a fraternal insurance society established in Chicago to provide death benefits to its members.
- Even though she had never attended a convention of the Order and was not involved with its politics, Margaret was willing to oppose the decision of the chairwoman to award herself a lifetime appointment.
- "I didn't know much about the organization, I knew nothing of its politics, but I knew the principle of election for life was wrong, un-American, autocratic."
- Margaret went to the convention and challenged the lifetime appointment; for her effort, she was expelled from the Order, slapped with an injunction, and introduced to the legal system; it was her first taste of adversarial politics.
- Later, when the Order offered to reinstate her if she would simply apologize, Margaret left the hall and its "mob" behind.
- The Chicago Teachers Federation was established in 1897 toward the end of a major economic depression that had rocked America during the 1890s.
- The school system was the city's largest employer and required the biggest share of the budget, even though teachers earned less than unskilled workers.
- In addition, Chicago was rapidly growing as immigrants from Greece, Poland and Italy stampeded to the Midwestern Mecca for employment.
- Margaret believed that the survival of democracy in America rested upon organized teachers, which she called the "fifth estate."
- She defined democracy as "freedom of activity directed by freed intelligence," and was increasingly concerned about the concentration of wealth into the hands of the few.
- Margaret believed that the "fifth estate" must play a role in the war being waged by the privileged against the people in the lower classes.

Life at Work
- Under Margaret Haley's leadership, the Chicago Teachers Federation fought for better pay, better conditions, and the right of "the teacher to call her soul her own."
- She was opposed to the "factorization" of the schools and the constraints placed on teachers by bureaucracies.
- And, since nearly 75 percent of America's teachers were women, she wanted them to have a seat at the decision-making table—even though only a tiny percentage of women were eligible to vote in general elections.

Margaret was one of Chicago Teachers Federation's five district vice presidents.

- Women made up a small percentage of administrators, and their power decreased with each higher level of authority.
- Their deportment was closely watched; their work in the schoolroom was not only scrutinized, but rigidly controlled.
- Teacher autonomy—always limited—was on the decline, and teachers resented it.
- In urban districts, teachers had the advantage of numbers, and thus cities became the centers for the teachers' associations that eventually grew into unions.
- In Chicago, Margaret and Catherine Goggin of the Chicago Teachers Federation rallied their peers for improved pay, retirement benefits and tenure.
- Margaret was teaching at the Hendricks School in the rough Stockyards district on Chicago's South Side when the Chicago Teachers Federation was organized in 1897.
- Because many teachers considered teaching a genteel, white-collar occupation, joining a union was an anathema to them.
- Margaret was less squeamish.
- Unlike the traditional state teachers' organizations which annually held respectable meetings to pass resolutions, the Chicago Teachers Federation was designed for battle in the courts and the political system for teacher tenure and improved salaries as a means of increasing the quality of teaching applicants.
- Margaret joined the Chicago Teachers Federation in 1898, and was one of the organization's first district vice presidents, just in time to challenge the Harper Commission.
- William Rainey Harper, president of the University of Chicago, headed a commission that proposed a complete restructuring of the Chicago school system.
- The Harper Report called for increased power for the superintendent, the instilling of corporate-like efficiency in the schools, the reduction of the School Board's size, the increase of "experts" in educational leadership positions, and the introduction of a salary system based on merit that favored male high school teachers and administrators over the mostly female elementary school teachers.
- In addition, the Harper Commission promoted the concept of issuing 99-year land leases on school property, which were not subject to taxation.
- This was at a time when school revenues and salaries were falling because the tax base of Chicago was not expanding quickly enough to keep pace with the growing number of schoolchildren.
- Once revealed, the 99-year lease plan looked like another of Chicago's corrupt kickback schemes in which everyone was rewarded except the city and its schoolchildren.

- The tax fight launched Margaret's career as she helped the public link tax reform and corporate arrogance with declining school budgets.
- Her efforts shone a spotlight on five major utility and streetcar companies, and returned $600,000 in tax dollars back to the schools.
- After the Chicago teachers turned back the tax-free land grab by business, *Review of Reviews* reported that "A very great lesson lies in the fact that this splendid triumph over hideous fraud and corruption has now been carried through by energetic women school teachers."
- Then, in 1902, the Chicago Teachers Federation made a second critical move—it linked its activities to a traditional union—The Chicago Federation of Labor—composed of working class men who had the right to vote based on their gender.
- The Chicago Teachers Federation's use of the courts and effective political campaigns to impact change got them branded as the most militant of the teachers' organizations.
- Their activities shocked the Chicago establishment and many teachers.
- Margaret preached from every forum that school reform was fundamental to social reform.
- By 1904, Margaret clambered onto the national stage as president of the Teachers Federation when she became the first elementary school teacher to speak before the National Education Association at the St. Louis Convention.
- Her speech, "Why Teachers Should Organize," demanded that more women have leadership roles at the local and national levels of teachers' unionization.
- In 1905, the teachers were able to elect a city mayor sympathetic to their plight; Margaret joined a "kitchen cabinet" of advisors to assist the mayor—resulting in three women among the first seven appointees.
- The women teachers of Chicago were finding their voice.
- It also meant that the Chicago Teachers Federation was tying its fortunes to city politics.
- Chicago Mayor Edward Dunne, like Margaret, favored the municipal ownership of streetcar lines and the principle of popular control.
- During Dunne's first two-year stint as mayor, the power of "administrative progressives" over teachers diminished.
- By the time Dunne left office, the Chicago Teachers Federation had built a national reputation for aggressive support of teachers.
- Margaret repeatedly challenged the establishment of Chicago and the traditional role of women.
- It made the men she opposed furious.
- When she challenged one male speaker at a national conference, he retorted, "Pay no attention to what the teacher down there has said. I take it she is a grade teacher, just out of her classroom at the end of the school year, worn out, tired out, and hysterical. I have repeatedly said these meetings held at this time of year are a mistake. If there are any more hysterical outbursts after this, I shall insist these meetings be held at some other time of year."
- Then, pointing his finger at Margaret, he said, "Chicago is no criterion for other parts of the country...Chicago is a morbid, cyclonic and hysterical place that is in no way representative of the rest of the country."

Chicago Mayor Dunne supported Margaret's ideas.

Life in the Community: Chicago, Illinois

- The rapidly growing Chicago boasted a population of three million people, over 70 percent of whom were foreign born or the children of foreign-born parents.
- "It is a veritable Babel of languages," a Frenchman observed. "It would seem as if all the millions of human beings disembarking year after year by the shores of the United States are consciously drawn to make this place their headquarters."
- After the fire of 1871, Chicago rebuilt its commercial center buildings with brick, stone and concrete—the consequence of a city ordinance passed in the wake of the great inferno.
- Nationwide, Chicago was known as a railroad center; within its limits the elevated rail system effectively linked workers to factories in different parts of the city.
- The rise of activity among women, both professional and recreational, drove the demand for more simplified clothing; working women, particularly those in the cities, were a prominent part of the consumer culture fostered by women's magazines and those who advertised in them.

- Mass-produced versions of the latest styles and clothing were increasingly available and affordable to the working class.
- Previously, there had been a marked difference between the dress of working women and that of the upper class; by 1907, the key distinction of a well-off patron was quality, not design.
- Marshall Fields, Chicago's leading department store, encouraged workers of all ethnic and economic stations to visit the store, and distributed rules to the sales force stipulating that they be "polite to rich and poor alike."
- While projecting this egalitarian attitude, department stores also reinforced the notions of bourgeois good taste and propriety, emphasizing the correct clothes for every occasion.
- Chicago also boasted hundreds of nickelodeons, or moving picture theaters, most of which were basically converted street front stores.
- Across the country, 10,000 of the tiny theaters had been opened to meet demand; most films lasted less than 10 minutes but enjoyed a high level of audience participation, including laughing, cheering and boisterous commentaries.
- Approximately 19 percent of Chicago's manufacturing workforce was female, typically women in their teens and early twenties earning money to supplement their families' income before they married.
- By 1907, Chicago was teeming with newcomers from Southern and Eastern Europe, especially Greece, Italy and Poland; their arrival was in direct competition with earlier immigrants from Northern and Western Europe, particularly Germany, Ireland and Scandinavia.

HISTORICAL SNAPSHOT
1907

- The first Montessori school and daycare center for working class children opened in Rome

- The Second Hague Peace Conference was held

- A record 1.2 million immigrants arrived in the United States; Congress raised the head tax on immigration to $4

- *Harper's Weekly* warned of "nickel madness," referring to the growing popularity of nickelodeons throughout the country

- The passenger liner *RMS Lusitania* made its maiden voyage from Liverpool, England, to New York City

- The average salary of an American worker was $495 a year; teachers earned $453 a year, while the average factory worker earned $598 per year

- Ringling Brothers bought out Barnum & Bailey as the former continued to grow in popularity and size; railroad caravans carried 1,000 performers or more

- Guglielmo Marconi initiated commercial transatlantic radio communications between his high-power long-wave wireless telegraphy stations in Clifden, Ireland, and Glace Bay, Nova Scotia

- The Forest Preservation Act set aside 16 million acres in five states

- The Protestant Episcopal Convention condemned the removal of "in God we trust" from new gold coins

- Professional baseball player Honus Wagner won his fifth batting title

- Residents of New York City's Lower East Side, eager to read the news in their own language, had more than 50 newspapers and periodicals published in Yiddish

- Surgeons discovered that patients recovered faster and with fewer complications if they became mobile shortly after surgery

- The Diamond Sūtra, a Buddhist scripture from 868 CE, was discovered in the Mogao Caves and dated as the earliest example of block printing

- Lee DeForest invented the triode thermionic amplifier, which began the development of electronics as a practical technology

- Popular songs included, "When a Fellow's on the Level with a Girl That's on the Square," "I'd Rather Be a Lobster Than a Wise Guy," and "I Just Can't Make my Eyes Behave"

Selected Prices

Automobile, Graham Roadster......... ....$850.00

Baseball Calendar................ ....$0.30

Bookcase.............. ....$18.25

Castor Oil Tablets, Box..$0.10

Dental Filling..$1.00

Iron Stove.............. ....$19.50

Motor Oil, Gallon................. ....$0.60

Rolltop Desk... ....$37.50

Stockings, Women's..$0.25

Tooth Cleanser, Tube................. ....$0.25

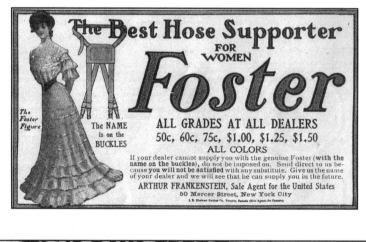

How the Rest of the World Goes to School, "Teachers' Everyday Plans," F.A. Onen Publishing Company, 1907:

In the west this is the age of children. Children have been loved in all ages; but never before have children been so considered, so studied. New systems of education have been carefully devised for them. Their amusement, pleasure, and dress have been as great a study as have those of the adults.

Free schools, free textbooks and commodious buildings are the rule in the United States and wherever her power has extended. And really, is it not wise? We may try to reform the criminal, elevate the degraded, but to really want to do anything for a nation, we must begin with the children.

It is through the study of them, too, that we learn to understand other peoples, for the grown-ups look upon us with the eyes of suspicion in cold distrust, but child nature is essentially the same the world over, trusting and frank, and unconscious; not even racial difference raises any barrier between them and us.

Whenever the ruling class has come into power, the first thought has been to investigate the schools and model them on the plan of their own.

In Hawaii, people were essentially children in nature, living in houses of leaves, and stems and grasses, as are the birds. Their lives were as free and happy and careless as the birds' until the missionary and the schools came.

Hawaiian children are the heritors of little or no literature, and yet they speak and write—those of them who can write—in the language of poetry. They are apt pupils of nature in the land where the flowers flaunt their splendid beauty and thousands of coffee trees lift their handsome heads packed with fragrant scarlet berries.

The people express themselves in many superlatives and with much force and directness.

But education does not agree with Polynesians, at least not Western education, for they were being educated away and the race is rapidly decreasing. The curriculum of the modern school seems not intended for this tropical flower used only to their open air and the warm water of the southern seas. Hawaiian parents never coerce their children, and enforced obedience seems like hothouse flowers.

The Hawaiian children excel in music and poetry, and are very deft in feather work and doing things that are useful in that southern climate.

They are adept swimmers, many of the children swimming to school, with their few garments held in one hand as they paddle along with the other. They are very careful of their bright, pretty clothes.

Continued

How the Rest of the World Goes to School . . . (Continued)

Sometimes the teacher and the children sit under the shadow of the pepper tree or beneath the sandal woods. Most of the teachers are men, and if they are natives, they often bring their children to school and tend to them, for in Hawaii the men monopolize many branches of work we associate with women. Men tend all the babies and children—the little they need tending—while the mothers go riding or visiting.

The President's Letter to the American School Children

To the School Children of the United States:

Arbor Day (which means simply "Tree Day") is now observed in every State in our Union—and mainly in the schools. At various times from January to December, but chiefly in this month of April, you give a day or part of a day to special exercises and perhaps to actual tree planting, in recognition of the importance of trees to us as a Nation, and of what they yield in adornment, comfort, and useful products to the communities in which you live.

It is well that you should celebrate your Arbor Day thoughtfully, for within your lifetime the Nation's need of trees will become serious. We of an older generation can get along with what we have, though with growing hardship; but in your full manhood and womanhood you will want what nature once so bountifully supplied and man so thoughtlessly destroyed; and because of that want, you will reproach us, not for what we have used, but for what we have wasted.

For the nation, as for the man or woman and the boy or girl, the road to success is the right use of what we have, and the improvement of present opportunity. If you neglect to prepare yourselves now for the duties and responsibilities which will fall upon you later, if you do not learn the things which you will need to know when your school days are over, you will suffer the consequences. So any nation which in its youth lives only for the day, reaps without sowing, and consumes without husbanding, must expect the penalty of the prodigal, whose labor could with difficulty find him the bare means of life.

A people without children would face a hopeless future; a country without trees is almost as hopeless; forests which are so used that they cannot renew themselves will soon vanish, and with them all their benefits. A true forest is not merely a store house full of wood, but, as it were, a factory of wood, and at the same time a reservoir of water. When you help to preserve our forests or to plant new ones, you are acting the part of good citizens. The value of forestry deserves, therefore, to be taught in the schools, which aim to make good citizens of you. If your Arbor Day exercises help you to realize what benefits each one of you receives from the forests, and how by your assistance these benefits may continue, they will serve a good end.

THEODORE ROOSEVELT
The White House,
April 15, 1907.

Planting Suggestions

The proper season for planting is not everywhere the same. Where spring is the best season—north of the thirty-seventh parallel generally—the right time is when the frost is out of the ground before budding begins.

The day to plant is almost as important as the season. Sunny, windy weather is to be avoided; cool, damp days are the best. For this reason it is well to leave the date for Arbor Day unfixed. All exercises are better deferred until the planting is done.

Trees cannot be thrust into a rough soil at random and then be expected to flourish. They should be planted in well-worked soil, well enriched. If the trees cannot be set out immediately after being secured, the first step is to prevent their roots drying out in the air. This may be done by standing the roots in a "puddle" of mud or "heeling-in" the trees by burying the roots deep in fresh earth.

In planting, they should be placed from two to three inches deeper than they stood originally. Fine soil should always be pressed firmly—not made hard—about the roots, and two inches of soil at the top should be left very loose, to act as a mulch to retain the moisture.

Small seedlings may be secured easily and cheaply. If these are set out in good numbers after the pattern of a commercial plantation, they will become in due time a true forest on a small scale. No matter how few the trees, they may be made to illustrate planting for some useful purpose.

The scope of planting may sometimes be broadened by securing permission for the children to plant a small block of trees in some field unsuited for crops, and in this way the work can be done just as it would be done on a larger scale by the forester.

Outside the scope of the actual planting, it is well to bear in mind that Arbor Day is not the only day in the year on which trees deserve to be remembered and cared for. They need care throughout the season. Watching the plantation thrive under the right treatment greatly adds to the educational value of the work, and to its success, which should be its best lesson.

It is all important that the plantation should serve as a model of what can be accomplished along these lines. Then, when the children are grown men and women, they will find great satisfaction in the work of their school days.

Approved:
James Wilson,
Secretary.
Washington, D.C., March 28, 1907.

To win rudimentary justice, women had to battle with brain, with wit, and sometimes even with force. If you happen to be born wanting freedom for yourself, for your group, for people at large, you had to fight for it and you had to fight hard. Those of us who were flown on the frontier of the war for human rights had little choice of weapons or battleground. We had to make our own slings and arrows. If we have won with them anything of lasting value and, in a way, I think we have, it was because we knew that we were never fighting for ourselves alone. Always with us marched the army of the silent, but poor, the oppressed, the shackled. If we faltered, we had to remember them and keep on fighting.

—The Autobiography of Margaret Haley

God seems to have made woman peculiarly suited to guide and develop the infant mind, and it seems...very poor policy to pay a man 20 or 22 dollars a month for teaching children the ABCs, when a female could do the work more successfully at one third of the price.

—Littleton School Committee, Littleton, Massachusetts, 1849

"Teachers Favor Flogging, Say Corporal Punishment Is Necessary for Discipline," *The New York Times*, December 12, 1907:

That corporal punishment is a necessity in the public schools to protect the women teachers from degrading insults, the children from the demoralizing influence of bad companions, and to save, if possible, the few bad boys from utter ruin by the only power they will understand was the unanimous voice of the school Principals and Commissioners who met at the call of the Public Education Association at the house of Mrs. James A. Scrymser, 107 West Twenty-first Street, last evening. The subject for discussion was the conditions that have led to the demand for corporal punishment.

The speakers also acknowledged frankly that corporal punishment is actually in use in the public schools, brought about by conditions that make it practically unavoidable. "The grossness of insult to which the women teachers suffer I could not recite in your presence," said John Doty, Principal of the Rivington Street school. "They suffer daily from indignities to which I do not think any human being could submit and keep their temper and their hands off the perpetrator. That is the very worst kind of corporal punishment; it is not punishment, but retaliation, but I do not blame the teacher.

"I asked President Burlingham of the Board of Education what he would do if a boy of fourteen did thus and so to him. 'I would knock him down,' he answered. Then think of the effect of this disrespect for the law upon the other children.

Continued

"Teachers Favor Flogging . . . (Continued)

"In 1872 or 1873, when corporal punishment was given up, we had two methods of redress, expulsion or elimination by a process of stipulation. In 1894, when the compulsory education law was put in force, we lost that power, and I tremble to think what would happen if the law was really enforced. It is that which has led to the present conditions in the schools. All punishment is more or less corporal. The reform school is corporal punishment, and to my mind a flogging does less harm. There is no corporal punishment for men, but if a man resists arrest he is clubbed until he submits. Surgery does not cure, but it saves life and gets rid of the evil, that good may come.

We cannot leave punishment to the parents. I have known a father to knock his boy down and kick him in the ribs until I took him away. Flogging should only be resorted to in a few instances, but I have never known any punishment by God or man that was not based on the corporal."

Commissioner Nathan Jones, Chairman of the committee to investigate the subject of corporal punishment, told of the difficulty there had been even in having the commission appointed against the wishes of the City Superintendent. He told of a personal experience, where a young woman teacher in one of the schools had been sent to him by her Principal. One of her boys had used such vile language to her that she had felt obliged to punish him, and had gone to the Commissioner as a matter of self-protection to tell him the story.

"I thought if that were the case with her," said the Commissioner, "there must be many others. Of all the Superintendents to whom I have written to ask about corporal punishment, the majority have been overwhelmingly in favor of it. The others have said that if they did not have corporal punishment, there must be some method to preserve discipline.

Commissioner McDonald read extracts to be presented to the Board of Education asking for corporal punishment. William McAndrew of the Washington Irving High School said that he was theoretically and sentimentally opposed to corporal punishment, but from his experience with boys' schools he considered it necessary.

In a letter from Miss Lida Williams, she said: "The chief cause of the demand for the return of corporal punishment is the persistent lessening by the Board of Education and the Superintendents of the authority of the school Principal, a consequence of the effort to administer every detail of this enormous system from 500 Park Avenue.

"There is a fourth right that a boy has besides that of life, liberty and the pursuit of happiness: that is the right to be led by compulsion or persuasion to obey where it is for his own usefulness and happiness."

The Public Education Association was not represented among the speakers for corporal punishment.

1916: Teacher of Immigrant Children

Teacher Emily Standhope strove to Americanize the Greek, Italian, and Russian immigrants in her Brooklyn classroom, by forcing them all to speak English.

Life at Home

- Emily Strandhope heard the call at an early age; in retrospect, the vision arrived while she was at the open-air market not far from her home in Brooklyn, New York.
- She was 15 and had been sent to the market for some carrots, cabbage and flour.
- None were in sight, and when she asked the vendor, he replied in German that he didn't understand her request; she turned to the next vendor and he, too, spoke no English.
- That's when Emily decided that she was being called to Americanize the immigrant hordes flocking to the United States.
- Fixing the immigrant problem would save America from the anarchists and Bolsheviks, and the best way to do that was to teach the "foreign parts" out of their heads.
- The quicker they learned to speak nothing but English, the better off everyone would be.
- From 1870 to 1916, 27 million immigrants arrived at America's shores to find work, education and opportunity.
- The lure of American-style education was so great that, on days after a steamship landed in New York Harbor, the city's schools would often experience an enrollment hike of 125 pupils.
- Education was necessary if the American way of life was to be preserved.
- Emily attended college at Columbia with this goal in mind.
- There, she learned that the emerging idea called "kindergarten" could not only educate the very young, but also serve as a

Emily Strandhope
Americanized immigrants.

substitute for the moral training not taught to the children by their parents in the slums of New York.

- Under this theory, children could be taught in school disciplines such as cleanliness, politeness, obedience and regularity; some schools even installed showers to meet the needs of the dirty, neglected unban children.

- These steps were all necessary, experts said, because among the immigrants, critical influences like the family, church and community had collapsed.

Immigrants lived in poor, neglected neighborhoods.

- Emily knew in her heart that the child who lived for years in the misery of a crowded tenement home would become too comfortable with corruption and immorality as an adult.

- She was, in effect, saving America from itself, and was often disappointed that her friends did not fully comprehend how important her work was, and how much she was sacrificing for the country.

- She didn't hesitate to scrub a child clean when he arrived dirty, she washed children's hair to reduce lice infestations, and she regularly swatted children on their backsides when she heard them speaking in their native language.

- Emily was one of five children born in Upstate New York in 1880.

- Her parents owned so many books—possibly as many as 300—the neighbors used the Strandhope home as a lending library.

- Emily always made sure every book was returned on time—sometimes without a lot of finesse.

- Early in her career, she had read *The Atlantic Monthly* that called for adoption of business organization by schools.

- The author identified the ideal teacher as one who would rigidly "hew to the line."

- His ideal school was a place strictly adhering to rigid routine, and repeatedly stressed in his article a need for "unquestioned obedience."

- Emily did not wish to be well liked by her students—popularity was a dangerous game that helped no one; she was going to Americanize the foreigners before they took over.

- While her parents were enormously proud, her sisters thought her a fool.

- When she was 24, she turned down a marriage proposal from

Emily forced all children to speak English.

Emily's students adhered to rigid routines and did not question her.

a solid working man so she would not have to give up teaching—as married women were expected to do.

- Now, at 36, she was an "old maid" with no prospects on the horizon.
- At least with the onset of World War I, Europe had radically reduced the number of new immigrants coming to America; now was the time to pull the welcome mat, extinguish the symbolic welcome flame on the Statue of Liberty, and deal with what they had already.
- One of the answers was kindergarten and the chance to "straighten the crooked sticks" while they were young.
- Emily had even helped several young children by changing the spelling of their names to make them more American; when one parent objected, Emily told her "it was for her own good."
- The first public school kindergarten in the United States opened in St. Louis, Missouri, in 1873, with the specific purpose of dealing with urban poverty.
- Forty-three years later, the educational reform movement had evolved, and now included the improvement of parenting skills—especially those of the urban poor immigrant mothers.

Life at Work

- Emily Strandhope knew in her bones that the Gary Plan was destined to fail in New York City, where the student population was diverse, multiple languages were embedded in the culture, and the children were less manageable.
- First established in 1906 in Gary, Indiana, the Gary Plan curriculum kept students in motion; children moved from class to class, learned automobile repair and took physical education classes.
- Superintendent William Wirt wanted his students to be busy.
- He viewed the self-sufficient family farm as containing all of the characteristics necessary for a student's development, particularly vocational training, physical activity, and character growth.
- Work and productivity characterized rural life, and Wirt believed that the rapid urbanization occurring in the early twentieth century threatened the rural values necessary for the total development of children.
- Wirt maintained that the public schools should provide an oasis to instill the values of family, work and productivity among urban students and produce an efficient, orderly society of solid, productive citizens.
- He pioneered nature classes, animal care and husbandry, an auto mechanics shop and businesses to run.
- All the space was used all the time; he called it "Work-Study-Play."
- Gary students helped to run the school from the print shop to the cafeteria.
- Wirt's goal was to "make every working man a scholar and every scholar a working man."

- Emily considered it an invitation to bedlam; children learned best when they were sitting still, facing forward and paying attention.
- When their hands got too busy, the brain went dead.
- Besides, if farming was so great, why were so many people flocking to the cities?
- There was only enough time to help the promising ones, she declared proudly, and that is how she wanted to spend her time—no matter what crazy fad some status-seeking superintendent had foisted on the public.

Children learned best when they were sitting still.

- She had learned to read people's characters at an early age.
- Now that she had taught for more than 16 years, she could spot a loser from across the room.
- Classes with 45 children were too big, and making teachers instruct in only one subject robbed the teacher of the opportunity to engage the whole student.
- While the Gary Plan was still being tested on children, it was merchandised from the newsstand, pulpit, and lecture circuit, lauded in administrative circles, and soundly praised by John and Evelyn Dewey in their 1915 book, *Schools of Tomorrow.*
- It was quickly adopted as gospel by the proponents of the scientific management movement, while *Elementary School Teacher* in 1912 published a piece titled, "Elimination of Waste in Education."
- Teaching, it said, was slated to become a specialized scientific calling conducted by pre-approved agents of the central business office.
- Classroom teachers would teach the same thing over and over to groups of traveling children; special subject teachers would deliver their subjects to classes rotating through the building on a precision time schedule.
- Early in 1914, the Federal Bureau of Education endorsed the Gary Plan, which was installed in dozens of schools in Brooklyn.
- New York City parents, especially the guardians of the city's Jewish students, staged a spontaneous rebellion against extension of the Gary Plan.
- A program that looked like a complete and comprehensive education in Gary, Indiana, looked like a government-paid training program for New York City factory workers.
- In addition, the size of the schools envisioned by the Gary Plan would reduce the personal touch and turn neighborhood schools into education factories.
- New-fangled ideas about education were not going to produce moral, educated children—only strict discipline would do that.
- And Emily was sure—without question—that she had been called to Americanize the filthy masses and protect America's shores from foreign invaders.

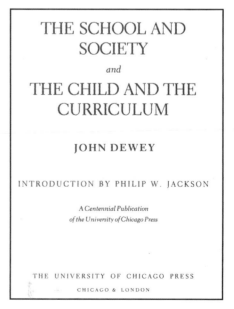

THE SCHOOL AND
SOCIETY

and

THE CHILD AND THE
CURRICULUM

JOHN DEWEY

INTRODUCTION BY PHILIP W. JACKSON

*A Centennial Publication
of the University of Chicago Press*

THE UNIVERSITY OF CHICAGO PRESS
CHICAGO & LONDON

Life in the Community: Brooklyn, New York

- The Dutch were the first Europeans to settle in the area on the western end of Long Island, also inhabited by a Native American people, the Lenape.
- The Dutch lost the area they called Breuckelen in the British conquest of New Netherland in 1664; over time, the name evolved from Breuckelen, to Brockland, Brocklin, Brookline, Brookland and, eventually, Brooklyn.
- During the first half of the nineteenth century, Brooklyn experienced significant growth along the economically strategic East River waterfront across from New York City; Brooklyn's population expanded more than threefold between 1800 and 1820, doubled again in the 1820s, and doubled yet again during the 1830s.
- Then, in 1854, the City of Brooklyn annexed the City of Williamsburg, an event that allowed Brooklyn to grow from a substantial community of 36,236 to an influential city of 96,838.
- The building of rail links, such as the Brighton Beach Line in 1878, heralded explosive growth, and, in the space of a decade, Brooklyn annexed the towns of New Lots in 1886; Flatbush, Gravesend, and New Utrecht in 1894; and Flatlands in 1896.
- The Brooklyn Bridge, completed in 1883, linked Manhattan to Brooklyn, and in 1894, Brooklyn residents voted by a slight majority to join with Manhattan, The Bronx, Queens, and Richmond (later Staten Island) to become the five boroughs of the modern New York City.
- But Brooklyn continued to maintain a distinct culture.
- Many Brooklyn neighborhoods were enclaves where particular ethnic groups and cultures predominated.
- When the Williamsburg Bridge opened in 1903, it was the largest suspension bridge in the world.
- Five years later, in 1908, the city's first subway began running trains between Brooklyn and Manhattan; in 1909, the Manhattan Bridge was completed.

Brooklyn, New York

HISTORICAL SNAPSHOT
1916

- Ebbets Field opened in 1913, and the Brooklyn Dodgers, formerly known as the Bridegrooms and then the Trolley Dodgers, had a new home
- During World War I, Paris was bombed by German zeppelins for the first time
- In the court case of *Brushaber v. Union Pacific Railroad*, the U.S. Supreme Court upheld the national income tax

- The Royal Army Medical Corps staged the first successful blood transfusion using blood that had been stored and cooled
- Tristan Tzara "founded" the art movement Dadaism
- Emma Goldman was arrested for lecturing on birth control
- The Baltimore Symphony Orchestra staged its first concert
- President Woodrow Wilson sent 12,000 troops over the U.S.-Mexico border in response to Pancho Villa leading about 500 Mexican raiders against Columbus, New Mexico, in an attack that killed 12 U.S. soldiers
- The light switch was invented by William J. Newton and Morris Goldberg
- The U.S. Marines invaded the Dominican Republic
- During the secret Sykes-Picot Agreement following the conclusion of World War I, Britain and France agreed how to divide Arab areas of the Ottoman Empire into French and British spheres of influence
- The *Saturday Evening Post* published its first Norman Rockwell cover
- President Wilson signed a bill incorporating the Boy Scouts of America
- In Seattle, Washington, William Boeing incorporated Pacific Aero Products, later named Boeing
- German agents caused the Black Tom explosion in Jersey City, New Jersey, an act of sabotage destroying an ammunition depot and killing at least seven people
- Woodrow Wilson signed legislation creating the National Park Service
- D. W. Griffith's film *Intolerance: Love's Struggle Through the Ages* was released
- Margaret Sanger opened the first U.S. birth control clinic, a forerunner of Planned Parenthood
- The 40-hour work week began in the Endicott-Johnson factories of western New York
- Woodrow Wilson narrowly defeated Republican Charles E. Hughes
- Republican Jeannette Rankin of Montana became the first woman elected to the U.S. House of Representatives
- Woodrow Wilson married Mrs. Edith B. Galt in Washington
- Oxycodone, a narcotic painkiller closely related to codeine, was synthesized in Germany
- The Summer Olympic Games in Berlin, Germany, were cancelled
- Ernst Rüdin published his initial results on the genetics of schizophrenia

Selected Prices

Automobile, Franklin Runabout $1,900.00

Campbell's Condensed Soup, Can...$0.12

Cookware, Aluminum, 25 Pieces..$10.95

Doll $0.98

Doublemint Gum, 25 Pkgs...$0.73

Food Jar, One Gallon $10.00

Rum, Bacardi, Fifth..$3.20

Theater Ticket, including War Tax $2.20

Victrola..$125.00

Woman's Hose, Artificial Silk..$0.35

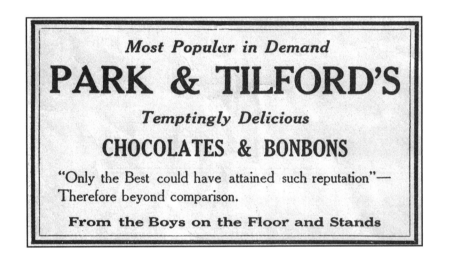

Most Popular in Demand

PARK & TILFORD'S

Temptingly Delicious

CHOCOLATES & BONBONS

"Only the Best could have attained such reputation"—
Therefore beyond comparison.

From the Boys on the Floor and Stands

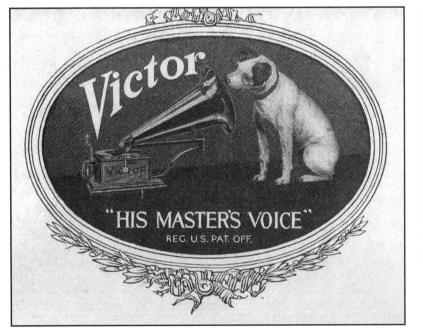

Letter to the Editor: "The Gary Plan: A Backward S," Isidore Springer, Principal, Public School 25, Brooklyn, *The New York Times*, January 6, 1915:

Very few educational movements have aroused so much interesting discussion among the public and education circles as the Gary Plan. We find editorials and newspapers advocating very strenuously its adoption. Directors of educational associations seem to find it a cure-all for all educational ills. In view of this constant agitation, I believe it is time to consider the Gary Plan, not in the light of partnership, but in view of educational history and practice, and seek to find whether this movement or plan is in harmony with the trend of educational thought during the past two decades.

I do not wish to be considered as an opponent of the Gary Plan, nor an exponent of the Ettinger or any other plan. It is simply my purpose to consider this plan in light of the various educational movements that had been discussed and proved worthy to be incorporated as a part of the educational program. I beg, therefore, to make a brief summary of the various movements that have been occupying the public attention and discussion for the past 20 years: to note, if possible, the common tendency or meaning; to examine, in such a light, the Gary Plan, and so determine whether this plan is a step forward and therefore in harmony with the main currents of educational history, or whether, on the contrary, this plan is not an about-face to what has gone before and practically nullifies educational progress for the past 20 years.

The graded class, which was called into being by the organization of large city schools, presented many problems which soon demanded solution. An attempt to solve the problem of mass instruction, with its attendant evils of disregard of the individual, was by formation of special classes, such as the "C" classes, or, English to foreign classes; "E" classes, classes which should help the backward pupils; and the ungraded classes, which would take care of the mentally unfit. A further attempt at this solution took the form of the organization in every class of groups, and the provision of the educational busy work for the members of the group not reciting.

In 1912, the Committee of Inquiry of the Board of Estimate and Apportionment began an investigation of the city schools with a view of determining wherein these schools were inefficient and uneconomical. This inquiry had been called forth by the then public discussion as to the prevalence of overage and retarded children in schools of the city of New York. It will be remembered by even the general reader that this question of overage became so heated as to, at times, assume an acrimonious stage. Conferences were called by the city superintendent, various committees were appointed, and important progress was made to solve the problem of retardation. It was seen that retarded and overage children were an economic loss to the city, and the prevention of retardation would result in a gain to the city, both economically and socially. The committee appointed by the Board of Estimate and Apportionment presented a report that showed that part-time and overcrowded classes were causes of retardation.

Continued

Letter to the Editor . . . *(Continued)*

If we examine carefully, then, these various movements which have been deemed worthy of being incorporated as part of the educational practice of the day, I think it will be found that all these agitations seemed to have a basis, whether consciously or not, in a desire that the interests of society are best served when the needs and capacity of the individual are considered and developed....

In other words, the past two decades will be known in educational history as the period of the individualization of instruction.

Now let us consider the relation of the Gary Plan to this movement. The Gary Plan calls for the economical and wider use of the school plan by providing for schools of large size and large numbers of children in each class. Fundamentally considered, the Gary Plan is a plan for part-time schools, with many of the objectionable features of part-time schools culminating by incorporating ancillary activities, such as swimming pools, libraries, shops, etc. The Gary Plan does not present a single innovation in school methods or show a new approach toward individual instruction, but is simply a departmental schedule so drawn up as to accommodate two groups of classes in one building, a scheme which was attempted for many years in New York under the part-time school.

The Gary idea, and planning for large schools, from 64 to 128 classes, creates such a tremendous educational machine that the individual is lost. The direct relation between the supervisor in the class is reduced to a minimum. The close personal touch that should exist between principal and children must disappear. The supervisor becomes administrative officer, a business manager. The school becomes an educational factory.

The greatest danger, however, is the overcrowding of classrooms. The question of the number of children in the class that makes for efficient instruction has been the subject of a number of experiments recently. It has been proved almost conclusively that the ideal class should have 30 to 35. The Gary Plan, fundamentally a plan of economy, calls for classes of 45 and more. The possibility of a close study of the individual with the view of determining his needs and issues, teaching, instead of becoming an art based on scientific pedagogy, degenerates into the peddling of information....

Finally, the Gary Plan, however attractive it may be made, is a double session plan, or part-time plan, and therefore brings with it the attendant evils of retardation and overage. Our evaluation of the Gary Plan leads us to the conclusion that it is a distinct backward step in educational history. The problems for retardation and overage which promised to be solved again become in imminent danger. The process of individualized education, the process of the study of the individual, to know his capacities, and to adopt himself to the service of society according to its needs, is halted, and American education becomes reactionary because of a policy of financial entrenchment.

"Working Women and Wages," *The Outlook*, March 29, 1913:

The employment of girls and women in factories, department stores, and all such out-of–the-home industries is comparatively new, says *Life*. "It has nearly all come with the immense development of machinery during the last two generations and with the demand for cheap labor which has followed. Commercial organizations such as has given us the department stores is a form of machinery and has come along with all the other machines," *Life* adds.

At present, girls are the cheapest article in the labor market, and are used enormously in industrial exploitation. If it gets around that girls have a potential value to society which makes it uneconomic to use them up in service and scrap them like worn-out machines, it may raise hob with a lot of industries that are run by cheap girl-power at present.

When Jane Addams enlisted in the Progressive Movement sometime prior to the formal opening of the last presidential campaign, says the Los Angeles *Express*, her critics demanded that she confine her activities to the field of accredited philanthropy. "Her answer to these critics was an appeal for relief for the victims of an industrial system that refused to take account of the right of working girls and children to food, shelter, and safety." The Progressive National platform calls for "minimum wage standards for workingwomen to provide a living wage in all industrial occupations." But the New York *Sun* warns us that "a generous concern for the underpaid or the unfortunate should not blind the great mass of us to the fact that any artificial system of wages must result in cruel displacements of labor."

"Vocational or Trade Schools," *Croonborg's Gazette of Fashions*, August 1915:

In this country, broad, educational systems are in a transitional stage. The best schools are discarding the narrow traditions of the past and are adjusting their activities to the needs of the present. The old subjects with the exception of the Three R's are being changed to meet new conditions which confront a nation of workers.

A careful examination of the records of those who have graduated from the grammar schools will show that a very small percentage enter into the High Schools, and their destination may be classified as 1) business, 2) trades, 3) domestic life. Greatly changed social conditions have transformed what were formerly parental obligations into school obligations.

These changed conditions have led the Legislatures and School Boards to revive their systems, in order that the rising generations may be enabled to fit themselves with a trade or profession which will bring them a competency ample and sufficient to take them through life.

There was a time when a boy or a girl was enabled to serve an apprenticeship with those who are qualified to teach them a trade or profession, but that is a thing of the past, and today we are made aware that the average tradesmen or mechanic has neither the inclination nor the time and patience, and more often than not, the means, to do this great work. Furthermore, we have learned that the best method of education is that laid down in our public school system where all partake of the same source and are paid for out of one common purse.

The citizen is awake to this, and with that in mind, the systems are being made over to conform with the needs of the hour. This work should have the endorsement of every employer and employee giving such assistance and aid to those interested with this work.

First, find out the ideas in the child of tender age, and then put them in operation through manual training. This may be described as the means of education through the hand and eye by work with tools and materials of industry. This will bring up the pace and attitude of those different branches of industry.

Second, this should be followed by the occasional work in higher grades with the result that when graduation takes place, the pupils are apt to go to work as soon as the law allows, and take with them what will be of use through life, viz., "the ability to earn their living no matter where they may be, and not be turned down and out and doomed as unskilled laborers."

Much thought and attention must be given to the subject during the next few years, and we as Merchant Tailors can do a large share of this work, by doing it in each locality, wherever that may be.

Yours truly,
Harry Fisher

1917: Creator of Campbell's Kids

A graduate of the Philadelphia School of Design for Women, Grace Wiederseim created the Campbell's Kids for the company's streetcar advertising campaign.

Life at Home

∞ Born October 14, 1877, Viola Grace Gebbie was the third daughter of George Gebbie, a lithographer, who was Philadelphia's first art printer and the father of seven.

∞ Gebbie had emigrated from Scotland in 1862.

∞ After landing in Quebec and working in upstate New York for a short time, he arrived in Philadelphia, listing his occupation as a bookseller in his immigration papers; he was naturalized in 1869.

∞ Gebbie was a Scots Presbyterian; Grace's mother, Mary Jane Fitzgerald, was a strict Catholic.

∞ All six of the Gebbie girls attended Catholic schools.

∞ Grace grew up in a sophisticated environment of art publishing; her father's library held many belles-lettres and Greek and Roman classics, many illustrated.

∞ Her sisters and niece, Mary A. Hays Huber, who authored a comic strip of her own, *Kate and Karl*, all had drawing talent.

∞ Growing up, the sisters learned from each other and from an older relative; drawing cartoon figures was simply another way to amuse each other.

∞ Early education was in private and church schools, including the Convent of Notre Dame, Philadelphia, and the Convent of Eden Hall, Torresdale, Pennsylvania.

∞ Grace was 15 years old when her father died in 1892.

∞ Three years later, Grace began her formal art training from the Philadelphia School of Design for Women, where Robert Henri was a faculty member.

Artist Grace Wiederseim created the "Campbell Kids."

∞ Grace Gebbie enrolled in Henri's Antiques class, described in the College Catalogue as "Drawing from the antique, artistic anatomy, composition, Crayon portraits."

∞ The school was founded to prepare women for a successful career in industrial design at a time when "No nice girl should go to art school."

∞ She married for the first time in 1900 to Theodore Wiederseim, an advertising executive for a Philadelphia streetcar company.

Life at Work

∞ Grace Gebbie Wiederseim's artistic career began at a young age, with her freelancing as a commercial artist by the time she was 18 years old.

∞ Often her drawings depicted small-fry characters with round faces, pug noses and full figures that resembled Grace herself.

∞ Campbell's, founded in 1869 by Joseph A. Campbell and Abraham Anderson, an icebox manufacturer, originally produced a line of canned tomatoes, vegetables, jellies, soups, condiments, and minced meats.

∞ Rapid industrialization of America's cities had transformed the rural economies; food was now being grown a long distance from its consumers.

∞ This demanded that less perishable foods be created, capable of surviving the ever-widening distances separating the farm from the urban dinner table.

∞ Campbell and Anderson believed that canned foods were the answer.

∞ Their cannery was located between the fertile fields near Camden, New Jersey, and nearby Philadelphia, a regional transportation hub.

∞ Campbell's was especially known for its canned beefsteak tomatoes that exemplified a blending of Anderson's tinsmith skills with Campbell's farming background.

∞ The company's big break came in 1897.

∞ Dr. John T. Dorrance, a chemist with degrees from MIT and Göttingen University, Germany, developed a commercially viable method for condensing soup by halving the quantity of its heaviest ingredient: water.

∞ Dorrance had recently returned from Europe, where he had developed his taste for Continental soups.

∞ Franco-American and the Hutchins Company were both making ready-to-eat soups with some success, while Borden had perfected the process for evaporating milk.

Campbell's began with a few products, including canned tomatoes, jellies, and soups.

∞ Dorrance reasoned that if Campbell's was able to create a condensed ready-to-eat soup, the product would be cheaper to ship, take less room in the store and could be sold for less to the busy housewife.

∞ Within a year of the invention, the Joseph Campbell's Preserve Company was selling five varieties of condensed soups, all easily identified by its can's bright red and white color scheme.

∞ Herberton Williams, a Campbell's executive, had convinced the company to adopt the look based on the crisp colors of the Cornell University football team's uniforms.

∞ By 1900, the soups were awarded the Gold Medallion for Excellence from the Paris international Exposition.

∞ Campbell's wanted to attract the attention of women who had started to become streetcar regulars.

∞ The National Biscuit Company had its recognizable figure in Zu Zu the ginger snap clown, Sunny Jim hawked the wares of Force Cereal, and Nipper the listening dog was permanently positioned at the horn of a phonograph manufacturer.

∞ At her husband's urging, Grace Wiederseim designed two plump and adorable little children for a series of streetcar ads in 1904; thus was born the "funny babies" as she called them, known to the world as the Campbell's Kids.

∞ Her rosy-cheeked, cherub-faced youngsters were an immediate hit for the streetcar line and Campbell's.

∞ Their first magazine appearance was in the *Ladies' Home Journal* in 1905.

∞ Before long, the beloved Kids were everywhere—in books, on pajamas, post-cards, games, dishes, banks, as dolls, and much more.

∞ And every American child wanted to be a Campbell's Kid.

∞ The sales of Campbell's products soared behind the creative marketing force of Grace's unsigned portraits of American life.

∞ In 1905, the company was advertising "21 kinds of Campbell's Soup—16 million sold in 1904."

∞ The year 1904 was also when Grace had made her mark on the company known for its $0.10 cans of soup.

∞ Campbell's had invested heavily in advertising since its inception, a proclivity that only accelerated with the success of the ubiquitous "Campbell's Kids."

∞ The "Kids" had no individual names, nor were they of any determinative age.

∞ There was no set number of Campbell's Kids, nor was their relationship to each other ever explained.

∞ Yet they symbolized the ideal picture of health; intuitively, Grace's pudgy tots proclaimed Campbell's Soup's quality and wholesomeness.

∞ The company received so many requests for posters of the streetcar ads featuring the Campbell's Kids, it decided to fulfill every request, charging just $0.15 per poster—the cost of postage.

∞ The first Campbell's Kids doll was issued in 1909, followed quickly by a second doll created by the E.I. Horsman Company in 1910.

∞ Two years later, both the Sears, Roebuck and Montgomery Ward catalogs featured the cute dolls.

∞ They were sold by the thousands for $1.00 each.

∞ That same year, Campbell's added the word "Soup" to its corporate name, an acknowledgement of the role soup products played in the company's profitability.

∞ Next came pictures of the pudgy toddlers on postcards and bridge tallies and even lapel pins, which declared "I am a Campbell's Kid."

∞ Under Grace's direction, the Kids began giving etiquette lessons to children and

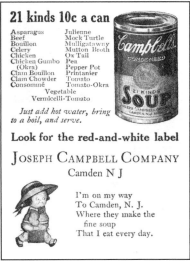

21 kinds 10c a can

Asparagus	Julienne
Beef	Mock Turtle
Bouillon	Mulligatawny
Celery	Mutton Broth
Chicken	Ox Tail
Chicken Gumbo (Okra)	Pea
	Pepper Pot
Clam Bouillon	Printanier
Clam Chowder	Tomato
Consommé	Tomato-Okra
Vegetable	
Vermicelli-Tomato	

Just add hot water, bring to a boil, and serve.

Look for the red-and-white label

JOSEPH CAMPBELL COMPANY
Camden N J

I'm on my way
To Camden, N. J.
Where they make the
fine soup
That I eat every day.

Housewives spent long hours sewing the Campbell dolls.

advised housewives on domestic matters through company-published book-lets like *Help for the Hostess.*

∞ Meanwhile, the Campbell's Kids, as depicted in company-paid advertising, were actively testing early versions of the automobile, the airplane and the telephone.

∞ Campbell's girls demanded the right to vote; Campbell's boys put on Charlie Chaplin mustaches and pretended to be in the movies.

∞ Through it all, Grace continued creating.

∞ Early on, Grace created comics for the *Philadelphia Press* entitled *Bobby Blake* and *Dolly Drake.*

∞ As her work in cartooning expanded, Grace developed *The Terrible Tales of Captain Kiddo* in collaboration with her sister, Margaret G. Hayes.

∞ In the midst of this, Grace divorced her first husband in 1911 and married Heyward Drayton III.

The Campbell Kids.

∞ While the Joseph Campbell Company was busy using Grace's clever illustrations to sell soup to the nation, Grace Drayton continued to illustrate for various magazines.

∞ In 1913, she created a new character, Dolly Dingle, to appear in the popular publication *Pictorial Review.*

∞ With her shoe-button eyes and baby curls, Dolly Dingle instantly skipped into the hearts of the American public.

∞ Soon, Grace would create more than 200 paper dolls in the Dolly Dingle series, printed in full color in the *Pictorial Review.*

∞ Dolly Dingle's adventures included traveling around the world to visit children of distant lands, including such characters as Beppo and Prince Dalim Kumar.

∞ These foreign friends came complete with costumes and symbols of their native lands.

∞ Travel by steamer had never been easier, and even the most stay-at-home Americans were often turned into globetrotters visiting Egypt, Rome, and the Holy Land.

∞ As 1916 came to a close, with the shadow of American involvement in World War I looming, Grace began to relinquish control of her "funny babies" after 12 years to concentrate on Dolly Dingle.

∞ By that time, the Campbell's Kids were so critical to the image of the company, Roy Williams of the *Philadelphia Public Ledger* was hired to take over the main drawing duties, leaving Grace more time to create.

Life in the Community: Philadelphia, Pennsylvania

∞ The history of Philadelphia, Pennsylvania, goes back to 1682, when the city was founded by William Penn.

∞ Philadelphia quickly grew into an important colonial city, and during the American Revolution was the site of the First and Second Continental Congresses.

∞ At the beginning of the nineteenth century, Philadelphia was one of the first U.S. industrial centers boasting a variety of industries.

Philadelphia was an important colonial city, and one of the first U.S. industrial centers.

∞ Following the Civil War, Philadelphia's population grew from 565,529 in 1860 to 674,022 in 1870.

∞ By 1876, the city's population stood at 817,000.

∞ A large portion of the growth came from immigrants, mostly German and Irish.

∞ In 1870, 27 percent of Philadelphia's population had been born outside the United States.

∞ By the 1880s, immigration from Russia, Eastern Europe, and Italy started rivaling immigration from Western Europe.

∞ Philadelphia's major industries of that era were the Baldwin Locomotive Works, William Cramp and Sons Ship & Engine Building Company, and the Pennsylvania Railroad.

∞ There were numerous iron- and steel-related manufacturers, including Philadelphia-owned iron and steel works outside the city, most notably the Bethlehem Iron Company.

∞ The largest industry in Philadelphia was textiles.

∞ Philadelphia produced more textiles than any other U.S. city, and in 1904, textiles employed more than 35 percent of the city's workers.

∞ The cigar, sugar, and oil industries also had an economic impact on the city.

Major department stores lined the city's Market Street.

∞ During this time, the major department stores—Wanamaker's, Gimbel's, Strawbridge and Clothier, and Lit Brothers—sprang up along Market Street.

∞ In the beginning of the twentieth century, Philadelphia had taken on a poor reputation.

∞ *Harper's Magazine* commented: "The one thing unforgivable in Philadelphia is to be new, to be different from what has been."

∞ Along with the city's "dullness," Philadelphia was known for its corruption.

∞ The Republican-controlled political machine, run by Israel Durham, permeated all parts of city government.

HISTORICAL SNAPSHOT
1917

∞ The University of Oregon defeated the University of Pennsylvania 14–0 in college football's 3rd Annual Rose Bowl

∞ German saboteurs set off the Kingsland Explosion at Kingsland, New Jersey, leading to U.S. involvement in World War I

∞ President Woodrow Wilson called for "peace without victory" in Europe before America entered World War I

∞ An anti-prostitution drive in San Francisco attracted 27,000 people to a public meeting; 200 houses of prostitution were closed

∞ The World War I Allies intercepted the Zimmermann Telegram, in which Germany offered to give the American Southwest back to Mexico if Mexico declared war on the United States; America declared war on Germany

∞ The Original Dixieland Jazz Band recorded their first commercial record, which included the "Dixie Jazz Band One Step"

∞ The Jones Act granted Puerto Ricans United States citizenship

∞ The U.S. paid $25 million for the Danish West Indies, which became the U.S. Virgin Islands

∞ The first Pulitzer Prizes were awarded to Laura E. Richards, Maud Howe Elliott, and Florence Hall for their biography, *Julia Ward Howe;* Jean Jules Jusserand received the first Pulitzer for history for his work *With Americans of Past and Present Days*; and Herbert Bayard Swope received the first Pulitzer for journalism for his work for the *New York World*

∞ The Silent Protest was organized by the NAACP in New York to protest the East St. Louis Riot as well as lynchings in Texas and Tennessee

∞ An uprising by several hundred farmers against the newly created World War I draft erupted in central Oklahoma and came to be known as the Green Corn Rebellion

∞ At Vincennes outside of Paris, Dutch dancer Mata Hari was falsely accused by the French of spying for Germany and executed by firing squad

∞ President Woodrow Wilson used the Federal Possession and Control Act to place most U.S. railroads under the United States Railroad Administration, hoping to more efficiently transport troops and materiel for the war effort

Selected Prices

Campbell's Condensed Soup, Can.. $0.12
Campbell's Tomato Soup, Can.. $0.10
Cookware, Aluminum, 25 Pieces..$10.95
Doll.. $0.98
Doublemint Gum, 25 Pkgs... $0.73
Food Jar, One Gallon $10.00
Hershey's Chocolate Bars, 24... $0.98
Instant Coffee $0.10
Pep-O-Mint Life Savers, Roll $0.05
Victrola $125.00

"Have Modern Children Lost Knack of Play, as Famous Artist Claims?" *Pennsylvania Daily News*, June 30, 1930:

Grace Drayton, world-famous artist of *Child Life*, says the sophistication of modern life has crept into even the tiniest tots until they're missing the fun that's due them, in other words, the children of today don't know how to play.

"The good 20th century slogan of 'Give them what they want' is spoiling American's childhood," Mrs. Drayton, creator of Dolly Dimples and Bobby Bounce, declared recently.

"And in the case of children as well as grown-ups the slogan should be changed, to 'Give them what they THINK they want.' For most of us think we want something when all we need is better ideas.

"Years ago toys began to get realistic and lose their play charm. Dolls stopped having great big eyes and pinky complexions. Baby dolls that used to be cunning little dimpled darlings began to look like real newborn babies. Their heads are flat, their bodies are red, and most of them have faces screwed up in an expression of disgust, dismay, and despair that should be reflected in their little girl mothers' faces when they see the trick Santa Claus played on them."

Commercial Canning Timeline

1795

Napoleon offered 12,000 francs to anyone who could devise a way of preserving food for his army and navy.

1809

Nicolas Appert of France devised an idea of packing food into special "bottles," like wine.

1810

Nicolas Appert was awarded the 12,000-franc prize from the French Government after he invented the method of preserving food through sterilization; Appert published the *Book for all Households*, which was translated into English and published in New York.

Peter Durand of England received a patent from King George III that included pottery, glass and tinplated iron for use as food containers.

1812

Thomas Kensett of England established a small packing plant in New York to can oysters, meats, fruits and vegetables in hermetically sealed containers.

1818

Peter Durand introduced his tinplated iron can to America.

1819

Thomas Kensett and Ezra Gagett started selling their products in tinplate cans.

1825

Kensett received an American patent for tinplated cans.

1830

Huntley and Palmer of England began selling biscuits and cakes in decorated cans.

1846

Henry Evans introduced dies to increase production speeds tenfold.

1847

Allan Taylor patented a machine for stamping cylindrical can ends.

1849

Henry Evans was granted a patent for the pendulum press, capable of making a can end in a single operation; production speeds improved from five or six cans per hour to 50-60 per hour.

1856

Gail Borden was granted a patent on canned condensed milk.

continued

Commercial Canning Timeline *(continued)*

1858
Ezra J. Warner of Waterbury, Connecticut, patented the first can opener

1866
E.M. Lang of Maine was granted a patent for sealing tin cans by dropping bar solder in measured drops on can ends.

J. Osterhoudt patented the tin can with a key opener.

1870
William Lyman patented a can opener with a rotating wheel, which cut along the top rim of the can.

Hinged-lid tin cans were introduced.

1875
Arthur A. Libby and William J. Wilson of Chicago developed the tapered can for canning corned beef.

Sardines were first packed in cans.

1877
The simplified "side seamer" for cans came into use.

1880-1890
Automatic can-making machinery debuted.

1892
Tobacco cans were introduced.

1894
AMS Machine Company began manufacturing locked double-seam cans.

1898
George W. Cobb Preserving Company perfected the sanitary can.

1901
The American Can Company was formed.

1909
Tuna canning began in California.

1914
Continuous ovens, used to dry inked tinplate, were introduced.

1917
The Bayer Company introduced pocket-sized cans for aspirin.

Key-opening collar-cans for coffee were introduced.

Food Brand and Product Introductions

1872
- Blackjack chewing gum

1876
- Premium soda crackers (later Saltines)

1881
- Pillsbury Flour

1885
- Dr Pepper

1886
- Coca-Cola

1887
- Ball-Mason jars

1888
- Log Cabin Syrup

1889
- Aunt Jemima pancake mix
- Calumet Baking Powder
- McCormick spices
- Pabst Brewing Company

1890
- Knox Gelatine
- Libby introduces keys on its cans of meat
- Lipton tea

1891
- Del Monte
- Fig Newtons
- Quaker Oats Company

1893
- Cream of Wheat
- Good & Plenty
- Juicy Fruit gum

1894
- Chili powder

1895
- Shredded coconut
- Triscuit

1896
- Cracker Jack
- Michelob beer
- S&W canned foods
- Tootsie Roll

1897
- Campbell's Condensed Soup

- Campbell's Tomato Soup
- Grape-Nuts
- Jell-O

1898
- Nabisco
- Nabisco graham crackers
- Shredded Wheat1899
- Wesson oil

1900
- Chiclets
- Cotton candy
- Hershey's chocolate bar

1901
- Instant coffee

1902
- Barnum's Animal Crackers
- Karo corn syrup

1903
- Pepsi
- Best Foods
- Canned tuna
- Sanka
- Sunshine Biscuits

1904
- Banana split
- Campbell's Kids
- Campbell's pork and beans
- Canada Dry ginger ale
- Peanut butter
- Popcorn

1905
- Epsicle (later Popsicle)
- Holly Sugar
- Royal Crown Cola

1906
- A1 Sauce
- Bouillon cube
- Kellogg's Corn Flakes
- 1907
- Hershey's Kisses

1908
- Dixie cup
- Hydrox
- Monosodium glutamate

continued

Food Brand and Product Introductions *(continued)*

1909
∞ Quaker puffed wheat and rice
∞ Tillamook Cheese
1910
∞ Tea bag
1911
∞ Crisco
∞ Mazola Corn Oil
1912
∞ Cracker Jack prize
∞ Hamburger buns
∞ Hellmann's Mayonnaise
∞ Life Savers
∞ Lorna Doone Shortbread Cookies
∞ Morton Salt
∞ Ocean Spray Cranberry Sauce
∞ Vitamin pills
∞ Whitman's Sampler
∞ Oreos
1913
∞ Campbell's Cream of Celery Soup
∞ Peppermint Life Savers

1914
∞ Doublemint gum
∞ Fruit cocktail
∞ Morton Salt girl
1915
∞ Processed cheese
∞ Pyrex bakeware
1916
∞ Fortune cookie
∞ Kellogg's All-Bran Cereal
∞ Mr. Peanut
∞ Orange Crush
1917
∞ Clark Bar
∞ Moon Pie
1918
∞ Campbell's Vegetable Beef Soup
∞ Contadina Tomato Sauce
∞ French dip sandwich
∞ Welch's first jam, Grapelade

"Like Washington, ere deeds are done,
With forethought I prepare.
I feed my troops on *Campbell's Soups*
So let the foe beware!"

"Liner *Cymric* Is Torpedoed off Irish Coast, Great White Star Vessel Was Bound to Liverpool from New York," *The New York Times*, May 9, 1916:

LONDON, May 8—The 13,000-ton White Star Line steamship *Cymric*, which for some time has been engaged in freight service, has been torpedoed by a German submarine, according to advices received here.

The *Cymric* left New York April 29 with an enormous cargo of war munitions. As she usually makes the voyage from New York to Liverpool in ten days, she was therefore within a day or two of her destination. It is considered probable, in the absence of definite details, that the disaster to the *Cymric* occurred off the west coast of Ireland, but whether on the northerly or southerly route cannot be stated.

The fate of the steamship is not yet known, although an early message received in London reported that the *Cymric* was sinking. The crew aboard numbered about 100 men, but the steamer carried no passengers.

The dispatch filed at Queenstown would seem to indicate that the *Cymric* had been attacked off the southwest or south coast of Ireland, possibly not far from where the *Lusitania* went down.

When the *Cymric* sailed from this port on April 29 she carried a crew of 110 officers and men and one of the largest cargoes of munitions of war yet shipped. None of these men is definitely known to be an American, although it was said unofficially yesterday that there were probably twenty Americans among them. J. J. MacPherson, the British Vice Consul in charge of shipping, said that eight new men were shipped on the *Cymric* for her last voyage, and that none of these was American. During the vessel's stay here twelve of her crew deserted and these eight were shipped to replace them.

In addition to the regular crew, three officers and two seamen of other British vessels, who had been stranded in this port, were being sent home.

According to the line's officials, the *Cymric* was in their service, denial being made that she had been taken over by the British Government. There was a very small amount of commercial goods shipped on the vessel, practically the entire cargo consisting of more than 18,000 tons of munitions and other war materiel. While no intimate details of the munitions could be obtained yesterday, the manifest showed that the *Cymric* carried:

continued

"Liner *Cymric* Is Torpedoed off Irish Coast, Great White Star Vessel Was Bound to Liverpool from New York," *(continued)*

8 cases of firearms.

13 cases of guns.

80 cases of rifles.

820 cases of Gaines (gun covers).

590 cases of primers.

2,163 pieces of forgings.

11,049 cases of empty shells.

300 cases of cartridge cases.

40 cases of aeroplanes and parts.

81 cases of tractors and parts.

62 cases of lathes.

7,554 barrels of lubricating oil.

60 cases of steel tubes.

107 cases of copper tubes.

1,768 plates of spelter.

20 cases of gun parts.

6 cases of bayonets.

624 cases of rubber boots and shoes.

220 cases of fuse heads.

7 cases of empty projectiles.

122 cases of forgings.

8,600 cases of cartridges.

6,720 cases of fuses.

18 cases of automobiles.

1,247 cases of agricultural machinery.

1,231 bundles of shovels.

831 bales of leather.

400 reels of barbed wire.

21,908 bars of copper.

1,056 cases of brass rods.

Captain F. E. Beadnell, who has been in the service of the White Star Line for more than twenty years and who was formerly commander of the *Baltic*, was in command of the *Cymric*.

The vessel was built by Harland & Wolff, Ltd., in Belfast, and was launched in 1898. She has a gross tonnage of 13,370 and is 585 feet long, with a beam of 64 feet and a depth of about 38 feet.

Never a fast vessel, the *Cymric* is rated as a ten- or eleven-day ship, and was one day from port at the time it was reported that she was sinking. For the last six weeks she has not carried passengers, and when in that service, only had accommodations for one class. The *Cymric* has had several narrow escapes from submarines during her previous voyages. On March 28, 1915, she was less than twenty miles away from the *Falaba* when the latter was torpedoed, having sailed a short time before that vessel. Captain Beadnell received the *Falaba*'s call for help, but was forced to obey the Admiralty instructions and refrain from going to her assistance.

On Sept 26, 1915, when the *Cymric* reached here, members of her crew said that she was escorted into Liverpool by a cruiser and two torpedo boats, and announced that they believed that the Hesperian was torpedoed in mistake for their vessel, as both looked alike.

When the Cymric arrived here on Jan. 23, 1916, carrying $100,000 in gold and $26,250,000 in American securities, Captain Beadnell said that he had received a wireless warning shortly after clearing from Liverpool, that there were German submarines about and warning him to be on the lookout. This warning came from the Admiral at Queenstown, and the Cymric was met by three heavily armed patrol boats, which escorted her for more than fifty miles, or to the end of the danger zone. On that trip she carried a number of passengers.

"Milledgeville Citizens Take Part in Funeral of Aged Negress," *Atlanta Constitution*, January 12, 1910:

Milledgeville, Ga., January 11 (Special). For the second time in the recent history of Milledgeville has a negro been buried with some of our most prominent white citizens acting as pallbearers. In both instances, it was the funeral of an old colored mammy; this time it was Aunt Amy Latimer. The pallbearers were Judge G. T. Whilden, recorder; Dr. J. E. Kidd, W. W. Stembridge, George H. Brantley, L. H. Andrews, C I. Morris. Last Sunday, Dr. B. J. Simmons, one of the most successful negroes of this state, was buried in this city. He had accumulated some $20,000 in the last 15 years from the practice of medicine. He represented all the most that a progressive man of his race had accomplished in this community. The white people of this city did not ignore his success. He received considerable consideration in many ways as an evidence that his ability was recognized. Quite a number of our citizens attended his funeral, but it safe to say that there is no comparison to be made of the feelings of the white people over the passing away of these two members of another race. Aunt Amy had accumulated little or nothing. It was not what she had, but what she was and what she had been that opened the hearts of her white friends and made them mindful of her even after death. Aunt Amy had been in the valley and shadow with many a good mother in this community. Her tender, humble sympathy and gentle services were not to be forgotten. Her voice had first announced the arrival of many a bouncing boy or girl. The white women sent wreaths and roses.

1919: Hair Care Business Owner

Harlem native Sarah Walker became one of the richest women in America when her hair-straightening product launched her successful hair-care business.

Life at Home

∞ Sarah Breedlove McWilliams Walker was 37 years old before she launched her hair care business that made her one of the richest black women in America.

∞ She was born on the Burney plantation in Delta, Louisiana, in 1867 to Owen and Minerva Anderson Walker, former slaves who worked as sharecroppers on the cotton plantation.

∞ Sarah was the first in her family to be born outside of slavery.

∞ The shack in which the family lived had no windows, no water, no toilet, one door and a dirt floor.

∞ Built from cottonwood logs gathered on the plantation, the cabin had a fireplace used for cooking and warmth that dominated one wall of the one-room structure.

∞ The shanty's other prominent feature was the bedstead topped with a homespun mattress sack stuffed with Spanish moss, gathered from trees in the area.

∞ Though now sharecroppers and no longer slaves, the Breedloves and young Sarah still lived in a dangerous and hostile environment.

∞ Venomous snakes and mosquitoes, the latter of which caused diseases such as malaria and yellow fever, were always lurking in the sweltering, swampy climate of the Delta.

∞ From the day she was born, Sarah Breedlove spent nearly every moment with her parents.

∞ As a baby, she was strapped to her mother's back while the latter worked in the fields.

∞ At the age of four, Sarah had learned to work alongside her parents drilling holes in the field where she carefully dropped cotton seeds.

Sarah Walker founded a successful hair care business.

∞ Each year she received material for her one sackcloth dress from the plantation owner.

∞ Sarah had no time to attend school even if one existed; instead, she learned to pick cotton and pick it well.

∞ An orphan at age seven, she had few options and was moved across the Mississippi River to Vicksburg, Mississippi, with her sister Louvenia and her sister's abusive husband Jesse Powell in 1876.

∞ Life in Vicksburg was hard for the Breedlove sisters; work was scarce and the shanty in which they lived was crowded.

∞ After the birth of Louvenia's son Willie, her husband became increasingly hostile; there was never enough money or food to sustain the growing family.

∞ To escape the volatile situation in her sister's home, Sarah became a live-in domestic worker for a white family who provided her with meals, lodging and a small salary.

∞ Too young to cook, she laid fires, dusted, mopped, washed dishes, scoured pots and pans, changed bed linens, polished boots and took in washing and ironing.

∞ In 1882, at age 14, she married Moses McWilliams and left her domestic position to work as a laundress.

∞ "I married at the age of 14 in order to get a home of my own," Sarah explained years later.

∞ In the 1880s, machines were taking over the laundry business even in Vicksburg, where a new Chinese laundry advertised the newest vacuum-type washing machines.

∞ Sarah realized she could not compete with the speed and productivity of the steam laundries, so she found other ways to please her customers: reliability and professionalism.

∞ Sarah Breedlove McWilliams gave birth to a daughter she named Lelia on June 6, 1885; just two years later she found herself a widow and a single parent.

∞ After the sudden death of her husband, who was rumored to be one of 95 black men lynched nationwide in 1888, she left Vicksburg for St. Louis, Missouri, where her brother Alexander was a barber who lived in the mostly black Mill Creek Valley section of the city.

∞ The steamboat trip up the Mississippi River consumed a week and cost $4.00 for a mother and child.

∞ St. Louis was a city filled with black entrepreneurs, including nearly 300 black barbers who shaved their white customers daily.

∞ Within a decade, the barbering business would dramatically change after King Gillette introduced the easy-to-use safety razor, designed for home use.

∞ The two-story tenement apartment in which she lived with her brother and her young daughter was a one-room affair which served as a kitchen and sleeping room.

∞ She soon took a job as a laundress.

∞ A survey by the St. Louis public schools showed that of 5,076 black parents, 22.6 percent worked as laundresses and 42.6 percent were laborers.

∞ White steam laundry owners considered blacks particularly suited to the task, given their legendary tolerance for heat and sweltering conditions.

Sarah was married at 14 years old.

∞ The work required Sarah to stand over hot tubs of boiling water all day stirring the laundry with a long stick, a task demanding great strength and stamina.

∞ Sarah was making a $1.50 a day when she began her new career in hair care products at age 35; she was living on $468 a year.

∞ After she deducted $8.00 a month for rent and $3.00 a week for food, she was left with $216 a year for fuel, medicine, transportation, clothing, church donations and incidentals.

Life at Work

∞ Sarah Breedlove McWilliams was on the edge of becoming entirely bald when she was introduced to Annie Turnbo hair care products for black women.

∞ Annie Turnbo's agents sold her brand of hair straightener door-to-door.

∞ For years, like many African-American women, Sarah had shampooed her hair only monthly, less often in the wintertime, and suffered from acute dandruff, lice, eczema and psoriasis.

∞ In addition, she had used harsh lye soaps, goose fat and meat drippings to straighten her hair; the use of lye and sulfur had burned her skin and destroyed her hair follicles, resulting in hair loss.

∞ To hide her condition, Sarah often wore a scarf in the fashion she had learned on the farm.

Sarah's job as a laundress was physically demanding.

∞ As a woman with African features, Sarah was reminded regularly that white skin and shiny straight hair were far more prized than black skin and coiled, kinky hair.

∞ Even within the black community, long, straight hair denoted prosperity and beauty, while poor hair care marked a woman as coming from the country, unsophisticated and uneducated.

∞ Eager to cure her baldness, Sarah had tried a variety of concoctions, including several that promised to simultaneously grow and straighten her hair.

∞ Most failed miserably.

∞ But after using the Pope-Turnbo Wonderful Hair Grower made by Annie Turnbo and experiencing miraculous results, Sarah joined the army of women selling Pope-Turnbo products door-to-door and quickly became their leading saleswoman.

∞ As part of her front-porch sales pitch, Sarah told the story of how the Wonderful Hair Grower had changed her life.

∞ The Pope-Turnbo promotional literature made the connection between beautiful hair and prosperity very clear.

∞ "Clean scalps mean clean bodies. Better appearance means greater business opportunities, higher social standing, cleaner living and beautiful homes," the brochure said.

∞ Turnbo's competitors hawked hair straighteners and shampoos with names such as "Kinkilla," "Kink-No-More" and "Straightine."

∞ The Boston-based Ozono promised in its advertisements to take the "Kinks out of Knotty, Kinky, Harsh, Curly, Refractory, Troublesome Hair."

∞ Some products were so patently dangerous or useless that black-owned newspapers refused to carry their advertising.

∞ Most black intellectuals, including Booker T. Washington, disdained most of the hair straightening products sold to Negro women.

∞ But that had little impact on Sarah's success in St. Louis or Denver, when she took her sales operation farther west.

∞ In July 1905, with $1.50 in savings, 37-year-old Sarah moved to Denver, where she worked as a cook for druggist E.L. Scholtz and moonlighted selling Turnbo's products.

Women had the freedom to vote.

∞ Even though the state of Colorado's entire population of 540,000 people was smaller than the city of St. Louis, Sarah smelled opportunity in the mining town..

∞ She used $0.25 of her $1.50 savings to buy business cards advertising Pope-Turnbo Wonderful Hair Grower, now available in Denver; as orders arrived, Sarah reinvested the profits in more advertising.

∞ She also found the city welcoming: women could vote and there was less racial animosity toward African-Americans, although the Chinese, whose population was increasing dramatically, were despised.

∞ Then Scholtz suggested that she provide him with a sample of the product so that it might be analyzed.

∞ Sarah was soon mixing chemicals for a formula of her own and a new company was launched, featuring a wide variety of hair care products.

∞ Later she would say that the magical concoction came to her in a series of dreams brought by a man with very specific instructions; competitor Annie Turnbo thought otherwise.

∞ In 1906, Sarah married C.J. Walker and soon developed her own line of hair care products under the name Madam C.J. Walker; that year she tripled her income to $3,652.

∞ For the next 18 months, Sarah and her husband demonstrated and sold their products throughout the South, systematically canvassing the region where 90 percent of the nation's African-Americans still lived.

∞ In each city they would contact the Baptist or African Methodist Episcopal (AME) Church, rent the best house they could afford, introduce themselves to the local black fraternal organizations, arrange a demonstration at the church or lodge, hold classes to train agents, take orders for Madam C.J. Walker's Wonderful Hair Grower and then travel to the next place.

∞ "All the people who know me are just wild about my hair," Sarah was told by one customer; "I have to take it down and let them see and feel it for themselves. I tell you, I am quite an advertisement here for your goods."

∞ In the summer of 1907, the volume of orders had become so great Sarah decided to relocate the business to Pittsburgh, whose 16 rail lines offered convenient shipping nationwide—a critical component of her mail-order business.

∞ In 1908 Madam Walker earned $6,672, nearly twice the previous year's earnings; one year later she took home $8,782, attracting the attention of the Pennsylvanian Negro Business Directory, which called her "one of the most successful businesswomen of the race in this community."

∞ When women saw her photo and heard her life story, they clamored to take her course and sit for treatments; for thousands of maids and laundresses, Sarah symbolized the progress possible even for black women without a formal education.

∞ After two and a half years in Pittsburgh, the peripatetic Madam Walker was ready to relocate again, this time to Indianapolis, where a small article in the *Indianapolis Recorder* described her as "the noted Hair Culturalist."

∞ Advertisements placed by Sarah advised women "calling for treatments will kindly bring comb, brush and two towels"; consultations were free, while scalp treatments cost $1.00 and tins of her Wonderful Hair Grower sold for $0.50 each.

∞ There she built a manufacturing facility, employed three dozen women and constructed a beautiful six-bedroom house for herself; her income exceeded $10,000.

∞ Indianapolis was the nation's largest inland manufacturing center, with banks willing to finance startup companies.

∞ The city's central location also gave Sarah access to Chicago and Cincinnati as well as to her Southern and Eastern markets.

∞ Press notices preceded her arrival in Indianapolis as she toured the city in her chauffeur-driven $1,500 Pope-Waverly electric runabout that captured lots of attention.

Success of Madam C.J. Walker led her to larger cities.

∞ Following the opening of her factory, her sales soared to $250,000 annually and Sarah could legitimately claim to have the largest black-owned company in the United States.

∞ And still she hustled for more business, attending dozens of black-sponsored conventions and gatherings to lecture on hair care.

Sarah donated $1,000.00 to build a YMCA in Indianapolis.

∞ The restless Madam Walker stayed on the prowl for new customers, always adding to her commissioned workforce of 950 saleswomen.

∞ She personally trained agents throughout the South and designed their own advertising, even as her marriage to C.J. Walker was disintegrating.

∞ She also discovered the power and pleasure of philanthropy.

∞ In 1911, when the concept of building YMCAs for black youth was in its infancy, Sarah stepped forward to accept the challenge laid down by Sears and Roebuck executive Julius Rosenwald to build a YMCA in Indianapolis.

∞ Sarah made a pledge of $1,000, setting the standard for others, especially in the white community, to match.

∞ *The Indianapolis Freeman* declared her to be "The First Colored Woman in the United States to Give $1,000 to Colored YMCA Building" and featured her in an article that was read throughout the nation.

- ∞ Next, she became involved with the National Association of Colored Women, where she met and helped support Mary McLeod Bethune, a proponent of the need for the education of black girls.
- ∞ Sarah's $5,000 donation to the NAACP Anti-Lynching Campaign was the largest in the Campaign's history.
- ∞ She also joined a delegation that traveled to Washington to protest the blight of lynching and President Woodrow Wilson's silence on the matter.
- ∞ Moved by men and women willing to better themselves, Sarah promoted a Valentine's Day charity benefit for Indianapolis's only black harpist—a 15-year-old girl who had lost her mother at the age of nine.
- ∞ In addition, she supported family members, including her daughter who worked in the business, a sister-in-law, four nieces, as well as her elder sister.
- ∞ But despite her best efforts, including her continuing business success and her philanthropic donations, African-American thought leader Booker T. Washington continued to ignore her and her company—largely because of his disdain for hair straightening products.
- ∞ As a diversion from business, Sarah often attended movies to watch silent romances, Westerns and comedies often featuring entrepreneurs who had found success.
- ∞ The movie theaters also propelled her to leave Indianapolis for New York after the owner of the Isis Theatre arbitrarily increased ticket prices from $0.10 to a quarter "for colored people"; Sarah was insulted by the racism and vowed to move.
- ∞ During 1914 and 1915, she traveled extensively, especially out West, giving lectures on hair care and making donations, particularly scholarships to worthy students.
- ∞ Often, especially in California, Sarah had more invitations for speaking engagements than she had time; everywhere she went she trained new agents, sold Wonderful Hair Grower and laid the groundwork for new business.
- ∞ By the time Sarah moved her operation to Harlem in New York City, she employed 10,000 commissioned agents, making her the largest employer of black women in America.
- ∞ They were organized into Walker Clubs that rewarded their members based on who raised the most money for charities well as the highest total sales.
- ∞ By 1916, she had real estate investments in Indiana, Michigan, Los Angeles and Oklahoma; her federal tax returns reflected that her business and real estate interests provided a net worth of $600,000.
- ∞ Even though Sarah moved into a beautifully refinished brownstone on 136 Street W. and Lenox Ave., she saw the flood of poor, undereducated women in need of her services throughout Harlem.
- ∞ For women seeking something other than domestic or factory work, Madam C.J. Walker offered an alternative: selling Walker's Scientific Scalp Treatment for the chance to earn between $15 and $40 per week.
- ∞ And for working women, making the most money of their lives, Sarah offered an urban, modern look for $1.75 per tin.
- ∞ Her goal, she said repeatedly, was to grow hair and confidence.
- ∞ Potential agents were tempted by written testimonials: "It is a Godsend to unfortunate women who are walking in the rank-and-file that I had walked. It's helped me financially since 1910. We have to been able to purchase a home and overmeet our obligations."

∞ Despite the luxury she had created for herself in New York City, Sarah spent the last three years of her life traveling for the war effort to encourage the patriotic service of Negro men and train additional agents.

∞ On several occasions her travels were halted by nervous exhaustion and failing health.

∞ For her final crusade, Sarah returned to the question of lynching, armed with a report that said 3,200 people had been lynched in America between 1889 and 1918; the vast majority were black men, and almost all were in the South.

∞ In 1918 alone, 63 African-Americans, including five women, as well as four white men, had been lynched.

∞ To that cause alone she pledged $5,000, one of many charitable gifts she made "to help my race."

Harlem, New York.

Life in the Community: Harlem, New York

∞ Until the early 1870s, Harlem had been a distant rural village of mostly poor farmers in the northern end of Manhattan Island.

∞ But at the end of that decade, with the launching of the city's first elevated train, Harlem became the city's first suburb.

∞ Soon thereafter, contractors built opulent brownstones, and Harlem became known for its many mansions.

∞ An expansion of the Interborough Rapid Transit Line brought a second wave of growth, principally fueled by Irish and Jewish families.

∞ But when the overheated real estate market collapsed in 1905, West Harlem was saturated with vacant apartments, which became the home of middle-class blacks eager to escape the tenements of the Tenderloin and the San Juan Hill districts.

∞ In 1911, the prosperous St. Philip's Episcopal Church, an all-black congregation, engineered a million-dollar real estate transaction in Harlem that became the symbolic beachhead for the black presence.

∞ Three years later, when Sarah gave her first serious thoughts to a New York move, Harlem was home to 50,000 African-Americans.

∞ A National Urban League report said, "Negroes as a whole are...better housed in Harlem than any other part of the country."

∞ At the same time, a large influx of African-Americans were being pushed from the South by the floods of 1915 and the boll weevil infestations in 1916.

∞ Many were pulled to Northern cities, including New York City, where they found employment at factory jobs left vacant when the two-decade-long flood of European immigrants was halted by the beginning of World War I.

∞ Many African-Americans found they could make as much as $8.00 a day in a Northern city after a lifetime of making only $0.40 a day farming in the South.

∞ Churches, black newspapers, YMCAs and groups like the National League on Urban Conditions sprang up.

∞ Manhattan's population topped two million and claimed bragging rights to the world's tallest buildings, from the 60-story terra-cotta Woolworth building on Broadway and Park to the 50-story Metropolitan Life Insurance Building.

African Americans found decent factory jobs in New York City.

Historical Snapshot
1919

∞ The Eighteenth Amendment to the United States Constitution, authorizing Prohibition, went into effect despite a presidential veto

∞ The World War I peace conference opened in Versailles, France

∞ Bentley Motors was founded in England

∞ The League of Nations was founded in Paris

∞ The Seattle General Strike involving over 65,000 workers ended when federal troops were summoned by the State of Washington's Attorney General

∞ Oregon placed a $0.01 per gallon tax on gasoline, becoming the first state to levy a gasoline tax

∞ Congress established most of the Grand Canyon as a National Park

∞ The American Legion was formed in Paris

∞ Eugene V. Debs entered the Atlanta Federal Penitentiary in Georgia for speaking out against the draft during World War I

∞ Edsel Ford succeeded his father as head of the Ford Motor Company

∞ The University of California opened its second campus in Los Angeles, initially called the Southern Branch of the University of California (SBUC); it was eventually renamed the University of California, Los Angeles (UCLA)

∞ Albert Einstein's theory of general relativity was tested and confirmed by Arthur Eddington's observation of a total solar eclipse in Principe, and by Andrew Crommelin in Sobral, Ceará, Brazil

∞ Congress approved the Nineteenth Amendment to the United States Constitution, which would guarantee suffrage to women

∞ The U.S. Army sent an expedition across the continental United States to assess the condition of the Interstate Highway System

∞ Race riots occurred in 26 cities

∞ The first NFL team for Wisconsin—the Green Bay Packers—was founded by Curly Lambeau

∞ Hit songs included "Swanee," "Baby, Won't You Please Come Home?" and "When the Moon Shines on the Moonshine"

∞ President Woodrow Wilson suffered a massive stroke, leaving him partially paralyzed

∞ Robert Goddard proposed using rockets to send a vehicle to the moon

∞ Conrad Hilton spent his $5,000 life savings on the Mobley Hotel in Frisco, Texas

∞ The first Palmer Raids were conducted on the second anniversary of the Russian Revolution; over 10,000 suspected communists and anarchists were arrested in 23 U.S. cities

Selected Prices

Dress Pattern $0.10

Farmland, per Acre $20.00

Gin, Fifth.. $2.15

Hair Color $0.25

Hair Curlers.. $0.25

Hair Pins $0.05

Phonograph Record.. $0.65

Radium Water, 50 24-Ounce Bottles................................. $25.00

Shampoo $0.33

Travelers' Checks $0.50

BEAUTY IS AN ASSET CULTIVATE IT

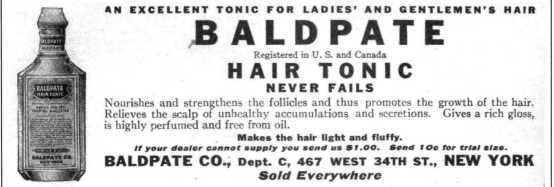

AN EXCELLENT TONIC FOR LADIES' AND GENTLEMEN'S HAIR

BALDPATE

Registered in U. S. and Canada

HAIR TONIC

NEVER FAILS

Nourishes and strengthens the follicles and thus promotes the growth of the hair. Relieves the scalp of unhealthy accumulations and secretions. Gives a rich gloss, is highly perfumed and free from oil.

Makes the hair light and fluffy.

If your dealer cannot supply you send us $1.00. Send 10c for trial size.

BALDPATE CO., Dept. C, 467 WEST 34TH ST., NEW YORK

Sold Everywhere

Advertisement, "Asbestos—the only rock on which plants thrive,"
***Leslie's Weekly*, November 15, 1919:**

Industry thrives most where waste is least. And since the development of Asbestos has gone hand in hand with the saving of heat, power and friction, this mineral of wonderful qualities has played an important part in Industrial Conservation.

It is the base of all efficient heat insulation—the necessary *other* 15% in 85% magnesia.

It is, as well, the basic material in the most efficient of friction reducing packings.

As roofings it has qualities of durability and fire-resistance that no other material can approach.

And in innumerable other forms it works miracles of industrial economy that a decade ago would have seemed impossible.

For more than half a century the Johns-Manville Company has steadily grown with the growth of industrial demand for Asbestos.

The Johns-Manville asbestos mines are the largest in the world. In the Johns-Manville plants every Asbestos product is produced under super advantages both of experience and equipment. The Johns-Manville sales-organization, operating through branches in all large cities, is an engineering organization as well, carrying a helpful practical Service, that varies to meet each new requirement but always has for its object—Conservation.

"He Deposits $500 a Month!"

The wisest among my race understand that the agitation of questions of social equality is the greatest folly, and that progress in the enjoyment of all the privileges that will come to us must be the result of severe and constant struggle rather than of artificial forcing.

—Booker T. Washington, speech, 1895 Atlanta Cotton States and International Exposition

"Ragtime Millionaire," popular at the 1904 St. Louis World's Fair:

I'm a ragtime millionaire,
I've got nothing but money to spend;
Automobiles floating in the breeze,
I am afraid I may die of money disease,
Don't bother a minute about what those white folks care;
I am a ragtime millionaire.

"Not Color but Character," Nannie Helen Burroughs, *Voice of the Negro*, 1904:

What every woman who bleaches and straightens out needs, is not her appearance changed, but her mind changed. If Negro women would use half the time they spend on trying to get white, to get better, the race would move forward apace.

"Whisky Sold as Hair Tonic. Detectives in Sailors' Uniforms Arrest Bronx Barber," *The New York Times*, March 14, 1918:

Detectives Ferguson and Albrecht of the newly created Division of National Defense of the New York Police Department put on naval uniforms yesterday and visited the barbershop of Nicholas Serra at 1019 East 170th street, the Bronx, where they found several blue-jackets having bottles filled with "hair tonic" from a large-sized demijohn.

In their turn, Ferguson and Albrecht both presented bottles and asked for "hair tonic." After making sure by sampling it that the "hair tonic" was cheap whiskey, the two detectives drew automatic revolvers and told Serra that he was under arrest. Five barbers in the shop had razors in their hands, but made no effort to interfere with the detectives. Serra was later arraigned before United States Commissioner Hitchcock and released on bail of $500.

"I wonder if he's going to be ill"

"Wealthiest Negress Dead. Mrs. C.J. Walker, Real Estate Operator, Made Fortune in Few Years," *The New York Times*, May 26, 1919:

Mrs. C.J. Walker, known as New York's wealthiest negress, having accumulated a fortune from the sale of so-called anti-kink hair tonic and from real estate investments in the last 14 years, died yesterday morning at her country estate at Irvington-on-Hudson. She was proprietor of the Madam Walker hair dressing parlors at 108 West 136th Street and other places in the city. Her death recalled the unusual story of how she rose in 12 years from a washerwoman making only $1.50 a day to a position of wealth and influence among members of her race.

Estimates of Mrs. Walker's fortune have run up to $1,000,000. She said herself two years ago that she was not yet a millionaire, but hoped to be some time, not that she wanted the money for herself, but for the good she could do with it. She spent $10,000 every year for the education of young negro men and women in Southern colleges and sent six youths to Tuskegee Institute every year. She recently gave $5,000 to the National Conference on Lynching.

Born 51 years ago, she was married at 14, and was left a widow at 20 with a little girl to support. She worked as a cook, washerwoman, and the like until she had reached the age of about 37. One morning while bending over her wash she suddenly realized that there was no prospect on her meager wage of laying away anything for old age.

She had often said that one night shortly afterward she had a dream and something told her to start a hair tonic business, which she did, in Denver, Col., on a capital of $1.25.

In a few years she had accumulated a large sum, and invested in real estate in the West and South and in New York State, nearly all the property greatly increasing in value. She then owned a $50,000 home in the northern part of this city, which some years ago she gave to her daughter, Mrs. Lelia Walker Robinson, associated with her in business.

In 1917 Madam Walker completed at Irvington, on the banks of the Hudson, a mansion which cost $250,000, and since then had made her home there. The house, which is one of the showplaces in the vicinity, is three stories high and consists of 30 or more rooms. She had installed in this home an $8,000 organ with furnishings, including bronze and marble statuary, cut glass candelabra, tapestries, and paintings, said to be of intrinsic beauty and value.

"$25 for 'Gouging' Soldier. Barber Fined for Charging $4.60 for a Haircut and Shave," *The New York Times*, May 15, 1919:

It cost Arthur Stading, a barber employed in a shop at 138 West 34th Street, $25 yesterday for the various operations he performed on the unsuspecting head of Cecil Bell, a former member of the Third Anti-Aircraft Machine Gun Battalion, who has just returned from overseas.

Bell entered the barber shop last Monday morning for a haircut, shave "and trimmings." When the barber got through he got a check for $4.60. Bell paid it without a murmur, being unfamiliar with the ways of metropolitan barbers, but his comrades told him that he had been overcharged, so he obtained a summons and Stading was arraigned in Jefferson Market Court before Magistrate Corrigan yesterday morning.

Stading protested that he was only carrying out the instructions of the proprietor, and showed an itemized bill, which included $2 for a "peroxide steaming" and $1 for "mange treatment."

"Have you got the mange?" inquired Magistrate Corrigan of Bell.

"No," replied the soldier. "I didn't ask for the treatment. I didn't know what they were putting on my head."

"This is an outrage," said the court. "That mange cure can be bought for 20 cents a gallon. We have frequent complaints of overcharging from the barber shops and it appears that they have one price for civilians and another for soldiers. If I had the proprietor here I would fine him $100. As it is, I will fine you only $25. That shave and haircut and a lot of superfluous treatment will cost you just $20.40."

Thereupon the magistrate complimented Bell on his initiative in having the barber brought to court.

"Art in Eyebrows," *The New York Times*, May 11, 1919:

Lovers in these days might well write sonnets to their ladies' eyebrows—supposing sonnets were a twentieth-century form of love-making—the eyebrows of the girl of today are works of art. The delicately arched eyebrow, which physiognomists might consider to stand for delicacy of character, means nothing now, for its owner may be naturally a beetled-browed damsel. The round-eyed expression of innocence it gives her is not the work of nature but of her hairdresser.

For the last five or six years there has been more or less experimentation with the eyebrows, but it has not been until this year that the practice of toning down eyebrows that are too heavy or giving the girl who wishes it an eyebrow which appears delicately penciled has become comparatively general. A shampoo, a hair wave and treatment of the eyebrows are now all in a single day's work. Shaving is sometimes practiced, but that is not considered as desirable as the use of a pair of tweezers. A little cold cream is put on before the operation and a simple astringent after it and it can be classed as a minor operation. Where the eyebrows are heavy and scattering, trimming up in this way gives a trim, clean look to the face without altering the expression. The delicately arched eyebrow, where it does not belong, turns the wearer into a different person. There may be a general doubt as to its being an improvement, but there are enough people who like it to make it a regular business for the hairdresser. It does not require doing very frequently; the time differs with different people. Ordinarily, eyebrows pulled with tweezers make their appearance again in about two months.

"Asks $5,000 for Red Hair. Miss Gottdank Sues When Peroxide Fails to Make Tresses Golden," *The New York Times*, January 4, 1917:

The efficacy of peroxide as a hair bleach was brought into question before Supreme Court Justice Erlanger and a jury yesterday when Miss Katie Gottdank, 16 years old, of 230 Second Street, asked $5,000 damages from Julius Kalish Inc., Grand Street druggists. Miss Gottdank complained that, in trying to transform herself from a maiden with hair of chestnut hue into a blonde, she lost part of her hair, and what she had left became brick red.

The plaintiff testified that, when she used one bottle of peroxide without seeing evidence of blondness, the manager of the drug concern advised her to try more, and she kept on doing it until she had poured the contents of five bottles over her locks. She exhibited a shoebox full of hair which, she said, had fallen out during the treatment.

The defendant contended that the plaintiff had failed to prove that the injury to her hair was due to the peroxide and offered to prove that peroxide alone could not cause the hair to become brittle and break off. Miss Gottdank's grandfather, Carl Weisshar, a barber and wig-maker, was called as an expert witness for the young woman, but he was unable to qualify because he admitted that he knew nothing about the effect of peroxide on hair. Justice Erlanger took under consideration a motion to dismiss the complaint because of lack of proof that the young woman's loss of hair was due to the peroxide.

1921: Teacher of German Immigrants

Mildred Gambon of Minneapolis required all her second grade students—German immigrants included—to act like Americans, and punished them for speaking German in her classroom.

Life at Home

- Mildred Gambon knew in her bones that the time of reckoning had finally arrived.
- After years of having to listen to her students jabber in a foreign language, English-only instruction was going to be the law of the land.
- Thirty-four states had passed, or were considering, legislation mandating English instruction.
- German was not even a pretty language; why in the world would second- and third-generation immigrants cling to something so foreign to the American way?
- Now they couldn't talk behind her back and call her ugly names.
- Nope—those days were over.
- Without English, they would never be real Americans, she knew in her heart, so why did they keep speaking German?
- Well, it was out of their hands now: English-only instruction was on the horizon and they couldn't do a thing about it.
- Mildred had lost count of the number of children who had arrived at her first-grade class without a world of English on their breaths.
- Their parents had not bothered to Americanize them properly, and proudly spoke only German at home.

Mildred Gambon taught English to German immigrants.

- She wouldn't have handicapped her three children in that way.
- She never ceased to be amazed at the way some parents treated their children.
- During the century preceding the First World War, a well-established German-language culture existed in America that formed the readership of a vast array of German-language newspapers and publications.
- America's reaction to these German-cultural enclaves was mixed.
- While some states mandated English as the exclusive language of instruction in the public schools, Pennsylvania and Ohio in 1839 were first to permit German to be used as an official alternative.
- Some public and many private parochial schools, primarily in rural areas, taught exclusively in German throughout the 1800s.
- In a few large cities, such as Baltimore, Cleveland, and Cincinnati, bilingual public schools were available.
- According to the 1910 Census, in a total U.S. population of 92 million, nine million people in the country still spoke German as their dominant language.
- Following the onset of the First World War in Europe, the power erosion of German-Americans accelerated, especially after America entered the war in 1917.
- Rocks were thrown through the windows of the Germania State Bank in South Carolina; the name "frankfurters" gave way to the term "hot dogs," and works by German composers—living and dead—were erased from the upcoming season of classical music.
- The ban of German hit some groups particularly hard.
- For the Missouri Synod Lutherans, the war and postwar hysteria discouraged the teaching of Lutheran Bible exegesis in German.
- In the words of the state legislature of Nebraska in April 1919: "No person, individually or as a teacher, shall, in any private, denominational, parochial or public school teach any subject to any person in any language other than the English language."
- One state representative spoke for many when he said, "If these people are Americans, let them speak our language. If they don't know it, let them learn it. If they don't like it, let them move…."

Life at Work

- Mildred Gambon had to admit that many German families were trying especially hard to become Americans now that the American doughboys had smashed Germany's dreams of world domination.
- German-Americans, especially immigrants, were blamed for the aggression of the German Empire; in many places, speaking German was seen as unpatriotic.
- Some families Anglicized their last names (e.g., from Schmidt to Smith, Schneider to Taylor, Müller to Miller, etc.), and German disappeared nearly everywhere from the public arena.
- Mildred was now able to fully implement her "sink or swim" program—total submersion, she called it privately—that required her first- and second-graders to learn English and how to read simultaneously.
- One of her sons had returned with scarred lungs from fighting in France during World War I— the result of German mustard gas—and it was about time someone paid for his disability.
- Her first-grade class of 27 included five German-speaking-only students—four boys and one girl.
- On day one, she placed the five in the back corner near the punishment stick and told them to be silent.
- It was their job to learn English, and she was not about to hold the rest of the class back.
- She had an obligation to her other students, and saw no reason to penalize the majority for the faults of the few.
- For two weeks, the terrified girl cried quietly and then disappeared.
- The quietest boy was moved to the slow class, and three boys learned enough to pass the first semester.
- Besides, it was obvious to anyone with a brain that humanity could be improved by encouraging the ablest and healthiest people to have more children.
- If America was to be a great nation, it needed positive breeding.

Mildred required her first and second graders to act like Americans.

- It was time more people supported Charles Fremont Dight, a physician in Minneapolis who launched a crusade to bring the eugenics movement to Minnesota.
- He believed that the state should actively improve the stock within its borders through eugenics education, changes in marriage laws, and the segregation and sterilization of what he called "defective" individuals.
- The issue of multiple languages had ricocheted across public opinion throughout American history.
- As a result of the Louisiana Purchase in 1803, the United States acquired French-speaking populations in Louisiana.
- Following the Mexican-American War, the United States acquired about 75,000 Spanish speakers in addition to several indigenous language-speaking populations.
- In 1849, the California Constitution recognized Spanish-language rights.
- In 1868, the Indian Peace Commission recommended English-only schooling for Native Americans.
- In 1878-79, the California Constitution was rewritten: "All laws of the State of California, and all official writings, and the executive, legislative, and judicial proceedings shall be conducted, preserved, and published in no other than the English language."
- In the late 1880s, Wisconsin and Illinois passed English-only instruction laws for both public and parochial schools.
- By 1896, under the Republic of Hawaii government, English became the primary medium of public schooling for Hawaiian children.

- After the Spanish-American War, English was declared "the official language of the school room" in Puerto Rico.
- In the same way, English was declared the official language in the Philippines, after the Philippine-American War.
- During World War I, widespread sentiment against the use of the German language in the U.S. included removing books in the German language from libraries.
- The Nomenclature Act of 1917 authorized the renaming of 69 towns, suburbs or areas that had German names.
- ProEnglish, the nation's leading advocate of "Official English," summarized their belief that "in a pluralistic nation such as ours, the function of government should be to foster and support the similarities that unite us, rather than institutionalize the differences that divide us. Therefore, ProEnglish "works through the courts and in the court of public opinion to defend English's historic role as America's common, unifying language, and to persuade lawmakers to adopt English as the official language at all levels of government."

- Another "Official English" advocate group, U.S. English, summarized their beliefs: "The passage of English as the official language will help to expand opportunities for immigrants to learn and speak English, the single greatest empowering tool that immigrants must have to succeed."
- Most states had enacted laws that required the use of English in specific situations, such as in testing for occupational licenses.
- During World War I, the idea of expulsion as an alternative to assimilation was frequently discussed; in 1916, the National Americanization Committee, which had close ties to the Federal Bureau of Education, sponsored a bill in Congress to deport all aliens who did not apply for citizenship within three years.

Life in the Community: Minneapolis, Minnesota
- Minneapolis and Saint Paul are collectively known as the "Twin Cities," and fostered a rivalry during their early years, with Saint Paul being the capital city and Minneapolis becoming prominent through industry.
- The term "Twin Cities" was coined around 1872 after a newspaper editorial suggested that Minneapolis could absorb Saint Paul.
- Residents decided that the cities needed a separate identity, so people coined the phrase "Dual Cities," which later evolved into "Twin Cities."
- Minnesota became a part of the United States as the Minnesota Territory in 1849, and became the thirty-second state on May 11, 1858.
- After the upheaval of the Civil War and the Dakota War of 1862, the state's economy started to develop when natural resources were tapped for logging and farming.

- Minnesota became an attractive region for European immigration and settlement as farmland.
- Minnesota's population in 1870 was 439,000; this number tripled during the two subsequent decades.
- The Homestead Act in 1862 facilitated land claims by settlers, who regarded the land as being cheap and fertile.
- The railroad industry, led by the Northern Pacific Railway and the Saint Paul and Pacific Railroad, advertised the many opportunities in the state and worked to get immigrants to settle in Minnesota.
- In 1890, the railroad, now known as the Great Northern Railway, started building tracks through the mountains west to Seattle. Other railroads, such as the Lake Superior and Mississippi Railroad and the Milwaukee Road, also played an important role in the early days of Minnesota's statehood.
- The power of the waterfall first fueled sawmills, but later it was tapped to serve flour mills.
- In 1870, only a small number of flour mills were in the Minneapolis area, but by 1900, Minnesota mills were grinding 14 percent of the nation's grain.
- Advances in transportation, milling technology, and water power combined to give Minneapolis dominance in the milling industry.
- Technological improvements led to the production of "patent" flour, which commanded almost double the price of "baker's" or "clear" flour, which it replaced.
- Pillsbury and the Washburn-Crosby Company became the leaders in the Minneapolis milling industry.

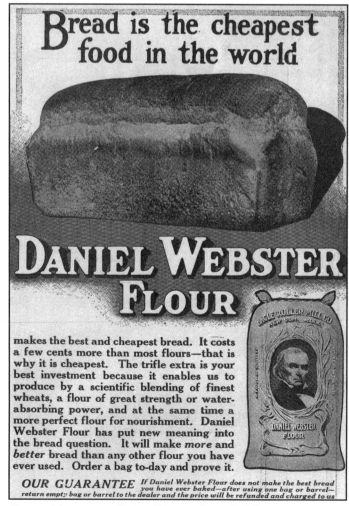

Competition among flour mills was fierce in Minnesota.

HISTORICAL SNAPSHOT
1921

- The first religious radio broadcast was heard over station KDKA AM in Pittsburgh, Pennsylvania

- Henry E. Huntington bought Gainsborough's *The Blue Boy* and Reynolds' *Portrait of Mrs. Siddons* for $1 million

- Books included John Dos Passos' *Three Soldiers*; *Symptoms of Being Thirty-Five* by Ring Lardner; *The Outline of History* by H.G. Wells, and *Dream Psychology* by Sigmund Freud

- The DeYoung Museum opened in Golden Gate Park, San Francisco

- The Mounds candy bar, Eskimo Pie, Betty Crocker, Wise potato chips, Band-Aids, table tennis, and Drano all made their first appearance

- The Allies of World War I Reparations Commission decided that Germany was obligated to pay 132 billion gold marks ($33 trillion) in annual installments of 2.5 billion

- The Emergency Quota Act was passed by Congress, establishing national quotas on immigration

- Cigarette consumption rose to 43 billion annually despite its illegality in 14 states

- A Massachusetts jury found Nicola Sacco and Bartolomeo Vanzetti guilty of first-degree murder following a widely publicized trial

- The first vaccination against tuberculosis was administered

- Researchers at the University of Toronto led by biochemist Frederick Banting announced the discovery of the hormone insulin

- Adolf Hitler became Führer of the Nazi Party

- Harold Arlin announced the Pirates-Phillies game from Forbes Field over Westinghouse KDKA in Pittsburgh in the first radio broadcast of a baseball game

- Sixteen-year-old Margaret Gorman won the Atlantic City Pageant's Golden Mermaid trophy to become the first Miss America

- Literature dealing with contraception was banned; a New York physician was convicted of selling *Married Love*

- Centre College's football team, led by quarterback Bo McMillin, defeated Harvard University 6-0 to break Harvard's five-year winning streak

- Albert Einstein was awarded the Nobel Prize in Physics for his work with the photoelectric effect

- During an Armistice Day ceremony at Arlington National Cemetery, the Tomb of the Unknowns was dedicated by President Warren G. Harding

- Hyperinflation was rampant in Germany after the Great War, where 263 marks were needed to buy a single American dollar

Selected Prices

Alarm Clock..$2.50

Apartment, Sacramento, Five Rooms $70.00

Bathing Suit, Men's $5.00

Carpet Sweeper...$5.00

Crib $17.50

Handkerchiefs, Dozen..$1.80

Hen...$25.00

Hotel Room, New York, per Day $3.00

Poker Set, 100 Chips...$6.25

Typewriter, Remington..$60.00

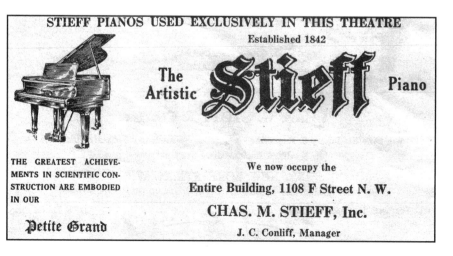

We have room for but one language in this country and that is the English language, for we intend to see that the crucible turns our people out as Americans, of American nationality, and not as dwellers in a polyglot boarding house.

—President Theodore Roosevelt, 1907

Letter to the Editor, *Forward*, New York, 1907:

Worthy editor,

Allow me a little space in your newspaper and, I beg you, give me some advice as to what to do.

There are seven people in my family, parents and five children. I am the eldest child, a 14-year-old girl. We have been in the country two years and my father, who is a frail man, is the only one working to support the whole family.

I go to school, where I do very well. But since times are hard now and my father earned only five dollars this week, I began to talk about giving up my studies and going to work in order to help my father as much as possible. But my mother didn't even want to hear it. She wants me to continue my education. She even went out and spent $10 on winter clothes for me. But I didn't enjoy the clothes, because I am doing the wrong thing. Instead of bringing something in the house, my parents have to spend money on me.

I have a lot of compassion for my parents. My mother is now pregnant, but she still has to take care of the three borders we have in the house. Mother and father work very hard and they want to keep me in school.

I am writing to you without their knowledge, and I beg you to tell me how to act. Hoping you can advise me, I remain your reader.

ANSWER: The advice to this girl is that she should obey her parents and further her education, because in that way she will be able to give them greater satisfaction than if she went out to work.

"Courses Offered in the Second Term, State Normal School," Virginia Teacher, March 1921:

113. Elementary Education

The first 25 days of the course will be based on LaRue's *The Science and Art of Teaching*. Topics: nature teaching; method as determined by the nature of the child; method as related to the teacher; teaching as conditioned by subject matter; administrative organization of schools; specific school problems, the first day, the daily program, children's textbooks, attendance, grading, children's monthly reports, promotion; how to get acquainted with school and regulations; how to get needed repairs and equipment; how to get a school library; monthly and term reports to superintendents; duties of teachers to children, the community, politicians, to fellow teachers, to superior officers, to profession.

116. Methods in Reading for Primary Grades, First Year

General topic for term, the introduction of the child to reading. Topics: meaning of reading; elements in reading, problems in beginning reading, the best approach, units of reading, material. (A.) children's poems, (D.) stories, (C.) nature, (D.) plays and games, (E.) school activities; mechanical elements, essentials in phonic study, drill, devices; relationship between oral and silent reading in first grade; critical study of primers and first readers, including those which are on the State list.

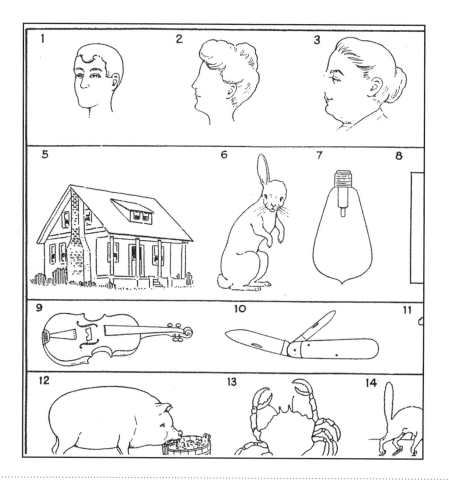

"English Only in Schools," *Mills County Tribune* (Glenwood, Iowa), March 20, 1919:

The bill of Representative Dean of Osceola County requiring that English only be used in the public and private schools of Iowa for elementary instruction passed the House Wednesday noon by a vote of 63 to 40, after being amended to permit the use of foreign language for religious worship or instruction. The bill as passed reads as follows:

"That the medium of instruction in all secular subjects taught in all of the schools, public and private, within the state of Iowa should be the English language, and the use of any language other than English in secular subjects in said schools is hereby prohibited; provided, however, that nothing herein shall prohibit the teaching and studying of foreign languages as such, as part of the regular school course in any such school in all courses above the eighth grade."

EDITORIAL: America or Americans, *Twin Falls Daily News* (Idaho), February 9, 1919:

The action by the Idaho Legislature in adopting Sen. John D. Robertson's bill making it a felony to hoist, carry or display a red flag or other emblem of anarchy, will be endorsed by every loyal citizen of the state and nation who believes with the late Col. Theodore Roosevelt that there should be in this country only one flag and one language.

It is in order now for the Idaho lawmakers to follow the lead of Washington and some other states in adopting a measure to abolish the study of the German language from our public schools. No adequate excuse has existed for the introduction of the study of German into our curriculums. It is of service and value to not one in 100 pupils who are instructed in it, and it enfolds no treasure of literature, or sciences that would suffer its translation into the English language. Only upon easygoing, unsuspecting Americans could the harbor for enemies within our boundaries have a potent implement for insidious propaganda afforded by the foreign tongue has been imposed.

If a foreign language must be taught in our schools, let it be Spanish, which is the language of the southern hemisphere, or French, which is so thoroughly established that, reports tell us, many of the sessions incidental to the peace conference are carried on in that tongue. At least some satisfactory reason must be found than can be induced to the language of the enemy.

Another thing, and one perhaps more essential than the eradication of the red flag for the elimination in the enemy tongue, is a necessity for greater caution and care being used in the selection of the textbooks in our schools. A cursory examination of some of the textbooks here for use in American schools yielded the trail of the propagandist.

Determined and relentless warfare must be waged against foreign graphs in the development American ideals wherever they are to be found.

America must be made safe for Americans.

1927: Jazz Singer & Dancer

Born into poverty, blues singer Florence Mills of Harlem became known as the "Queen of Happiness" for her beautiful singing voice and innovative jazz and tap dancing moves.

Life at Home

- Known as the "Queen of Happiness," Florence Mills, born Florence Winfrey, captivated the public with her enchanting song "I'm a Little Blackbird Looking for a Bluebird," and her stage performances in *Shuffle Along*.
- The song was created by Tin Pan Alley songwriter George W. Meyer, who also wrote the music for the songs "For Me And My Gal," "If You Were the Only Girl in the World" and "Where Did Robinson Crusoe Go With Friday on Saturday Night?"
- When Florence died at age 31, more than 150,000 people came to her funeral; kings sent flowers, Americans—black and white—mourned, and Harlem came to a standstill.
- The youngest of three daughters of John and Nellie Winfrey, Florence was born into extreme poverty on January 25, 1895.
- Both her parents were born in slavery in Amherst County, Virginia, and worked in the tobacco industry.
- When tobacco farming tanked, the family moved from Lynchburg, Virginia, to Washington, DC, where her father worked as a day laborer and her mother took in laundry.
- Both parents were illiterate.
- Florence grew up in the streets of Goat Alley, Washington, DC's infamous slum, where she demonstrated natural gifts as a singer and dancer which brought her to the attention of an international audience.

Blues singer Florence Mills was one of the most prominent entertainers of the 1920s, before her untimely death at age 31.

- At age five, she won prizes for cakewalking and buck dancing, and was awarded a bracelet by the wife of the British ambassador for entertaining her international guests from the diplomatic corps.
- By age seven, Florence was a regular performer in theaters and private homes, and rapidly developed a name for herself on the vaudeville and burlesque circuits.
- Some of her earliest roles were as a "pickaninny" or "pick" in white vaudeville, then as a sister act on the black popular entertainment circuit.
- It was a tough life for a small child, playing small venues all over the country, putting in endless hours rehearsing, and traveling.
- The high point of her childhood was her appearance in the road company production of Bert Williams and George Walker's *Sons of Ham*, in which she sang "Miss Hannah from Savannah."

Florence's parents were born into slavery and the tobacco industry.

- As a result, the traveling white vaudeville team of Bonita and Hearn hired her.
- Florence then moved to New York with her mother and sisters, and by age 14 had organized a traveling song-and-dance act with her sisters known as the Mills Sisters.
- From then on, Florence Mills was the name she used instead of Florence Winfrey.
- Florence was innovative: skilled in all varieties of jazz and tap dance, she was especially renowned for her "acrobatic" and "eccentric" dancing, some of which she learned from her husband U.S. "Slow Kid" Thompson, the originator of "slow motion dancing" and one of the earliest practitioners of Russian dancing or "legomania."
- Her lessons in tap came from her close personal friend Bill "Bojangles" Robinson when she was living in Chicago in 1916-1917.
- At the same time, new opportunities were developing for the artistic black community—long a victim of humiliating discrimination and Jim Crow laws.
- White promoter Otto Heinemann and his company OKeh Records were struggling to get established; Heinemann was willing to try anything when he asked Cincinnati's young black singer Mamie Smith to cut a record.
- For the premiere recording, Smith sang "That Thing Called Love" and "You Can't Keep a Good Man Down," backed by the house orchestra—to keep the record from sounding "too colored."
- This was quickly followed by the recording of "Crazy Blues" and "It's Right Here for You (If You Don't Come Get It, 'Taint No Fault of Mine)," this time accompanied by a five-piece black band known as the Jazz Hounds.
- The result was impressive and possibly the first actual blues recording by a black artist with black accompaniment.
- Within a month, 75,000 copies of "Crazy Blues" had been sold in Harlem record shops; in only seven months, national sales topped one million copies.
- Mamie Smith and her band were pure gold; everything they recorded sold immediately.
- Smith made more than $100,000 in recording royalties alone; in addition, she was making between $1,000 and $1,500 a week in the large theaters in New York and Chicago.
- As a result, record companies scrambled to sign new blues singers; Columbia Records even bragged that it had "more colored artists under exclusive contract than any company today."
- Black Swan Records, produced for Pace Phonograph Company of New York, advertised itself as the "only genuine colored record. Others are only passing for colored."

Life at Work

- Florence Mills's big break came in 1921 with *Shuffle Along*, the off-Broadway hit show that introduced syncopated song and dance to White America.
- Florence luxuriated in the music and lyrics by black songwriters Noble Sissle and Eubie Blake.
- When the show opened in New York, it was an immediate hit.
- Writer Langston Hughes believed *Shuffle Along* initiated the Harlem Renaissance and inaugurated the decade when "the Negro was in vogue."
- Florence's uninhibited singing and dancing stunned the audiences.
- She was paid $125 per week.
- "We were afraid people would think it was a freak show and it wouldn't appeal to white people," said Eubie Blake. "Others thought that if it was a colored show, it might be dirty."
- Sissle and Blake first joined forces as members of the World War I "Hell Fighters" Jazz Band of the 369th Infantry led by James Reese Europe.

The off-Broadway hit Shuffle Along *introduced syncopated song and dance to white America.*

- They transformed an old sketch named "The Mayor of Jimtown" into a lively musical featuring hit songs such as "I'm Just Wild About Harry" and "Love Will Find A Way," combined with energetic dancing.

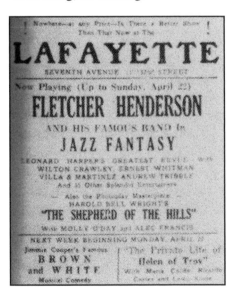

- After *Shuffle Along*, Lew Leslie, a white promoter, hired Florence to appear in a revue at the Plantation Club that featured Florence and a wide range of black talent including visiting performers such as Paul Robeson.
- The show—which charged a $3 admission—introduced white audiences to the ebullient, fast-paced rhythms of black music.
- Edith Wilson and the Jazz Hounds served as Florence's house orchestra.
- Florence was paid $200 per week.
- In 1922, the nightclub act was converted into a Broadway show called *The Plantation Revue*, and Florence was positioned to become one of the first black female performers to break into the racially restricted show business establishment.
- She was paid $500 per week, for no fewer than 35 weeks a year.
- Civil rights crusader Bert Williams believed that Florence would accomplish more than he had: "This is once where the pint is better than the quart."
- Florence did it all: she sang blues, "hot jazz" and ballads, plus she danced, acted, and was an accomplished comedian and mime.
- Luminaries such as Jelly Roll Morton, James P. Johnson and Willie "The Lion" Smith helped dub her "The Queen of Jazz."

- Composer Irving Berlin said that if he could find a white woman who could sing like Florence, he would be inspired to write a hit a week.
- Writer James Weldon Johnson wrote, "The upper range of her voice was full of bubbling, bell-like, bird-like tones. It was a rather magical thing Florence Mills used to do with that small voice in her favorite song, 'I'm a Little Blackbird Looking for a Bluebird,' and she did it with such exquisite poignancy as always to raise a lump in your throat."
- But that did not change the fact that the set where she performed was fashioned like a pre-Civil War southern plantation featuring a large watermelon slice, whose seeds were electric lights, and a bandanna-coifed black woman flipping pancakes.
- Nonetheless, Florence brought the house down with the naughty song, "I've Got What It Takes But It Breaks My Heart to Give It Away"; Edith Wilson performed her showstopper in the same revue: "He May Be Your Man, But He Comes to See Me Sometimes."
- Florence was reported to be the "highest-salaried colored actress on the American stage."
- The Great White Way was not solely white anymore.
- On opening night for the second, 1922-1923 season, the audience included Charlie Chaplin, Irving Berlin and Irene Bordoni.
- One of the new songs added to the second season, "Aggravatin' Pappa," became a radio hit—by Sophie Tucker; by the end of the year, a dozen female singers had recorded Florence's new song.
- When Sir Charles B. Cochran began looking for attractions for the London stage, he invited the Plantation Company to the Pavilion in the spring of 1923, despite a newspaper headline reading, "Nigger Problem Brought to London."
- The show that Cochran devised was called *Dover Street to Dixie*; it was staged with an all-English cast in the first half and featured Florence and the Plantation cast in the second half.
- It proved so successful that issues of race were soon forgotten.
- The Prince of Wales was said to have seen the show numerous times; Florence became so popular that she was to London what Josephine Baker was to Paris.
- Composer Duke Ellington wrote a musical portrait for Florence called "Black Beauty"; she was featured in *Vogue* and *Vanity Fair* and photographed by Bassano and Edward Steichen.
- In 1923, upon her return to New York, Florence received an invitation to appear in the Greenwich Village Follies annual production—the first time a black woman was offered a part in the major white production.
- She was also offered a contract to join the Ziegfeld Follies but turned it down.
- She elected to stay with Lew Leslie to create a rival show with an all-black cast.
- She felt she could best serve her race by providing a venue for an entire company of actors and singers; "If in any way I have done anything to lift the profession, I am unconscious of it, and it was done only for love of my art and for my people."
- Florence enjoyed a triumphant return.
- Her popularity knew no bounds—she was now an international star.
- Florence and her husband bought a new house—a five-story brownstone in the middle of Harlem—and furnished it with carpets imported from China and a music box that played records without rewinding.

Florence and her husband filled their new house with fine and expensive furnishings.

- *Dover Street to Dixie*, which had thrilled in London, became *Dixie to Broadway* when it opened in New York on October 29, 1924, with a brand-new slate of songs.
- Advertisements proclaimed Florence to be "The World's Greatest Colored Entertainer: The Sensation of Two Continents."
- One critic said, "The vital force of the revue proceeds from the personality of Miss Mills."
- In 1926, when Leslie produced *Blackbirds*, Florence had achieved her goal of creating a major all-black revue with the opening of this show at the Alhambra Theatre in Harlem.
- The show then moved to London's Pavilion Theatre and enjoyed 276 performances.
- Exhausted from so many successive performances, Florence went to Germany to rest, but her condition did not improve.
- In 1927, she returned to New York to a royal welcome and decided to have an appendectomy she had put off for too long.
- On October 24, 1927, she entered the hospital for the operation.
- One week later, on November 1, 1927, Mills died.
- She believed that every white person pleased by her performance was a friend won for the race.
- Florence Mills's funeral brought over 150,000 people out onto the streets—the largest such gathering in Harlem's history.

Life in the Community: Harlem, New York
- Harlem was defined by a series of boom-and-bust cycles, with significant ethnic shifts accompanying each one.
- Black residents began to arrive en masse in 1904, the year the Great Migration began by Southern blacks fleeing poverty, few opportunities and aggressive enforcement of discriminatory Jim Crow laws.
- In the 1920s, the neighborhood was the locus of the "Harlem Renaissance," an outpouring of artistic and professional works without precedent in the American black community.

Manhattan Field and the Harlem River.

- Harlem earned a reputation as the Mecca for jazz and blues.
- Venues like the Cotton Club and the Apollo Theater made stars out of entertainers such as Duke Ellington, Cab Calloway, Ella Fitzgerald, James Brown, Michael Jackson, and D'Angelo and Lauryn Hill.
- Harlem began life as a haven for European immigrants and citizens of European descent.
- Initially attracted by its fertile soil and location, Dutch settlers founded Harlem in 1658.
- Governor Peter Stuyvesant named the town Nieuw Haarlem after a city in Holland—British immigrants renamed it Harlem.
- Harlem's economy in the early days was based on agriculture until the railroad and Manhattan street system brought industry to the area.
- A housing boom in the 1890s produced an overabundance of houses, and by 1903, builders opened their doors to tenants of all colors and races.
- Entrepreneur Philip Payton and his company, the Afro-American Realty Company, actively recruited black families and almost single-handedly ignited the migration of blacks from their previous New York neighborhoods, the Tenderloin, San Juan Hill and Hell's Kitchen.
- The move by black residents to northern Manhattan was partially driven by fears of anti-black riots that had occurred in the Tenderloin in 1900 and in San Juan Hill in 1905.
- By 1910, Harlem had a population of around 500,000, of whom 50,000 were African-American and 75,000 were native-born whites; the rest were immigrants from Ireland, Germany, Hungary, Russia, England, Italy and Scandinavia.
- During World War I, expanding industries recruited black laborers to fill new jobs.
- By 1920, central Harlem was 32.43 percent black; between 1920 and 1930, 118,792 white people left the neighborhood and 87,417 blacks arrived.

School band in Harlem.

HISTORICAL SNAPSHOT
1927

- The first transatlantic telephone call was made from New York City to London
- The U.S. Federal Radio Commission began to regulate the use of radio frequencies
- In New York City, the Roxy Theater was opened by Samuel Roxy Rothafel
- The first armored car robbery was committed by the Flatheads Gang near Pittsburgh, Pennsylvania
- The Great Mississippi Flood of 1927 affected 700,000 people in the greatest natural disaster in U.S. history
- Philo Farnsworth transmitted the first experimental electronic television pictures
- *To The Lighthouse* was completed by Virginia Woolf
- The Academy of Motion Picture Arts and Sciences was founded
- Saudi Arabia became independent of the United Kingdom under the Treaty of Jedda
- Charles Lindbergh completed the first solo non-stop transatlantic flight from New York to Paris in the single-seat, single-engine monoplane *Spirit of St. Louis*
- Mount Rushmore was dedicated with promises of national funding for the carving
- The Columbia Phonographic Broadcasting System, later known as CBS, was formed and went on the air with 47 radio stations
- A treaty signed at the League of Nations Slavery Convention abolished all types of slavery
- *The Jazz Singer*, a movie with sound, ushered in "talkies" in the United States
- Leon Trotsky was expelled from the Soviet Communist Party, leaving Joseph Stalin with undisputed control of the Soviet Union
- The Holland Tunnel opened to traffic as the first Hudson River vehicular tunnel linking New Jersey to New York City
- After 19 years of Ford Model T production, the Ford Motor Company unveiled the Ford Model A, available in four colors, with a self-starter
- The musical play *Show Boat*, based on Edna Ferber's novel, opened on Broadway—one of 268 plays on Broadway
- Harold Stephen Black invented the feedback amplifier
- Sears, Roebuck and Co. distributed 15 million catalogues to American homes
- Arthur H. Compton won the Nobel prize in physics for his discovery of wavelength change in diffused x-rays
- The Voluntary Committee of Lawyers was founded to bring about the repeal of Prohibition in the U.S.
- Hit songs included "Ol' Man River," "Can't Help Loving Dat Man," "I'm Looking Over a Four Leaf Clover," "The Best Things In Life Are Free" and "Me And My Shadow"
- The world population reached two billion

Selected Prices

Bath Salts, Jar $1.50
Bathtub...$29.95
Cigarette Case $11.72
Dress, Crepe..$49.50
House Paint, Gallon..$2.15
Incense and Burner $1.00
Iron..$4.45
Oil Heater $4.95
Refrigerator, Ice Capacity 100 Pounds....................$56.95
Toilet...$6.95

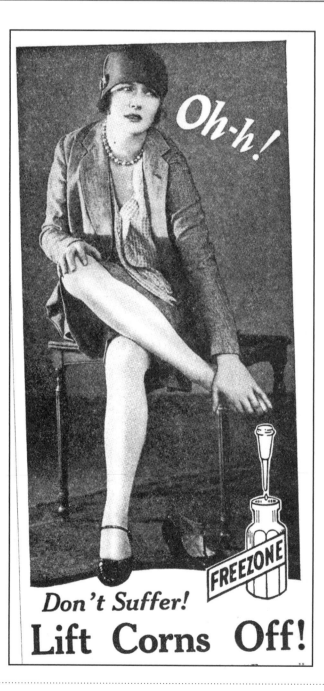

It's Radio Time!

Fine programs on the air tonight and every night. More big special events coming soon.

You'll own a Radiola eventually; why not enjoy it now?

RADIOLAS as low as $78. Convenient terms arranged.

The Corley Company inc.

THE PATRICIAN GOLD BAND REED SUITE, No. A-100—*created by* A. L. RANDALL COMPANY

A NEW and delightful American Period in furniture is now established. Randall Gold Band Reed and Fibre Furniture has achieved new beauty, cheer, and comfort for every room in the home. An infinite variety in design and covering affords selection to harmonize with every decorative scheme and architectural style, even to the pure colonial. In suites, dav-enport beds, or single pieces, Randall Gold Band Reed and Fibre Furniture strikes a new note of charming grace in the home, the club or the hotel.

See it at the better stores or write for our book, "The New American Period in Furniture."

A. L. RANDALL COMPANY, Chicago, Illinois

RANDALL *Reed&Fibre* Furniture

TRADE MARK

THE ONLY FURNITURE TRADE-MARKED WITH THE GOLD BAND OF QUALITY
Copyright 1923, by A. L. Randall Company

Florence Mills's description of her own dancing:

"I never know what I'm going to do. Perhaps I'm the black Eva Tanguay: I don't know. And I don't care. I just go crazy when the music starts and I like to give the audience all it craves. I make up the dances to the songs beforehand, but then something happens, like one of the orchestra talking to me, and I answer back and watch the audience without appearing to do so. It's great fun. Something different at every performance. It keeps me fresh. Once in New York, I fell down, literally. Did the split. The audience thought I was hurt. I heard some sympathetic expressions. So I got up and started to limp comically. It got a burst of applause. Then I winked and that got another hand. So the producer ran backstage and asked me to keep it in. I did for several nights, but other things happened and I forgot. I never remember just what to do. I'm the despair of stage managers who want a player to act in a groove. No groove for me. The stage isn't large enough for me at times. But it is during the midnight performances that I let out the most. We all do. Not that we overstep the conventions, you understand. But it's just the feeling that it's after hours, I suppose. And we whoop it up."

"Colored Singing," *Variety*, **1923:**

Colored singing and playing artists are riding to fame and fortune with the current popular demand for "blues" disc recordings, and because of the recognized fact that only a Negro can do justice to the native indigo ditties, such artists are in great demand.

Mamie Smith is generally credited with having started the demand on the Okeh Records. Not only do these discs enjoy wide sales among the colored race, but they caught on with the Caucasians. As a result, practically every record-making firm, from the Victor down, has augmented its catalog with special "blues" recordings by colored artists.

As a result of this "blues" boom and demand, various colored publishers are prospering. Perry Bradford and the Clarence Williams Music Company are among the representative Negro music men cleaning up from the mechanical royalties with the sheet music angle negligible and almost incidental. No attention to professional plug-in is made; these publishers are concentrating on the disc artists.

"Paul Robeson on the English Stage," Marie Seton, 1958:

Something happened in Drury Lane Theatre on the night when *Show Boat* opened there in April 1928. Leaving their five-month-old Pauli in the care of Essie's mother, Mrs. Goode, the Robesons had sailed again for England for Paul to appear as Joe the Riverman in Jerome Kern's musical of Edna Ferber's Book. Robeson sang "Ol' Man River" and everything else in *Show Boat* was forgotten by both audience and critic. His was the voice of a man speaking in the midst of a puppet-show. The audience did not realize that what moved them was the fusion point where real experience is transmitted into art.

As the weeks passed and more and more people went to see *Show Boat*, the impact of Robeson was like a chain reaction. The first to "discover" him were the smart Mayfair set who went in search of the latest sensations and inaugurated new fashions, but soon the country people who came to London for the "season" were telling their friends to go to Drury Lane. Then, the elderly, frowsty people who go to matinees began talking about Robeson's voice. Soon, the "intelligentsia" of Bloomsbury and Chelsea, who seldom deigned to go to musical comedies, were discussing him. At last, young people from Chapham and Tooting could be heard talking about him from the tops of buses on the Underground. Like many other Londoners, I went to see *Show Boat* shortly after it opened. I remembered Robeson's name from reviews I had read of *Emperor Jones*, but I not seen the O'Neill play.

When the curtain rose, *Show Boat* began to unfold according to the traditional mechanics of romantic musical plays. Only the setting was different—a steamboat plying the Mississippi River. Jerome Kern's musical was pleasant and tuneful; but 24 hours after leaving the theatre, the romance based on Edna Ferber's story faded in one's memory. It was surprising that there seemed to be no dramatic buildup to the entrance of this new star, Paul Robeson.

The scene shifted from the ship's steamboat to the wharf. Suddenly, one realized that Joe the Riverman was Robeson, the silent figure endlessly toting bales of cotton across the stage—a black man with grayed hair moving about like a walk-on, an extra—in life, the man who is overlooked because his role is to work and serve. Suddenly, Joe the Riverman filled the whole theatre with his presence. Robeson began to speak in song. He sang about the flowing Mississippi, and the pain of the black man whose life is like the eternal river rolling towards the open vastness of the ocean:

> "Tote that barge and lift that bale,
> You get a little drunk
> And you lands in jail.
> I gets weary and sick of trying,
> I'm scared of livin' and feared of dyin'…."

> The expression on Robeson's face was not that of an actor.
> "I'm scared of livin' and feared of dyin'…."
> The pathos of Robeson's voice called up images of slaves and
> overseers with whips. How had a man with such a history risen?

The creation of jazz by black artists gave this country a language that it was searching for, and gave it a rhythmic identity, and so it makes perfect sense that the composers would use this inventive language and rhythm for the theater.
—George C. Wolfe, director

"The Turn of the Tide, What's Going On in the World," *McCall's*, April 1928:

Under the masterly direction of Prince Otto von Bismarck and Count Helmuth von Moltke, the greatest military machine ever devised by man sprang into being during the '60s and '70s of the last century. In order to make this machine yet more potent, a doctrine of "blood and iron" was proclaimed. The State—social, political, and industrial—was molded into a compact organization for its successful enlargement by means of war, and Denmark, Austria and France successively succumbed to its irresistible force.

Bismarck, in his wisdom, halted to allow his Fatherland to consolidate and become accustomed to the sudden change from a kingdom to an empire. What might have happened had Bismarck lived and held his power no man may say, but the direction of German affairs fell into less capable hands and disaster came. The deed was done and the consequences were to follow.

While in Germany war had become glorified, the balance of Europe was terrified by this new menace to peace. Fear led the Great Powers, in self-protection, to form an iron circle around the dreaded borders of this great military state.

Through the bitterness of defeat in the Great War came salvation, not alone for the German people, but, perhaps, for Europe as well. Today, the tide has turned in the nation formerly the protagonist of ruthless and relentless war, and has become an earnest advocate of disarmament and peace. Germany has gone so far as to announce her intention to accept the optional clause in the World Court making obligatory peaceful settlements of international disputes of judicial character. In Geneva, the voice of Germany constantly is raised on behalf of every measure having for its purpose conciliation as opposed to war. The terms of reproach heretofore leveled at her by opponents are now used against other nations less yielding in the cause of disarmament and compulsory arbitration.

It may be of interest for Americans to know that the wartime ambassador from Germany to the United States—Count von Bernstorff—is one of the foremost leaders in the movement for general disarmament and the abolition of war. Together with the German Minister for Foreign Affairs—Gustafson Stressemann—he has represented Germany at the League of Nations' conferences and has gone further than almost any delegate in his demands for measures to secure the peace of Europe.

Those, from long habit, still critical of Germany see in her a sinister purpose. It is said that she is restrained by the Versailles Treaty from having a large army and navy, and that she is actuated not so much by a change of heart as by a change in circumstance. But it may well be that the German people are awakened to the truth that peace has more possibilities for their welfare than war, and if they lead as fervently in the direction of peace as they formerly did for war, the ultimate result will not alone be of advantage to Germany, but to all of Europe as well.

There is a tremendous urge among the small nations of Europe against war. This feeling has never been so strong as now. The fear of another catastrophe like that of 1914-1918 hangs over them. This dread is one of the most marked results of the Great War. It is a shadow that can never be wholly lifted during the lives of this generation.

While the forebears of the American people came almost wholly from Europe, it is difficult for us to think in terms of Europeans. From the dawn of history until now, the fear of aggressive wars has haunted them. From the tribal raids of the misty past all through the ages, we find the same story. Civilization has hewn its way with the sword. The cost, the misery, and the mental anguish are beyond computation. And in our day of supposed enlightenment came the greatest holocaust of all. The madness of it is just beginning to make an impression sufficiently strong to give the world hope.

1928: Purity for Silent Films Advocate

Carla Mufson, convinced that Hollywood was corrupting America's youth, monitored movies for the Woman's Christian Temperance Union from her hometown of Topeka, Kansas.

Life at Home

- The last of 11 children, Carla Mufson almost died at birth.
- Barely breathing when she emerged from the womb, she was set aside while the doctors concentrated on saving the life of her 38-year-old mother.
- From that day forward, everyone agreed, Carla was serious, determined and headstrong.
- Early on she decided that a quality education was more valuable than a farmer-husband, who might harbor a love of intoxicating drink like her father.
- So, despite much discouragement and little support at home, Carla finished 11 years of school, then one year in a secretarial college.
- Although she had never unchained her secret dream of holding a four-year degree from a large university, she remained easy to work with, even on those days when she was convinced that she was smarter than most of the men at the County Bank, where she had worked for 20 years.
- At 48, she knew that attending more college was an opportunity that had passed for her.
- So she spent several afternoons each week counseling scores of promising young girls to pursue a degree in something other than an MRS.
- She had come to believe that even in the liberated 1920s, men still sang most of the songs and women were still expected to hum along in unison.

Carla Mufson monitored movies for the Women's Christian Temperance Union.

Carla and her 10 siblings grew up in the family home in Topeka, Kansas.

Many young women were counseled by Carla to pursue college careers.

- It was while working with the smartest girls in Topeka, Kansas, that she discovered the power of moving picture shows for good and for evil.
- Several very well-raised, bright young ladies would skip tea and conversation to view the latest movie.
- At first, Carla consented to attend the movies as a way to understand this rudeness.
- Her first film experience was *Safety Last,* a wild comedy featuring Harold Lloyd, a lovable country hick with an ingratiating smile and large black glasses.
- Because it was a six-reeler, Carla had enough time to calm her nerves in a darkened room full of strangers and grow accustomed to the flashing titles, organ music, and even the comical plot.
- Halfway through, she realized that she had laughed herself silly.
- What a marvelous experience! How intoxicating an influence on the souls of impressionable girls, she thought!
- That was four years earlier.
- Since then she had feasted on the scenes in *The Hunchback of Notre Dame,* was horrified by the murder of Trina in the movie *Greed,* reveled in the comedy of Charlie Chaplin's *The Gold Rush* and walked indignantly out of a dozen others.
- She was convinced that immoral content in movies should be edited out before young people could see it.
- Besides, if movies in general were not controlled, their romanticized thirst for blood would soon get us into another Great War.
- Many of the patrons she saw in the movies were working class people whose emotions, she felt, were more easily inflamed and who shouldn't be wasting their money anyway.
- After she presented herself to the Woman's Christian Temperance Union and stated her goals, the women there were more than happy for her to monitor movies that came to town.
- They gave her a list of movie guidelines issued by the movie industry, knowing that right-thinking people understood that these rules were just the beginning.
- As a result, Carla began to watch three movies each week, but never with the young ladies she had sworn to protect.
- What would she do and what would her young girls think if an unmarried couple engaged in a passionate embrace?
- It would just be too embarrassing.
- Everyone knew, thanks to the new science, that film images moved straight from the eyes to the brain without interpretation or conscious reflection.
- People simply couldn't help their reactions to movies.

- This was why, in addition to her monitoring activities, she sought out the movie house managers when they came to the bank.
- Someone needed to tell them that morality was more important than money.

Life at Work

- Carla had seen enough movies to know that the alarm bells could not be rung loudly enough, especially with movies like *The Wind*.
- She sat watching it in a darkened theater, surrounded by men and women she had never met, whose voices were stirred to a fevered pitch by an unmarried couple in a kissing embrace that lasted forever.
- Moreover, she was astonished that actress Lillian Gish would act that way, especially when she was driven to commit the sin of murder within the harsh landscape of Texas.
- Without a doubt, the film was capable of unleashing ungovernable spirits among the youth and must be edited if it was to be shown in Kansas again.
- The ladies of The Woman's Christian Temperance Union had been lobbying to restrict the violence and immorality of films for years; obviously, more needed to be done.
- It was a big job; since 1912 nearly 10,000 films had been produced.
- In the 1890s, the Woman's Christian Temperance Union had become interested in the monitoring of movies at the dawn of the fledgling industry.
- Their first goal was the creation of pure motion pictures useful for educational and moral reform, followed quickly by the establishment of an appropriate environment within the nickelodeons and picture palaces.
- They even got an agreement from Thomas Edison that his movie studio would not promote drinking scenes.

Harry Landgon and Joan Crawford in TRAMP, TRAMP, TRAMP, *1926.*

- Mostly, they had to settle for modifying the content of immoral or wrongheaded films distributed in their region.

Lars Hanson and Lillian Gish in THE WIND, *1928.*

- Many fretted that movies were taking the place of the mother as the primary teacher of young children.
- This fear had been vindicated many times.
- After the 1910 Johnson-Jeffries heavyweight fight, in which black boxer Jack Johnson defeated the "Great White Hope," champion Jim Jeffries, race riots erupted all over the United States.
- Immediately, the WCTU noted that "unwonted elation among the more ignorant negroes" caused poor whites to become violent.
- They petitioned Congress to ban films of prize fights; officials in nine states and in scores of racially mixed cities quickly barred prize-fight films.
- By 1912, a federal law banned films featuring a prize fight.
- In 1915 the U.S. Supreme Court ruled that motion pictures could be regulated because they were not art, but instead were created only to make money; thus, the First Amendment did not apply.
- Kansas created a Board of Review shortly thereafter.
- The WCTU also worked community by community in an attempt to convince theater owners not to show unwholesome movies, especially on Sundays, when many children where there.
- In 1922, as a direct result of the reformers' work, the Motion Picture Producers and Distributors Association hired Will Hays, a former Postmaster General, to regulate itself.
- After a short period of elation, the WCTU was soon disappointed because he would not meet their level of purity.
- Many came to believe that the $150,000 annual salary paid to Will Hays was a down payment on his soul.
- In 1925 the National WCTU disbanded the Department of Purity in Literature and Art and formed a Motion Picture Department to get censorship laws passed.
- That's when Carla Mufson became involved in screening movies.
- Though at first it was intimidating to say a movie needed changes, she knew that her work had an impact in both Topeka and a five-state region.
- Because of the high cost of changing movie prints, one state's demand for change often resulted in the distribution of the edited version to the entire region.
- In Kansas, the film reviewers often deleted drinking scenes from movies, making the Kansas WCTU a powerful voice for censorship.
- These deletions also included scenes of white women in physical danger at the hands of villainous, leering Chinamen, German spies, and Mexican assaulters.
- Chastity was paramount and views of miscegenation were to be avoided, as were scenes of black men looking at a woman's figure.
- Nationally, the WCTU was focused on federal regulation, especially when movies with sound were being advertised.
- Without a doubt, every decent woman in America knew that the movie moguls would try to make more money by adding dirty words to their films.
- Movies filled with debauchery were destroying America's image abroad, said President-Elect Herbert Hoover after a Uruguayan editor told him that American movies were a "main obstacle to the proper understanding and esteem between the United States

and the South American countries" because they showed only "cabaret life, the sins of society and crime."

- After all the horrors of World War I, every tool, including movies, should be marshaled toward the cause of international alliances to prevent another devastating war.

Life in the Community: Topeka, Kansas

- The Kansas State Board of Review took an active role in monitoring the moral content of films, forcing movie makers to adapt the film state by state, based on the sensitivities of the state boards.
- After watching the 1920 film *The House of Blindness,* the Kansas board of review demanded that the pivotal scene in which Dora was forced to drink poison be removed.
- As a result, that section of the film wound up on the cutting room floor, although it was untouched in other states.
- Kansas was not alone in its attempt to control the potentially "debasing" new medium; Virginia, Maryland, New York, Pennsylvania and Ohio, as well as approximately 50 cities, had also created boards to review and censor movies.
- Approval guidelines included the review of subtitles, spoken dialogue, songs, other words or sounds, folders, posters and advertising materials to make sure they were "moral and proper."

Al Jolson in THE JAZZ SINGER, *1927.*

The Kansas State Board of Review had the power to remove movie scenes that "corrupted morals."

- When the board viewed films, it was looking for moving picture shows that were "cruel, obscene, indecent or immoral, or such as tend to debase and corrupt morals."
- All films to be shown in the state had to be first passed by a board of three censors.
- This board had the power to remove any scenes that corrupted morals.
- The board also could ban films completely.
- After being reviewed and edited, the film was tagged with a unique serial number that allowed it to be distributed for public showing.
- Penalties for showing unauthorized films ranged from a substantial fine to 30 days in the county jail.
- The State Board of Review met with substantial resistance from the motion picture industry, which was forced to pay for both the initial review and any subsequent edits.
- Motion picture companies spent significant sums lobbying legislators and trying to influence local elections.
- Some movie houses even recruited and then promoted anti-censorship candidates on the big screen itself.
- The first rating system was started in Chicago in 1914, when an official restricted attendance to the movie *The Scarlet Letter* to only persons over the age of 21.
- Even though women in the community supported its showing, the official frankly admitted that he did not know how to explain to his 15-year-old daughter the meaning of the scarlet "A," which was so central to the plot.
- Afterward, movies restricted to those over 21 were issued "pink permits."

Gloria Swanson in QUEEN KELLY, *1928.*

Historical Snapshot
1928

- The German dirigible *Graf Zeppelin* landed in Lakehurst, New Jersey, on its first commercial flight across the Atlantic
- Future President Herbert Hoover promoted the concept of the "American system of rugged individualism" in a speech at New York's Madison Square Garden
- Three car mergers took place: Chrysler and Dodge; Studebaker and Pierce-Arrow; and Chandler and Cleveland
- The Boston Garden officially opened
- The first successful sound-synchronized animated cartoon, Walt Disney's *Steamboat Willie* starring Mickey Mouse, premiered
- The first issue of *Time* magazine was published, featuring Japanese Emperor Hirohito on its cover
- Peanut butter cracker sandwiches, Rice Krispies, Philco radios, quartz clocks and the Oxford English Dictionary all made their first appearance
- North Carolina Governor O. Max Gardner blamed women's diet fads for the drop in farm prices
- *Bolero* by Maurice Ravel made its debut in Paris
- George Gershwin's musical work *An American in Paris* premiered at Carnegie Hall in New York
- The clip-on tie was created
- Real wages, adjusted for inflation, had increased 33 percent since 1914
- Nationalist Chiang Kai-shek captured Peking, China, from the communists and gained United States recognition
- Aviator Amelia Earhart became the first woman to fly across the Atlantic Ocean from Newfoundland to Wales in about 21 hours
- The first all-talking movie feature, *The Lights of New York,* was released
- Fifteen nations signed the Kellogg-Briand Peace Pact, developed by French Foreign Minister Aristide Briand and U.S. Secretary of State Frank Kellogg; also known as the Pact of Paris, it outlawed war and called for the settlement of disputes through arbitration
- Actress Katharine Hepburn made her stage debut in *The Czarina*
- Scottish bacteriologist Alexander Fleming discovered the curative properties of the mold penicillin
- *My Weekly Reader* magazine made its debut
- Ruth Snyder became the first woman to die in the electric chair

In its first show to feature a black artist, the New Gallery of New York exhibited works by Archibald Motley

- Bell Labs created a way to end the fluttering of the television image
- President Calvin Coolidge gave the Congressional Medal of Honor to aviator Charles Lindbergh

Selected Prices, 1928

Airplane, Single-Engine	$2,000.00
Automobile, Packard Convertible	$4,150.00
Baby's Play Suit	$0.59
Chauffer's Outfit	$78.00
Comforter, Lamb's Wool Filling	$21.00
Hot Water Heater	$55.00
Luggage, Set of Five	$26.95
Maternity Corset	$6.95
Toothpaste, Listerine	$0.25
Tuition and Board at Cornell University, per Year	$1,400.00

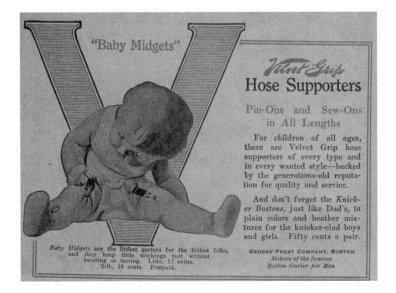

Film Industry Timeline

1889

Thomas Edison was commissioned to build the first motion-picture camera, named Kinetograph.

1894

The Edison Corporation established the first motion picture studio, nicknamed the Black Maria, a slang expression for a police van.

The first Kinetoscope parlor opened at 1155 Broadway in New York City, where spectators were charged $0.25 to watch films.

1895

In France, Auguste and Louis Lumière invented the Cinématograph, a combination camera and projector.

1896

The Edison Corporation produced *The Kiss*, the first film ever made of a couple kissing; the short 20-second film, with a close-up of a kiss, was denounced as shocking and pornographic by some early moviegoers and caused the Roman Catholic Church to call for censorship.

1901

With the arrival of electricity, Broadway set out white lights stretching from 13th to 46th Streets in New York City, inspiring the nickname "the Great White Way."

1903

Edison Corporation's Edwin S. Porter directed the first Western, *The Great Train Robbery*, which lasted 12 minutes.

The courts ruled that a film did not have to be copyrighted frame-by-frame, but rather that it could be covered in its entirety by one copyright submission.

1904

The 35 mm film width, and a projection speed of 16 frames per second, were accepted as an industry standard.

1905

In Pittsburgh, the first movie theater opened, named a nickelodeon after the cost of admission, a nickel, and the Greek word for theater, "odeon."

1906

The Keith organization began converting vaudeville theatres into motion picture houses and encouraged parents to send their children there after school was over.

1907

The Saturday Evening Post reported that daily attendance at nickelodeons exceeded two million nationwide.

The Chicago Daily Tribune denounced nickelodeons as firetraps and tawdry corrupters of children.

The first film makers arrived in Los Angeles, which offered a favorable climate and a variety of natural scenery.

Bell and Howell developed a film projection system.

1908

About 9,000 nickelodeons were open across the country.

1909

The New York Times published the first movie review, a report on D. W. Griffith's *Pippa Passes*.

The New York Times coined the term "stars" for prominent movie actors.

continued

Timeline . . . *(continued)*

1909

The Motion Picture Patents Company (MPPC) was formed and became a holding company for all of the patents belonging to the film producers who were members.

The MPPC agreed to submit its films to the Board of Censorship, which had been established by the People's Institute of New York City to head off state and local censorship efforts.

1910

Thomas Edison introduced his kinetophone, which made talkies a reality more than a decade later.

The first movie stunt featured a man jumping from a burning balloon into the Hudson River.

1911

Pennsylvania became the first state to pass a film censorship law.

Credits began to appear at the beginning of motion pictures.

1912

Photoplay debuted, the first magazine for movie fans.

Motion pictures began to move out of nickelodeons and into real theaters as movies became longer, more expensive and featured more stars.

1913

America's first feature-length film dealing with sex was *Traffic in Souls,* a "photo-drama" exposé of white slavery at the turn of the century in New York City.

1914

Charlie Chaplin played the role of the Little Tramp, his most famous character.

Winsor McCay released *Gertie the Dinosaur,* the first animated cartoon.

1915

D. W. Griffith released *The Birth of a Nation,* which introduced the movie techniques of the narrative close-up and the flashback; the film ignited controversy over its depiction of the Civil War and Reconstruction era.

The Bell & Howell 2709 movie camera allowed directors to film close-ups without physically moving the camera.

The Board of Censorship became The National Board of Review.

Movie sex goddess Theda Bara's role as a worldly, predatory woman who stole a married man away from his wife and child in *A Fool There Was* earned her the title of "the wickedest woman in the world."

A Free Ride, the earliest-known silent stag or pornographic film, was released.

1916

Charlie Chaplin signed on with Mutual Studios for an unprecedented $10,000 a week.

continued

Timeline . . . *(continued)*

1917

The Lincoln Motion Picture Company, the first African-American-owned studio, was founded.

1919

Charlie Chaplin, D. W. Griffith, Douglas Fairbanks Sr., and Mary Pickford established United Artists in an attempt to control their own work.

Felix the Cat first appeared.

Cecil B. DeMille's film *Male and Female* included a semi-nude scene of actress Gloria Swanson disrobing in preparation for a lavish bath in a sunken tub.

1920

Actress Yvonne Gardelle appeared naked during a Garden of Eden prologue sequence in *The Tree of Knowledge*.

1921

The Sheik, starring Rudolph Valentino, was released.

Charlie Chaplin produced *The Kid*, which featured Jackie Coogan.

Comedian Roscoe "Fatty" Arbuckle was arrested for the alleged rape and murder of 25-year-old actress Virginia Rappe during a wild party in San Francisco, reinforcing the public's image of Hollywood as scandalous.

1922

Hollywood censored itself by creating the Motion Picture Producers and Distributors of America (MPPDA).

Movie director William Desmond Taylor was found murdered in Los Angeles with a bullet in his back; dozens of potential starlets were suspects.

1923

German shepherd Rin Tin Tin became film's first canine star.

Cecil B. DeMille's first version of *The Ten Commandments* featured the largest set ever constructed in movie history up to that time; the "City of the Pharoah" was 120 feet tall and 720 feet wide, with massive Egyptian statuary weighing one million pounds.

The Hollywood sign, spelled HOLLYWOODLAND, was built for $21,000.

1924

Walt Disney created his first cartoon, *Alice's Wonderland*.

1925

Ben-Hur, which cost a record-setting $3.95 million to produce, included a segment featuring rows of bare-breasted flower girls dancing in a pageant procession as they tossed flowers to the crowd lining the street.

The first in-flight movie, a black-and-white silent film titled *The Lost World*, was shown in a WWI converted bomber during a 30-minute flight near London.

1926

Leading man John Barrymore starred in *Don Juan* with Mary Astor and Estelle Taylor, a film that included 127 kisses.

continued

Timeline . . . (continued)

1927

Popular vaudevillian Al Jolson marked the end of the silent movie era when he spoke the line: "Wait a minute. Wait a minute. You ain't heard nothing yet!" in *The Jazz Singer.*

A sound-on-film system called Movietone was developed in which the sound track was placed onto the actual film next to the picture frames, rather than on a separate synchronized disc, as in Vitaphone.

Motion picture film became standardized at 24 frames per second.

The Hays Office issued a memorandum, "Don'ts and Be Carefuls," a code of decency telling the studios 11 taboos to avoid, including profanity, "licentious or suggestive nudity," illegal traffic in drugs, any inference of sex perversion, white slavery, miscegenation, sex hygiene and venereal diseases, scenes of actual childbirth, children's sex organs, ridicule of the clergy, and willful offense to any nation, race or creed.

Paramount released a film titled *It* featuring sexy starlet Clara Bow as a lingerie salesgirl, who soon became known as the "It Girl."

1928

Walt Disney introduced *Galloping Gaucho* and *Steamboat Willie*, the first cartoons with sound.

The Academy Awards were awarded for the first time; *Wings* won Best Picture.

"Movies Foster Crime, Canon Chase Charges," *The New York Times,* January 2, 1928:

The motion picture screen for the past 25 years has been a school of crime, according to Canon William S. Chase, who took the affirmative in a debate at the Ingersoll Forum, 113 West Fifty-seventh Street, last night on "Should There Be Federal Supervision of Motion Pictures?" Dr. Wolf Adler upheld the negative.

"Did you notice that in his account of his dreadful crime, Hickman said it was his habit to see motion pictures daily?" Canon Chase asked.

He said the movies were a menace to the children of the world, and to the furtherance of world peace. By representing American life in a false light, he charged that motion pictures aroused the antagonism of other countries and created much ill feeling by portraying foreigners as villains and Americans as heroes.

Because moving pictures are run by interests with the sole purpose of making money, he urged that the government supervise the movies so as to further the best moral and political interests of the public.

Dr. Adler said he had no admiration at all for movies, but he did not believe there should be censorship or supervision, because all censorship was bad.

"If you start censoring motion pictures, you will soon begin regulating literature, the stage and every other activity of life," he said. "The movies do not influence morals for the worst. They merely reflect morals as they are by showing the realities of life. If they are immoral, they are an effect of immorality, not a cause. Federal control will not be of any use because it cannot abolish things as they are."

If the movies have tended to foster warlike tendencies, he continued, it is because they are used by every nation as propaganda against other nations.

Popular Movies:

1927			1928
The Jazz Singer	Camille	The Last Command	Street Angel
Wings	The Way of All Flesh	The Racket	The Singing Fool
Napoleon	Love	The Crowd	The Mysterious Lady
The King of Kings	The Unknown	Sadie Thompson	The Circus
Flesh and the Devil	The General	Steamboat Willie	The Docks of New York
The Night of Love			

The movies constitute much of the education of many. . . . Shall this (movie industry) education produce graduates of the type of the 14-year-old murderers, of the Leopold-Loeb super-intellectuals criminal breed, of the flapper who is a potential mother and may reproduce more of the same, of the foreigner, the fool and the traitor who consider the Eighteenth Amendment a joke and laugh at the Stars and Stripes?

—Harriett Pritchard, director of the WCTU Department of Purity in Literature and Art, 1925

We believe mechanically perfect, artistically beautiful, morally clean motion pictures are one of the best-known means of preserving and transmitting to future generations the best ideals and institutions of our generation. We believe the best in the life of any people presented by the silver screen to the whole people will popularize that best. . . .The motion picture industry through constant production of the worst has failed to transmit the best. We believe federal regulation is required to change the situation.

—Speech by Maude M. Aldrich of Oregon, chairperson of the
National Woman's Christian Temperance Union's
Department of Motion Pictures, November 21, 1928

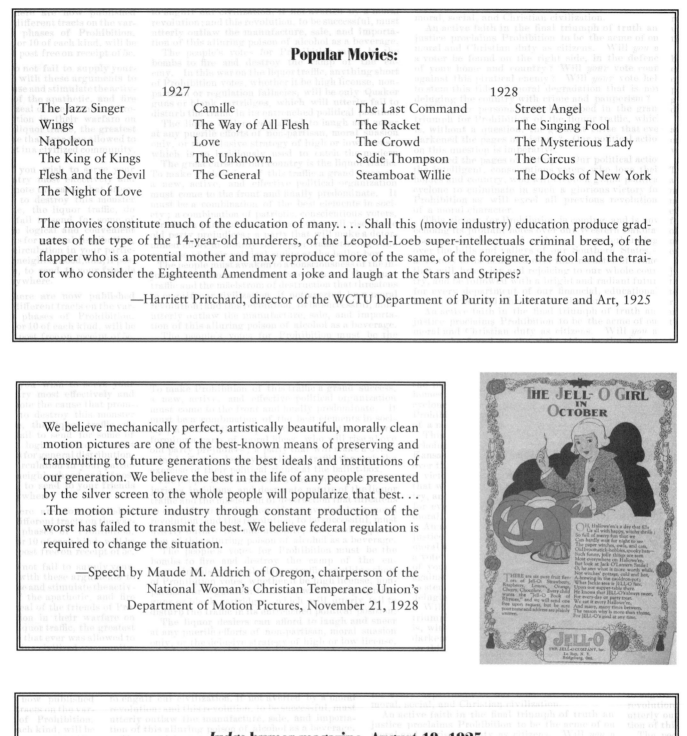

***Judge* humor magazine, August 19, 1925:**

And now they say a thing is "Catzy!" meaning marvelous, wonderful, etc. Where do these expressions come from, anyway? It's obvious "Catzy" descended from "The Cat's Meow," but what massive brain originated that—and why? Maybe the bird that names Pullman cars started all these expressions.

"Film Men Attack Morality Drives," *The New York Times*, January 28, 1928:

Various suggestions to improve the motion picture and means to overcome the exhibitor's difficulties in obtaining desirable films were discussed yesterday at the fourth annual Conference of the National Board of Review of Motion Pictures at the Waldorf. Delegates representing Better Film Committees condemned morality drives and the like and urged intelligent selection of pictures as opposed to the methods of reform groups.

Discussing a community plan to encourage the high type of motion picture, Professor Leroy E. Bowman of the Department of Social Science at Columbia [said] that the best pictures "can be evolved only through intelligent selection by the interested public and not through censorship, moralism or monopoly. It is the plan of common effort and of common sense as opposed to the narrow, moralistic and monopolistic plans that have been proposed in various quarters."

Professor Bowman praised the National Board of Review as the only extensive agency in the country on which reliance can be placed to express the interest and wishes of the public "because it approaches the problem from a natural, human point of view without bureaucratic censorship."

"The only thing the matter with movies is the audience," Ida Clyde Clarke, lecturer and author, told the delegates.

"The American public is tabloid-minded and has the tabloid soul," she said. "It wants a stimulant for its atrophied or undeveloped emotions and prefers to take it undiluted and unrefined."

Dr. Horace M. Kallen of the New School for Social Research traced the history of censorship, the psychological foundation of which, he said, is based on the three emotions—"fear, greed and a sense of shame."

Morality drives, he declared, originate in the emotions of persons who feel certain that the evils they would correct will not hurt them but might have a harmful influence on others.

Dr. Kallen warned the audience "to make sure that the vague and uncertain rules laid down are not used as instruments of competitive oppression within the industry.

"Certain types of prohibitions," he said, "have been recently adopted by the picture industry which involve affecting the sense of shame with respect to sex. It is necessary to make sure that there is not some psychopathic influence in the work of censorship within the industry."

Countries we have long characterized as 'heathen' have taken active steps against American movies. Even Turkey has forbidden children under 15 years of age to attend movies 'to protect young Turks from the demoralizing effects of American-made films.' The infidel nation is aroused to save its children from the Christian nation. . . . Will Hays said in a recent speech in Berlin 'the worldwide distribution of films fills an important part in making people in different lands understand each other,' but Sir Hesketh Bell (former Governor of Uganda) says, "Nothing has done more to destroy the prestige of the white man among the colored races than these deplorable pictures."

—Helen A. Miller, New York State Director of Motion Pictures, 1926

1933: School Librarian

After doing research at her local library in Danville, Virginia, Laura Hargrove was so impressed by the information the library held that she became a librarian.

Life at Home

- Laura Hargrove grew up in bustling Danville, Virginia, and had always wanted to be a telephone operator, a job that would pay well, give her prestige and make her father proud.
- The fourth of five girls, Laura knew early that her father had desperately wanted her to be a boy.
- When she could barely walk, she learned to carry tools to her father as he repaired cars, and later was his congenial companion during the long walks he liked to take along the Dan River.
- Considered the plain daughter by nearly everyone, Laura knew she would work for a living—at least until she was married, if anyone asked her.
- Telephone operating was considered a respectable, white collar occupation for unmarried, mostly native-born women; the Bell Telephone System, along with its subsidiaries, had become the largest employer of women in the United States.
- In the years just before the Great War, local businesses routinely paid telephone operators a $50 Christmas bonus to guarantee better phone service; by the time Laura applied for a job as a telephone operator in 1928, scientific management ideas and systematized work processes had been rigidly put in place.

Laura Hargrove's unexpected love for libraries led her to becoming a librarian.

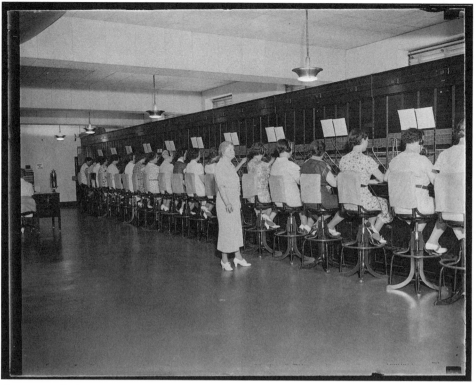

Laura worked as a telephone operator before discovering her passion.

- Bonuses were out, while elaborate manuals covering any situation were in.
- Some offices had as many as 15 operators sitting at an exchange; Danville had six, not counting the chief operator, who stood behind them and evaluated their ability to follow rules quickly and courteously.
- Laura was proud to tell her dad that she had been promoted to senior operator after only a year; the job was essentially the same, but the pay was higher.
- She credited her success to studying the operator's manual and knowing how to handle every situation; her employers were also impressed by her diction and ability to pronounce numbers and words clearly.
- By her third year on the job, she could anticipate whom the caller was attempting to connect with and answer questions before she was asked.
- No chitchat was allowed, but her supervisor—a second cousin on her mother's side—trusted her to help customers even when it meant breaking the strict rules of the manual.
- Bell Telephone was the only company in the area that provided its employees with sick pay.
- For the girls who worked the textile mills, Laura was considered lucky because she dressed nicely, didn't get lint in her hair during work hours, and was performing an indispensable public service.
- She was happy to have made her father proud; that's why the visit to the library was so unsettling—and exciting.
- Her supervisor had asked her to research a local business, and she was told she had all afternoon to complete her work.
- With plans of finishing early and purchasing an ice cream cone on the way home, Laura set to work reading books, magazines and newspapers provided by the librarian.
- The librarian seemed to know everything—where to find the information and how to compile it; she appeared organized, flexible and resourceful.
- It was a life-changing day; for the rest of the month, Laura found an excuse to visit libraries as often as possible—even volunteering to do research.
- She had found a place that was capable of feeding her curiosity and enhancing her knowledge.

- To learn more, she began using the "Reading With a Purpose" courses provided by the Carnegie Corporation which were distributed through the nation's library system.
- Each "course" was a short volume introducing a specific subject with specifically recommended books and commentary on that subject.
- She sampled English Literature, Alexander Meiklejohn's Philosophy, and Everett Martin's Psychology.
- In all, a total of 54 courses had been prepared: topics included foreign languages, classics, English, history, mental hygiene, and journalism. Nationwide, the librarian was being viewed no longer as "the jealous guardian of sacred treasures almost too sacred to be touched by the hand of the vulgar" but rather "the enthusiast inflamed with missionary zeal."
- The prospect thrilled Laura and horrified critics.
- After a few months, the librarian—an older woman who had grown up with Laura's mother—asked Laura why she didn't think about becoming a librarian herself.
- She obviously liked to do the work, and with her sharp mind would be able to guide others; the woman even volunteered to train her in the special skills and techniques of being a librarian.
- "You are already curious, detailed and tenacious," Laura was told. "Now all you need are a few tricks of the trade."
- Besides, the increasing number of high schools in the area had spawned the need for librarians in the public school system.
- It didn't pay as well as the telephone company, but it might be the answer to a deep desire to do more with her life.
- The thought elicited an emotion that surprised her.
- In the nineteenth century, the rise of school libraries was intertwined with the rise of public libraries.
- In 1835, New York State allowed school districts to use tax funds to purchase library books, and in 1839, the local districts were permitted to establish district libraries.
- By 1876, 19 states—nearly half the number of states in the Union—passed laws allowing school libraries to be developed.
- By 1913, the U.S. Office of Education reported about 10,000 public school libraries, many doubling as community libraries.

Life at Work

- It was pure celestial music to Laura's ears to hear state education leader C. W. Dickinson announce at the annual meeting of the Virginia Education Association that libraries were a high priority in Virginia.
- She had already applied for a job as the Danville High School librarian; friends had told her the job was hers, but it had not been formally offered.

- Dickinson said, "If I were allowed to name the single requisite for effective school-library service, my unhesitating choice would be the school librarian, one who has a vision of the increasingly important role which the library must play in the modern, progressive school and who has the personality and professional training to make her vision a reality."
- The successful school librarian, he said, needs the professional training required of both teacher and librarian; she must use tact, sympathy, initiative, patience, and much common sense to win the position of leader among the teachers.

- Her knowledge of the course of study and the contents of the basic textbooks must be proved to teachers by helpful suggestions as to how they may make wider use of library materials.
- "It is most important to the librarian to secure the friendly support and cooperation of the teachers at the very beginning of the school term," he said.
- The ability to select materials wisely is important, he told the assembled audience.
- Knowledge of children's books and children's literature should have been gained by wide reading and practical work with them as a student teacher in the model school library.
- William Learned, staff member of the Carnegie Foundation and author of the book *The American Public Library and the Diffusion of Knowledge* (1924), had prophesied that the city library had the potential to "be an institution of astonishing power—a genuine community university bringing intelligence systematically and persuasively to bear on all adult affairs."
- If properly organized nationwide, "it would immediately take its place as the chief instrument of our common intellectual and cultural progress."
- Learned continued, "We cannot abandon our education at the schoolhouse door; we must keep it up through life; the success of a democracy depends upon an educated and intelligent citizenship."
- Laura believed in her heart that democracy could last on just one condition: getting everyone educated.
- Three days after the library conference, Laura was offered the position of librarian at the high school.

Life in the Community: Danville, Virginia

- Danville, Virginia, located on the south side of the commonwealth, was proud of its national reputation as a tobacco and textile center.
- Boasting a population of 30,500, Danville was recognized for its 48 manufacturing plants, with investing capital of $21 million capable of producing new business revenues of $52 million a year.
- The city was home to 10 tobacco auction warehouses which employed 319 people and represented annual sales of $11.8 million.
- The city advertised itself as the "Gateway to the industrial section of the Piedmont," providing "good schools, good health, good government, good people—all combining to make a good city."
- The Clarke Electric Company declared in its advertisements that electricity was one of the greatest services to all of mankind, making it possible to offer the Frigidaire automatic refrigerator.

Danville, Virginia

- In 1728, Colonel William Byrd visited the area as a member of the joint commission to establish the exact boundary between Virginia and North Carolina, and declared it to be the "Land of Eden."
- During the American Revolution, soldiers gathered in the area to witness sturgeon leaping high into the air at Wayne's Falls on the Dan River.
- Danville was founded by an act of the legislature in November 1793, and incorporated in 1833.
- By 1856, the Richmond and Danville Railroad was established to transport tobacco and other agricultural products.
- Danville largely escaped the destruction of the Civil War, though it did serve as the last capital of the Confederacy.
- With the fall of Petersburg, Virginia, in April 1865, Confederate President Jefferson Davis and his Cabinet were forced to evacuate Richmond and retreated to Danville.
- The executive offices of the Confederacy were then maintained in an old school building on Wilson Street until word of General Robert E. Lee's surrender reached Danville on April 10.
- During Reconstruction, the city was occupied by Wright's Sixth Army Corps and became the military district until the end of the "re-adjuster movement" in 1883.
- With the aid of steam power to operate hydraulic tobacco presses, Danville enjoyed prosperity in the run-up to the new century.
- At one time, 24 independent tobacco manufacturers engaged in making cigarettes, chewing tobacco and smoking tobacco.
- Many carried the Danville name—further promoting the city.
- Textile mills added to the industrial base of the community, particularly the manufacture of yarns.
- According to a 1933 special report by the *Danville Register*, the city "turned the corner of the new century on two wheels, and has been rapidly forging ahead ever since, nearly doubling its population and increasing its manufacturing output by 85 percent since 1900."
- During America's entry into the Great War, Danville continued to prosper; the Liberty Loan quotas assigned to the city were always oversubscribed, and its Red Cross was one of the most active in the South.
- The city's textile industry supplied clothing and materials essential to the success of the Allied cause, while Danville itself provided its share of soldiers.
- In the early days, when most of the highways were terra-cotta ribbons stretching over hill and dale, it was a day's journey to Greensboro, North Carolina.
- With the advent of the automobile and good roads, the 45-mile journey took only a few hours.

Danville Yarnworks employees were part of the city's growing textile industry.

HISTORICAL SNAPSHOT
1933

- Construction of the Golden Gate Bridge began in San Francisco Bay
- Congress voted for independence for the Philippines, against President Hoover
- The Twentieth Amendment to the United States Constitution was ratified, changing Inauguration Day from March 4 to January 20, starting in 1937
- *The Lone Ranger* debuted on the radio
- The New York City-based Postal Telegraph Company introduced the first singing telegram
- In Miami, Florida, Giuseppe Zangara attempted to assassinate President-elect Franklin D. Roosevelt; Chicago Mayor Anton J. Cermak was killed
- *Newsweek* was published for the first time
- *King Kong*, starring Fay Wray, premiered at Radio City Music Hall in NYC
- Mount Rushmore National Memorial was dedicated
- President Franklin Roosevelt proclaimed, "The only thing we have to fear, is fear itself."
- Frances Perkins became U.S. Secretary of Labor and the first female Cabinet member
- Dachau, the first Nazi concentration camp, was opened
- The Civilian Conservation Corps was established to relieve unemployment
- Karl Jansky detected radio waves from the Milky Way Galaxy, leading to radio astronomy
- The Tennessee Valley Authority was created
- The Century of Progress World's Fair opened in Chicago
- Walt Disney's *Silly Symphony* cartoon *The Three Little Pigs* was released
- The first drive-in theater opened in Camden, New Jersey
- The first electronic pari-mutuel betting machine was unveiled at the Arlington Park race track near Chicago
- The first Major League Baseball All-Star Game was played at Comiskey Park in Chicago
- Army Barracks on Alcatraz was acquired by the Department of Justice for a federal penitentiary
- Albert Einstein arrived in the United States as a refugee from Nazi Germany
- The Civil Works Administration, designed to create jobs, was launched
- The Dust Bowl in South Dakota stripped topsoil from desiccated farmlands
- The Twenty-first Amendment officially went into effect, legalizing alcohol in the U.S.
- The first doughnut store, Krispy Kreme, opened in Nashville, Tennessee

Frances Perkins was the first female Cabinet member.

Selected Prices

Bed Sheet $0.65

Bell Telephone, NY to London, Three Minutes..............................$30.00

Book, *Popular Chemistry*...$0.50

Electric Washer $79.85

Ice Box $18.75

Lawn Mower..$5.49

Mattress..$4.65

Microphone $1.00

Motor Oil, Gallon...$0.49

Percolator $1.00

lieve it or Not!
10 cents is all you pay for these Rayon Hose

HOTEL DANVILLE, DANVILLE, VA.

Danville's Newest and Most Modern Hotel

Wishes full measure of success to the industrial survey project and offers every possible co-operation in the development of this good city.

ALL FOR DANVILLE
AND
DANVILLE FOR ALL
When In Danville Stop at the Hotel Danville
"Danville's Only Fireproof Modern Hotel"

Question to Carl Milam, secretary of the American Library Association, from H. L. Woolhiser, city manager in Illinois, during a 1933 radio broadcast called *How to Reduce the Library Budget*:

Wages are down, and the incomes from every business and every property have been drastically reduced. In many cases the income from property is not sufficient to pay taxes, much less living expenses of the owner.... In a time of depression we have to stop considering what is good for a well-organized social structure and consider what is necessary for continued existence of the people. In my town, we have been spending $90,000 per month for poor relief and that is not enough. Our public library spends about the same amount each year. Suppose we are reduced to the necessity of eliminating one of these functions; which will it be, Mr. Milam?

The public library is maintained by democratic society in order that every man, woman, and child may have the means of self-education and recreational reading.

—Standards for Public Libraries, 1933

The Library and Adult Education, Alexander Meiklejohn, 1924:

Democracy is education..... Insofar as we can educate the people, insofar as we can bring people to understanding of themselves and of their world, we can have a democracy. Insofar as we cannot do that, we have got to have control by the few.

Survey of Danville and Pittsylvania County, P. H. Batte, 1928:

The first and only industrial survey ever made of Danville and Pittsylvania County comes at a time when Danville's future appears brighter than ever. The new spirit of Danville is in line with the new progressive spirit of the Old Dominion, and Danville, one of Virginia's oldest cities, charted 136 years ago, is presenting today a comprehensive survey of her realization of past ambitions, as well as her objective of future greatness.

Danville is a good city—solid as the Rock of Gibraltar. Unlike many ambitious cities, Danville is out of its experimental stage. Confidence in the future is just led by marvelous achievements in the past.... This city, like many others, may not fully appreciate the many other industries because of the unusual size of their largest industry. The cotton mills have 467,000 spindles and are equal to 24 of the average-size North and South Carolina cotton mills. The number of bails of cotton consumed in 1927 was 91,569, or 46,439,753 pounds. The production in yards was 158,565,440, in miles 90,094, or enough cotton to go around the world 3 1/2 times.

Continued

Survey of Danville and Pittsylvania County, . . . (Continued)

Danville has many other large industries. The Danville Knitting Mills, manufacturers of stable and fancy hosiery, is the largest knitting mill in Virginia. This mill was organized in 1899 by Danville citizens, and enjoys a tremendous business. Then we have a number of other substantial industries, such as the Morotock Manufacturing Company, manufacturers of overalls, children's suits and men's work pants; the Anderson Brothers Consolidated Company, manufacturers of tropical linen suits, overalls and work shirts; the Dan City Silk Mills, manufacturers of broad silks; Boatwright Furniture; the Westbrook Elevator Manufacturing Company; Dan Valley Mills, manufacturers of flour; and the Waddill Printing Company.

The tobacco industry has been another great factor in the development of Danville. Since 1869, the market has shown a steady yearly increase in tobacco handled here. Danville is recognized throughout the world as the premier tobacco market. It offers better facilities, more experienced tobacconists, and all-round marketing conditions unlike any other market in the United States....

The modern Danville offers the advantages of a well-planned city. In its desire to grow, it reflects a spirit infused with progressive ideas.... Danville is not a "one industry" city. On the other hand, the city has 48 thriving industries engaged in the manufacturing and tobacco industry. If anyone should ask the writer to give some of the chief contributory factors in the development of Danville, he would put at the top of the list "Type of Citizens." Men of character, vision, ability and all-round progressive citizens have made Danville the kind of town men like to do business in. The largest industries of Danville were founded by and are still directed by home men and money.

Survey of Danville and Pittsylvania Co.

"Library on Wheels Takes Books to Readers," *The New York Times*, June 24, 1934:

Booklovers living in rural parts or outlying districts of the city, far from a branch of the public library, need not despair of obtaining reading material. The "traveling library" has been put into operation for the purpose of circulating books in the more sparsely populated regions of the country which do not warrant the installation of regular branch libraries.

One such library on wheels [was] designed by H. J. Gumpolt, bursar of the New York Public Library, and R. E. Rohne of the Expando Company of Chicago.... Its outward appearance resembles that of any other commercial vehicle except for the books which line both sides.

Through specially constructed mechanical contrivances, the side walls of the bus are expanded 13 inches, the roof is raised 11 inches, at the same time exposing the side panels which supply

Continued

"Library on Wheels Takes Books to Readers," ... (Continued)

additional light and ventilation to its interior. A tire box at the rear of the car is lowered and becomes a platform with steps on either side, giving access to the librarian's window.

Every inch of the interior is ingeniously utilized. There are facilities for carrying 2,000 books each trip. The compact arrangement leaves sufficient room for the selection of books by 15 persons at a time.

According to Mrs. Ruth E. Wellman, head of the extension division of the New York Public Library, the traveling library has proved a successful venture. There are 8,000 enrolled readers, most of them young people. The bus takes a different route each day, stopping for an hour at each station.

"First Free Library in the United States Observes Its 100th Birthday," *The New York Times*, April 2, 1933:

PETERBOROUGH, N.H.—The 100th anniversary of the first free public library in the United States to be supported by taxation is to be observed this spring and summer by the people of this town, where on April 9, 1833, the Peterborough Town Library, by vote, was declared "free" to every citizen.

During the week of April 9, the Peterborough churches, clubs and schools will commemorate the event, and the Peterborough Stamp Club is sponsoring a cachet that will be mailed out on the library's anniversary. It will bear the stamp of one of New Hampshire's most famous sons, Daniel Webster. On August 22, the people of Peterborough will take further recognition of America's first free library when it will give a special program with members of the New Hampshire Library Association and others as guests.

The movement to establish the Peterborough Town Library resulted from the division of the State Literary Fund, established in 1821 and raised by an annual tax on the capital stock of banks for an endowment of the State University. This project was abandoned, and a little later on this money was divided annually among the towns of the State of New Hampshire "for the support of common free schools, or other purposes of education." Peterborough was the first town to realize the significance of the later clause and the educational importance of a free library.

In 1833, Rev. Abiel Abbott, D. I., then Minister of the Peterborough Unitarian Church, with others, conceived the idea of a free library, which was carried into execution. Since April 9, 1833, by vote at the Peterborough annual town meeting, the library was owned and wholly supported by an annual town appropriation.

The catalog of America's first free library made its appearance in February 1834. It was written in longhand by the Rev. Dr. Abbott, and a copy is still in existence. This was followed

Continued

"First Free Library in the United States Observes
Its 100th Birthday," ... *(Continued)*

in 1837 by a catalog printed by John Prentiss of Keene, a 16-page pamphlet, listing 579 volumes. In 1834, the policy of keeping open Sundays was adopted and this has been continued without interruption down to this day.

The library had many religious books 100 years ago, but others were not overlooked, and on the shelves were found the lives of Bonaparte and Mohammed, the travels of Capt. Cook and of Lewis and Clark. For fiction, one could read Robinson Crusoe, the works of Goldsmith, Miss Edgeworth or Washington Irving. There were, also, a number of books for the young.

Miss Susan N. Gates was the first woman librarian of the library supported entirely by taxation, and to her fell the honor of making the first individual gift of money to the library. It was $20 and represented her entire salary for eight months.

In 1873, the lot upon which the library stands was purchased by 10 public-spirited men, who contributed $77 apiece. The present library was built in 1892 through the generosity of Mrs. Nancy S. Foster of Chicago, George S. Morison of New York, and William H. Smith of Alton, Ill.

1936: Olympic Swimmer

Raised at the ocean's edge in Florida, Katy Rawls was determined to win medals in both swimming and diving at the summer Olympics in Berlin, Germany.

Life at Home

- In the 1932 Olympics, Katherine Rawls captured a silver medal in the three-meter springboard diving competition.
- With the 1936 Olympics looming, Katy had her sights set on winning medals in both swimming and diving.
- Her chances were good.
- Raised in Florida, Katy started swimming when she was two, began diving at seven, set a world record in the 300-meter individual medley at 13 and won an Olympic medal in diving at 14.
- The oldest in a family of swimmers and divers, Katy and her two sisters were collectively known in Florida as the "Rawls diving trio."
- The children also put on exhibitions as the "Rawls Water Babies."
- Water sports were a natural aspect of growing up in Florida.
- Family stories included Katy's fearlessness on a 25-foot-high platform as a second-grader, and competing at age 13 at the 1931 National Swimming Championships in Bronx Beach, New York.
- Even before the competition in New York, stories began circulating about her athletic prowess.
- She swam freestyle events from sprints to the mile, considered the individual medley her best event, set records in the breast stroke, and dove from both the platform and the springboard.
- But when she arrived for the 300-meter individual medley competition in New York, all spectators saw was a tiny girl, eager to swim one of the most difficult events.
- The individual medley required the swimmer to backstroke for one-third of the distance, breast stroke for a third, and freestyle over the remaining distance.

Katy Rawls' goal was winning not one, but two, Olympic events.

Although Young, Katy proved she deserved a spot on the Olympic team.

- Her principal competitor was superstar Eleanor Holm, the reigning queen of racing who had been winning with frustrating regularity.
- Katy not only won the race, but beat the world record previously set by Eleanor Holm herself.
- The next day Katy enhanced her reputation further by beating champion Margaret Hoffman in the 220-yard breast stroke.
- A year later, as a competitor in 1932 Olympics, Katy was the youngest team member by four years.
- To make the team, she traveled to Jones Beach located on Long Island in New York, site of the U.S. Olympic trials.
- Told by her coach to conserve her energy and aim for a third place finish during the trials of the 200-meter breast stroke, Katy finished a disappointing fourth and failed to qualify.
- Undaunted, she rowed across the water to where the springboard diving competition was underway.
- There she upset champion Georgia Coleman—by a razor thin scoring margin—to win the competition and qualify as an Olympic diver.
- Then she returned to the Casino Pool, a saltwater facility in Fort Lauderdale where she attended high school, before setting out for the Olympics in California.
- Competing in her first international meet, Katy dove well enough against the world's finest in 1932 Olympics in Los Angeles to capture the silver medal—edged out by American Georgia Coleman.
- Georgia captured the springboard diving gold by executing a flawless two and a half front somersault, the first woman to perform the feat in Olympic competition.
- Soon afterwards the International Swimming Federation banned dives it thought too daring for women, including the two and a half somersault.
- That fall, Katy defeated Georgia Coleman in the national championships, one of her four victories during the championship—the maximum number possible in one meet.
- In addition to the springboard diving event, Katy won the 200-meter breast stroke, the 880-yard freestyle and the 300-meter individual medley.
- Katy was hailed as a member of a new youth movement that also included 17-year-old Dorothy Payton.
- As she prepared for the 1936 Olympics, Katy was named *The New York Times* favorite in seven of the nine events in the upcoming Nationals, depending on which she chose to compete in.

Katy and her competitors dove well.

Life at Work

- Faced with the difficult task of making the 1936 Olympic team in both swimming and diving, Katy Rawls chose to concentrate on the freestyle event—her favorite, since the individual medley was not an Olympic event—and springboard diving.
- During tryouts in July at the Astoria Park pool, New York, Katy performed a spectacular layout front somersault dive that gave her an early edge over fierce competition.
- She also executed a forward one and a half with ease.
- Thirty minutes later, she was off the diving platform and preparing for the freestyle event.
- Katy took an early lead and won the event, but had to fight to hold her position in the final five yards of the race.
- She became one of eight athletes to capture a spot that first day.

Katy enjoyed competing.

- Katy also became the only athlete—male or female, runner, swimmer, jumper, fencer or equestrienne—to compete on two distinctly separate Olympic teams before reaching the age of 20.
- Champion swimmer Eleanor Holm Jarrett wasn't so lucky.
- During the nine-day voyage to the Olympics in Berlin, Germany, aboard the *SS Manhattan,* Jarrett, now married and accustomed to an active social life, ignored the strict curfews instituted by the American Olympic Committee.
- Jarrett attended an on-board party that lasted until six in the morning, and continued to drink in public, despite being warned to tone down her behavior.
- Before the ship landed, U.S. officials voted to remove Jarrett from the team, even though she was the defending champion and the favorite to win the backstroke events.
- The decision to dismiss Jarrett caused chaos throughout the swim team.
- At the games themselves, the tradition of the Olympic torch relay before the games was introduced as a way of defining the modern Olympic experience and promoting the new Germany.
- German filmmaker Leni Riefenstahl originally requested that all the torchbearers run entirely in the nude in homage to the athletes of the ancient Olympia.
- The runners preferred to remain dressed.
- The 1936 Olympics also was the first to place the top three finishers in each event on a tiered podium to receive their medals, while the national anthem of the gold-medal winner was played over the loudspeaker.
- Other firsts included freestyle swimmers being allowed to start from diving blocks, and the addition of basketball to the Olympic program.
- In the final basketball game, the United States beat Canada 19-8 in a contest played outdoors on a dirt court in driving rain so severe the teams could not dribble the ball.
- Americans swept the women's springboard diving competition, but not in the order Katy had planned.
- Thirteen-year-old Marjorie Gestring dove flawlessly to become the youngest woman in history to win a gold medal.
- Katy, in a repeat of the 1932 Olympics, captured silver.
- Swimming was even a greater disappointment for Katy.
- As predicted by ousted team member Eleanor Holm Jarrett, the American women were bested by the Dutch who set a new world record.
- Katy finished a distant seventh, but the United States fared well overall.

- American Jesse Owens, one of 10 African American athletes and part of a 66-man track and field squad, won four gold medals in the sprint and long jump events.
- Colorado farm boy Glenn Edgar Morris won gold in the Decathlon.
- Rower Jack Beresford won his fifth Olympic medal, and his third gold.
- The U.S. eight-man rowing team from the University of Washington won the gold, coming from behind to defeat the Germans and Italians with Adolf Hitler in attendance.
- Thanks to extensive preparation, Germany fared better in the games than they did four years earlier.

Life in the Community: Berlin, Germany

- The 1936 Olympic Games in Berlin were carefully scripted long in advance by its German organizers.
- The 1916 Olympics were scheduled to take place in Berlin but WW I caused a change in location, so one could say that the Germans had been preparing for 20 years.
- Prior to canceling events in Berlin, the Reichstag voted to subsidize the Berlin games, the first time such costs were borne by government rather than the private sector.
- Several non-European cities offered to host the 1916 games, including Cincinnati, who promised a half million dollars to help build the stadium and bring European athletes to America but, ultimately, the 1916 games were canceled.
- Germany, as well as several other "aggressor nations," was barred from the 1920 and 1924 Olympics games as unfit for peace-loving enterprises.
- The 1928 the Olympics in Amsterdam included Germany, as well as an American team under the tutelage of Gen. Douglas MacArthur, who considered the games to be a kind of "war without weapons."
- The 1932 Olympic Games in Los Angeles represented the second time the event had been held in the United States.
- The first was in 1904 in St. Louis, Missouri, which was not well attended internationally or remembered fondly.
- Los Angeles was determined to put the city on the map for something other than moviemaking.
- To defray housing costs in the midst of the Depression, Los Angeles created an Olympic Village for men where lodging cost two dollars per day instead of the seven, by more expensive nearby hotels.
- In the Baldwin Hills overlooking the Pacific Ocean, Olympic Village was the perfect setting for movie stars such as Douglas Fairbanks and Will Rogers to walk the grounds signing autographs.
- Women athletes, including the American women's swim team, were assigned to the Chapman Park Hotel downtown.
- Fearing that European athletes would boycott the American Olympics because of the high transportation costs, organizers negotiated, for Olympic participants, a 20 percent discount for transatlantic travel and 40 percent discount for railroad travel within the United States.
- To support its 69 athletes and defray expenses, the Brazilian team attempted to sell bags of coffee at ports along the way at 50 cents a bag.
- They raised enough for 24 members of the team to leave the ship and compete when it reached its destination.
- More than 100,000 people attended the opening ceremonies and the crowds remained respectable for all 14 days of competition.
- The Los Angeles games were the first Olympics to turn a profit, which was approximately $150,000.

- The United States dominated the Olympics, winning 41 gold medals.
- Germany won only three golds, behind Italy, Sweden, Finland, Japan, Hungary and France.
- Newly installed German Chancellor Adolf Hitler denounced the 1932 Olympic Games as a "plot of Freemasons and Jews."
- German Olympic organizers took detailed notes to prepare for the 1936 games, including design of the sports complexes, transportation, housing, publicity, broadcasting, even investigating a Los Angeles department store's claim that its clerks spoke every language represented at the games.
- German newspaper *Volkischer Beobachter,* noted, "Blacks have no place in the Olympics . . . this is a disgrace and a degradation to the Olympic ideal without parallel, and the ancient Greeks would turn over in their graves if they knew what modern man were doing with their sacred national games."
- In 1936, for the first time in modern history, an international protest movement was founded against the designated city of Berlin.
- American Jewish groups branded the Berlin games as the "Nazi Olympics," and wanted the Olympics moved from Germany or for America to boycott the event.

Adolf Hitler's Germany was a contested location for the Olympics.

- Black-owned newspapers pointed out that it is hypocritical for American sports officials to demand equal treatment for German Jews when discrimination against black athletes was accepted at home.
- The movement forced some German reforms, and by the time the games started, only Spain was missing, due to the Spanish Civil War then underway.
- Germany undertook a massive building project including a new stadium that required 2,600 workers to build.
- The Olympic Village in Berlin had its own movie theater, shops, full-sized gymnasium, running track, soccer field, swimming pool and Finnish sauna.
- Every national taste in food was accommodated, including pork for the Czechs, rye bread and blueberries for the Finns, and raw fish and soy sauce for the Japanese.
- Coca-Cola was sold outside the official venues, but German health officials insisted that a warning about its caffeine content be stated on every bottle.
- As in Los Angeles, the Olympic Village was for male athletes only, and the women were housed in a dormitory with tiny rooms near the stadium.
- On opening day, 170 buses brought the athletes to the sports complex, where the airship *Hindenburg* cruised back and forth across the stadium trailing an Olympic banner from its gondola.
- An overflow crowd of 110,000 spectators jammed Olympic Stadium on opening day with 49 nations represented, up from 37 in 1932.
- With great ceremony, the Olympic flame was brought to the stadium by a torch relay from its the starting point in Olympia, Greece.
- Track and field competition, the centerpiece of the modern Olympic Games, dominated the first week of competition and served as a showcase for American star Jesse Owens.
- African American men and women captured 13 medals in track and field, accounting for 83 of America's 107 points in that division.
- These games were the first to have live television coverage by the German Post Office, which broadcast over 70 hours of coverage to special viewing rooms throughout Berlin and Potsdam.

HISTORICAL SNAPSHOT

1936

- Dust storms stripped farmlands of all vegetation in Kansas, Oklahoma, Colorado, Nebraska and the Dakotas

- Lewis Meyer won his third Indianapolis 500 in nine years with an average speed of 109 mph

- Margaret Mitchell's book *Gone with the Wind* sold a record one million copies in six months

- The popular magazine *Literary Digest* predicted that incumbent President Franklin D. Roosevelt would lose the presidential election to Alf Landon

- Jay Berwaner, winner of the Heisman Trophy, was the first pick in the inaugural National Football League draft

- Hit songs included, "I've Got You Under My Skin," "Is It True What They Say About Dixie?," "The Night Is Young and You're So Beautiful" and the "WPA Blues"

- The Boulder Dam, built on the Colorado River, was completed, creating the world's largest artificial reservoir and enough power for 1.5 million people

- The Associated Press began a weekly college football list of the nation's top 20 schools based on a poll

- The first successful helicopter flight was made

- The baseball Hall of Fame inducted its first class: Ty Cobb, Honus Wagner, Babe Ruth, Christie Matheson and Walter Johnson

- Heavyweight German boxer Max Schmeling defeated Joe Louis in 12 rounds

- Polls indicated that 67 percent of Americans favored birth control

- Cleveland Indians rookie pitcher Bob Feller made his first start, striking out 15 St. Louis Browns in a 4-1 victory

- *The Green Hornet* radio show debuted and *The Phantom* made his first appearance in U.S. newspapers

- In violation of the Treaty of Versailles, Nazi Germany reoccupied the Rhineland

- Bruno Richard Hauptmann, convicted of kidnapping and killing Charles Lindbergh III, was executed in New Jersey

- The Santa Fe Railroad inaugurated the all-Pullman *Super Chief* passenger train between Chicago, Illinois, and Los Angeles, California

- Stress was first recognized as a medical condition

Selected Prices

Automobile, Reo	$795.00
Bed and Mattress	$14.95
Bloomers	$0.23
Electric Heater	$1.00
Highway Flare Torches, Dozen	$24.00
Shave Cream	$0.25
Tire	$2.95
Typewriter, Underwood	$49.50
Vacuum Cleaner	$28.95
Wristwatch, Elgin	$33.25

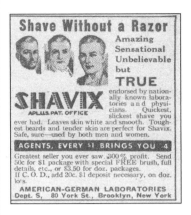

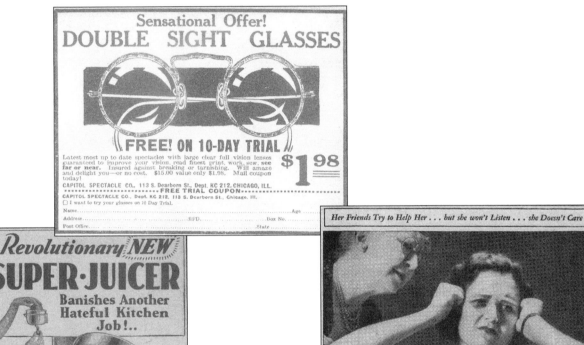

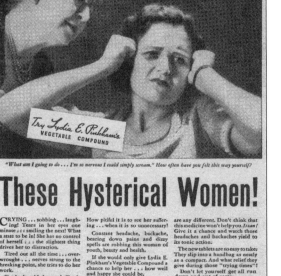

"Sister Acts in Swimming Give Sport Plenty of Life," Harry Grayson, *The Lowell Sun* (Massachusetts), July 27, 1935:

Had the gentleman in the bowler hat who asked the Floradora girl the famous question, "Are there any more at home like you?" been a witness at the national women's AAU swimming championships, he would've found that there are quite a few more, but they didn't stay home, but quite the contrary, swarmed on Manhattan Beach, New York, to help keep the laurels in the families.

There were the Rawls sisters, of Fort Lauderdale—bobbed-haired Katherine, Evelyn, and the youngest and curly-haired Dorothy.

There were the Brooklyn sisters, Elizabeth and Erna Kompa, and the now famous Hoeger girls, of Miami, 11-year-old, 73-pound Mary, the youngest person to ever win a national title of any kind; Ruth, and Helen.

But perhaps it's just as well for mermaids of other lands that Lenoe Kight of Homestead, Pennsylvania, hasn't a sister who swims anywhere near as well as she does. For between stocky Miss Kight, the freestyle luminary who has succeeded the record-wrecking Helene Madison, and the sister acts, women's swimming in America has been swept to its topmost height.

Katherine Rawls, only slightly less formidable than Miss Kight as an all-around star, won the 300-meter individual medley and the 220-yard breast stroke.

The crop-haired, 18-year-old miss has combined with her sisters to win 260 trophies, much to the delight of their father W. J. Rawls, a wholesale produce man.

Like Katherine, Dorothy Rawls, 14, and Neville, 16, are phenomenal backstroke competitors. It was by defeating Eleanor Holm in the backstroke to win her first title that Katherine first attracted widespread attention.

The three Rawls girls have been swimming since they can remember. The gentleman in the bowler no doubt would have agreed that three was quite enough, but would have learned that another Little Rawl Miss Peggy, 8, swan dives, as does Sonny, 10.

The Kompa girls are rising young exponents of the backstroke. They make the finish of 220-yard backstroke strictly a family affair, with Elizabeth barely beating Erna.

The latter only a few days previous had claimed a corner on backstroke fame by shattering a world 220-yard record as old as Mary Hoeger twice in as many days in a New York invitational meet in which she also cracked two American marks.

"Father of Youthful Diver Tells Story of Her Career,"
The Salt Lake Tribune, August 13, 1936:

Only three years ago, at a municipal plunge in Omaha, Nebraska, Marjorie Gestring, then 10 years old, learned to swim—in a very few minutes.

But not until later did she give promise of the diving talent which carried her to the springboard championship in the Olympic games in Berlin Wednesday. She was a puny baby and took gymnastic training on the advice of physicians.

William Gestring, insurance broker, father of the 13-year-old blonde wisp, told about her career after receiving news of her victory.

In addition to her diving virtuosity, she is fairly accomplished at the piano, having given two recitals.

The family was on a vacation visit in Omaha when she learned to swim. That same day, however, her mother, Mrs. Beta Gestring, sent for a music teacher, and a bargain was perfected. For each half-hour Marjorie practiced piano, she would be permitted an hour in the swimming pool.

Within three months, coach Pete Windel in Omaha boasted that exhibitions and a series of radio talks Marjorie made from the poolside in a city park increased the plunge's receipts $400 a week.

Back in Los Angeles, Marjorie continued her diving under the tutelage of coach Fred Cady, now in Berlin. To him, Gestring gave most of the credit for her having won 10 state championships.

She and her mother, who accompanied her to Berlin, will visit the latter's parents in Sweden before returning in time for Marjorie to reenter school, Gestring said.

"Japanese Take Big Lead Over Water Rivals," Gayle Talbot, *Ogden Standard-Examiner* (Utah), August 9, 1936:

The Japanese and Dutch dominated the first day of Olympic swimming competition today, leaving a string of broken records in their wake, and submerging America's hopes to a new all-time low.

The preliminary round saw the little brown men and women establish themselves as exuberant favorites in the men's 100-meter event.

America qualified its two great dash men, Peter Fick of New York and Art Lindegren of Los Angeles, 100-meter semifinal, while all three of its entries in the women's 100, Katherine Rawls, Fort Lauderdale, Florida, Olive McKean, Seattle, Washington, and Bernice Laip, Newark, New Jersey, all survived the opening round. But there didn't look like a winner in the bunch.

In the women's breast stroke, Uncle Sam's flashers finished fifth, fifth, and fourth in three rousing heats.

"Kitty Rawls Trails As New Mark Is Made," *Chester Times* (Pennsylvania), August 10, 1936:

Bearing out the pessimistic predictions of Mrs. Eleanor Holm Jarrett, Dutch women swimmers took the honors in the hundred-meter freestyle event today, with Katherine Rawls, leading American entry, fading out to wind up in seventh place.

As Mrs. Jarrett foresaw, the race went to Rita Mastenbrock of Holland in the new Olympic record time of 1.05.9 with Miss Campbell of the Argentine second in 1.06.4 and Fraulein Arendt of Germany third at 1.06.6.

"Youthful Marjorie Gestring Leads Sweep of Girls Diving Event,"
Salt Lake Tribune, August 13, 1936:

America swept back into the Olympic picture Wednesday when the University of Washington sweepswingers cracked the Olympic record for eight-oared crews wide open, Jack Medica and Marjorie Gestring hung up unexpected triumphs in aquatic competition, and the basketball and boxing teams chalked up new successes.

Surprised by the power of Great Britain, the Huskies from the American Far West stroked by ailing Don Hume had to come from behind to win their trial heat and lower the Olympic record for the 2,000-meter distance to 6.00.8.

Medica lowered the Olympic 400-meter freestyle record to 4.44.5 in scoring an unexpected victory over Shumpel Uto of Japan, while Miss Gestring beat out her teammates Katherine Rawls and Dorothy Poynton Hill for springboard diving honors.

Letter from Swedish International Olympic Committee member Sigfrid Edstrom to Avery Brundage, head of the American International Olympic Committee:

It seems there is some agitation from the American Jews. . . . I cannot understand the reason for this agitation. I understand it's on account of the persecution of the Jews but as to the sport this persecution has not been allowed. Already at the Congress of Vienna in June last year the International Olympic Committee was assured from the highest authorities that there would be no trouble for Jewish athletes in connection with the Olympic Games. Even German Jews would be allowed on the German team. . . .

It is too bad that the American Jews are so active and causing so much trouble. It is impossible for our German friends to carry on the expensive preparations for the Olympic Games if all this unrest prevails. . . .

As regards the persecution of the Jews in Germany, I am not at all in favor of said action, but I fully understand that an alteration had to take place. As it was in Germany, a great part of the German nation was led by the Jews and not by the Germans themselves. Even in the USA the day may come when you will have to stop the activities of the Jews. Many of my friends are Jews so you must not think I am against them, but they must be kept within certain limits.

"Owens Defeats German Sprint Stars Handily," *Salt Lake Tribune*, August 13, 1936:

Jesse Owens, star of the United States Olympic track team, Wednesday night equaled the world 100-meter dash record of 10.3 but disappointed 8,000 spectators by broad-jumping only 7.02 meters (23 feet and 1/2 inches) in losing to Wilhelm Leichum of Germany, who jumped 7.25 meters (23 feet, 9 7/16 inches) in an international track meet.

Displaying Olympic speed despite his third straight night of barnstorming, Jesse outraced two Germans, Gerd Hornberger and Borchmeyer, by two and three yards in the 100.

1939: Pianist & Arranger

At 13 years-old, Mary Lou Williams was a jazz pianist and arranger in her own right, writing for Tommy Dorsey and Benny Goodman, with Louis Armstrong one of her biggest fans.

Life at Home

- Jazz pianist Mary Lou Williams was fittingly described by one critic as "the swingingest female alive."
- In partnership with Andy Kirk, Mary Lou also was a pioneer of the smooth simplicity and extended solo riffs that came to be known as Kansas City jazz.
- Born Mary Elfreida Scruggs in 1910, Mary Lou was one of 11 children who moved to Pittsburgh when she was five or six years old.
- Mary Lou, who sat on her mother's lap as the latter played the organ, began playing the piano for money at neighbors' houses when she was seven, sometimes earning $20 to $30 a day with her skills.
- In the fifth grade, she displayed her ability to produce an unaided perfect pitch when she substituted for a mislaid pitch pipe.
- When Mary Lou was 10 years old, the fabulously rich Mellon family paid her $100 to play piano for a party and brought her to the event in a chauffer-driven limousine.
- And when she was 11, Mary, who occasionally sat in with the Earl Hines Band, was asked at the last minute to substitute for the regular pianist on a touring show, *Hits and Bits.*
- Since there was no written score, a member of the cast hummed all the tunes for her on the day of the performance; she performed flawlessly.
- For the next two summers, she traveled with the show and returned to Pittsburgh in the fall for school.
- The travel schedule, especially trips to Harlem, brought her into contact with popular groups like McKinney's Cotton Pickers and Duke Ellington's Washingtonians.
- She played with both bands and proved that she could do more than simply keep up.

Mary Lou Williams was a jazz pianist with fans all along the East Coast – including Louis Armstrong – by the time she was 13 years old.

- By the time she turned 13, she was a veteran musician with fans all along the East Coast.
- One of those fans was future husband and saxophonist John Williams, whose combo joined *Hits and Bits* in 1924.
- When Seymour and Jeanette, a top vaudeville team on the Orpheum circuit, proposed that John Williams could join their circuit, he insisted on taking Mary Lou along.
- "Cut her hair and put pants on her!" shouted Seymour in response. "We cannot have a girl in the outfit."
- After she played the piano, Seymour changed his mind and she stayed with the act until it broke up a year later.
- Another major salute to her talent came that same year when she was only 15.
- One morning at 3 a.m., when she was jamming with McKinney's Cotton Pickers at Harlem's Rhythm Club, Louis Armstrong entered the room, paused to listen, then "Louis picked me up and kissed me."
- John and Mary Lou were married in 1926 when she turned 16.
- Together they toured the South with her own small band until John joined Clouds of Joy in 1928.
- A year later they moved to Kansas City for a steady job at the Pla-Mor, one the city's top ballrooms; for the next seven years they worked out of Kansas City, Missouri.
- "Kaycee was really jumping," Mary Lou said. "So many great bands have sprung up there or moved in from over the river. It attracted musicians from all over the South and Southwest."

Louis Armstrong at the piano.

Life at Work

- Kansas City was a wide-open town, firmly under the control of political boss Tom Pendergast, who ignored the national Prohibition against alcohol sales, while promoting gambling and other vice in the city.
- "Naturally, work was plentiful for musicians," Mary Lou Williams said.
- Talented musicians flocked to the town—where the music never went to bed—to play in after-hours jam sessions with established musicians like Herschel Evans, Coleman Hawkins and Lester ("Prez") Young.
- "We didn't have closing hours in those spots," Mary Lou said. "We'd play all morning and half through the day if we wished, and, in fact, we often did. The music was so good we seldom got to bed before midday."
- By the 1930s, Kansas City jazz was recognized as a unique sound with its preference for a 4/4 beat that made it more relaxed and fluid.
- New York had developed its own swinging jazz sound, Chicago was recognized as a center for jazz, and the crossroads community of Kansas City owned its own distinctive sound.
- Extended soloing fueled by a culture whose goal was to "say something" with one's instrument also marked Kansas City jazz as distinctive.
- At times, one "song" could be performed for several hours, with the best musicians often soloing for dozens of choruses at a time.
- Constructed around a 12-bar blues structure, rather than the eight-bar jazz standard, the style left room for elaborate riffing by individuals or pairs.
- And since the big bands in Kansas City also played by memory, composing collectively rather than sight-reading, the KC style was often looser and more spontaneous.
- It was a sound that suited Mary Lou's musical skills.
- Critics wrote of Mary Lou, "If you shut your eyes, you would bet she was a man."

Clouds of Joy's success was a direct result of the songs that Mary Lou wrote and arranged for them.

- *Time* magazine said she played "the solid, unpretentious, flesh-&-bone kind of jazz piano that is expected from such vigorous Negro masters as James P. Johnson."
- For a decade, Andy Kirk's Clouds of Joy and Mary Lou were inseparable.
- She wrote most of its arrangements, and many of them such as "Roll 'Em" and "Froggy Bottom" quickly became classics among jazz players.
- One week she got down 15 scores and, all told, she provided the Clouds of Joy with 200 arrangements, including "Walkin' and Swingin'," "Twinklin'," "Cloudy'," and "Little Joe from Chicago."

Wherever they played, tickets to see Clouds of Joy always sold out.

- During a recording trip to Chicago, Mary Lou recorded "Drag 'Em" and "Night Life" as piano solos.
- The records sold briskly, lifting Mary Lou to national prominence.
- Soon afterwards, she also began playing solo gigs and working as a freelance arranger for Earl Hines, Benny Goodman, and Tommy Dorsey.
- Mary Lou and the Clouds of Joy also scored another hit with "Until The Real Thing Comes Along,"—an exceptional achievement in the midst of a national Depression—thanks to the development of jukeboxes.
- Suddenly, their sound was coming from every bar; when they played live, thousands of music lovers had to be turned away.
- At times they would perform "Real Thing" half a dozen times per show because the demand was so great.
- But the lugubrious ballad was a departure from KC swing, and the critics made sure the musicians knew it.
- In 1937, she produced *In the Groove*, a collaboration with Dick Wilson, and Benny Goodman asked Mary Lou to write a blues number for his band.
- The result was "Roll 'Em," a boogie-woogie piece based on the blues, which followed her successful "Camel Hop," Goodman's theme song for his radio show sponsored by Camel cigarettes.
- Goodman wanted Mary Lou to write for him exclusively, but she refused, preferring to freelance.
- She was accustomed to making her own path.

Life in the Community: Kansas City, Missouri

- Kansas City, Missouri, which straddles the border between Missouri and Kansas at the confluence of the Kansas and Missouri rivers, was incorporated in 1850 with a population of 1,500.
- Throughout the 1840s, the population of the Town of Kansas swelled as it increasingly became a vital starting point on the Oregon, Santa Fe, and California trails for settlers heading West; rail travel came to Kansas in 1847.
- The first newspaper and telegraph service were established in the Town of Kansas in 1851.
- In 1889, with a population of around 130,000, the town adopted a new charter and changed its name to Kansas City as it became the second-busiest train center in the country, trailing only Chicago.
- The Kansas City Stockyards became second only to Chicago's in size, and the city itself was identified with its famous Kansas City steak.
- The Pendergast era, under Democrat big city bosses James Pendergast and Tom Pendergast from 1890 to 1940, ushered in a colorful and influential era for the city.

Mildred Bailey was one of the first successful non-Black jazz singer in Kansas City.

- During this period, the Pendergasts declared that national Prohibition was meaningless in Kansas City, and the Kansas City boulevard and park system was developed.
- American aviator Charles Lindbergh helped lure the newly created Transcontinental & Western Airline—later TWA—to locate its corporate headquarters in Kansas City because of its central location, making Kansas City a hub of national aviation.
- During the later part of the Golden Age of Aviation—the 1930s and 1940s—TWA was known as "The Airline Run by Flyers."
- When Prohibition finally was repealed in 1933 by means of the Twenty-first Amendment, little changed in Kansas City.
- The first Kansas City band to achieve a national reputation was the Coon-Sanders Original Nighthawk Orchestra, a white group which broadcast nationally in the 1920s.
- Kansas City was a national crossroads resulting in a mix of cultures; transcontinental trips by plane or train often required a stop in the city.

The Chesterfield Club was one of many popular jazz clubs in Kansas City.

- Jazz musicians associated with the style were born in other places but got caught up in the friendly musical competition among performers that could keep a single song being performed in variations for an entire night.
- Members of the Big Bands would perform at regular venues earlier in the evening, and go to the jazz clubs later to jam for the rest of the night.
- Clubs were scattered throughout city, but the most fertile area was the inner city neighborhood of 18th Street and Vine.
- Among the clubs were the Amos 'n' Andy, Boulevard Lounge, Cherry Blossom, Chesterfield Club, Chocolate Bar, Dante's Inferno, Elk's Rest, Hawaiian Gardens, Hell's Kitchen, the Hi Hat, the Hey Hey, Lone Star, Old Kentucky Bar-B-Que, Paseo Ballroom, Pla-Mor Ballroom, Reno Club, Spinning Wheel, Street's Blue Room, Subway and Sunset.

HISTORICAL SNAPSHOT

1939

- The Hewlett-Packard Company was founded
- Amelia Earhart was officially declared dead two years after her disappearance while attempting to fly around the world
- *Naturwissenschaften* published evidence that nuclear fission had been achieved by Otto Hahn
- Adolf Hitler ordered Plan Z, a five-year naval expansion effort intended to create a huge German fleet capable of crushing the Royal Navy by 1944
- Hitler prophesied that if "Jewish financers" started a war against Germany, the result would be the "annihilation of the Jewish race in Europe"
- The Golden Gate International Exposition opened in San Francisco, and the 1939 World's Fair opened in New York City
- Sit-down strikes were outlawed by the Supreme Court
- In Bombay, Mohandas Gandhi began a fast protesting against British rule in India
- Students at Harvard University demonstrated the new tradition of swallowing goldfish to reporters
- British Prime Minister Neville Chamberlain gave a speech in Birmingham, stating that Britain will oppose any effort at world domination on the part of Germany
- African-American singer Marian Anderson performed before 75,000 people at the Lincoln Memorial in Washington, DC, after having been denied the use of both Constitution Hall by the Daughters of the American Revolution, and of a public high school by the federally controlled District of Columbia
- John Steinbeck's novel *The Grapes of Wrath* was published
- Billie Holiday recorded "Strange Fruit," the first anti-lynching song
- *Batman*, created by Bob Kane, made his first comic book appearance
- Major League Baseball's Lou Gehrig ended his 2,130 consecutive games played streak after developing amyotrophic lateral sclerosis (ALS)
- Pan-American Airways begins transatlantic mail service with the inaugural flight of its *Yankee Clipper* from Port Washington, New York
- The *St. Louis*, a ship carrying 907 Jewish refugees, was denied permission to land in Florida after already having been turned away from Cuba, and was forced to return to Europe, where many of its passengers later died in Nazi death camps during the Holocaust
- The National Baseball Hall of Fame and Museum was officially dedicated in Cooperstown, New York
- The 1st World Science Fiction Convention opened in New York City
- The sculpture of Theodore Roosevelt's head was dedicated at Mount Rushmore
- Albert Einstein wrote to President Franklin Roosevelt about developing the atomic bomb using uranium, leading to the creation of the Manhattan Project
- MGM's classic musical film *The Wizard of Oz*, based on L. Frank Baum's novel, and starring Judy Garland as Dorothy, premiered
- As World War II began in Europe with Germany's attack on Poland, the United States declared its neutrality
- Gerald J. Cox, speaking at an American Water Works Association meeting, publicly proposed the fluoridation of public water supplies in the U.S.
- Nylon stockings went on sale for the first time
- *Hedda Hopper's Hollywood* premiered on radio with Hollywood gossip columnist Hedda Hopper as host
- La Guardia Airport opened for business in New York City
- General Motors introduced the Hydra-Matic drive, the first mass-produced, fully automatic transmission, as an option in 1940 model year Oldsmobiles

Selected Prices

Camera, Kodak	$20.00
Coca-Cola	$0.25
Home Movie, 16 mm	$8.75
Movie Camera	$49.50
Movie Ticket	$0.25
Nylons	$1.95
Pocket Telescope	$1.00
Seat Covers, Sedan	$5.85
Toothpaste	$0.25
Wall Clock	$6.98

SWEET and LOW

You can compare a bowl of Kellogg's Corn Flakes to a lullaby. These crisp, delicious flakes are an excellent sleep-inducer these warm evenings. They're satisfying and easily digested. Result — you sleep sweetly and arise cheerfully.

Try a bowl of Kellogg's after that late party. They're sold every place where you can buy food.

Nothing takes the place of

Kellogg's

CORN FLAKES

Catch it! WITH **Contax**

The Candid Camera of Unlimited Scope

Quick as a flash, and under the most trying conditions, Contax will enable you to take such pictures as you never took before!—Candid, true-to-life photos full of character and human interest, fast-action, sport-shots, portraits, close-ups of birds, etc.—Any picture, anywhere, any time—indoors or out, in daylight or ordinary artificial light.

Zeiss Lenses and automatic range-finder-focusing produce needle-sharp negatives with all the detail and tone values that make a picture "sing."

ZEISS IKON Contax is now available in two models, Contax I (black) and a new Contax II (Chromium), which at slightly higher price offers new features and advantages. At leading dealers.

Write for Literature
CARL ZEISS, Inc., Dept. C
485 Fifth Ave., New York
728 So. Hill St., Los Angeles

NEW **Kodak BANTAM SPECIAL**

A brilliant, distinctive miniature camera . . .

"The New York World's Fair Music Festival," Olin Downes, *Etude Music Magazine*, May 1939:

A visitor from Cape Town, South Africa, who was taken for a preview through the New York World's Fair grounds, was heard to exclaim in a kind of neo-Mayfair accent, "My word, one couldn't begin to see all this in a lifetime." The reason for this, doubtless, is that highly experienced and energetic men behind the huge project realized that Canadians who will visit the World's Fair would be presented with an enormous variety of appeals—high-brow, low-brow, broad-brow and narrow-brow—something representative of everything under the sun, for everyone under the sun.

One might say that the same dimensions and characteristics apply to the music programs arranged and still being arranged for the World's Fair. In fact, these dimensions are so extensive that, even though I have been surrounded with them since the beginning, I'm still bewildered by their size. They've long since left the boundaries of the Fair itself.

This reminds me of the story of a colored man named Esau, who worked upon the campus of a little Southern college in a town invisible upon the map. At the time of the Chicago Fair, he was enraptured by the posters in the railroad station so as to take his savings to venture upon the long trip. Practically none of the colored folks had ever been more than three miles from town. When he left, every worker from the neighboring plantations was at the station to see him off. He was gone a month. Colored picture postcards of the Fair thrilled his friends. When he came back, an anxious and excited crowd was on hand to greet him. The president of the college asked the traveler what he liked best at the Fair. Esau scratched his head, meditated, and then said, "Well, Massa Boss, you see when I got to Chicago I just got so busy I never did get time to get to the fairgrounds."

As a matter of fact, the plans for the music of the Fair, as now outlined, will very properly be devoted to concerts and operas in New York City itself. About one-half of the celebrations will be upon Manhattan Island and one-half at the fairgrounds. As projected, the first six months of the fair season (May 1 to November 1) will include so many important occasions that one can confidently predict that it will be the most significant musical festival the world has ever known....

We have given a suggestion as to the participation of some foreign governments. It may be interesting to know that several countries overseas recognize the importance of music as a glorified expression of national ideals, and therefore these countries have arranged to engage great American symphony orchestras to play the music of their famous composers at a distinguished series of concerts given under the auspices of these countries. The plans are so far-reaching that I can give here only a sketch. Two performances of the New York Philharmonic Symphony Orchestra are certain, and six to 10 are possible. Poland has engaged this great orchestra for a Polish program Monday third; and Roumania has engaged it for May 5. Roumania has also engaged the Philadelphia Orchestra from May 14 to 16, to be conducted by the eminent Roumanian composer George Enesco. Czechoslovakia, Brazil, Switzerland, Finland, Argentina, and other nations are now negotiating for similar engagements with American orchestras. Practically all of the leading American orchestras have been invited to come to the Fair, and many have accepted.

There was usually something worth hearing in town in those days, even if Pittsburgh was not one of the jazz centers. One Saturday night I went to the theater on Frenchtown Avenue where all the Negro shows were booked. But I hardly noticed any part of the show; my attention was focused on a lady pianist who worked there. She sat cross-legged on the piano, cigarette in her mouth, writing music with her right hand while accompanying the show with a swinging left! Impressed, I told myself, "Mary, you'll do that one day." And I did, traveling with Andy Kirk's band in the 1930s on one-nighters.

—Mary Lou Williams

Recorded Popular Songs: 1939

- "Over the Rainbow"
  (Judy Garland)

- "God Bless America"
  (Kate Smith)

- "Three Little Fishies"
  (Kay Kyser)

- "When the Saints Go Marching In"
  (Louis Armstrong)

- "Moonlight Serenade"
  (Glenn Miller)

- "Beer Barrel Polka"
  (Will Glahe)

- "Sunrise Serenade"
  (Glenn Miller)

- "Says My Heart"
  (Red Norvo)

- "Little Brown Jug"
  (Glenn Miller)

- "South of the Border (Down Mexico Way)" (Shep Fields)

- "Jeepers Creepers"
  (Al Donohue)

- "If I Didn't Care"
  (Ink Spots)

- "Wishing (Will Make It So)"
  (Glenn Miller)

- "And the Angels Sing"
  (Benny Goodman)

- "Deep Purple"
  (Larry Clinton)

- "Heaven Can Wait"
  (Glen Gray)

- "They Say"
  (Artie Shaw)

- "Stairway to the Stars"
  (Glenn Miller)

- "Scatter-Brain"
  (Frankie Masters)

- "At the Woodchopper's Ball"
  (Woody Herman)

"Mary Lou Williams With Andy Kirk Band," *Cumberland Evening Times* (Maryland), **July 13, 1937:**

Mary Lou Williams is featured with Andy Kirk's Orchestra Thursday evening at Crystal Park. She is known as "America's Sweetheart of the ivories," and the most talked about "swing" pianist in the orchestral world. She's the girl that swings the band. She makes the piano speak in a language to which every dance responds…an unusual personality…she's America's foremost femme stylist of the piano.

Mary Lou Williams is the gal that makes all of Benny Goodman, Lou Armstrong, and Bob Crosby's special swing numbers.

1945: High School Teacher

War-time high school teacher Martha Deaton was convinced that the lack of adequate space and supplies, and family and stress, would leave her students unprepared for post-war America.

Life at Home

- When Martha Deaton took a long look at her ninth-grade history class, she had but one conclusion: America's schools were one of the primary casualties of the current World War.
- Thirty-nine students were crammed into a space designed for 28; children in shock over the recent deaths of brothers and fathers were being asked to dispassionately study the Peloponnesian War; rationed food, blaring headlines of even more fighting, and a total lack of qualified teachers were ever present.
- In her senior American history class, overcrowding was less an issue: within a week, two young men volunteered for the Army, while three more boys were anticipating their induction notices.
- And now that Martha was also teaching a class in world literature—to cover for a teacher whose son was recently wounded— her preparation time had doubled and her one free period had vanished.

Teaching during war time was challenging for high school teacher Martha Deaton.

- The same war that had disrupted family life and heightened emotional tensions had placed an additional responsibility on schools to guide the younger generation toward self-reliance.

- Between 20,000 and 25,000 teaching positions had been abandoned in the name of patriotism and war, resulting in overcrowded classrooms and dispirited teachers.
- Martha began her teaching career on the farm when, at the age of four, she corralled a gaggle of chickens into one end of the barn where she proceeded to teach them to count.
- Grades went unrecorded as the hens scratched their way to giggly, gleeful success.
- The second of four children, Martha learned to read when she was three, preached a "youth sermon" at church on her seventh birthday, and tutored eighth-graders in math when she was only 10.
- Martha's mother constantly talked about her precocious daughter; Martha's father, a structural engineer, rarely spoke at all, yet made prodigious efforts to attend piano recitals, district-wide writing contests and school plays.
- Martha attended a local teacher's college on a scholarship, fell in and out of love several times before discovering Mr. Right, and accepted her first job as a special education teacher in one of the toughest schools in Ohio.
- There she learned a lifetime's worth of lessons about standing her ground and looking beyond stereotypes; the administration had been ordered by the Board of Supervisors to institute the program.
- Martha's principal wanted the program to fail, Martha to quit, and the handicapped children to go away from his school.
- He received his wish, with a twist: after a year the principal was asked to leave, while Martha and the children stayed.
- She then tried teaching third-graders, followed by a stint with seventh-graders before finding her home with high school teenagers, whose influence on cultural and economic society was being recognized, advertised and highlighted in every major newspaper.
- Now that high school graduation rates had jumped from 10 percent in 1900, when high schools were in their infancy, to 30 percent in 1930, Martha thought that the 50 percent now being attained would go even higher.
- Already a greater emphasis was being placed on the teens.
- *Seventeen*, an American magazine for teenagers created in 1944, was squarely aimed at young girls and women.
- Article headings such as "What You Wear" and "Having Fun" were clearly aimed at expanding the American consumer market beyond adults.

Life at Work

- Thirty-one-year-old Martha Deaton wished that the foreman at the Cincinnati weapons plant would stop recruiting teachers to work in the factory.
- Plainly, women with teaching degrees could do more to service the cause of peace by staying in the schools.
- Besides, once the war ended—as it surely would one day—the factories would turn their backs on women again; it happened after World War I and it would happen this time, too, Martha believed.
- The only time women received any respect was when men needed something.
- More than any war in history, World War II was a battle of production.
- After all, the Germans and the Japanese had had a 10-year head start on amassing weapons, so rapid production of military equipment was essential to victory, and women were the last labor reserve.
- When President Franklin D. Roosevelt asked in 1940 for 50,000 airplanes a year, critics lampooned the goal, but by 1944, the U.S. was producing 120,000 planes annually.
- Half of the aircraft were built in plants where more than half of the employees were female; ammunition plants, shipyards and equipment factories recorded similar gender employment.

- To meet the aggressive goals, industry recruited educated, middle-class housewives who had never dreamed of working outside the home.
- They were willing to serve their country, but not under dirty, dangerous conditions.
- First-generation immigrant women spurned the environment thrust upon them; working conditions improved for all and harsh disciplinary techniques were abandoned for more positive incentives.
- Shortages were so acute, women were recruited from surrounding states and counties to fill job openings and were provided buses for commuting or dormitories for those who needed housing.
- In some rural locations, the new women workers had never used telephones or flush toilets, but their pay gave them access to independence, skills and confidence they had never experienced before.
- In 1940, 12 million women were working; five years later there were 19 million in the workforce.

Martha Deaton, right, with a student.

- It was time for firsts for many women—including teachers who benefited from the competitive atmosphere for workers.
- For more than 100 years, school boards—mostly composed of men—had imposed onerous rules on teachers' behavior—including where they could live, how they might socialize, the color of the clothes they could wear and how ashes from the schoolhouse fire must be removed.
- Women who married often had to stop teaching; married teachers who became pregnant were asked to step down.
- Now that industry was sniffing around for help, married women were suddenly acceptable and some school boards even made exceptions for childbirth.
- One national survey showed that 39 percent of school superintendents approved of the marriage prohibitions for teachers and 52 percent disapproved.
- But if highly vocal, tax-paying citizens opposed married teachers, many superintendents found it too risky to confront them.
- Men were considered the breadwinners and a wife's pay purely supplemental.
- It was generally believed that teachers were more likely than blue-collar women to be married to white collar men, and as such, had more economic flexibility to resign their jobs when they married.
- Some middle-class husbands simply would not allow their wives to work.
- In October of 1939, there were virtually no teaching jobs available nationwide; by October 1943, 7,000 jobs went unfilled and 57,000 had been filled by teachers who could not meet regular certification.
- U.S. Commissioner of Education John W. Studebaker said that during the course of the national emergency, as many as 115,000 teachers had left the nation's classrooms to help the war effort in one way or another.

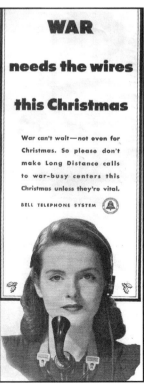

U.S. Commissioner of Education John Studebaker, standing, worried that recruiting teachers for the war effort resulted in understaffed schools and overcrowded classrooms.

- "Every community can testify to the competent and unselfish job teachers have done both at their posts and in voluntary wartime tasks of rationing, salvaging and bond sales. But the fact remains that at this critical time in our history, between 20,000 and 25,000 positions have been abandoned and thousands of classes are overcrowded."
- Rights had come begrudgingly slowly to teachers.
- The question of whether married women could still teach was litigated in 1937 when a New Jersey tenured teacher was asked to sign a contract that reduced her pay to a level designated for married teachers; the State Supreme Court ruled the classification "unreasonable and thus invalid."
- Society as a whole believed women could be superior teachers, especially for the lower grades, because of biological predestination and the natural affinity for children.
- Ironically, motherhood was often the reason a teacher was asked to step aside.
- A bevy of studies concerning the competence of married women scrutinized everything from the number of sick days they could have to what they did on Saturdays, the number of dependents, their service participation, and whether eighth-graders liked them more than single women.
- Teachers found "no distinct differences in social, recreational, and professional life of married and single women as teachers."
- Yet reformers saw working women as dangerous to the family ideal, while feminists considered employment a prerequisite for female independence.
- What was also true was that the higher the visibility of a job, the more likely it was to encounter societal discrimination; considerably less was said about female factory workers and domestics.

- Suddenly, the war presented female teachers with a unique bargaining position; once shortages occurred, teachers' viewpoints became more important.
- Martha had faced similar challenges through the years, and though they were not pleasant, she had been allowed to continue teaching.
- She was also determined that her daughter would not be subjected to similar economic discrimination.
- If men could change the rules when a war necessity dictated, they could keep the reforms once the danger had passed.
- After World War II broke out, Wellesley College assistant professor of education Isabel Stephens studied the opportunities provided by teaching versus the expanded job market.
- For college-educated women, she found five reasons to leave the field of education: 1) lack of community support, 2) lack of intellectual interchange, 3) petty gossip in the schools, 4) a system where scientific efficiency was valued over ideas, 5) the practice of firing women if they married.

Life in the Community: Cincinnati, Ohio

- At the dawn of the 1940s, Cincinnati was the 14th biggest city in the United States, bustling with life and still proud of its title as the Gateway to the West.
- During World War II, gas and rubber were tightly rationed for everyone in the United States, and in Cincinnati, the streetcar became a popular means of transportation.
- Rationing seemed to suit the people of the Queen City, and the 1940s in the tri-state area were constantly hopping with development, art and culture.
- Cincinnati sweetheart Doris Day was just beginning her famous career in the city in the 1940s, performing as a vocalist for local bands and building her reputation just as the city was beginning to fade.
- Cincinnati's public schools ranged from nursery schools to a municipal university.
- In addition, several elementary and 16 parochial high schools and academies were scattered throughout the city, along with two Catholic colleges in three theological schools—Catholic, Protestant, and Jewish.
- Settled in 1788, by the early nineteenth century, Cincinnati was the first American boomtown in the heart of the country and rivaled the larger coastal cities in size and wealth.
- As one of the first major inland cities, Cincinnati earned a reputation as "the first purely American city."
- It was originally named "Losantiville" from four terms, each from a different language, meaning "the city opposite the mouth of the Licking River."
- In 1790, Arthur St. Clair, the governor of the Northwest Territory, changed the name of the settlement to "Cincinnati" in honor of the Society of the Cincinnati, of which he was a member.
- The Society honored General George Washington, who was considered a latter-day Cincinnatus, the Roman farmer who was called to serve Rome as dictator, an office which he resigned after completing his task of defeating the Aequians in no less than 16 days, and was considered the role model dictator.
- Cincinnati was incorporated as a city in 1819; the introduction of steam navigation on the Ohio River in 1811 and the completion of the Miami and Erie Canal helped the city grow to 115,000 residents by 1850.
- To protect its growth, the city began paying men to act as its fire department in 1853, creating the first full-time, paid fire department in the United States and the first in the world to use steam fire engines.

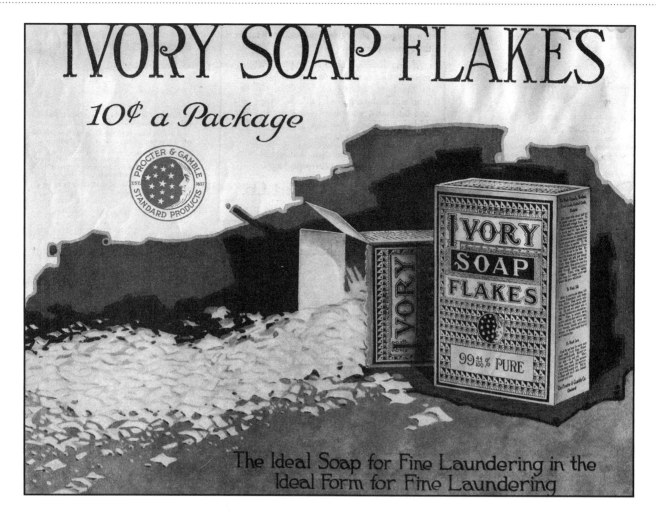

- Six years later, in 1859, Cincinnati laid out six streetcar lines, making it easier for people to get around the city.
- By 1872, Cincinnatians could travel on the streetcars within the city and transfer to railcars for travel to the hill communities.
- The Cincinnati Red Stockings, a baseball team whose name and heritage inspired the Cincinnati Reds, began their career in the nineteenth century as well, and became the first professional team in the country in 1869.
- In 1879, Procter & Gamble, one of Cincinnati's major soap manufacturers, began marketing Ivory Soap. It was marketed as "light enough to float."
- By the end of the nineteenth century, with the industrial shift from steamboats to railroads, Cincinnati's growth had slowed considerably and was surpassed in population and prominence by Chicago.
- Cincinnati weathered the Great Depression better than most American cities of its size, largely because of resurgence in river trade, which was less expensive than rail.
- The rejuvenation of the downtown area began in the 1920s and continued into the next decade with the construction of Union Terminal, the post office, and a large Bell Telephone building.
- The flood of 1937 was one of the worst in the nation's history; afterwards, the city built protective flood walls.

HISTORICAL SNAPSHOT
1945

- Franklin D. Roosevelt was inaugurated to an unprecedented fourth term as president
- In the Philippines, 121 American soldiers and 800 Filipino guerrillas freed 813 American POWs from the Japanese-held camp at Cabanatuan City
- The Soviet Union agreed to enter the Pacific War against Japan once hostilities against Germany were concluded
- President Roosevelt, Prime Minister Winston Churchill, and Soviet leader Joseph Stalin held the Yalta Conference
- Chile, Ecuador, Paraguay, and Peru joined the United Nations
- In the Battle of Iwo Jima, approximately 30,000 U.S. Marines landed on Iwo Jima
- Dutch diarist Anne Frank died in the Bergen-Belsen concentration camp
- The film *Les Enfants du Paradis* premiered in Paris
- American B-29 bombers attacked Tokyo with incendiary bombs, killing 100,000 citizens
- The 17th Academy Awards ceremony was broadcast via radio for the first time; the Best Picture award went to *Going My Way*
- American bombers numbering 1,250 attacked Berlin
- Sylvester the cat debuted in *Life with Feathers*
- Adolph Hitler, along with his wife Eva Braun, committed suicide on April 30, 1945
- President Roosevelt died suddenly at Warm Springs, Georgia; Vice President Harry S. Truman became the thirty-third president
- Rodgers and Hammerstein's *Carousel* opened on Broadway
- Poet and author Ezra Pound was arrested by American soldiers in Italy for treason
- The Trinity Test, the first test of an atomic bomb, used about six kilograms of plutonium and unleashed an explosion equivalent to that of 19 kilotons of TNT
- Winston Churchill resigned as prime minister after his Conservative Party was soundly defeated by the Labour Party in the 1945 general election
- The United Nations Charter was ratified by the U.S., the third nation to join the new international organization
- The Zionist World Congress approached the British government to discuss the founding of the country of Israel
- Emperor Hirohito announced Japan's surrender on the radio; the United States called that day V-J Day for Victory over Japan
- Writer Arthur C. Clarke advanced the idea of a communications satellite in a *Wireless World* magazine article
- The Detroit Tigers won the baseball World Series against the Chicago Cubs
- At Gimbels Department Store in New York City, the first ballpoint pens cost $12.50 each

Selected Prices

Ashtray $8.50

Automobile, De Soto $2,200.00

Deep Freezer $225.00

Fountain Pen $15.00

Home Permanent Kit...$1.40

Radio Phonograph..$199.95

Record Cabinet...$13.50

Records, Four 12" $4.72

Silk Stockings $0.98

Wrenches, Set of Six...$2.85

"Education," *1944 Britannica Book of the Year*, 1944:

The Shortage of Teachers

The shortage of teachers, which had already begun to make itself felt in 1942, increased during 1943, when it was estimated that more than 100,000 teachers had left the profession to join the armed forces or to enter defense industries. It was anticipated that this number would continue to grow, particularly since steps were not taken immediately to adjust teachers' salaries to the increasing cost of living. With 40 percent of the teachers receiving less than $1,200 a year and 8 percent less than $600 a year, the temptation to enter well-paid positions in defense industries could not be resisted. The exodus of teachers was in the main from rural and village schools; teachers who left the urban schools were chiefly those whose special training was needed in defense industries and by the armed forces. The effect on all schools—rural and urban—was serious. In rural schools it was estimated that about 6,000,000 pupils would be taught by inexperienced teachers, assuming that the schools were open at all. In urban schools, serious difficulties were encountered in replacing teachers of mathematics, chemistry, physics, and industrial and physical education. The War Manpower Commission, as a result of pressure brought to bear upon it by school officials and educational associations, declared teaching an essential occupation and sought, under its stabilization plan, to regulate the transfer of teachers from one position to another for increased pay. Nevertheless, the turnover of teachers was nearly double that of any normal year (189,000 as compared to 95,000).

In an effort to check the migration from the profession, a variety of schemes were tried. Attention was directed to the importance of education in a democracy; parent-teacher associations conducted publicity campaigns among the public and among teachers; promises of better conditions of service, tenure and old-age security were made; promising candidates were encouraged to enter the profession; and emergency training classes were established for inexperienced teachers or for those who had been out of the profession for some time and wished to help during the emergency....

The Exodus From School

It was estimated by the middle of 1943 that at least 2,000,000 boys and girls between the ages of 14 and 18 had left school to enter wage-earning occupations, and that of these, 25 percent were under 15. This was a consequence of the labor shortage and the high wages which could be earned after a very short period of training. To some extent, the disruption of school organization due to the shortage of teachers and lax enforcement of compulsory attendance laws may have exercised some influence. The situation became sufficiently serious for the War Manpower Commission, the Children's Bureau of the Department of Labor, and the U.S. Office of Education to issue an announcement to urban communities stating that "The first obligation of school youth is to take advantage of their educational opportunities in

Continued

"Education,". . . *(Continued)*

order that they be prepared for citizenship and for service to the nation … school authorities, employers, parents and other interested parties should recognize the obligation to safeguard the physical and intellectual development of youth." The Educational Policies Commission of the National Education Association issued a similar recommendation: "School attendance until graduation is the best contribution to the war effort which school age youth can make." Both groups urged that arrangements be made to combine part-time work in war occupations with the continuation of regular schooling until high school graduation. Not only was the academic education of youth being sabotaged, but young workers were being exploited and were not being paid the "wages paid to adult workers for similar job performances."

Federal Aid for Education

The effort to secure federal aid for education, which began during World War I, was continued during 1943, but was again defeated. Since 1917, the need for federal aid to implement the American ideal of equality in educational opportunity was believed by some educators to be greater than ever. The war revealed differences in educational provisions in the country as never before. Under the selective draft systems, large numbers of draftees were shown to be wholly or functionally illiterate, and another large number were rejected on physical grounds. The shortage of teachers revealed the low standards of remuneration which prevailed in the country.

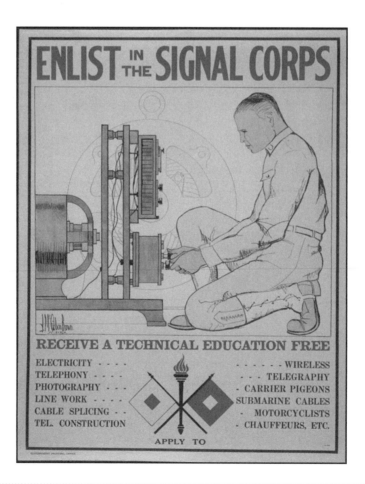

> ### "Bible Teacher for Elementary Schools Named,"
> ### *The Asheville Times* (North Carolina), January 14, 1946:
>
> Miss Mary Ann Dendy of Weaverville has been elected teacher of Bible for Asheville elementary schools and will assume her duties tomorrow, it has been announced.
>
> A graduate of Weaverville high school and Mars Hill College, Miss Dendy received a bachelor of arts degree in religious education from Erskine College, Due West, South Carolina, in 1945 and did graduate study work in Bible at Columbia Seminary in Decatur, Georgia....
>
> Miss Dendy's appointment was announced by L. T. New, chairman of the Bible in the Schools executive committee.
>
> Mr. New pointed out that the committee launched a campaign last August to raise funds to make employment of a fourth Bible teacher for the city schools possible, and that, since a teacher was not available for the first semester of school work, the $1,006 raised from the campaign was held in trust until a teacher could be obtained.

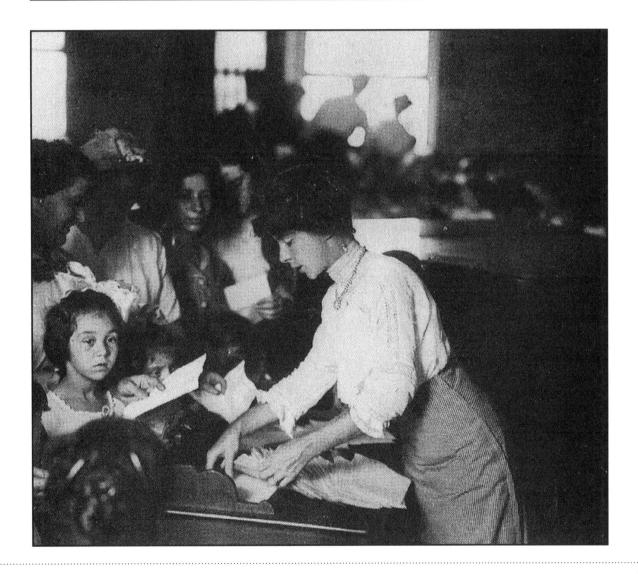

"Major Problems: Teacher Shortage," *Waukesha Daily Freeman* (Wisconsin), September 10, 1949:

Any discussion of the problems facing schools must start, of course, with the teacher shortage. For in the final analysis, the teacher is the school; the teacher is the curriculum.

A district may have an excellent building and the finest equipment available, but if the teacher is poor, the school is poor. On the other hand, a good teacher can often provide a good school despite numerous handicaps.

Because the nearest state Teachers College has virtually stopped preparing rural teachers, we here in Waukesha County have been very seriously hampered by the teacher shortage. The recruitment of teachers has become one of the major duties of the county office. After tremendous efforts throughout the summer, we finally filled all vacancies. But then our real problems began, for many of these new teachers were unprepared and must be given detailed, continuous guidance in educational policies and methods. Thus, in addition to being an employment bureau, the Office of County Superintendent has become a sort of a mobile college for on-the-job training of teachers.

This year, we have in the county 66 special emergency permit teachers, which is the same number as last year. This would indicate that we are holding our ground, but in reality we are not, and unless conditions change suddenly it will probably be several years before the supply of teachers balances the demand, especially in the elementary field.

Our factory superintendents complain that the high turnover of workers impairs and slows down production. This is, of course, true, but the turnover of a Waukesha industry comparable in size to our school system was only 20 percent last year, whereas the turnover of teachers in our county was 33 percent.

It is, therefore, clear that the problem of labor shortage is much more intensive in education than in industry. It is also more serious, for the production by the schools of an inferior product has a much more dramatic and lasting effect upon our civilization than the production by industry of an inferior motor or refrigerator.

In fact, we have ample evidence to support the argument that the teacher shortage is one of the most perplexing problems facing America today.

The Handicapped Child

It is fitting and proper that we improve the education of normal children, but at the same time we must not neglect the mentally and physically handicapped. These children who, through the force of circumstances, are not able to meet the standards set up for normal boys and girls need special attention for their own sake and for the sake of society in general.

Years ago, when Dr. G. O. Banting was president of the Wisconsin Education Association, he made a significant speech on this problem at the State Teachers Convention. In his speech he pointed out that just as one weak rail can wreck the midnight express, so one misguided boy can bring chaos to humanity.

Continued

"Major Problems . . . *(Continued)*

For years, the State of Wisconsin has appropriated a large sum of money to eight cities in the employment of special teachers of handicapped children. Through action on the last legislature, these funds are now available to counties. Under this new arrangement, several counties are employing or taking the steps to employ special teachers. Here in our county we need:

1. A speech correctionist to work with stutterers, children with cleft palates, etc.
2. A specially trained instructor to assist mentally retarded children and establish and supervise opportunity rooms.

As the state bears three-fourths of the cost of these workers, and as the problem of the handicapped child is becoming more and more acute in our overcrowded schools, Waukesha County cannot for long put off the employment of such educational specialists.

"We Stick Our Neck Out," *Predictions of Things To Come*, March, 1943:

- Dried eggs will become an increasingly important food commodity.
- Women's fashion reflecting an African influence will be promoted next fall.
- If and when razor blades are rationed, American men will cultivate beards and mustaches.
- Because of the increasing number of women engaged in war work, the wearing of slacks will become more and more popular.
- Metal and plastic screw caps for tubes of drug and toilet goods will shortly be replaced by caps made of tough, fibrous stock covered at the end with a printed label.
- The Alcan Highway (which is the official name of the new Alaska-Canada highway that has just been completed) will become, after the war, one of the greatest tourist attractions of the age. Scenery, as well as the hunting and fishing en route, will be incomparable.
- Most colleges will drop intercollegiate football next fall for the duration.
- Next summer, the percentage of women who will go stockingless will increase many times.
- Rudolph Hess will be put on trial after the war, but not until then. It will be one of the most sensational trials in the history of the world.
- Pennies will be made of steel and coated with zinc to release copper for war industries as soon as Congress passes permissive legislation.
- Double movie features will decline, especially during the war. The government is discouraging them, because there is a shortage of film and because it wishes to increase the use of one-reel films which contribute towards civilians' morale and the war effort.

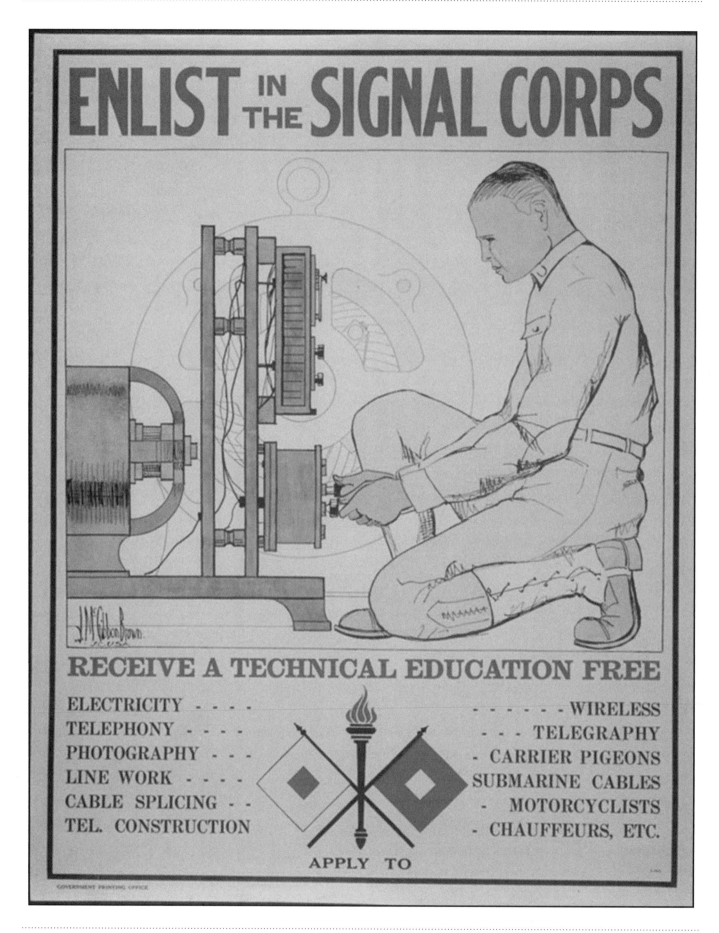

1945: US Navy Lieutenant

Radcliffe College PhD graduate Mary Sears used her knowledge of marine tides to help the U.S. Navy invade enemy islands during World War II, and help overcome that institution's all-male prejudices.

Life at Home

- In the opening months of the Second World War, U.S. Naval commanders had to overcome two well-established traditions: a distrust of academic types and women in the Navy, especially on ships.
- Born in 1905 and raised in rural Wayland, Massachusetts, outside Boston, Mary took responsibility for raising her two younger siblings in the years after her mother died in 1911.
- When she graduated from Windsor School in Boston in 1923, her classmates believed she was destined for a political career representing the farm bloc in Congress, since she knew everything there was to know about farming, especially raising Guernsey cows.
- At Radcliffe College, Mary planned to study Greek before she was encouraged by her stepmother, a Radcliffe graduate, to explore other subjects.
- A class in biology led to two summers in Bermuda studying corals that triggered a lifetime pursuit of collecting specimens.
- Her pursuit of marine invertebrates channeled her towards a major in zoology, traditionally a male-only path, symbolized by the absence of any women's bathrooms in Harvard's Museum of Comparative Zoology where she spent most of her study time.

Lt. (Dr.) Mary Sears overcame prejudices in the U.S. Navy.

- In 1927, Mary received a bachelor's degree, graduating magna cum laude, and was elected to Phi Beta Kappa; a master's from Radcliffe followed in 1929.
- Her thesis, "The Deep-Seated Melanophones of the Lower Vertebrates," earned her a doctorate in 1933 and served as the foundation for her career in biological oceanography.
- Her next step was employment at the recently opened Woods Hole Oceanographic Institute, where she worked until the early years of the war.
- By then the Navy was eager to embrace new technology; the first few years of the war had been costly and sometimes disastrous.

As a student, Sears enjoyed the study of biology.

- Several island invasions had gone badly, thanks to out-of-date tidal charts and too little knowledge, the result of which was thousands of American soldiers killed.
- Defeating the Germans and the Japanese was going to be difficult.
- World War II, which was clearly shaping up to be a truly technological battle, needed advanced and exact scientific knowledge.
- In addition, the demands of a two-ocean campaign placed enormous pressure on the Navy to rapidly develop new scientific capability.
- Throughout the 1930s, the U.S. Congress had refused to approve funds for oceanographic research by the Navy while the Japanese had assiduously charted the waters of the Pacific Ocean.
- When in early 1942 the War Manpower Commission found itself unable to supply a sufficient number of men, it turned to unorthodox personnel—women.
- Barnard College Dean Virginia C. Gildersleeve remarked, "If the Navy could possibly use dogs or ducks or monkeys, the admirals would probably prefer them to women."
- American women with scientific skills had little incentive to join the Navy or the other services.
- Unlike women in Britain and the Soviet Union, U.S. women were not subject to compulsory military service.
- In fact, the creation of the U.S. draft in September 1940 had taken many young male scientists and mathematicians away from their positions in industry and academia, which opened the way for women in the jobs left behind.
- Not that the list of highly trained women was large.
- Before the war, few women graduated with technical degrees of any sort; fewer than a dozen a year graduated in engineering during the late 1930s.
- Even the Navy's name for the women's organization expressed its ambivalence: WAVES—Women Accepted for Volunteer Emergency Service.

Life at Work

- Shortly after the Japanese attack on Pearl Harbor in December 1941, Dr. Mary Sears made her scientific skills available to the United States Navy.
- Based on the needs—and the financing—of the Navy, the Woods Hole Oceanographic Institute was alive with new projects.
- The collaboration of the Navy and Woods Hole Oceanographic Institute was initially a marriage of convenience that brought money, new equipment and the opportunity to explore untraditional topics.

Sears was determined to make a good impression when she enlisted for WAVES.

- Often, different scientifically oriented organizations worked on only parts of any given project, with the Navy itself pulling the final project together.
- Mary's first assignment was investigating ways to reduce the level of marine life fouling on ships' bottoms, a natural phenomenon that reduced the overall speed of warships—potentially endangering the crew.
- To satisfy the needs of the Navy, Mary created a catalog on barnacles and other organisms that played a part in fouling; this was the first step towards inventing a solution.
- By then Mary was an accomplished oceanographer with little actual experience at sea; even Woods Hole prohibited women from sailing on research vessels because of a lack of "facilities" for women.
- While a graduate student, she had worked at Harvard University with Dr. Henry Bigelow, a founder and the first director of the Woods Hole Oceanographic Institute.
- She began working summers as a planktonologist in 1932, one of the first 10 research assistants to be appointed to the staff at the Institute.
- Although Woods Hole had been a mostly summer-only operation through the 1930s, Mary was named in 1940 as a planktonologist on a year-round basis.
- During this time, she also served as a research assistant at Harvard, a tutor at Radcliffe and an instructor at Wellesley College.
- In 1941, she served at Pisco Bay in Peru as Grant and Faculty Fellow for Wellesley College's Committee on Inter-American Cultural and Artistic Relations.
- When Mary felt called to leave the Institute and join the WAVES, initially the shy, small woman failed a medical exam because of an earlier bout with arthritis.
- But the Old Boy network that she understood so well, and her scientific skills, overcame the bureaucratic hurdles, and she was offered a position as a first lieutenant, junior grade.

- Her first assignment was to head the Oceanographic Unit of the newly formed U.S. Navy Hydrographic Office, whose chief responsibility was the making of navigational charts for use on combat ships.
- The data produced by the Hydro unit were considered "an essential instrument of war" when provided to fleet and shore-based aircraft "in direct combat operations."
  - The need was tremendous.
  - When Mary arrived in June 1943, there were already 43 enlisted WAVES at Hydro with 85 due in July and a projected goal of 250 by September.
  - The need for data was so great, the Hydro unit operated three shifts a day, seven days a week.
  - Mary's team of 12 women and three men included an expert on barnacles, an oceanographic research librarian, the former curator of crustaceans at Harvard University's Museum of Comparative Zoology, an algologist, a limnologist, and Mary served as the planktonologist.
  - The Naval Hydrographic Office was created in 1854 with a focus on ocean bottom mapping for more accurate navigational charts.
  - By the 1930s, the Navy's interest was primarily around submarine warfare and the newly developed sonar technology.
  - Understanding ocean properties such as temperature distribution, pressure, salinity, and bottom characteristics was essential to predicting how sound would travel in the water.
  - Mary's work led to the publication of *Submarine Supplements to the Sailing Directions*, which predicted the presence of thermoclines in certain waters, areas of rapid temperature change in the water column which cause refraction and bending of sound waves.

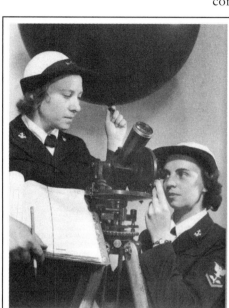

Sears joined a growing number of enlisted women.

- Thus, the Navy learned that submarines could effectively hide under thermoclines, avoiding detection by ship-mounted sonar devices.
- Naval oceanography was also interested in such diverse subjects as current drift for search and rescue operations and floating mines, surf predictions for amphibious landings, and the turbulent effects of sea and swell waves on moored mines.

The Hydro team worked around the clock laying out navigational charts.

- Marine biology was also an interest, since bioluminescent plankton activated by ship wakes could be used to locate ships in the dark, certain organisms contributed to ambient marine noise that inhibited sonar operations, large kelp growths fouled amphibious landing craft, and certain marine organisms degraded mine mechanisms.

- During the course of the war, the Oceanographic Unit was expanded into a division, and Mary was promoted to lieutenant commander.
- Mary also worked on improving tidal predictions and inventing new ways to mathematically forecast conditions.
- The Navy became ruefully aware of its shortcomings after the battle of Tarawa, when an inaccurate tidal prediction stranded an amphibious group of Marines on a reef, where they were cut to pieces by shore-based Japanese machine gunners.
- Mary further refined her tidal predictions and wave refraction charts to recommend an alternate attack route for the planned amphibious assaults on Luzon and various islands around Okinawa.
- The most taxing of her responsibilities, which were centered primarily in the Pacific and Indian Oceans, was the constant demand for intelligence reports concerning hydrographic factors affecting a possible invasion.
- The reports were always urgently needed for immediate strategic and tactical planning for amphibious operations in the Pacific.
- Her reports, she understood, would impact the lives of thousands; often her best available information on sea and swell in the Indian Ocean came from a Dutch publication written in 1896.
- Time pressure was particularly acute "whenever Roosevelt and Churchill got together," Mary said.
- Often the "pursuit of impossible perfection" had to be abandoned in favor of "quickies" that required her to work all night.
- Her best source of information was provided by the Japanese, who surveyed the ocean and published extensive tracts about Asian waters in the years leading up to the war.
- She also received intelligence by reading the logs of military ships and the gathering of tidal data by sailors.
- Ultimately, Mary's assignment was to draw information from many sources to form an intricate mosaic from which the planners in Washington could form their battle plans.
- During the first months of 1944, the Oceanographic Unit was asked for reports on Sakhalin, the Kuriles and northern Hokkaido, while at the same time the Unit was developing ocean current charts for "certain Pacific areas" as well as bottom settlement charts for Java, the Makassar Strait, Cam Ranh Bay to Cape Varella, and Singapore Strait to the Banka Straits.
- The success of the Oceanographic Unit's work was best illustrated by the Allied landings on Luzon in the Philippines.

American troops were in need of new intelligence.

- The surf was low in the western part of the Gulf in Western Luzon, making it the most attractive location for an invasion; for that reason it was also most heavily fortified by the Japanese.

Better charts enabled the Navy to make safe and tactically successful landings ashore.

- Employing weather data and wave refraction charts, Mary and her team recommended that the invasion take place in the eastern part of the Gulf where it was also safe to come ashore.
- Her recommendations launched the successful Philippine invasion, which had been captured 37 months earlier by the Japanese.
- Ironically, the closer the Americans got to the Japanese homelands, the easier Mary's work became—"as we are able to use the very complete data published by Japanese scientists before Pearl Harbor."

Life in the Community: Woods Hole, Falmouth, Massachusetts

- In 1927, a National Academy of Sciences committee concluded that it was time to "consider the share of the United States of America in a worldwide program of oceanographic research."
- The committee's recommendation for establishing a permanent independent research laboratory on the East Coast to "prosecute oceanography in all its branches" led to the founding in 1930 of the Woods Hole Oceanographic Institute.
- A $3 million grant from the Rockefeller Foundation supported the summer work of a dozen scientists, construction of a laboratory building and commissioning of a research vessel, the 142-foot ketch *Atlantis*, whose profile forms the Institute's logo.
- The Institute was located at Woods Hole, located in the town of Falmouth, Massachusetts, at the extreme southwest corner of Cape Cod, where scientific research had been conducted since 1871.

- The term "Woods Hole" referred to a passage for ships between Vineyard Sound and Buzzards Bay known for its extremely strong current, approaching four knots.
- Historically, Woods Hole's harbor had allowed the area to emerge as a center for whaling, shipping, and fishing during the eighteenth century.
- At the end of the nineteenth century, Woods Hole was the home of the Pacific Guano Company, which produced fertilizer from bird dung imported from islands in the Pacific Ocean, the Caribbean, and the coast of South Carolina.
- After the firm went bankrupt in 1889, Long Neck—the peninsula on which its factory was located—was renamed Penzance Point and was developed with shingle-style summer homes for bankers and lawyers from New York and Boston.
- Woods Hole Oceanographic Institute grew substantially in the late 1930s to support defense-related research, and during World War II expanded dramatically in staff and scientific stature.
- Over the years, Woods Hole scientists have been credited with seminal discoveries about the ocean.

HISTORICAL SNAPSHOT
1945

- The Red Army liberated the Auschwitz and Birkenau death camps
- American soldiers and Filipino guerrillas freed 813 American POWs from the Japanese-held camp at Cabanatuan City, Philippines, following the invasion of the islands
- Eddie Slovik was the first American soldier since the Civil War to be executed by firing squad for desertion
- Thirty thousand U.S. Marines successfully invaded Iwo Jima and raised the American flag
- Dutch teenager Anne Frank died of typhus in the Bergen-Belsen concentration camp, Lower Saxony, Germany
- American B-29 bombers attacked Japan with incendiary bombs; Tokyo was fire-bombed, killing 100,000 citizens

- The Seventeenth Academy Awards ceremony was broadcast via radio for the first time; Going My Way won the award for Best Picture
- Berlin was attacked by 1,250 American bombers; Adolf Hitler ordered that all military installations, machine shops, and transportation and communications facilities in Germany be destroyed
- President Franklin D. Roosevelt, while serving his fourth term, died suddenly at Warm Springs, Georgia; Vice President Harry S. Truman became the thirty-third president of the United States
- The American war correspondent Ernie Pyle was killed by Japanese machine gun fire on the island of Ie Shima off Okinawa
- Rodgers and Hammerstein's Carousel, a musical play based on Ferenc Molnár's Liliom, opened on Broadway
- Heinrich Himmler offered a German surrender to the Western Allies, but not to the Soviet Union; Western Allies rejected any offer of surrender by Germany other than an unconditional one
- British Lancaster bombers dropped food into the Netherlands to prevent the starvation of the civilian population
- Adolf Hitler and his wife of one day, Eva Braun, committed suicide as the Red Army approached the Führerbunker in Berlin
- Poet Ezra Pound was arrested by American soldiers in Italy for treason

continued

HISTORICAL SNAPSHOT *(continued)*
1945

- A Japanese balloon bomb killed five children and a woman near Bly, Oregon, the only people killed by an enemy attack on the American mainland during World War II
- Winston Churchill resigned as the United Kingdom's prime minister after his Conservative Party was soundly defeated by the Labour Party
- The U.S. B-29 Superfortress Enola Gay dropped an atomic bomb, code-named "Little Boy," on Hiroshima, Japan, and the B-29 Bomber Bockscar dropped another, code-named "Fat Man," on Nagasaki, Japan
- The Zionist World Congress approached the British government to discuss the founding of the country of Israel
- The final official surrender by Japan was accepted by Supreme Allied Commander General Douglas MacArthur and Fleet Admiral Chester Nimitz
- Mohandas Gandhi and Jawaharlal Nehru demanded that all British troops leave India
- Arthur C. Clarke advanced the idea of a communications satellite in *Wireless World* magazine
- The first ballpoint pens went on sale at Gimbels Department Store in New York City for $12.50 each
- John H. Johnson published the first issue of the magazine Ebony
- Telechron introduced the "Musalarm," the first clock radio.
- War trials against 24 Nazi war criminals began at the Nuremberg Palace of Justice
- Assembly of the world's first general purpose electronic computer, the Electronic Numerical Integrator and Computer (ENIAC), was completed
- At the Mayo Clinic, streptomycin was first used to treat tuberculosis

Selected Prices

Ashtray $8.50
Automobile, De Soto $2,200.00
Barbell $8.95
Electric Food Liquidizer $35.00
Home Permanent Kit...$1.40
Manicure Set...$15.00
Mattress $54.50
Radio Phonograph $199.95
Record Cabinet $13.50
Wrenches, Set of Six $2.85

Pre-War Full
Swing Skirt

Wartime Soft
and Slim Line

Pre-War Full
Waist Silhouette

Wartime Fitted
Waist Silhouette

"Navy Redoubles Effort In WAVE Enlistments," *Long Beach Independent* (California), November 16, 1943:

Fearing that Italy's capitulation and successful aggressive action on many fronts may cause complacency and letdown in volunteers for the Women's Reserve, the Navy Department issued instructions to the Office of Naval Officer Procurement to redouble efforts to effect enlistment of more WAVES.

Rear Admiral I.C. Johnson, in charge of the WAVE program for the 11th Naval district, called upon his staff and members of the Navy recruiting services to give wide dissemination to the need for women in the Navy now.

"The Navy's war has just begun. Additional men will be needed to man ships taken from the enemy. Shore-stationed blue jackets will be called upon to go into the combat duty at sea, and WAVES must replace these men in vital jobs ashore," Gen. Johnson said.

"Inventions Can Win the War: Have You an Idea That Might Help?" *Popular Science*, October 1942:

In the summer of 1940 Goering's airmen, flushed with their victories in Norway, Belgium, Holland, and France, swept over Britain. There they were met and thrown back by some 3,000 R.A.F. flyers. Several factors played a decisive part in that historic defeat. The heroism of the young men in the Hurricanes and Spitfires was one of them. But heroism does not enable a flyer to see that attacking plane in the dark. There was also a technological factor—the British were equipped with a radio location device by which, in effect, they could see their enemies at night. Without it they would have been unable to bring them down in such vast numbers as to make Goering hesitate—and when he hesitated he was lost.

This is a sample of the part invention is playing in the war. Until recently the radio locator could not even be mentioned in print; even now it can be no more than mentioned. But it is a fact that without this particular unpublicized invention, the British might well have gone down to defeat. Dr. Vannevar Bush, speaking recently on "Science and National Defense," said the "radio detection, developed by a group of devoted British scientist working from 1935 on, at times without much encouragement, offset the element of surprise. This one development may have saved the Isle of Britain."

Dr. Bush should know; besides being president of the Carnegie Institute of Washington, he is director of the Office of Scientific Research and Development, our chief coordinator in the field of organized worktime invention. It takes some coordination. Before the war, out of 170,000 manufacturing companies in the United States, only 1,800 maintained research laboratories, and of those, only a few hundred were big ones. The number of industrial research workers did not exceed 33,000. As Herbert Hoover never tired of pointing out, we were not doing enough research. As a result, now that we are at war, we do not have nearly enough trained scientists to work on the problems which the Army and Navy are pressing for an immediate solution. Needless duplication must be avoided, and that is one responsibility of the Office of Scientific Research and Development and its subsidiary, the National Defense Research Committee, headed by Dr. J.B. Corrigan, who sidelined as the president of Harvard University. Another is to make sure that the most urgent things are done first, and the results of research in one field are articulated with those in the others.

The NDRC officials are responsible for the bulk of the non-medical scientific work required in connection with the war effort. Yet it has no laboratories and does no research of its own. Research projects go to existing laboratories—a model of 100 percent subcontracting. At last advisories, it had over 450 research projects operating under contract, involving the technical facilities for some of the most important university and industrial laboratories in the country.

continued

"Inventions Can Win the War: Have You an Idea That Might Help?" *(continued)*

Every one of these 450 projects is highly confidential. The men working on various problems, although all of them have been investigated and approved by the Federal Bureau of Investigation, are not told of other problems that were allocated to other groups, unless these are so closely related as to be effectively one. Scientific candor, the free exchange of information, are all washed up during the war. A few key officials at the top necessarily know everything that is going on.

"COME OUT OF THAR, WILLIE! YOU'VE PLAYED AIR RAID SHELTER LONG ENOUGH FOR ONE DAY!"

"Germany Sees Us in a Grotesque Distortion Mirror," Thomas Kernan, *Reader's Digest*, August 1944:

When the war is finished, when we have flown our flags above bomb-wrecked Unter den Linden, we shall still face a real problem: the penetration of the German mind.

Goebbels' Propaganda Ministry has so indoctrinated the German mind that the German people do not see with their eyes, or hear with their ears, or even consider it worthwhile bothering to listen to anything the outside world has to say.

I spent 13 months interned at Baden-Baden in Germany. My opportunities for news were exactly those of a German citizen. I was permitted to subscribe to newspapers from Germany and German-occupied places—France, Belgium, Holland, and Italy. I listened to radio broadcasts prepared for Germans and the German-dominated peoples. I was free to compare notes and hold discussions with my fellow internees, many of them newspaperman and diplomats.

By profession a publishing and advertising man, I made it my business to follow the course of German interior propaganda, and to observe the functioning of the machine Dr. Goebbels has brought to sinister perfection.

Goebbels has kept Germans well-informed on favorable military news and misinformed about America. Day by day, bit by bit, we pieced together the image of America in the German mind, and it was rather like looking at oneself in a distortion mirror. The Germans think our liberty a joke. They want no part of our Republican ideas. Everything we are, everything we stand for, has been misrepresented to them with such a plausible twist that, while it is recognizably American in fact, it is completely false in its conclusions.

Goebbels made the most of the opportunity to churn out violent hatred with the stepped-up bombings of German cities by English and American planes. European cities are closely built. Whenever we wish to destroy a railroad junction or a bridge or a plant, we are sure to hit also the homes of the vicinity and a church or two. Goebbels began to teach the Germans that our planes aimed only at non-military targets, and that their job was to do away with the cultural and charitable institutions in Germany. Repeated a hundred times, photographed thousands of times, the theme of an Anglo-American assault on Europe's ancient culture has finally sunk deep into the thoughts of the German people.

In March 12, 1943, an Allied armada passed over us on the way to Stuttgart, released one bomb over Baden and burned up a Catholic church. This was the only bomb dropped on the Baden Valley during our 13-month stay. Because the church was a large one, prominent on a hill, no one will ever be able to persuade the local people the bomb was an accident. Again, a great 6,000-bed hospital in Frankfurt is out in the country, removed from any other buildings. It was totally destroyed by a recent raid, undoubtedly mistaken for some other target. Among the important buildings entirely destroyed or badly damaged are the cathedrals at Cologne, Trier, Aachen and Munster, and all the leading churches and museums of Munich.

When one tells a German that, after all, the Germans did the same thing to London in the winter of 1940-41, he looks at you with blank astonishment, for

continued

"Germany Sees Us in a Grotesque Distortion Mirror," *(continued)*

he never heard of it. He seems honestly ignorant of the Luftwaffe's tragic toll in England, and he actually believes that it was England, not Germany, that began the bombing of cities.

Unfortunately, German control over the press of occupied countries is so complete that even France accepts this propaganda scheme to some extent. Perhaps the most unfortunate incident of all involved the bringing down of an American plane which had been nicknamed by its crew "Murder, Inc." We know that American plane crews christen their ship with whatever name strikes their fancy—Hot Mama, Leaping Lizzie, Fancy Pants, or the like. Such a thing is unthinkable to the literal-minded Germans. To them "Murder, Inc." was an official designation for an American bomb, destined to kill German women and children....

More dangerous is what I might call the "black propaganda" against America, in the form of vicious books and photographs. These play up anything that is in bad taste or scabrous in our vast land, and sell very inexpensively.

One book reproduces a handsome series of OWI posters called "The Highest Standard of Living in the World" and "The American Way," and opposite them are authentic photos showing bums loitering under the Chicago elevated, destitute old men at soup kitchens in New York, the living quarters of sharecropper Negroes. In Germany, where low-cost housing is a fetish and where the psychopathic bum is kept in a concentration camp out of the public sight, these photos give a sad impression of America....

Liberal friends of mine in the United States often say, "Oh, if only our message could get through to the Germans! If only they knew about the Atlantic Charter and the Four Freedoms!"

I regret to report that the German public knows all about the Atlantic Charter and has heard many times about Mr. Roosevelt's Four Freedoms. It is part of Goebbels' technique to reveal our idealistic documents to the Germans, in full and immediately, but with the counterblast of ridicule that disposes of them at once in the German mind.

The Atlantic Charter was dismissed as vague, impractical idealism, a "seaborn rehash," of President Wilson's points. Goebbels blared, "You caught us once in 1918 with your fine phrases; you can't catch us again.

Mary Sears paved the way for female naval officers.

1948: Baseball Player

Jane Shollenberger of Racine, Wisconsin, threw a baseball harder than most boys, but was accepted for her athletic ability only when women were needed to boost morale during the war.

Life at Home

- Jane "Jeep" Shollenberger had been thrown out of half a dozen ball parks in her 17 years—for being a girl.
- Her father began teaching her to throw a baseball when she was eight, alongside two older brothers who saw no reason to coddle their little sister.
- When their father wasn't looking, her oldest brother Hank would fire baseballs at her head to make her leave the field.
- As a consequence, she became a superb defensive player.
- Her other brother would pitch baseballs to her high and inside, then tease her unmercifully if she bailed out of the batter's box to avoid the pitch.
- Jeep's only option was to hit scorching line drives back to the pitcher's mound.
- Line drives that forced her brother to jump out of the way were always a plus.
- Jeep, nicknamed for her height and ruggedness, finally landed a spot on the Industrial Softball League.
- The men didn't run her off because she was good and "they used to think I worked there," Jeep said.
- As tall as most of the men she played with, Jeep struggled to fit in.
- After a game her teammates were never sure whether to kiss her or buy her a beer.
- The war changed everything.
- Suddenly, the men were all enlisting, neighbors were preparing for an invasion and women were being told they needed to work outside the home.
- Factory work—the bane of any nice girl's plan—became respectable and patriotic.
- One day she received two important letters

Jane Shollenberger was a shoe-in for the new women's professional baseball team.

Fans came to see the women field . . .

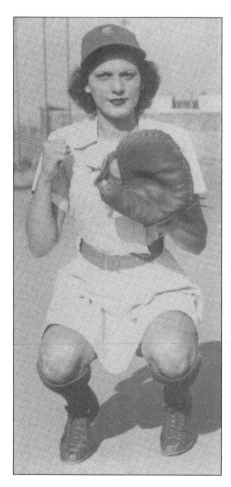

. . . catch . . .

- The first was from her brothers, who were soldiers since 1942
- The second invited Jeep to play in the All-American Girls Baseball League (AAGBL).
- America needed its morale lifted and women were the answer.
- Baseball owner P. K. Wrigley had received word from President Franklin D. Roosevelt that the 1943 Major League baseball season might be suspended due to manpower shortage.
- He wanted Wrigley to do something to keep the game of baseball going until the men got home from service.
- Athletes such as Jeep Shollenberger were needed for the war effort.
- She was thrilled!
- The newly fashioned league was to be a blend of women's softball and men's baseball.
- Wrigley joined forces with Branch Rickey and several small-town entrepreneurs to create the first professional baseball league for women.
- He used Hall of Fame players Dave Bancroft, Max Carey, and Jimmie Foxx as managers to draw interest in the league.
- That first year, in 1943, the league played a game that was a hybrid of baseball and softball.
- The ball was 12 inches in circumference, the size of a regulation softball (regulation baseballs are nine to nine and a quarter inches).
- The pitcher's mound was only 40 feet from home plate, closer even than in regulation softball and much closer than the baseball distance of 60 feet, six inches.
- Pitchers threw underhand windmill, like in softball, and the distance between bases was 65 feet, five feet longer than in softball but 25 feet shorter than in baseball.
- Major similarities between the AAGBL and baseball included nine-player teams and the use of a pitcher's mound.

. . . and pitch.

- Over time, the rules were gradually modified to more closely resemble baseball.
- The ball shrank from season to season, the mound was moved back to 60 feet, the base paths were extended to 85 feet and overhand pitching was allowed.
- Runners were allowed to lead off and steal.
- The new game was faster and more exciting for the fans.
- Thirty scouts were hired to find the most outstanding softball players all over the United States and Canada.
- Four teams were started in the AAGBL's first season in 1943.
- In 1944, the All-American Girls Baseball League expanded to six teams.
- Jeep was told she could earn $65 a week playing in the new league.
- She didn't hesitate and traveled by herself to try out with 200 women in Wrigley Field in Chicago.
- For a country girl from Indiana, Chicago was a wonderland of sights, particularly the Cubs' home field.
- After she made the team, she went to Helena Rubinstein classes every morning and practiced baseball every afternoon.
- As she was told repeatedly, "Mr. Wrigley wants ladies, not tomboys."
- The teams generally played in Midwestern cities and frequently moved based on attendance and ownership changes.
- The uniforms were a belted, short-sleeved tunic dress with a slight flare of the skirt.
- Rules stated that skirts were to be worn no more than six inches above the knee, a requirement Jeep routinely ignored so she could run more comfortably.
- A circular team logo sewn on the front of each dress completed the look.
- As a part of the League's "Rules of Conduct," short hair was forbidden and players were required to wear lipstick at all times.
- Fines for not following the League's rules of conduct were $5.00 for the first offense, $10.00 for the second, and suspension for the third.

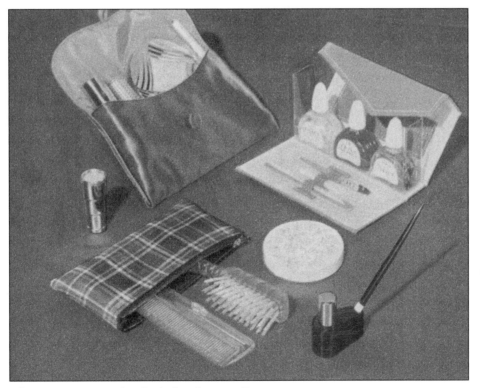

Players were required to look their best at all times.

Life at Work

- Jane "Jeep" Shollenberger's first season was a dream come true.
- She was getting paid to play ball every day.
- Her position was left field, and she was hitting .290.
- The League assigned managers, players and chaperones to teams to balance the talent and make play more competitive.
- Jeep's friends and teammates were traded in mid-season to maintain that balance.
- The regular season ran from mid-May to the first of September and the team that won the most games was declared the pennant winner.
- Jeep's team finished in the middle of the pack, but drew big crowds wherever they played.
- Jeep especially enjoyed honoring her brothers overseas before each game when the entire team lined up in a human "V" for Victory formation.
- Published records showed that the first year's attendance was 176,612 fans, and the press was uniformly amazed at how well the women played ball.
- Indeed, the role of women was changing throughout America in response to the war.
- Women by the thousands had left their homes to support the war effort by taking factory jobs, making munitions and other military machinery.
- This change in traditional attitudes toward women ushered in the acceptance of female professional ball players.
- Going to the ballpark was popular entertainment, and ballpark owners capitalized on the patriotic mood of the country by emphasizing the "All-American Girl" image.
- In effect, the players were symbols of "the girl next door" in spikes.
- The players also played exhibition games to support the Red Cross and the armed forces, and visited wounded veterans at Army hospitals.
- Season two began in Peru, Illinois, with 120 girls, and six managers.
- All League personnel were housed either at the Peru Hotel or at the St. Francis Hotel in Peru's twin city, LaSalle.
- There was access to three baseball diamonds, swimming pools and a gym and the Ruth Tiffany School was contracted to run the nightly charm school.
- The emphasis was on integrating a healthy mind and body, and included the art of walking, sitting, speaking, social skills, clothing selection and make-up application.
- Jeep was in the batting cage at spring training when she learned she had been traded to the Kenosha Comets.
- She never felt comfortable with her new team and thought about quitting, but the thought of returning to mill work kept her playing.
- By 1946, the eight teams in the League were playing 110 games per season, and Jeep was traded to the Racine Belles in Wisconsin.
- To add more excitement to the game, League rules introduced sidearm pitching, which allowed the ball to be delivered toward the batter from a different angle.
- The rule change was decimating the League, as dozens of players found the newly approved pitch impossible to hit.
- Jeep adjusted quickly and found the sidearm delivery helped her clobber more balls with authority.
- At the beginning of each season, Jeep got to know the other girls and helped select nicknames—Bird Dog, Ryecrispe, Curley, or Little Cookie—then it was down to the serious business of winning ball games and avoiding injuries.
- The schedule of 110 games per season required the teams to play single games six days a week, plus double headers on Sundays.
- The only time off was rained-out games, which were made up by playing double headers.

Each team in the League was frequently on the road, playing 110 games per season.

- Right after a game, the team boarded a bus, often arriving in a new city just in time to play the next game.
- The pay schedule was from $55.00 to $125.00 per week.
- By 1948 Jeep was one of the top paid players in the League, earning $125 weekly during the season.
- Expenses were paid by the team, including $2.25 per day for meals.
- In 1948, the League drew a record 910,000 fans for the 10-team League.
- Jeep was having a great year.
- Racine was in a race for the championship, Jeep was in a serious romance with a businessman she had met in Racine, and the major leagues were getting restaffed with quality players.
- Fans had a choice of which league to follow—men's or women's—and some sportswriters thought the women's League could survive, even if the Negro leagues were on their last legs.
- Several women were mentioned as possible players in major league baseball, igniting debates on whether men and women should play together.
- Jeep just wanted to win a championship.
- As the season came to a close she was hitting .315, playing errorless on defense and emerging as a team leader.
- Then came the marriage proposal.
- He was handsome, educated, employed at Johnson's Wax and he loved her even though she was not a traditional girl.
- In the last four games of the season Jeep hit .408 and she had won her championship.
- Within weeks Jeep and her fiance began looking for a house.

Jane's fiancee.

Jane loved her job but looked forward to buying a house and becoming a wife.

Life in the Community: Racine, Wisconsin

- Located on the edge of Lake Michigan, Racine, Wisconsin had its roots in manufacturing and shipping.
- One of the first products manufactured there was fanning mills, machines that separated wheat grain from chaff.
- In 1872 one the world's first automobiles was built there by Dr. J. W. Cathcart, as was the Pennington Victoria tricycle.
- In 1887, malted milk was invented in Racine by English immigrant William Horlick.
- The garbage disposal was invented in 1927 by architect John Hammes of Racine, who founded the company InSinkErator.
- Johnson's Wax, whose headquarters were designed in 1936 by Frank Lloyd Wright, held a large corporate presence.
- And it was home to the Racine Belles, and its live, play-by-play coverage of every home game was an innovation for the League.
- Racine was a blue collar town, ready to cheer for its blue collar team.
- Historically, women in sports were supposed to be women first, athletes second.
- Every effort was made to blend the Racine Belles into both.
- Thanks to the work ethic of the women, the play was exciting and the fans enthusiastic.
- The public liked its girls to be strong and athletic.
- The arrival of the widely publicized "athletic girl" at the turn of the twentieth century had previously brought walking, riding, motoring, cycling, and playing athletic games by women to the forefront.
- It also exposed the paradox of women's sports: how to remain feminine while being athletic.
- Ironically, it was the wealthy women of America who led the way, mostly through social and country clubs where they participated in archery, croquet, tennis and golf.
- It was generally believed that individual sports, as opposed to team sports, were less demanding and more conducive to graceful female physical movements.

- But still, upper-class women were required to show restraint when competing and usually wore full-length dresses including tight-laced corsets.
- A true lady would never consider swinging a mallet between her legs to achieve an accurate croquet shot or drive a tennis ball with an overhand slam.
- Refined sports like archery and tennis did not violate the boundary between proper women and women of other classes.
- The bicycle changed all that.
- The "wheel" allowed all women, especially the middle class, greater freedom to exercise, to ride astride the vehicle wearing shorter, more comfortable skirts, and the independence to go where they pleased.
- Basketball provided women with their next opportunity for freedom of movement and aggressive competition, emerging in the teens as most popular team sport for women.

Babe Didrikson was a sports phenomenon.

- In most cases women played on class teams or in physical education classes, although a substantial number of colleges formed varsity teams.
- By the 1920s the growth of women's athletics spawned numerous female sports heroes such as 20-year-old Sybil Bauer, who broke the men's record in the backstroke, and Gertrude Ederle, who swam the English Channel.
- Stories about female tennis stars became common in the daily sports pages of newspapers—an emerging trend in itself.
- Then came athlete extraordinare Babe Didrikson, who broke Olympic world records in five separate track and field events in the 1930s and then captured headlines as an amateur and professional golfer.
- By the 1930s working-class women discovered sports sponsored by churches, city recreation departments and industrial leagues.
- At the Hawthorne Works of the Western Electric Company in Chicago alone, 500 women participated in bowling, 127 in horseback riding and 96 in rifle shooting.
- Women's softball in particular took the nation by storm.
- In 1946 *The New York Times* estimated 600,000 women's softball teams had been formed to play before 150 million spectators.

Teams in the League were close-knit.

HISTORICAL SNAPSHOT
1948

- Warner Brothers showed the first color newsreel, selecting the Tournament of Roses Parade and the Rose Bowl
- Indian pacifist leader Mahatma Gandhi was assassinated by Nathuram Godse
- The Lions football team was purchased by a Detroit syndicate for $200,000
- The innermost moon of Uranus was discovered by Gerard Kuiper
- Dick Button became the first American to win a figure skating championship in the Olympics
- The Hells Angels motorcycle gang was founded in California
- President Harry Truman signed the Marshall Plan, officially the European Recovery Program (ERP), which authorized $5 billion in aid for 16 countries after World War II
- The 1948 Arab-Israeli War erupted
- The Berlin Blockade began
- Citation won the $117,300 Belmont Stakes to become the eighth horse to win racing's Triple Crown
- The Basketball Association of America expanded to 12 teams when four teams joined from the National Basketball League
- The Negro National League was dissolved, leaving the 10-team Negro American League as the only segregated baseball association remaining
- President Truman initiated a peacetime military draft amid increasing tensions with the Soviet Union and signed Executive Order 9981, ending racial segregation in the armed forces
- Homerun king Babe Ruth died at age 53 from throat cancer
- Heavyweight champion Joe Louis knocked out Joe Walcott in his twenty-fifth defense of his title and then retired

Selected Prices

All-American Girls Baseball Player Salary, per Week . . . .$40-$100
Baseball Player Jackie Robinson's Salary, per Year $17,500
Baseball Player Joe DiMaggio's Salary, per Year $90,000
Baseball Player Ted Williams' Salary, per Year $125,000
Deodorant $0.39
Face Cream $1.39
Hand Cream $1.50
Motorcycle Goggles $3.49
Sunglasses $6.95
Television, General Electric $189.95

OPEN UP AN **OREO** CREME SANDWICH AND TAKE A LICK!

no *other* chocolate cookie sandwich has the luscious creamy filling of OREO CREME SANDWICH

Nabisco loves cookies! that's why they make 'em so good!

Two mouth-melting chocolate cookies filled *lavishly* with rich vanilla fondant . . . that's an OREO CREME SANDWICH you're loving! It makes a wonderful dessert . . . a perfect between-

9-419-M

It does help in times like these

All you need to do to relieve the tension of a World Series game is to ask the butcher boy for a package of

Beech-Nut GUM

"Always Refreshing"

Women's Baseball Timeline

1866

The first organized women's baseball teams in the U.S. were started at Vassar College.

1867

The Dolly Vardens of Philadelphia became the first professional black women's team.

1875

The first women's baseball game for which fans were charged and women players were paid occurred between the Blondes and the Brunettes in Springfield, Illinois.

1876

The Resolutes developed uniforms which included long-sleeved shirts with frilled high necklines, embroidered belts, wide floor-length skirts, high button shoes and broad striped caps.

1890s

Women's "Bloomer Girls" clubs, with an average of three males on them, barnstormed the U.S. and played men's town, semi-pro, and minor league teams; Rogers Hornsby, dressed as a woman, got his start with a Bloomer Girls' team.

1898

Lizzie Arlington became the first woman to sign a professional baseball contract; she signed with the Philadelphia Reserves.

1904

Amanda Clement was the first woman to be paid to umpire a baseball game.

1908

The U.S. baseball national anthem, "Take Me Out to the Ball Game," was inspired by and written about a young girl's love of the game.

1911 to 1916

The St. Louis Cardinals were owned by Helene Britton.

1920s

Philadelphia had factory teams for women, women's leagues, and the Philadelphia Bobbies for non-working women.

1928

Lizzie Murphy became the first woman to play for a major league team in an exhibition game.

1930s

Women baseball players toured internationally, played junior baseball, and signed minor league contracts.

1934

Olympic hero Babe Didrikson pitched exhibition games for the Athletics, Cardinals, and Indians.

1943

The All-American Girls Baseball League (AAGBL) was started by Philip Wrigley, owner of the Chicago Cubs and Wrigley's Chewing Gum.

1946

Sophie Kurys set the stolen base record for the AAGBL with 201 stolen bases in 203 attempts.

1947

The Racine Belles of the AAGBL started the Junior Belles baseball program; 100 girls tried out and 60 were selected to play on four teams.

1948

After five years of play, the AAGBL started throwing pitches overhand instead of underhand.

RULES OF CONDUCT

THE RULES OF CONDUCT FOR PLAYERS AS SET UP BY THE ALL-AMERICAN GIRLS PROFESSIONAL BASEBALL LEAGUE

THE MANAGEMENT SETS A HIGH STANDARD FOR THE GIRLS SELECTED FOR THE DIFFERENT CLUBS AND EXPECTS THEM TO LIVE UP TO THE CODE OF CONDUCT WHICH RECOGNIZES THAT STANDARD. THERE ARE GENERAL REGULATIONS NECESSARY AS A MEANS OF MAINTAINING ORDER AND ORGANIZING CLUBS INTO A WORKING PROCEDURE.

1. Always appear in feminine attire when not actively engaged in practice or playing ball. This regulation continues through the playoffs for all, even though your team is not participating. At no time may a player appear in the stands in her uniform, or wear slacks or shorts in public.

2. Boyish bobs are not permissible and in general your hair should be well groomed at all times with longer hair preferable to short hair cuts. Lipstick should always be on.

3. Smoking or drinking is not permissible in public places. Liquor drinking will not be permissible under any circumstances. Other intoxicating drinks in limited portions with after-game meal only, will be allowed. Obscene language will not be allowed at any time.

4. All social engagements must be approved by chaperone. Legitimate requests for dates can be allowed by chaperones.

5. Jewelry must not be worn during game or practice, regardless of type.

6. All living quarters and eating places must be approved by the chaperones. No player shall change her residence without the permission of the chaperone.

7. For emergency purposes, it is necessary that you leave notice of your whereabouts and your home phone.

8. Each club will establish a satisfactory place to eat, and a time when all members must be in their individual rooms. In general, the lapse of time will be two hours after the finish of the last game, but in no case later than 12:30 a.m. Players must respect hotel regulations as to other guests after this hour, maintaining conduct in accordance with high standards set by the League.

9. Always carry your employee's pass as a means of identification for entering the various parks. This pass is NOT transferable.

10. Relatives, friends, and visitors are not allowed on the bench at any time.

11. Due to shortage of equipment, baseballs must not be given as souvenirs without permission from the Management.

12. Baseball uniform skirts shall not be shorter than six inches above the knee-cap.

continued

RULES OF CONDUCT . . . *(continued)*

13. In order to sustain the complete spirit of rivalry between clubs, the members of different clubs must not fraternize at any time during the season. After the opening day of the season, fraternizing will be subject to heavy penalties. This also means in particular; room parties, auto trips to out of the way eating places, etc. However, friendly discussions in lobbies with opposing players are permissible. Players should never approach the opposing manager or chaperone about being transferred.

14. When traveling, the members of the clubs must be at the station thirty minutes before departure time. Anyone missing her arranged transportation will have to pay her own fare.

15. Players will not be allowed to drive their cars past their city's limits without the special permission of their manager. Each team will travel as a unit via method of travel provided for the League.

FINES OF FIVE DOLLARS FOR FIRST OFFENSE, TEN DOLLARS FOR SECOND, AND SUSPENSION FOR THIRD, WILL AUTOMATICALLY BE IMPOSED FOR BREAKING ANY OF THE ABOVE RULES.

CHARM SCHOOL

FOREWORD

When you become a player in the All-American Girls Baseball League you have reached the highest position that a girl can attain in this sport. The All-American Girls Baseball League is getting great public attention because it is pioneering a new sport for women.

You have certain responsibilities because you, too, are in the limelight. Your actions and appearance both on and off the field reflect on the whole profession. It is not only your duty to do your best to hold up the standard of this profession but to do your level best to keep others in line.

The girls in our League are rapidly becoming the heroines of youngsters as well as grownups all over the world. People want to be able to respect their heroines at all times. The All-American Girls Baseball League is attempting to establish a high standard that will make you proud that you are a player in years to come.

We hand you this manual to help guide you in your personal appearance. We ask you to follow the rules of behavior for your own good as well as that of the future success of girls' baseball.

In these few pages you will find many of the simple and brief suggestions which should prove useful to you during the busy baseball season. If you plan your days to establish an easy and simple routine, so that your meals are regular and well balanced, so that you have time for outside play and relaxation, so that you sleep at least eight hours each night and so that your normal functions are regular, you will be on the alert, do your job well and gain the greatest joy from living. Always remember that your mind and your body are interrelated and you cannot neglect one without causing the other to suffer. A healthy mind and a healthy body are the true attributes of the All-American girl.

BEAUTY ROUTINES

Your ALL-AMERICAN GIRLS BASEBALL LEAGUE BEAUTY KIT should always contain the following:

Cleansing Cream	Mild Astringent
Lipstick	Face Powder for Brunette
Rouge Medium	Hand Lotion
Cream Deodorant	Hair Remover

You should be the best judge of your own beauty requirements. Keep your own kit replenished with the things you need for your own toilette and your beauty culture and care. Remember the skin, the hair, the teeth and the eyes. It is most desirable in your own interests, that of your teammates and fellow players, as well as from the standpoint of the public relations of the League that each girl be at all times presentable and attractive, whether on the playing field or at leisure. Study your own beauty culture possibilities and without overdoing your beauty treatment at the risk of attaining gaudiness, practice the little measures that will reflect well on your appearance and personality as a real All-American girl.

I. SUGGESTED BEAUTY ROUTINE
"After the Game"
Remember, the All-American girl is subjected to greater exposure through her activities on the diamond, through exertion in greater body warmth and perspiration, through exposure to dirt, grime and dust and through vigorous play to scratches, cuts, abrasions and sprains. This means extra precaution to assure all the niceties of toilette and personality. Especially "after the game," the All-American girl should take time to observe the necessary beauty ritual, to protect both her health and appearance. Here are a few simple rules that should prove helpful and healthful "after the game."

1. Shower well and soap the skin.
2. Dry thoroughly to avoid chapping or chafing.
3. Apply cleansing cream to face; remove with tissue.
4. Wash face with soap and water.
5. Apply skin astringent.
6. Apply rouge moderately but carefully.
7. Apply lipstick with moderate taste.
8. Apply eye makeup if considered desirable.
9. Apply powder.
10. Check all cuts, abrasions or minor injuries.

If you suffer any skin abrasion or injury, or if you discern any aches or pains that do not appear to be normal, report them at once to your coach/chaperone or the person responsible for treatment and first aid. Don't laugh off slight ailments as trivialities because they can often develop into serious infections or troublesome conditions that can handicap your play and cause personal inconvenience. See that your injuries, however slight, receive immediate attention. Guard your health and welfare.

continued

BEAUTY ROUTINES . . . *(continued)*

II. ADDITIONAL BEAUTY ROUTINE
"Morning and Night"
In the morning, when you have more time to attend to your beauty needs, you will undoubtedly be enabled to perform a more thorough job. Use your cleansing cream around your neck as well as over the face. Remove it completely and apply a second time to be sure that you remove all dust, grease and grime. Wipe off thoroughly with cleansing tissue. Apply a lotion to keep your hands as lovely as possible. Use your manicure set to preserve your nails in a presentable condition and in keeping with the practical needs of your hands in playing ball.

A. TEETH
Not a great deal need be said about the teeth, because every All-American girl instinctively recognizes their importance to her health, her appearance and her personality. There are many good tooth cleansing preparations on the market and they should be used regularly to keep the teeth and gums clean and healthy. A regular visit to a reliable dentist is recommended and certainly no tooth ailment should be neglected for a moment.

B. BODY
Unwanted or superficial hair is often quite common and it is no problem to cope with in these days when so many beauty preparations are available. If your have such hair on arms or legs, there are a number of methods by which it can be easily removed. There is an odorless liquid cream which can be applied in a few moments, permitted to dry and then showered off.

C. DEODORANTS
There are a number of very fine deodorants on the market which can be used freely all over the body. The most important feature of some of these products is the fact that the fragrance stays perspiration proof all day long. These deodorants can be used especially where excess perspiration occurs and can be used safely and effectively without retarding natural perspiration. The All-American girl is naturally susceptible because of her vigorous activities and it certainly pays dividends to be on the safe side. Deodorant keeps you fresh and gives you assurance and confidence in your social contacts.

D. EYES
"The Eyes Are the Windows of the Soul"
The eyes indicate your physical fitness and therefore need your thoughtful attention and care. They bespeak your innermost thoughts; they reflect your own joy of living or they can sometimes falsely bespeak the listlessness of mind and body. Perhaps no other feature of your face has more to do with the impression of beauty, sparkle and personality which you portray.

A simple little exercise for the eyes and one which does not take much time can do much to strengthen your eyes and add to their sparkle and allure. Turn your eyes to the corner of the room for a short space of time, then change to the other corner, then gaze at the ceiling and at the floor alternately. Rotating or rolling your eyes constitutes an exercise and your eyes will repay you for the attention that you give to them. There are also vitamins prescribed for the care of the eyes. Drink plenty of water and eat plenty of vegetables. We all know well that the armed forces found carrots a definite dietary aid to eyesight. Use a good eyewash frequently and for complete relaxation at opportune moments, lie down and apply an eye pad to your eyes for several minutes.

continued

BEAUTY ROUTINES . . . *(continued)*

E. HAIR
"Woman's Crowning Glory"
One of the most noticeable attributes of a girl is her hair, woman's crowning glory. No matter the features, the clothes, the inner charm or personality, they can all suffer beneath a sloppy or stringy coiffure. Neither is it necessary to feature a fancy or extravagant hairdo, because a daily program for the hair will help to keep it in healthful and attractive condition.

Neatness is the first and greatest requirement. Arrange your hair neatly in a manner that will best retain its natural style despite vigorous play. Off the diamond, you can readily arrange it in a softer and more feminine style, if you wish. But above all, keep your hair as neat as possible, on or off the field.

Brushing the hair will help a great deal more than is realized. It helps to stimulate the scalp which is the source of healthful hair growth. It develops the natural beauty and luster of the hair. And it will not spoil the hairdo. When brushing, bend over and let your head hang down. Then brush your hair downward until the scalp tingles. Just a few minutes of this treatment each day will tend to keep your scalp in fine condition and enhance the beauty of your "crowning glory."

F. MOUTH
Every woman wants to have an attractive and pleasing mouth. As you speak, people watch your mouth and you can do much, with a few of the very simplest tools, to make your mouth invitingly bespeak your personality. Your beauty aids should, of course, include an appropriate type of lipstick and a brush. They should be selected with consideration and care. With your lipstick, apply two curves to your upper lip. Press your lips together. Then, run your brush over the lipstick and apply it to your lips, outlining them smoothly. This is the artistic part of the treatment in creating a lovely mouth.

Patient practice and care make perfect. Open your mouth and outline your own natural curves. If your lips are too thin to please you, shape them into fuller curves. Now, use a tissue between your lips and press lightly to take off excess lipstick. If you wish to have a "firmer foundation," use the lipstick a second time and use the tissue "press" again.

Caution: Now that you have completed the job, be sure that the lipstick has not smeared your teeth. Your mirror will tell the tale and it is those little final touches that really count.

G. HANDS
The hands are certainly among the most expressive accouterments of the body; they are always prominent and noticeable and while feminine hands can be lovely and lily white, as described in the ads, the All-American girl has to exercise practical good sense in preserving the hands that serve her so faithfully and well in her activities. Cleanliness and neatness again come to the fore. Your hands should be thoroughly cleaned and washed as frequently as seems desirable or necessary, and especially after games, they should be cleaned to remove all dust and grime. Soap and water and pumice will do this job to perfection. Then a protective cream should be applied to keep hands soft and pliable and to avoid cracks and overdryness. Your nails should be gone over lightly each day, filing to prevent cracks and splits, oiling for the cuticle.

The length of your nails, of course, depends largely upon the requirements of your play. Keep them neat and clean and your hands will always be attractive.

continued

BEAUTY ROUTINES . . . *(continued)*

H. FACE
"All Beauty Comes from Within"
To the All-American girl, who is exposed to the elements, to the sun, to the wind and to the dust, it is most essential that every precaution be taken for the care of the skin. It should be covered with a protective substance of cream or liquid, depending entirely upon whether your skin is dry or oily. If it is dry, the cream type is recommended and if it is oily, you should use the liquid type. A good cleansing cream can serve as a cleanser, a powder base, a night cream and also a hand lotion. It is a good idea to have such an allaround utility cream on hand at all times and to use it regularly for these purposes.

I. FOR YOUR COLORING
It depends on your particular complexion and whether you have an abundance of natural color tones or need very little coloring. You can determine this in keeping with good taste to acquire the necessary results. People who are naturally pale, of course, need the coloring to help their complexion

III. CLOTHES
Clothes, of course, have always been one of woman's great problems and it might seem so to the All-American girl. However, with the exercising of good taste, the All-American Girls Baseball League player can solve her problem in a tasteful manner and without great expense, without being encumbered with too great a wardrobe for the summer months. The accent, of course, is on neatness and feminine appeal. That is true of appearances on the playing field, on the street or in leisure moments. The uniforms adopted by the League have been designed for style and appeal and there is a tremendous advantage to the girl and to the team which makes the best of its equipment.

From the standpoint of team morale, there is a real "lift" noticeable in the smartly turned out and neatly arrayed aggregation. And from the public appeal standpoint, it is surprising how the crowd will respond to the team that appears on the field with a neatness and "snap" in its appearance. The smart-looking teams invariably play smart ball and you can add to your own drawing power and crowd appeal by looking the part of a ball player on the field. Wear your cap and keep it securely in place. Keep your uniform as clean and neat as possible. Always secure your stockings so that they are smooth and neat and remain in place. Keep your shoes clean and shining. And see if you don't feel better and play better ball.

VICTORY SONG
co-written by La Vonne Paire-Davis and Nalda Phillips

Batter up! Hear that call!
The time has come for one and all
To play ball. For we're the members of the All-American League,
We come from cities near and far.
We've got Canadians, Irishmen and Swedes,
We're all for one, we're one for all,
We're All-American.

Each girl stands, her head so proudly high,
Her motto Do Or Die.
She's not the one to use or need an alibi.
Our chaperones are not too soft,
They're not too tough,
Our managers are on the ball.
We've got a president who really knows his stuff,
We're all for one, we're one for all,
We're All-Americans!

All-American Girls Baseball League, 1948 Results

Eastern Division
Grand Rapids Chicks (77-47)
Muskegon Lassies (66-57)
South Bend Blue Sox (57-69)
Fort Wayne Daisies (53-72)
Chicago Colleens (47-76)

Western Division
Racine Belles (76-49)
Rockford Peaches (74-49)
Peoria Redwings (70-55)
Kenosha Comets (61-64)
Springfield Sallies (41-84)
Play-off Champions: Rockford Peaches

1955: Founder of Scholarship Program

One of the richest women in America, Dee-Dee Kliebard used her fortune to create a scholarship program for talented New Jersey college-bound girls.

Life at Home

- Her real name was Jesse Elaine Torrey Kliebard, but everyone called her Dee-Dee.
- Through the years the origin of her nickname had changed dozens of times—predicated on Dee-Dee's mood and the circumstances at hand.
- For years, she told friends that her first words were "Dee-Dee" instead of "dada."
- In high school, after her mother died leaving behind a fortune amassed in the condiment industry, she claimed Dee-Dee was her mother's middle name.
- To her dates in the 1930s, she shyly "confessed" that a previous boyfriend had christened her Dee-Dee based on the new method of measuring brassiere cup size.
- By the time her aristocratic father died in 1945 when Dee-Dee was 35, she started telling anyone who asked that the moniker had started out as "darling daughter" and evolved into Dee-Dee.
- When Dee-Dee reached the age of 45—10 years after her father had died—she made an evaluation of her life.
- She was rich—that was clear.
- Her mother's ketchup fortune had been carefully invested, which, in combination with her architect father's real estate holdings, made her one of the wealthiest women in New Jersey.

Dee-Dee Kliebard founded a scholarship for college-bound girls.

- She had been married once—for 31 days—which she noted to friends was not enough time to use up a whole bar of soap.
- Her ex-husband liked her money and loved other women, a combination that failed to stir Dee-Dee's passion.
- Her time at Sweet Briar College lasted longer—three semesters—where she acquired a taste for Kentucky bourbon, tall men with Southern accents, and the rousing music played at country honky-tonks—any one of which could get her suspended from school.

Head of Sweet Briar College, left, from which Dee-Dee was expelled.

- Three out of three was worthy of immediate dismissal, especially when a 1948 red Chevrolet coupe was added to the mix.
- After several years of touring Europe, learning to fly a plane, and a near-death experience to Antarctica, Dee-Dee had an epiphany.
- She realized that she was simply a custodian of the oodles of money sitting in her accounts; wealth had been given to her so she could help others.
- But as she had known most of her life, the world was full of hopeless causes eager to be rescued by her wealth.
- The key was picking out the recipients before they knew they were being examined.
- That way, the least and the lost would have just as good a chance to get help.
- Her goal was helping young women get an education, including graduation from high school and an opportunity to attend college—no matter their financial condition.
- The creation, fostering and growth of universal, free high school education was one of America's successes.
- Until the late 1800s, an eighth-grade education was customary for most Americans; in 1870, only two percent of 17-year-olds had received a high school diploma.
- In 1875, a lawsuit was filed in Kalamazoo, Michigan, affirming the right of towns to use taxes to support the village high school.
- Thanks to expanded taxing power, hundreds of new buildings were erected nationwide; by 1910 the percentage of high school graduates had increased to nine percent, of which 60 percent were female.
- Progressively more and more cities expanded the opportunities for its citizens to go beyond the completion of the eighth grade.
- In 1940, more than half the U.S. population of all ages had completed no more than that, and only six percent of males and four percent of females had completed four years of college.
- Immediately after the Second World War, the high school graduation rate attained 70 percent.
- But clearly, in the postwar environment of the 1950s, a high school education was not going to be enough; college would be vital for American world leadership.

- Dee-Dee believed that women should be included in the educational bonanza underway thanks to the thousands of men being educated through the G.I. Bill.
- Women, simply because they were not called up to be soldiers, should not be thrown on the economic trash heap.
- Therefore, she decided that she would find, select and finance the next generation of female leaders by giving a large number of women the opportunity to compete independently in the world—supported by a fully paid four-year scholarship to the college of their choice.

Unless supported by rich families, many women were not given the opportunity to attend a four-year college.

- Many, if not most, college educations prior to 1900 were privately financed, and thus, only open to the wealthy; despite that, both men and women born prior to 1910 had attended college in almost equal numbers.
- But women, who were almost universally enrolled in two-year teachers' colleges, were expected to resign their teaching jobs when they married—which devalued the educational experience.
- The number of students from the working classes who could raise the tuition was usually kept in check by the expenses of living during the years of study.
- A typical family could not afford educating a son, let alone a daughter, even if the education itself was free.
- After World War II, more working-class students were able to receive a degree, resulting in the inflation of education and an increased middle class.

Life at Work

- The idea of creating a scholarship program for talented New Jersey girls was so exciting; Dee-Dee Kliebard could not sleep at night.
- At first, she hired a team of educators and charity professionals to help her select the first crop of recipients from Trenton, New Jersey.
- The educators talked in theories and carefully coded messages, and the others mostly talked with their hands.
- Both groups quickly decided that they could succeed best if they told her little, believing that her millions did not make her an expert.
- Undaunted, Dee-Dee ordered books and met with experts to decide the purpose of education: to get a job, to create better citizens, to establish a foundation for lifetime learning, to find a mate, or to develop a business network.
- Educational theories abounded; everyone had opinions but no one had the answer.

The first recipients of Dee-Dee's scholarships were chosen without her input.

- Should education stick to the basics? Should the curriculum be broad and wide to excite the interests of students? Should students be divided by potential or class or IQ to make the classroom more efficient?
- Then there were the questions concerning the role of administrators versus teachers, and even disputes between colleges and high schools over how students could be best prepared for the challenges of life.
- The first 10 girls were selected without Dee-Dee's input.
- When she met with the winners, most understood little about Dee-Dee's aspirations for them, and most could not pronounce her last name during the congratulatory reception.
- In addition, most looked like the daughter she never had, fully understood what to do during a formal tea, and planned to attend Ivy League schools.
- Dee-Dee managed to wait until the last recipient had left before she fired everyone in sight.
- The sanctimonious educators and experts had not listened to her at all.
- Her scholarships were to be about opportunity for those who were struggling—not the perpetuation of the ruling, wealthy class.
- America had made tremendous educational progress in the prior 55 years, and Dee-Dee planned to accelerate that achievement, even if she had to interview every high school principal in the state of New Jersey personally.
- In 1900, 50 percent of children five to 19 were enrolled in school; by 1930, the enrollment rate was 69 percent, and by 1955, enrollment stood at 86 percent of eligible children.
- The number of girls in school and the percentage of African-Americans were also in the mid-80s.

- The number of days devoted to school was also increasing: from 78 days per year in the decades after the Civil War compared to an average 152 days in 1950.
- The illiteracy rate, which was at 10.7 in 1900, had fallen to 2.2 percent.
- At the same time, many educators had declared that 20 percent of students were being well served by the college entrance programs, and 20 percent were gaining benefit from vocational classes.
- But the remaining 60 percent of high school students should be educated and prepared for the working world, marriage and supporting democracy through life-adjustment classes.
- Dee-Dee wondered how many of her potential recipients were being hidden by the new system, and how many believed they were not college bound because they couldn't afford more education.
- This time, Dee-Dee hired three teachers and one principal to be her advisors.
- She invited them to her home for a week of training and then visited the first eight schools with each one of her teacher-investigators.
- Then she turned them loose to find 25 girls capable of changing the world.
- Under no circumstance were the investigators allowed to discuss where the money originated; Dee-Dee didn't want to experience back channel lobbying efforts and planned to swear each girl to secrecy after her selection.
- After seven months, she was presented with the candidates, each driven to Dee-Dee's home with her parents for a personal interview.
- Dee-Dee was terrified that she would not know what to ask, but found the process pleasing and the high school seniors enchanting.
- Two of the girls had given up on going to college, even before they entered high school; the grades of three more were marginal and six had not started applying to schools.
- What they had in common was spunk and a mentor.
- In nearly every case, a teacher, coach or principal had spotted potential hidden from the rest of the world.
- Of the 25 candidates, Dee-Dee selected 23 for full scholarships.
- One girl bragged that she had a trust fund and didn't need anyone else's money, while another confessed that she was pregnant and not planning to attend college for a while.
- After that, Dee-Dee decided that future classes would also contain 23 winners, and that each year she would stage a reunion of "her girls" to celebrate their successes.
- A total of 19 college students returned in 1955 to receive their second year's tuition and scholarship money.
- One of her favorites, a tall dark-haired Italian who was attending Sweet Briar College, even brought a small bottle of Kentucky bourbon that tasted as good as Dee-Dee remembered.

Nineteen of 23 first year scholarship girls returned for their second year's tuition.

Life in the Community: Trenton, New Jersey

- The first New Jersey settlement, which would become Trenton, was established in 1679 by Quakers, who were being persecuted in England at this time; North America provided the perfect opportunity to exercise their religious freedom.
- By 1719, the town adopted the name "Trent-towne," after William Trent, one of its leading landholders who purchased much of the surrounding land.
- During the Revolutionary War, the city was the site of the Battle of Trenton, George Washington's first military victory.
- On December 26, 1776, Washington and his army, after crossing the icy Delaware River to Trenton, defeated the Hessian troops garrisoned there.
- After the war, Trenton was briefly the national capital in November and December of 1784.
- The city was considered as a permanent capital for the new country, but the Southern states favored a location south of the Mason-Dixon Line.
- Trenton became the state capital in 1790, but prior to that year the Legislature often met here.
- Growth was rapid throughout the nineteenth century as Europeans came to work in the city's pottery and wire rope mills.
- Trenton was a major industrial center in the late nineteenth and early twentieth centuries, earning the slogan "Trenton Makes, The World Takes" for its role in the manufacture of rubber, wire rope, ceramics and cigars.

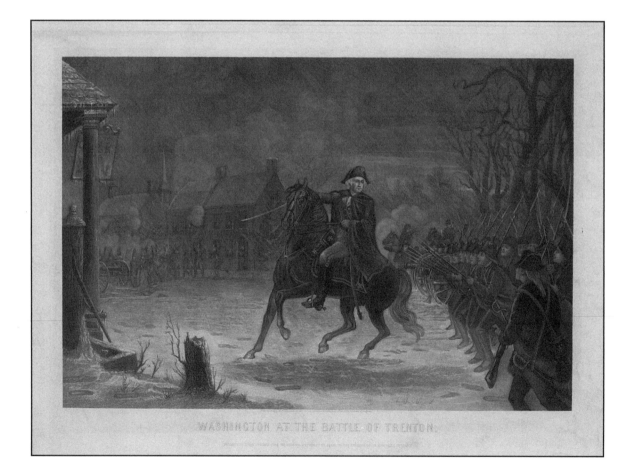

WASHINGTON AT THE BATTLE OF TRENTON.

HISTORICAL SNAPSHOT
1955

- Marian Anderson became the first African-American singer to perform at the Metropolitan Opera in New York City

- The game Scrabble debuted

- Congress authorized President Dwight D. Eisenhower to use force to protect Formosa from the People's Republic of China

- Ray Kroc opened a McDonald's fast food restaurant (the company's ninth since it was founded in 1940), and oversaw the company's worldwide expansion

- Eisenhower sent the first U.S. advisors to South Vietnam

- The Broadway musical version of *Peter Pan*, which had opened in 1954 starring Mary Martin, was presented on television for the first time by NBC-TV with its original cast

- KXTV of Stockton, California, signed on the air to become the 100th commercial television station in the country

- Evan Hunter's movie adaptation of the novel *Blackboard Jungle* premiered in the United States, featuring the famous single, "Rock Around the Clock," by Bill Haley and His Comets

- The Salk polio vaccine received full approval by the FDA

- The TV quiz program *The $64,000 Question* premiered on CBS-TV with Hal March as the host

- *Lady and the Tramp*, the Walt Disney Company's fifteenth animated film, premiered in Chicago

- The first edition of the *Guinness Book of Records* was published in London

- *Gunsmoke*, *Alfred Hitchcock Presents*, and *The Mickey Mouse Club* all debuted on TV

- Disneyland opened to the public in Anaheim, California

- Racial segregation was outlawed on trains and buses in interstate commerce

- The Montgomery Improvement Association was formed in Montgomery, Alabama, by Dr. Martin Luther King, Jr., and other black ministers to coordinate a boycott of all city buses

- General Motors Corporation became the first American corporation to make a profit of over $1 billion in one year

Selected Prices

Acne Cream $0.59

Automobile, Chrysler New Yorker...$4,243

Face Powder..$1.38

License Plate $1.00

Mattress, Serta King Size...$79.50

Paneling...$47.00

Pocket Radio $75.00

Race Car Kit...$2.75

Railroad Fare, Chicago to San Francisco...$63.12

Razor Blades, 20 ....$0.79

"Teenomania," by Marion Walker Alvado, *Woman's Day*, September 1952:

I want to make it perfectly plain that I have nothing whatsoever against teenagers. Some of my favorite people are teenagers, including my oldest son. But I can't help wondering if there isn't currently much too much commotion about them.

I wonder if the teens haven't come to be considered too much an age apart, age completely different from any other. I wonder if the teenager isn't too continually in both the public and family limelight. And, at the risk of being put summarily in my place by the experts, I wonder if parents are those long-suffering clay pigeons of the shotguns in How-To-Bring-Up-Your-Children books about this particular stage in the offspring's development.

The teenager is a fairly recent discovery. Twenty years or so ago, if you were between 12 and 17, you were referred to rather vaguely as being "at that age" or "in between." There were no clothes designed especially for you; you wore little girl dresses until the waistlines were under your armpits, and then you were graduated abruptly into your mother's kind of clothes. If you were a boy, you were promoted to long pants when your legs got long enough. No one considered your patois amusing. No one considered your problems important. You were low man on the social totem pole.

This was a deplorable state of affairs and clearly needed improvement. But now the pendulum seems to have swung as far the other way. Today the teenager, also known as the teenster, the teener, the subdeb, the prep, and the Junior Miss, is a national celebrity. He, or she, is society's most publicized and pampered pet. Magazines feature his problems. Novels, plays, comic strips, movies, radio serials, and television programs are based on his escapades and his wit. Fashion experts vie to design his clothes. And the general public views him with a flattering mixture of affection that used to be reserved for collegians in a raccoon coat.

At home, a teenager used to be treated like an ordinary member of the family. Today it is considered de rigueur to treat him like visiting royalty. The family kitchen and the family living room should be at his instant disposal, the experts tell us. Authorities suggest that we remodel an entire section of the family residence for his exclusive use. According to the experts, it is a teenager's privilege to monopolize the family radio and the family telephone. It is also considered his privilege to monopolize practically all of his parents' time, effort, patience, energy, and attention.

You can always identify a teenager's parents. There is a stoop to their shoulders. There is a harried look in their eyes. "Isn't it awful!" They are likely to murmur hollowly when you happen to meet. "If you think that is strenuous," they warn you while your own children are still in pin-up lingerie, "just wait till they're teenagers!"

Yes, you can always identify teenagers' parents, that is, if you can catch up with them. They haven't time to come to dinner. They haven't time to play bridge, they have been warned of sinister evils that would befall their young unless they maintained an all cylinder program supervision and entertainment. They have been made to feel that they are failing in their

Continued

"Teenomania,". . . *(Continued)*

duty as parents unless they spend every possible moment conveying their children and their children's friends to movies, club meetings, ball games, and parties, and retrieving them afterwards.

This vogue of lionizing the teenager is based on good intentions. Its purpose is to give him a fair share of social prominence, to help him avoid some well-known pitfalls, and to help him solve the problems of growing up. But does it really accomplish what it sets out to do? In my opinion, it is being carried to such extremes, it creates new problems instead of solving old ones, in my opinion, and it's unfair to everyone concerned....

Keeping your teenagers happy and well adjusted is a commendable achievement. Keeping parents happy and well adjusted will never make sensational copy, but there are those among them who feel it deserves some thought.

From the very end of a very long limb, I should like to suggest that our whole conception of what the parent-child relationship should be is in serious danger of getting out of kilter. Years ago, duty to one's parents was a recurrent and silent topic of discussion. Today, nobody talks about duty to his parents. Today, everybody talks about duty to children. Parents are held responsible for every physical and emotional anomaly that children develop, for every mistake they make, for every problem they have to face. Years ago, children were virtually the slaves of parents. We seem to be progressing a good deal faster than the law demands toward the exact reverse.

Religion, morality and knowledge being necessary to good government and the happiness of mankind, schools and the means of education shall forever be encouraged.

—The Northwest Ordinances of 1787 that authorized grants of lands for the establishment of educational institutions

Annual Cost of University of Pennsylvania Undergraduate Schools:

1900
College and the Wharton School:
Tuition: $150
Minimum: Room and Board: $185; Text-books: $10
Maximum: Room and Board: $250; Text-books: $50

1930
College, School of Engineering and Applied Science (SEAS) and the Wharton School:
Tuition: $400, which included the General Fee
Room and Board: $520; Text-books: $35; Clothing and miscellaneous: $260

1955
College, College of Liberal Arts for Women, School of Engineering and Applied Science (SEAS), the Wharton School, the School of Nursing, and the School of Allied Medical Professions (SAMP)
Tuition: $800
General Fee: $135; Room and Board: $835; Books: $50

1956: Puerto Rican Factory Worker

Twenty-three year-old Annette Martinez left Puerto Rico to find work in New York City, after her brothers and sister found good jobs in Baltimore and Philadelphia.

Life at Home

- Annette Martinez was born in 1930 in Salinas, a small agricultural community on the southern coast of Puerto Rico, known for its sugar production.
- During the first half of the twentieth century, Puerto Rico was one of the leading producers of sugar for the United States and other countries.
- Annette's family made their living on the sugar plantations.
- Beginning in the 1940s, many sugar plantations were replaced by large foreign-owned industrial factories.
- This change meant a higher standard of living for some, but fewer plantation jobs for others.
- As a result of the decreasing agricultural jobs, many members of Annette's family began thinking about leaving Puerto Rico to find work.
- Emigrating to the United States was the natural first choice because Puerto Ricans had American citizenship and could work legally.
- During World War II, many American labor recruiters came to the island in search of cheap labor to replace the workers lost to the military draft.
- Annette's two older brothers were the first of her family to emigrate after being recruited by an American businessman to work in a toy factory in Baltimore, Maryland, in 1945.
- Then, a year later, in 1946, Annette's older sister Glenda left to work as a domestic servant for a wealthy family in Philadelphia.
- Although Annette wanted to follow her siblings, she didn't trust the American recruiters.
- Annette stayed in Puerto Rico, hoping that her brothers or sister could find her a stable job in America.
- In 1953, during a trip to San Juan to visit her cousins, 23-year-old Annette met an American family there on vacation.

Annette Martinez was 23-years-old when she left Puerto Rico.

Annette's family worked on sugar plantations in Puerto Rico.

Annette's parents and her brother.

Two sisters celebrate Annette's First Communion.

- The father, Mr. Santos, offered her a job working in his hotel in New York City.
- Annette trusted him because he had not come to Puerto Rico specifically to recruit workers.
- Soon after, she left Puerto Rico on a plane to New York.
- Annette was terrified to fly, but was encouraged by her sister, who told her about the views from the airplane window and the food service.
- The flight took six and a half hours and cost $44.00.
- Annette paid for the trip with money she had saved since she was 14, plus $20.00 her grandmother gave her before she died.
- With the help of Mr. Santos, Annette rented a room in one of the poorest sections of Manhattan, known as Spanish Harlem.
- She shared the apartment with two other Puerto Rican women.
- Annette had little money to live on, after sending most of her paycheck home to help support her family in Puerto Rico.
- Her neighborhood was largely made up of Puerto Ricans and immigrants from other Spanish-speaking countries.
- She found that many Puerto Rican customs and traditions were preserved in New York, and she was not as homesick as she had feared she would be.
- She found many familiar foods that she had eaten at home, such as rice and beans, pork, and beef.
- Much of her island's fresh fish and tropical fruit were harder to come by.
- Once in a while, Annette went out on the weekends dancing with her friends.
- In 1954, she met Wilfredo Rivera at a dancehall.
- Willy, as she called him, rolled cigars in his father's shop.
- After a short courtship, they were married.
- Her brothers and sister were not able to travel to New York for the wedding.
- Despite being very happy at getting married, Annette felt terribly sad that she had no family to share the happy day.
- After the wedding, Annette moved in with Willy and his family in the South Bronx.

- Their first son, Carlos, was born in 1955.
- Wilfredo's mother took care of the baby so that Annette could continue working.
- Annette continued to send money to her family in Puerto Rico every week.
- Though living with her husband's family was inexpensive and convenient, both Annette and Willy longed to be able to own their own home.
- They both saved most of what was left of their paychecks after living expenses and family obligations.
- Home ownership was considered important in Puerto Rican culture.
- Annette was content with her life, but missed her family.
- She was not able to take time off from work to visit her brothers in Baltimore or her sister in Philadelphia.
- She wrote to her parents in Puerto Rico often, but knew she would never see them again.

Life at Work

- Annette worked as a room maid for four months at the Santos's large hotel—La Calienda Casa.
- A neighbor told Annette about an opportunity to work as a sewing machine operator in a garment factory in downtown Manhattan.
- Although she didn't mind working at the hotel, the job in the garment factory seemed like a good idea.
- The factory workers were almost entirely Puerto Ricans, giving Annette the opportunity to work and socialize with people to whom she could easily relate.
- The factory job was also unionized.
- This was important because Puerto Rican workers were easily taken advantage of.
- Unfamiliar with American work practices and unable to speak English well, they were ill equipped to argue on their own behalf.
- The factory job paid more than her job at La Calienda Casa, a result of the collective bargaining agreements of the union.
- She made $0.75 per hour and sent $12.00 to $15.00 a week to Puerto Rico.
- Once she started saving for her own house, she sent a bit less, but still had to contribute to her husband's household.
- Despite the advantages, operating a sewing machine was very grueling work.
- The hours were long and Annette had to sit at her sewing machine for eight-hour stretches with only a few brief breaks.
- The factory was overcrowded with workers; the building was often too hot during the summer and too cold in the winter.
- Once, Annette fainted from heat exhaustion.
- To supplement her factory work, Annette often mended clothes at home to make extra money.
- She was grateful that her mother-in-law was able to help care for Carlos, allowing her to devote more hours to work.
- Her dream of being able to move out of the Riveras' house was always on her mind.

They lived with her husband's family.

While Annette was at work, her mother-in-law took care of Carlos.

Life in the Community: New York City

- Annette was part of the group of Puerto Ricans who came to New York during the "Great Migration" of the 1940s and 1950s.
- These individuals were needed to help replenish the workforce, as many of the city's more affluent residents relocated to the suburbs.
- New York City Mayor Robert F. Wagner, Jr. was in favor of Puerto Ricans settling in the city and encouraged businesses to recruit Puerto Rican workers.
- The part of the Bronx where Annette and Willy lived was predominantly Puerto Ricans but more middle class than the impoverished Spanish Harlem section.
- Their neighborhood was full of Puerto Rican families, shops and businesses.
- Annette did grocery shopping at a nearby *Bodega* where the owners spoke only Spanish.
- She found many of the foods, including fish and produce, that she used to buy in Puerto Rico.
- Before the birth of their son, Annette and Willy would often go dancing at the same dancehall where they had first met.
- They enjoyed the music of popular Puerto Rican artists Pedro Flores and Cuarteto Victoria.
- The couple were practicing Catholics and tried to attend mass as much as possible.
- Their busy work schedules often made it difficult to do so.
- Annette considered herself very lucky to have a wonderful husband and a healthy son.
- She thanked God every day that her new family lived in a relatively safe neighborhood.
- Despite her contentment, however, tensions often ran high between Puerto Ricans and the city's other ethnic immigrant groups.
- Many resented Annette because she, like most Puerto Ricans, already had American citizenship even before arriving in the United States.
- Annette often asked herself who she was: Puerto Rican or American?
- Despite her citizenship, she was often viewed as an outsider by many of the city's longtime residents.
- Annette and Willy's family often felt pulled in opposite directions, welcomed by businesses looking for cheap labor, but shunned by residents afraid that their neighborhoods were being taken over by 'Ricans.
- Annette sometimes felt other young mothers thought their babies superior to her son.
- She secretly wondered if Carlos would ever be accepted as American.
- Oftentimes, Puerto Ricans also felt divided amongst themselves.
- Willy's parents tried to strictly preserve the culture and traditions of Puerto Rico, while Annette felt it important to integrate into American life.
- This caused some hard feelings in the Rivera household.
- Another dividing issue among Puerto Ricans was language.
- Annette spoke English as a result of the government-mandated use of English in public schools when she was growing up in Puerto Rico.
- Many Puerto Ricans, including Willy's parents, who were from the rural parts of the island, didn't have the same exposure to English.
- They struggled with the language when they came to New York, adding to their reluctance to shed their Puerto Rican traditions.
- Due to the large number of non-English-speaking immigrants, the city created services to assist the Spanish-speaking population.
- New schools, and social and civic services were established and funded by all the city's taxpayers.
- This angered longtime residents who thought that everyone should be forced to speak English.
- But this conflict was not entirely a new problem.

- Ever since Puerto Rico was ceded to the United States following the Spanish-American War of 1898, Americans struggled with what to do with a colony that was largely non-white and entirely Spanish-speaking.
- During the first 20 years of American control, two different governmental policies were established.
- In the Foraker Act of 1900, the United States modeled its governmental style after that of the British Crown Colonies.
- Islanders would be citizens of Puerto Rico but not the United States.
- Beginning in 1902, there would be no tariffs on goods between Puerto Rico and the United States.
- The U.S. president would be responsible for the appointment of the island governor and its Supreme Court.
- The U.S. Congress would retain veto power over any laws in Puerto Rico.
- There will be an 11-member Executive Council named by the governor.
- The House of Delegates (35 members) would be elected by popular vote.
- Few were pleased with the Foraker Act.
- Wealthy Americans called it undemocratic, while Puerto Ricans proclaimed it not statehood, independence, or home rule.
- After the United States acquired the Virgin Islands, President Woodrow Wilson signed the Jones Act in 1917, which provided:
  - Puerto Ricans could freely travel to the U.S. mainland;
  - Puerto Ricans were U.S. citizens;
  - Although Puerto Ricans could not vote in federal elections and were not taxed, they could be drafted during wartime;
  - The Senate and House on Puerto Rico were elected by universal male suffrage until 1929, when women's suffrage was granted;
  - The governor, Supreme Court, and top officials were to be appointed by the president.
- The Jones Act was amended in 1947, granting Puerto Ricans the right to elect their own governor, but kept the U.S. Congress as the source of Puerto Rico's rights.
- In July 1950, Public Law 600 was signed which allowed the people of Puerto Rico to draft their own constitution.
- Puerto Rico was granted commonwealth status on July 25, 1952.
- This meant that Puerto Rico was self-governing on local matters, but required to pay federal taxes.
- Though not fully independent, Puerto Ricans could receive many benefits from their association with America, including social benefits such as food stamps.

HISTORICAL SNAPSHOT
1956

- The nation boasted 7,000 drive-in theaters
- The DNA molecule was photographed for the first time
- Teen fashions for boys included crew cut haircuts known as "flaptops"
- Procter and Gamble created disposable diapers sold under the name Pampers
- Ford Motor Company went public and issued over 10 million shares which were sold to 250,000 investors
- A survey showed that 77 percent of college-educated women married and 41 percent worked part-time, 17 percent full-time
- Boston religious leaders urged the banning of rock 'n' roll
- Eleven percent of all cars sold were station wagons
- For the first time the airlines carried as many passengers as trains did
- The last Union veteran of the Civil War died; he served as a drummer boy at 17
- Broadway openings included *Waiting for Godot, Long Day's Journey into Night, My Fair Lady, Bells Are Ringing* and *Separate Tables*

- After vowing never to allow Elvis Presley's vulgarity on his TV show, Ed Sullivan paid Presley $50,000 for three appearances
- Midas Muffler Shops, Comet, Raid, Salem cigarettes, La Leche League, Imperial margarine and women ordained as ministers in the Presbyterian Church all made their first appearance
- Don Larsen of the New York Yankees pitched the first perfect game in the World Series
- John F. Kennedy won the Pulitzer Prize for his book *Profiles in Courage,* a biography; *Russia Leaves the War* by George F. Kennan won in the U.S. History category
- In the art world, a canvas purchased in Chicago for $450 was discovered to be a Leonardo valued at $1 million
- Television premieres included *As the World Turns, The Edge of Night, The Huntley-Brinkley Report, The Price Is Right* and *The Steve Allen Show*
- Soviet Premier Nikita Khrushchev assailed past President Joseph Stalin as a terrorist, egotist and murderer
- Anti-Soviet demonstrations in Hungary were violently suppressed
- American colleges began actively recruiting students from the middle classes
- Martin Luther King, Jr. said, "Nonviolence is the most potent technique for oppressed people. Unearned suffering is redemptive."
- Hit songs included "Blue Suede Shoes," "Hound Dog," "Mack the Knife," "The Party's Over" and "Friendly Persuasion"
- European autos gained in popularity, including Volkswagens, Jaguars, Ferraris, Saabs and Fiats
- Ngo Diem was elected president of South Vietnam

Puerto Rican Immigration Timeline

1493

On his second voyage, Christopher Columbus discovered the Virgin Islands and Puerto Rico.

1509

Ponce de Leon was appointed governor of Puerto Rico.

1580

Imported European diseases virtually wiped out the native Indians of Puerto Rico.

1868

The Fourteenth Amendment to the United States Constitution was adopted which declared that all people of Hispanic origin born in the United States would be U.S. citizens.

A Puerto Rican decree freed all children born of slaves.

Puerto Rican insurrectionists, fighting for independence, were defeated by the Spanish.

1870

The Spanish government freed all the slaves it owned in Cuba and Puerto Rico.

1873

All slavery was abolished in Puerto Rico.

1875

The U.S. Supreme Court ruled that the power to regulate immigration was held solely by the federal government.

1892

Revolutionary organizations focused on independence were created in both Cuba and Puerto Rico.

1897

Spain granted Puerto Rico and Cuba autonomy and home rule.

1898

Following the Spanish-American War, Spain signed the Treaty of Paris, transferring Cuba, Puerto Rico and the Philippines to the United States.

The Foraker Act established a civilian government in Puerto Rico under U.S. dominance that allowed the Islanders to elect their own House of Representatives but did not permit Puerto Rico a vote in Washington.

1917

The Jones Act was passed extending U.S. citizenship to all Puerto Ricans and created two Puerto Rican houses of legislature, elected by male suffrage.

English was declared the official language of Puerto Rico.

Congress passed the Immigration Act of 1917, imposing a literacy requirement on all immigrants.

continued

Timeline . . . *(continued)*

1921
Limits on the number of immigrants allowed in the United States in a single year were imposed for the first time in the country's history.

1926
Puerto Ricans in Harlem were attacked by non-Hispanics fearful of the growing Puerto Rican population in New York.

1930
United States interests controlled 44 percent of the cultivated land in Puerto Rico.

U.S. capitalists controlled 60 percent of the banks and public services and all the maritime lines in Puerto Rico.

1933
The Roosevelt administration reversed the policy of English as the official language of Puerto Rico.

1934
During the early years of the Depression, 20 percent of all Puerto Ricans living in the United States returned to the island.

1940
An independent union was formed as the major labor organization in Puerto Rico.

1941
The Fair Employment Practices Act was passed, designed to eliminate discrimination in employment.

1944
Operation Bootstrap, initiated by the Puerto Rican government to meet labor demands in World War II, stimulated a major wave of immigration to the United States.

1946
The first Puerto Rican Governor, Jesus T. Pinero, was appointed by President Harry Truman.

1947
Approximately 20 airlines provided air service between San Juan, Puerto Rico, and New York

1950
The United States Congress upgraded Puerto Rico's political status from protectorate to commonwealth.

1954
The U.S. Supreme Court ruled in Hernandez v. Texas that Hispanic Americans and all other racial groups had equal protection under the Fourteenth Amendment to the Constitution.

Selected Prices

Bedroom Set, Walnut	$645.00
Coffee Maker, Percolator	$16.88
Lipstick, Cashmere Bouquet	$0.49
Mattress, Serta	$79.50
Nylons	$1.00
Paneling, 70 Panels	$47.00
Refrigerator	$259.00
Typewriter, Smith-Corona, Electric	$209.35
Vacuum Cleaner, Eureka	$69.95
Watch, Bulova	$59.50

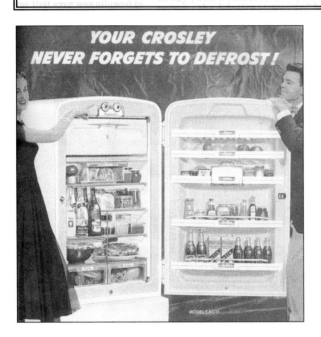

YOUR CROSLEY NEVER FORGETS TO DEFROST!

COLONIAL DESK — MODEL 121

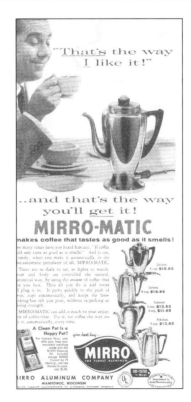

"That's the way I like it!"

..and that's the way you'll get it!

MIRRO-MATIC makes coffee that tastes as good as it smells!

MIRRO THE FINEST ALUMINUM

MIRRO ALUMINUM COMPANY
MANITOWOC, WISCONSIN

"Find Parasite Worms in Puerto Rican Children," *Tri-State Defender* (Memphis, Tennessee), November 21, 1959:

Worm infestation diseases, which were rarely seen in the Philadelphia area, are now being found in pre-school Puerto Rican children.

In a report of research done in an overcrowded Philadelphia neighborhood, Eugene N. Myers, Roberto Negron, and Hillard Pearlstein, medical students at Temple University School of Medicine, showed that almost 70 percent of children examined, who were born in Puerto Rico, had some kind of parasitic (worm) infestation.

The most common parasite in over half the Puerto Rican-born youngsters was *Trichocephalus trichiurus*, better known as the human whipworm, a thread-like parasite about one-quarter inch long. These worms cause weakness, anemia, and stomach pains.

Tested children who were born in the U.S., but who visited Puerto Rico, had a 57 percent incidence of parasites. As a control, the medical students studied 100 children who were born in the U.S., but who had not been to Puerto Rico. Of these latter children, in contrast, only 23 percent were infected.

When housing conditions were considered as a factor, worms were found in 90 percent of those who lived in overcrowded dwellings, as compared to 10 percent in non-overcrowded dwellings.

The study, which received the second place award at the recent Student American Medical Association Scientific Forum in Chicago was reported in the current (November) issue of the *New Physician*.

"Puerto Rico Adds 50 Industries," *The New York Times*, January 3, 1950:

SAN JUAN, P.R.—"Operation Bootstrap"—Puerto Rico's program initiated under Gov. Luis Munoz Marin to free this island from dependence on its sugar industry— is now showing results.

At Carolina, a few miles from here, Beacon Textiles is completing a $1.5 million plant that will start operations late in February. Near Bayamon, a short distance to the west, private capital from the States is putting up a $500,000 rayon mill, to be finished and equipped late in the spring. Meanwhile, the last machines are being installed in the big Textron mill at Ponce, on the south coast, and the first cloth has been run off in test production there, in preparation for regular operations early in March.

At Vega Baga, in north central Puerto Rico, Crane China's factory, which cost $1.5 million, now employs nearly 500 workers and will use 200 more when the training program is completed and full production of 25,000 dozen pieces weekly is reached.

At Guayanilla, near Ponce, a site has been chosen and preliminary details ironed out for the construction of an oil refinery that may represent an investment of nearly $20 million of private capital from the mainland.

continued

"Puerto Rico Adds 50 Industries," ... *(continued)*

Nearly a dozen new plants are in various stages of construction as the insular government presses its drive to industrialize this semitropical home of 2.2 million traditionally poor people.

Although there are some misgivings on the part of the operators of the sugar plants and plantations, who fear that in time the new factories will lure away too many of their workers, all admit that a new era has dawned in the midst of backward agricultural terrain.

Water power and better highways, new hotel and club facilities have come to the island as a part of the new dispensation. Most of the plants started under Government auspices to show what could be done there are working at capacity. The Government's cement plant is turning out one million barrels of cement a year, and finding a ready market for it in new housing, roads, business and factory construction.

The shoe factory at Ponce, after reaching a production of about 1,800 pairs daily to help supply a big part of the island's demand for $14 million worth of shoes a year, has been sold by the Puerto Rico Industrial Development Company to the Joyce interests of California as the first step in getting official industries into private hands.

Three bids are being considered by the development company for the Puerto Rico Clay Products plant, near here, and several offers are being weighed for the cement plant. The glass-bottle plant has made its first shipments to Central American countries. Only the paper-board plant has been listed as a failure.

The 50 new industries now operating or soon to start will give employment to about 8,000 persons, and will have an annual payroll of more than $8 million. Their output ranges from fur coats, jewelry and buttons to optical instruments and radio and television sets. The 25,000-spindle plant of Textile, perhaps the first of several planned by this company in Puerto Rico, will have a capacity of more than 10 million yards of "cotton print cloth gray goods" annually.

"Where to Go This Month," *McCall's*, February 1958:

Puerto Rico: One of the gayest of all pre-Lenten carnivals begins here on February 1 and continues through February 18. You may start out a spectator watching the passing parades of costumed celebrants, pageants, sailing regattas, coronations and other ceremonies, but before long you will probably catch the carnival spirit and don masks to join the street dancing, Battle of the Flowers, masquerade balls and parties at all the hotels.

"The World of Children," by Peter Cardozo, *Good Housekeeping*, February 1951:

Want to be a fairy princess? Small fry in Oakland, California, have discovered an exciting land of make-believe. The magic passwords? Oakland Costume Loan Service. Sponsored by the city's Recreation Department, this unique community service stocks over 10,000 costumes for holiday festivals, school pageants, amateur theatricals and any make-believe in which a girl becomes a fairy princess or a boy an Indian chief. Schools, church groups, playgrounds and other nonprofit organizations can rent costumes; a small fee covers the cost of laundering. Through the magic of colorful fabrics, needles, and thread, youngsters can be transformed into Puritan maidens, elves, Dutch folk with wooden shoes, gypsies, even knights in armor. Seven thousand costumes loaned each year!

Let's make ice cream. With miniature dairy plants set up right in the classroom, three million children will soon be "pasteurizing" milk and churning make-believe scoops of ice cream. Dairy-class Workit, a new teaching aid, includes cutout sheets of trucks and machinery the children can fold, paste together and assemble on a lithographed dairy layout. By adding the full-color background picture of the farm, a three-dimensional model of the dairy plant can actually be operated. A "textbook" tells youngsters how bottles of milk get to their doorsteps. Sponsored by the National Dairy Council, these Class Workits supplement field trips to farms, giving a realistic picture of the dairy industry at work.

continued

"The World of Children," . . . *(continued)*

Like a diamond in the sky. Twinkle, twinkle, Little Star! How I wonder what you are. . ." This year in New York, children are learning the scientific answer. They attend a series of heavenly talks now being given in the Theater of the Stars, at the Hayden Planetarium. Especially adapted for eight- to 14-year-olds, the Young People's astronomy course covers such topics as the sun, the planets, the moon, and the constellations. The purpose of the course: To acquaint junior astronomers with the wonders of the heavens and make them feel at home under the night sky. Each child who sits under the Planetarium's magic domed ceiling becomes a superman. He sees in seven seconds how the sky picture changes in a whole year; he can even take a trip to the moon and back!

Paper Pianos. Without leaving their desks, children in Public School 119 in New York City are learning to play the piano. Sounds impossible, but it isn't. Taking part in a "class piano" experiment, youngsters from eight to 12 spend 40 minutes a week learning to play the piano. Each child spreads out a three-octave piano keyboard. (These are made of paper, cost only $0.25.) While the teacher plays a simple melody on a real piano, the children will "play" it on their paper keyboard, following the notes and chords written on the blackboard. They sing the melody as they play, take turns at the real piano, give a recital at the end of the year. Teachers and students find group teaching (10 pupils at the same time) as satisfactory as private lessons; the children like to learn together.

NONSENSE VERSES

BY ALFRED I. TOOKE

Seventeen of Everything

There was a young lady with seventeen cats.
She went to the city to buy them some hats.
They picked out the prettiest ones they could find,
And wore them all home with the front part behind.
Before they got back they'd walked seventeen miles,
Met seventeen people with seventeen smiles,
And seventeen times had said, "How do you do!"
And seventeen people replied, "How are you!"

Now, one was a farmer with seventeen houses,
And seventeen chickens and seventeen cowses.
Said he, "I'm a farmer who does as he pleases,"
Then, milking the cows, he made seventeen cheeses.
The cats cut a cheese into seventeen pieces,
Had supper with all of their nephews and nieces,
Then took off the hats from their seventeen heads,
And went off to sleep in their seventeen beds.

1959: Hospital Workers' Strike Organizer

Union organizer Nidia Fernandez walked the picket line with her hospital co-workers in New York City to improve working conditions, despite personal financial hardship.

Life at Home

- Nidia Fernandez was born in 1930 in Paterson, the second-largest city in New Jersey.
- She was the second child and only daughter of Juan Fernandez and Alicia Juarez.
- Her mother's parents were born in New Jersey; her father's parents had immigrated to America from Puerto Rico.
- When Nidia was a toddler, her parents divorced and she moved to New York City with her mother and two brothers.
- As a single parent during the Great Depression, her mother struggled.
- To support the family, she worked at a cannery at night and as a waitress during the day; her father helped watch the children.
- Nidia enjoyed a close relationship with her grandfather, who called her "seven tongues" because she always talked so much.
- During the 1940s and the onset of the war economy, her family's financial situation improved.
- Nidia's mother remarried and became the owner of a restaurant and hotel visited by Japanese, Chinese, Jews, Filipinos, and Puerto Ricans.
- At age 16, Nidia dropped out of school to work.
- She and her mother were often at odds, mostly about the boys with whom Nidia associated.
- Nidia began spending more time with her biological father, who still lived in Paterson.

Nidia Fernandez led her hospital co-workers to better working conditions.

Nidia with her mother, brother and step-father.

- From him she learned to cherish the role unions played in helping workers gain their rights.
- In 1913 Paterson was the site of a major labor strike initiated by 800 broad silk weavers; they were soon joined by the ribbon weavers and the dry house workers. .
- The strike eventually affected 300 mill and dye houses, which employed 24,000 workers.
- Their demands included wage increases, the establishment of an eight-hour workday, and abolition of the four-loom system in broad cloth that required workers to service multiple looms.
- More than 2,000 workers allowed themselves to be arrested, flooding the jails and disrupting the courts.
- But after several months of bitter picketing, the English-speaking and better-paid workers returned to work, breaking the back of the strike.
- The experience taught Nidia that unions were the only way workers could gain the strength to demand a fair share, but only if they were well organized.
- She was shocked that most unions had been reluctant to accept women workers like herself.
- During the war years, the increased number of women in the nation's shops and factories posed a major problem for America's unions, many of which barred female members.
- But the gender restrictions fell quickly under the pace of World War II production demands.
- Both the government and women workers applied pressure to open the doors of the unions.
- The International Association of Machinists; the Molders and Foundry Workers; the Iron Shipbuilders and Helpers; and the Carpenters and Joiners admitted women soon after the attack on Pearl Harbor.
- In the fall of 1942, the intransigent International Brotherhood of Boilermakers admitted women to its membership for the first time in its 62-year history.
- By 1944, 11 national unions reported more than 40,000 women members.
- By the war's end, nearly all AFL and CIO unions had accepted women, although many local unions remained opposed to their admission.
- But the doors of many unions remained closed to women of color, including most blacks and Puerto Ricans.
- In 1948, Nidia took a job in a New York cafeteria, convinced that worker solidarity and clear demands would win the day.
- The prosperous economy of post-World War II America was creating many new jobs, but most of the best-paying jobs were going to men.
- After three months on her first job, Nidia demanded equal pay with men and bathroom break privileges.
- She was promptly fired as a troublemaker.

Life at Work

- In the winter of 1958, when Nidia Fernandez was approached about her participation in a new hospital worker's union, she asked a lot of questions.
- Twenty-nine, divorced and the mother of two, she was more cautious about where she spoke out these days.

- She had been a nursing assistant for three years at Mount Sinai Hospital in New York City; work was steady and predictable, although the pay was poor.
- Nonprofit or voluntary hospitals claimed that they generated so few revenues, they should not be expected to pay competitive wages.
- "A hospital is not an economic, industrial unit," declared Dr. Martin Steinberg, director of Mount Sinai. "It is a social unit. . . . Human Life should not be a pawn in jousting for economic gain or power."
- Most of the larger unions already had passed on proposals to organize legions of hospital workers, most of whom were black and Puerto Rican women.
- But Union Local 1199 had a long history of uniting diverse groups.
- Founded in 1932 by progressive pharmacists and clerks, 1199 and its leaders were guided by the slogan "An injury to one is an injury to all."
- Originally part of the Pharmacist Union of Greater New York, by 1936 it had become Local 1199, Retail Employees Union, a part of the Retail, Wholesale & Department Store Union, attached to the American Federation of Labor.
- As early as 1937, the predominantly Jewish union won a campaign in Harlem for the hiring of African American pharmacists using a seven-week strike.
- In 1958, when 1199 undertook a campaign to organize New York City's voluntary hospital workers, most traditional labor leaders marked it for failure.
- The workers, most of whom were women who did not like working together, earned about $32.00 a week with few or no benefits.
- Many were too poor to manage the economic stress of a protracted strike.
- All voluntary hospitals were exempt from labor laws because they were charitable organizations, another mark against a successful strike.
- The modest 5,000-member 1199 accepted the challenge almost by accident.
- A black porter at the Montefiore Hospital happened to compare his wages and conditions with those of a relative who worked as a porter in a Bronx pharmacy.
- The unrepresented hospital porter was being paid $36.00 for a 44-hour week, while the drugstore porter, who worked for a 1199-unionized pharmacy, was earning $72.00 for 40 hours.
- In addition, the unionized employee was covered by an employer-financed pension plan and health and welfare protection.
- Disturbed by the difference, the Montefiore porter assembled a group of co-workers and went to the 1199 for support.
- The union assigned Elliott Godoff, who was formerly with the teamsters, to organize the workers; Theodore Mitchell, a black drugstore porter, was named to assist.
- Their goal was to organize bedpan emptiers, dietary aides and laundry room workers, most of whom were underrepresented Latin American, black or Puerto Rican women, in New York City's hospitals.
- Within three months, 600 of the 800 workers had joined the union.
- The average wages were $34.00 to $38.00 a week for most; laboratory technicians received $50.00 to $55.00.
- The union invited the hospital to negotiate wages, benefits and union representation.
- The hospital declined, stating clearly and accurately that employees of voluntary hospitals were excluded from labor legislation protection.

Hospital workers met with union leaders.

- Petitions, telegrams and several meetings failed to move the hospital trustees.
- Even a much-sought-after union endorsement in *The New York Times* failed to persuade hospital administrators.
- The dam broke when, in December 1958, Montefiore workers voted overwhelmingly for 1199.
- Mount Sinai workers got into the act on March 6, 1959, when 800 workers boycotted the cafeteria in a lunch-hour demonstration.
- The workers, including Nidia, demanded that the hospital recognize the union.
- The hospital administrators issued a letter to employees that said that higher wages could only be created by higher hospital income and that the hospital was working with the city, insurers and other sources to get more money.
- Concerning strike threats, the letter asked, "Strike against whom? Our patients, sick people, children needing immediate medical care?"
- Mount Sinai's rank and file rejected the administration's arguments and voted, along with the employees of five other nonprofit hospitals, to walk out.
- In all, 3,500 workers, including elevator operators, orderlies, nursing aides, kitchen workers and other housekeeping employees, exchanged their jobs for the picket line.

Life in the Community: New York, New York

- When the New York hospital workers strike began, Nidia had no savings; she had been living paycheck to paycheck since her divorce five years earlier.
- Every morning of the strike she dressed carefully and joined her fellow strikers on the picket line.
- She was proud to walk the line every morning and yell at the strike-breaking scabs who had picked a pitiful paycheck over union solidarity.
- Nidia's sign declared, "Mount Sinai workers can't live on $32.00 a week. ON STRIKE. Please help us win."
- She was even proud that the newspapers described the picketers as "a bedraggled army"; at least they were standing for something.
- And she was invigorated when the same newspapers pointed out that the strikes made New York City's hospital workers the first employees in private, nonprofit hospitals in the nation to unionize.
- She never dreamed that the strike would last so long and attract national attention.
- For its part, the union leadership decried the "shameful working conditions" that "threaten the health of the infants and children of these workers . . . and breed juvenile delinquency, crime and violence."
- The Greater New York Hospital Association countered, "This is not a strike, but revolution against law and order."
- As far as Nidia was concerned, the secret weapon was the national attention the strike was attracting, thanks to its links with the civil rights movement.
- Starting in 1956, the union had solicited membership funds to support the Montgomery, Alabama bus boycott.
- As a result the union established a friendship with Dr. Martin Luther King, Jr., leader of the boycott.
- To rally public support, Local 1199 lined up backing from civil rights leaders like Dr. King, Bayard Rustin, A. Philip Randolph, and many elected officials and editorial writers.

- Dr. King, who described 1199 as his "favorite union," called the fight to raise wages for the $30.00-a-week workers a civil rights struggle.
- But links to Dr. King were only one of the workers' strengths.
- The hospital workers' strike also captured the attention of the traditional labor leaders.
- New York City Central Labor Council President Harry Van Arsdale saw the strike as a means of uniting the labor movement in the city.
- First, he participated in the marathon negotiating sessions with the hospital; then, he led 700 unionists in joining the picketers at Beth Israel Hospital.
- Nidia had been told repeatedly that the labor leaders themselves never walked the line; now she knew this strike would be successful.
- The bitter fight for recognition lasted 46 days; the poor, undereducated workers had not been broken as the men downtown on both sides of the issue had predicted.
- But in the end the union was not recognized, despite a New York judge's accusation that the hospital management's refusal to recognize the union was an "echo of the nineteenth century."
- Management only agreed to arbitration.
- The final agreement guaranteed "no discrimination against any employee because he joins a union"; a minimum wage of $1.00 an hour; wage increases of $5.00 a week; a 40-hour week; time and a half for overtime; seniority rules; job grades; and rate changes.

Dr. Martin Luther King's family supported his alliance with the hospital worker's union.

HISTORICAL SNAPSHOT
1959

- Alaska and Hawaii were admitted to the Union as the forty-ninth and fiftieth states
- American Airlines entered the jet age with the first scheduled transcontinental flight of a Boeing 707 from Los Angeles to New York for $301.00
- Arlington and Norfolk, Virginia, peacefully desegregated their public schools
- A plane crash claimed the lives of rock-and-roll stars Buddy Holly, Ritchie Valens and J. P. "The Big Bopper" Richardson
- The United States successfully test-fired a Titan intercontinental ballistic missile from Cape Canaveral
- The U.S. launched its first weather station, *Vanguard II*, into space
- The FCC applied the equal time rule to TV newscasts of political candidates
- Miles Davis recorded the album *Kind of Blue* with John Coltrane, Cannonball Adderly, Philley Joe Jones, Paul Chambers and Bill Evans
- The Barbie doll was unveiled at the American Toy Fair in New York City by the Mattel Toy Company for $3.00
- The *USS Skate* became the first submarine to surface at the North Pole
- NASA announced the selection of America's first seven astronauts for the Mercury program: Scott Carpenter, Gordon Cooper, John Glenn, Gus Grissom, Wally Schirra, Alan Shepard and Donald Slayton
- "The Battle Of New Orleans" by Johnny Horton peaked at number one on the pop singles chart and stayed there for six weeks
- Congress authorized food stamps for poor Americans
- The first telephone cable linking Europe and the United States was laid
- Television's *The Twilight Zone, The Untouchables, Rawhide* and *Bonanza* all premiered
- The Guggenheim Museum, designed by Frank Lloyd Wright, opened in New York City
- The Rodgers and Hammerstein musical *The Sound of Music* opened on Broadway
- The film *Ben-Hur,* starring Charlton Heston, had its world premiere in New York
- The first color photograph of Earth was received from outer space

Selected Prices, 1959

Automobile, Ford Thunderbird $4,222.00
Candygram, Western Union, Pound $2.95
Chandelier, Crystal $425.00
Child's Jeans $1.64
Hamburger, Burger King Whopper $0.37
Lawn Sprinkler $16.95
Movie Projector $89.95
Scotch, Chivas Regal, Fifth $8.06
Stereo $129.95
Transistor Pocket Radio, Zenith $75.00

Labor Timeline

1910
A bomb destroyed a portion of the Llewellyn Ironworks in Los Angeles, where a bitter strike was in progress.

1911
The Supreme Court ordered the AFL to cease its promotion of a boycott against the Bucks Stove and Range Company.

The Triangle Shirtwaist Company fire in New York City resulted in the death of 147 people, mostly women and young girls working in sweatshop conditions.

1912
Women and children were beaten by police during a textile strike in Lawrence, Massachusetts.

The National Guard was called out against striking West Virginia coal miners.

1913
Police shot three maritime workers during a strike against the United Fruit Company in New Orleans.

1914
The Ford Motor Company raised its basic wage from $2.40 for a nine-hour day to $5.00 for an eight-hour day.

Five men, two women and 12 children died in the "Ludlow Massacre" when company guards attempted to break a strike at Colorado's Ludlow Mine Field.

A Western Federation of Miners strike was crushed by the militia in Butte, Montana.

1915
Labor leader Joe Hill was arrested in Salt Lake City on murder charges and executed 21 months later despite worldwide protests and two attempts to intervene by President Woodrow Wilson.

Twenty rioting strikers were shot by factory guards in Roosevelt, New Jersey.

The Supreme Court upheld "yellow dog" contracts, which forbade membership in labor unions.

1916
A bomb set off during a "Preparedness Day" parade in San Francisco killed 10 and resulted in the conviction of Thomas J. Mooney, a labor organizer, and Warren K. Billings, a shoe worker.

Riots erupted during a strike at Everett Mills, Everett, Washington; local police watched and refused to intervene, resulting in the death of seven workers.

Federal employees won the right to receive worker's compensation insurance.

1917
Vigilantes forced 1,185 striking copper miners in Bisbee, Arizona, into manure-laden boxcars and "deported" them to the New Mexico desert.

The Supreme Court approved the Eight-Hour Act under the threat of a national railway strike.

Industrial Workers of the World (IWW) organizer Frank Little was lynched in Butte, Montana.

Federal agents raided the IWW headquarters in 48 cities.

1919
United Mine Worker organizer Fannie Sellins was gunned down by company guards in Brackenridge, Pennsylvania.

Looting and violence erupted in Boston after 1,117 Boston policemen declared a work stoppage to gain union representation.

continued

Timeline . . . *(continued)*

1919

Three hundred fifty thousand steel workers walked off their jobs to demand union recognition.

IWW organizer Wesley Everest was lynched after a Centralia, Washington IWW hall was attacked by Legionnaires.

Approximately 250 "anarchists," "communists," and "labor agitators" were deported to Russia, marking the beginning of the so-called "Red Scare."

1920

The U.S. Bureau of Investigation began carrying out the nationwide Palmer Raids, seizing labor leaders and literature to discourage labor activity.

Seven management detectives and two coal miners were killed in the Battle of Matewan in West Virginia.

1922

Violence resulted in the deaths of 36 people during a coal miners' strike in Herrin, Illinois.

1924

Congress approved a child labor amendment to the U.S. Constitution; only 28 of the necessary 36 states ratified it.

1925

Two company houses occupied by non-union coal miners were blown up by labor "racketeers" during a strike against the Glendale Gas and Coal Company in Wheeling, West Virginia.

1926

Textile workers fought with police in Passaic, New Jersey, during a year-long strike.

1930

Labor racketeers shot and killed contractor William Healy, with whom the Chicago Marble Setters Union had been having difficulties.

One hundred farm workers were arrested for their unionizing activities in Imperial Valley, California.

1931

Vigilantes attacked striking miners in Harlan County, Kentucky.

1932

Police killed striking workers at Ford's Dearborn, Michigan plant.

1933

Eighteen thousand cotton workers went on strike in Pixley, California.

1934

During the Electric Auto-Lite Strike in Toledo, Ohio, two strikers were killed and over 200 wounded by National Guardsmen.

Police stormed striking truck drivers in Minneapolis who were attempting to prevent truck movement in the market area.

A strike in Woonsocket, Rhode Island, directed at obtaining a minimum wage for textile workers, resulted in over 420,000 workers striking nationwide.

1935

The Committee for Industrial Organization (CIO) was formed to expand industrial unionism.

1937

General Motors recognized the United Auto Workers Union following a sit-down strike.

continued

Timeline . . . *(continued)*

1937

Police killed 10 and wounded 30 during the "Memorial Day Massacre" at the Republic Steel plant in Chicago.

1938

The Wages and Hours Act was passed, banning child labor and setting the 40-hour work week.

1939

The Supreme Court ruled that sit-down strikes were illegal.

1941

Henry Ford recognized the United Auto Workers.

The AFL agreed that there would be no strikes in defense-related industry plants for the duration of the war.

1944

President Franklin D. Roosevelt ordered the army to seize the executive offices of Montgomery Ward and Company after the corporation failed to comply with a National War Labor Board directive regarding union shops.

1946

Packinghouse workers nationwide went on strike.

Four hundred thousand mine workers struck.

The U.S. Navy seized oil refineries to break a 20-state postwar strike.

1947

The Taft-Hartley Labor Act, curbing strikes, was vetoed by President Harry Truman but overridden by Congress.

1948

Labor leader Walter Reuther was shot and seriously wounded by would-be assassins.

1950

President Truman ordered the U.S. Army to seize all the nation's railroads to prevent a general strike.

1952

President Truman ordered the U.S. Army to seize the nation's steel mills to avert a strike; the order was later ruled to be illegal by the Supreme Court.

1955

The two largest labor organizations in the U.S. merged to form the AFL-CIO, with a membership estimated at 15 million.

1956

Columnist Victor Riesel, a crusader against labor racketeers, was blinded when a hired assailant threw sulfuric acid in his face.

1959

The Landrum-Griffin Act passed, restricting union activity.

The Taft-Hartley Act was invoked by the Supreme Court to break a steel strike.

The person who is unorganized because of a racial bar or discrimination of any kind is a threat to the conditions of those who are organized. Anyone who is underpaid, who has substandard conditions, threatens the situation of those in unions.

—AFL President George Meany, 1955

Men make history and not the other way around. In periods where there is no leadership, society stands still. Progress occurs when courageous, skillful leaders seize the opportunity to change things for the better.

—Former President Harry S. Truman, 1959

"Victims of Charity," Dan Wakefield, *Nation*, March 14, 1959:

A Negro lady from the nurses' aides' department spoke up to say: "We're doing pretty good in our department, but a lotta people are afraid—they think they're gonna be fired. And some of the nurses told the girls they shouldn't join a union because then the hospital would be like a 'business.'"

The others hooted, and one voice raised above the rest to say, "It's all right for the nurses to talk; they get plenty and they don't want us to get it."

A lady from the kitchen staff raised her hand and reported that "the ladies in the cafeteria say they get paid mostly by tips and the union can't help them. One of the supervisors said the union can't help us, we'll still have to work no matter what the union does. Well, all I know is when I see those people making $32.00 a week, I'm ready to join anything."

A.H. Raskin, *The New York Times*, May 29, 1959:

They seem determined to carry on indefinitely. THEY say they are tired of being "philanthropists" subsidizing the hospitals with their labor. One girl picketer said: "Whenever we feel disheartened, we can always take out the stub of our last paycheck and get new heart for picketing." She pulled out her own and showed that it came to $27.00 in weekly take-home. . . .

Financial hardship has been a part of their life so long that the prospect of higher pay is less of a goal for many than the pivotal issue of union recognition. They feel for the first time that they "belong" and this groping for human dignity through group recognition is more important than more cash.

"6-Hospital Strike Delayed 2 Weeks, Union Bars Walkout Today After Hospitals Agree to Consider Fact Finding," Ralph Katz, *The New York Times*, April 22, 1959:

A strike of nonprofessional employees at six voluntary hospitals, scheduled for 6 a.m. today, was deferred last night for two weeks. The union agreed to put off action while the hospital boards of trustees considered a fact-finding formula.

The development was announced by Mayor Wagner at 11 p.m. after a series of conferences at City Hall with union and management representatives. Earlier it appeared the strike was inevitable.

Talks had begun at 10 a.m. yesterday. By 8 p.m. it appeared that Local 1199 of the Retail Drug Employees Union would proceed with plans to call out its membership among the hospitals' 4,550 nonprofessional employees. The union claims 3,450 of the workers as members.

At issue is the union demand for recognition as collective-bargaining agent. The two-week delay was offered, the Mayor said, because five of the six hospitals are Jewish institutions. The Jewish High Holy Days of Passover begin at sundown tonight.

Nidia Fernandez helped hospital workers unite.

1964: Black Artist Producer

White, married, mother of two Estelle Stewart Axton was an unlikely record producer, but she and her brother created Stax Records—the South's premier label for black artists.

Life at Home

- Estelle Stewart Axton was white, 40 years of age, a former schoolteacher, and married with two children.
- She was working as a bookkeeper at Union Planters Bank in Memphis, Tennessee, when she agreed to mortgage her house to buy a $2,500 one-track Ampex Recorder.
- Her business partner and brother, Jim Stewart, hardly fit the record producer mold, either.
- He worked in the bond department of a rival bank and played fiddle in several swing bands.
- He found much more pleasure in the latter.
- But together, they created Stax Records, a label that would challenge the supremacy of Motown Records in Detroit.
- Stax was home to Otis Redding, Rufus Thomas, Booker T and the MGs, and Isaac Hayes.
- Estelle was born September 11, 1918, in Middleton, Tennessee, and grew up on a farm.
- She moved to Memphis as a schoolteacher, married Everett Axton, and was working in a bank when, in 1958, her brother Jim Stewart asked for help in developing an independent record label he planned to call Satellite Records.
- He wanted to issue recordings of local country and rockabilly artists.
- All he needed was $2,500 to buy a recording machine, and in exchange, Estelle would be his partner.

Estelle Steward Axton was an unlikely record producer for black artists.

- When Estelle talked to her husband about it, his response was, "No way!"
- But the more she thought about the concept, the more she liked it.
- Eventually, she convinced her husband that they should remortgage their house and, in 1959, she joined Satellite as an equal partner.
- Initially, the brother and sister pair set up shop in an abandoned, rent-free grocery store in a small community 30 miles from Memphis.
- At the time, the newspapers were full of headlines concerning the new *Sputnik*, the Russian satellite that had become first manmade object in space.
- It appeared to represent the future, so they named the company Satellite Productions, which attracted a trademark lawsuit and resulted in a name change to Stax Records, comprising the first two letters in their last names, Stewart and Axton.

Estelle created Stax Records with her fiddle playing brother, who became her business partner.

- The following year, Estelle and Jim discovered the unused Capitol Theatre in a black Memphis neighborhood and turned it into a recording studio and record shop; the cost was $150 a month.
- Once the studio was set up, they opened a record shop next-door in a space that formerly housed the theater's candy counter; Estelle kept her day job at the bank.
- To get inventory for the store, Estelle took orders for records from her coworkers at the bank, then went to Poplar Tunes, the largest record store in town, bought the records for $0.65 and resold them for $1.00.
- Initially, the record store kept the Stax Records studio afloat.
- None of their early records were successful, that is, until popular black disc jockey Rufus Thomas came to the studio to pitch some ideas with his 16-year-old daughter, Carla, in tow.
- That day they previewed "'Cause I Love," written by Rufus Thomas, and convinced Estelle and Jim to record and distribute it.
- Rufus Thomas's most successful recording had been an answer song, created in response to a Big Mama Thornton's "Hound Dog," titled "Bear Cat" and released in 1953; "Hound Dog" would later be successfully covered by a white singer named Elvis Presley.
- About 15,000 copies later, Atlantic Records head Jerry Wexler offered $1,000 for the right to distribute "Cause I Love" nationally—giving the studio some exposure, some cash and its white owners of Stax a sense of the potential of black music.
- Their recording studio itself had acoustical drapes handmade by Estelle, a control room built on the movie theater stage, insulation on the one outside plaster wall to reduce echo, and baffles made with burlap hung from the ceiling.
- The end result was a very live recording environment issuing a reverberation effect similar to that of the concert hall; this would become an important component of what was later known as the Stax Sound.

Life at Work

- Stax Records' big break came when Rufus and Carla Thomas returned to the station with another idea, another song.

- "As soon as Jim and I heard that song, we knew it was a hit. It's funny, when you hear a song, you know if it's got something in it that will sell," Estelle said.

- With the $1,000 they had received from Atlantic Records, Stax Records recorded "Gee Whiz, (Look at His Eyes)" and established itself as a hit-maker.

- Carla Thomas, who commandeered the title of Queen of Memphis Soul, grew up in the projects, in close proximity to Palace Theater on world-famous Beale Street.

- The talented Thomas first became a member of the high school-oriented Teen Town Singers in 1952 at the age of 10.

- Thomas was responsible for not only attending classes and completing her schoolwork, but she also had to attend rehearsals on Wednesdays and Fridays after school and then perform at the radio station on Saturday.

- Somehow she found the time to write "Gee Whiz" when only 16, using a 32-bar AABA pop song structure.

- Sales of "Gee Whiz" began slowly in 1960, but just as Thomas was in the midst of her first year at Tennessee A&I University in Nashville, the success of the single propelled her into the visual spotlight as she performed on *American Bandstand*.

Carla Thomas – Queen of Memphis Soul – and Stax Records both became stars with song Gee Whiz.

- The song provided a launching pad to Thomas's first album, and gave Stax Records national exposure and label recognition; Atlantic also signed on to handle distribution.
- Estelle's next hit arrived courtesy of a neighborhood group, the Mar-Keys, playing "Last Night," an instrumental played by a racially integrated R&B group that included Estelle's son; when the band toured, its members were all white.
- The song was played on WLOK radio before it became a record, generating enormous interest in the Memphis area; however, Jim Stewart was reluctant to take time to cut a record.
- Estelle, known as Lady A, finally got it into the marketplace by pleading, cussing and finally betting $100 it would be a hit; she knew that the kids could "twist" to the record.
- Memphis Radio station WHBQ introduced the record to white audiences and played it over and over before it went national and Estelle collected her $100.
- The neighborhood surrounding Stax Records would adopt the Soulsville moniker and honor performers such as Aretha Franklin, Johnny Ace, and James Alexander of the Mar-Keys.

Stax recorded Last Night *by the Mar-Keys, a neighborhood group that included Estelle's son.*

- Stax sounds were different from its rival Motown in Detroit, whose urban, smooth sounds were more polished.
- "Once you crossed the Mason-Dixon line and got down to Memphis," "Rufus Thomas said, "it was altogether different."
- In 1959, a young black songwriter named Berry Gordon Junior formed Motown for the purpose of aggressively marketing black rock 'n' roll to a white audience.
- Motown turned out hit records in an assembly line fashion—each one technically perfect, efficiently marketed, and designed to have a broad crossover appeal.
- Motown carefully supervised the repertoire of its acts and required them to take classes in diction, stage presence, and choreography.
- As a result, Gordy developed headliner acts such as Diana Ross and the Supremes, the Temptations, and Michael Jackson of the Jackson Five.
- Estelle and Jim's system was less formalized and more prone to an occasional misfire.
- Stax also became one of the most successfully integrated companies in the country—from top management and administration to its artists.
- "We didn't see color," Estelle said, "We saw talent."
- By 1963, Stax was releasing two or three records per month and four or five albums per year; even so, Stewart still worked for the bank.

Songwriter Berry Gordon, Jr. formed Motown Records.

- All the while from her perch at the record store, Estelle led impromptu songwriting sessions on new releases by competitors.
- Every word was parsed by the music crowd as thoroughly was if it were an ancient manuscript.
- The elements of a song's appeal were identified and then analyzed to determine why they worked.
- At the same time, jazz great Phineas Newborn Jr. might drop by and play the piano for hours while David Porter, who worked across the street bagging groceries, was learning the craft of songwriting.
- Saturdays were set aside for musicians, amateur and professional alike, to audition—establishing yet another link to the community.
- Singer Otis Redding got his start at Stax with "These Arms of Mine," recorded at the end of another band's recoding session; Rufus Thomas continued his string of hits with "Walking the Dog," which he wrote while watching an attractive woman dance one night.

Stax Records connected to the community by holding impromptu songwriting sessions and auditions for amateurs and professionals alike.

- In 1963, three albums were issued by Stax: Gus Cannon's "Walk Right In," (also covered by the Rooftop Singers), an artist's anthology titled "Treasured Hits From the South," and Rufus Thomas's "Walking the Dog."
- The bottom line profits of Stax in 1964 were steady but unspectacular, with a majority of its records being sold to black customers through inner-city mom-and-pop record stores.
- Meanwhile, Motown Records was in its ascendancy with the Supremes, Mary Wells, the Miracles, the Temptations, and Stevie Wonder all topping the pop charts.
- In Detroit, Motown based its image around "Hitsville, U.S.A." while Stax was based on being "Soulsville, U.S.A."
- One of Stax's assets was its ability to grow talent.
- When impoverished musician Isaac Hayes began hanging out, Stax's system made room for the talented youngster with the miraculous ear and special knowledge of arrangement.
- And when Hayes combined his talents with Otis Redding's, they became ambassadors to the Memphis Sound.
- Estelle wouldn't have it any other way.

Otis Redding got his start at Stax with These Arms of Mine.

Life in the Community: Memphis, Tennessee

- Majestically perched on a bluff on the eastern bank of the Mississippi River, Memphis had long been a land apart.
- While Tennessee consisted of rolling hills that nurtured country music, Memphis was as flat as the Delta and historically a breeding ground for classic blues, black gospel, and rockabilly.
- The city had long served as a stopping-off point for large numbers of travelers—black and white—mesmerized by the great migration to St. Louis or Chicago.
- Urban by definition, Memphis was still rural in mindset as the 1960s unfolded.
- The city was musically known as both the nurturing ground for the Pentecostal music of the Church of God in Christ and the sophistication of Big Band blues led by BB King.
- Out of this polyglot grew Memphis Soul, defined as stylish, funky, uptown soul music, a sultry style produced at Stax and Hi Records, using melodic unison horn lines, organ, bass, and a driving beat on the drums.
- When Jim Stewart and Estelle Axton converted that old movie theater into a recording studio at the corner of McLemore Avenue and College Street, they gave witness to the level of homegrown talent in the area.
- Their record store became one of the hipper local hangouts, attracting musicians, songwriters, and vocalists, all eager to hear the latest sounds.
- "I think there would have been no Stax Records without the Satellite Record Shop," Booker T. Jones, of Booker T. and the MGs. "Every Saturday I was at the Satellite Record Shop—that's where I went after school; I got to go in there and listen to everything."
- The shop also served as a testing ground for new recordings; Estelle often played recently recorded demo tapes to the record shop patrons.
- Their reactions often determined whether the new record would be changed, dumped or promoted heavily.
- Hi Records was started by three Sun Studio musicians—Ray Harris, Bill Cantrell, and Quentin Claunch—as well as Joe Cuoghi, one of the owners of Poplar ("Pop") Tunes, a local record store.
- Hi Records' early releases were primarily rockabilly.
- Just as the Mar-Keys' "Last Night" helped Stax, the success of Bill Black's Combo changed Hi from a rockabilly label to an instrumental powerhouse during the early 1960s.

Memphis, Tennessee.

HISTORICAL SNAPSHOT
1964

- In the first meeting between leaders of the Roman Catholic and Orthodox churches since the fifteenth century, Pope Paul VI and Patriarch Athenagoras I met in Jerusalem
- In his first State of the Union Address, President Lyndon Johnson declared a "War on Poverty"
- Surgeon General Luther Leonidas Terry reported that smoking may be hazardous to one's health (the first such statement from the U.S. Government)
- Thirteen years after its proposal and nearly two years after its passage by the Senate, the Twenty-fourth Amendment to the Constitution, prohibiting the use of poll taxes in national elections, was ratified
- General Motors introduced the Oldsmobile Vista Cruiser and the Buick Sport Wagon
- The Beatles, having vaulted to the Number 1 spot on the U.S. singles charts for the first time with "I Want to Hold Your Hand," appeared on *The Ed Sullivan Show*, and were seen by an estimated 73 million viewers, launching the mid-1960s "British Invasion" of American popular music

- The Supreme Court ruled that congressional districts must be approximately equal in population
- Muhammad Ali beat Sonny Liston in Miami Beach, Florida, and was crowned the Heavyweight Champion of the World
- Teamsters President Jimmy Hoffa was convicted by a federal jury of tampering with a federal jury in 1962
- In *New York Times Co. v Sullivan*, the Supreme Court ruled that, under the First Amendment, speech criticizing political figures cannot be censored
- The first Ford Mustang rolled off the assembly line at Ford Motor Company
- A Dallas, Texas, jury found Jack Ruby guilty of killing John F. Kennedy assassin Lee Harvey Oswald
- Merv Griffin's game show *Jeopardy!* debuted on NBC
- The Beatles dominated the top five positions in the Billboard Top 40 singles in America: "Can't Buy Me Love," "Twist and Shout," "She Loves You," "I Want to Hold Your Hand," and "Please Please Me"
- Three high school friends in Hoboken, New Jersey, opened the first BLIMPIE restaurant
- The Rolling Stones released their debut album, *The Rolling Stones*
- The New York World's Fair opened to celebrate the 300th anniversary of New Amsterdam being taken over by British forces and renamed New York in 1664
- John George Kemeny and Thomas Eugene Kurtz ran the first computer program written in BASIC (Beginners' All-purpose Symbolic Instruction Code), an easy-to-learn, high-level programming language
- College students marched through Times Square and San Francisco in the first major student demonstration against the Vietnam War
- Three Civil Rights workers—Michael Schwerner, Andrew Goodman, and James Chaney—were murdered near Philadelphia, Mississippi, by local Klansmen, cops, and a sheriff
- President Johnson signed the Civil Rights Act of 1964 into law, legally abolishing racial segregation in the United States
- At the Republican National Convention in San Francisco, presidential nominee Barry Goldwater declared that "extremism in the defense of liberty is no vice," and "moderation in the pursuit of justice is no virtue"
- The Supreme Court ruled that, in accordance with the Civil Rights Act of 1964, establishments providing public accommodations must refrain from racial discrimination
- Cosmic microwave background radiation was discovered
- Dr. Farrington Daniels's book, *Direct Use of the Sun's Energy*, was published by Yale University Press
- The first Moog synthesizer was designed by Robert Moog

Selected Prices

Air Conditioner	$455.00
Beer, Schlitz, Six-Pack	$0.99
Calculator, Remington	$189.50
Camera, Kodak Instamatic	$240.00
Girdle	$11.00
Record Album	$5.98
Refrigerator-Freezer	$300.00
Shoes, Men's Leather	$13.80
Slide Projector	$149.50
Watch, Timex	$9.95

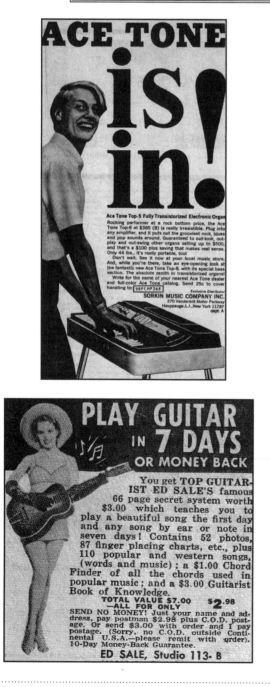

"The Stax Story Part Six, Porter and Hayes Producers," *Hit Parader*, February 1968:

Isaac Hayes and Dave Porter have written about 150 songs together for Stax artists and also produced most of them. So far their most successful collaboration has been with Sam and Dave on songs like "Hold On, I'm Coming" and "Soul Man"; in addition, Isaac plays piano on his own sessions in many of the other Stax sessions.

Isaac was born in 1942 on a farm in Covington, Tennessee, and raised by his grandparents who worked as sharecroppers. His mother died when he was an infant and he never saw his father. When Isaac was seven, the family moved to Memphis. He won several music scholarships, but he couldn't afford to buy an instrument, so he took the vocal training. He had to drop out of school to help support the family, and took singing jobs in local nightclubs where he also taught himself to play piano. Gradually, he worked into full-time gigs and met Dave.

Dave was born in Memphis in 1942, one of nine children. He grew up never knowing what his father looked like. "It was just my mother and a bunch of kids. I ran around barefoot and we were so poor it hurt." He sang in church regularly and wrote a class poem in the sixth grade. He formed a singing group in high school and wrote original songs—"which were really horrible." Then he got a job in a grocery store across from Stax and watched the musicians coming and going. In his spare time he sang in nightclubs and hung out around the Stax studio. "Then I met Isaac. We worked as a duet and wrote 30 straight flops, but we learned a lot."

HP: Who writes the lyrics and who writes the melodies?

Dave: Normally I write the lyrics and Hayes comes up with the melodies.

HP: Do you ever work with Steve Cropper?

Dave: Yes, we do. Steve's a tremendous writer himself. We get together with Steve on arrangements.

Isaac: Sometimes the three of us work together or we work with Steve individually.

HP: Who are the main singers you produce?

Dave: Sam and Dave, Carla Thomas, Johnny Taylor, some of Otis Redding, Mabel John, Rufus Thomas, Jean and the Darlings, a new group we have. We've also been working with some new songwriters, Homer Banks and Alan Jones, and a girl named Betty Crutcher. They're very good.

HP: Do you write songs with particular artists in mind?

Dave: Normally we tailor-make songs for a particular person. We block out all other things so that we can find a trait that the artist can protect the best.

Isaac: If we write something for another Stax artist, we present it to the producer in charge. Maybe we'll give something to Booker T., who produces William Bell.

HP: What's the difference in writing material for Johnny Taylor and Sam and Dave?

Isaac: With Sam and Dave, we have to create excitement in the material. With Johnny, the material has to be more subtle.

Dave: Johnny is selling 100 percent message. He's capable of getting any message over. So we concentrate on that. With Sam and Dave, we concentrate on sound, gimmicks as well as message.

HP: Sam and Dave must do a lot of improvising on your material.

Dave: Not necessarily. When we write a song, we include ad-libs. This keeps the message together. This gives the audience a chance to grasp everything.

Isaac: We'll throw in little phrases they can use on the side. Once they get the song down, they naturally use their own interpretation when they're delivering the tune.

HP: Isaac, you play piano on a lot of things, don't you?

Isaac: Yes. I play piano on all the records Dave and I produce. I'm on quite a few others, too. Wilson Pickett cut "99 1/2" and "634-5789" down here, and I played on those. I'm on Albert King's records. I also play piano and organ with the Monkeys. Booker T. usually plays organ on all the records, but sometimes we switch. Booker's playing is slower and smoother than mine.

HP: Were both of you born in Memphis?

Isaac: I've been in Memphis since I was seven, but I was born a few counties away. I came to Stax three or four times with bands and vocal groups trying to sell records. I played saxophone at the time. I finally got on as a session man. Porter came to me and we worked together in nightclubs as a team. I used to work in a meatpacking plant but I got laid off. I joined a band and decided to stick with it until I made it.

Dave: I was born in Memphis and I've been here all 25 years. I lived in the neighborhood of Stax since its inception. Stax started about five years ago, and I was one of the first artists on the label, with a record that didn't do anything. I sang on a corny R&B thing called "Old Gray Mare." It was one of the first records cut here. Hayes came in on a few sessions, and when we talked, we found many similarities in our thoughts. We decided to try it as a team. Before I came to Stax, I was working across the street in a grocery store pushing carts, and at night I sang in nightclubs.

HP: Describe how your work is different from Holland Dozier at Motown?

Isaac: I really don't know how they work or what the formula is, but it seems to me they do have a formula. We try to make our tunes more natural.

Dave: The truth is, we work with a formula, too. We have a plan. We know what to look for on any tune we write. Before we okay an idea, it must possess the things we're looking for. We count on the rhythm and the naturalness of it, whereas Holland and Dozier, which we admire to the fullest, seem to go more for sound. They have strong lyrics, but they're going for a specific sound. We hope our things sound good, too, but we concentrate on the natural feelings. There might be a mistake here and there, but if it feels good, we leave it in.

Isaac: We regard a mistake as being natural. We put ourselves into the stories we're writing. I also make my music complement the words.

HP: What's your favorite song that you've produced as a team?

Dave: "Hold On, I'm Coming" by Sam and Dave.

Isaac: That's my favorite, too.

"Music: Folk Music Revival," Robert Shelton, folk music critic, *Encyclopedia Yearbook*, 1964:

In 1963, folk music entrenched itself as an established part of the popular music industry of the United States. Attendance at folk concerts reached record proportions; nearly one out of every three pop music discs had some folk flavor, and the term "hootenanny" became a household word.

The current revival of interest in folk music stems from 1957, when the Kingston Trio burst on the scene. There had been earlier waves of popularity in the cities and among collegians in folk music, which is actually the oldest form of music in the world.

The largest previous revival had been during World War II, when such names as Leadbelly, Burl Ives, Josh White, Richard Dyer-Bennet, Woody Guthrie, and Susan Reed dominated the scene. Another spurt occurred in 1950 with the popularity of Pete Seeger and the Weavers in the North and Hank Williams in the South.

But by 1963, the picture had changed considerably. The chief impetus probably came from the American Broadcasting Company's *Hootenanny* television show. The program, which started as a half-hour musical visit to various college campuses during the spring of 1963, received favorable notice from the critics and grew to an hour by autumn.

With as many as 11 million people watching the *Hootenanny* show on Saturday night, the impact of the mass audience was irrefutable. It immediately reflected itself in the establishment of a "hootenanny craze"—touring companies of that name, dozens of records. Besides the rather low-level "folk music" the show—and its offshoots—offered, the craze had its good side effects. It obviously affected the record turnout for Newport Folk Festival of July.

The television show and the Newport Folk Festival represent the two polarities of American folk music. *Hootenanny* has come to represent the most commercial, least probing and most superficial approach to the folk song. The Newport Festival dealt in folk music of integrity, performances that spoke as musical expression as well as social document of a high order. The festival, which has its counterparts in programs at the University of Southern California, Chicago, Cornell and elsewhere, stressed traditional, little-known, authentic singers in performance, workshops and panels. The television show is primarily run for profit, has become embattled with either an outright boycott or indifference by major performers in the field, chiefly because of its overt blacklisting of Pete Seeger as well for its low esthetic concept....

Between these two poles lies American folk song, a commercial product and artistic product. It can be heard in the bright and urbane stylings of Peter, Paul and Mary, the only pop music group ever to have had three discs among the nation's top five simultaneously. It can be heard in the purling, sensuous voice of Joan Baez, singing the ancient ballad of the Anglo-Scots-American tradition. It can be echoed in the angry, passionate poetry of the newest major star of the folk cosmos, Bob Dylan, the songwriter who reflects a growing tension of social protest in his music. It is in the contemporary folk songs of the many followers of Dylan. It is the songs of the Negro integration battler, chanting "We Shall Overcome" in the South.

1965: Psychologist & Head Start Champion

Psychologist Susan Walton Gray challenged the belief that a child's genes were his destiny, and her work inspired Head Start, designed to help poor preschool children succeed in school.

Life at Home

- Susan Walton Gray was born December 5, 1913, to a wealthy family in the small town of Rockdale in Maury County, Tennessee, about 70 miles southwest of Nashville.
- She was the second of three children.
- The family was originally from New England, where it had a tradition of iron manufacturing stretching back to the 1700s.
- Her uncle, J. J. Gray Jr., owned the Rockdale Iron Company, a pig iron furnace that owned a patented process.
- Her father, Dan R. Gray, Sr., practiced falconry and raised basset hounds; Susan lived around much poverty, especially among African-Americans.

Susan Gray's work inspired the Head Start program.

- In later years she would describe her childhood as living in a "feudal society" centered around her uncle's blast furnace.
- Her father was highly individualistic, and she didn't feel pressure to assume traditional female roles.

- "I got the notion as a little child I was just as good as anybody."
- The Grays sold their furnace in 1926 as part of a $30 million merger, and Susan's parents moved into a house in Mount Pleasant, about eight miles northeast of Rockdale.
- She enrolled in Randolph-Macon Woman's College in Lynchburg, Virginia, in the early 1930s, in the midst of the Great Depression.
- She recalled feeling very guilty when an economics professor said, "the trouble with you young ladies is that you don't think an intelligent thought can ever be achieved by someone with dirty fingernails."

Susan attended Randolph-Macon Woman's College.

- From then on, she became concerned about social injustice.
- Susan majored in the classics—Latin and Greek—but she also liked math and biology, and took some psychology courses.
- She was intrigued by the work of Mary Margaret Shirley, a psychologist who was writing "The First Two Years," an important work in developmental psychology.
- She graduated with her bachelor's degree in 1936 from the school and taught fourth grade in public schools, but soon realized that was not what she wanted to do for the rest of her career.
- She decided to pursue a higher degree, and was encouraged by some friends and mentors to study psychology.
- Susan came to George Peabody College for Teachers in Nashville, where she earned her master's degree in 1939 and a doctoral degree in developmental psychology in 1941.
- She taught for four years at Florida State College for Women in Tallahassee during World War II, and published research on the vocational aspirations of young black children.
- After the war, the president of Peabody recruited her to return and build the psychology department.
- When she joined the faculty in 1945, she was the only psychologist at the school—male or female; a second woman psychologist arrived in 1958.
- Her most famous work was the Early Training Project, born of her need to have a program where graduate students from Peabody could perform research, her belief that psychologists should perform socially useful work, and the concern of the superintendent of Murfreesboro schools over a decline in achievement scores of black children.
- She never married or had children of her own—not uncommon in her day when a woman's choice was between a career and family.
- "I don't know whether I feel good about it or not," she said in later years.
- She was elected president of the Southeastern Psychological Association in 1963, the first woman to hold this post.
- She was very much a Southern lady, but she had a strong will and great intellectual curiosity—she always asked probing questions.
- She took an interest in photography, and shot thousands of photos of subjects ranging from children living in poverty in Appalachia to close-ups of flowers.

- An Episcopalian, she served tea and cookies in the afternoons; with her knowledge of Latin and Greek, she would play games using obscure words with her colleagues.
- Despite her proper manner, she drove a sporty Ford Thunderbird in the early 1960s; one of her graduate students recalled that Susan received speeding tickets more than once on her frequent drives between the campus in Nashville and Murfreesboro, 33 miles away.

Life at Work

- Susan Gray said her career path was more a matter of serendipity than planning.
- According to colleague Penny Brooks, "The timing of her work was perfect. The crack in the door was the need for a program for the War on Poverty. And it was the '60s—a time when there was growing emphasis on the social environment as the cause of all ailments.... The Civil Rights Movement was raising awareness of people who were disadvantaged, and these factors aligned to make it a time of hope—race and income are not necessarily destiny.... Enter the Early Training Project. It showed that early training and intervention could make important differences in the future of children."
- A nationwide survey of October 1964 enrollments found that nursery schools were predominately private and generally beyond the reach of low-income families.
- Most kindergartens were public, but were absent in many areas.
- The U.S. Health, Education and Welfare Department released its report in August 1965.
- "Large numbers of American youngsters who are most in need of a hand up in the early stages of the educational processes are not getting it," said Wilbur J. Cohen, who was then the department's acting secretary.
- Among five-year-olds nationwide, the percentage enrolled in kindergarten or other grades hovered around 20 percent from the 1920 through the 1940 Census.
- But five-year-old enrollments rose to 35 percent in 1950, and 45 percent in 1960.
- The South as a whole had a 23 percent enrollment rate for five-year-olds in 1960, while the rate for other regions ranged from 53 percent to 58 percent.
- The rate was 20 percent in Tennessee in 1960.
- Peabody professors Julius Seeman, Raymond Norris, and Susan started Peabody's doctoral program in school psychology in 1957, and

Susan believed that many children in her kindergarten classes were disadvantaged by poverty and social disabilities.

won a federal grant to support this emerging branch of education training.
- In 1959, Susan started an experimental preschool program called the Early Training Project.
- Many educators at the time believed that a child's intelligence was innate and could not be changed by training.
- Susan believed that poverty and other social disabilities held back children; she believed a child's "educability" could be enhanced by early education of the child and training for parents.

- Contrary to considerable thinking of the times, children from poor families weren't destined to fail, and they could reach their full potential with careful help.
- Four- and five-year-olds from poor, mostly black neighborhoods in Murfreesboro attended a summer school.
- Others involved with the program made regular visits to the children's homes and worked with mothers to share their skills in preschool education.
- In Columbia, Tennessee, a town near where Susan grew up, researchers created a control group to identify a similar group of preschoolers and chart how well they performed over the years with no intervention.
- Susan carefully measured the progress of these students as they started school, and also charted changes within families.
- Her research showed that children from poor families had a better chance of success when they started the first grade if they had participated in a well-designed preschool.
- She also found those around the child—mothers and siblings—also benefited as the methods diffused through families and neighbors.
- "We have been struck by great strengths in most of the homes we have visited," Susan wrote. "One is the deep, underlying concern of the parents for their children. Not only do they have the same goals and aspirations as more affluent parents, they also have a deep reservoir of potential for improving their lives…. This deep concern for the welfare of their children and latent ability to cope with life's demands provide the opportunities for an intervention program working with mothers, a program designed to enable them to become more effective as teachers of their young children.
- "Home visiting is not a panacea for the problems of low-income families in present-day society," she wrote. "Still, if we can enable parents to become more effective educational change agents, we thereby make a lasting contribution toward improved lifestyles and general welfare in such low-income homes, and toward a more satisfying future life for their children."
- Research similar to the Early Training Project was being done by several other researchers across the country.
- Twelve such teams formed a consortium in the early 1960s to be able to pool their data to test their findings more rigorously.

Home visits helped mothers help their children.

- President Lyndon Johnson had launched a series of federal programs called the "War on Poverty." In 1964, Sargent Shriver, who was in charge of the new agency overseeing the programs, joined his wife, Eunice Kennedy Shriver, on a visit to Tennessee to present a grant at Peabody for another program and to visit the Early Training Project.
- Only a year before, Eunice's brother, President John F. Kennedy, had been assassinated in Dallas.
- Susan drove the Shrivers to Murfreesboro in her Ford Thunderbird, along with another Peabody psychologist, Carl Haywood, who recalled that they visited facilities and homes where the preschool experiment had been taking place.
- The Shrivers thought they had seen children who were "mentally retarded," but Haywood said the children were picked only for their poverty status—social impediments, not physical ones.
- On the flight back, Sargent Shriver turned to his wife and remarked on the success of the Early Training Project.
- "I could do this with regular children all across America," he said.
- The Shrivers credited that visit as a crystallizing moment for the inception of Head Start; the program was approved by Congress that year, and the first summer program began in 1965.
- Head Start's first program lasted eight weeks in July and August of 1965, involving 561,000 children ages four and five at 13,344 centers across the country.
- The program's first year cost $95 million: 90 percent from federal grants and 10 percent from local matches.
- The centers employed more than 40,000 teachers and other professionals.
- Assistance also came from 45,000 neighborhood residents, most of whom were paid the federal minimum wage of $1.25 an hour, and about 250,000 volunteers.
- Later Susan wrote: "A start has been made for these young people and others like them, but there is still far to go before such young people as a group can realize the potential that is within them."

Life in the Community: Nashville, Tennessee
- Head Start was founded as America passed through its most turbulent years of the Civil Rights Movement.
- One of the program's motives was to give disadvantaged children, many of them minorities, a better chance to succeed in school as they were desegregated.
- It was part of a pantheon of anti-poverty programs launched as part of Johnson's Great Society Program, whose underlying philosophy said that discrimination and poverty were preventing schools from the proper development of human talent.
- To tackle the issue of poverty in America, Congress passed the Economic Opportunity Act of 1964 and the Elementary Education Act of 1965.
- Contained in the Economic Opportunity Act were both Job Corps and Head Start.

Young girl in Head Start program.

- Head Start was seen as a way for children of the poor to enter the social-sorting process of school on more equal terms with children of the middle class.
- Job Corps focused on one of the three areas of emphasis: unemployment and delinquent youth; disadvantaged students for whom education did not provide equality of opportunity; and ways to break the cycle of poverty.
- In many parts of America, race and poverty were intertwined.
- The Civil Rights Movement in Tennessee was more peaceful than in many Southern states, but the road was long and difficult.
- Nashville was one of the crossroads of the movement.
- Tennessee had been a slave state before the Civil War.
- In 1866, one year after the war's end and the abolishment of slavery, the state enacted a law requiring separate school systems for white and black children.
- Laws expanding and stiffening segregation were passed into the 1930s.
- In many counties, it was difficult for blacks to register to vote, and families faced reprisals if they tried.
- Highlander Folk School, founded in east Tennessee in 1932, worked mostly with labor unions for its first 20 years in its efforts to foster education among adults to increase their power in their communities.
- By 1951 it began shifting to establishing "Citizenship Schools" to teach blacks to read and write so they could register to vote.
- Many people who would become prominent in the early Civil Rights Movement attended sessions at Highlander.
- Among them was Rosa Parks, shortly before she and others organized the Montgomery, Alabama, bus boycott in 1955.

Guy Caraway plays guitar at student workshop at Highlander Folk School.

HISTORICAL SNAPSHOT
1965

- President Lyndon B. Johnson unveiled his "Great Society" during his State of the Union address
- *Ranger 8* crashed into the moon after a successful mission of photographing possible landing sites for the Apollo program astronauts
- Some 3,500 U.S. Marines arrived in South Vietnam, becoming the first official American combat troops there
- Cosmonaut Aleksei Leonov left his spacecraft *Voskhod 2* for 12 minutes and became the first person to walk in space
- NASA launched the first two-person crew, Gus Grissom and John Young, into orbit around Earth
- Martin Luther King, Jr. and 25,000 civil rights activists successfully ended the four-day march from Selma, Alabama, to the Capitol in Montgomery
- The world's first space nuclear power reactor, *SNAP-10A*, was launched by the United States; the reactor operated for 43 days
- The first Students for a Democratic Society (SDS) march against the Vietnam War drew 25,000 protestors to Washington, DC
- U.S. troops were sent to the Dominican Republic by President Johnson "for the stated purpose of protecting U.S. citizens and preventing an alleged Communist takeover of the country," thus thwarting the possibility of "another Cuba"
- Forty men burned their draft cards at the University of California, Berkeley, and a coffin was marched to the Berkeley Draft Board
- Muhammad Ali knocked out Sonny Liston in the first round of their championship rematch with the "Phantom Punch" at the Central Maine Civic Center in Lewiston
- The U.S. spacecraft *Mariner 4* flew by Mars, becoming the first spacecraft to return images from the Red Planet
- Bob Dylan elicited controversy among folk purists by "going electric" at the Newport Folk Festival
- President Johnson signed the Voting Rights Act and the Social Security Act establishing Medicare and Medicaid
- The Watts Riots ripped through Los Angeles
- The Beatles performed the first stadium concert in the history of rock, playing before 55,600 people at Shea Stadium in New York City
- Congress passed a law penalizing the burning of draft cards with up to five years in prison and a $1,000 fine
- Yale University presented the Vinland map, sparking considerable controversy
- Cuba and the United States formally agreed to start an airlift for Cubans who wanted to come to America
- American generals called for an increase in the number of troops in Vietnam, from 120,000 to 400,000

Selected Prices

Crib, Portable $22.95

Drill, Black & Decker $10.99

Film, 35 Millimeter Color Slide...$2.49

Food Processor...$39.95

Hat, Pillbox $4.97

Pepsi, Six-Pack $0.59

Radio, Portable Transistor..$12.95

Socket Set, 57-Piece..$56.95

Tape Player, 8-Track $67.95

Watch, Timex $9.95

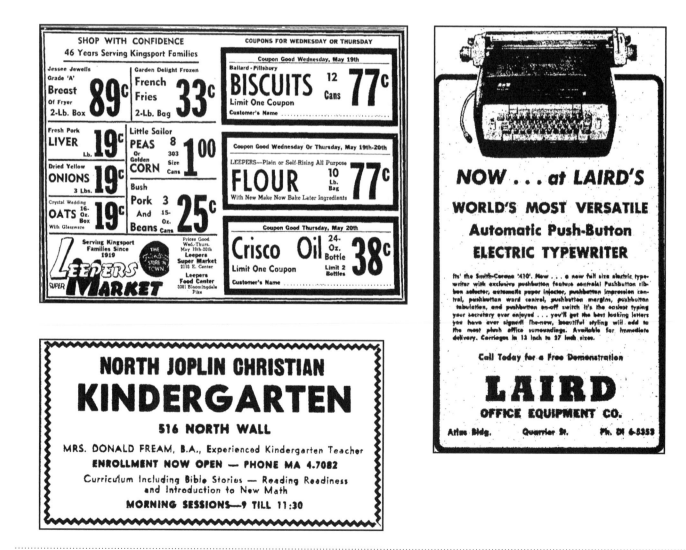

"The Kindergarten," Elizabeth Palmer Peabody, *The New York Times*, August 12, 1873:

The Kindergarten is a method of caring for, developing and instructing little children between the ages of three and eight years, invented or found out by the great German pedagogue, Friedrich Froebel (1782-1852), and which is taught by the most intelligent teachers—indeed, we believe, by all who have any knowledge of it—regarded as a step in education as important to the happiness and development of little children, and their preparation for the more enlightened education of these days, as the telegraph and railroad are to the convenience and successful prosecution of modern commerce.

We do not propose to give a detailed explanation of Froebel's system, but only to say that it keeps the child from books and places him in the hands of an intelligent and loving teacher, whose duty and object it is to repress nothing in the child, but to guide and direct all its energies so that every movement of play shall be both physically and morally, also a movement of discipline and development.

For this purpose, Froebel put into the hands of the teacher a series of inventions made by himself, consisting of building blocks, material for braiding, embroidery, and platting, clay for modeling figures, etc.... With these the child is taught to play in such a manner as to become, during those early years, practically acquainted with all geometrical forms, their lines, angles, planes, and faces, and with many mechanical and scientific facts and principles, while it also acquires manual facility and skill, with judgment in the use of material for the production of all forms of use and beauty.

The child, through all this discipline and development, is conscious only of playing with the most delightful toys. The teacher plays with the child—not in a purposeless, haphazard way, but by a series of carefully devised exercises, all of which tend to lead the child as it plays also to observe and reflect upon the things which are offered to its observation.

Plays of a certain kind are accompanied by music, and this most soothing and agreeable agency might perhaps be called the foundation of the Kindergarten.

Continued

"The Kindergarten,". . . *(Continued)*

Books are entirely withheld from the child, and all of its operations of mind are left to be free and voluntary. It undergoes no drudgery, but is led to ask questions and derive instruction by the presentation to its mind of interesting objects concerning which the teacher, having prepared herself beforehand, is full of requisite information. Whoever has observed his own mental operation knows that knowledge is acquired with vastly greater ease and effect when the mind is seeking specific information about some concrete thing. This is more true of children than adults—indeed, the child learns in no other way at first.

The object of the Kindergarten by Froebel, for a somewhat whimsical and yet perfectly just reason, is that it treats the little child as the wise gardener treats the plant—bringing to its aid everything that can promote growth, and requiring nothing from it which is not natural to its immature state.

"Head Start Project May Bring Changes to America's Education," *Delta-Democrat-Times*, Greenville, Mississippi, November 4, 1965:

NASHVILLE, Tenn.—The impact of the federal government's hastily conceived Project Head Start may already have caused a permanent alteration in the entire structure of American education, an article in the new magazine *Southern Education Report* said today.

This suggestion by some educational observers was noted by writer Erwin Knoll in a survey of the vast program's activities during the past summer. The SER article is titled "Hasty 'Landmark.'"

The preschool training program, Knoll wrote, "has already established itself, in the view of many observers, as the most formidable weapon in the arsenal of the federal War on Poverty." But its proponents, he said, believe it will reach far beyond the lives of the nation's poor.

Head Start "has encountered its share of administrative problems and political controversy," the article said, including racial conflict in the South, religious friction in the Middle West, salary disputes in New York and enrollment difficulties in Alaska.

"Nonetheless," Knoll [wrote], "the program has enjoyed broader support than most other aspects" of the government's antipoverty campaign.

Knoll's report appeared in the second issue of *Southern Education Report*, published bimonthly in Nashville under a grant from the Ford Foundation to the Southern Education Reporting Service. The objective, fact-finding enterprise is directed by a board of Southern educators and editors.

Head Start's summer program enrolled 561,000 children in communities around the country. As the session drew to a close at the end of August, President Johnson called it "a landmark, not just in education, but in the maturity of our own democracy," and announced the program would be extended on a year-round basis.

Continued

"Head Start Project May Bring Changes to America's Education,". . . *(Continued)*

Dr. Julius B. Richmond, dean of the medical faculty at the State University Upstate Medical Center in Syracuse, New York, and director of Project Head Start, said:

"Even at this early date, we can say that gains of the children in widely varying programs have exceeded the expectations of our planning committee. Since the child development centers are comprehensive in nature, we have seen improvement in nutrition and health, and vocabularies have shown striking improvements. The children have gained confidence in their relations with people, and they are much richer in their understanding of the world around them.

"Many long-term observers of the development of young children have been somewhat surprised at the apparent effectiveness of our programs, particularly in view of their brevity. They tend to attribute much of this success to the small groups (a pupil-teacher ratio of 15-to-1) and to the teacher assistants and aides who helped to provide individual attention."

Delegates to the White House Conference on Education in July said Project Head Start presaged a nationwide commitment to universal public preschool education. Reporting on the discussion in a panel session on early childhood education, James E. Allen Jr., New York state commissioner of education said:

"The continuation of Head Start and other such preschool programs was deemed essential. The incorporation of such programs into regular school programs was considered to be highly desirable, with the provision that the co-operation and involvement of the entire community and its whole resources be continued. And paramount in the deliberations on the subject of preschool education was an all-pervading feeling that the momentum of Head Start should not be lost."

"Education 1963," Fred M. Hachinger, Education Editor,
The New York Times Encyclopedia Yearbook, **1964:**

In 1963 the battle between the two rival U.S. teacher organizations came to boiling point—with indications of important consequences to public education. The relatively small (80,000 members) American Federation of Teachers (AFL-CIO) in its public meetings attacked the giant (860,000 members) National Education Association. The AFT used as its major success story the tough stance of the New York City Local United Federation of Teachers, which, as the official bargaining agent for the city's 43,000 teachers, has taken credit for unprecedented increases. In fact, the country's largest city has, in collective bargaining and under the threat of teachers' strikes, given pay increases which give most teachers $1,500 more money over a three-year period in addition to their regular salary.

The NEA, under such pressure, stiffened its back. While opposing strikes in theory, it has put teeth into its substitute weapon—sanctions—to a point where it's hard to tell the instruments apart. The threat of sanctions against an entire state—Utah—gave the NEA a substantial victory, including both immediate pay increases and the promise of further improvements based on an impartial commission report. As for the general education scene, the contest between the labor union and the quasi-professional organization has had this important effect: it has made teachers more aggressively determined to have a voice in local and state affairs related to school policy.

Continued

"Education 1963,"... *(Continued)*

On a different level, the American teacher also became a matter of spirited debate: the question as to how well or badly today's teachers are prepared was aired in two publications. James D. Koerner, long a critic of teachers' colleges and a leading member of the Council for Basic Education, which is often identified with Adm. Rickover's approach to the schools, wrote an extensive critique, *Miseducation of American Teachers* (Houghton Mifflin Co.). He documented much shabby teaching in so-called education courses and called for substantial improvement of the teacher training curriculum.

After such rough treatment, it came as a major surprise when Dr. James D. Conant, usually a far more gentle critic of public education, presented a far more dramatic prescription for change in his long-awaited book *The Education of American Teachers* (McGraw-Hill Book Company). The former Harvard president, author of the already historic *Conant Report (1959) on The American High School Today*, asked for abolition of existing state certification rules. He urged substitution instead of three major control elements: direct responsibility for the quality of teachers on the part of colleges and universities which train them; greater responsibility for selection and on-the-job training of teachers on the part of local school boards; and supervision of what Conant wants to make the heart of teacher certification—practice teaching—on the part of state education authorities. In addition, Dr. Conant would not allow credits for salary increases based on completed "educational courses." He urged recruiting of teacher-training candidates among the upper third of each year's high school graduating class.

The third great controversy—integration—continued, but a new element was added when the issue shifted notably to the Northern cities and suburbs. The problem there—in contrast to legal segregation in the South—was that of de facto segregation in areas with Negro concentration in housing. In many cities, including New York and Chicago, the issue led to picketing and even school boycotts. Dr. James E. Allen, Jr., New York State education commissioner, asked all school districts to report to him on plans to deal with de facto segregation. He attempted to define the problem by warning that any school in which the non-white population exceeds 50 per cent should be considered as being in danger of being segregated. The problem was particularly difficult to solve in some cities—Chicago, Washington, and at least the New York boroughs of Manhattan—where the total white enrollment represents a minority.

Finally, the year brought a somewhat milder controversy over the ruling of the Supreme Court, on June 17, that no state or locality may require Bible reading or the Lord's prayer as a religious exercise in the public schools. The controversial impact of this emotion-charged issue was somewhat softened by two factors: the court had prepared the ground with a decision, a year earlier, that it was unconstitutional for any state agency, such as a school board or Board of Regents, to write or prescribe a prayer for use in the schools; the court also made it clear that study of the Bible, with proper discussion, is a legitimate part of public education and should be encouraged.

1969: Co-founder of SIECUS

Dr. Mary Calderone, head of Sex Information and Education Council of the U.S., believed in educating elementary school children about human sexuality despite strong opposition.

Life at Home

- Nationwide, one school district after another was embroiled in angry arguments over sex classes being promoted by Dr. Mary Steichen Calderone through the organization she headed, Sex Information and Education Council of the U.S. (SIECUS).
- Even though the National Education Association had passed a resolution strongly affirming its support of the courses, communities in 35 states were debating the role of the public school in sex education.
- The arguments were not new to Mary; she had championed the cause for more than a decade dating to a time when sex was simply not discussed in public.
- The current controversy revolved around how specific the information should be, to what ages it should be taught, and who should be teaching children about health and human development, including human sexuality.
- As an outspoken advocate for sex education in the public schools, Mary promoted the concept that human sexuality was a multifaceted and vital part of a healthy life that should not be hidden under a shroud of secrecy or limited to smutty magazines.
- Born in Paris on July 1, 1904, Mary never lacked for intellectual stimulation.
- Her bohemian childhood was experienced at the feet of her father, photographer Edward Steichen; her uncle, poet Carl Sandburg; and many of the leading artists of the day.

Mary Calderone was an outspoken advocate for sex education in public schools.

- When Mary was six, she berated the family friend and sculptor Constantin Brâncuşi for his horizontal-headed bird pieces, which, she said, would undoubtedly hinder the bird from singing.
- Brâncuşi listened respectfully to the tike and afterward only sculpted birds with more upturned heads.
- Dancer Isadora Duncan asked Mary's father to let the girl join her dance troupe.
- Mary attended the Brearley School in New York City for her secondary education before entering Vassar College, graduating in 1925 with an A.B. in chemistry.
- At graduation, Mary decided to go into theatre and studied for three years at the American Laboratory Theater.
- She married actor W. Lon Martin and had two daughters, Nell and Linda.
- She abandoned acting and divorced in 1933.
- During this period, Mary underwent two years of Freudian analysis.
- In 1934 she took courses at Columbia University Medical School, placing her daughters Nell, eight, and Linda, six, in boarding school in Massachusetts.
- Nell died the next year of pneumonia, plunging her mother into the deepest and most bitter emotional crisis of her life.
- She spent that summer recovering at her father's place in Connecticut.
- "I don't really know what I did except hate the world for taking my child," she said. "Then I felt suddenly that if I reached my hand backward and forward in time, hundreds of thousands of other mothers who had lost children would touch me. I was just one of many."
- "Nell was very much like me," Mary said. "She looked like me and had a powerful personality. I had to come back the week after she died and take my exams. A week later I had a hysterectomy scheduled. That was some three-week period."

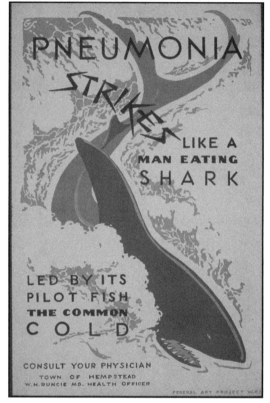

Mary's daughter died from pneumonia.

- In 1939, she received her diploma from the University of Rochester Medical School, and three years later took a master's in public health at Columbia.
- There she met her second husband, Dr. Frank Calderone, who later served as chief administrative officer of the World Health Organization.
- They married in 1941 and had two daughters.
- Mary worked as a physician in the Great Neck, New York public school system.
- In 1953, Mary joined the staff of the controversial Planned Parenthood Federation of America as its Medical Director.
- Her biggest success at Planned Parenthood came in 1964, when she overturned the American Medical Association's policy against physicians disseminating information on birth control, and transformed contraception into part of mainstream medical practice.
- At the same time, letters kept arriving at Planned Parenthood asking questions, not just about sex, but sexuality in general.
- Mary came to the realization that sex education was sorely lacking from American society.
- She believed that her work should not be limited to preventive measures against pregnancy, but should integrate human sexuality into the field of health.
- That would require a new organization and a renewed commitment.

Life at Work

- Looking for new challenges, Dr. Mary Calderone co-founded the controversial Sex Information and Education Council of the U.S. (SIECUS), which served teachers, therapists and other professionals. Mary's insistence that sex education should begin as early as kindergarten did not impress religious conservative groups like MOMS (Mothers Organized for Moral Stability) and MOTOREDE (Movement to Restore Decency), who branded her the leader of the "SIECUS stinkpot." Nevertheless, her crusade for sexuality education with a "positive approach and moral neutrality" was launched.
- Although adamant about sexual freedom, she believed that the sex act should be ultimately reserved for marriage, and that sexuality found its peak expression through the "permanent man-woman bond."
- Her extensive work popularizing sexuality education was compared to Margaret Sanger's campaign for birth control and Rachel Carson's support of the environment.
- The human child is sexual even before birth, Mary said during lectures across the nation.
- "We know now that the penis erects in the uterus. And when the infant is born, the parents immediately begin to communicate to the child that it is a boy or a girl. For example, fathers are more gentle handling baby girls. Gender identity is fixed by the age of two.
- "Finally, there is the disapproving attitude of the parents toward the child's discovery that his body is pleasurable.
- "Parents reflect our sexophobic society."
- The 1960s were the launching ground for the wave of controversy over sex education in U.S. schools, but as early as 1912, the National Education Association (NEA) called for teacher training programs in sexuality education.
- In 1940, the U.S. Public Health Service strongly advocated sexuality education in the schools, labeling it an "urgent need."
- In 1953, the American School Health Association launched a nationwide program in family life education.
- Two years later, the American Medical Association, in conjunction with the NEA, published five pamphlets that were commonly referred to as "the sex education series" for schools.
- By 1968, Mary was condemned by the John Birch Society as "an aging sexual libertine."
- She was picketed in Oklahoma: "Tulsa's Shame! Calderone Came!" read one placard.
- Fears about what sex education might do to schoolchildren spread to some parents and church groups.
- "I expected someone to take a potshot at me," she says of those early days.
- A bestselling 1968 pamphlet, *Is the School House the Proper Place to Teach Raw Sex?*, targeted SIECUS, calling Mary the "SIECUS Sexpot" and claiming that she wanted to undermine Christian morality and corrupt children.
- Support for sexuality education among public health officials and educators did not sway its opponents; battles raged between conservatives and health advocates over the merits and format of sexuality education in public schools.

Parents and church groups protested against sex education in schools.

- They contended that Mary's promotion of sex education in schools was encouraging a premature and unhealthy participation in sex and usurping the role of parents in guiding their children's lives.
- Her reply was that if parents were doing their job properly, there would be no need for school-based sex education.
- Sex education programs were described by the Christian Crusade and other conservative groups as "smut" and "raw sex."
- The John Birch Society termed the effort to teach about sexuality "a filthy Communist plot."
- Phyllis Schlafly, leader of the far-right Eagle Forum, argued that sexuality education resulted in an increase in sexual activity among teens.
- Sex education programs in public schools proliferated, in large part due to newly emerging evidence that such programs did not promote sex but, in fact, helped delay sexual activity and reduce teen pregnancy rates.
- By the 1960s, the United States was experiencing a powerful and widely publicized sexual revolution following the introduction of the birth control pill.
- The classes took two routes: abstinence education supporters insisted that the best way to help with teen sexuality problems was to teach them not to have sex at all.
- If girls did not participate in sex, then they couldn't become pregnant and were dramatically less likely to get a sexually transmitted disease (STD).
- The supporters of abstinence claimed that not only would abstinence prevent harmful psychological presumptions, but would build skills designed for improving a relationship.
- The second approach focused on safe sex teachings.

Evidence proved that sex education programs helped delay sexual activity and reduce teen pregnancy.

- These advocates, including Mary, insisted that since many kids would still decide to have sex, it was more effective to teach them ways to protect themselves while doing so.
- At the same time, she had an expansive view of intimacy.
- During a lecture at Syracuse University's Institute for Family Research and Education, Mary said, "You must remember that, for most people, until very recently, sex was something you did in bed, preferably in the dark in one position ... and fully clothed."
- The students laughed appreciatively.
- Then she said, "You know there is a word ending in 'k' which means intercourse. Do you know what it is?"
- Several in the class gave the obvious answer.
- She then asked, "How about 'talk'? That is sexual intercourse. We never talk to each other as nonsexual people. I am not talking to you as a nonsexual person. I am well aware of my sexuality and very happy with it."
- She stated that parents should not punish their children for doing the things that are part of being human.
- Even though masturbation was considered unhealthy and dangerous when Mary was growing up, most doctors now viewed it as not only acceptable but desirable.
- "What you do is socialize. You teach that these are private things for the child alone. Then when he's older, sex will be with someone else whom he'll choose. Later, parents can teach children how to give and receive love because that is the real role of the family—not just providing shelter, food, education and recreation."
- It was as though she had been trained her entire life for this moment.
- Her theatrical and medical training, coupled with her dignity, poise and authoritative voice, helped her to get her message across that children are born sexual beings and remain so until they die, and that people of all ages need and deserve a proper sexual education.
- Sex education in the schools should start in kindergarten, she said.
- Modern children, she insisted, were in desperate need of sex education because they were sexually vulnerable: ''devoid of chaperones, supervision, rules and close family relations and subject to onslaughts of commercial sexual exploitation."

American Education Trends
- As the 1960s came to a close, America's schools had been handed additional, society-based burdens from endemic segregation, illegal drugs and entrenched poverty.
- Teachers and administrators increasingly inherited the problems that swirled in the community—outside the schoolhouse door.
- Often this expectation was created without the consent of the school or proper training of the teachers.
- In the 1960s, schools were seen as one of the primary weapons in the war on poverty by both politicians and the inner-city families struggling for a larger piece of the American pie.
- Americans came to question the ideology in the institutions of public education; issues of income inequality, teen pregnancy and drug use were laid at the feet of U.S. schools and their teachers.
- Critics questioned whether equality of education was enough to hurt the quality of opportunity for all.
- Teacher unionization, collective bargaining, judicial decrees, student rights and community control competed for time in the classroom.
- Liberals and conservatives argued for alternative structures: vouchers, performance contracting, radical decentralization, free schools, alternative schools, home schools.

- Teachers were deserting the profession in large numbers because of low pay and the downward spiraling of morale.
- Classes were overcrowded, more and more communities were embracing double sessions, and affluent parents were losing confidence in the public schools, fueling a dramatic enrollment increase in private schools.
- Educators focused public attention on the need for growing American talent as a weapon in the Cold War with the Soviet Union.
- As the nation's poor moved to urban areas to seek opportunity, the nation's white middle class—along with their children—fled the cities; Cleveland experienced a drop in white population of 26.5 percent during the decade, Chicago's white middle class declined by 18.6 percent, and St. Louis decreased 31.6 percent in its white residents.
- In its ruling concerning *Brown v. Board of Education*, the Supreme Court reiterated its belief in the "importance of education to our democratic society" as "the very foundation of good citizenship."
- In its ruling, the Court said schooling "is a principal instrument in awakening the child to cultural values, in preparing him for later professional training, and in helping him to adjust normally to his environment. In these days, it is doubtful that any child may reasonably be expected to succeed in life if he is denied the opportunity of an education."

Student plaintiffs from throughout the South came forth in Brown vs. Board of Education.

HISTORICAL SNAPSHOT
1969

- The Soviet Union launched *Venera 5* toward Venus
- *Led Zeppelin I*, Led Zeppelin's first studio recorded album, was released
- Richard Milhous Nixon succeeded Lyndon Baines Johnson as the thirty-seventh U.S. president
- After 147 years, *The Saturday Evening Post* ceased publication
- Elvis Presley recorded his landmark comeback sessions for the albums *From Elvis in Memphis* and *Back in Memphis*
- A blowout on Union Oil's Platform spilled approximately 100,000 barrels of crude oil into a channel and onto the beaches of Santa Barbara County in Southern California, inspiring Wisconsin Senator Gaylord Nelson to organize the first Earth Day in 1970
- The Beatles gave their last public performance, on the roof of Apple Records; the impromptu concert was broken up by the police
- Two cosmonauts transferred from *Soyuz 5* to *Soyuz 4* via a spacewalk while the two crafts were docked together—the first time such a transfer took place
- In *Tinker v. Des Moines Independent Community School District*, the Supreme Court ruled that the First Amendment applied to public schools
- In a Los Angeles court, Sirhan Sirhan admitted that he killed presidential candidate Robert F. Kennedy
- NASA launched *Apollo 9* to test the lunar module
- In Memphis, James Earl Ray pleaded guilty to assassinating Martin Luther King, Jr.
- The novel *The Godfather* by Mario Puzo was published
- Dr. Denton Cooley implanted the first temporary artificial heart
- The Harvard University Administration Building was seized by nearly 300 students, mostly members of the Students for a Democratic Society
- An American teenager known as 'Robert R.' died in St. Louis, Missouri, of a baffling medical condition later identified as HIV/AIDS
- *Apollo 10*'s lunar module flew to within 15,400 miles of the moon's surface
- President Nixon announced that 25,000 U.S. troops would be withdrawn from Vietnam
- The Stonewall riots in New York City marked the start of the modern gay rights movement in the U.S.
- Edward M. Kennedy drove off a bridge on his way home from a party on Chappaquiddick Island, Massachusetts, killing Mary Jo Kopechne, a former campaign aide to Robert F. Kennedy
- An estimated 500 million people worldwide watched in awe as Neil Armstrong took his historic first steps on the moon
- The Woodstock Festival was held in upstate New York, featuring some of the top rock musicians of the time
- The first automatic teller machine in the United States was installed in Rockville Centre, New York

Selected Prices

Air Conditioner, 8,000 btu $189.95

Blender, Proctor $13.49

Camera, Polaroid...$50.00

Bread, Loaf $0.20

Gas, Gallon $0.35

Dishwasher...$119.25

Milk, Gallon $1.10

New House...$40,000

New York City Ballet Ticket $4.95

Slide Projector, Kodak $80.00

"Sex Education Opponents Blast Back," Marilyn Baker, *Montclair Tribune* (California), November 13, 1969:

In this final installment of the sex education series, the spotlight is focused on those who adamantly oppose sex education, and why they feel it is wrong and what they base such opinions on, when voicing them.

Perhaps the most outspoken local critic of sex education is the Stanhope family, Clayton and Cleo Stanhope, and their 10-year-old daughter Susan.

All three have written letters, branding sex education in the least attractive terms, with Stanhope himself declaring that such education does little but cause the problems it allegedly corrects.

Mrs. Stanhope felt that past installments of the series were "a smooth cover-up job for sex education" primarily because the medical terminology for the sex organs was not spelled out in newspaper articles.

She added that such medical terms are apparently "A-OK for the toddlers" in the opinion of this reporter, hence, felt that such terms should be published in the newspaper "for those old fogey adults who never had the opportunity to delve into sex at such a tender age."

Stanhope himself based his blast on sex education on the fact that some 10-year-old children preferred baseball to sex education philosophy or other older pursuits.

His comment was, "Would these sex-crazed, meddling adults allow that to present 10-year-olds the same opportunities that young boys had without indoctrinating them with a mess of sex facts that can do nothing but wreck their young lives."

Ten-year-old Susan Stanhope took exception to a statement made via a letter to the editor which claimed "sex is NOT a communist plot and neither is sex education."

The youngster demands that "the burden of proof is on the writer's shoulders ... his proof should be forthcoming."

The statement from 10-year-old Susan Stanhope was her belief that the series was "just spouting the liberal clichés which one reads in the daily or weekly one-sided newspapers."

Another opponent of sex education is Dr. Richard Parlour and his wife Liz.

Dr. Parlour has prepared a six-page statement, which he titled "The Case Against Family Life Education," issued September 27 of this year.

In his statement, Parlour claims the title "family life education" was "cleverly chosen" to delude the American public about the actual subject matter.

Continued

"Sex Education Opponents Blast Back," ... *(Continued)*

Parlour brands as "fallacious and proven unsound" what he terms is the basic philosophy of family life education, that philosophy being "children should not be taught what to think; instead they should be given all this information so they can think for themselves."

"[This] is the philosophy that has created a generation of unhappy, confused, rebellious youth who have achieved their mark with record rioting, suicide, addiction, sexual promiscuity, epidemic venereal disease and rejection of everything established, even the good things," according to Parlour's statement.

Parlour believes that the classroom family life series undermines the "indoctrination process that parents should have established at home."

In another tack, Parlour also challenges the actual need for sex education, asking "How much is the life of an ordinary person enriched by reading *The Kinsey Report?*"

He adds, "Only rudimentary sexology is really necessary for adult mental health. The importance of sex in healthy living is an American obsession."

The doctor adds that "knowledge about sound family life is sorely needed," but does not feel this family life study should include the manner in which a couple beget a family.

Rather, Parlour supports "the time-honored and proven curriculum for children of reading, writing, and arithmetic, taught to the tune of the hickory stick."

"*The Kinsey Report on Women,* Long-Awaited Study Shows They Are Not Very Interested in Sex," Ernest Havemann, *Life,* August 24, 1953:

Shortly after Dr. Alfred Kinsey published his famous 1948 report on women's sex habits, he got a letter from a woman who hit a particularly shrill note in feminine indignation. The whole study, she complained, was a foolish waste of Dr. Kinsey's time; reading the book was a total waste of hers. For all the book did was prove what she and every other right-thinking woman had known all along, to wit, that "the male population is a herd of prancing, leering goats."

In his new report on women, to be published September 14, Dr. Kinsey quotes this letter with some amusement. Turns out, however, that the letter is only another proof that many a truth is spoken in jest, deliberate or unconscious. The letter, like James Thurber's sardonic title *The War between Men and Women,* like Peter Arno's cartoon of the woman reading the report on men and asking with horrified sympathy, "Is there a Mrs. Kinsey?" is a fairly accurate reflection of what can now be reported as one great message of the Kinsey sex studies.

Continued

"*The Kinsey Report on Women*, Long-Awaited Study Shows They Are Not Very Interested in Sex," ... (*Continued*)

The surprise in the first Kinsey report, if any, was that man's sexual appetite starts earlier, is stronger and lasts further into old age than some people believed. The surprise in the new report, and it will come as a genuine surprise to most people including the various counselors and psychologists who have pretended the greatest knowledge in the field, is that the average woman's sexual appetite starts later and is considerably weaker than anyone has guessed. The optimists who took for granted that the world is just so well organized that for every male sex urge there must also be a female urge have been in gross error. The new Kinsey book demonstrates that, to the average woman, the average man must indeed seem, simply by virtue of his own physique and glandular system and through no fault of his own, like a "prancing, leering goat." To the average man, the average woman must seem, simply by virtue of her own physiology and through no coyness or stubbornness of her own, disinterested, unresponsive and sometimes downright frigid. So completely different are male and female sexual appetites and tastes, says Dr. Kinsey, it is almost a miracle that "married couples are ever able to work out a satisfactory sexual relationship."

The message, to be sure, will not immediately be apparent to the casual reader of *Sexual Behavior in the Human Female*, and there is indeed considerable danger that it may be lost amidst the turmoil of shock and controversy that is sure to follow publication. The 5,940 interviews obtained by Dr. Kinsey and his assistants constitute a sort of mass confession that American women have not been behaving at all in the manner in which their parents, husbands and pastors would like to think, and doubtless a great many people will even be loath to believe that Dr. Kinsey has got his facts straight. (He can only reply that if he and his assistants, who have now devoted 40 man years to the job of gathering interviews, cannot obtain the truth, the world will never have it.)

What the Kinsey figures show, in the way of bare statistical trees, which may in some cases be mistaken for the forest, is that a great revolution in American women's sex habits occurred in the 1920s. "Flaming youth" was no mere catch phrase; the young men returned from World War I, their girlfriends who were starting a mass move into higher education, and the adolescents who followed their precepts behaved quite differently from the generation before them. Part of the change, Dr. Kinsey believes, was due to the wide popularity of such frank commentators as Sigmund Freud and Havelock Ellis. Part of it was due to the fact that in World War I camps and barracks, a great many upper-class young man, reared under strict moral standards, were thrown into contact for the first time with young men in the lower classes, where the unmarried male's pursuit of the female has always been regarded with a certain amount of equanimity. The young men discovered a much more casual attitude toward sex than they had ever dreamed of—and they passed it on the young women of their class.

One of the great issues of this era is the question of how to reframe our moral values in terms relevant to the needs and conditions of a world that grows more complex and demanding every day. Many of the moral dilemmas relate in one way or another to sexual behavior within, as well as outside, marriage.

—Dr. Mary Calderone, 1968

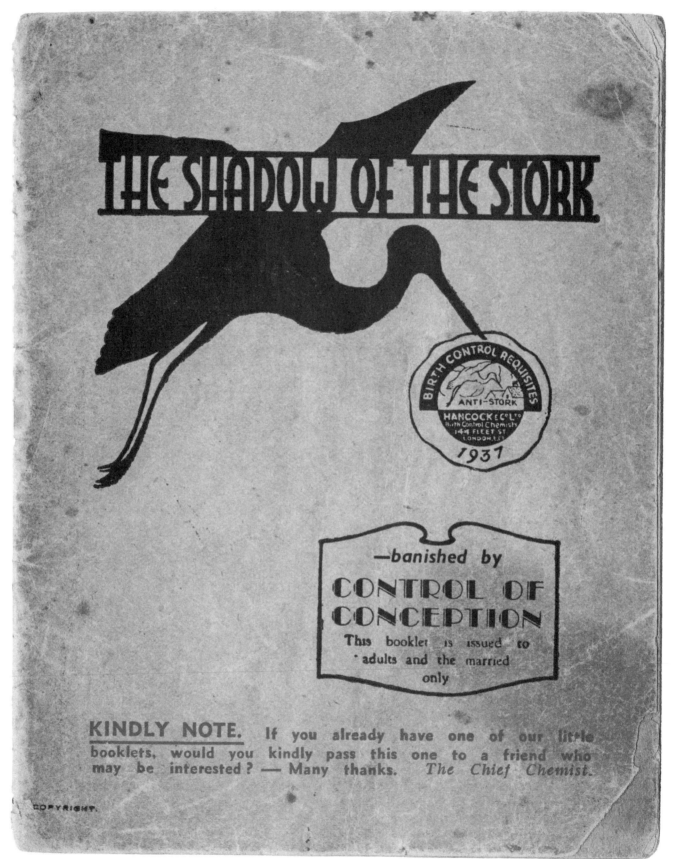

This pamphlet from 1937 directed sex information to married couples only.

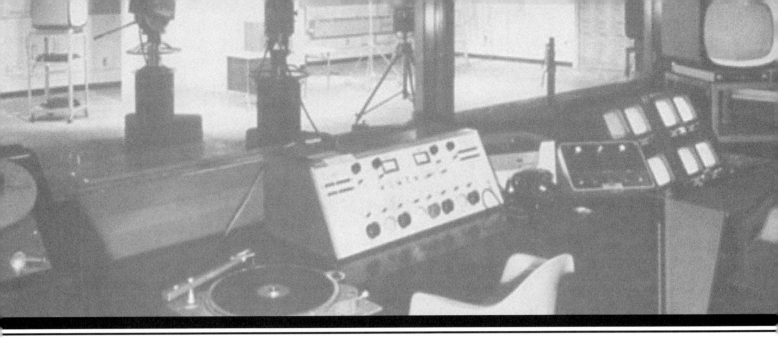

1970: Executive Director of CTW

Joan Cooney's passion for broadcasting TV for preschool children that was both educational and entertaining helped put *Sesame Street* on the air.

Life at Home

- Joan Ganz Cooney was born November 30, 1929, in Phoenix, Arizona, to a wealthy banking family with both Jewish and Catholic heritage.
- Her grandfather, Emil Ganz, was a German Jew who came to America just before the Civil War, moved to Georgia and fought with the Confederate Army.
- After the war, he moved west and settled in Phoenix, where he opened a liquor store and later became president of a local bank.

Joan Cooney's passion about educational TV, helped put Sesame Street on the air.

- He was a Democrat who was elected mayor of Phoenix three times.
- Joan's mother, Pauline Reardon Ganz, was a Catholic from Michigan; her father, Sylvan Cleveland Ganz, was president of his father's bank for 44 years.
- "I was raised in the most conventional way," Joan said, "raised to be a housewife and mother, to work in an interesting job when I got out of college, and to marry at the appropriate time, which would have been 25."

- Joan grew up within a "country-club atmosphere," but she became concerned about poverty in high school.
- She was inspired by Father James Keller, a Maryknoll priest who founded The Christophers, a group that encouraged people to use their God-given talents to make a positive difference in the world.
- The movement borrowed an ancient Chinese proverb: "It's better to light one candle than to curse the darkness."
- She went to the Dominican College of San Raphael, a Catholic college in California, but transferred to the University of Arizona, where she graduated with a bachelor's degree in education in 1951.
- Joan had no interest in teaching.
- So right after college, she and a friend moved to Washington, DC, to work as clerks using a typewriter to create letters and other documents for the State Department.

Joan was an enthusiastic 23-year old when she moved to New York.

- "I just wanted to see what it was like to live in Washington and work for the federal government."
- She returned to Phoenix for a year to work on the local newspaper, *The Arizona Republic*, and save money for her next goal: moving to New York City.
- Her mother said: "You know you are a big fish in a little pond in Phoenix; why do you want to be a little fish in a big pond?"
- Joan's response: "How do you know I won't be a big fish in a big pond?"
- Joan was 23 when she arrived in New York in the fall of 1953.
- "When I came to New York I thought I would probably work in print, but of course this great new medium of television was blossoming."
- Her newspaper work helped her get an entry-level job in RCA's publicity department, which quickly led to her getting a job making $65 a week writing summaries of soap operas for the NBC television network.
- In 1954, she stepped up to a job as a publicist for U.S. Steel Corporation on their show, *The U.S. Steel Hour* (ABC, 1953-55; CBS, 1955-63), which aired a variety of critically praised dramas.
- She was aware of the emergence of educational television, and became "obsessed" with being part of it.
- "It just hit me as exactly what I wanted to do with my life," she said.
- "I wanted to see the medium do constructive things, and I could see that that was really the way."
- When WNDT, Channel 13, established a public television station in New York in 1962, she jumped at the opportunity to join, even though she knew it meant a cut in pay.
- She tried to get a job as a publicist, but the general manager said they didn't need publicists; they needed producers, particularly one for a weekly live debate show called *Court of Reason*.
- She had no experience as a producer, but was undeterred.
- She told the general manager: "I don't know all the people personally that you would have on the air, but I know what the issues are and I know who the people are who espouse what positions on what issues. I can do that show."

- She was hired—and her yearly pay fell from $12,000 at U.S. Steel to $9,000 on Channel 13.
- "I had a thousand dollars in the bank," she said; "I figured I would … need a hundred dollars more a month to live, but by the time I ran out of money, I would get a raise, and that's just the way it worked out."
- Joan graduated to short documentaries.
- One of her suppliers for ideas was Tim Cooney, director of public relations for the New York City Department of Labor.

Joan's documentary was used to train Head Start teachers.

- He called her in 1964 to alert her to an experimental reading program underway with four-year-olds in Harlem.
- This experiment—like one being conducted by psychologist Susan Gray in Tennessee—would become a model for the inception of Head Start that year.
- Joan met with researchers Lillian and Martin Deutsch and produced a documentary called *A Chance at the Beginning*.
- After Head Start was launched, the federal program bought 125 prints of the documentary to use as training films for their teachers.
- Joan married Cooney in February 1964.
- Her June 1965 documentary called *Poverty, Anti-Poverty and the Poor* caught the attention of Jack Gould, an influential television critic for *The New York Times*.
- He described the format as similar to a "teach-in" held earlier in Washington, DC, joining public officials, experts and the general public.
- "The floor participants queued up before microphones in the aisles and let fly with statements, criticisms, challenges and, occasionally, questions."
- By early 1966, Joan said she "had become absolutely involved intellectually and spiritually with the Civil Rights movement and with the educational deficit that poverty created; I was not necessarily focused on young children, though."
- That moment came at a dinner party she held at her apartment in February 1966.
- For the next three years, she was involved in a swirl of activity that would bring together the educational experts, television artists and the money that would enable the launch of the first season of *Sesame Street* in 1969-70.

Life at Work

> "Sunny day, keeping the clouds away
> On my way to where the air is sweet.
> Can you tell me how to get,
> How to get to Sesame Street?"
>
> —Opening lines of the *Sesame Street* theme song composed by
> Joe Raposo and Jeff Moss

- Many Americans were hoping for sunshine and sweetness as the 1969-70 television season opened, and what little there was came from an improbable source: a new television show for preschoolers called *Sesame Street*.

- The show first aired as the Vietnam War and protests against it were reaching a feverish pitch.
- Four protesters were shot and killed on the campus of Kent State University in Ohio in May 1970.
- It was also a time when interest in preschool education was high and disdain for popular television intense.
- "The timing was incredible," Joan said. "Every night the TV set brought you bad news. Finally, it was as if the public was saying 'So do something!' to the TV set, and one day they turned on the TV set and the TV set did something. And everyone understood that, for a change, TV was doing something.
- "There was huge idealism because we were trying to reach inner-city children as well as others."
- The way to *Sesame Street* had begun in the early 1960s when Joan met Lloyd N. Morrisett, who would become the show's co-creator.
- Morrisett was a psychologist and executive at the Carnegie Corporation of New York, which was established by steel mill owner Andrew Carnegie in 1911 "to promote the advancement and diffusion of knowledge and understanding."
- Morrisett was about the same age as Joan.
- He moved to New York in 1959 to work for Carnegie, one of the nation's biggest private funders for educational and social improvement programs.
- He and Joan met a couple years later.
- In the early 1960s, Carnegie became increasingly interested in funding programs that would help children from poor households be successful in school.
- While several projects were funded, all were experiments involving only a few hundred children.
- Morrisett and his wife, Mary, were bemused and not a little worried when they woke up 6 a.m. on a Sunday morning in 1965 and found their three-year-old daughter, Sarah, had turned on the television herself and was intently watching.
- Even more concerning was that the only thing on the screen at that hour was what was a test pattern—a still image that was broadcast when the network was "off the air."
- For Morrisett, it helped reinforce his belief in the "the utter fascination that little kids had with television."
- He brought up the subject at a dinner party hosted by Joan and her husband in February 1966.
- As they chatted, Lloyd Morrisett asked: "Do you think television could be used to teach children?"
- "Lloyd talked about the possibility of Carnegie financing … a little three-month study," Joan said, "where [an] investigator would go around the country talking to various child development people.
- "I didn't know until that moment that I would be interested," Joan said. "I suddenly saw that this was a way of making television do something for the people that needed the help."
- With a $15,000 Carnegie grant to WNDT to cover Joan's salary and expenses, she traveled around the country from June to October 1966 talking with educators and child development psychologists.
- Joan left public television station WNDT in early 1967 and became an employee at Carnegie, where she would continue to shape the show.
- This was just a few years after the 1965 launch of Head Start, and in the peak of the "preschool moment."
- Educators, researchers and parents were keenly interested in early childhood education, not only as a way to help all children succeed in school, but especially to help children from impoverished backgrounds overcome their social obstacles.
- And the poor included a disproportionate number of black households.
- The preschool movement coincided with the Civil Rights movement.
- While Joan knew little about preschool educational theories, she, like many white liberals, supported the efforts of blacks to end segregation and gain equal footing in all spheres of life, from education to housing.

- But specifically targeting minority children had its own dangers.
- Louis Housman, a former commercial TV executive and a federal government advisor on the project, said a minority-oriented show would draw the ire of black parents who would consider it "demeaning" and "patronizing," while driving away the white, middle-class audience.
- Joan and Morrisett were continually asked by potential backers whether television could teach.
- She and Morrisett believed it could.
- After all, preschoolers were memorizing television commercials for products ranging from bread to beer.
- Joan decided that, while the creative people would be the final judges of what went on the air, they would work closely with educators and researchers to test and improve the show at every step.
- They enlisted funders to a show that would be an experiment.
- By early 1968, Joan and Morrisett had lined up $8 million in funding for a two-year experimental project that would produce six months of programs for the 1969-70 season.
- Half came from federal government sources, including $650,000 from Head Start.
- The rest came from Carnegie, the Ford Foundation, and other private sources; Carnegie's $1.5 million grant was one of its largest ever.
- With the funding in place, Carnegie announced in March 1968 the creation of the Children's Television Workshop with Joan as its executive director.
- Joan took to heart a key piece of advice from a public television executive: Keep the goals for the program simple and modest.
- "We would teach the alphabet, the recitation of the alphabet, recognition of letters, recognition of numbers when you see them, certain sounds of letters; because we were phonetic, we believed that phonics was the way to go, that learning the sounds of letters was useful."

Sesame Street's Big Bird taught the alphabet to a pre-school audience.

- Joan had hired David D. Connell as executive producer.
- Connell had the same role for 12 years with the company that produced *Captain Kangaroo*, an hour-long children's television show on CBS since 1955.
- How would the show's producers know if they were truly engaging the preschoolers?
- The researchers would watch them.
- Young actor James Earl Jones caught the attention of the test audiences by reciting the alphabet slowly in his deep voice.
- Each letter appeared above his head a moment before Jones pronounced it, and researchers saw the value of repetition as the kids began to shout each letter before Jones said it.
- The insert made it into the show's second episode in 1969.
- The show's street scenes were originally filmed without any puppets—a move intended to clearly separate the show's "real" parts from "fantasy" ones.
- But researchers saw kids' attention fall away on the street scenes, and pick up only when the show switched to animation or puppets.
- "So it turned into a street where Oscar can come out of a trash can or Big Bird can come wandering by," Connell said.
- Jim Henson and his Muppets were hired for the project in 1968, and the Muppets multiplied with researchers' suggestions.
- Suggestion: Children ought to be taught that it's okay not to be happy all the time, and not to be pleasant all the time.
- Result: Oscar the Grouch.
- Suggestion: Show a child being smarter than the adults, so that you're modeling smart kids.
- Result: Bert and Ernie.
- Suggestion: Show a child as a child is—awkward and forever asking questions.
- Result: Big Bird.
- One of the last elements to fall into place was the show's name.
- The Muppets acted out the tortured naming process in a promotional video shown to potential funders in 1968.
- After a board of grousing Muppets came up with a name spanning a few dozen words, Kermit the Frog said, "Why don't you call your show 'Sesame Street.' You know, like 'open sesame.' It kind of gives the idea of a street where neat things happen."
- After the first season, the workshop released a study finding that 90 percent of preschoolers surveyed in a poor neighborhood in Brooklyn had seen *Sesame Street* in its first season.
- The 611 children surveyed lived in households with TV sets, and did not go off to daycare or nursery schools.
- Of them, 60 percent saw the show at least once a day.
- Separately, the independent Nielsen Rating Service estimated that half of the nation's 12 million children ages three to five had watched *Sesame Street* in its first season.
- Studies of 120 children in Maine, New York, and Tennessee showed thinking and reading skills improved more among preschoolers who watched the show compared with those who did not.
- The show won an Emmy award in 1970 for Outstanding Achievement in Children's Programming.
- And there were other signs of success.
- "Rubber Duckie," Ernie's signature tribute song to his beloved bathtub toy, reached No. 16 on Billboard's "Hot 100 Singles" chart in 1970.
- The song was nominated for a Grammy Award for Best Recording for Children, but it lost to *The Sesame Street Book & Record*, which included the song.
- And the weekly news magazine *Time* featured *Sesame Street* in its November 23, 1970, issue.
- "When Big Bird hit the cover of *Time*, I knew we had something that would last forever," Joan said.
- The Workshop didn't want to depend on government for funding.

- Most foundations like Carnegie made large grants to start up projects, expecting that recipients would find their own funds to continue the programs—usually government funds.
- The Workshop sought a new funding model for *Sesame Street*.
- By April 1970, Joan was talking about selling books and records to reinforce the show's lessons—and raise money.
- That month, the Children's Television Workshop broke away from its parent, National Educational Television, and became a non-profit company with Joan as its president.

Life in the Community: Racial Controversy

- While *Sesame Street* allowed the public to meet the Muppets, it also brought them into a world that was urban and integrated.
- A cast with educated black men and women in prominent roles might have escaped the notice of preschool viewers, but it was one of the most noticeable aspects of the show to older children and adults—both black and white—who had grown up with their own notions of racial identity.
- "It was the first show that really worked at integration—not only black and white men and women, but Muppets and human beings," Joan said.
- "It was a show that really taught kindness to one another."
- The racially mixed cast scared public officials in Mississippi.
- The state was one of the last to start an educational television network, and its first station in the state went on the air February 1, 1970, in Jackson, the state capital.
- Shortly afterward, the state legislature voted to spend $5.3 million to establish stations across the state.
- But the all-white state commission overseeing educational television voted to postpone showing *Sesame Street* even though it cost the state no money to air it.
- *The New York Times* carried a short news story noting that the commission chairman, Jackson banker James McKay, was the son-in-law of Jackson's former mayor, Allen Thompson.
- "Mr. Thompson is president and leading spokesman for FOCUS, a new group in Mississippi that is seeking to re-establish the principle of 'freedom of choice' in public schools."
- But the most telling aspect of the outcry was that some of the loudest voices were Mississippians.
- Newspaper editorials blasted the decision, and WDAM, a commercial station in Jackson, said it would offer airtime for *Sesame Street* if the commission didn't reverse its decision when it met again later that month.
- *The Delta Democratic-Times*, a family-owned newspaper in Greenville whose editor was Hodding Carter III, published two editorials languidly eviscerating the commission for the blocking of Big Bird.
- The May 5 editorial read: "We are penalized again, and our children more than adults, by the official determination to pretend that reality doesn't exist."
- On May 12, the Carters, who were longtime Democrats, took another tack: a tongue-in-cheek appeal to the Republican sensibilities of some of its readers.
- The editorial noted *Sesame Street* had the seal of approval from Republican Vice President Spiro Agnew.
- The editorial suggested, "white Mississippians, who like what he has to say about left-wing intellectuals, radical youths and school busing," should embrace the show and claim victory in the name of President Nixon's goal of bridging the generation gap.
- "We can't think of a bigger gap than between our three-year-olds' world and our own."
- And, by following Agnew, "radicals in the kindergarten would be thwarted."
- In late May, the commission met again and reversed its decision.

HISTORICAL SNAPSHOT
1970

- Pan American Airways offered the first commercially scheduled 747 service from John F. Kennedy International Airport to London's Heathrow Airport
- Black Sabbath's eponymous debut album, often regarded as the first heavy metal album, was released
- A jury found the Chicago Seven defendants not guilty of conspiring to incite a riot, in charges stemming from the violence at the 1968 Democratic National Convention; five of the defendants were found guilty on the lesser charge of crossing state lines to incite a riot
- The Nuclear Non-Proliferation Treaty went into effect, after ratification by 56 nations
- The United States Army charged 14 officers with suppressing information related to the My Lai massacre in Vietnam
- Postal workers in a dozen cities went on strike for two weeks; President Richard Nixon assigned military units to New York City post offices
- The first Earth Day proclamation was issued by San Francisco Mayor Joseph Alioto
- Congress banned cigarette television advertisements, effective January 1, 1971
- Paul McCartney announced that the Beatles had disbanded as their twelfth album, *Let It Be*, was released
- An oxygen tank in the *Apollo 13* spacecraft exploded, forcing the crew to abort the mission and return in four days
- The U.S. military invaded Cambodia to hunt out the Viet Cong; widespread, large antiwar protests erupted in the U.S.
- Four students at Kent State University in Ohio were killed and nine wounded by Ohio National Guardsmen during a protest against the incursion into Cambodia
- The U.S. promoted its first female generals: Anna Mae Hays and Elizabeth P. Hoisington
- *Venera 7* was launched and became the first spacecraft to successfully transmit data from the surface of another planet
- The Women's Strike for Equality took place down Fifth Avenue in New York City
- Elvis Presley began his first concert tour since 1958 at the Veterans Memorial Coliseum in Phoenix, Arizona
- The first New York City Marathon took place
- Guitarist Jimi Hendrix died in London of drug-related complications
- *Monday Night Football* debuted on ABC
- In Paris, a Communist delegation rejected President Nixon's October 7 peace proposal for the Vietnam War as "a maneuver to deceive world opinion"
- Garry Trudeau's comic strip *Doonesbury* debuted in approximately two dozen newspapers in the U.S.
- The crash of Southern Airlines Flight 932 killed all 75 on board, including 37 players and five coaches from the Marshall University football team
- The Soviet Union landed *Lunokhod 1* on the moon—the first roving remote-controlled robot to land on a natural satellite
- The North Tower of the World Trade Center was topped out at 1,368 feet, making it the tallest building in the world
- Alvin Toffler published his book *Future Shock*

Selected Prices

Automobile, Gremlin $2,196.00

Calculator, Electric Printing...$1,495.00

Circular Saw..$27.77

Electric Shaver $13.97

Guitar, Electric $199.95

Ketchup, Hunt's, 14 Ounces $0.22

Refrigerator, Frigidaire $208.00

Rider Mower $352.95

Router..$34.95

Whiskey, Seagram's, Fifth $5.79

Editorial: "No to Sesame Street," *The Delta Democrat-Times*, Greenville, Mississippi, May 5, 1970:

It is not hard to sympathize with officials at Mississippi's educational television commission. They know the state's political and ideological realities, know that suspicious critics are closely examining everything they do and know that what the legislature gave this year it can take away next year. But when caution gives way to what appears to be panic at the first sign of possible controversy, a logical question arises. Exactly what is ETV supposed to be for?

The question must be asked because of the ETV commission's decision not to run *Sesame Street*, an educational show aimed at preschool children.

Sesame Street is an extraordinary venture in the use of television to do a serious job of educating young children rather than merely entertaining them, although it educates through a skillful blend of entertainment, psychology, color and sound teaching methods. Tests have repeatedly shown that the show, sponsored by several foundations through The Children's Television Workshop, does a successful job. One test suggested that children who had watched the show over a six-week period showed 2.5 times as much progress as children who had not.

But Mississippi's ETV commission won't be showing it for the time being because of one fatal defect, as measured by Mississippi's political leadership. *Sesame Street* is integrated. Some of its leading cast members are black, including the man who does much of the overt "teaching." The neighborhood of the "street" is a mixed one. And all that, of course, goes against the Mississippi grain.

It doesn't matter that integration in the schools is now a reality in Mississippi, and segregation is against the law of the land in virtually every field, including housing. Commercial television may portray this fact, but educational television, a state-controlled venture, may not. Thus, we are penalized again, and our children more than adults, by the official determination to pretend that reality doesn't exist.

There is no state which more desperately needs every educational tool it can find than Mississippi. There is no educational show on the market today better prepared than *Sesame Street* to teach preschool children what many cannot or do not learn in their homes. But "we decided it would be best to postpone it in the early days of ETV because some of the legislators might be offended," an ETV commission spokesman told *Democrat-Times* Jackson correspondent Ed Williams.

Mississippi ETV's officials maintain that *Sesame Street* is not being banned, but only postponed. Nevertheless, it is fairly apparent that those who run from anticipated pressure today are not very likely to show backbone when real pressure is applied. As in the case of the ETV decision not to show the award-winning documentary, *Hospital*, deciding against running *Sesame Street* seems to indicate that Mississippi ETV will settle for safe mediocrity every time. If that proves the case, there are strong reasons to ask whether the tax money which is being appropriated for educational television would not better be rediverted to the public schools. There, at least, the realities of 1970 cannot be avoided and the needs are immense.

Editorial: "Agnew Likes It," *The Delta Democrat-Times*, Greenville, Mississippi, May 12, 1970:

Vice President Spiro T. Agnew has a wide following among white Mississippians, who like what he has to say about left-wing intellectuals, radical youths and school busing.

Sesame Street does not have much following in Mississippi's educational television commission.

But the vice president thinks *Sesame Street*, the highly acclaimed educational television show for three- to five-year-olds, is one of the few examples of good television fare on the scene today.

Somehow there ought to be a way to get the vice president and the ETV commissioners together. The commissioners could reverse their earlier decision to reject showing *Sesame Street*, the vice president could laud their action, and his many followers would echo his support.

That way, everyone would win. The vice president, speaking for the "silent majority," would give a majority on the ETV commission enough nerve to risk displeasure from state politicians when they allow *Sesame Street* on the air. That would be a victory for our children and for common sense.

But it would also be a victory for the Nixon administration. Bridging the generation gap has suddenly become one of its major priorities, and we can't think of a bigger gap than between our three-year-olds' world and our own. Knowing that their vice president cares about the level of television they are offered would do wonders for the preschoolers' appreciation of this administration, and thus by indirection[,] of all authority. Radicals in the kindergarten would be thwarted. The American way would be upheld.

And all because the vice president likes *Sesame Street*.

"*Sesame* Showing Would Be Blunder, Officials Say," Ed Williams, Capitol Correspondent, *The Delta Democrat*-Times, Greenville, Mississippi, May 12, 1970:

JACKSON—Showing the widely praised children's program *Sesame Street* on Mississippi educational television at this time would be a political blunder, according to two members of the state ETV commission who asked not to be identified.

The major reason: Only during the last session did the state legislature begin to show solid support for the ETV project, and scheduling *Sesame Street*, with its racially mixed cast and its Ford Foundation funding, would give intransigent ETV opponents another weapon in future battles.

The ETV commission discussed scheduling the program twice, sources said—in January and on April 17. They decided by an informal vote that the program should not be scheduled now. "We decided it would be best to postpone it in the early days of ETV because some of the legislators might be offended," one commission member said.

"Some of the educators on the commission were a little timid," another member said: "You know they have a colored man and a colored woman—who, by the way, speak excellent English—and they have all these little children around them, some black, some white." The fear of legislative disapproval of the key roles played by blacks "was the primary reason we decided to look at it a little longer," he said.

An article in *PTA Magazine* for May 1970 called the program "a sensation in Mississippi," but for different reasons.

Sesame Street had its genesis in a study conducted by Mrs. Joan Cooney, a producer of award-winning TV documentaries in New York. The study, funded by the Carnegie Corp., sought to discover what role television could play in the education of preschool children.

After the study, Carnegie joined with the Ford Foundation and the U.S. Office of Education to fund the Children's Television Workshop in 1968. Other major sponsors were the Corporation for Public Broadcasting, the Markle Foundation, and Project Head Start.

Children's Television Workshop gathered a variety of experts—child-development specialists, psychologists, educators, TV producers, film makers, advertising men, book illustrators, and audience researchers. They approached the idea of using television for preschool education with many questions. How much can you expect preschool kids to learn about numbers, letters of the alphabet, people, places, animals? How can the child's interest in new and varied things be stimulated? What format would hold the child's attention?

Their answers are displayed in *Sesame Street*.

Continued

"*Sesame* Showing Would Be Blunder, Officials Say," . . . (*Continued*)

The setting is a typical American city street. It has a sidewalk, apartment houses, a newspaper-candy store, mailbox, trees, and an excavation site. A wall of doors of various colors surrounds the excavation site. The doors open to transport the children of *Sesame Street* to adventures at farms, lakes, mountains, the seashore. The residents of Sesame Street are children, black and white.

PTA Magazine said tests in daycare centers in several states indicate *Sesame Street* is a valuable educational tool. In several skills—recognizing letters, numbers and geometric forms; in sorting out and classifying groups—children who watched the program over a six-week period showed 2.5 times as much progress as children who hadn't watched the program.

Sesame Street has all the elements which make a prime target for legislative opponents of ETV. Recall some of the arguments made against the $5.3 million ETV appropriation in the state House of Representatives:

—Rep. Tullius Brady of Brookhaven warned of ETV's "subtle influence on the mind" and noted that the Ford Foundation has a "great deal of influence in educational television, and it has been used for evil purposes, for the most part."

—Rep. Malcolm Mabry of Dublin noted the federal money involved in ETV, and said "if you think the federal government is not going to eventually control what it subsidizes, you're very slow to learn."

Sesame Street had its nationwide debut last November. It is offered free to ETV stations, and about 95 per cent of them use it. Mississippians aren't shielded from the program. ETV stations in Memphis, New Orleans, and the state ETV network of Alabama show the program, and it seeps across the state line into Mississippi. The ETV commission isn't against *Sesame Street*, some members say.

"There's no question in my mind that it will be on ETV in Mississippi," one said. "But right now I don't think one program is worth risking what we're trying to build in this ETV system. By not showing this program now, the only people we're depriving are the ones around Jackson. We won't have the statewide system set up until at least the fall of next year. We haven't banned *Sesame Street*—we just decided this isn't the proper time to put it on the air."

The ETV commission is made up of the State Superintendent of Education, the head of the Junior College Division in the State Department of Education, a member of the State College Board, and four persons appointed by the governor.

All the members are white.

"Educational TV, Still Young, Still Trying," John Horn,
***The Progressive*, February 1966:**

The state of educational television (ETV) in the United States recalls one of Fred Allen's comments on program ratings. "It's possible to get a minus rating," the comedian said. "Nobody listens to your program, but one guy out in Albuquerque goes around knocking it." A bitter critic of selected sampling and the broadcasting industry's uses of the technique, Allen fired off many such barbs. As an analogue applied to educational television, the quip is slightly exaggerated.

It is not true that no one is listening to and looking at ETV. Nearly 100 stations bring ETV programs within the reach of an estimated 50 million Americans. But the actual audience that tuned in is highly selective, which is as ETV wants it. Some five million individuals watch more than one hour a week. In vivid contrast, the average family among the 55 million families who have access to the almost 600 commercial television stations clocks the staggering total of more than five hours of viewing per day.

Continued

"Educational TV, Still Young, Still Trying," . . . *(Continued)*

In other ways, too, ETV is relatively inconsequential. The commercial television industry—three national networks and 575 stations—reported $1.8 billion in total broadcast revenues last year and $415.6 million in pretax profits. That commercial television profit could keep going the operations of all of ETV for eight years. It would be enough to finance the 100 ETV stations and program-producing National Educational Television (NET) network, sometimes called "the bicycle network" because it is not interconnected electronically as the commercial network stations are. ETV tapes and films are shipped and shared. Being non-commercial, ETV is happy to break even.

The 1964 television budget of the medium's top advertiser—Procter & Gamble's $140,736,000—could have supported three ETV station-network complexes with $20 million left over for mad money. The sum spent by television's fiftieth largest sponsor—Royal Crown Cola's $8,001,000—was almost exactly equal to the 1964 budget of NET, the central production facility of educational television.

Program production costs are just as ludicrously disparate.

NET, a far more lavish spender than any of its stations, splurges up to $20,000 to produce a one-hour program. ETV stations can keep their costs extremely low. WNDT, New York, put on the 1964 Emmy-winning series, *The Art of Film*, for a total of $150 a week in out-of-pocket expenses, which included a modest honorarium for the host, Stanley Kauffmann, film critic for *The New Republic.*

Commercial television's bill, in contrast, averages about $50,000 for a half-hour program. But it has often shot to the heady heights of a half a million and more for network extravaganzas such as *Hedda Gabler*, starring Ingrid Bergman, and *My Name is Barbra*, the 1965 Barbra Streisand special.

In a medium overwhelmingly devoted to entertainment, ETV deals with education, enrichment and enlightenment. Although television, in the words of advertising executives, is the greatest sales medium devised by man's genius, ETV sells no commercial products. In the field of mass communications, it appeals only to minority audiences.

ETV is a marvel of perversity and a triumph of sheer survival. Just what is it that makes it something of value?

In the materialistic jeweler's eye of modern affluent America, nothing. To those who step to the music of a different drummer, everything. ETV's informational and cultural programming during prime evening hours offers American viewers a choice, an alternative to the rampant commercialism, standardized comedy, violence and superficiality that dominate commercial television....

ETV is a second chance for American broadcasting.

Continued

"Educational TV, Still Young, Still Trying," . . . *(Continued)*

The first chance, leased to private enterprise with FCC reins held so loosely as hardly to be felt, has reached a dead end. At the times when most people watch, their commercial television choice is held down to virtually one level—that of the comic book—with their range of choice limited to westerns, soap operas, situation comedies, spy stories, and variety shows.

"Television in the main is being used to distract, delude, amuse and insulate us," Edward R. Murrow said in a 1958 speech that still rings true. "We are protecting the mind of the American public from any real contact with the menacing world that squeezes in upon us.... There is a great and perhaps decisive battle to be fought against ignorance, intolerance, and indifference. The trouble with television is that it is rusting in the scabbard during a battle for survival." He was speaking, of course, about commercial television.

The principal accolade for the far-sighted concept of ETV's potential should go to Frieda Hennock, the thoughtful, liberal FCC commissioner who alone, in July 1949—the FCC "freeze" of station construction while priorities were studied—proposed the reservation of certain television channels for education. Educational groups that had been alerted to what was at issue, including agencies of the Ford Foundation, successfully pleaded before the FCC and won 242 channels for non-commercial educational television when the freeze was lifted in April 1952.

The growth of educational television was understandably slow. An investment of more than $50 million in properties had to be made, and operating funds collected. The first ETV station, KUHT, Houston, went on the air on May 12, 1963. One hundred ETV stations have now been established. From the beginning, the Ford Foundation was the prime organizer, creating committees, agencies, and the Educational Television and Radio Center (which eventually became NET); raising funds; establishing stations; getting them on the air and keeping them there.

Since 1951, the Ford Foundation has given a total of $96.8 million to ETV. Three-fourths of NET's $8 million annual operating cost is borne by the same unflagging source. The Foundation has earmarked $10 million more to provide, over the next four years, matching grants to the public-supported community ETV stations as a stimulus to their own fundraising efforts.

The unevenness of NET's output betrays dispersion of responsibility among diverse sources. Outside firms, program underwriters, individual stations and the NET staff are all in the producing act. Strong leadership, minimum standards, and definite direction are yet to be established.

The loose confederacy nevertheless has yielded good, even great programs, especially those produced for NET by WGBH-TV, Boston, operated by the WGBH Educational Foundation. The Foundation is a partnership of Harvard, the Massachusetts Institute of Technology, the Boston Symphony, and the Lowell Institute, a century-old pioneer in adult education.

Continued

"Educational TV, Still Young, Still Trying," . . . *(Continued)*

A major pioneering contribution of WGBH-TV and of NET was the station's coverage, for the network, of the American Negro's civil rights struggle of 1963. The Boston station was first on the airwaves with quality programs on the subject, programs that aired the views of Negroes and whites, and of official and unofficial leaders from Roy Wilkins to Malcolm X. Following NET's spring lead on the big domestic story of the year, the commercial television networks scheduled their own programs on civil rights before the summer was over, notably NBC-TV's three-hour prime-time Labor Day special.

Prodding the commercial networks was an achievement, but more important was influencing national policy on civil rights. A key event took place after a group of Negroes met in New York City in May 1963 with Attorney General Robert F. Kennedy, who represented [his brother] President John F. Kennedy. Both sides left the meeting frustrated and depressed, feeling they had not really understood each other. James Baldwin, who was present, went to a studio within a few hours to tape a WGBH-TV interview. He was furious that he and his friends had failed to convince the Attorney General of urgency of the problem. Baldwin's impassioned speech was telecast May 28. The eloquent 40-minute television plea—that the future of the Negro and of America "is entirely up to the American people, whether or not they are going to face and deal with and embrace the stranger whom they maligned so long"—persuaded the Kennedys, as the abortive meeting had not, and was a factor leading to President Kennedy's moral commitment of America to equality for all in his speech of June 10.

Coverage of the civil rights story of 1963 remains NET's high-water mark, the time it came closest to its stated objective: "To provide a national program service that tangibly contributes (1) to the knowledge and wisdom of the American people on subjects crucial to their freedom and welfare, and (2) to the continuing cultural growth and renewal that are vital in any healthy society."

Such enterprise on "crucial subjects" has not been exhibited since. The controversy over escalation of the war in Vietnam, demonstrated by a rising tide of protest in the United States, was the big story of 1964. NET muffed or dodged it, except for the telecast of a Washington, DC, teach-in. So did commercial television until late summer, when CBS and NBC finally scheduled major documentaries whose principal contribution was detailing of the Johnson administration's position.

In the NET cultural area, a wide variance of quality persists, with far too many embarrassing examples of amateurism and pretension getting on the air. Muddled in execution as it is, ignored by the big audience, existing hand-to-mouth on handouts, displaying more potential than performance, and unsure of direction or survival—ETV still remains a promise of better television to come. Educational television is America's only hope for a second broadcasting chance, a chance to raise the quality of television at least a few notches above the level of comic books.

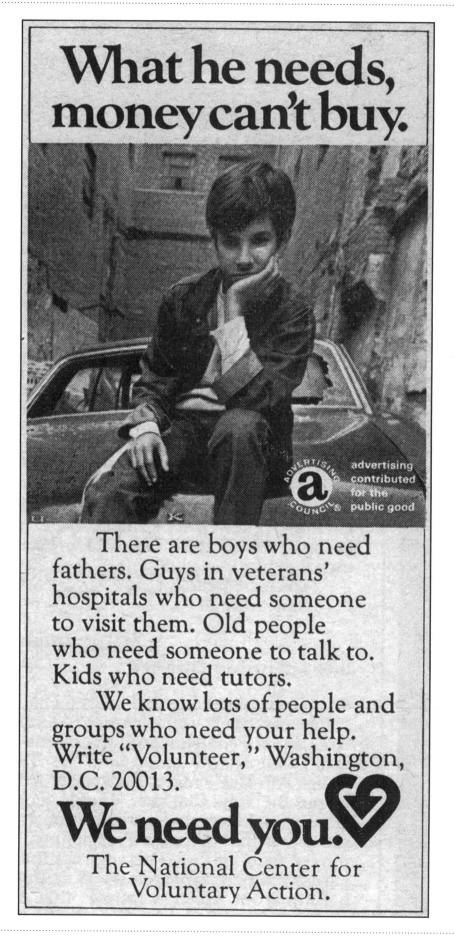

1972: Grateful Dead Deadhead

Melissa Goldberg, disenchanted by the "establishment's" hypocrisy and authoritarianism, became a full-fledged deadhead at the Grateful Dead concert in San Francisco.

Life at Home

- Melissa Goldberg first fell under the spell of the Grateful Dead at the Monterey Pop Festival.
- Even though the Grateful Dead were sandwiched between the Who's Pete Townshend's guitar-smashing finale and Jimi Hendrix's electric guitar explosion, the Dead's long, intricate riffs captured Melissa's attention.
- Two months earlier she had abruptly left home and college behind in Madison, Wisconsin, to be part of the 1967 Summer of Love celebration well underway in San Francisco, California.
- Her father, a heart surgeon, and her mother, an English literature professor, had insisted that they knew what was best for their 19-year-old daughter.
- Melissa disagreed.
- She knew in her heart that now was the time to discover the rest of the world.
- She had grown up happy and well cared for in Madison; she even looked forward to the harsh winters when her snow-covered neighborhood felt at peace with itself.
- Then came the Vietnam War and America's invasion of that Asian country.
- Vietnam was but the first of many crimes that she had discovered during her freshman year: the virtual slavery of Negroes in Mississippi, the corruption of the industrial military complex, and the nation's materialistic obsession that robbed poor countries of opportunity.
- Melissa even came to realize that her parents—who had attended her every dance recital and piano performance—were part of the problem.

Melissa Goldberg became a full-fledged Deadhead at the Monterey Pop Festival.

- She had been raised by the enemy.
- Even the cold winters seemed oppressive now.
- To prove her purity, she gave away all her possessions to the Salvation Army while home from college one weekend.
- Her father's response was swift and clear: He took away her car, further proving that America's ruling class was willing to do anything to crush rebellion.
- So initially, she let her parents catch her smoking marijuana.
- They first threatened to take her to the police: "I will not have illegal drugs in my house," her father had shouted as loudly as he could.
- Then they invited a friend for dinner, who turned out to be a psychiatrist intent on "letting her talk."
- She had no interest in discussing her internal hurts with a moldy old friend of her mother; besides her boyfriend was more than willing to share his stash of dope, drive her where she wanted to go, and even give her a place to stay if her parents threw her out of the house.
- The last major fight had been about the boy she was dating.
- They didn't think he was good enough for her.
- On that count, they were right.

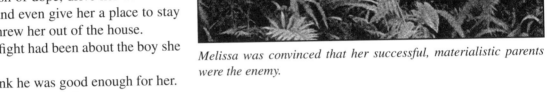

Melissa was convinced that her successful, materialistic parents were the enemy.

- Although he had initially agreed—enthusiastically, in fact—to accompany her to the West Coast, when it came time to leave he proved to be as spineless and undependable as her parents had predicted he would be.
- Only one semester short of graduation from the University of Wisconsin in engineering, he elected to finish school, vowing all the while to join her the minute he got his degree.
- Melissa had no—zero—interest in waiting for a guy who could not be spontaneous and free.
- So she took to the road traveling by thumb—catching rides when she could and walking when she couldn't.
- Melissa needed 13 days of hitchhiking to reach California, detouring at one point to New Mexico because the trucker was going that way, and then San Diego before reaching San Francisco.
- When she arrived, she was penniless, having given her money away to needy people along the way, and without a place to sleep.
- At the time, Melissa arrived in San Francisco's Haight-Ashbury district—Ground Zero for hippie culture—the Grateful Dead were a local phenomenon referenced often by TV commentators and bus operators ferrying middle-class tourists through Hippie City.
- The hippie hop tour through Haight-Ashbury was advertised as "The only foreign tour within the continental limits of the United States."
- The band was even photographed on their front porch for *Time* magazine's "Summer of Love" issue, making their abode a hippie White House of sorts.
- Melissa was quickly welcomed into a commune housed in a shabby chic Victorian that was exploring the emerging concepts of blending free love and free-form music.

Life on the Road

- To Melissa Goldberg, the Summer of Love in 1967 seemed to be one endless party.
- Everyone was either high on mescaline, grass or LSD; friends were living in tepees along the Big Sur, high school runaways were flocking to big harvest pot parties while she played bongos and drank red Mountain wine at all-night parties.
- As Melissa told friends back home, "it was the undressed rehearsal" for a changed world.
- When a British film crew from the BBC attempted to capture the essence of a "hippie party," they had to stop filming because there were too many naked party people.
- The footage was too risqué to be broadcast.
- Melissa had originally gone to the Monterey Pop Festival because the Jefferson Airplane and the Mamas & the Papas where there, but left in love with the Grateful Dead.
- The Grateful Dead, melded together in 1965, pioneered an eclectic style that fused elements of rock, folk, bluegrass, blues, reggae, country, jazz, psychedelia, and space rock.
- The Dead started their career as the Warlocks, a group formed in early 1965 from the remnants of a Palo Alto jug band called Mother McCree's Uptown Jug Champions.
- The first show under the new name Grateful Dead was in San Jose, California, in December 1965, at one of Ken Kesey's Acid Tests.

San Francisco's Haight-Ashbury district was Ground Zero for hippie culture.

- In January, the Dead appeared at the Fillmore Auditorium in San Francisco and played at the Trips Festival, an early psychedelic rock show.
- Charter members of the Grateful Dead were: banjo and guitar player Jerry Garcia, guitarist Bob Weir, blues organist Ron "Pigpen" McKernan, the classically trained bassist Phil Lesh, and drummer Bill Kreutzmann.
- The name "Grateful Dead" was chosen from an old dictionary, which defined "Grateful Dead" as "the soul of a dead person, or his angel, showing gratitude to someone who, as an act of charity, arranged his burial."
- The band's first LP, *The Grateful Dead*, was released on Warner Brothers Records in 1967.
- But their first live performance at the Monterey Pop Festival was unscheduled.
- Melissa awoke from sleep after midnight to discover an impromptu concert underway with Eric Burdon of the Animals singing "House of the Rising Sun" with Pete Townshend of The Who playing lead guitar.
- This was followed by jam sessions combining the talents of The Grateful Dead's Jerry Garcia, The Byrds, Jimi Hendrix, David Crosby, and the Jefferson Airplane.
- Once the official festival began, Melissa got to hear Country Joe and the Fish sing antiwar ballads, Otis Redding mesmerizing with his energy, and Jimi Hendrix playing his Stratocaster with his teeth and then setting the guitar on fire.
- But Melissa's personal showstopper was Jerry Garcia and the Grateful Dead.
- Live performances featured long musical improvisations that made every concert unique; "Their music," wrote Lenny Kaye, "touches on ground that most other groups don't even know exists."
- She especially appreciated the Dead's decision to "borrow" nearly one million dollars' worth of Fender audio equipment to perform another free concert, this time in San Francisco.
- Even after the equipment was returned, the authorities failed to see the humor in the situation.

- Melissa desperately wanted be part of this world, where people threw off theories concerning music just as casually as her mother discussed Jewish holiday recipes.
- The idea of the moment was three-dimensional sound; the goal was for every instrument to be in stereo by fashioning every guitar and every drum set to have a right and left channel, so the audience could hear everything.
- Most bands thought this concept was technologically impossible.
- Melissa's chance to meet Jerry Garcia came because of a water balloon fight among several members of the band.
- Melissa took half a dozen blows—soaking her from head to toe—when Garcia rescued her and they started to hang out, even after the Dead were busted for pot possession and harder drugs began to circulate.

After meeting Jerry Garcia, Melissa was ready to join the band's tour.

- And Melissa was unquestionably ready to join the caravan of fans when the Quick and the Dead Tour started in January 1968; the concept of the Dead spreading their vibe to the whole country was simply awesome.
- Melissa figured she was attached to the greatest show on Earth: a hippie Buffalo Bill show jammed with young, freaked-out American rock 'n' roll music.
- They took a song and turned it into a sound journey—one that sometimes had to be altered on the band's albums.
- The Grateful Dead's almost seamless, continuous soundtrack had to be cut into pieces because record companies paid royalties based on the number of tracks on an album, not the number of minutes recorded.
- Melissa trailed the Dead every step of the way; if they were playing, she was in the audience.
- She wasn't alone: One of the more unique customs of the Deadhead community was to go on tour with the band.
- Deadheads typically quit their jobs and left everything behind to follow the band from venue to venue, seeing as many shows as possible.
- The parking lot scene before and after a show resembled a street fair, complete with the sounds and smells one might expect.

The Grateful Dead held a news conference after their drug bust.

- It was the "show before the show" and where friends met afterwards to exchange thoughts on the night's experience and to make plans to meet later on in the tour.
- Deadheads from around the country converged on what was known as "Shakedown Street," the main row of venders (Deadheads with goods to sell or barter with), which over the years reached mythical proportions.
- Melissa bought and sold homemade tie-dyed clothing and hemp jewelry.
- All the while, Deadheads sat around playing acoustic guitars, banging out deafening rhythms in drum circles, throwing Frisbees, or sleeping to recoup energy for that night's show.
- Different songs filled the air; once the gates opened, the experience simply moved inside.
- To keep track of her travels, Melissa kept a journal of the shows she attended, decorated with ticket stubs, pictures of friends at the shows, hand-drawn pictures, and most importantly, setlists!
- Melissa became fanatical about the setlist as a written record of the songs played (in order) during a show.
- Some Deadheads scribbled them on ticket stubs, matchboxes, or envelopes—usually in the dark—during the show.
- But Melissa was meticulous.
- She knew her setlists were part of the living legacy of the Grateful Dead and the Deadhead community.
- It wasn't always easy: Unlike most bands, the Dead didn't always end their songs.
- Often, she found, they simply segued into another song.
- Several times an entire set was nothing more than several songs played continuously.
- These song pairings encouraged a setlist shorthand that joined songs with an arrow.
- For this reason, some familiar song pairings were condensed: "China Cat Sunflower" followed by "I Know You Rider" would be written as "China/Rider," while "Scarlet Begonias" followed by "Fire on the Mountain" was recorded as "Scarlet/Fire."
- When she lost the bound notebook in a police raid, she took it as a sign that it was time to return home.
- Besides, the health of original band member Pigpen had deteriorated to the point that he could no longer tour with the band; his final concert appearance was June 17, 1972, at the Hollywood Bowl.
- On June 18, 1972, Melissa made a long-distance phone call; she had not seen her parents in five years.

Life in the Community: San Francisco, California
- The flower child or hippie movement started around 1965 in San Francisco and spread across the United States, Canada, and parts of Europe.
- Inspired by the Beats of the fifties, who declared themselves independent from the "authoritarian order" of America, the Haight-Ashbury "anti-community" rested on a rejection of American commercialism.
- Haight residents eschewed the material benefits of modern life, encouraged by the distribution of free food and organized shelter by the Diggers, and the creation of institutions such as the Free Clinic for medical treatment.
- Psychedelic drug use became but one means to find a "new reality."
- According to Grateful Dead guitarist Bob Weir, "Haight-Ashbury was a ghetto of bohemians who wanted to do anything—and we did—but I don't think it has happened since. Yes, there was LSD. But Haight-Ashbury was not about drugs. It was about exploration, finding new ways of expression, being aware of one's existence."
- An all-volunteer army of hippies flocked to San Francisco, congregating near the corner of Haight Street and Ashbury Street, where the world got its first view of this unique group.
- The place came to be known as the Haight-Ashbury district, where average Americans took bus tours to view the flower child phenomenon.
- Average Americans were shocked by their hair, clothing, drug experimentation and alternative lifestyles, even though most hippies were young people from prosperous middle-class homes.
- The Haight-Ashbury district was in the very center of San Francisco and incorporated Golden Gate Park.
- Musicians in the Jefferson Airplane, the Grateful Dead, and Janis Joplin's band Big Brother and the Holding Company all lived a short distance from the famous intersection.
- The prelude to the Summer of Love was the Human Be-In at Golden Gate Park on January 14, 1967, billed as a "gathering of tribes."

- Haight-Ashbury's own psychedelic newspaper, the *San Francisco Oracle*, commented: "A new concept of celebrations beneath the human underground must emerge, become conscious, and be shared, so a revolution can be formed with a renaissance of compassion, awareness, and love, and the revelation of unity for all mankind."
- The gathering of approximately 30,000 like-minded people made the Human Be-In the first event that confirmed there was a viable hippie scene.
- This was followed by the term "Summer of Love," when thousands of hippies gathered there, popularized by hit songs such as "San Francisco (Be Sure to Wear Some Flowers in Your Hair)" by Scott McKenzie.
- A July 7, 1967, *Time* magazine cover story on "The Hippies: Philosophy of a Subculture," and an August CBS News television report on "The Hippie Temptation" exposed the hippie subculture to national attention and popularized the Flower Power movement across the country and around the world.
- The ever-increasing numbers of youth making a pilgrimage to the Haight-Ashbury district overwhelmed and alarmed the San Francisco authorities, whose public stance was that they would keep the hippies away.
- The mainstream media's coverage of hippie life in the Haight-Ashbury district drew youth from all over America, especially after writer Hunter S. Thompson labeled the district "Hashbury" in *The New York Times Magazine*.

During the Summer of Love, hippies flocked to Haight-Ashbury.

HISTORICAL SNAPSHOT
1972

- President Richard Nixon ordered the development of a Space Shuttle program
- World War II Japanese soldier Shoichi Yokoi was discovered in Guam, where he had spent 28 years in the jungle
- Shirley Chisholm, the first African-American congresswoman, announced her candidacy for president
- The HP-35, the first scientific handheld calculator, was introduced with a price of $395
- *Mariner 9* transmitted pictures from Mars
- U.S. airlines began mandatory inspections of passengers and baggage
- Phonorecords were granted U.S. federal copyright protection for the first time
- The Soviet unmanned spaceship *Luna 20* landed on the moon and returned to Earth with 1.94 ounces of lunar soil
- President Nixon made an unprecedented eight-day visit to the People's Republic of China and met with Mao Zedong
- North Vietnamese negotiators walked out of the Paris Peace Talks to protest U.S. air raids
- The *Pioneer 10* spacecraft became the first artificial satellite to leave the solar system
- The 92nd U.S. Congress sent the proposed Equal Rights Amendment to the states for ratification
- *The Godfather* was released in cinemas in the U.S.
- The United States and the Soviet Union joined some 70 nations in signing the Biological Weapons Convention, an agreement to ban biological warfare
- The Boston Marathon officially allowed women to compete for the first time
- The fourth anniversary of the Broadway musical *Hair* was celebrated with a free concert in Central Park
- Nixon ordered the mining of Haiphong Harbor in Vietnam
- The first financial derivatives exchange, the International Monetary Market (IMM), opened on the Chicago Mercantile Exchange
- Wernher von Braun retired from NASA, frustrated by the agency's unwillingness to pursue a manned trans-orbital space program
- Five White House operatives were arrested for burglarizing the offices of the Democratic National Committee in the Watergate Complex in Washington, DC
- Jane Fonda toured North Vietnam, during which she was photographed sitting on a North Vietnamese anti-aircraft gun
- Comedian George Carlin was arrested by Milwaukee police for public obscenity, for reciting his "Seven Words You Can Never Say on Television" at Summerfest
- The United States launched *Landsat 1*, the first Earth-resources satellite
- U.S. health officials admitted that African-Americans were used as guinea pigs in the Tuskegee Study, "Untreated Syphilis in the Negro Male"
- Eleven Israeli athletes at the 1972 Summer Olympics in Munich were murdered after eight members of the Arab terrorist group Black September invaded the Olympic Village; five guerillas and one policeman were also killed in a failed hostage rescue
- During a scientific meeting in Honolulu, Herbert Boyer and Stanley N. Cohen conceived the concept of recombinant DNA, which opened the door to genetically modified organisms
- The Dow Jones Industrial Average closed above 1,000 (1,003.16) for the first time
- Atari kicked off the first generation of video games with the release of their seminal arcade version of Pong, the first video game to achieve commercial success
- *Apollo 17* landed on the moon, and Eugene Cernan became the last person to walk on the moon, after he and Harrison Schmitt completed the third and final extravehicular activity
- The U.S. ban on the pesticide DDT took effect

Selected Prices

Bathroom Scale	$17.99
Food Processor	$39.99
Hair Dryer	$3.88
Home, Six Rooms, Flushing, NY	$48,500
Ice Bucket	$80.00
Maternity Top	$8.00
Radio, AM	$6.99
Stereo Cassette System	$400.00
Watch, Woman's Movado	$925.00
Woman's Jumpsuit	$32.00

The Touchhead's Guide to the Grateful Dead:

The language of the Deadhead community is sometimes confusing and incomprehensible to the outsider or newbie (a Deadhead who has just "gotten on the bus"). Some language has evolved over the years through the use of mind-altering chemicals, through endless hours of conversations with other Deadheads in the parking lot before shows, and in the venues themselves. Some of the language has come about due to necessity, such as the need to alert others to the sudden appearance of law enforcement. Some of the more colorful dialect that is heard among Deadheads, especially at shows, includes:

- tripping on DNA: Going to a show with a member of your family.
- tour rats: Hardcore Deadheads who travel from show to show, live in the parking lot during a tour, earn money by selling homemade goods, or wait for a miracle ticket.
- miracle ticket: An extra ticket given to another Deadhead without a ticket free of charge.
- wooks: Hardcore backwoods hippies who attend shows wearing nothing but a pair of dirty shorts.
- ick: Tour slang to describe the common bacterial or viral infections resulting from undernourishment and overexposure while on tour.
- spin: To copy a tape.
- puddle: A larger-than-average-size dose of LSD.
- noodling: The description of the band's searching excursions during jams and solos.
- benji: A hundred-dollar bill used in case of emergencies. I think these exist in folklore alone.
- bugment: The music being so intense it makes your eyes bug out.
- crisp: A soundboard tape that has no saturation or hiss.
- the Pepto pink: Bob Weir's painfully pink guitar.
- teef: To steal something small and of no significance.
- de-reek: Getting rid of "truck mouth" with mouthwash or a breath mint.
- puppied: Being so relaxed that you want to snuggle with somebody.
- spinning madly: The copying of several tapes.
- biscuit shows: Good shows in out-of-the-way venues only the most hardcore Deadheads attend.
- family: Friends that are Deadheads.
- get on the bus: The moment people realize they are Grateful Dead fans.

As stated previously, Deadheads can often be found frantically writing down names of the songs during shows. Many years ago, Deadheads started using setlist shorthand in their setlists. Some examples of this setlist shorthand are found throughout the Deadhead community:

- BIODTL: Beat It On Down the Line
- FOTD: Friend of the Devil
- GDTRFB: Goin' Down the Road Feelin' Bad
- GDTS: Grateful Dead Ticket Sales
- NFA: Not Fade Away
- NSB: New Speedway Boogie
- TLEO: They Love Each Other
- WALSTIB: What a Long Strange Trip It's Been
- PITB: Playing in the Band

Line Donkeys, Deadheads that enter the venue with a backpack filled with food, books, clothing, etc., are a source of irritation at shows. Line Donkeys hold up the line, as all bags and purses are emptied, checked, and repacked before being admitted through the gates. Line Donkeys can easily add an extra 20 minutes to the entrance process if more than one are in line. Wedgers, the adult version of "budgers" found in elementary school, are also held in low regard. Lines will explode in choruses of displeasure when wedgers try and slime into the line.

"Letter to the Editor: Back in His Room," *Berkeley Barb*, March 28, 1969:

An open letter from Rocky Raccoon concerning Caravan North '69:

Dear Friends,

Hundreds of letters and phone calls have come into the BARB office since an article explaining tentative plans for "Caravan North '69" first appeared several weeks ago.

The enthusiastic letters of inquiry came from all over the nation. I was able to answer only a handful of them personally. The BARB has given me space to answer the rest of you in this fashion.

The original plan called for a caravan of roughly 300 cars and 1,000 hip people to leave Seattle June 1 to settle in Alaska. The Caravan would travel over 1,523 miles of gravel road to the destination. Other turndown pioneers would join the group at a staging area in the Fairbanks vicinity before heading for the wilds of interior Alaska to establish a community from scratch.

As the time draws near, planners have been overwhelmed with details of such a giant undertaking. First, we've been unable to get title to adequate land. Second, in order to feed, house and care for 1,000 people, a smooth organization has to be set up in Fairbanks.

The BARB article got some mileage in Alaska, too, when a Fairbanks radio station picked it up and based a news story on it. The reaction there was not entirely friendly.

A lot of good work has been started. But not enough has been done, in my opinion, to pull the thing off successfully this summer.

I have decided not to return to Alaska during 1969. Probably by next summer, the plan could be carried out properly. But my decision need not put a damper on Caravan North '69 if there are still a number of people who want to go as a group, and if there is someone willing to get behind it as a driving force.

After eight years in Alaska and now several months in San Francisco, several factors make me think it is best for me to stay on this side of Canada this summer.

1. So much is happening here that is exciting. Farm communes in New Mexico, Colorado, and other rural areas with plenty of room and a climate less harsh than Alaska's are tremendously appealing.

2. Obtaining title to adequate land in Alaska can best be done from that end. That is why a small group (hopefully with a little bread and not too many children to feed the first winter) could accomplish this for a larger body to follow.

3. Many of those who have written for information indicate they have no money, no craft (with which to earn a living), and only a foggy idea of what Alaska is really like. It takes $200 a person to cross the border from the U.S. and Canada. Jobs are sometimes scarce. People can sometimes be uptight.

In short, I don't want to be responsible for a possible fiasco, and I believe the idea needs more work on both ends: San Francisco and Fairbanks. I will help to work this end, but looking ahead to the summer of 1970.

If someone feels like being Brigham Young and wants to lead the children forth into the wilderness this summer, then I would like to speak to this brother. Meanwhile, I am checking out communes in New Mexico and California for myself.

If you want to go to Alaska, you're on your own unless you hear from Brigham.

Love and peace,

Rocky Raccoon

"Poll Reveals Significant Marijuana Use at Tulane," *The Tulane Hullabaloo*, November 3, 1967:

Thirty-one percent of the 200 students answering a HULLABALOO poll report they've used marijuana at one time, although only seven percent say they use it frequently.

But there was little difference noted in the poll between the percentages of male and female students who have tried marijuana; the poll showed a regular increase of use with age in both sexes. One out of six freshmen, six out of 10 juniors, and over 70 percent of graduate students responding to the poll said they had used marijuana at least once.

These figures are significantly higher than the national percentage of marijuana use by college students reported in a Gallup poll published in the November Reader's Digest. That poll, which covered 426 American colleges, indicated that only six percent of the nation's college students have ever used marijuana.

Of the students answering the Gallup poll, 51 percent said they did not even know a single student who had tried marijuana, and estimated that only four percent of those on the campus and 13 percent of all college students have tried marijuana or LSD.

The Gallup poll also showed that the majority of American college students were "reluctant" to try drugs and generally disapprove of those students who use marijuana or LSD.

On the Tulane campus, however, 59 percent of those responding to the poll felt that the use of marijuana should be legalized.

"Pot, according to scientific evidence, is less harmful to the body than tobacco and nicotine. Banning it is as ridiculous as the Prohibition laws in the 1920s, because of the increase in use of the drug," commented one student.

"Advertisement: To Commemorate the New Grateful Dead Album, We Present Our Pigpen Look-Alike Contest (Part Two)," *Berkeley Barb*, May 30, 1969:

To be downright brutal about it, Part One of our Peter Pan look-alike contest that we laid on you a few weeks back is a bust. Not that there weren't plenty of entries. There've been plenty. But so far, no one has, via black-and-white color photograph, captured the panache, the bravado, the insouciance—the true and the utter raunch of Mr. Pen.

Just to have a mustache doesn't make it.

Just to have long hair doesn't make it.

Blondes don't make it.

Photos with no name and address don't make it.

And the pigmy from Venice (California) who wrote that "contests suck" doesn't make it.

Now, because (1) in our heart of hearts we know there is a Pigpen look-alike in this world of ours, (2) the Grateful Dead have a new album called *Aoxomoxoa*, and deserve an ad, and (3) we need all the diversion we can get here in Burbank, the Box Top and Party Games Department has voted to extend the current deadline for the Pigpen look-alike contest and make it easier to enter.

1976: Inventor of Liquid Paper

Bette Graham of San Antonio, Texas, combined her inventiveness, and need to type without mistakes on her new electric typewriter, to invent Liquid Paper.

Life at Home

∞ Born in 1924 in Dallas, Texas, but raised in San Antonio, Bette Claire McMurray was strong willed, talkative and sometimes considered a discipline problem at school.

∞ Her artist mother owned a knitting shop and her father ran an auto parts store.

∞ When only 17 years old, she dropped out of Alamo Heights High School to marry her high school sweetheart, Warren Nesmith, just before he went off to war.

∞ Ten months later, their son Michael, who would be famous in the 1960s as a member of the music group the Monkees, was born in 1943.

∞ When her husband returned from war, their marriage rapidly fell apart, and by 1946 Bette found herself divorced and the single mother of a three-year-old.

∞ Putting aside her love of art, Bette talked her way into a job as a secretary even though she didn't know how to type.

∞ The firm liked her energetic spirit and agreed to send her to secretarial school to learn typing.

∞ By 1951, Bette had moved to Dallas and worked her way up to the role of executive secretary at Dallas Bank and Trust, when the company introduced new IBM electric typewriters.

∞ Bette, who still struggled to type an entire page without a single mistake, found that the new carbon film ribbons on the machines made matters worse; they did not erase well and corrections simply made a mess.

∞ Electric typewriters had come into widespread use after World War II, and even though the new machines made typing easier, making corrections with a pencil eraser was nearly impossible.

Bette Nesmith Graham combined craftiness, business know-how, and necessity to invent Liquid Paper.

∞ Betty grew tired of having to retype the entire page because of a single error or typo.

Bette was tired of retyping a whole page to fix one mistake.

∞ That's when she drew inspiration from the artists decorating the bank's front windows at Christmastime.

∞ To earn extra money, Bette was helping to dress the bank window when she noticed that the artists painting the glass corrected their imperfections by painting another layer over them.

∞ If erasures were unnecessary on glass, why should they be required on paper?

∞ Bette then went home and attempted to mimic the artists' techniques by mixing up a white, water-based template paint which she applied with a thin paintbrush to cover her typing errors.

∞ It worked beautifully.

∞ Experimenting in her kitchen, she learned how to mix her special formula to match the exact shade of stationery.

∞ Her boss never noticed the correction paint on his documents, and for five years she kept her invention largely to herself.

∞ Eventually, word spread throughout the bank; other secretaries were willing to pay for a bottle of the mistake fixer.

∞ Working over her kitchen sink, Bette prepared the first batch of "Mistake Out" in 1956, which she had bottled with the help of her son and his friends.

∞ The reaction was enthusiastic, and the recipe for Bette Nesmith's Mistake Out continued to evolve; customers wanted the liquid to be thicker and dry faster.

∞ Unable to afford a chemist, she recruited a person who worked in the office supply store, her son's high school chemistry teacher, and a friend from a paint-manufacturing company to help her perfect her product.

∞ Experiments were conducted using an aging mixer on her kitchen counter.

∞ Nightly she mixed, bottled and shipped the product, now called Liquid Paper, after a full day at the office.

∞ She struggled to keep up with orders totaling hundreds of bottles per month from her garage.

Life at Work

∞ Being a full-time secretary and part-time entrepreneur was both exciting and exhausting for Bette Nesmith Graham.

Liquid Paper went from part-time job to family breadwinner.

∞ At one point, she attempted unsuccessfully to persuade IBM to market her invention.

∞ Knowing that women were not viewed as capable entrepreneurs, she signed her letters to the company "B. Nesmith" to disguise her gender.

∞ In her spare hours, she visited office supply stores to interest them in her correction fluid.

∞ Then, in 1958, Bette unexpectedly received an opportunity to market her product full-time after she had made a serious mistake on a letter she typed and sent out.

∞ She was fired on the spot.

∞ Suddenly, Liquid Paper was her only means of support; her $300-a-month salary, which had been used to support the family and develop the correction fluid, was gone.

∞ Luckily, a brief but glowing description of her product in an office trade magazine produced 500 orders from across the United States.

∞ *The Secretary* magazine followed up with a favorable report and more orders poured in.

∞ General Electric Company placed the first single large order for over 400 bottles in three colors—four times her monthly production.

∞ Despite these successes, in 1960 her company's expenses exceeded its income.

∞ But the increase in sales for IBM electric typewriters worldwide—and superb word of mouth advertising—were spurring the need for liquid paper correcting fluid.

∞ In 1961, a decade after she had invented liquid paper, Bette hired her first full-time employee.

∞ Help also came from a new husband, Robert Graham, who joined her in the business in 1962.

∞ Together they traveled throughout the South and West demonstrating their magic product.

∞ In 1963, Liquid Paper increased its weekly production tenfold from 500 to 5,000 bottles.

∞ Three years later, the company was selling 40,000 bottles per week, and moved its operations into a 10 by 26-foot metal shed Bette had built in her backyard.

∞ There the bottles were filled, labels attached and distribution handled.

∞ By 1968, the company was grossing $1 million annually and constructing its own automated factory.

∞ Bette's kitchen sink was no longer large enough to keep up with demand.

∞ The new factory, designed by Bette, included a daycare center for her employees to accommodate the needs of working mothers.

∞ Raised in the Methodist Church but having converted to Christian Science in 1942, Bette gave credit to her religion for her success.

∞ To that end, her corporate statement of policy emphasized egalitarian thinking and proclaimed that the company was built to foster the cultural, educational and spiritual development of its employees.

∞ Company committees comprised a cross-section of employees.

∞ Every aspect of the new factory was designed to encourage communication between those who worked in the office complex and those in the plant.

∞ Her belief that women brought a more caring culture to the male-dominated business world was demonstrated by the fish pond included in the company greenway and the company library.

∞ In 1971, the number of bottles sold surpassed five million.

∞ By 1975, Liquid Paper Corporation had built an international headquarters in Dallas capable of producing 500 bottles a minute.

∞ But the sweet taste of success was tempered by her deteriorating relationship with her husband, Robert Graham.

∞ With their marriage ending and their messy divorce, Bette decided to retire in 1975, leaving her husband to run the company she had built.

Bette's business was growing, while her home life was deteriorating.

∞ Shrewdly, Bette remained the majority stockholder.

∞ Almost immediately, she regretted her decision to retire.

∞ Her ex-husband eliminated the cherished Statement of Policy and changed the format for Liquid Paper to deprive her of many of her royalties.

∞ Bette then launched a fight for control of the company.

∞ A self-proclaimed feminist, Bette also established in 1976 a foundation designed to educate "mature" women in business practices.

Life in the Community: San Antonio, Texas

∞ San Antonio, the second-largest city in Texas, was famous for Spanish missions and the Alamo.

∞ San Antonio's economy depended upon attracting thousands of tourists annually and the strong military presence, including Fort Sam Houston, Lackland Air Force Base, and Randolph Air Force Base.

∞ Early Spanish settlement of San Antonio began as a means to reassert Spanish dominance over Texas from the nearby French in Louisiana.

∞ In 1719, the Marqués de San Miguel de Aguayo made a report to the king of Spain proposing that 400 families be transported from the Canary Islands, Galicia, or Havana to populate the province of Texas.

∞ San Antonio grew to become the largest Spanish settlement in Texas, and for most of its history, the capital of the Spanish—later Mexican—province of Tejas.

∞ The Battle of the Alamo took place from February 23 to March 6, 1836.

∞ The outnumbered Texian force was ultimately defeated, with all of the Alamo defenders seen as "martyrs" for the cause of Texas' freedom.

∞ "Remember the Alamo" became a rallying cry in the Texian Army's eventual success at defeating Santa Anna's army.

∞ In 1845, the United States annexed Texas and included it as a state in the Union, which led to the Mexican-American War.

∞ During the war, the population of San Antonio was reduced by almost two-thirds, or 800 inhabitants; by 1860, at the start of the Civil War, San Antonio had grown to a city of 15,000 people.

∞ In 1877, the first railroad reached San Antonio and the city was no longer on the frontier.

∞ At the beginning of the twentieth century, the streets of San Antonio's downtown section were widened to accommodate streetcars and modern traffic, with many historic buildings destroyed in the process.

∞ The city continued to experience steady population growth, and boasted a population of just over 650,000 in the 1970 Census.

You no longer have to choose between tape dictation and belt dictation.

HISTORICAL SNAPSHOT
1976

∞ The Cray-1, the first commercially developed supercomputer, was released by Seymour Cray's Cray Research.

∞ Super Bowl X: The Pittsburgh Steelers defeated the Dallas Cowboys 21-17 at the Orange Bowl in Miami, Florida

∞ The United States vetoed a United Nations resolution that called for an independent Palestinian state

∞ *Live from Lincoln Center* debuted on PBS

∞ The New Jersey Supreme Court ruled that coma patient Karen Ann Quinlan could be disconnected from her ventilator; she remained comatose and died in 1985

∞ Apple Computer Company was formed by Steve Jobs and Steve Wozniak

∞ The Jovian-Plutonian gravitational effect was reported by astronomer Patrick Moore

∞ The U.S. Treasury Department reintroduced the two-dollar bill as part of the Bicentennial celebration

∞ The punk rock group the Ramones released their first self-titled album

∞ In the Indianapolis 500, Johnny Rutherford won the rain-shortened race

∞ A car bomb fatally injured *Arizona Republic* reporter Don Bolles, who was investigating the mafia

∞ The Boston Celtics defeated the Phoenix Suns 128-126 in triple overtime in the NBA Finals at the Boston Garden

∞ The National Basketball Association and the American Basketball Association agreed to merge

∞ In *Gregg v. Georgia,* the U.S. Supreme Court ruled that the death penalty was not inherently cruel or unusual and constitutionally acceptable

∞ U.S. cities celebrated the 200th anniversary of the Declaration of Independence

∞ The first class of women were inducted at the United States Naval Academy

∞ The *Viking 2* spacecraft landed at Utopia Planitia on Mars, taking the first close-up color photos of the planet's surface

∞ The Copyright Act of 1976 extended copyright duration for an additional 20 years in the United States

∞ The Cincinnati Reds swept the New York Yankees to win the 1976 World Series

∞ *Hotel California* by the Eagles was released

∞ The first laser printer was introduced by IBM, the IBM 3800

Selected Prices

Apron	$12.00
Baby Walker	$10.88
Blazer, Woman's	$50.00
Computer, IBM	$1,795.00
Copier	$2,995.00
Desk, Executive	$139.95
Food Processor	$99.99
Tobacco Pipe	$18.75
Typewriter, Manual	$89.95
Wrinkle Cream	$15.00

History of Office Equipment

By 1900, nearly 100,000 people in the U.S. were working as secretaries, stenographers, and typists in an office. The average worker was employed for 60 hours per six-day work week. Specialized training was available for people who wished to study office skills.

Copiers

The mimeograph machine of the 1890s increased the number of copies that could be made from a few to a hundred, using a "master." But the only way to copy an original after it had been made was to retype, redraw, or re-photograph it.
The first photostat machine was developed before World War I, but it was too expensive, too big, and required a trained operator.

After World War II, 3M and Eastman Kodak introduced the Thermo-Fax and Verifax copiers into the workplace. The office models were relatively inexpensive and easy to use, but their special paper was expensive and turned dark over time.

Chester Carlton's discovery of the effect of light in photoconductivity led to the success of the Haloid Xerox 914 machine in 1960.

Typewriters

The first typewriter to be commercially successful was invented in 1867 by C. Latham Sholes, Carlos Glidden, and Samuel W. Soule in Milwaukee, Wisconsin.
The patent was sold for $12,000 to Densmore and Yost, who made an agreement with E. Remington and Sons to commercialize the machine as the Sholes and Glidden Type-Writer.

Remington began production of its first typewriter in 1873, in Ilion, New York, using the QWERTY keyboard layout, which was slowly adopted by other typewriter manufacturers.

Unfortunately, the typist could not see the characters as they were typed, giving life to the "visible typewriters" such as the Oliver typewriters, which were introduced in 1895.

continued

History of Office Equipment *(continued)*

By 1910, the manual typewriter had achieved a standardized design, including the invention of the Shift key, which reduced the number of required keys by half.

In 1941, IBM announced the Electromatic Model 04 electric typewriter, featuring the concept of proportional spacing. By assigning varied rather than uniform spacing to different-sized characters, the Type 04 recreated the appearance of a printed page, an effect that was further enhanced by a typewriter ribbon innovation that produced clearer, sharper characters on the page.

IBM introduced the IBM Selectric typewriter in 1961, which replaced the typebars with a spherical element (or typeball), slightly smaller than a golf ball, with reverse-image letters molded into its surface. The Selectric used a system of latches, metal tapes, and pulleys driven by an electric motor to rotate the ball into the correct position and then strike it against the ribbon and platen. The typeball moved laterally in front of the paper instead of the former platen-carrying carriage moving the paper across a stationary print position.

Dictating Equipment

Early attempts to transform Thomas Edison's early phonograph equipment into a dictation machine were a dismal failure in the late 1800s.

But practitioners of Scientific Management believed that dictating letters into a machine would cut the cost of producing a letter and make the executive more creative. Numerous attempts were made to popularize dictaphones, which were cumbersome to use.

It took magnetic tape in the 1950s to make dictating practical. Then letters, memos and bright ideas could be captured by tape recorders and played back easily.

Ballpoint Pen

The first patent on a ballpoint pen was issued on October 30, 1888, to John Loud, a leather tanner, who made a writing implement to write on the leather he tanned. Although the pen could be used to mark rough surfaces such as leather, it proved to be too coarse for letter writing and was not commercially exploited.

In the period between 1904 and 1946, there was intense interest in improving writing instruments. In the early inventions, the ink was placed in a thin tube whose end was blocked by a tiny revolving ball that did not always deliver the ink evenly and often smeared.

László Bíró, a Hungarian newspaper editor, frustrated by the amount of time wasted in filling up fountain pens and cleaning up smudged pages, designed in 1938 a new type of pen that used fast-drying printer's ink in a pressurized cartridge.

During World War II, U.S. businessman Milton Reynolds saw a Biro pen in a store in Buenos Aires and began producing the Biro design without a license as the Reynolds Rocket. The first ballpoint pens went on sale at Gimbels department store in New York City on October 29, 1945, for $12.50 each.

"A Tale of the Monkees," *Pacific Stars & Stripes*, September 26, 1968:

Between skirmishes, I chatted with Mike Nesmith and learned that the Monkees consider it "a moral victory" that their television series wasn't renewed for next season.

The Monkees will appear in Tokyo October 3-4 at the Budokan Hall.

"We couldn't have gone through another season with the series," he said. "We were in the middle of a political struggle and, although we didn't precipitate any of it, we got a bad press. Now we've instituted an open-door policy to talk to anyone, anytime. This is a moral victory for us," Mr. Nesmith said

They will continue together as a group, of course.

"Now we'll be able to do the things the way we want to," Nesmith says. We each have our own style. Peter is understatement, quieter, melodic; Mickey is ragtime, old-fashioned; Davy is Broadway, mohair tuxedo, and I'm hard-driving West Coast rock, and our albums will have a bit of each."

He says the "pop music establishment" is down on them, possibly out of jealousy, and that they haven't received the recognition they deserve as musicians. But he believes, with time, that will change and they will be appreciated.

"People think we are tools of the establishment," he says, "but we're not. We're really the truest expression of iconoclastic youth today."

Their personal lives have, naturally, changed considerably since the lightning struck. Nesmith has adjusted beautifully to the problems of fame and fortune.

"The solution," he says, "is to realize what you can and cannot do. I learned early that I can go into Denny's for a hamburger. But I've found quiet, out-of-the-way places where I can go. It may cost me $50 to get in, but I have privacy."

"Paper Restoring: A Scary Business,"
The New York Times, May 3, 1975:

When Margo Feiden is scared, she shares her fears with her clients. As she talks, "somehow things come together," and, as in the fairytales, everything turns out happily in the end.

Well, you may ask, just what does Margo Feiden do that inspires such foreboding? Now that you've asked, here's the answer. She's a paper restorer and preserver, a profession not usually thought of as scary, probably because it's a profession not usually thought of it all.

The scary part of her work comes when it's necessary to reduce paper almost to its liquid state, and although the work isn't always suspenseful, it is frequently strange.

"Would you believe it is easier to fix something that's ripped than something that has been creased?" Miss Feiden asked somewhat rhetorically.

Miss Feiden, who is also Mrs. Stanley R. Goldmark, began her unusual work almost by accident. She was an art collector and art dealer (and still is), and noticed that, although age was being blamed for stains and discoloration, Rembrandt etchings were often in better condition than modern works.

"I began noticing that more drawing and etchings were stained when they were covered by a mat and framed, than those that remained unframed, and the theory that age was accountable for damage just didn't make sense to me," she said.

After reading everything available on the subject, experimenting and finally making her own paper in a bathtub, Feiden reached the conclusion that a hefty percentage of artwork requiring restoration had been damaged by improper framing. Now, with almost 12 years of experience behind her, her conclusions have solidified.

"Mats made of cardboard contain acids that attack paper," she said. "And some adhesives for holding mats or pictures in place promote the growth of damaging molds and fungi."

Feiden, who has done work for the graphics department of Sotheby Parke Bernet and a number of well-known collectors, restores documents, marriage licenses, works of art and books. She just finished working on a document (a receipt for their pay) signed by five of the men who signed the Declaration of Independence.

1983: Anti-Nuclear Weapons Advocate

Anna Delgado became involved in the Anti-Nuclear Weapons Movement through her activity in rallies held to freeze the growth of nuclear weapon stockpiles.

Life at Home

- Though only 21 years old, Anna Delgado had spent the last two years actively working for the nuclear freeze movement—an effort to stop the development of weapons that could potentially destroy the world's population.
- As a result, she had seen the inside of a jail for the first time, had long political talks with her parents and found a cause she felt was worth fighting for.
- Throughout the Cold War, the United States had been competing with the Soviet Union to develop thousands of Intercontinental Ballistic Missiles, or ICBMs, capable of delivering nuclear warheads across the world.
- This growth in potential nuclear destruction disturbed Anna, and she vehemently disagreed with the media's assertion that the growth of nuclear weapons was a method for peace.
- The United States was currently promoting new weapons to maintain the peace, such as the MX missile and the Space Defense Initiative.
- The MX missile would allow the United States to send 10 nuclear warheads in one missile halfway around the world with deadly accuracy.
- The Space Defense Initiative—a satellite system that would destroy incoming missiles attacking America—was nicknamed "Star Wars" and attacked by critics as unlikely to succeed.

Anna Delgado worked for the nuclear freeze movement.

- This was in addition to the thousands of Minuteman missiles already in place and prepared to be launched at targets around the world in the event of a nuclear attack.
- While attending the University of Pennsylvania, Anna first got involved in the nuclear movement by participating in several rallies intended to persuade the U.S. and other governments to freeze the number of nuclear weapons.
- Finding the time to participate in protests was a challenge—her obligations to her college coursework in elementary education and her part-time job left little time to be involved in the movement.
- But by attending the protests, she discovered a strong connection to what her parents believed in and the need to thwart the growing war establishment.
- Both her mother and father had protested the Vietnam War, especially after her older brother went "missing in action" in 1972.
- She vividly remembered attending anti-war rallies with her mother a decade earlier.
- Regretfully, it did nothing to help bring her brother back home.
- At nuclear weapons rallies, Anna carried one of her two protest picket signs designed by her father: "End the Arms Race NOW!" and "Women for Peace."
- Anna saw this movement as a "New Abolitionist Movement" and was proud of being part of a national effort.
- This concept was reinforced when she read a *Rolling Stone Magazine* article on the subject in March.
- At the protest rallies off-campus in the city, Anna was one of the youngest protesters; the vast majority were working professionals 10 or 20 years older, often with families.
- Also at these rallies were religious people, especially those with Christian backgrounds, who viewed the development of nuclear weapons as immoral.
- Some of the older protestors had worked to elect politicians in Congress who would support a bilateral freeze of nuclear weapons with the Russians and stop the proliferation of nuclear devices, weapons, and generating plants, all nicknamed "nukes."

- During the prior year's elections, these activists worked nationwide to support candidates in 45 election races in the House of Representatives on this issue.
- Pro-freeze candidates won 36 of the races.
- Over 1,500 different peace groups across the country were backing the freeze.
- Yet the majority of Americans still believed that the best way to be safe from Communist domination was to build the biggest weapons.
- At the rallies Anna attended in Philadelphia, she was often confronted by supporters of the government's nuclear arms policy, who called her a "dupe of the Kremlin."
- They insisted that the American Pro-Freeze rallies were hurting the United States' effort to negotiate with the Soviets.
- They were also called "freezeniks," along with other references of being communists and traitors to America.
- During one of the protests, an older woman told Anna about a women-only protest at the Seneca Army Depot in New York planned for the summer.
- The summer protest was called the Women's Encampment for a Future of Peace and Justice and would operate from July 4 to Labor Day.

- Through the summer, the encampment would condemn the nuclear weapons the U.S government was storing on-site, including the Pershing cruise missiles for shipment to Western Europe.
- The location was also chosen for its close proximity to Seneca Falls, where the first women's rights convention occurred in 1848.
- Anna knew immediately that she wanted to participate.
- With help from friends, she arranged to sublease her apartment during the summer and saved money to cover expenses for six weeks.
- Anna packed her Ford Pinto with camping gear, her "comfy" sleeping pillow, her protest signs, several changes of clothes, three milk gallon jugs of water, four cartons of Virginia Slims cigarettes and three grocery bags full of rice, beans and canned vegetables.
- By the end of June, Anna left her parents' home in Columbia, Maryland, and traveled to Romulus, New York—the location of the women's encampment.

Life at Work

- When Anna Delgado arrived in Romulus, New York, at the Women's Encampment for a Future of Peace and Justice, the grounds were already full of women from all over the United States.
- Many saw this protest as a way to protect their families from nuclear war, but others supported a range of feminist and peace issues.
- Some believed that women-centered protests enabled the world to see women as the caretakers of the world and of families.
- All women were encouraged to volunteer for many duties; Anna decided to help prepare the vegetarian meals for the attendees during her stay.
- The opening day of protest on July 4 was full of excitement and debate.

- One early controversy was whether to accept an American flag from a local community leader for the women to fly on the encampment property.
- Many of the women were conflicted because the American flag held mixed symbols of militaristic nationalism and of benevolence.
- Some felt that an international peace camp should not fly any nation's flag.
- The women decided not to fly the flag, but to permit the women to create their own flags the size of a pillowcase to hang on a clothesline.
- The local community did not receive the decision favorably.
- Anna was thrilled with the first day's activities, which started with approximately 500 women gathered to pledge their allegiance to the earth, for the life it provides and for peace and beauty for all.

- Later she and the others followed a Buddhist woman beating her drum while they walked slowly, chanting "All we are saying is give peace a chance."
- As the women marched past the Seneca Army Depot gate, they planted two rose bushes—one red, one white—as symbols of life.
- Later, the women lined up holding up their hands in a triangular shape known as a "yoni," or ancient goddess symbol, which became the sign of the women's resistance to the Depot.
- Four local veterans planted little American flags by the two rose bushes outside the depot, saluted and walked away.
- The opening day's protest was peaceful and viewed as a successful beginning.
- Peaceful protest continued daily at the Seneca Army Depot with other symbols that showed the strength of women.

- Women formed in circles or webs—both signs of unification, strength, and the world's connectivity.
- The interconnected web was painted on a number of the structures around the camp.
- In another symbolic act, the protestors tied onto the Army Depot's fence possessions they did not want to lose in the event of a nuclear war.
- Items included photos of families and children.
- Anna tied a number of webs to the fence with photos of her parents, her friends and the family dog.
- She wanted to put her missing brother's photo on the fence, but she was afraid of losing one of her few remaining mementos of him.
- Anna shared her grief of losing her brother in Vietnam with some of the friends she made at camp; they encouraged her to hold on to the photo until he was found.
- Over the next couple of weeks of protests, hundreds of women arrived to condemn the nuclear weapons on the base.
- Over time, the women expanded their civil disobedience by climbing over the Seneca Army Depot's fence to protest.
- Anna was a bit hesitant at first to participate in this aggressive form of protest.
- The women who climbed over were arrested by military police and detained on the post, fingerprinted, photographed and given letters barring them from re-entering the property.
- Anna climbed over the fence one hot summer morning.
- Immediately she was arrested by a military police sergeant and handcuffed while chanting "Peaceful women wanting peace."
- After a couple of hours of military arrest, Anna was fingerprinted and awarded her "bar letter" prohibiting her from re-entering the site.
- Anna was excited and immediately went to a pay phone to call her parents about the arrest, receiving her bar letter and the good she was doing for the world.
- They were happy for her but cautioned her not to do anything that would hurt her professionally in the long run.
- After the call, she jumped up and down with glee.
- She now had documented proof that her protests were impacting the military, and it further validated her efforts in the Freeze Movement.

Life in the Community: Seneca, New York

- Local residents in the Seneca, New York area had issues with the women protesters.
- Some tried to welcome the women but received little community support.
- Residents were also concerned about the added cost and attention the protest brought to the community and feared that it might cause the closure of the military base.
- Anna and the women did not want the base to close, but to be used for something peaceful to the community.
- Regardless of how often the protesters communicated this message, the residents were worried that jobs would be lost.
- Times had been tough and didn't need to get tougher.
- Also, the community was shocked by the broad feminist nature of the protests, which ranged from nuclear weapons to sexuality, religion and the concerns of oppressed women.
- A large number of the residents were simply offended by the alternative lifestyles the women were supporting and viewed the protest as un-American.
- Anna often spent time discussing these concerns with the other women: Would the locals come to see their point of view or should the women attempt to improve relations with the local community?
- Most in the discussion agreed that there was little that could be done to improve the situation.
- The community's wariness exploded during a planned 15-mile feminist walk from Seneca Falls to the Peace Camp on Saturday, July 30.
- The women communicated this planned march to local officials along the route, including the town of Waterloo near the women's encampment.
- On that Saturday, when Anna and hundreds of women entered Waterloo, they wore white bibs printed with historically important women's names, such as Elizabeth Cady Stanton and Susan B. Anthony.
- At the Waterloo Bridge, they encountered 300 local residents waving American flags with a 20-foot banner in front saying, "Many Men and Women Have Earned the Right for Anyone to Protest in America. Respect Them, Our Flag, and Our Country."
- Some of the local residents were holding American flags or cardboard signs that said, "Go Home," "We're Proud to Be Americans," and "Pinko Lesbians, Go Home."
- They were also chanting "America" and screaming at the women, "Go home" and "Go protest in Russia."
- The local citizens' counter-protest blocked traffic and the flow of the women marchers for a period of time.
- Local law enforcement was fearful of a riot at the bridge.
- Anna was concerned; she had never seen so much anger and hatred from those who opposed her.
- Instead of trying to cross the bridge, the women decided to stop and sit in the road.
- Many of the women were becoming angry at the comments and expletives coming from the bridge.
- Within a short time, both sides were yelling at each other.
- The moment became extremely frightening when a man with a rifle approached the women.
- Fortunately the police apprehended the man and arrested him immediately.
- After two hours of tension between the two groups, the officers instructed the women to leave and return to the encampment.
- The women refused because the local citizens, not the women, were illegally blocking the road.

- The police disagreed.
- A number of the women, including Anna, held their ground until the police dragged them away and arrested them.
- As each was hauled away, the local citizens cheered and encouraged the police.
- The authorities charged 53 women from the encampment for disorderly conduct at the bridge.
- The only local resident arrested was the man with the rifle.
- Because there was little space in the sheriff's department jail, a makeshift jail was established at a school away from Waterloo in Seneca County.
- It was stuffy, confusing and maddening.
- The women supported each other during the next several days while in prison at the school.
- Anna thought about calling her parents for help, but the other women convinced her that she had done nothing wrong and should go free.
- Each day when she thought she should call, she decided to wait one more day.
- She even thought of trying to escape as two women did while imprisoned at the school.
- After several days, the local authorities dropped all charges on the women.
- While Anna was under arrest, approximately 2,000 women protested at the Seneca Army Depot.
- Over 200 were arrested for peacefully trespassing onto the federal property.
- Upon returning to the women's encampment, Anna heard rumors that the locals may cause further harm to the women.
- Rumors of bombings or burnings were bruited for a couple of days.
- With all the excitement and stress over the past several weeks, Anna's time at the camp came to an end.
- She decided to head home and prepare for her final year at the University of Pennsylvania and the next confrontation with the military establishment.

Historical Snapshot
1983

- The musical *Annie* was performed for the last time after 2,377 shows in New York City
- President Ronald Reagan proclaimed 1983 "The Year of the Bible"
- A special commission report of the U.S. Congress was critical of the practice of Japanese internment during World War II
- IBM released the IBM PC XT
- President Reagan called the Soviet Union an "evil empire" and made his initial proposal to develop technology to intercept enemy missiles called the Strategic Defense Initiative, dubbed "Star Wars"
- The first non-American Disney theme park opened in Japan as Tokyo Disneyland
- The U.S Embassy in Beirut was bombed, killing 63 people
- Maine schoolgirl Samantha Smith was invited to visit the Soviet Union by its leader Yuri Andropov after he read her letter in which she expressed fears about nuclear war
- *Stern* magazine published the "Hitler Diaries," which were later found to be forgeries
- *Pioneer 10* became the first manmade object to leave the solar system
- Sally Ride was first American woman in space on the space shuttle *Challenger*
- A Soviet jet fighter shot down Korean Air Flight 007, killing all 269 passengers and crew on board, when the commercial aircraft entered Soviet airspace
- Soviet military officer Stanislav Petrov averted a worldwide nuclear war by refusing to believe that the United States had launched missiles against the USSR, despite the indications given by his computerized early warning systems
- A suicide truck-bombing destroyed the United States Marine Corps barracks at Beirut International Airport, killing 241 U.S. servicemen
- The United States invaded Grenada
- President Reagan signed a bill creating a federal holiday to honor civil rights leader Martin Luther King, Jr.
- McDonald's introduced the chicken McNugget
- Popular films included *Star*

I'D RATHER BE PLAYING SCRABBLE. Brand Crossword Game

America's Favorite Crossword Game

SCRABBLE® is the registered trademark of Selchow & Righter Co., Bay Shore, NY for its line of word games and entertainment services

Selected Prices, 1983

Apartment, Chicago, Two Bedroom, Month	$489.00
Attaché Case, Leather	$89.99
Car Stereo, Sanyo	$179.99
Golf Clubs, Wilson, 11-Piece	$219.99
Men's Leather Driving Gloves	$17.00
Skateboard	$59.99
Sofa, 80-Inch, Fabric	$1,495.00
Video Disc Player	$539.00
Video Tape, Maxell	$13.49
Wristwatch, Rolex	$2,725.00

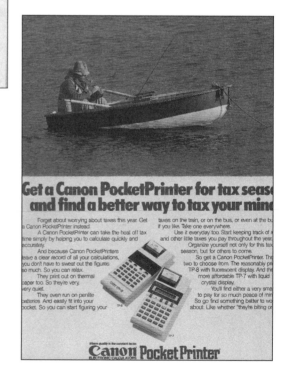

Nuclear Weapons Protest Timeline

1957

The Committee for a SANE Nuclear Policy was founded and published an advertisement in *The New York Times*.

1958

The USSR announced a unilateral halt to atmospheric nuclear tests; the United States responded with a one-year testing moratorium.

The National Student Council for a SANE Nuclear Policy was organized.

1960

A SANE rally in Madison Square Garden, New York, attracted 20,000 to hear Eleanor Roosevelt, Norman Cousins, Norman Thomas, A. Philip Randolph, Walter Reuther, and Harry Belafonte call for an end to the arms race.

1961

SANE hosted an eight-day, 109-mile march from McGuire Air Force Base in New Jersey to U.N. Plaza attended by 25,000 to petition President Kennedy to maintain a moratorium on testing in the atmosphere.

The arms race intensified as the Soviet Union resumed atmospheric testing of nuclear weapons; the United States resumed underground testing.

1962

The U.S. conducted above-ground testing of nuclear weapons.

After photographs showed Soviet missile bases under construction in Cuba, the United States established an air and sea blockade of Cuba and threatened to invade unless the bases were dismantled.

Dr. Spock was recruited as a national sponsor of the SANE pro-freeze movement.

Graphic Artists for SANE was organized, including Jules Feiffer, Ben Shahn, and Edward Sorel.

1963

President John F. Kennedy signed the Limited Test Ban Treaty in which Britain, the Soviet Union, and the United States agreed to outlaw nuclear weapons tests in the atmosphere, underwater and in outer space.

1964

China detonated its first atomic weapon.

1966

The first French atomic bomb was tested at Muruoa Atoll.

The U.S. Minuteman ICBM (intercontinental ballistic missile) entered service.

1967

The Outer Space Treaty banned nuclear weapons from being placed on any celestial body, or in orbit around Earth.

The Treaty of Tlatelolco created a Latin America nuclear-weapons-free zone.

China detonated its first hydrogen bomb.

1968

France tested its first hydrogen bomb at Fangataufa Atoll in the South Pacific.

1969

SANE produced ads attacking anti-ballistic missiles (ABMs): "From the people who brought you Vietnam."

President Richard M. Nixon announced plans to deploy a missile defense system called "Safeguard" to protect U.S. ICBM fields from attack.

continued

Timeline ... *(continued)*

1969

Preliminary Strategic Arms Limitation Treaty (SALT) talks took place in Helsinki, Finland.

1970

The U.S. deployed the first missile with multiple independently targetable re-entry vehicles (MIRVs).

1971

The first Poseidon submarine-launched ballistic missiles were introduced by the U.S.

1972

President Nixon and General Secretary Leonid Brezhnev signed the Anti-Ballistic Missile (ABM) Treaty, the Strategic Arms Limitation Treaty (SALT) and the Interim Agreement on Strategic Offensive Arms in Moscow.

SALT II treaty negotiations began.

1974

India tested a low-yield nuclear device under the Rajasthan desert.

The Threshold Test Ban Treaty (TTBT), which limited nuclear test explosions to under 150 kilotons, was signed in Moscow.

President Gerald Ford and General Secretary Brezhnev signed the Vladivostok Accord, agreeing to limit the number of strategic launchers and MIRV launchers.

1976

President Ford and General Secretary Brezhnev signed the Underground Nuclear Explosions for Peaceful Purposes (PNE) Treaty.

1977

The United States successfully tested a neutron bomb, whose lethal effects come from the radiation damage caused by the neutrons it emits.

Peace groups launched a national Campaign to Stop the B1 Bomber by restricting congressional allocations.

1978

The United States cancelled development of the neutron bomb.

1979

The Three Mile Island nuclear power plant near Harrisburg, Pennsylvania, suffered a partial core meltdown.

The SALT II Treaty was signed in Vienna, Austria.

A mysterious flash detected by a U.S. satellite was determined to be from a clandestine nuclear explosion by South Africa.

Peace groups began a national STOP-MX Missile Campaign.

1980

The first of many nuclear freeze resolutions were approved in western Massachusetts.

A referendum against MX missiles was approved in Nevada.

1981

Israeli aircraft destroyed Iraq's Osirak reactor, thought to be producing materials for an Iraqi nuclear device.

President Reagan unveiled plans for a record $200 billion military budget funded through cutbacks in social programs.

The Nuclear Weapons Freeze Campaign was founded in D.C.

continued

Timeline . . . *(continued)*

1982

One million protestors gathered in New York City for a peace and disarmament march; a sister rally attracted 100,000 in Pasadena, California.

More than 10 million voters approved nuclear freeze referenda in eight states.

Strategic Arms Reduction Talks (START) began in Geneva, Switzerland.

1983

The Nuclear Freeze resolution passed the U.S. House of Representatives.

Hollywood for SANE published an ad in *Variety* magazine signed by over 250 celebrities including Jack Lemmon, Burt Lancaster, James Earl Jones, Sally Field, Jean Stapleton, Shirley MacLaine, Anne Bancroft and Ed Asner.

"Women Plan Arms Protest Upstate," Suzanne Daley, *The New York Times*, June 27, 1983:

Romulus, NY June 24—Beside a small farm on Route 96 here in the Finger Lakes Region, a sign says: Women's Encampment for a Future of Peace & Justice"....

A group of women bought the 52-acre farm in May and hopes to attract hundreds of women here this summer to use the farm's fields as a camping ground and assembly area for antinuclear demonstrations.

Adjoining the land is the target of the protest—the Seneca Army Depot, an 11,000-acre ammunitions storage site that is widely assumed to contain nuclear weapons. The Army will not comment on this....

The prospect of such a protest has set the Army to building fences, hiring extra caviling guards and holding meetings to ease the concerns of workers. It has also caused a great deal of anxiety in this town of about 2,000 residents....

Mr. Zajac [Town Supervisor] who thinks the women "have a beautiful dream but have bitten off more than they can chew," says he has many concerns. They range from the town's limited water supply to its lack of a police force to having only one judge....

"We aren't equipped to deal with this," Mr Zajac went on. "The women say: 'We're not trying to bother you. Our beef is with the federal government.' But they've already caused a hardship with all the worrying. They say that by the end of the summer we'll all be great friends but if that happens, I'll sit in this office and eat my hat."

Like the commander of the Army Depot and the sheriff, Mr. Zajac says he feels frustrated because the women maintain they have no leader and are sometimes vague in describing what they plan to do.

"Nothing is clear," said Mr. Zajac, "They don't know, so we don't know how many people will show up. We aren't so much worried about them, although I want to tell you that the prospect of breaking up 300 mothers is awesome—but what about the others who will be attracted to this sort of thing. Maybe motorcycle gangs—who knows?"....

One of the three paid workers at the farm, Barbara Reale, 23 years old, who studied economics at Cornell University and has since worked for several peace organizations, said the farm would have campsites ready to accommodate about 350 people. Some fields will be kept available to handle any overflow attendance....

The encampment, said Miss Reale, is being sponsored by a large assortment of individual women and women's groups. Contributors, she said, include such groups as the American Friends Service Committee, a Quaker pacifist group; the New England War Tax Resistance; Church Women United; Nuclear Weapons Facilities Network; the Rochester Peace and Justice Education Center; and the Women's International League for Peace and Freedom....

Several of the women on the farm cite instances of people who have been friendly to them—a bar down the road gave a refrigerator, some local women have brought pies or homemade bread. But there are people in town who are angry that their way of life may be changed this summer.

"They aren't going to do anything but raise our taxes," said Milly Todd.... "We are going to have to pay for more protection for them and for ourselves. I don't think they have any idea what they are doing to a small town. We don't even dare go away on our summer vacation. If people are coming in here by the droves, who knows what will happen?"

Copyright 1983. Reprinted by permission of The New York Times, New York, NY

No
War
Toys

"200 Protesters Seized by M.P.s at Army Depot, 1,900 Women in a Rally Against Nuclear Arms," *The New York Times*, August 2, 1983:

ROMULUS, N.Y., Aug 1 (AP)—Military policemen arrested more than 200 women this afternoon as about 1,900 women protesting nuclear arms rallied at the Seneca Army Depot.

The protesters were jeered by more than 200 flag-waving counter-demonstrators, mostly local residents, who chanted, "Go Home."

With an Army helicopter overhead, the military policemen spread razor-sharp wire along 200 yards of fence to prevent the women from climbing it. But many of the women climbed over the fence into the arms of military policemen and were arrested.

"The message we are giving is that we are peace-loving women," said Connie McKenna, a spokesman for the protesters. She said the women had wanted to plant trees, gardens and rose bushes inside the depot. Some of the women have been spending the summer at the Women's Encampment for a Future of Peace and Justice, near the depot in the Finger Lakes region.

Planners for the rally said it was called to demand a halt in the United States plans to deploy Pershing 2 and Cruise missiles later this year. The demonstrators believe that the base is an arsenal for nuclear weapons. The Army refuses to confirm or deny the presence of nuclear weapons at the Seneca Army Depot or any other site.

The Seneca County Sheriff's Department was being assisted in handling the demonstration by 100 sheriff's deputies from nearby counties.

Reagan's Case Against the Freeze, Excerpts from a speech by President Ronald Reagan to the Los Angeles World Affairs Council on March 31, 1983:

The freeze concept is dangerous for many reasons. It would preserve today's high, unequal and unstable levels of nuclear forces and, by so doing, reduce Soviet incentives to negotiate for real reductions.

It would pull the rug out from under our negotiators in Geneva, as they have testified.

After all, why should the Soviets negotiate if they've already achieved a freeze in a position of advantage to them?

Also, some think a freeze would be easy to agree on, but it raises enormously complicated problems of what is to be frozen, how it is to be achieved, and verified. Attempting to negotiate these critical details would only divert us from the goal of negotiating reductions for who knows how long.

The freeze proposal would also make a lot more sense if a similar movement against nuclear weapons were putting similar pressures on Soviet leaders in Moscow.

As former Secretary of Defense Harold Brown has pointed out: The effect of the freeze "is to put pressure on the United States, but not on the Soviet Union."

Finally, the freeze would reward the Soviets for their 15-year buildup while locking us to our existing equipment, which in many cases is obsolete and badly in need of modernization. Three-quarters of the Soviet strategic warheads are on delivery systems five years old or less. Three-quarters of the American strategic warheads are on delivery systems 15 years old or older. The time comes when everything wears out. The trouble is it comes a lot sooner for us than for them. And, under a freeze, we couldn't do anything about it.

"Circle of Fire," based upon a song by Linda Hirschorn, sung by the Women's Encampment for a Future of Peace and Justice:

Chorus

Circle for survival, circle for the right
Not to disappear into the everlasting night
Circle for survival, circle for the right
Not to disappear into the everlasting night

Circle all the bases, circle day and night
Enclose them in a wall of sacred strength and sight
Let the people see them for what they really are
Let the people know they threaten our home star

Chorus

Circle all the strip mines, circle day and night
Circle all the people, lend them all our might
Circle all the rapists, the men and their machines
Circle all the ones who take away our dreams

Chorus

Circle all the pueblos, keep them safe from harm
Circle native people with hearts and minds and arms
They're fighting for their homelands, what little they have left
It's up to us to help them rectify the theft

Chorus

The circle is our weapon, the circle is our tool
The circle is our heartspace, the circle is our school
The circle is our kiva, the circle is our truth
The circle is our power against the ones who rule

Chorus

Keep the Pacific Independent and Nuclear free

1983: Microphone Boom Operator

Twenty-three year-old Maggi Taylor and her husband, a foreign correspondent, left Australia for NYC, where she became a legal immigrant and successful boom operator.

Life at Home

- Maggi Taylor was born in 1943 in Sydney, New South Wales, Australia; her sister Jenny was born two years later.
- Her parents split up shortly after Jenny's birth; her mother, with her two daughters, moved in with her parents.
- Her mother left for long periods of time to find work, and "Margaret" and her sister were left almost entirely in the care of their grandmother.
- Maggi was sent to boarding school at age 12, and although she came home for holidays and summer break, The Glennie School for Girls, in Toowoomba, Queensland, was her home until she graduated at age 18.
- Although she was a very bright and friendly girl, Maggi almost always felt alone.
- After graduation, and against her mother's wishes, she defiantly ran off and married Richard, a young writer she had met just a year before while on school break.
- It was 1962, and Maggi and Richard moved to New Zealand, where he had a job; she found work there on a radio station, something an inexperienced young woman could not have done in Australia.
- New Zealand needed educated workers of all kinds, and businesses were willing to hire women.
- The job away from home helped prepare her for her move to America in 1966.
- Since childhood, Maggi had been called by her given name, Margaret.

Maggi Taylor left Australia when she was 23.

Glennie School for Girls, Queensland.

Maggi and Richard in NYC.

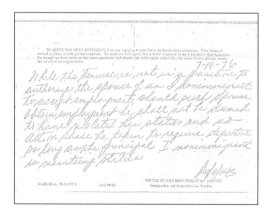

INS gave Maggi permission to work in America.

- On her first day in New York, when asked her name, she said, "It's Maggi"; she knew right then that America was the beginning of a new life.
- As a foreigner in a foreign land, she could truly be herself—not her mother's daughter, not the lonely girl in boarding school, and not just her ambitious husband's wife.
- Twenty-three-year-old Maggi and husband Richard lived in New York, where Richard worked as a foreign correspondent from 1966 to 1968, and then both returned home to Australia.
- It wasn't until she was back in Australia, faced with the old familiar attitudes and inhibitions, that Maggi realized she wanted to return to America.
- Then in 1973, after five years away from the United States and her first taste of America, to Maggi's delight, Richard was again assigned to New York.
- As a foreign journalist, he entered the country on an H-1 visa, giving him the right to work and stay in the U.S.
- Spouses, mostly wives of H-1 workers, were technically visitors, but were given a complimentary H-2 visa, so that they would not have to exit and re-enter the country every six months to renew a visitor's visa.
- The H-2 visa was not exactly a working visa, but near enough.
- A much-Xeroxed copy of a notice from the Immigration and Naturalization Service (INS) circulated among the wives that stated that as long as the H-1 visa holder was legally employed, the INS permitted the spouse to work, too.
- Through her connections with the Australian community, Maggi got a job in the Australian Consul as a receptionist.
- She then worked at the UN for United Nations English Language Radio, which eventually led to her career as a boom operator in the film and television industry.
- When in 1980, after seven years in America, Richard returned to Australia, Maggi chose to remain behind.
- Since the late 1970s, Maggi and Richard had been navigating very rocky marital terrain.
- Maggi often worked late on a movie or television shoot or was on location for days, sometimes weeks at a time.
- As a news reporter, Richard had a schedule that was even more erratic and which included lots of out-of-town trips and lots of hotel bars.
- Richard was becoming an alcoholic, and there were other women.
- After his trips, often marked by unaccounted-for absences from his hotel room, Richard would return home contrite, affectionate, and determined to tell almost all to soothe his conscience, regardless of how much it hurt Maggi.
- She forgave him each time and they drifted back to their fractured home life.
- In the spring of 1980, Richard quit his job in order to work full-time on a novel.
- He had a publisher and a contract, but the writing wasn't going well; he said he needed to devote more time to the writing.
- He said he needed to be alone.
- Soon afterward, in June, he left for Newport, Rhode Island, where he met Joan, a visiting, well-off Australian widow.

- She was there enjoying the sunny days; it was, after all, winter in Australia, but she planned to go back to Sydney at the end of August.
- Maggi was working on a film in New Hampshire, and she and Richard talked on the phone every couple of days and even met up when she could get a day off.
- She sensed that something was wrong—more wrong than usual.
- He said the writing wasn't going very well.
- At the end of August, Richard returned to New York, but within a month he left for Australia, claiming research for his book.
- While paying the past month's phone bill, Maggi noticed an unusual number of calls to an unknown number in Australia.
- She called the number and got Joan and Richard at the other end.
- After many heart-wrenching calls back and forth, he and Maggi decided to separate; with or without Joan, he wanted to stay in Australia.
- With or without Richard, Maggi wanted to stay in America.

At United Nations English Radio.

Life at Work

- By the time Maggi and Richard Taylor decided to break up, she found that she was surprisingly relieved, and realized that she did not want him to come back.
- She had started building a career and a life, and in his absence, she realized that she had been lonelier when they were together than she was now.
- She began the long, arduous, and expensive process to get a work permit and then a Green Card so that she could stay in America on her own as a permanent legal immigrant.
- This legal journey would take many letters of inquiry, many phone calls, many forms to fill out, a second set of lawyers, a trip back to Australia, and four years of appointments and paperwork to reach her goal.
- Because of the nature of her work, there were more than the normal delays; she often had to be out of town on location for a shoot, and had to postpone appointments.
- Sometimes she spent 14 straight hours on the set, and could do nothing when she got off work but sleep.
- She never knew on the job how long a sequence would take, or how many takes it would require.
- A missed appointment could mean a long wait before another could be scheduled; government bureaucracies, she came to understand, did not operate on "show biz" time.
- She had to wait for downtime between shoots to write letters, fill out forms, and meet with lawyers or government officials.
- The process dragged on.
- To start the process, she first needed to submit an Application for Alien Employment Certification to the U.S. Department of Labor, Employment and Training Administration; this application had to identify a potential employer and describe the job to be performed.
- Maggi checked all of her film connections and The National Association of Broadcast Engineers and Technicians (NABET) bulletin board; she needed a Sound Man looking for an assistant.
- She heard through the grapevine that Joseph Neeland was looking for someone with multimedia sound experience.
- She had worked on a free-lance project with him in the past, and he was willing to be her sponsor and ready to offer her a full-time job as his assistant.
- He needed a boom person with production skills, and she fit the bill.

- Along with the application, she had to show proof that extensive recruitment efforts made by Neeland had produced no qualified U.S. workers.
- He was required to advertise the position in a newspaper of general circulation, such as The New York Times, to run for three consecutive days (not on a Saturday).
- She also had to post the same ad on the NABET bulletin board, and had to formally apply for the job herself.
- She then had to include a copy of the ad, and all of the responses, with her application to the Department of Labor.
- The application required a full job description, work hours and salary.
- The description read: "Applicant must be responsible for correlating materials, processing and dubbing in cassette production. Responsible for supervising transfer of sound material, editing and mixing. Must be familiar will all aspects of sound recording, including studio, motion picture and video techniques, post-production, signal processing editorial procedures, boom work and equipment maintenance."
- The position paid $15,000 per year.
- Her labor certification was filed with the Department of Labor in November 1981, and she was hired by Neeland, using her complimentary H-1 visa, based on her H-2 visa, while she waited.
- She was advised that she should expect to wait another year for permanent residence status, and her application for preference status would have to be submitted to the Immigration Service and to the American Consul in Australia.
- When she was called for a visa appointment, she had to leave the U.S. and report to the American Consul in Sydney.
- She had to produce her birth certificate; the Police/Character Clearance Certificate, attesting that she did not have a police record; and a set of her Non-Criminal Fingerprints taken in New York.
- She also needed four copies of a recent photograph, 1½ x 1½ inches, and an update of her job offer, written on her employer's business stationery, and notarized.
- It was a long and costly process, involving lawyers.
- Maggi also had to have a medical examination, including X-rays and blood tests, from a physician who had been approved of in the consular district.
- When everything was in order, her papers were stamped and accepted; her health was perfect, and her past good citizenship was certified—plus, her interview went very, very well.
- She had been coached on what to say to immigration officials, advised to cover up her tattoos—she had several—and had to provide a clean police record from Australia.
- Because of the time difference between the U.S. and Australia, Maggi spent one whole night on the phone (at great expense), and finally got a promise from someone in the police department to send a fax saying that she did not have a police record.
- On the day of the interview she remembered to wear slacks and a turtleneck sweater with long sleeves, and a pleasing smile.

Maggi had a successful career as a boom operator.

- Once Maggi's application for alien labor certification was accepted, she was free to work and live in the U.S.
- Thanks to her past work in radio, and the fact that she had apprenticed on the set of *Contract on Cherry Street,* Maggi continued to get work as a boom operator while she applied for a Green Card.
- A boom operator is an assistant of the production sound mixer.
- The principal responsibility of the boom operator is microphone placement, often using a "fishpole" with a microphone attached to the end.
- Sometimes, when the situation permitted, the boom operator used a "Fischer boom," a special piece of equipment that the operator stands for more precise control of the microphone at a much greater distance away from the actors.

- The boom operator also placed wireless microphones on actors when necessary.
- The boom operator was part of the film's crew, employed during the production or photography phase for the purpose of producing a motion picture.
- Crew are distinguished from cast, consisting of the actors who appear in front of the camera or provide voices for characters in the film.
- The crew is also distinct from the production staff, consisting of producers, managers, their assistants, and those whose responsibility falls in pre-production or post-production phases, such as writers and editors.
- Communication between production and crew generally passes through the director and his/her staff.
- Medium to large crews are generally divided into departments with well-defined hierarchies and standards for interaction and cooperation among the departments.
- Other than acting, the crew handles everything in the photography phase: props and costumes, cameras, sound, lighting, sets, and special effects.
- Caterers (known in the film industry as "craft services") are usually not considered part of the crew.
- Within a short time, Maggi gained a reputation for excellence and was soon in great demand.
- *Eddie and the Cruisers,* an independent, underground hit, was one of her first feature films; she also worked on the full first season of *Law & Order.*
- Maggi had to put in long hours on various film sets, often six days a week during intensive shooting, and traveled wherever she was needed.
- In 1980 she worked on *Imposters,* directed by Mark Rappaport, which was presented at the Museum of Modern Art's New Directors/New Films series.
- She worked on TV commercials, including ones for BMW and Jumping Jack Shoes, and even an independent horror film, *You Better Watch Out,* starring Brandon Maggart and Jeffrey DeMunn.
- She worked on the American segments of foreign films, traveling to Philadelphia, Ohio and Canada.
- As a woman in a man's business, she knew it was important to establish a reputation of being not only good at her job, but also reliable and available.
- Her made-for-TV movies included *Summer,* part of the Edith Wharton Project for PBS, shot in Keene, New Hampshire, and *We're Fighting Back,* a TV movie based on the Guardian Angels with Ellen Barkin.
- Maggi traveled to Minnesota for the videotaping of a performance for television of *The Wonderful World of Oz,* which was produced by the Children's Television Theatre Company, staged at the Guthrie Center in Minneapolis.
- In 1983 she did *Over the Brooklyn Bridge,* directed by Menahem Golan and starring Elliott Gould, Margaux Hemingway, Sid Caesar and Shelley Winters.

Life in the Community: New York City
- Maggi Taylor found a small apartment in Manhattan on East 22nd Street.
- Although she kept in touch with the friends she had made in the foreign press and the Australian Consul when she had first arrived with Richard, she quickly made friends in the film industry, and spent most of her free time with them because of the odd hours they all worked.
- New York as a city was once again reinventing itself.
- In Greenwich Village, Tower Records was attracting 6,000 to 8,000 customers on an average Saturday to shop, watch MTV on 17 large video screens and learn about emerging groups like Human Sexual Response.
- The New York City Council was addressing potential birth defects by requiring liquor stores, bars and restaurants to post signs saying that pregnant women who drink alcohol were in danger of harming their babies.
- All of this while many New York 11th grade students were sitting through interdisciplinary seminars on "Nuclear Issues."

Historical Snapshot
1983

- Psychologists reported increased marital stress due to computer preoccupation, which was creating computer widows and widowers
- The per-capita personal income in New York was $12,314; in Mississippi it was $7,778
- The first artificial heart recipient, Barney Clark, died after 112 days
- After four years of major losses, the automotive industry rebounded and appeared to be on the road to financial recovery
- The top movies of the year included *Terms of Endearment, The Right Stuff, The Big Chill, Silkwood, Return of the Jedi, Flashdance, Mr. Mom, The Year of Living Dangerously, Yentl,* and *Wargames*
- Actress Jennifer Beals established a new fashion trend in the movie *Flashdance* by wearing clothing with holes and tears
- Anti-drunk driver campaigns were credited with a reduction in automobile accident fatalities for the year
- Television premieres included *The A-Team, Wheel of Fortune, Night Court,* and *Webster*
- *A Chorus Line* became the longest-running show in Broadway history with a record 3,389 performances
- The Supreme Court upheld a Florida law denying high school diplomas to students who failed a literacy test
- Firsts for the year included the hatching of a California condor in captivity, fingerprinting of infants, the first black mayor of Chicago, the first woman in space and a female Secretary of Transportation
- MTV was received in 17.5 million homes and credited with reviving the record industry
- The National Basketball Association contract was the first in sports to include revenue sharing with players
- Martin Luther King, Jr. became the first person since George Washington whose birthday was declared a national holiday
- The Supreme Court reaffirmed its 1973 *Roe v. Wade* decision affirming a woman's constitutional right to an abortion
- Degas' painting *Waiting* sold for $3.7 million—a record price for an Impressionist's work, while Mary Cassatt's *Reading Le Figaro* sold for $1.1 million
- The report *A Nation at Risk* warned, "The educational foundations of our society are presently being eroded by a rising tide of mediocrity that threatens our very future as a nation and our people"
- More than 100 million people watched *The Day After,* a made-for-TV film about a nuclear attack on Lawrence, Kansas

Australian Historical Timeline

40,000 BCE

Aboriginal tribes are believed to have arrived in Australia.

1606

The Dutch ship *Duyfken,* under Captain Willem Janszoon, explored the western coast of Cape York Peninsula; it was the first recorded landfall by a European on Australian soil.

1770

Captain James Cook claimed Australia for Britain; he was the first explorer and navigator to map Newfoundland, the first European to make contact with Australia and the Hawaiian Islands, and the first to circumnavigate New Zealand.

1788

The first fleet from England arrived in Australia and founded the first European settlement and penal colony.

An English settlement was founded at Norfolk Island.

1792

The first United States ship, the *Philadelphia,* entered the Australian port in Sydney.

1829

The whole of Australis was claimed as a British territory, and the settlement of Perth was founded.

1833

American merchants opened trading branches.

1836

The U.S. opened the first United States Consul in Sydney with the appointment of James Hartwell Williams, who arrived to take office in 1839.

1850

The University of Sydney was founded.

1851

Gold was discovered, and several thousand Americans arrived in Australia during the 1850s.

1891

A national Australian Convention adopted the name The Commonwealth of Australia and drafted a constitution.

1895

"Waltzing Matilda," Australia's most widely known folk song, was written by poet and nationalist Banjo Paterson.

1901

Australia became a federation free of England.

continued

Timeline . . . *(continued)*

1902

The Franchise Act guaranteed women the right to vote in federal elections, but excluded most non-European ethnic groups, including Aboriginal people.

1914

Australia entered the First World War.

1915

Surfing was introduced to Australia by Hawaiian Duke Kahanamoku, who gave an exhibition of wave riding at the Freshwater Life Saving and Surf Club.

1920

The airline Qantas was founded.

1939

Australia entered the Second World War.

1940

Scientists under Howard Florey developed penicillin.

1945

Howard Florey, Ernst Boris Chain, and Alexander Fleming shared the Nobel Prize for Medicine for the extraction of penicillin.

Australia became a founding member of the United Nations.

1950

Australian troops fought in Korea and against the communist insurgency in Malaya.

1956

Melbourne held the Summer Olympics.

1962

Indigenous Australians gained the right to vote in all states except Queensland.

Australia entered the Vietnam War.

1964

The Beatles toured Australia.

1965

Indigenous Australians gained the right to vote in Queensland.

1971

Neville Thomas Bonner was the first Indigenous Australian to be elected to the Parliament of Australia.

1973

The Sydney Opera House opened.

1983

Australia won the America's Cup, the most famous and prestigious prize in the sport of sailing, and the oldest active trophy in international sport.

Selected Prices

First-class Postage Stamp	$0.15
Gas, Regular, One Gallon	$1.25
Milk, One Gallon	$2.16
Butter, One Pound, Land O' Lakes	$1.99
Bacon, Half Pound	$1.39
Aspirin, Bayer, 100 Count	$1.49
Laundry Detergent, Tide, 49-Ounce Box	$1.89
Sewing Machine, Kenmore	$159.95
Washing Machine, Kenmore, Large	$289.00
DeLorean DMC-12 Sports Car	$25,000.00

"27 Spots Raided After an Inquiry on Immigration," By Lindsey Gruson, *The New York Times*, February 10, 1983:

The United States Immigration and Naturalization Service last night raided 27 Manhattan restaurants, night-clubs and massage parlors after obtaining warrants for 24 people on charges of attempting to bribe immigration officers, officials said.

Paul Shechtman, an Assistant United States Attorney for the Southern District of New York, said he could not say how many people were arrested.

Two other suspects are accused of smuggling illegal aliens into the United States through Canada, Mr. Shechtman said. Last night's actions culminated a one-and-a-half-year Immigration Service undercover investigation, dubbed Operation Handlebars, into attempts by illegal aliens to obtain permanent residency cards by bribing officials of the Immigration Service, Mr. Shechtman said. . . .

About a dozen people were taken into custody when several uniformed immigration officers raided the Sam Bok Korean Restaurant and Bar at 127 West 43rd Street, several diners said. The restaurant was one of the first businesses raided in last night's operation.

"I was sitting there waiting for someone to ask if I wanted coffee when our waiter walked by in handcuffs," said Geraldine Brooks, a graduate student at Columbia University who was in the restaurant at the time of the raid.

When Miss Brooks, an Australian, asked the officers whom she should pay for her dinner, one officer asked to see her visa. "Luckily I was applying for a visa to Russia this afternoon and had my papers and passport with me or I would have spent the night in jail," she said.

Historical Census Statistics on the Foreign-born Population of the United States Population Division, U.S. Bureau of the Census

- The 1850 census was the first in which data were collected on the birth place of the population.
- From 1850 to 1930, the foreign-born population of the United States increased from 2.2 million to 14.2 million, reflecting large-scale immigration from Europe.
- From 1930 to 1950, the foreign-born population of the United States declined from 14.2 million to 10.3 million, or from 11.6 percent to 6.9 percent of the total population.
- Immigration rose during the 1950s and 1960s, but was still low, then dropped slowly to 9.6 million in 1970, a record low of 4.7 percent of the total population.
- Since 1970, the foreign-born population of the United States has increased rapidly due to large-scale immigration, primarily from Latin America and Asia.
- The foreign-born population rose from 9.6 million in 1970 to 14.1 million in 1980.
- As a percentage of the total population, the foreign-born population increased from 4.7 percent in 1970 to 6.2 percent in 1980.

Australians Living in the United States

1960	22,209
1970	24,271
1980	36,120

Comments from Recent Immigrants

I had been in the U.S. a few days and my fiancé and I planned a dinner with some of his friends who were eager to meet me. The restaurant was rather noisy and during the course of the evening I stood up and informed them quite loudly I was going to the toilet. There was a slight pause, as all at the table looked at me in shock. I can only imagine what they must have thought; in America "going to the toilet" is like saying you are going to the dunny or the bog house.

—Cathy

I was in horror when my hubby's friend and his son, after an enjoyable evening, told us they were going to go shag. I am used to the term "go shag" meaning to go and have sex. Apparently in Texas, to "go shag" means to leave.

—Mandy

In the USA, a fanny is a rear end, and in Australia a fanny is the front end of a lady's anatomy. Try not to get the two mixed up! So, when you're in the USA, wear your fanny pack on your butt!

—Sam

I was complaining to some American colleagues about how rigid the co-op board of my apartment building is, specifically about a rule forbidding pot plants above a certain height on the balconies. They were astounded that I was allowed to have pot plants at all. After some clarification, I found that in the U.S., there's a big difference between "pot" plants and "potted" plants.

—Katherine

Australian Products Available in America

- Sheepskin and wool boots and slippers, as well as leather gore-sided boots.
- Felt hats made from a blend of rabbit and hare fur.
- Waterproof coats and hats and other outdoor all-weather clothing.
- Australian wool fleece, especially bred for hand spinning and weaving.
- Art: Aboriginal art, including bark paintings and carvings. Photographs of Aboriginal rock art.
- Artifacts: Aboriginal artifacts, including boomerangs, swords, spears, shields.
- Didgeridoos, one of the world's oldest wind instruments; all sizes of beginner to professional models available.
- Tea Tree Oils: Medicinal and cosmetic products made from *Melaleuca alternifolia* trees. Known anti-fungal and antibiotic.
- Foods: Australian foodstuffs, including lollies, Nestle Milo bars, Arnott's Biscuits (Australian cookies), Vegemite (a salty sandwich spread), Australian teas, including invigorating Australian morning tea, subtly sippable Australian afternoon tea, and more.

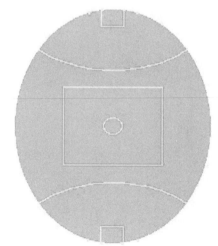

Australian football players and oval field.

Popular Music in Australia
Online: The Australian Government Culture and Recreation Portal

- Like rock music, popular, or pop music had its origins in the 1950s and 1960s, and is one of Australia's most successful musical exports.

- Australian pop music has been going strong, with stars such as Little Pattie, who made it big after she was spotted by talent scouts at the Bronte Surf Club in 1963.

- Her first hit was "He's My Blonde-Headed Stompie-Wompie Real Gone Surfer Boy." In 1966, at just 17 years of age, she was the youngest entertainer to play to Australian troops in Vietnam.

- During the 1960s other performers, such as Col Joye, the Bee Gees, Normie Rowe, and the Seekers also became well known for their tunes and (mostly) clean-cut images.

- Many of these bands or individual performers are still performing today. Helen Reddy rose to international success with her pop anthem, "I Am Woman." When she wrote the song in 1972 she tapped into the growing feminist movement.

- Like so many Australian artists of the time, and since, Helen Reddy moved to the United States before finding the fame she sought.

- The Bee Gees are an example of an Australian pop group that achieved international success as singers, songwriters, and performers. The brothers, Barry, Robin, and Maurice Gibb emigrated to Australia from Britain as children. They lived in Brisbane and recorded many of their early songs in Sydney.

- After relocating to the U.K. in 1967, they produced dozens of songs that made it to the top of the charts in the U.S., England and Australia, including their late 1970s hits "How Deep is Your Love," and "Stayin' Alive." They also wrote many hits for other successful artists.

- Two Australian pop musicians who are considered ambassadors for the Australian pop industry are John Farnham and Olivia Newton-John.

- John Farnham's first notable recording was "Sadie the Cleaning Lady" (1968). It was the largest-selling single by an Australian artist of the 1960s.

- Olivia Newton-John's first major success was in 1974 with the single "I Honestly Love You," which was a hit in the U.K. and the U.S. In the U.S., Olivia Newton-John branched off into country music.

- In 1974, she was awarded the Country Music Association's Female Vocalist of the Year. She then starred in *Grease* and *Xanadu*. In 1981, she had a number one pop hit in the U.S. with the single "Physical."

Maggi's Grandfather's Grandfather, Clancy

Poet and nationalist Banjo Paterson, who wrote Australia's most widely known folk song, "Waltzing Matilda," in 1895, also wrote "Clancy of the Overflow," a poem based on James Clarence Clancy D'Arcy Webster, Maggi's grandfather's grandfather.

Clancy of the Overflow
By Banjo Paterson

I had written him a letter which I had, for want of better
Knowledge, sent to where I met him down the Lachlan, years ago,
He was shearing when I knew him, so I sent the letter to him,
Just "on spec," addressed as follows, "Clancy, of the Overflow."
And an answer came directed in a writing unexpected,
(And I think the same was written with a thumb-nail dipped in tar)
'Twas his shearing mate who wrote it, and verbatim I will quote it:
"Clancy's gone to Queensland droving, and we don't know where he are."

In my wild erratic fancy visions come to me of Clancy
Gone a-droving "down the Cooper" where the Western drovers go;
As the stock are slowly stringing, Clancy rides behind them singing,
For the drover's life has pleasures that the townsfolk never know.

And the bush hath friends to meet him, and their kindly voices greet him
In the murmur of the breezes and the river on its bars,
And he sees the vision splendid of the sunlit plains extended,
And at night the wond'rous glory of the everlasting stars.
I am sitting in my dingy little office, where a stingy
Ray of sunlight struggles feebly down between the houses tall,
And the foetid air and gritty of the dusty, dirty city
Through the open window floating, spreads its foulness over all.

And in place of lowing cattle, I can hear the fiendish rattle
Of the tramways and the buses making hurry down the street,
And the language uninviting of the gutter children fighting,
Comes fitfully and faintly through the ceaseless tramp of feet.

And the hurrying people daunt me, and their pallid faces haunt me
As they shoulder one another in their rush and nervous haste,
With their eager eyes and greedy, and their stunted forms and weedy,
For townsfolk have no time to grow, they have no time to waste.

And I somehow rather fancy that I'd like to change with Clancy,
Like to take a turn at droving where the seasons come and go,
While he faced the round eternal of the cash-book and the journal
But I doubt he'd suit the office, Clancy, of "the Overflow."

1985: Classical Singer

Classically trained singer Carleen Cahill's career spanned from singing at the New York City opera to teaching and performing in upstate New York.

Life at Home

- Carleen Rose Cahill was born in Detroit, Michigan, in 1951.
- She was first exposed to music through her parents, who would play 78 rpm records of swing and big band music.
- Her family would often dance and sing along to the music of Benny Goodman and Glen Miller, and Carleen actually sang before she spoke.
- Carleen sang in the school chorus as early as she could remember, and had her first solo—the third verse of "The Battle Hymn of the Republic"—in the fourth grade.
- Carleen's first instrument was the violin, which she started playing in fifth grade, after seeing her school's orchestra play *The Nutcracker Suite.*
- Carleen used a family violin that belonged to her grandmother, but it did not have any strings.
- She practiced finger positions and "played" on that stringless instrument for almost a year.
- When her teacher saw Carleen practicing finger positions on the edge of her desk, she encouraged Carleen's mother to put strings on her violin.
- As she got older, Carleen became increasingly interested in the rock music of the 1960s—including the Beatles, Chuck Berry, and the Rolling Stones—becoming a lifelong Beatles fan.
- Carleen's brother bought her a guitar for her sixteenth birthday, which she played in local bands, especially Joni Mitchell songs.

Classically trained singer Carleen Cahill thrived in New York City's opera scene.

- Although she continued to play guitar and violin throughout high school, she discovered that singing brought her the most pleasure.
- Singing had always felt very natural to her, and she sang it all while growing up—pop, rock, church, classic and folk, but not opera.
- In fact, she did not enjoy opera at all during high school.
- After high school, Carleen worked in an insurance company as a secretary.
- She also sang in a folk trio after work, performing at coffeehouses and making very little money.
- Her sister persuaded her to go to college to pursue a music career.
- Carleen got her Bachelor's of Music in Voice Performance at Western Michigan University in Kalamazoo, several hours west of Detroit—close enough to her family, but far enough to be on her own.

Make-up was important in transforming performers into many operatic roles.

- Studying music in college in the early 1970s was not terribly common.
- There were fewer career resources, and students had to figure out—by themselves—the practical aspects of how to become professional musicians.
- In college, Carleen discovered her love of opera and her ability to perform.
- Her music department put on three full-scale opera performances per year—a lot for a school of its size—giving Carleen the opportunity to experience a variety of musical styles, and to discover how much she enjoyed working as part of a team with the other cast and crew members.
- She found that she never got nervous when singing with other people in an opera production.
- As a voice performance music major, she was also required to study four languages: Spanish, French, Italian and German.
- During her college years, she sang with the Muskegon Symphony for $200, and with the Detroit Symphony for the experience.
- Upon graduating college, her goal was clear—to train as a classical singer.
- Carleen took the next step and got her Master's of Music in Voice Performance from the University of Michigan in Ann Arbor.
- In graduate school, Carleen performed six full-scale operas, which she added to her professional repertoire, as: the mother in E. Humperdinck's *Hansel and Gretel*; Donna Elvira and Donna Anna in Mozart's *Don Giovanni*; the widow in F. Lehar's *The Merry Widow*; Rosalinda in J. Strauss' *Die Fledermaus*; and Musetta in Puccini's *La Bohème*.
- Opera required much more than just singing; the best performers needed to act, be physically fit, have a good sense of timing, and the ability to work well with a cast and crew.
- Carleen paid her way through graduate school by singing at local church ceremonies for $50 per event, and by her permanent position as the church soloist.

In college, Carleen performed the leading role in Falstaff *by Verdi.*

Life at Work

- Armed with her Master's of Music in Voice Performance, Carleen Cahill moved to New York City in 1975 to pursue a classical singing career—a necessary career move for a classical singer.
- Upon arriving in New York, Carleen waitressed to support herself and her continued studies with a professional voice teacher—another necessary career decision that cost $50 per lesson.
- Professional voice teachers in New York required students to audition before being accepted to study in their studios.
- Carleen auditioned and was accepted into the studio of a teacher who was recommended by her professors in graduate school.
- The teacher was very strict, and would not let Carleen audition for anything for a year and a half.
- Once Carleen began auditioning for parts, however, she had great success and began performing often in and around New York.

Carleen with her sister, mother and brother after a graduate school performance.

- Her work at this time included three different roles with the Bronx Opera (Donna Anna in Mozart's *Don Giovanni*, Susannah in Carlyle Floyd's *Susannah*, and Violetta in Giuseppe Verdi's *La Traviata*).
- She also sang as the soprano soloist in Handel's *Judas Maccabeus* in the New York City's Choral Festival, and was engaged by Boris Goldovsky to sing for several of his numerous lectures at the Metropolitan Museum of Art lecture series on opera.
- Three years after arriving in New York, Carleen took her career to the next level by engaging a professional management company.
- The management company helped Carleen get high-level performing jobs, such as the soprano soloist in Beethoven's *Ninth Symphony* at the Saratoga Arts Festival, Musetta in Puccini's *La Bohème* with the Houston Grand Opera Festival, and Nedda in Ruggiero Leoncavallo's *I Pagliacci* with the New York City Opera Touring Company.

Conductor Boris Goldovsky engaged Carleen to sing at his opera lecture series at the Metropolitan Museum of Art

- Once professionally managed, Carleen was able to support herself exclusively with music, even though the management company typically took 15 percent of her paycheck for opera roles and 20 percent for oratorio and orchestral work.
- Carleen often got jobs through the international opera circuit that regularly traveled to New York to hold auditions for shows in other cities.
- The representatives of the opera companies in this circuit often cast performers based on very specific—and sometimes non-talent-related—criteria.
- For example, if a company had already found an especially tall woman to play the female lead, they would open auditions for the male lead to only tall men.
- Carleen's management company arranged for her to audition for suitable parts, one of her favorite being Violetta in Verdi's *La Traviata*.
- Once she got a role, Carleen would travel to the city of the performance for one to two months of rehearsals and shows.

- This gave her an opportunity to travel around the world and make many new friends and colleagues.
- The opera circuit was also a steady source of income, and compensation per show was $2,000-$8,000, depending on the size of the company.
- Carleen performed all over the country and abroad, including with opera companies in San Francisco, New Orleans, Austin, Phoenix, Seattle, Geneva, and Buenos Aires.
- Her favorite performance was as Mimi in Puccini's *La Bohème*, performed in Maracaibo, Venezuela; the audience sat in the aisles and sang along to all of the opera choruses.
- She also accepted roles with smaller opera companies, depite less pay; this was a way to try out new roles in a smaller and often more forgiving arena before performing them in a larger city.
- It was just such a role that led her to upstate New York, where she fell in love with the area's natural beauty and relaxed pace.
- In 1980, she bought a house in Hillsdale, New York, and began splitting her time between city and country.

Playing Mimi in La Boheme, *in Venezuela, was one of Carleen's most memorable performances.*

Life in the Community: Hillsdale, New York

- While Carleen enjoyed living in New York City and traveling around the world to perform, this lifestyle prevented her from putting down roots.
- In 1980, The Columbia County Opera Company was founded by a wealthy opera lover from New York looking to recreate the country opera experience that was popular in his native England.
- The small opera company offered an intimate performance environment, and produced a series of outdoor concerts set against the scenic backdrop of beautiful upstate New York.
- While the year-round population of the area was small, the community's proximity to the city made it a popular tourist destination, and the Columbia County Opera's audience was accustomed to top-rate performances.
- Despite its beautiful location and proximity to New York City, however, it was difficult for the opera company to attract top-rate performers, mostly because they couldn't meet big city salaries, which could be as much as $2,000-$5,000 higher per show.
- Despite less money, the Columbia County Opera Company was exactly what Carleen was looking for—more time in the country combined with her passion for music.
- In 1981, she performed in their second season, and again in 1982, in Mozart's *L'oca del Cairo* and *La Finta Giardiniera*.
- In 1983, Carleen married Joseph, the Italian repairman who often came to fix her less-than-dependable country phone service, ending her city/country lifestyle.
- In Hillsdale full-time, Carleen had fewer musical opportunities than in New York, but she enjoyed living in one place and being involved in the community.
- She began teaching voice at the local music school.
- She also became an adjunct music professor at a nearby college.
- Some of her students were involved in school plays for which Carleen enjoyed helping them rehearse, and was often in the front row on opening night.

Carleen as Rosalinda in J. Strauss' Die Fledermaus.

Carleen and husband Joseph.

HISTORICAL SNAPSHOT
1985

- In Hollywood, the charity single "We Are the World" was recorded by USA for Africa
- Minolta released world's first autofocus single-lens reflex camera
- The Food and Drug Administration approved a blood test for AIDS, used to screen all blood donations in the United States
- *Amadeus* won Best Picture at the 57th Academy Awards
- WrestleMania debuted at Madison Square Garden
- Coca-Cola changed its formula and released New Coke, only to reverse itself in the face of an overwhelmingly negative response
- The FBI brought charges against the heads of five Mafia families in New York City
- Thomas Patrick Cavanaugh was sentenced to life in prison for attempting to sell stealth bomber secrets to the Soviet Union
- John Hendricks launched the Discovery Channel
- Route 66 was officially decommissioned
- *Back to the Future* opened in American theaters and became the highest grossing film of 1985
- The Greenpeace vessel *Rainbow Warrior* was bombed and sunk in Auckland Harbor by French Directorate-General for External Security (DGSE) agents
- Live Aid concerts in London and Philadelphia raised over £50 million for famine relief in Ethiopia
- Nintendo Entertainment System, including the Super Mario Bros. pack-in game, was released
- The comic strip *Calvin and Hobbes* debuted in 35 newspapers
- Microsoft Corporation released Windows 1.0
- President Ronald Reagan sold the rights to his autobiography to Random House for a record $3 million
- The Ford Taurus and Mercury Sable went on sale
- NeXT was founded by Steve Jobs after he resigned from Apple Computer
- The Tommy Hilfiger brand was established
- DNA was first used in a criminal case

Selected Prices

Bicycle, Aero Urban Cowboy	$600.00
Briefcase, Leather	$565.00
Camcorder	$994.00
Coca-Cola, Two-Liter	$1.00
Doll, Playskool	$24.97
Ice Cream, Dove Bar	$1.45
Martini for Two	$1.08
Modem	$119.95
Synthesizer, Yamaha	$188.88
Walkman, Sony	$19.95

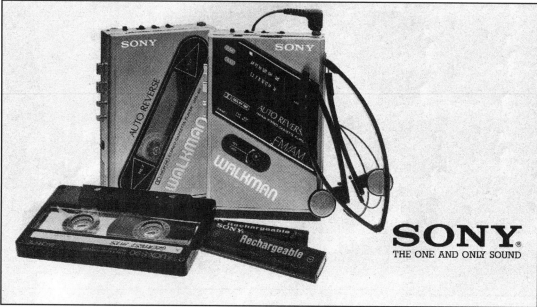

"Opera: Premiere of *Rinaldo* at Met," Donald Henahan, *The New York Times*, January 21, 1984:

It was a night of important debuts, some long delayed, at the Metropolitan Opera. The most important and most delayed was that of George Frideric Handel, none of whose more than 40 operas had ever been produced by the company before his 273-year-old *Rinaldo* found its way to the stage Thursday night. The production, borrowed almost intact from Canada's National Arts Center, might have astonished or perplexed him in some ways, but he probably would have found it as entertaining, ultimately, as most of the audience at this premiere obviously did.

Transporting a Handel opera from its Baroque setting to a modern house the size of the Met presents enormous problems, many of which this attractive production solves. The edition, edited by Martin Katz, was a conflation of Handel's several versions, expertly cut and trimmed to suit modern conditions.

Above all, however, the Handel opera demands important voices capable of handling the breathtaking coloratura and exhausting repetitions that figure so greatly in the opera seria genre. The Met had Samuel Ramey, for one, making his first appearance with the company as the Saracen warrior Argante. Mr. Ramey, who sang for years at the New York City Opera without attracting the Metropolitan's attention, went off to Europe several seasons ago and that apparently gave him the credentials necessary to impress the Met's casting department. At any rate, he made a tremendous impression with his powerful, pliable bass voice, particularly at his dazzling first entry in a wonderfully Baroque chariot. After throwing a big, steely tone out into the house in that aria, "Sibilar gli angui d'Aletto," he opened the following scene with a dulcet "Vieni, o cara, a consolarmi," demonstrating his great vocal as well as expressive range.

As brilliant a success in her own gentle way was Benita Valente as Almirena. Miss Valente actually drew one of the night's most sustained ovations with her plaintive and affecting aria rejecting the Saracen's advances, "Lascia ch'io pianga."

Marilyn Horne, in the title role, sounded a bit dry of throat and tired at first, but she warmed up for her vengeance aria to end Act I in a blaze of vocal pyrotechnics. On the whole, the evening did not find her in absolute top form, but Miss Horne's second best is anybody else's triumph. She ran out of breath at times in the final act's grand battle aria, which would have severely tested the powers of a steam boiler. Handel seldom wrote one note where 10 or 20 would do. She also contributed one of the premiere's more apparent flubs when she made a false start at one point in the finale. The house broke out in laughter and Miss Horne herself lost a desperate battle to keep a straight face.

Able, intermittently splendid performances also were turned in by Edda Moser (Armida), Dano Raffanti (Goffredo) and Diane Kesling (A Mermaid).

Along with technically polished singing, any Baroque opera needs spectacular stage effects if it is to come anywhere close to the spirit of that age of grand theatrical gestures. Mark Negin, making his debut as set and costume designer, provided a great deal of childish delight with a charming fire-breathing dragon, a waterfall of plastic ribbons, towers that opened out to become gardens—and the other way around—and scenes that magically transformed themselves in clouds of fog.

Frank Corsaro, in another of the evening's delayed debuts, directed the action with his usual ingenuity, but wisely stayed out of the way while sheer heroic vocalism was the point. Because of the rigidity of Baroque conventions, he was often hard put to find ways to keep things looking lively as singers spun out their florid repetitions and da capo arias. After Argante took a couple of turns around the stage in his chariot to fill up the time between verses, for instance, the novelty of that device wore out.

Two other welcome debuts added to the evening's satisfactions. Mario Bernardi, who early this season conducted the City Opera's beguiling *Cendrillon* (also a Canadian import, you remember), led this *Rinaldo* with great verve as well as sensitive concern for the singers.

Top Singles: 1985

1. "Careless Whisper," Wham!
2. "Say You, Say Me," Lionel Richie
3. "Separate Lives," Phil Collins and Marilyn Martin
4. "I Want to Know What Love Is," Foreigner
5. "Money for Nothing," Dire Straits
6. "We Are the World," USA for Africa
7. "Broken Wings," Mr. Mister
8. "Everybody Wants to Rule the World," Tears for Fears
9. "The Power of Love," Huey Lewis and the News
10. "We Built This City," Starship
11. "St. Elmo's Fire," John Parr
12. "Can't Fight This Feeling," REO Speedwagon
13. "Crazy for You," Madonna
14. "Easy Lover," Phillip Bailey and Phil Collins
15. "Everytime You Go Away," Paul Young
16. "Don't You (Forget About Me)," Simple Minds
17. "Take on Me," a-ha
18. "Party All the Time," Eddie Murphy
19. "Everything She Wants," Wham!
20. "Shout," Tears for Fears
21. "Alive and Kicking," Simple Minds
22. "I Miss You," Klymaxx
23. "Sea of Love," Honeydrippers
24. "Cool it Now," New Edition
25. "Part-Time Lover," Stevie Wonder
26. "Saving All My Love for You," Whitney Houston
27. "Sussudio," Phil Collins
28. "Oh Sheila," Ready for the World
29. "A View to a Kill," Duran Duran
30. "One More Night," Phil Collins
31. "Cherish," Kool & the Gang
32. "Heaven," Bryan Adams
33. "The Heat Is On," Glenn Frey
34. "Raspberry Beret," Prince and The Revolution
35. "You're the Inspiration," Chicago
36. "If You Love Somebody Set Them Free," Sting
37. "Miami Vice Theme," Jan Hammer
38. "Freeway of Love," Aretha Franklin
39. "Don't Lose My Number," Phil Collins
40. "Never," Heart
41. "Things Can Only Get Better," Howard Jones
42. "The Boys of Summer," Don Henley
43. "Rhythm of the Night," DeBarge
44. "We Don't Need Another Hero," Tina Turner
45. "We Belong," Pat Benatar
46. "Loverboy," Billy Ocean
47. "All I Need," Jack Wagner
48. "One Night In Bangkok," Murray Head
49. "Never Surrender," Corey Hart
50. "Lovergirl," Teena Marie

I've said that playing the blues is like having to be black twice. Stevie Ray Vaughan missed on both counts, but I never noticed.

Personal Essay
B.B. King

"Michael Jackson Inks Multimillion-Dollar Deal With Pepsi," *Rolling Stone*, June 19, 1986:

Whether or not it's the choice of a new generation, Pepsi's definitely generating a ton of money for Michael Jackson. Over the next three years, Jackson will make at least three commercials for Pepsi as part of the most lucrative advertising deal ever negotiated between a celebrity and a corporation: the singer will make $10 million.

Jackson and his brothers earned roughly $5.5 million when they appeared in two Pepsi commercials in 1984 and signed a tour-sponsorship deal with the soft drink company. In the new deal, Jackson is committed to producing two pieces of original music for the new ads. The singer's manager, Frank DiLeo, said that a song from Jackson's upcoming LP, due this fall, may also be used for one of the commercials. Jackson will film a minimum of two spots plus a Spanish-language ad. Pepsi plans to show the commercials worldwide and will premiere the first one in early 1987.

Under the terms of the deal, Jackson will be involved in writing the spots, choosing the directors, and designing the visuals. The contract also calls for Jackson to become a "creative consultant" for Pepsi in 1988, at which point he will direct a commercial itself. And while it is not definite Pepsi would be the sponsor of any forthcoming Jackson tour, Pepsi USA President Roger Enrico said that "whatever activities Michael does in support of his new album, we will be involved...."

Enrico estimates that the cost of the Jackson ad campaign, including production cost and airtime, "will be well in excess of $50 million." He has no doubt Michael is worth the price. The 1984 ads are credited with sharply boosting Pepsi sales. "My judgment is that these amounts of money, which seemed to be huge, do in fact payoff," Enrico said.

Jackson reportedly does not drink Pepsi himself and will not even hold the product in his hand for the ads, but, according to Pepsi spokesman, a truckload of the beverage is dropped off at his house every week.

"The Rod Stewart Concert Video, Video News," *Rolling Stone*, June 19, 1986:

Rod Stewart has one of the biggest egos in the music business, and every ounce of it is on display in the Rod Stewart Concert Video. There's not a moment when he's not swaggering, strutting and preening as he dominates the screen.

If he weren't having so much fun, this would be completely repellent. But Stewart seasons his posing with a sense of glee that, combined with the driving precision of his band, produces an unexpectedly entertaining show.

The cassette opens with an audio-visual bio that's just short enough to avoid being boring. Stewart begins the concert footage with a string of his hits starting with "Infatuation" and proceeding to "Tonight's the Night," "Young Turks," and "Passion." Between songs, he shows a reedy, easygoing magnetism that helps this tape escape the tedium that dogs most concert tapes.

"The New Lure of the Neighborhood," Nancy McKeon,
New York Magazine, June 17, 1985:

Only a few years ago, New York retailing mostly meant Saturday's Generation shopping in the Cellar while filling up the Gaps. But now, in the full bloom of the boutique age, with Benettons around every corner, shopping is becoming a neighborhood thing.

Outside of the city, discounters are nibbling at the bottom line of big stores. But in New York, where shoppers still trek regularly to Macy's, Bloomingdale's, and the other emporiums, it's the smaller retailers who are increasingly taking the initiative by creating "shopping centers" in residential neighborhoods, each with its own personality. There's the glossy Madison Avenue strip, now stretching into the Eighties, and raffish West Broadway in SoHo, the Fast Fashion of Columbus Avenue, and the energetic funk of NoHo. Chelsea's sprouting too: Gear, a home-fashion wholesaler, just opened on Seventh Avenue, and the neighborhood's major anchor, Barneys, will open its new women's store next winter, by which time Benetton's "superstore" will have opened down the block. The East Village has its own batch of offbeat boutiques and even lower Third and Fifth Avenues are bubbling over with new food and clothing shops.

The big stores are undeniably having their problems. April was the eleventh straight month of depressed sales—down 3.5 percent from April 1984, the largest monthly decline since August 1976, according to the monthly spot check of New York department stores by *The New York Times*.

New Yorkers have more opportunity to shop than ever before—retailing is increasingly a seven-day-a-week business. So the scramble for the customer's dollar has never been quite so intense. And when the target is the affluent consumer, the challenge to the retailer is novel. "Basically," says Ellen Fine, who owns the Fine Design store in the Flatiron district, "everybody has everything they need already," leaving the stores to compete for discretionary purchases.

Some of New York's big retailers have suggested that the younger consumers no longer think of the large stores as weekend entertainment. A cruise up Columbus or Madison or West Broadway certainly reinforces that impression: one big-store executive acknowledges that new shopping streets have siphoned off many of the recreational shoppers, and that the "intensity" of the weekend traffic isn't what it once was.

Meanwhile, the other major retailers are courting consumers by becoming "promotional," creating one-day sales and offering regular merchandise at short-term discount prices. The frequency of these price cuts, and the fact that regular prices are often pumped up so that items can be offered at significant reductions, has had negative results. The strategy has frequently led to sales increases in the short run but shrinking profits. In the longer term, it has trained customers to be cynical about the regular prices and to wait for sales.

These problems may be cyclical, of course, but the big stores are experiencing difficulties that just won't go away. Twenty years ago, says consultant Arlene Hirst, the innovative stores concentrated on developing private-label fashions, a fondly remembered example being the "Parisiennes" collection at Lord & Taylor, adapted from the Paris originals. Then came the designer era. Stores began promoting names that soon became international brands and, unfortunately for the stores that launched them, widely available. Now there's rekindled interest in private-label programs, with their potential for greater profits (items that are exclusive to one store can be comparison-shopped only in the most general way).

At the same time, the department stores are trying to produce excitement and increase store traffic by extending the designer-boutique formula to non-fashion areas, often asking manufacturers to share the expense of building discrete "environments." Ralph Lauren in domestic linens, Esprit in casual sportswear, Mikasa and Fitz & Floyd in china, even Macy's Metropolitan Museum of Art shop, are examples of the trend.

In big stores, manufacturers and importers are cooperating. But at street level, they're in hot competition. Many of the boutiques on Madison, Columbus, and West Broadway—Tahari, Laura Ashley, Hot House ceramics, Crabtree & Evelyn toiletries, MGA sportswear, and coming soon to Columbus, Murjani—are actually retail outlets owned, franchised, or licensed by manufacturers. They're joining the risky retail world in order to capture a bigger chunk of the dollar than plain old wholesalers get.

The feast-or-famine nature of retailing hasn't stopped developers from packing their projects with stores or from trying to mall the island of Manhattan. Like fast-food outlets, malls are essentially a suburban phenomenon that needs time to work its way into New Yorkers' daily routines.

Despite their problems, malls will continue to proliferate, mostly because builders want them. Still, there are growing pains. Trump Tower is the most successful, but it has had a couple of casualties, Fila and Loewe. Park Avenue Plaza's elegant specialty stores—like Chartwell Booksellers and Darabin Ltd., a haberdasher for executive women—remain semi-hidden treasures. Herald Center, trying hard to be uptown in the heart of Herald Square, is only a little more than half rented. And South Street Seaport's sales are only as good as the weather on any given weekend.

New York City is home to the New York City Opera and the Metropolitan Opera House.

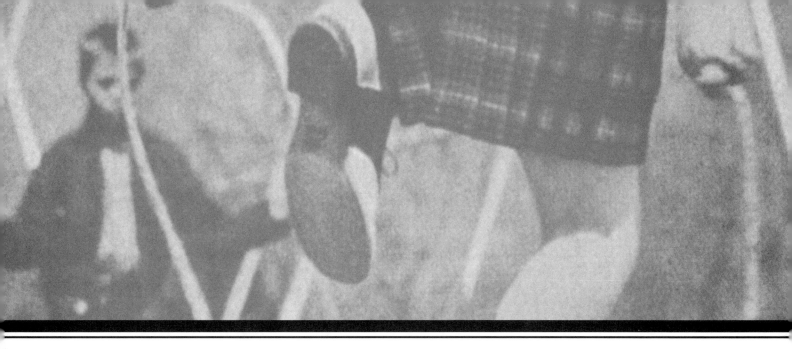

1992: High School Athlete & Scholar

Florida high school student Gayle Warwick used Title IX to buck the trend of male-dominant sports by earning letters in five different sports and three state championships.

Life at Home

- Gayle Warwick had heard all the excuses before; they were disappointedly familiar to what her older sister, mother and grandmother had been told.
- "Playing sports with boys was not only unfeminine but proof of lesbianism."
- "Female athletes were physically unattractive and weren't asked out on dates."
- "Competitive sports would harm reproductive organs as well as a woman's chances of marriage."
- "Girls were too selfish to play team sports; their hearts were too small, tempers too short."
- Girls' teams had to raise their own money through bake sales or carwashes.
- Girls' teams could not afford new uniforms and could only practice when the boys did not "need" the gym.
- Only the newest and worst referees were assigned to the girls' games.
- Cheerleaders received more attention than female athletes.
- If the boys' program was cut so that girls could have a team, the entire school would be mad—any decline in the boys' achievements would be the girls' fault.

Gayle Warwick bucked the trends by excelling in sports, science and math.

- Girls played in empty gymnasiums; even parents wouldn't watch their daughters compete.
- Born in 1972—the year Title IX of the Education Amendment was enacted—Gayle was a natural athlete who wanted to take advantage of the law that had changed women's athletics.
- Her older sister had helped blaze the trail in Tampa, Florida, by playing on the boys' soccer team and starring on the newly created girls' squads.
- When it was Gayle's turn to explore the various benefits of playing on girls-only soccer and field hockey teams, she choose to play them both.
- Her father understood; her mother was sure it would end badly.
- In addition to soccer, Gayle wanted to participate in volleyball, track and softball.
- But as important, she also demanded a space in the advanced classes in science and math—avenues that had been considered "boys' activities" and discouraged for girls—prior to Title IX.
- Although Title IX had ushered in athletic opportunities for thousands of girls like Gayle, its

impact was far wider, having erased the boys-only label that had been attached to certain academic disciplines, job opportunities and extracurricular activities.
- Hailed as one of the great achievements of the Women's Movement, Title IX states: "No person in the United States shall, on the basis of sex, be excluded from participation in, be denied the benefits of, or be subjected to discrimination under any education program or activity receiving federal financial assistance."

By the 1990s, more females were participating in organized sports.

- Gayle considered the law to be "gender-neutral" and not a "gift" to girls like some grown-ups liked to say.
- Title IX simply eliminated the special privileges historically given to boys by providing girls with equal access to higher education, career education, education for pregnant and parenting students, employment, a healthy learning environment, math and science, standardized testing, technology, and laws against sexual harassment.
- Title IX covered all state and local agencies that received federal education funds, including approximately 16,000 local school districts, and 3,200 colleges and universities.
- Prior to the passage of Title IX in 1972, some tax-supported colleges did not admit women, athletic scholarships were rare, and math and science were realms reserved for boys.
- Girls were encouraged to become teachers and nurses, but not doctors or principals; women rarely were awarded tenure and even more rarely appointed college presidents.
- Sexual harassment was excused because "boys will be boys," but if a student became pregnant, her formal education ended.
- Before Title IX, female athletes at the University of Michigan sold apples at football games so that they could compete for the school, which did not have a budget for women, and female gymnasts at the University of Minnesota had to rely on their male counterparts to provide them with leftover tape.
- Graduate professional schools openly discriminated against women; being female was seen as a pre-existing condition that made them unqualified.

Life at School

- Gayle Warwick was voted the school's most athletic student in her senior year, having earned letters in five different sports and earned three state championships.
- The athletic fields on which she played were considerably better than those provided to her older sister, and the referees who called the games actually liked working the girls' games, without considering it a "punishment."
- In 1972, fewer than 295,000 girls participated in high school varsity athletics, accounting for just 7 percent of all varsity athletes.
- In 1992, female participation exceeded one million, including the traditional male sports of wrestling, weightlifting, rugby, and boxing.
- Parents eagerly watched their daughters on the playing fields, courts, and on television; Gayle's father scheduled his work around her soccer and field hockey games.
- But as far as Gayle was concerned, her greatest achievement was a full-ride scholarship offer from Duke University in Durham, North Carolina, to study biochemistry, not to mention the scholarships offered to her by Florida State, Vanderbilt, and Virginia Tech to play field hockey.

- She had tried to do both sports and biochemistry, and played for Duke's field hockey team her freshman year, but realized that her real interest was in lab research.
- Now a junior with half a dozen science classes under her belt, she had fallen in love with the exploratory study of essential fatty acids such as omega-3s and the role they played in the human inflammatory system.

Gayle loved to work in the science lab.

- Considerable information had already emerged concerning infant brain development and fatty acids.
- Now, if science could link omega-3s to the body's inflammatory receptors, Gayle was convinced the impact on medicine would be huge.
- She was convinced this opportunity would have passed her by without Title IX; her success was exactly the result the bill's sponsors had intended.
- The first person to introduce Title IX in Congress was its author and chief Senate sponsor, Senator Birch Bayh of Indiana.
- At the time, Senator Bayh was working on numerous constitutional issues related to women's rights, including the Equal Rights Amendment, to build "a powerful constitutional base from which to move forward in abolishing discriminatory differential treatment based on sex."
- But he was struggling to get the ERA out of committee, and the Higher Education Act of 1965 was on the floor for reauthorization.
- On February 28, 1972, Senator Bayh introduced the ERA's equal education provision as an amendment.
- In his remarks on the Senate floor, he said, "We are all familiar with the stereotype of women as pretty things who go to college to find a husband, go on to graduate school because they want a more interesting husband, and finally marry, have children, and never work again. The desire of many schools not to waste a 'man's place' on a woman stems from such stereotyped notions. But the facts absolutely contradict these myths about the 'weaker sex' and it is time to change our operating assumptions.
- "While the impact of this amendment would be far reaching, it is not a panacea. It is, however, an important first step in the effort to provide for the women of America something that is rightfully theirs—an equal chance to attend the schools of their choice, to develop the skills they want, and to apply those skills with the knowledge that they will have a fair chance to secure the jobs of their choice with equal pay for equal work."
- When President Nixon signed the bill, he spoke mostly about desegregation through busing, which was also a focus of the signed bill, but did not mention the expansion of educational access for women he had enacted.
- Opposition from established men's athletics emerged quickly and powerfully,
- Senator Bayh spent the next three years keeping watch over Health, Education & Welfare (HEW) to formulate regulations that carried out its legislative intent of eliminating discrimination in education on the basis of sex.
- When the regulations were finally issued in 1975, they were contested, and hearings were held by the House Subcommittee on Equal Opportunities on the discrepancies between the regulations and the law.
- Senator John Tower had already tried to reduce the impact of Title IX in 1974 with the Tower Amendment, which would have exempted revenue-producing sports from Title IX compliance.

Title IX gave girls an alternative to cheerleading.

- More than 20 lawsuits had been filed challenging the law.
- When HEW published the final regulations in June 1975, the National Collegiate Athletic Association (NCAA) claimed that the implementation of Title IX was illegal, even though America's colleges and universities were given an additional three years to comply.
- Despite the regulatory delays, the concept behind Title IX began having an impact, even in sporting venues not under the aegis of Title IX.
- The Boston Marathon began officially accepting women contestants in 1972; in 1992, 1,893 entrants—nearly 20 percent—in the race were female.
- Women had hardly been welcomed with open arms.
- When Katherine Switzer, a 20-year-old Syracuse University junior, showed up to run the Boston Marathon in 1967, her goal was to prove to her coach that she was capable of running 26.2 miles.
- Women were not allowed to officially run the marathon, but no one had any reason to question "K. V. Switzer" as her name appeared on the application.
- In the middle of the race, Jock Semple, a Boston Marathon official, jumped off a truck, ran toward Switzer and shouted, "Get the hell out of my race."
- Another female athlete, Marge Snyder, said, "I played on my Illinois high school's first varsity tennis team from 1968 to 1970. We were 56-0 over my three years. We were permitted to compete as long as we made no efforts to publicize our accomplishments and personally paid for our uniforms and equipment."
- For Gayle, the celebration of Title IX also embraced a number of less tangible victories, including a study that showed a direct correlation between increased athletic participation and reduced obesity rates.
- In addition, athletics in high school had taught her how to be a member of a team—a valuable skill, for someone determined to collaborate on major science discoveries—and how to handle the personal disappointment of a bad game or a close loss.
- School athletics had given her a strong body frame, which added to her confidence and allowed her to take risks that translated into opportunities.
- "It's a different world now," Gayle told her parents, "and just imagine the opportunities that will be open to my children."

Life in the Community: Tampa, Florida

- Located on the Gulf of Mexico, Tampa, Florida, experienced dramatic growth during the second half of the twentieth century as both a retirement and vacation destination.
- Once inhabited by indigenous peoples, notably the Tocobaga and the Pohoy, Tampa was briefly explored by Spanish explorers in the early sixteenth century, but there were no permanent American or European settlements within the current city limits until after the United States had acquired Florida from Spain in 1819.
- "Tampa" may mean "sticks of fire" in the language of the Calusa, a Native American tribe, and be a reference to the many lightning strikes that the area receives during the summer months.
- Other historians claim the name means "the place to gather sticks."
- In 1824, the Army established a frontier outpost near the mouth of the Hillsborough River, which provided protection to pioneers from the nearby Seminole population.
- Tampa grew slowly until the 1880s, when railroad links, the discovery of phosphate, and the arrival of the cigar industry jumpstarted Tampa's development.
- In 1891, Henry B. Plant built a lavish 500+ room, quarter-mile long, $2.5 million eclectic/Moorish Revival-style luxury resort hotel called the Tampa Bay Hotel among 150 acres of manicured gardens along the banks of the Hillsborough River.
- The resort featured a race track, a heated indoor pool, a golf course, a 2,000-seat auditorium, tennis courts, stables, hunting and fishing tours, and electric lights and telephones in every

Luxury hotel in Tampa emphasized the city's importance in the early 1900s.

room, plus the first elevator in town and exotic art collectibles which Plant had shipped in from around the world.

- Tampa became an important city by the early 1900s and adopted the mantle of "Cigar Capital of the World" long before production peaked in 1929, when over 500 million cigars were hand-rolled in the city.
- During the Depression, profits from the bolita lotteries and Prohibition-era bootlegging led to the development of several organized crime factions in the city.
- The era of rampant and open corruption ended in the 1950s, when the Senator Kefauver's traveling organized crime hearings resulted in sensational misconduct trials of several local officials.
- During the 1950s and 1960s, Tampa saw record-setting population growth spurred by major expansion of the city's highways and bridges, bringing thousands into the city and spawning two of the most popular tourist attractions in the area—Busch Gardens and Lowry Park.
- In 1956, the University of South Florida was established in North Tampa, spurring major development in this section of the city.
- The biggest recent growth in the city was the development of New Tampa, which started in 1988 when the city annexed a mostly rural area of 24 square miles between I-275 and I-75.
- Tampa was part of the metropolitan area most commonly referred to as the Tampa Bay Area that was part of the Tampa-St. Petersburg-Clearwater, Florida Metropolitan Statistical Area (MSA) that embraced 2.7 million residents, making it the fourth-largest in the Southeastern United States, behind Miami, Washington, DC, and Atlanta.
- That population supports a number of sports teams, such as the Buccaneers of the National Football League, the Lightning of the National Hockey League, the Rowdies of the North American Soccer League and the Rays in Major League Baseball.

The Gregg Typing
Keyboard Wall Chart

HISTORICAL SNAPSHOT
1992

- Singer Paul Simon toured South Africa after the end of the cultural boycott
- A Miami, Florida, jury convicted former Panamanian ruler Manuel Noriega of assisting Colombia's cocaine cartel
- Acquittal of four police officers in the Rodney King beating criminal trial triggered massive rioting in Los Angeles that lasted for six days, resulting in 53 deaths and over a $1 billion in damages
- The Space Shuttle *Endeavour* made its maiden flight as a replacement for a lost Space Shuttle
- The first World Ocean Day was celebrated, coinciding with the Earth Summit held in Rio de Janeiro, Brazil
- Boris Yeltsin announced that Russia would stop targeting cities in the U.S. and its allies with nuclear weapons, while George H. W. Bush announced that the U.S. and its allies would discontinue targeting Russia and the remaining communist states
- Iraq refused a U.N. inspection team access to the Iraqi Ministry of Agriculture, said to have archives related to illegal weapons activities
- Nirvana's *Nevermind* album was No. 1 in the U.S. Billboard 200 chart, establishing the widespread popularity of the Grunge movement of the 1990s
- Farm Aid Live took place in Irving, Texas, hosted by Willie Nelson; artists performing included John Mellencamp, Neil Young, and Paul Simon
- The Disney animated movie *Aladdin* was the highest-grossing picture of the year; *Unforgiven* captured the Academy Award for Best Picture
- Dr. Mae Jemison became the first African-American woman to travel into space, aboard the Space Shuttle *Endeavour*
- The average price of gas was $1.05 per gallon
- Green tea was discovered to contain an important anti-cancer agent
- Walter Annenberg donated more than 50 Impressionist paintings worth $1 billion to the Metropolitan Museum of Art in New York City
- Operation Julin was the last nuclear test conducted by the U.S. at the Nevada Test Site
- After performing a song protesting alleged child abuse by the Catholic Church, Sinéad O'Connor ripped up a photo of Pope John Paul II on *Saturday Night Live*, sparking controversy
- NBC Television selected Jay Leno to replace late night talk show host Johnny Carson
- The Church of England voted to allow women to become priests
- A coalition of United Nations peacekeepers led by the U.S. was formed to provide humanitarian aid and establish peace in Somalia
- Extremist Hindu activists demolished Babri Masjid—a sixteenth-century mosque in Ayodhya, India—leading to widespread violence, including the Mumbai Riots, in all killing over 1,500 people

Selected Prices

Alarm Clock..$9.99

Car Seat...$65.00

Christmas Tree, Artificial...$124.99

Comforter...$26.88

Lawn Mower..$289.00

Leggings...$15.00

Light Bulb, Halogen..$8.96

Microwave Oven..$99.00

Shower Curtain $19.77

Videotape, Three Blank..$8.49

"High School Football: At Elizabeth High School, It's a Matter of Getting From Here to There," Robert Lipsyte, *The New York Times*, November 27, 1992:

ELIZABETH, N.J.—The sounds and rhythms change at Elizabeth High School as the squeaky slap of leather on hardwood replaces the meaty thud of colliding bodies. The football season ended yesterday and practice begins for the girls' and boys' basketball teams today.

But for the coaches, the purpose of all this noise and sweat remains the same: keep the 4,300 students of New Jersey's largest high school interested and involved until they are prepared to escape this tough port city of 110,000, to college or to meaningful work.

Most coaches here believe, perhaps self-servingly, that a successful athletic program is the secular church of this predominately Hispanic and black school, even for those who only worship. And that the coaches, overwhelmingly white men, are the ministers of a higher order.

Basketball brings particular promise and pressure. The boys' coach, Ben Candeloni, is routinely expected to field a powerhouse. He has sent players to major colleges and the National Basketball Association. The girls' coach, Shannon Luby, may have a harder job: persuading historically oppressed young women from minority groups to assert themselves, even as she fights her own Title IX battles in a department that would prefer a man in her job.

Continued

"High School Football: . . . (Continued)

The pressure is still on the football coach, Jerry Moore, who must repay the kids from whom he demanded a season of intensity and pain. He has to help them get into colleges that will pay them to play. The recruiters have been lumbering through the halls all week.

Of his 22 seniors, Moore figures he has six blue-chippers who will quickly go to major schools, another four or five who will be harder sells and another half-dozen who won't be placed, in prep schools or junior colleges, much before February.

The star, six-foot-five-inch linebacker DuLayne Morgan has already been offered admission by Duke, and may also consider North Carolina, U.C.L.A., Rutgers, Florida State, Syracuse, Michigan, and Notre Dame. DuLayne had 980 on the college boards as a junior and a 3.25 average in the advanced honors program. He was rated one of the top 25 prospects in the country.

But there are young men who need Moore to persuade a college to take a chance, to understand that uneven play or erratic grades or low body weight reflects problems that may only be solved by being away at college, away from a violent home, a drunken mother, secure in a place offering three meals a day and a sense of worth.

Moore says that his team, which ended its season yesterday with an anticlimactic 13-12 loss to Cranford, was his most talented ever. So why did it end the season with a 5-4-1 record and two losses to archrival Union?

"Could have been the coaching," snapped Moore, who was pleased to be reminded that he had lost his quarterback and his tailback before the season began and had to depend on the remarkable though raw gifts of a 14-year-old freshman, Al Hawkins. Quarterback Hawkins suffered a sprained shoulder in the next-to-last game, but should be ready to throw his 85-mile-per-hour fastball for the baseball coach, Ray Korn, this spring.

The school's brassy, classy marching band, which often gives the impression that it thinks football is the sideshow to its performance, didn't win the big one, either, finishing third overall in its group at a big competition three weeks ago at Giants Stadium. But its crowd-pleasing "Carmen" routine won best music award.

At Elizabeth, however, victory is often measured not by winning and losing, but by survival, what Jerry Moore calls "getting from here to there," a phrase that has informed his coaching for the past 20 years.

In 1972, as a 30-year-old basketball coach at a suburban, predominately white Somerville High, Moore was far more authoritarian and his West Virginia twang was more pronounced.

When a group of black students defied the principal and stormed out of school to protest what they considered unequal racial treatment, Moore warned his basketball team that anyone who joined the demonstration would never again play for him.

Continued

"High School Football: . . . *(Continued)*

Moore's best player, a black guard named Ken Hayes, said: "Coach, I have to go out because those are the people I pass on the way home. You can help me here, but every day I got to get from here to there."

When Moore hesitated, Hayes said, "If you let me go, I'll bring everybody back into school in 30 minutes."

Moore says now: "I always reflect back on that day. Look at the decision I was forcing on those black players. Give up a shot at a major college scholarship or go against the people in their community. How can I do that?

"My kids at Elizabeth, some of them walk two miles past shootings and drug deals, they have to go from here to there every day, and you got to be sure you don't make too many rules that get in the way of their survival."

Twenty years ago, Moore defied his principal and sent Ken Hayes out to join the demonstration. Hayes, who went on to college ball and is now a law enforcement officer, brought the protesters back inside within 20 minutes. They met with the administration, and the conflict subsided.

"To this day I don't know who was right in all that," says Moore. "I only know it turned me around. When I deal with a kid, I always think first, he's got to get from here to there. How can I stay out of his way? How can I help him get there?"

Letters, *Syracuse Herald Journal* (New York), October 6, 1992:

Enough is enough
When I first read about the boy who was playing girls' field hockey, I kind of laughed. When I heard he might not be able to play anymore, I didn't laugh. Isn't the NHL's Tampa Bay Lightning giving a 20-year-old female a fair chance? Yes, they are. Aren't the men of the NHL physically bigger, stronger? Yes, there are woman who can play with men in the men's game; the boy who wants to play on a girls' field hockey team has to be examined by weight, age, height and be okayed by panel of judges. This is ludicrous. I'm tired of hearing about women's equal rights. Let's put it this way: Holland Patent, you are now much better team and Tampa Bay isn't.

—P. Coleman, Syracuse

Female athletes deserving
Should males be allowed to compete in primarily female sports and vice versa? If considered as a "right," there can be no doubt that the potential to ruin female sport dictates disapproval of any such mandate.

Continued

Letters, . . . *(Continued)*

In professional sports, male golfers and tennis players could dominate on the women's tour and this sort of thing should not be allowed.

A better way to phrase the question: should upward mobility be allowed for female athletes? For the gifted and competitive-minded female athletes, often the outlets available are more recreational than competitive.

Should the female athletes be allowed to test themselves by moving to more competitive levels? Of course they should.

Males do not belong in women's sports, but allowing women to compete in men's sports is necessary, not only to provide outlets where none exist for female athletes, but also to allow females to test themselves through performance.

—Don Gates, North Syracuse

Stick to their own teams
Should boys be allowed to play on girls teams, and vice versa? Certainly NOT.

Feminism or civil rights are not justifiable reasons in the world of sports from the amateur to the professional.

Fifteen-year-old Greg Crumb playing for the Holland Patent High School field hockey team is absurd. It's happened in other school areas, but approval makes a mockery of sports. The object of varsity sports in schools is two divisions. How can one take pride in being, say, the best girls' team if a boy is on the team?

Would you permit a girl in your school to wrestle against boys? Would there be different rules? How does a boy grasp a girl in the chest or crotch? And vice versa?

Football? How can a girl compete against hulking 250-pounders? Boxing: Forget it. Girls would be cut to shreds. And in other contact sports—lacrosse, basketball and soccer—girls or women wouldn't stand a chance.

—Lou Defichy

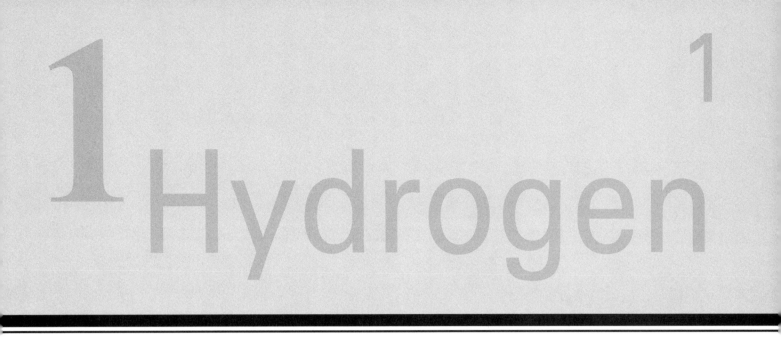

1994: Hydrogen Fuel Cell Visionary

Theater major Marie Moffett became a mechanic in Macon, Georgia, to earn money, and discovered that her true passion was working toward pollution free, hydrogen fuel cell cars.

Life at Home

∞ During Marie Moffett's sophomore year at Oglethorpe University in Atlanta, she applied for a summer job building theater sets; the only other position open required her to repair cars.

∞ Necessity followed form and function, and she soon became a mechanic who spent as much time as possible under the hood of a car, wistfully dreaming of how to make automobiles as efficient as possible.

∞ She imagined a car that didn't use vanishing fossil fuels to function, but was capable of fast starts, long-distance travel and high style.

∞ The car of the future should be both smart and sexy, she believed.

∞ A decade later—in 1990—she decided the answer was hydrogen fuel cells that emitted only vapor out the tailpipe.

∞ Hydrogen fuel cells made possible a car that was largely pollution-free, was not dependent on fossil fuels, was cheap to run, and most important—because it had no engine or traditional transmission—could be designed a million new and different ways.

∞ The car she envisioned wasn't exactly a car but the underpinnings of one, sort of a skateboard that encased the car's power and control system, which could be kept for decades while customers shuffled car bodies as tastes changed.

∞ And the bodies, too, would be radically different, with the windshield extending all the way down to the floor, if desired, because the car's essential systems are kept underfoot.

∞ The brake pedal and accelerator could be replaced with electronically controlled steering using hand grips on the wheel.

Marie Moffett invested her time and money in her vision of a hydrogen-fueled car.

∞ But it was not going to be easy: similar to the early days of autos in 1900, there was a race among France, Germany, and the United States; Japan had its own $11 billion initiative called New Sunshine to be the leader in hydrogen power.

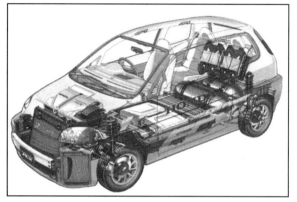

The car of the future would have interchangeable bodies, and a power source that could last for decades.

∞ Marie fully expected that the blending of technologies would result in a hybrid using both hydrogen and electricity initially.

∞ She knew, taken together, the technologies would move the automobile from the machine age to the digital age and result in a car that emitted no carbon dioxide.

∞ By then, she had earned a master's degree in engineering and gone to work designing the car of the future—and repairing cars for her mechanically challenged brothers.

∞ Marie was the last of seven children; her older sister was 26 years old when she was born.

∞ She was so much younger, Marie was treated like a talkative house pet who could be dragged to every adult event without a thought; hers was a resource-filled childhood jammed with events and adventures that required Marie to grow up quickly if she wanted to keep up.

∞ As a result, she knew few children her age and joined an adult theater group when she was 12; at 16 she entered college, and at 26, she was convinced she was being called to help solve the world's energy crisis.

∞ Four years later, reports of acid rain, dying forests and global warming all cried out for a carbonless solution to America's energy needs.

∞ She first dabbled with the potential of solar energy, then thermal, then wind, before discovering the potential of hydrogen fuel cells.

∞ Hydrogen—an invisible, tasteless, colorless gas—is the most abundant element in the universe, and when combined with a fuel cell, highly efficient.

The challenge was to efficiently and economically harness hydrogen as a fuel source.

∞ Fuel cells are electrochemical engines that combine hydrogen and oxygen in a flameless process to produce electricity, heat and pure, distilled water.

∞ The hydrogen fuel cell operated similarly to a battery: it had two electrodes, an anode and a cathode, separated by a membrane; oxygen passed over one electrode and hydrogen over the other.

∞ The hydrogen reacted to a catalyst on the electrode anode that converted the hydrogen gas into negatively charged electrons (e-) and positively charged ions (H+).

∞ The electrons flowed out of the cell to be used as electrical energy.

∞ The hydrogen ions moved through the electrolyte membrane to the cathode electrode where they combined with oxygen and the electrons to produce water; unlike batteries, fuel cells never run out.

∞ The problem with hydrogen as an energy source was devising an economical way of making the fuel and how to efficiently store it in a tightly controlled container.

∞ The first fuel cell was conceived in 1839 by Sir William Robert Grove, a Welsh judge, inventor and physicist who mixed hydrogen and oxygen in the presence of an electrolyte and produced electricity and water.

∞ The invention, which later became known as a fuel cell, didn't produce enough electricity to be useful.

∞ In 1889, the term "fuel cell" was first coined by Ludwig Mond and Charles Langer, who attempted to build a working fuel cell using air and industrial coal gas.

∞ In the 1920s, fuel cell research in Germany paved the way to the development of the carbonate cycle and solid oxide fuel cells of today.

∞ In 1932, engineer Francis T. Bacon began his vital research into fuel cells.

∞ Early cell designers used porous platinum electrodes and sulfuric acid as the electrolyte bath.

∞ Using platinum was expansive, and sulfuric acid was corrosive.

∞ Bacon improved on the expensive platinum catalysts with a hydrogen and oxygen cell using a less corrosive alkaline electrolyte and inexpensive nickel electrodes.

∞ It took Bacon until 1959 to perfect his design, when he demonstrated a five-kilowatt fuel cell that could power a welding machine.

∞ In October of 1959, Harry Karl Ihrig, an engineer for the Allis-Chalmers Manufacturing Company, demonstrated a 20-horsepower tractor that was the first vehicle ever powered by a fuel cell.

∞ During the early 1960s, General Electric produced the fuel cell-based electrical power system for NASA's *Gemini* and *Apollo* space capsules.

∞ The Space Shuttle's electricity was provided by fuel cells, and the same fuel cells provided drinking water for the crew.

∞ NASA funded more than 200 research contracts exploring fuel cell technology, bringing the technology to a level now viable for the private sector.

∞ The first bus powered by a fuel cell was completed in 1993, and several fuel cell cars were being built in Europe and in the United States.

Life at Work

∞ For Marie Moffett, hydrogen represented the space-age fuel of the future, so drawing upon her theater experience and her passion for a new energy policy, she traveled the nation telling the hydrogen energy story and personally investing in ideas that excited her.

∞ "The Space Shuttle already used hydrogen fuel cells to provide on-board electricity and drinking water; BMW operated experimental buses using fuel cells.

∞ And one of the leading firms working on hydrogen-powered cars had developed its technology to provide energy underwater.

∞ Energy Partners, based in West Palm Beach, Florida, was founded by John H. Perry, Jr., a former newspaper and cable television owner who introduced computerized typesetting into the newsroom.

∞ In the 1960s, Perry began producing small manned submarines for the offshore oil industry, eventually cornering 90 percent of the market.

∞ He also built the hydrogen fuel cell-powered Hydrolab, in which astronauts trained underwater for the weightlessness of space, and began to experiment with fuel cells in submarines.

∞ "The fuel cell," he told Marie, "is the silicon chip of the hydrogen age."

∞ Speaking to college groups, business forums and economic developer conclaves on behalf of Energy Partners and hydrogen fuel cells became an all-consuming job.

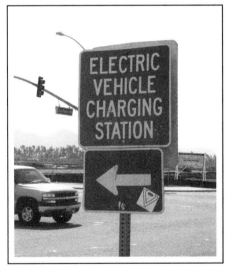

An electric car could be quickly recharged at stations across the country.

∞ America needed to understand the potential of this energy source, she told her brothers and sisters when she moved back to Atlanta to take advantage of the city's airport, rail and road transportation.

∞ She quickly learned that the explosion of the *Hindenburg* cast a pall over hydrogen, and the words "fuel cell" caused considerable confusion.

  ∞ Fuel cells were bulky and very expensive, until the development of proton exchange membranes, or PEMs for short.

  ∞ A PEM was a type of Teflon that looked like a regular sheet of transparent plastic.

Unfortunately, hydrogen often was thought of in connection with the 1937 Hindenburg disaster.

  ∞ When treated with platinum as a catalyst, it split hydrogen and separated out its electrons to form electricity.

  ∞ A series of PEM's stacked one on top of another like layers of meat in a sandwich produced a fuel cell that was light, small and potentially cheap enough to use in a car.

  ∞ After all, hydrogen can be burned in an internal-combustion engine.

  ∞ BMW, Mercedes-Benz, and Mazda all had prototype internal-combustion cars working on hydrogen fuel, but when used instead to produce electricity in a fuel cell, it will take that same car twice as far.

  ∞ A fuel cell in an electric car could increase its range to about 400 miles, and reduce its recharge time to two or three minutes.

Marie realized technology was not standing in her way, but marketing and economics were.

  ∞ Energy Partners planned to build a "proof of concept" car, rather than a production prototype, running on two hydrogen fuel cells.

  ∞ With it, Marie hoped to demonstrate that such cars can be ready for the mass market by the end of the decade, rather than 20 years from then, as most experts predicted.

  ∞ One of the many advantages of hydrogen as an energy carrier was fuel flexibility: hydrogen can be made from just about anything.

  ∞ It could be reformed either aboard the car or at the service station from methanol, ethanol or natural gas.

∞ It could even be produced by using solar power to electrolyze water.

∞ It seemed the perfect fantasy: a car running basically on sun and water.

∞ But outside Munich, Germany, an experimental power plant was already producing hydrogen from solar power and water.

∞ Solar technology may have been nowhere near the stage where it could power a family car directly, but its potential to power the car indirectly, by producing hydrogen, had now been established.

  ∞ The problem was building a market—at the right price—that was big enough to justify the large production runs that would make electric cars more economical.

  ∞ Marie came to realize it was economics, not science, that dominated this whole issue.

  ∞ The hydrogen-powered cars had to be affordable, which was even trickier when gasoline was cheaper than bottled water.

  ∞ Department of Energy studies indicated that fuel cells cost $141 per kilowatt; the car industry believed fuel cell engines couldn't compete with conventional ones until they cost less than $50 a kilowatt.

  ∞ Ford Motor Company said it could mass-produce hydrogen cars once 10,000 natural gas-reforming pumps at $250,000 to $1.5 million each were installed at filling stations around the country.

Marie's dream is that everyone would own a vehicle with a fuel cell engine.

∞ Marie continued to bet on the future, making 50 speeches a year while investing $1.6 million of her own money.

Life in the Community: Atlanta, Georgia

∞ Atlanta, Georgia, the capital and most populous city in the state, with a metropolitan population approaching six million.

∞ Like many areas in the Sun Belt, the Atlanta region had experienced explosive growth since the 1970s, thanks to its role as a primary transportation hub of the Southeastern United States, including highways, railroads, and airports.

∞ It was an industrial legacy dating back to the Civil War, when Atlanta served as a vital nexus of the railroads and hence a hub for the distribution of military supplies.

∞ On September 7, 1864, Union General William T. Sherman ordered the city's civilian population to evacuate, then torched the buildings of Atlanta to the ground, sparing only the city's churches and hospitals.

∞ In 1868, the Georgia State Capital was moved from Milledgeville to Atlanta because of the latter's superior rail transportation network; it was the fifth location of the capital of the State of Georgia.

∞ On December 15, 1939, Atlanta hosted the film premiere of *Gone with the Wind*, the epic film based on Atlanta's Margaret Mitchell's best-selling novel *Gone with the Wind*.

∞ "Several stars of the film, including Clark Gable, Vivien Leigh, Olivia de Havilland, and its legendary producer, David O. Selznick, attended the gala event, which was held at Loew's Grand Theatre.

∞ When the date of the Atlanta premiere of *Gone with the Wind* approached, Hattie McDaniel, who had played Mammy, told director Victor Fleming she would not be able to go, when in actuality she did not want to cause trouble because of the violent racism in Atlanta at the time.

∞ During World War II, companies such as the Bell Aircraft Company and the manufacture of railroad cars were dedicated to the war effort.

∞ Shortly after the war, the Federal Centers for Disease Control and Prevention was founded in Atlanta.

∞ During the 1960s, Atlanta was a major organizing center of the Civil Rights Movement, with Dr. Martin Luther King, Jr., Ralph David Abernathy, and students from Atlanta's historically Black colleges and universities played major roles in the movement's leadership.

∞ Two of the most important civil rights organizations, the Southern Christian Leadership Conference and the Student Nonviolent Coordinating Committee, had their national headquarters in Atlanta.

∞ Despite racial tension during the Civil Rights era, Atlanta's political and business leaders labored to foster Atlanta's image as "the city too busy to hate."

∞ In 1961, Atlanta Mayor Ivan Allen, Jr., became one of the few Southern white mayors to support desegregation of his city's public schools.

∞ African-American Atlantans demonstrated their growing political influence with the election of the first African-American mayor, Maynard Jackson, in 1973.

∞ In 1990, Atlanta was selected as the site for the 1996 Summer Olympic Games, and undertook several major construction projects to improve the city's parks, sports facilities, and transportation.

∞ By the 1990s, Atlanta was so unruly it was considered to be an archetype for cities experiencing rapid growth and urban sprawl.

∞ Unlike most major cities, metropolitan Atlanta does not have any natural boundaries, such as an ocean, lakes, or mountains, that might constrain growth.

HISTORICAL SNAPSHOT
1994

∞ The North American Free Trade Agreement (NAFTA) was established

∞ In Detroit, Michigan, Nancy Kerrigan was clubbed on the right leg by an assailant, under orders from figure skating rival Tonya Harding's ex-husband

∞ The Superhighway Summit was held at UCLA, the first conference to discuss the growing information superhighway

∞ President Bill Clinton and Russian President Boris Yeltsin signed the Kremlin Accords, which stopped the preprogrammed aiming of nuclear missiles toward each country's targets, and also provided for the dismantling of the nuclear arsenal in Ukraine

∞ In South Carolina, Shannon Faulkner became the first female cadet to attend The Citadel, but soon dropped out

∞ Byron De La Beckwith was convicted of the 1963 murder of Civil Rights leader Medgar Evers

∞ Edvard Munch's painting *The Scream* was stolen in Oslo

∞ Aldrich Ames and his wife were charged with spying for the Soviet Union by the U.S. Department of Justice

∞ In *Campbell v. Acuff-Rose Music, Inc.*, the Supreme Court ruled that parodies of an original work are generally covered by the doctrine of fair use

∞ *Schindler's List* won seven Oscars including Best Picture and Best Director at the 66th Academy Awards, hosted by Whoopi Goldberg

∞ The journal *Nature* reported the finding in Ethiopia of the first complete *Australopithecus afarensis* skull

∞ Kurt Cobain, songwriter and front man for the band Nirvana, was found dead, apparently of a single, self-inflicted gunshot wound

∞ The Red Cross estimated that hundreds of thousands of Tutsis had been killed in the Rwanda massacre

∞ Nelson Mandela was inaugurated as South Africa's first black president

∞ Nicole Brown Simpson and Ronald Goldman were murdered outside the Simpson home in Los Angeles, California; O.J. Simpson was charged in the killings

∞ The 1994–1995 Major League Baseball strike ended the 1994 MLB season

∞ President Clinton signed the Assault Weapons Ban, which banned the manufacture of new weapons with certain features for a period of 10 years

∞ The first version of Web browser Netscape Navigator was released

Selected Prices

Alarm Clock $9.99
Car Seat $65.00
Christmas Tree, Artificial $124.99
Comforter $26.88
Lawn Mower $289.00
Leggings $15.00
Light Bulb, Halogen $8.96
Microwave Oven $99.00
Shower Curtain $19.77
Videotape, Three Blank $8.49

"Next in Car Fuel: Hydrogen," *Cedar Rapids Gazette*, February 8, 1993:

Hydrogen power is the Holy Grail of clean energy; it doesn't pollute and it's universally available. But until recently, it's been too expensive for widespread use.

Now, a Florida company has invented a simplified fuel cell that can eliminate the internal combustion engine and run a car on hydrogen, and Energy Partners, Inc., says it's just the beginning.

"We think we can have an economically competitive car by the end of the century," says owner John Perry, Jr., who runs Perry Oceanographics. "Eventually this could replace all fossil fuels." The company's experimental hydrogen-fueled "Green Car" is scheduled to be unveiled in March.

Company vice president Mitch Ewan briefed this staff of environmentally oriented Vice President Al Gore before the election, he said, and the company has also worked closely with Sen. Tom Harkin, (D-Iowa), a strong supporter of hydrogen as a nonpolluting power source.

A fuel cell, although it sounds like some type of battery, is actually an electrochemical engine. It takes a fuel, hydrogen in this case, and pumps it through a chemically impregnated plate, generating an electrical current and the system's only waste product—water vapor.

And unlike internal combustion engines, it has no moving parts.

Energy Partners has supplied NASA with material for its Space Shuttle fuel cells, but the technology used in space is too cumbersome for widespread use on Earth, Perry says.

So the company set out to design a fuel cell that could be mass-produced in a factory. The company's fuel cell eliminates heat and hard-to-handle chemicals that make fuel cells unsuitable for most mundane uses, replacing them with a simple plastic sheet impregnated with chemical chains and platinum.

By the year 2000, Perry believes, the price of a fuel cell car engine could be down to about $3,000 and would last twice as long as gasoline engines. And cars are not the only use. Eventually, a television-sized hydrogen fuel cell can supply all the power needed by an average home.

There are several problems, Ewan says. To further reduce the size and weight, the company is working with the California designer to install fuel cells in a flying wing. The aircraft would use solar power to produce the hydrogen and could theoretically stay in the air for two years.

Fuel cell production requires far tighter tolerances than current engines, which means the manufacturing process must have very high precision.

Another problem is storing the hydrogen. The Green Car gets a respectable 120 miles per tank, but that's not enough for most consumers. So the company is working on techniques of absorption—adhesion to a surface that would bind the hydrogen gas to solid materials in the tank.

If it works, a full-sized van could eventually get 1,500 miles per tank, says Ewan.

"Gasoline Pollution Is Serious, Too," Marvin Legator and Amanda Daniel, *Galveston Daily News*, June 8, 1996:

Question: How safe is our gasoline? It is my understanding that one of the major sources of pollution is gasoline. How dangerous is gasoline, and what can we do about it?

Answer: Gasoline is a complex chemical mixture containing more than 1,000 possible substances. Gasoline vapors are released at bulking installations, refineries, during tank and barge transportation and when refueling automobiles at service stations.

According to the U.S. Environmental Protection Agency, approximately 40 percent of all gasoline releases occur during refueling. Gasoline represents a major source of exposure to the general population of toxic substances, including several known carcinogens such as benzene and butadiene.

Most experts agree that it's likely gasoline will be the dominant motor vehicle fuel well into the next century, although General Motors has developed an electric vehicle that is currently showing at select stops throughout the country.

This automobile uses no gasoline, no water and no spark plugs. It runs on a battery which remains charged for approximately 70 miles. This is a step in the right direction, and with further development may be the automobile of the future.

"EPA Unveils Plan to Reduce Acid Rain," *Salina Journal*, October 30, 1991:

The Environmental Protection Agency on Tuesday unveiled its plan to curb acid rain by forcing utilities to cut sulfur oxide emissions by 40 percent this decade.

EPA Administrator William Reilly estimated that the proposed rules would cost $4 billion annually by the year 2000. They will lead to sharp increases in electricity rates in the areas of the country that have the dirtiest coal-burning power plants, he said.

The new rules are expected to push up electricity rates about 1.5 percent nationwide, but much higher in some areas, Reilly said. He maintained the higher cost "will be more than offset" by the environmental benefits from controlling acid rain.

The proposed regulations, which are expected to be made final early next year, implement the Clean Air Act passed by Congress last year.

Acid rain is the name given to the industrial pollution that may be carried long distances in the atmosphere before returning to the earth as rain, snow, or soot, killing aquatic life. Sulfur dioxide emissions, mainly from coal-burning power plants in the Midwest, are a major cause of acid rain.

1999: Standardized Testing Skeptic

New York City elementary school teacher Viola Chadusky felt that the movement toward higher standards and tougher tests focused on measuring the wrong things.

Life at Home

- Viola Chadusky was born in Syracuse, New York, on September 17, 1959.
- She was a bright, vivacious girl who grew up wanting to make a difference in the world.
- As a college student, she chose the classroom as a place to start.
- Viola's mother, Anna Fisselbrand, was from nearby Manlius, where the family had lived for generations.
- Anna became a registered nurse and went to work in 1956 at the State University of New York's Upstate Medical Center, where she met Alfred Chadusky, an accountant at the hospital; they married in 1958.
- Al had grown up in Rochester and graduated from Columbia College in New York City in 1955.
- By the time Viola turned five, she had a sister, Anna, and a brother, Tom.
- Viola's parents sent her to a private kindergarten, then to a Catholic school in first grade.
- She was so excited before her first day at school she had trouble going to sleep.
- Girls wore a uniform consisting of a plaid, pleated skirt and a white blouse; boys wore black pants, a white shirt and a plaid bowtie.
- Viola was a good student and liked to play teacher with her siblings.
- Whenever she was alone, she read.

Teacher Viola Chadusky questioned the value of standardized testing.

- When her friends came over, they played with Barbie dolls or talked about the Beatles; her best friend Marcia liked Paul, but Viola liked John.
- Soon their musical interests drifted to the Monkees, who had their own television show from 1966 to 1968.
- The intrigue of the made-for-television band was heightened by the fact that the show debuted in color.
- Until then, television shows were almost always in black and white, and color television sets were just becoming available.
- Marcia's parents were the first on the block to get a color TV, so Viola stopped by often.
- Her parents decided in 1969 that it was too expensive to send their kids to Catholic schools, and enrolled them in public schools in the fall.
- For the first time, Viola had to choose what to wear to school each day.
- She didn't think much about "what she wanted to be when she grew up" as she moved from junior high into high school in 1973; she was more interested in hanging out with her friends.
- When they got together, she was often the one to steer them into their evening plans, and had a quick wit and a loud laugh.
- In a group, she wasn't always the one who talked the most, but when she spoke, people listened.
- Viola continued to read, and in tenth grade had an English teacher, Molly Peacock, who opened up her mind to authors new and old.

In Catholic school, Viola didn't think about what to wear.

Source: LOC # LC-USF34-083610-C

- When Viola first read Shakespeare, she was struck by the oddness of how words were spelled and strung together.
- But as Mrs. Peacock helped untangle the language, Viola marveled as she began to understand English as it was spoken in the 1600s.
- She read John Steinbeck's *The Grapes of Wrath*, in which she saw stark choices faced by many in the Great Depression.
- Watching Mrs. Peacock orchestrating her classroom through lively discussions led Viola to consider teaching as a career.
- While Viola had always earned good grades, she didn't consider herself very smart.
- But when she took her college aptitude tests in her junior year, she was surprised at having scored near the top, with especially high marks in English. Everyone else seemed to be able to write their papers effortlessly, while her first drafts were as painful as pulling fingernails.
- Second and third drafts were another matter; by that point, she could whip her words into shape.
- Her high scores were a big help in getting her a scholarship to New York University, which her family would not have been able to afford otherwise.

- She decided to major in education.
- Some of her classes were extremely dull and filled with a mind-numbing amount of jargon that she believed was more a way of showing status than conveying ideas.
- Her classes became more interesting as she entered her junior year, and her ability to write, speak and use her natural leadership skills helped her excel.
- During her senior year, she did an internship in a third-grade classroom in a New York public elementary school.
- It was an eye-opening experience.
- She met students who couldn't read, some who couldn't even speak English.
- Many were being raised by single mothers, or grandparents, who lacked the skills or time to help them.
- "I'm not in Syracuse anymore," Viola said to herself.
- She was hired in the fall of 1981 to teach fourth grade at a public school in New York City.
- During her first year of teaching, she came home many days and cried.
- The range of students' backgrounds and abilities was dizzying.
- Some of the brightest seemed bored, and she felt she wasn't doing enough to help those who were struggling.
- Discipline problems were constant.
- Administrators didn't seem to care, except when they dropped in to observe her class.
- Many of her fellow education graduates dropped out after their first year of teaching, but Viola persevered.
- As she talked with other teachers, she learned to focus better on her students by not carrying the guilt of all their failings.
- She did the best she could, which turned out to be pretty good, indeed.
- Her writing talent was a help, but she listened closely to other teachers, and when she could, she watched their techniques.
- A few of the other teachers were mediocre, but despite the school's failings, most of the teachers were committed and effective.
- Viola emphasized reading in her classroom, especially nonfiction.
- She kept lists of all the books students were reading during the year, helped organize book clubs, and arranged reading partners so her students could talk about what they read.
- As the years passed, she gained the respect of her peers, and even the administrators.
- She received recognition for her work at the end of her fifth year of teaching in 1997, and also completed her master's degree at the Teachers College of Columbia University in 1998, bumping up her pay to about $35,000 a year.

Life at Work

- Viola Chadusky accepted that standardized testing had always been part of teaching.
- However, she felt truly challenged when a movement for higher standards and tougher tests gained momentum in New York City in the mid-1990s.
- Viola often thought the tests were measuring the wrong things.
- Worse, the results tended to be used in ways for which the tests were not designed.
- On the other hand, she had seen from her students' work the paucity of their knowledge and the weakness of their skills.
- And, if nothing else, Viola had learned to work within the system to get the job done.
- Whatever tests the administration wanted, she would prepare her students for them.
- Most of her colleagues felt about the same way.
- Elementary schools already were under pressure from the city, with new and more stringent tests that could be used to fire principals or reassign teachers.

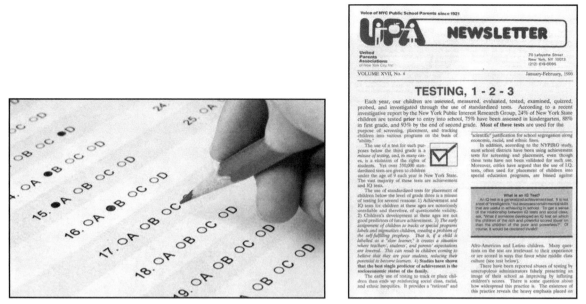

Standardized testing was becomming more important in 1999.

- But teachers' concerns about testing increased when they learned the State Board of Regents was planning to introduce a new, more rigorous set of language and math tests in 1999.
- Principals held long meetings with teachers in the fall of 1998 on what the new tests would mean.
- The old fill-in-the-blank test about a passage students had read was intended to measure minimum adequacy.
- About two-thirds of Viola's class had passed the test the previous year.
- Fourth-graders across the state would be taking three 55-minute tests over the course of three days starting January 12, 1999.
- This test differed from the usual in that it had an essay component.
- In one segment, students would read an excerpt and write a short essay; in another, teachers would read them a story, after which students would write an essay.
- The January 1999 test would be a practice run for students, but the next year it could be used to flunk and hold back fourth- and eighth-grade students.
- Viola's principal estimated that about 25 percent of the school's fourth-graders were in danger of failing.
- Although Viola didn't show her concern with her fourth-graders, she began spending more time on punctuation, rules of grammar, and—in anticipation of the stress—deep breathing exercises.
- She waited until November to describe the tests to her students.
- "They were stunned," she recalled.
- In the teachers' lounge, one third-grade teacher recounted how one of his borderline students had vowed "from now on I'll study more and I won't talk in class."
- The other teachers at the table laughed, but they also knew how devastating being held back would be on a child.
- Viola remembered the sleepless nights she had in her first years when she knew one of her children was going to be held back.
- She practiced with "Amos and Boris," a story about a mouse who is saved from drowning and carried home by Boris, a whale; years later, Amos finds Boris beached on the seashore and finds a way to return him to the sea.
- After reading the story, she told her students to jot down what each character did, and then to some of those words to write sentences describing the personality traits of the mouse and the whale.

- When two of her most worried students had done especially well, she praised them out loud.
- But many of her students didn't seem to grasp the task, and wrote garbled sentences.
- When Viola finally had a chance to retreat to the teachers' lounge, she could see that other teachers were worried, too.
- "They're not going to do their homework, and they know I can't make them," third-grade teacher Catherine Browne said. "I can't control what happens at home. I can't even reach a parent on the phone half the time."
- "Yeah," Viola said, "the public doesn't seem to get it. They look at our absentee rates and point their fingers at the schools. They wouldn't believe some of the reasons. I had one kid last year who skipped school so he could translate for his dad at the Immigration Office."
- The school remained open three hours in the mornings during most of the holiday break.
- About half the students attended the special sessions.
- In March, the results from the tests given back in January came in.
- Two-thirds of the fourth-graders at the school had flunked the English test, and it was only a small consolation to Viola that the failure rate in her classroom was 52 percent; she had hoped for at least a little more than that.
- She began thinking of new ways to teach that would strengthen her students' comprehension and writing skills.
- As much stress as the state test caused fourth-grade teachers, she heard even more complaints about the city's burgeoning schedule of multiple-choice tests.
- "And I don't know why they're so hot about these tests," a third-grade teacher said. "When was the last time anyone told kids to memorize the 50 states and their capitals? Not in the last 10 years. What's important is teaching the kids how to find the answers. Okay, they get them wrong half the time, but at least they're trying."
- At lunch, when fifth-grade teacher Henry Shekhanna said that the advocates of high-stakes testing would not be satisfied until they could put teachers' names and their performance scores on the school bulletin board, Viola said he was a crazy old man.
- "The union wouldn't stand for it," she said, "and even the regents would know it would backfire. People would never want to be teachers with that hanging over their heads."
- Henry, who was two years from retirement, had to have the last word: "That'll be yours to find out."

Life in the Community: New York City

- In 1995, big changes started happening in schools in New York City and across the state.
- By 1999, the number of tests students were required to take had increased, the tests became harder, and the stakes for failing higher.
- The changes started at the top.
- In 1995, the New York Board of Regents hired Richard P. Mills as its school superintendent, and Mayor Rudy Giuliani picked Rudy Crew as chancellor of New York City schools, the nation's largest school system, with more than one million students.
- Both Mills and Crew supported more stringent standards, more testing, and an end to "social promotion," the practice of promoting failing students from grade to grade so that they remain with their age group.
- New York became a leader in a national movement to set higher school standards and hold schools and students accountable to them through standardized tests.
- From 1993 to 1998, every state except Iowa had begun setting statewide standards.
- President Clinton wanted to create a national exam, and while states could use or ignore the federal test, it would set a national standard to allow parents, teachers and administrators to compare their schools with similar schools anywhere in the country where the national exam was adopted.

New York education leaders Rudy Crew, left, and Richard Mills supported stringent testing standards.

- Crew was able to convince the New York legislature to change a law to give him more power to appoint—and fire—superintendents of the system's 32 school districts—a move designed to curtail cronyism and make schools more accountable.
- He also negotiated a deal with the principals' union to end provisions providing lifetime job protection.
- But the biggest pressure on Crew was that New York City students weren't making the grade.
- They had lower test scores and higher dropout rates than students elsewhere in the state.
- And the pressure mounted.
- As Crew introduced new and tougher tests for students in the city, the state was imposing more stringent tests of its own.
- For Mills, a key piece for creating higher standards would be the New York State English Regents' Exam for seniors, who would have to hit a particular mark to graduate from high school.
- There were also new English tests for grades 4 and 8.
- "For teachers who have long been granted wide latitude in how they structured their lesson plans—especially those weaned on the flexible, child-centered approach popular since the 1960s—adapting to the new standards has required serious adjustment," *The New York Times* reported.
- The first round of the new state tests was set for Tuesday, January 12, 1999—one week after students returned from their holiday break.
- This would be a big change.
- With the old tests, fourth-graders read sentences or short passages, then filled in missing words from a list of multiple-choice answers.

- The new test, developed by a panel of 22 fourth-grade teachers, "moves from a focus on simple reading to an expectation that by the middle of fourth grade, pupils can understand and write about complex passages and about themselves, using correct spelling," *The New York Times* reported on the eve of testing.
- Mills expected the scores to be low because the standards were deliberately higher.
- Schools worked feverishly on writing exercises that fall, and offered special sessions during the holidays.
- The test's inauguration was inauspicious.
- There were complaints about late test deliveries and possible security breaches that might have given some schools an advantage.
- Also, bad weather closed dozens of schools.
- The test answers were scored by committees of teachers, after which the state released the results on May 25, 1999.
- Statewide, 48 percent of fourth-graders passed; in New York City only 33 percent passed.
- "This is an exercise in truth telling," Mills said. "Where do we go from here? We have to go up, obviously."
- An analysis by *The New York Times* showed that city students actually performed slightly better than others in the state when compared to similar groups based on poverty and homes where Spanish or another language other than English was used at home.
- Nevertheless, poor grades on the state test and city tests led Crew to send 35,000 failing students to summer school to give them another chance to pass their tests.
- The city's summer school program was strongly pushed by Mayor Giuliani, who argued that one way to improve schools was to get tough with failing students.
- But city officials flunked, too.
- The company that made the tests goofed in scoring them.
- In September 1999, the city announced that it had to revise results for citywide tests given in grades 3, 5, 6, and 7.
- The correct results showed higher scores, which meant the city had sent about 8,600 students to summer school by mistake.
- The display of incompetence in administering a student competency test was an embarrassment for Crew, even though the mistake was the vender's and was originally flagged by Crew's chief testing advisor.
- Relations between Giuliani and Crew had been worsening since April 1999, when the mayor proposed experimenting with school vouchers.
- Crew, who opposed vouchers because they diverted public money to private schools, fought the mayor's plan fiercely and defeated it.
- The testing problems and other issues made matters worse.
- On December 23, 1999, the city school board voted to end Crew's contract.

HISTORICAL SNAPSHOT
1999

- The Senate trial in the impeachment of President Clinton resulted in acquittal; he had been impeached by the House of Representatives
- In one of the largest drug busts in American history, the Coast Guard intercepted a ship with over 9,500 pounds of cocaine aboard, headed for Houston, Texas
- Rapper Big L was shot to death
- White supremacist John William King was found guilty of kidnapping and killing African-American James Byrd, Jr. by dragging him behind a truck for two miles
- The Supreme Court upheld the murder convictions of Timothy McVeigh for the Oklahoma City bombing
- The Roth IRA was introduced by Senator William V. Roth, Jr., as a retirement tool
- The 71st Academy Award for Best Picture went to *Shakespeare in Love*
- A Michigan jury found Dr. Jack Kevorkian guilty of second-degree murder for administering a lethal injection to a terminally ill man
- During the year, the Dow Jones Industrial Average closed above the 10,000 and 11,000 marks for the first time
- The World Trade Organization ruled in favor of the United States in its long-running trade dispute with the European Union over bananas
- Bill Gates' personal fortune exceeded $100 billion, based on the increased value of Microsoft stock
- In the Columbine High School massacre two Littleton, Colorado teenagers opened fire on their teachers and classmates, killing 12 students and one teacher, and then themselves
- Nancy Mace became the first female cadet to graduate from the Military College of South Carolina
- *Star Wars Episode I: The Phantom Menace* was released in theaters and became the highest-grossing *Star Wars* film
- The U.S. House of Representatives released the *Cox Report*, which details the People's Republic of China's nuclear espionage against the U.S. over the prior two decades
- Texas Governor George W. Bush announced he would seek the Republican Party's nomination for president
- Lance Armstrong won his first Tour de France
- USA soccer player Brandi Chastain scored the game-winning penalty kick against China in the FIFA Women's World Cup
- Off the coast of Martha's Vineyard, a plane piloted by John F. Kennedy, Jr. crashed, killing him and his wife Carolyn Bessette Kennedy and her sister Lauren Bessette
- *Mercury-Redstone 4* raised *Liberty Bell 7* from the Atlantic Ocean floor
- The last Checker taxicab was retired in New York City and auctioned off for approximately $135,000
- Viacom and CBS merged
- The New York Yankees swept the Atlanta Braves to win their twenty-fifth World Series baseball championship

Selected Prices

Automobile, Volvo Sedan $26,895

Bath Towel $24.00

Breadmaker..$129.99

Cell Phone..$49.99

Computer, Apple MAC Performa $2,699.00

Digital Camera...$800.00

Man's Belt, Italian Leather $42.00

Palm Pilot..$369.00

Wine Bottle Holder $150.00

Woman's Purse, Kenneth Cole...$148.50

"In New York, 'Whole Language' vs. 'The Test,'" Diane McWhorter, *The New York Times*, January 3, 1999:

GALLEON BEACH, Antigua— I've been getting the sweats here over making my nine-year-old daughter miss three days of school next week. (All the earlier flights back to New York were booked.) That means she'll have three fewer crucial days of cramming for the controversial new standardized test that all of New York State's public-school fourth graders must take, over three days, soon after our return.

During a recent siesta hour, Lucy attacked a sample test that she was assigned to practice over the holidays, stoically deconstructing a passage about a banana named Joey who regrets ending up in a bowl of cereal rather than a cream pie.

The Test represents an abrupt departure from the old multiple-choice format to an uncharted field of "inferencing," note-taking and essay writing. The students don't seem to be as exercised as their parents and teachers, who see The Test as yet another potentially punishing yardstick in the high-stakes meritocracy. Many in my cohort of two-career, college-educated families think their children are being treated as guinea pigs and worry that a poor test score, by disqualifying their kids from a good middle school, will start a long slide to Mudville.

But there's more at play here than New Yorkers' competitive neurosis. Many parents I know, even if their kids are in one of the "gifted" programs or other high-performance schools (that is, those with rich PTAs) are worked up because The Test will judge their children on skills that have never been a priority in school: what the Board of Education

Continued

"In New York, 'Whole Language' vs. 'The Test,'" . . . *(Continued)*

calls the "conventions" of grammar, spelling, punctuation, and even that hobgoblin of little hands, penmanship.

This brusque shift in testing protocol—and the heroic last-minute lengths to which teachers are going to accommodate it—suggests to me that The Test may be a stealth referendum on the "whole language" method that has been used to teach this generation of children to read and write. With its snubbing of phonics in favor of let-it-all-hang-out written expression through "invented spelling," whole language has long been a battleground in the larger culture war between the forces of tradition on the right and the proponents of fuzzywuzzy 60s-style self-actualization on the left.

But The Test has confused the ideological battle lines. Some of my fellow baby-boom parents, creatures of the 1960s (and victims of "See Spot run") for whom progressive education seemed invented, are not so sure which side of this particular conflict they're on. Our children's rampant run-on sentences and abuse of the apostrophe have made us nostalgic for the days of separate grades for form and content—indeed, for having grades at all—and make us question whether "conventions" can be converted into habit if they are introduced late in the process.

Yet perhaps the most alarming thing about The Test is that it seems to slight the real strength of our children's reformed education. Students who have been taught that writing is an evolutionary process of constant revision—Lucy's classroom "writing workshop" puts a piece through at least seven stages before it is "published"—are now expected to produce camera-ready essays to the ticking of a stopwatch.

Children who have been encouraged to reach beyond their grasp—to improvise the fancy words they did not know how to spell—are being directed toward a "conventional" middle. Lucy was told that if she wasn't sure how to spell the word "select," she should use "pick" or "choose" instead.

I haven't exactly found the practice tests a snap myself. I had trouble keeping all the characters straight in one story, a legend about how orchids came to grow on trees. (Every name seemed to begin with M and end with I.) And Lucy misread the key word as "orchard." It turned out she didn't know what an orchid was, having never received a corsage.

Still, she isn't staying up nights worrying about The Test. She did have trouble getting to sleep the first night we were here, but that was because she was upset about the poor people we saw while taxiing in from the airport.

The debate surrounding standardized testing continues.

2000: Lawyer Debating Prayer at School

Real estate lawyer Rita Willis took a stand against prayer in school when her daughter questioned being asked to recite the Lord's Prayer after the high school football game in Santa Fe, Texas.

Life at Home

- At 51 years old, Rita Willis was sure she was well past her rebel stage.
- Of course, when she went to law school in the early 1970s, she was considered a token female admission and a rebel of sorts.
- After all, the world seemed firmly convinced that only men were capable of coping with the rough-and-tumble world of "the law."
- "The law" appeared to rank above religion, presidential edicts, congressional mandates and the traditions of local practice.
- So, as she sat through the intoxicating world of constitutional law, she dreamed of fighting for the civil rights of the downtrodden and oppressed.
- Reality arrived quickly when she clerked for the first time at a major law firm where she was the lowest member of a very tall totem pole.
- Twelve-hour days of arcane research regarding commercial transactions hardly squared with her law school visions of glory.
- So after law school, marriage, and the birth of a child, Rita looked for an area of the law that balanced her love of legal precision and the tempo of her family.
- Real estate was booming in Macon, Georgia, as was the need for real estate lawyers.
- Real estate law paid reasonably well, was flexible enough to accommodate three very active children, and overall, it was an area of the law that was not festooned with conflict and controversy.
- Apparently, conflict was reserved for her personal life.

Real estate lawyer Rita Willis took a stand against prayer in school.

Prayer at a football game ignited a five-year court battle.

- Comfortable as a partner in one of Macon, Georgia's most respected law firms, Rita discovered that controversy could be thrust on anyone, at any age.
- And as a lifelong Episcopalian and choir member, she was shocked to discover that tackling the issue of school prayer would result in accusations that challenged her Christianity.

Life at Work

- The issue of prayer at school officially arose more than five years earlier when a student chaplain delivered a prayer over the public address system before a home varsity football game.
- Rita was at the game with her husband to support her youngest daughter, a cheerleader on the varsity squad.
- She stood with the rest, listened passively to the prayer delivered by a student, held her hand over her heart for the playing of the national anthem and cheered the team as they roared onto the field.
- The rhythm and pattern had been unchanged for 30 years.
- Only later, when a dozen teens gathered at Rita's home after the game, did she come face to face with the inequity of public prayer.
- An argument broke out about that evening's prayer.
- A junior girl of the Muslim faith said she didn't think it right for everyone in the entire stadium to be asked to pray to "Jesus Christ our Lord" for protection and guidance.
- The boys quickly told her to "shut up or go back home," which made the her cry, and made the other girls mad enough to berate the boys.
- Rita stepped in just as the disagreement reached a fevered pitch.
- Since 1962, she told them, the Supreme Court had consistently ruled that "Congress shall make no law respecting an establishment of religion."
- The Founding Fathers intended that no act of government—including laws governing public schools—should favor any one religion over others.
- That's hard to do, she said, because once someone mentioned God, Jesus, or anything even remotely "Biblical," he or she immediately pushed the constitutional envelope by "favoring" one practice of religion over all others.

- It may very well be that the only way not to favor one religion over others was not to favor any religion at all—a path now being chosen by many public schools already.
- The room was silent.
- "Shouldn't the majority rule?" her daughter asked to break the awkward silence.
- Rita knew that public opinion polls showed that a majority of people disagreed with the Supreme Court's religion-in-schools rulings and she told them so.
- Then she added, "While it's fine to disagree with them, it is not really fair to blame the Court for making them."
- The rulings were based on the way the Justices interpreted the First Amendment to the Constitution.

- The First Amendment spelled out America's guiding principles regarding religion, speech, press, assembly, and petition.
- Basically, it protected all Americans' right to worship as they wanted, to say what they wanted, to publish what they wanted, to gather in groups, and to make their concerns known to the government.
- It also prohibited the government from identifying with a particular religion, effectively separating church and state.
- Had the Supreme Court not been asked to interpret the Establishment Clause by private citizens, including some members of the clergy, they never would have done so.
- The Establishment Clause stated that Congress "shall make no law respecting an establishment of religion."
- "But," said Rita, "when you say, 'the majority rules,' does that include the majority that kept women out of law schools or medical schools or that said it was right for black people to ride in the back of the bus?"
- This time the room erupted into a flurry of questions and a few accusations of "Commie liberal talk."
- That's when Rita climbed out on the fragile limb that would support her life for the next five years.
- "Perhaps the most important job of the Supreme Court is to see to it that the will of the majority is never unfairly or hurtfully forced on the minority, and, that's a good thing because you never know when the minority might be you."
- All weekend she brooded over the conflict and what she had said.
- Her daughter seemed impressed with what had taken place.
- But Rita was unsure whether her daughter agreed with her comments or was simply pleased to see the boisterous boys shut down so effectively.
- When Monday arrived, Rita knew she had to act on her comments, so she made an appointment with the high school principal, a newcomer to Macon who might be sensitive to the needs of the students.
- In 1992, the Supreme Court had barred clergy-led prayers at graduation ceremonies, but there appeared to be unclear guidance about student-led prayer at football games.
- Her intent was to express her concerns and relate the weekend's events.
- But despite her best efforts, the first meeting went poorly.
- Early in the conversation, she casually mentioned the name of her law partner, and the principal immediately summoned his secretary to witness the remainder of the conversation.
- The second meeting involved the superintendent, the third a school district lawyer and the fourth was convened before the school board in open session.
- By the time she arrived home from the school board meeting, she was famous—or infamous.
- The 11 o'clock television news led with the word, "Prayer condemned as illegal by local attorney," beside an unflattering picture of Rita.
- The phone rang all night with calls that were mostly ugly and from people she didn't know.
- She attempted to take a low profile, but her timing was terrible.
- In Texas a case was brought by Mormon and Catholic students concerning the banning of prayer at football games.
- Nationally, school prayer became a hot topic once again.

Rita's daughter seemed impressed by her mother's stand.

- No matter what she said or how framed her answers, every media outlet in the South portrayed her as a godless spokeswoman for the Devil who wanted to rip prayer from the mouths of America's youth.
- During the lawsuit's five-year journey through the courts, Rita was vilified.
- After a time, the viciousness of the verbal assaults only served to remind her that the Constitution belonged to everyone, especially the Muslim girl who was verbally attacked by the boys that Friday night.
- In the intervening five years, her youngest daughter graduated from high school and college, her oldest daughter married and gave her a grandson, while her lawyer son took a job in Atlanta.
- Rita continually prayed for guidance and even joined a contemplative prayer group that gave her a measure of peace.
- And she began to explore the economic inequality of her community as a volunteer server at a local soup kitchen.
- By the time the courts ruled on the Texas prayer case, Rita was at peace with herself.
- But she could not keep from smiling at the results: the Supreme Court had ruled in favor of protecting the rights of America's minorities.

Life in the Community: Santa Fe, Texas

- In 1995 two families filed a lawsuit against the Santa Fe, Texas school district over prayer in school.
- Unlike that of Rita, the identity of the two families who filed the lawsuit, one Catholic and one Mormon, was sealed by the courts.
- Their lawsuit alleged that the school district's policy of allowing students to lead prayers at home football games violated the First Amendment by creating a religious atmosphere, and a lower court agreed in principle.
- A federal appeals court ruled that student-led prayers that were not limited to one specific religion and did not attempt to create converts were allowed at graduations, but banned before football games which the court said were not serious enough to be "solemnized with prayer."
- The school district responded to the lower court ruling by implementing strict guidelines banning pre-game prayer, and warned senior Marian Ward, elected by fellow students to deliver religious messages before football games, that she would be disciplined if she prayed.
- Ward's family filed suit in September, arguing that the guidelines violated her free speech rights.
- A U.S. district court judge agreed that the guidelines the school had written were unconstitutional and ruled that the school could not censor Ward's speech.
- So it was up to the Supreme Court to sort out all of the lower court rulings and make a decision.
- In the summer of 2000, the U.S. Supreme Court ruled 6-3 that public schools could allow student-led prayer before high school football games.
- The central question was whether allowing prayer violated the First Amendment's Establishment Clause, which stated that Congress "shall make no law respecting an establishment of religion."
- "We recognize the important role that public worship plays in many communities, as well as the sincere desire to include public prayer as a part of various occasions so as to mark those occasions' significance," Justice John Paul Stevens wrote for the majority.

- "But such religious activity in public schools, as elsewhere, must comport with the First Amendment," he added.
- The 4,000-student southern Texas school district, until 1995, had a policy in which students elected student council chaplains to deliver prayers over the public address system before the start of high school football games.
- While the lower courts were considering the legal challenge, the school district adopted a new policy under which student-led prayer was permitted but not mandated.
- Students were asked to vote on whether to allow prayers and to vote again to select the person to deliver them.
- A lower court retooled that policy to allow only non-sectarian, non-proselytizing prayer.
- An appeals court found the modified policy constitutionally invalid and the nation's highest court agreed with the appeals court, rejecting the argument that the pre-football prayer was an example of "private speech" because the students, not school officials, decided the prayer matter.

HISTORICAL SNAPSHOT
2000

- The arrival of the year 2000 failed to produce the predicted terrorist attacks, Y2K melt-downs or mass suicides among doomsday cults
- The last new daily *Peanuts* strip by Charles Schulz ran in 2,600 newspapers
- Two Austrian banks agreed to a $40 million settlement with an estimated 1,000 Holo-caust victims or their heirs for having confiscated their assets
- Time Warner agreed to be acquired by AOL in a merger valued at $162 billion
- The U.S. Supreme Court gave police broad authority to stop and question people who run at the sight of an officer
- Reports indicated that the number of Internet users in China had more than doubled over the last six months from 4 million to 8.9 million, most of them young, single men
- Nitrogen-based fertilizers were blamed for the rapid decline of the spotted frog in the Pacific Northwest
- The female-oriented TV cable channel Oxygen made its debut
- President Clinton proposed a $2 billion program to bring Internet access to low-income households
- A federal jury in Portland, Oregon, ordered abortion foes who had created "wanted" posters and a Web site listing the names and addresses of "baby butchers" to pay $107 million in damages
- Carlos Santana won eight Grammy awards, including album of the year for *Supernatural*
- Pope John Paul II begged for God's forgiveness for sins committed or condoned by Roman Catholics over the last 2,000 years, including wrongs inflicted on Jews, women and minorities
- CBS filmed the TV show *Survivor* on the Malaysian island of Pulau Tiga
- The Tribune Company bought the LA Times in a $6.5 billion merger with the Times Mirror Company
- More than 600 people set out on a five-day, 120-mile protest march to Columbia, South Carolina, to urge state lawmakers to remove the Confederate flag from the state house dome
- Judge Thomas Penfield Jackson ruled that Microsoft violated the Sherman Act by tying its Internet browser to its operating system
- The National Labor Relations Board ruled that graduate students who work as teaching assistants may organize a union
- Leaders of developing nations called for a "New Global Human Order" to spread the world's wealth and power
- In California, President Clinton created Giant Sequoia National Monument in Sequoia National Park to protect 328,000 acres of sequoias from timber harvesting
- The International Whaling Commission turned down requests from Japan and Norway to allow expanded whaling

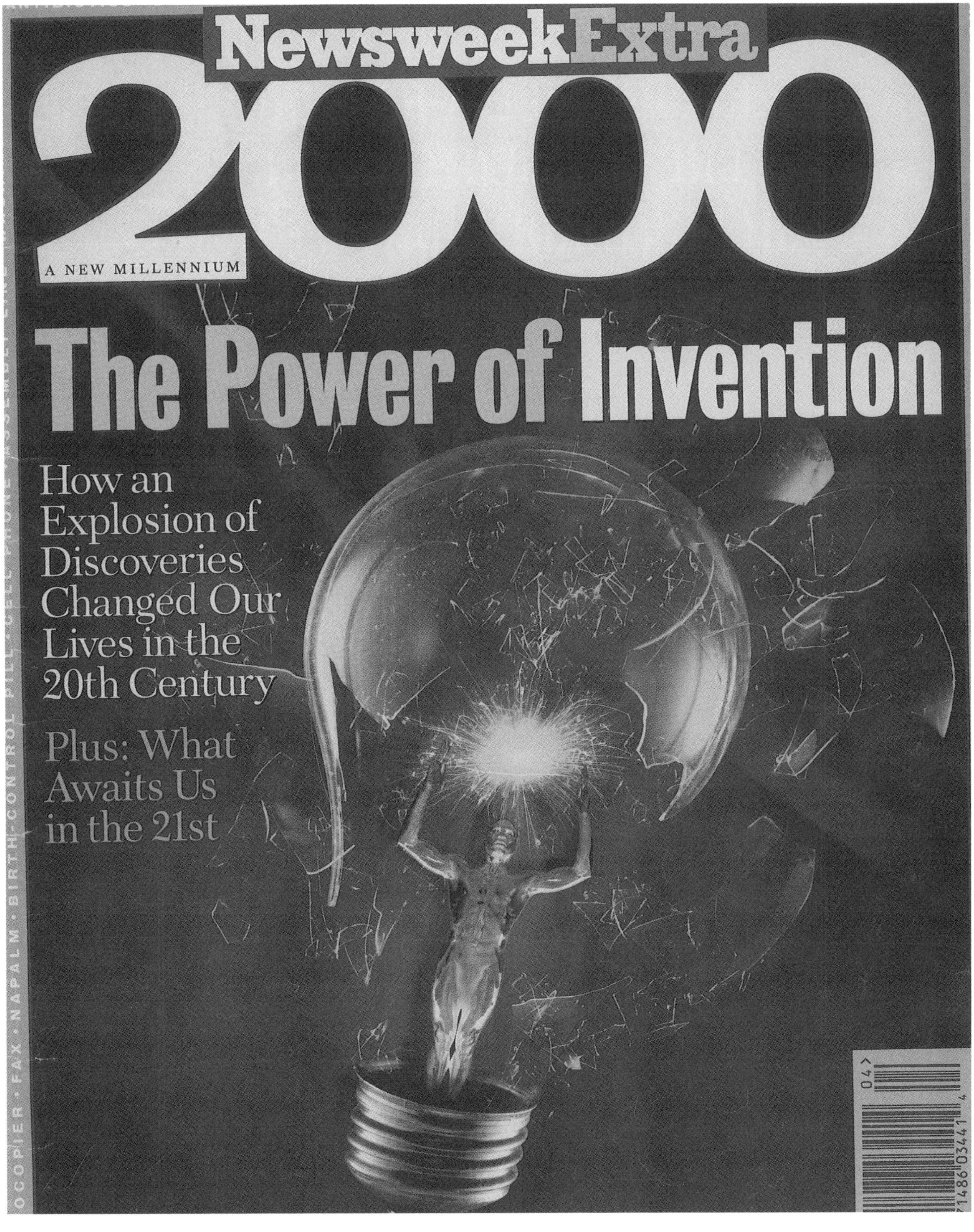

NewsweekExtra

2000

A NEW MILLENNIUM

The Power of Invention

How an Explosion of Discoveries Changed Our Lives in the 20th Century

Plus: What Awaits Us in the 21st

OCOPIER • FAX • NAPALM • BIRTH-CONTROL PILL • CELL PHONE ASSEMBLE LINE

Selected Prices, 2000

Blender, Oster	$80.00
Computer Desk	$999.00
Cordless Drill, DeWalt	$129.00
Diapers, Pampers, 40	$14.99
Digital Video Camera, Fisher	$899.99
iTunes Album	$16.99
Laser Eye Surgery, Lasik, per Eye	$599.00
Movie Ticket	$7.50
Treadmill, ProForm	$599.99
Weedwacker, Craftsman	$29.99

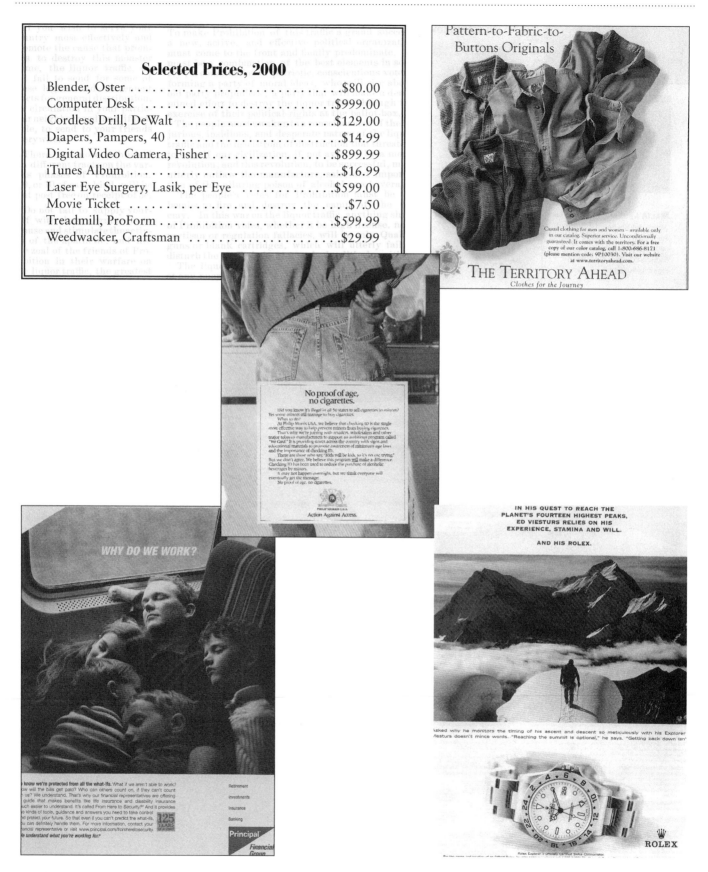

Timeline of Religion in Schools

1940

The Supreme Court ruled that a public school may require students to salute the flag and pledge allegiance even if doing so violated their religious beliefs.

1943

The Supreme Court overturned itself and ruled that no one can be forced to salute the flag or say the pledge of allegiance if it violates the individual conscience.

1948

The Supreme Court found religious instruction in public schools a violation of the Establishment Clause of the First Amendment and therefore unconstitutional.

1952

The Supreme Court ruled that release time from public school classes for religious instruction did not violate the Establishment Clause.

1962

The Supreme Court found school prayer unconstitutional.

1963

The Supreme Court ruled that Bible reading over the school intercom was unconstitutional.

The Supreme Court found forcing a child to participate in Bible reading and prayer unconstitutional.

1968

The Supreme Court ruled that states could not ban the teaching of evolution.

1980

The Supreme Court found the posting of the Ten Commandments in schools unconstitutional.

1985

The Supreme Court found that state laws enforcing a moment of silence in schools had a religious purpose and was therefore unconstitutional.

1987

The Supreme Court ruled that state law requiring equal treatment for creationism had a religious purpose and was therefore unconstitutional.

1990

The Supreme Court ruled that the Equal Access Act did not violate the First Amendment; public schools that received federal funds and maintained a "limited open forum" on school grounds after school hours could not deny equal access to student groups based upon religious, political, philosophical or other content.

1992

The Supreme Court found that prayer at public school graduation ceremonies violated the Establishment Clause and was therefore unconstitutional.

1993

The Supreme Court said that school districts could not deny churches access to school premises after hours if the district allowed the use of its building to other groups.

2000

The Supreme Court ruled that student-led prayer at a public high school athletic event violated the Establishment Clause and was unconstitutional.

"Defiant Prayers Surface on the South's Gridirons," by Erin McClam, *Atlanta Constitution*, September 23, 2000:

DALLAS, Ga.—The horns of the Paulding County High School marching band blew the last note of the national anthem, and there was silence. Then one voice, then another, then thousands.

Soon, the chorus dominated the modest stadium—asking this day for their daily bread, forgiving those who trespass against them, seeking to be led not into temptation but delivered from evil.

This recitation of "The Lord's Prayer" was simple but fundamentally defiant. Fans here compared themselves to Christian soldiers, fighting to save religion's place in schools before the courts strip it away.

The scene is being repeated on Friday nights, in varying forms but with an identical message, on the South's most hallowed battlegrounds—its football fields.

"People understand we are a religious nation," said the Rev. Curtis Turner, who brought his Baptist congregation from half a metropolis away to pass out copies of the prayer before Paulding County's game with arch-rival East Paulding. "It shouldn't be confined. What if we confine it? They'll do it like a smoking ban."

Turner's congregation, like others across the nation's Bible Belt, took offense with the Supreme Court's ruling this summer that amplified, student-led prayer approved by public school officials crosses the line in the separation of church and state.

Those leading the prayers are growing bolder every week, almost challenging the powers that be to stop them from praying.

Every Friday night this fall, Turner—who cuts an awkward figure in a dark suit and shiny necktie among football fans with pompoms and booster T-shirts—is leading his followers to a different game in metro Atlanta.

Each time, the church members pass out cards bearing "The Lord's Prayer" and encouraging fans to recite it after the national anthem. Each time, they claim they are fighting for God-fearing students who are losing their right to practice their religion in school.

"They've been intimidated," Turner said. "They're afraid to speak or pray. They think that prayer has been outlawed."

Church-state separatists argue that mass prayers in public, including school-sponsored events, infringe on the rights of religious minorities. Turner's caravanning prayers are "extremely inconsiderate," said Debbie Seagraves, executive director of Georgia's chapter of the American Civil Liberties Union.

"This is a group of people willing to stand up at a public school event, and very loudly over everyone else say, 'This is our prayer,' no matter what anybody else wants," she said.

But across the South, a region where devotion to football has been called religious itself, students and fans are bucking the high court's ruling, refusing to quiet their prayers.

In Alabama, most schools have replaced prayer with a moment of silence since the Supreme Court ruling. But Etowah County High School continues to broadcast students' prayers over the stadium public-address system.

"Number one, we think it's the right thing to do," principal David Bowman said. "And, number two, football is a contact sport where kids are apt to get hurt, and you need God on your side."

In rural South Carolina, a student body president took the press-box microphone at her school's football opener to lead fans in a pre-game prayer. In the face of a lawsuit threatened by the ACLU, other students at Batesburg-Leesville High School plan to sign up to lead prayers at future home games.

And in western Kentucky, high schools in two counties have no plans to stop holding public pre-game prayers. In another Kentucky town, a radio station broadcasting high school football is airing prayers before kickoff.

"The Christian people have rights, too," said Bob Kerrick, principal of Hancock County High School.

continued

"Defiant Prayers Surface on the South's Gridirons" . . . *(continued)*

The ACLU contends it is not opposed to private prayer in school. But huge masses reciting prayers in football stadiums are both disruptive and offensive to fans of other religions, Seagraves said.

"Suppose a group decided to stand up during 'The Lord's Prayer' and sing a rap song," she said. "Wouldn't the school consider that a disturbance? It's important we be considerate of each other's differences in society."

The Supreme Court decision does not outlaw prayer in school, by students or otherwise. But schools violate the Constitution when they advocate a "particular religious practice" by sponsoring amplified, student-led prayer.

Turner insists he is not promoting Baptism, or even Christianity, by leading the prayers in metro Atlanta. "The Lord's Prayer" is just what he knows best, he said, and members of other religions are free to pray to their gods at the same time.

Some of the pastor's followers believe the erosion of prayers in schools is responsible for the downfall of America's youth, including school shootings. They say schools bleached of religion are a sure sign of the country's moral destruction.

"Over 224 years, this has been part of our heritage. We can't rob the next generation of that," said Clint Andrews, 22, who passes out prayer cards with Turner's congregation. "They're trying to take away prayer altogether. So we're taking a stand. We're on the last straw. This is it, right here.

"Republished with permission of Atlanta Journal Constitution, from "Defiant Prayers Surface on the South's Gridirons," Erin McClam, September 23, 2000; permission conveyed through Copyright Clearance Center, Inc."

There is such a misrepresentation of what can and cannot be done. People say you can't pray in school. That is not true. People say you cannot read a Bible in school. That is not true. There is freedom of religion, and there is a division between religion and government.

—Dale Stuckey, chief counsel at the South Carolina
Department of Education, 1999

Remarks of Principal Jody McLoud before a Roane County High School football game, Kingston, Tennessee, on September 1, 2000:

It has always been the custom at Roane County High School football games to say a prayer and play the National Anthem to honor God and Country.

Due to a recent ruling by the Supreme Court, I am told that saying a prayer is a violation of Federal Case Law.

As I understand the law at this time, I can use this public facility to approve of sexual perversion and call it an alternate lifestyle, and if someone is offended, that's okay.

I can use it to condone sexual promiscuity by dispensing condoms and calling it safe sex. If someone is offended, that's okay.

I can even use this public facility to present the merits of killing an unborn baby as a viable means of birth control. If someone is offended, it's no problem.

I can designate a school day as Earth Day and involve students in activities to religiously worship and praise the goddess, Mother Earth, and call it ecology.

I can use literature, videos and presentations in the classroom that depict people with strong, traditional, Christian convictions as simple-minded and ignorant and call it enlightenment.

However, if anyone uses this facility to honor God and ask Him to bless this event with safety and good sportsmanship, Federal Case Law is violated. This appears to be inconsistent at best, and at worst, diabolical.

Apparently, we are to be tolerant of everything and anyone except God and His Commandments.

Nevertheless, as a school principal, I frequently ask staff and students to abide by rules that they do not necessarily agree with. For me to do otherwise would be inconsistent at best, and at worst, hypocritical. I suffer from that affliction enough unintentionally. I certainly do not need to add an intentional transgression.

For this reason, I shall render unto Caesar that which is Caesar's and refrain from praying at this time. However, if you feel inspired to honor, praise and thank God, and ask Him in the name of Jesus to bless this event, please feel free to do so. As far as I know, that's not against the law yet.

"Over 900 People Encircle School with Prayer Chain," by Stump Martin, *Chattanooga Times Free Press* (Tennessee), May 17, 1999:

Over 900 Rhea Countians "built a hedge" around Rhea County High School Sunday afternoon, seeking divine protection and a spiritual solution to the nation's problems.

It was the latest example of an increasing push to restore group prayer in public schools.

Organizers counted 950 people gathered at the high school's football stadium for prayer before being directed to join hands in a circle around the school. Billy Hall told the crowd, "We calculated it would take at least 800 to go all the way around the school; we have more than 900."

He told the group, "Your presence acknowledges the fact that the problems in this nation are not just social but spiritual. Yes, the family situation has deteriorated; yes, there is violence; yes, there are horrible things on TV. But they are symptoms, not the problem.

"We have got to acknowledge that there is a devil, and that Satan wants to get into the hearts and minds of people, especially young people. We are going to build a hedge of protection around our young people. We are going to ask the Lord to intervene in the lives of the children of this county."

Jeff Pewitt, who, with Mr. Hall, helped organize the program, told the crowd that members of their Sunday school class at New Union Baptist church near Dayton had talked about the shootings at Columbine High School in Colorado the Sunday following the tragedy. "The Lord put it on our hearts to do this."

Another example of the continuing drumbeat to restore structured prayer in public schools was on May 5 when the Hamilton County Commission sent a resolution to Tennessee's congressional delegation asking that they enact laws that would permit voluntary prayer in public schools.

The Rev. Marvin Morrison of Mission Ridge Baptist church in Rossville agreed. "For almost 200 years we had prayer in schools," he said. "During that time we became the greatest nation economically, morally and militarily that the world had ever known."

But then Madalyn Murray O'Hair, a committed atheist who founded the American Atheists in 1963, filed one of the lawsuits that prompted the United States Supreme Court to ban structured prayer in public schools. "Almost 40 years after," asks Rev. Morrison, "where are we?

"We may be good economically. And we may be OK militarily. But we're bankrupt morally," he said.

There are strong sentiments on both sides as the argument rages: If prayer is put back in schools, whose prayer will be used?

An April 14, 1998 advertisement paid for by the American Civil Liberties Union stated: "Official prayer sessions in public school seem like a good idea to many Americans, provided they get to choose the prayer. But in such a diverse society, how can one prayer satisfy every religious belief?"

Hedy Weinberg of the Tennessee chapter of the ACLU said the same people who accuse her organization of not being religious "are the same people we're protecting by being so staunch.

"We're not against an individual student having prayer in schools before they take an exam or if there is a crisis at home. But we don't want a student standing up in math class interrupting the rest of the class.

"The minute the government decides when you pray, to whom you pray, or where you pray, we have a problem," said Ms. Weinberg. "The (U.S.) Constitution reads that you can't entangle government in promotion of religious activities."

Reprinted with permission by the Chattanooga Free Press.

2001: Ultimate Frisbee Player

The daughter of athletic parents in Greenville North Carolina, Lola Martin excelled at many sports, but was most passionate about fast-growing ultimate frisbee, which showcased her athletic abilities.

Life at Home

- Lola Martin was raised in Greenville, South Carolina, the youngest of three children.
- Though her parents divorced when she was seven, she did not feel different from her classmates and enjoyed the opportunity to get to know both parents.
- Her father, as a basketball player, baseball player, and track runner in high school, encouraged all of his children to try different sports.
- Her mother, also athletically talented and a lover of the outdoors, encouraged her children to explore nature independently.
- As the youngest, Lola felt the need to keep up with her brother, three years older, and sister, seven years older.
- She started playing soccer at age eight on a coed team and soon joined a newly emerging all girls' team at age nine.
- An all girls' team was touted as progressive at the time, although other states had long ago created similar programs, making South Carolina a few steps behind even neighboring states like North Carolina and Georgia.
- She thought she would play soccer for the rest of her life, and did until her freshman year of college.
- In high school, she also played basketball, rock-climbed, and ran track and cross-country.
- In all, her teams won four state championships—one in soccer, one in basketball and two in track.
- She also found the time to play in one Ultimate Frisbee tournament, having been recruited for her ability to run and catch.
- Her previous experience with Ultimate Frisbee was at summer camp, where she enjoyed the constant movement but hated the tendency of the boys to rarely pass to the girls on the team.

Lola's love of sports stemmed from her parents.

Ultimate frisbee showcased all Lola's athletic abilities.

- But at the tournament she was able to showcase all her athletic talents and had a ball.
- She also realized how much there was to learn about the rules, the throwing motion, when to cut and when to huck the disc (throw long).
- Ultimate, as it was more appropriately termed (Frisbee is a brand name), involved a field similar to that of a football field (40 yards wide by 70 yards long with 25-yard end zones on either end).
- With seven players per team on the field at a time, the players' movements were a combination of soccer, basketball and football.
- The rules also mimic other sports: the need to establish a pivot foot was borrowed from basketball, the interference calls on receivers from football.
- In Ultimate, running with the disc was not allowed.
- Therefore, a team must move the disc down the field by throwing and catching with the eventual goal of catching the disc in the end zone to score.
- If the disc touched the ground during this progression, barring a foul, possession changed to the other team who then tried to score in the other end zone.
- Lola especially appreciated the multiple strategies that could be employed, including zone defenses, set plays on offense, various cutting strategies—all familiar because of her participation in basketball and soccer.
- The most unique aspect of the sport to Lola was the lack of official referees.
- Field conduct was regulated by "Spirit of the Game," a term used to describe each individual player's responsibility to uphold the rules and play with sportsmanship.
- Therefore, players must know all the rules of the game and call them when they felt there had been a violation.
- The opposing player had an opportunity to agree or disagree.
- There was a level of trust that each player would not cheat with rule calls to gain an unfair advantage.

- In higher-level games, official observers were used as passive referees; if there was a dispute on the field, the players asked the observer for his/her opinion, which was final.
- Since its conception, players have established the rules.
- Ultimate began with the invention of the disc, which World War II veteran Fred Morrison called the "Whirlo-Way" in 1948.
- By 1949 the disc was being marketed in the midst of the UFO craze as plastic flying saucers useful for tossing on America's beaches.
- Then, in 1955, Wham-O (best known for the hula hoop) provided national distribution and in 1957, the name Frisbee.
- By 1968 New Jersey high schools were experimenting with a variety of rules, and in 1972 Princeton and Rutgers Universities staged a collegian contest before 2,000 students.
- Also on hand were a local TV station, a reporter for *The New York Times* and a mention in *Sports Illustrated*.
- Twenty years later as many as 100,000 athletes were participating in organized games, mostly connected with colleges and universities.
- When Lola entered college, Ultimate was played in over 42 countries and was government sponsored in Sweden, Norway and Japan.

Life at Work

- Lola Martin entered college with high expectations.
- Her plan was to study hard and play college soccer; after a summer of intense training and weightlifting she was in superb shape.
- But after discovering the pitfalls of no social life and a disagreeable coach at a Division I Soccer varsity program, Lola searched for another athletic outlet.
- She remembered her one Ultimate Frisbee tournament and thought that developing her skills in a new sport would be fun.
- Soon, she was hooked.
- She also found that her switch from soccer to Ultimate was not uncommon; many new college Ultimate players migrated from sports such as soccer, basketball and volleyball.
- Her college's women's team was formed only three short years earlier.
- So Lola believed she would have an opportunity to help the program build on itself.
- At the end of her freshman year, she was elected captain for the following year and soon began gaining regional recognition for her aggressive play.
- She also discovered the difficulties that came with balancing a leadership position and rigorous university classes.
- While varsity players enjoyed the support of professional tutors and some sympathy from professors, Ultimate players practiced four to five times a week without similar support or recognition.
- She even found that most people thought her sport involved a dog, was some variation of golf, or that marijuana-smoking hippies were the only people that played.
- Though she enjoyed the liberal attitudes that the sport attracted, Ultimate was much more intense than the majority of people thought.
- When deciding on a major, she was naturally drawn toward teaching.
- She initially knew that she loved teaching, but was also drawn to the flexibility of scheduling, allowing her to play Ultimate when she pleased.
- Many of her older Ultimate role models were teachers and advised her as to which avenues to pursue to maximize her ability to play and complete her studies.

Lola loved to compete and was elected captain.

- With her increasing recognition, she was scouted by club teams in the area to play Ultimate outside of school.
- The club season was primarily from the middle of the summer through the fall, and the college season was mostly during the spring semester, though there were tournaments for both divisions all year.
- The club division was composed of open (men's), women's, mixed (coed) and masters' (men over 30) categories.
- Lola found herself recruited to play on mixed teams, but also one of the top women's teams in the country.
- With a lighter schedule her senior year, she switched from playing mixed to women's Ultimate, committing to coast-to-coast travel for tournaments and rigorous practice on the weekends.
- Because the women's team was not close by, she had to travel over two hours and would often stay at a teammate's house after practice on Saturday night before Sunday morning practice.
- She did not mind though; Ultimate was her life, and her best friends were her teammates.

The game was much more demanding than most people thought.

- By the end of her senior year, her team had qualified for nationals for the first time in school history, and she was being mentioned on blogs by people from across the country.
- Though her team did not finish strongly at nationals, she was honored in an awards ceremony as being voted the fifth best college player (called the Callahan award) in the U.S. and Canada by other female college players.
- She was pleasantly surprised, since East Coast players and players from smaller schools tended not to rank very high in other female players' minds.
- Shortly after she graduated, tryouts for her club team began, along with track practices, agilities workouts, and weekend practices, a never-ending cycle.
- Sometimes she felt overwhelmed.
- But then she picked up a disc and hucked it downfield and smiled to herself.
- She loved this sport.

Life in the Community: Greenville, South Carolina

- Greenville, South Carolina, was part of the Cherokee Nation's protected grounds after the Treaty of 1763, which ended the French and Indian War.
- No white man was allowed to enter, though some families already had settled just within the boundary, and white traders regularly crossed the area.
- During the American Revolution, the Cherokee sided with the British.
- After a campaign in 1776, the Cherokee agreed to the Treaty of DeWitt's Corner, ceding territory that includes present-day Greenville County to South Carolina.
- Originally called Pleasantburg, Greenville County was created in 1786.
- In the early to mid-1900s, with Greenville being known as the "Textile Center of the South," an Exposition Hall for the textile industries was built.
- Beginning in the 1970s, then-Mayor Max Heller spearheaded a massive downtown revitalization project.
- The first and most important step in changing downtown's image was the streetscape plan, narrowing the street's four lanes to two and installing angled parking, trees, and decorative light fixtures, as well as creating parks and plazas throughout downtown.
- As the largest city in the Upstate area, Greenville is home to theaters and event venues that regularly host major concerts and touring theater companies.
- Four independent theaters each present several plays a year, while the Greenville County Museum of Art is noted for its collections of work by Andrew Wyeth, Jasper Johns, Andy Warhol and Georgia O'Keeffe.
- Greenville's economy, formerly based largely on textile manufacturing, had been transformed by substantial investments by foreign companies.
- The city is the North American headquarters for Michelin and is the sole manufacturing location for BMW in the Americas.

HISTORICAL SNAPSHOT
2001

- Noah, a gaur, became the first individual of an endangered species to be cloned
- The U.S. Federal Trade Commission approved the merger of America Online and Time Warner to form AOL Time Warner
- Wikipedia, the online encyclopedia, was launched on the Internet
- President Bill Clinton awarded former President Theodore Roosevelt a posthumous Medal of Honor for his service during the Spanish-American War
- George W. Bush became the 43rd president of the United States
- The Baltimore Ravens defeated the New York Giants 34–7 to win their first Super Bowl title
- The submarine *USS Greeneville* accidentally struck and sank the Japanese fishing vessel *Ehime-Maru* near Hawaii
- The 73rd Academy Awards selected *Gladiator* as the year's Best Picture

- In The Netherlands, the Act on the Opening up of Marriage allowed same-sex couples to marry legally for the first time in the world since the reign of Nero
- *Soyuz TM-32* lifted off from the Baikonur Cosmodrome, carrying the first space tourist, American Dennis Tito
- The Colorado Avalanche won their second Stanley Cup
- The world's first self-contained artificial heart was implanted in Robert Tools
- FBI agent Robert Hanssen was arrested and charged with spying for Russia for 15 years
- NASCAR legend Dale Earnhardt died in a last-lap crash in the 43rd annual Daytona 500
- President George W. Bush limited federal funding for research on embryonic stem cells
- The U.S. Justice Department announced that it no longer sought to break up software maker Microsoft, and would instead seek a lesser antitrust penalty
- Almost 3,000 were killed in the September 11, 2001, attacks at the World Trade Center in New York City; the Pentagon in Arlington, Virginia; and in rural Pennsylvania
- The 2001 anthrax attacks commenced as letters containing anthrax spores were mailed from Princeton, New Jersey, to ABC News, CBS News, NBC News, the *New York Post,* and the *National Enquirer;* 22 people in total were exposed and five of them died
- Barry Bonds of the San Francisco Giants broke the single season home run record with 72 home runs for the year
- The U.S. invaded Afghanistan, with participation from other nations in retaliation for the September 11 attacks
- Enron filed for Chapter 11 bankruptcy protection five days after Dynegy canceled an $8.4 billion buyout bid, triggering the largest bankruptcy in U.S. history

Selected Prices

Advil, 50	$3.99
Binoculars	$29.99
Champagne	$15.99
Compass	$7.99
Dishwasher, Maytag	$429.00
Frisbee	$12.00
Pepper Grinder	$12.99
Pizza, Little Caesar's	$12.95
Sleeping Bag	$29.96
Tape Measure	$19.99

At Last,
a legitimate excuse for dancing with your cat.

Introducing a better kind of odor control.

Go ahead. Get your kitty groove on. And if anyone asks, say it's because you no longer have to worry about a smelly litter box thanks to New Fresh Step Crystals with odor locking action. It eliminates odors five times better than regular litter. And who could blame you for expressing the joy that only a fresh litter box brings?

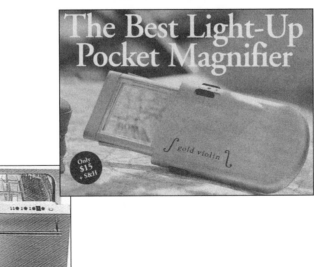

The Best Light-Up Pocket Magnifier

gold violin

Only $15 + S&H

It's the simple things we choose that change our lives.

"Bolts in Rocks Have Climbers Screaming from Mountaintops,"
Dean Starkman, *The Wall Street Journal,* June 11, 2003:

Patrick Seurynck was scaling a dangerous 400-foot granite cliff near Aspen, Colorado, last June when his partner above yelled down some disturbing news: "The anchors are gone!"

The 48-year-old Mr. Seurynck, who has been climbing rocks for 10 years, had just spent weeks drilling in place numerous stainless-steel bolts for securing ropes. He knew immediately what had happened: A bolt cutter had struck. He climbed down safely, fuming.

"It was just arrogant audacity," says Mr. Seurynck, still riled.

Whether to bolt or not is a smoldering question in rock climbing these days as the sport comes to grips with growing popularity. Once the domain of a scruffy few that embraced an ethic of self-reliance, conservationism and risk, rock climbing is being overrun by a new generation less connected to its daring past. The result: a culture clash on the rocks.

Traditional, or "trad," climbers favor passive protection gear metal nuts and spring-loaded retractable metal wedges called cams. These are slipped into cracks and then removed by the last climber to make an ascent. Climbers say newcomers put up permanent bolts merely to make hard climbs easier.

"They are entirely and utterly for the convenience of climbers, who, in my view, have just gotten incredibly lazy," says Richard Goldstone, a Poughkeepsie, New York, math professor, who has argued for fewer bolts in the Mohonk Preserve, a traditional climbing Mecca 80 miles north of New York.

The less-fastidious new-schoolers, sometimes called "sport climbers," dismiss the critique as elitist. They say bolted routes allow relatively safe climbs on even advanced routes and along the lines that otherwise could not be climbed at all. Besides, they say, bolts are becoming the norm. . . .

With at least 450,000 regulars now on the rocks in the U.S., up from 200,000 a decade ago, land managers fear that bolting is getting out of hand. "All of them are looking to prevent the proliferation," says Randy Kaufman, a National Park Service official. . . .

The nation's main rock-climbing group, the Access Fund, in Boulder, Colorado, is pro-bolt and favors leaving it up to climbers to decide when to place them. The group fears bureaucracy, so it is hoping the agencies provide "timely authorizations" for anchors, the spokesman says.

But a minority of climbers, including some big names in the sport, believe restrictions are needed. The anti-bolters echo the position of environmental groups that say permanent bolts degrade rock, look bad and allow climbers to disturb raptors' nests.

"'Ultimate Frisbee' Among Growing Outdoor Sports," Jennifer Anderson, Associated Press, *Kerrville Times* (Texas), September 7, 2000:

PORTLAND, Oregon: The plastic disc soars through the sky, tracing a long arc with a translucent glow before it floats for a frozen moment above the heads of two young men who leap to greet it.

Fwap! One claps the Frisbee between his hands while a player on defense lands on his feet and vows to knock it down the next time.

But there's no time for waffling.

"Stall one, stall two," he yells in Ultimate Frisbee lingo, counting the seconds his opponent has to fling the disc downfield in hopes of scoring the game point.

Before his defender can shout "stall three," he whips a hammer throw (Frisbee slang for a long vertical toss) into the end zone where a ponytailed teammate dives into the grass to catch it with her fingertips.

"Nice grab! Game!"

To these athletes, the familiar Frisbee that started as a toy more than 50 years ago has become a game enjoyed competitively by at least 100,000 people worldwide, about half in the United States.

Ultimate Frisbee—first played in 1968 by high school students in Maplewood, New Jersey—is a fast-paced non-contact sport that combines the speed of soccer, the objective of football and handling skills of basketball.

But what makes the sport unique is there is no referee, official scorekeeper or timekeeper.

Ultimate Frisbee relies on a "Spirit of the Game" rule, which, as defined in the game handbook, places responsibility for fair play on the player. It says that highly competitive play is encouraged, but never at the expense of the pure joy of the game.

"The people who play Ultimate really are virtuous people and play honestly," said Deana McMurrer, co-captain of Portland's only all-woman team, which last year took second place in the national tournament in San Diego and the world tournament in Scotland.

"It's a great quality that we can carry over to our lives."

Perhaps because of the game's emphasis on fun and fair play, Ultimate is especially embraced in the laid-back Pacific Northwest.

"The spirit of the game is alive and well here," said Mark Aagenes, Missoula, Montana-based coordinator for the Northwest region's Big Sky section, which includes Utah, Idaho, Montana, part of Wyoming and Alberta, Canada.

"People play because they like each other and want to have fun with it". . . .

"Frisbee Fans Get Fitness, Fun," *Winnipeg Free Press,* June 4, 2001:

It's just a round piece of plastic, but a Frisbee is the ultimate sport and fitness toy for growing fanatics like Jill Goddard.

Two nights a week, Goddard, a Toronto public health nurse, "hucks" and "backhands" a Frisbee at school and other fields, an oh-so-cool way to have fun, socialize and exercise.

Goddard is among Canadians who play Ultimate Frisbee, the trendy disc-throwing team sport that combines the nonstop running of soccer, the non-contact rules of basketball and the passing of football.

"You need to have good reflexes and you don't have to be a fitness freak, but you need a good cardiovascular base as there's lots of running around," the 28-year-old said before joining her coed team, the Limp Diskits, for a Monday night game against an opposing team at a Toronto high school.

A huck, as Ultimate jargon goes, is a long throw, and sometimes Goddard is guilty of a "swill," a bad throw.

But she was on a high after scoring three points in her team's 14-4 win to open the spring-summer season at the beginning of May, her first year in the Ultimate Frisbee adult coed league run by the Toronto East Sport Social Club. There are about 30 teams in two divisions, for beginners and advanced players.

Ultimate, sometimes called Frisbee football, is said to have been invented by New Jersey high school students in 1968 (although some say that it has its roots in Eastern colleges in the '50s). The Frisbee was conceived in 1948 by a California army pilot who molded plastic in the shape of pie tins, which kids and soldiers had been playing catch with decades. . . .

Ultimate has since become an international phenomenon, and there are world championships and competitive bodies like the U.S.-based Ultimate Players Association. The sport makes its debut as a medal sport in the 2001 World Games in Japan this August as the only self-officiated sport of the Games. There's also talk of it in the Olympics.

The beauty of Ultimate Frisbee is that it's a cheap form of fitness: all you need is a disc, which costs a few bucks, the players and a field . . .

"Ultimate is for people who want exercise, fresh air, to run around and blow off some steam after a hard day at work," said Michael Lichti, a coordinator for the Toronto East Sport Social Club, which charges $400 for a team with 10 players to join the league. "There's also the social aspect, meeting people on your own and on other teams."

After games, for instance, Goddard and her teammates go out for drinks and bites and to conduct a friendly game of postmortem.

"What I like is that Ultimate isn't as competitive as some of the other sports I do," says Goddard, who is also into running, hiking and paddling. "And most of the people in the league are of the same mindset, young professionals who are fit and into other sports, but who don't have the idea it's the be-all and end-all to win."

2006: Olympic Hockey Player

Jamie Hagerman, who learned to skate as a toddler, grew up to become a powerhouse hockey player in Lakeville Connecticut and a member of the 2006 Women's Olympic ice hockey team.

Life at Home

- Jamie Hagerman was born in 1981 in Deerfield, Massachusetts, the third child, with two older sisters, Casey and Kully; her younger sister Whitaker was born in 1987.
- Her parents both worked at the local preparatory high school, Deerfield Academy.
- Her father Dave was the head of athletics at the school, and her mother Parny was the director of admissions.
- Jamie's father was a hockey player at the University of New Hampshire and a hockey coach at Deerfield, so it was only natural that his children would play as well.
- Jamie hit the ice at age three.
- As she was learning to take her first strides on the ice, Jamie and her family relocated to another prep school, Hotchkiss School, in Lakeville, Connecticut.
- There, in the northwest corner of the state, she joined her first ice hockey team, becoming a "Cub" in Salisbury Youth Hockey.
- The Lakeville/Salisbury area had a small-town feel.
- The children with whom Jamie skated often attended the same school and church.
- Jamie attended the local public school, Salisbury Central School, up through eighth grade; just over 300 students attended the school.
- As she progressed through Salisbury Central, she also progressed through the different levels of youth hockey.
- After her three years as a Cub, she became a Mite, then a Squirt, Pewee, and finally a Bantam—spending about two years at each level.
- Jamie always made the "A" team—or the best team—at each level, going toe to toe with boys her age; she typically played right wing.

Jamie learned to skate as a toddler.

As a "cub," Jamie was the only girl on the Youth Hockey team.

- She was usually the only girl on her youth hockey team; her parents were careful not to point out her unique position on the team.
- Some of her favorite memories on the youth hockey team were playing on the frozen lakes in January with her Salisbury Youth Hockey teammates, who were also her best friends.
- In addition to playing in the youth hockey league, Jamie would practice with the Varsity girls' team at Hotchkiss School, which helped her become an even stronger player.
- The first time gender ever became an issue was when Jamie was 10.
- She was dressed in her hockey gear, eating at the dining hall at Salisbury School, where her dad was now working, when a boy walked up to her and said, "What are you doing?" She responded, "Going to hockey practice." The boy said, "Don't you know hockey is for boys and not for girls?"
- After graduating from Salisbury Central School, Jamie went to Deerfield Academy for high school from 1995 to 1999.
- While at Deerfield, she joined an all-girls' hockey team in Cromwell, Connecticut, called the Polar Bears, and also played on Deerfield's own girls' ice hockey, soccer and lacrosse teams.
- At Deerfield, she switched from playing right wing to defense.
- Starting at 14, she went to the USA Hockey camps, which were designed for the best hockey players, broken down by age groups.

Jamie loved playing with her friends on her neighborhood's frozen lake.

- Schoolwork at Deerfield did not come easy to Jamie.
- She had to work incredibly hard to master the subjects she was studying—if she didn't understand a topic or problem the first time, she'd try a second or third time until she eventually understood it.
- Her hard work endeared her to teachers at the time, and she became a top student at the school.
- By her senior year, she was captain of the hockey, lacrosse and soccer teams and was heading to Harvard to play hockey as well as lacrosse.
- Harvard was an essential step to her ultimate goal: to play hockey for the United States at the Winter Olympics.

Jamie was a natural at playing hockey.

Life at Work

- Jamie Hagerman thrived at Harvard.
- She loved her coaches and her teammates; in her freshman year, she was named to the conference All-Rookie team.
- Her second year at the school, she tore her anterior cruciate ligament, or ACL, during lacrosse practice.
- Her doctor told her she did not need surgery to play ice hockey since hockey is gentle on players' knees, but she could no longer play lacrosse.
- While she was at Harvard, she was once again selected to go to the USA camp for the best female players.
- At this level—the senior women's team—Jamie was being scouted for the Olympics.
- She also made it into the two critical tournaments a year—the Four Nations Cup in November, and the World Championships in April.
- She graduated from Harvard in 2003 and promptly moved to Canada to further her training for the Olympics.
- She was hoping to make one of the professional women's league teams in Canada.
- Only two Americans were allowed on each team, and there were eight teams in the country.
- In all, there were about 100 American girls fighting for those 16 spots.
- Jamie beat the odds and made a team in Toronto.
- She couldn't earn money in Canada for visa reasons, so she worked hard to save up money during the summer so she could financially survive the hockey season.
- When she headed up to Toronto, she was told by the team that she and the other American player needed to live with the Canadian Olympians until they got them their own house.
- The two women lived in an unfinished basement for four months—turning on the dryer at night to keep warm.
- Jamie moved back to the United States in April 2004 and made the World Championship Team, which brightened her hopes of making the 2006 Women's Olympic team.
- During this time, she moved back to Boston and worked as assistant coach on the women's hockey team at Harvard.
- She loved returning to her alma mater, her role as a coach, and the opportunity to stay in shape and practice for her possible Olympic bid.
- In the summer of 2005, she made the summer camp for the top 40 players in the country.

Jamie was excited to be a part of the Olympic team.

- Over the summer, the 40 Olympic competitor candidates were then cut to 25 hockey players.
- Those players then skated together from August to December, when the 25 were then cut to 20.
- Her family nervously awaited the announcement of the final roster outside the locker room of one of the exhibition games leading up to the Olympics.
- Jamie left the locker room in tears.
- Her parents thought the tears were because she did not make the team, but they were actually tears of joy—she was going to the Olympics.
- The 2006 Winter Olympic Games in Turin, Italy, were the third time women's ice hockey appeared in the Winter Games.
- Jamie and her team first played Switzerland and then Germany, beating both teams handily: 6-0 and 5-0, respectively.
- The third game against Finland was a bit tighter, but the United States came out on top, 7-3.
- After a three-day break, the women's hockey team headed into their semi-final game against Sweden.
- The United States had a 25-0 record against Sweden, so the odds were in their favor.
- The United States took the lead in the game, 2-0, with a goal in the first and second period each.
- But the Swedes caught up, scoring two goals little more than three minutes apart.
- Despite outshooting the Swedes 39-18, the United States could not get past the Swedish goalie Kim Martin, leaving the score tied through the third period and overtime.
- Now the teams were headed into a shootout.
- The United States failed to score during the shootout, and the Swedes scored their final two shots, leading them to victory and a spot in the finals against Canada.
- Brokenhearted at their loss, the United States gathered themselves for their bronze-medal game against Finland.
- Beating Finland 4-0, the United States team showed they could bounce back—playing stronger, with sharper passes and deft puck handling.
- Jamie and her teammates were awarded a bronze medal for their victory against Finland.
- Although she did not win the gold, it was a thrilling experience for Jamie to be on the Olympic team.
- It was also a special moment for her father, Dave.
- After playing goalie at the University of New Hampshire, her father was good enough to attend the U.S. National Team training camp, in preparation for the Olympics.
- Before he even got to go to the camp, he was drafted to fight in Vietnam.
- Jamie not only fulfilled her dream of going to the Olympics, but also her father's.
- After the Olympics, she discovered she had torn her ACL again.
- She knew she had injured herself during the Olympics, but decided to keep quiet about the injury so she wouldn't jeopardize her chances to make the team.
- She had surgery on her knee.
- After the big win at the Olympics, she headed to Washington, DC, to teach advanced placement psychology in high school.
- But hockey was not left behind.
- During the summer, she taught at ice hockey camps, sharing her Olympic story with a new generation of female skaters.

Life in the Community: Salisbury, Connecticut

- Salisbury, Connecticut, is located in the northwest corner of the state, on the borders of New York and Massachusetts.
- The town of Salisbury was incorporated in 1741, and it includes the villages of Salisbury and Lakeville, and the hamlets of Amesville, Lime Rock and Taconic.
- Salisbury is a rural area of rolling mountains, dotted with lakes and crisscrossed by the Housatonic River.
- During the Federal period, Salisbury was known for its iron production.
- Because the town was not near a river large enough to ship raw iron, the town instead handled much of the labor on their own—working the iron into wrought iron that was of such high quality it could be used for gun barrels.
- Salisbury iron became the choice iron for Connecticut's early nineteenth-century arms industry.
- Many of the arms were shipped South to be used by the Union army during the Civil War.
- Over the course of the twentieth century, Salisbury moved away from the iron industry and became a more upscale area, known as a weekend destination for New Yorkers.
- In 1999, Salisbury had a population of 3,977.

HISTORICAL SNAPSHOT
2006

- NASA's Stardust mission successfully returned dust from a comet
- United Airlines emerged from bankruptcy after being in that position since December 9, 2002, the longest such filing in history
- In Super Bowl XL, the Pittsburgh Steelers defeated the Seattle Seahawks 21–10
- The Blu-ray Disc format was released in the United States
- Massive antiwar demonstrations, including a march down Broadway in New York City, marked the third year of war in Iraq
- Warren Buffett donated more than $30 billion to the Bill & Melinda Gates Foundation
- The Military Commissions Act of 2006 was passed, suspending habeas corpus for "enemy combatants"
- A Pew Research Center survey revealed that 81 percent of Americans believed it was "common behavior" for lobbyists to bribe members of Congress
- More than a million immigrants, primarily Hispanic, staged marches in over 100 cities, calling for immigration reform
- Liquids and gels were banned from checked and carry-on baggage after London Metropolitan Police made 21 arrests in connection with an apparent terrorist plot to blow up planes traveling from the United Kingdom to the United States
- The International Astronomical Union defined "planet," demoting Pluto to the status of "dwarf planet" more than 70 years after its discovery
- Two stolen Edvard Munch paintings, *The Scream* and *Madonna,* were recovered in a police raid in Oslo, Norway
- President George W. Bush used the fifth anniversary of the September 11, 2001, attacks to emphasize the link between Iraq and winning the broader war on terrorism, asserting that "if we give up the fight in the streets of Baghdad, we will face the terrorists in the streets of our own cities"
- Google bought YouTube for $1.65 billion
- *Pirates of the Caribbean: Dead Man's Chest* became the fastest film in Hollywood history to reach the billion-dollar mark worldwide in box office receipts
- Former Iraqi leader Saddam Hussein was sentenced to death by hanging after an Iraqi court found him guilty of crimes against humanity
- Massachusetts enacted Universal Health Coverage, requiring all residents to have either public or private insurance
- PlayStation 3 and Wii were released in North America
- Smoking was banned in all Ohio bars, restaurants, workplaces and other public places

Stardust spacecraft

Collector tray to collect interstellar dust particles.

NO SMOKING

To report violations call
1-866-559-OHIO (6446)
in accordance with Chapter 3794
of the Ohio Revised Code.

Selected Prices

Beach Towel $20.00
Concert Ticket $40.00
Disposable Camera, Kodak $7.99
Gas Grill $134.99
Plastic Surgery, Liposuction $2,578.00
Private School, Hotchkiss, Annual $24,500
Radio/CD Player, Bose $499.00
Sirius Satellite Radio $100.00
Telephone, Motorola $79.95
Tires and Wheels $449.00

RE_INVENTING RADIO
Through_Innovation

MINI300PE

AM/FM Shortwave radio and flashlight

Compact and power-packed
- Multi-function LCD screen
- Clock, alarm, and sleep timer functions
- Receives 7 International Shortwave bands
- Telescopic and internal ferrite bar antennas
- Built-in speaker and earphone input
- 5 colors to choose from

Trends in Women's Hockey

- The first organized all-women's hockey game took place in Barrie, Ontario, in 1892, two decades before the formation of the National Hockey League.
- In 1894, a female club team formed at Queen's University in Kingston, Ontario, known as the "Love-Me-Littles," incurred the wrath of the school's archbishop, who did not want women to play.
- Within two years, teams had formed at McGill University and in the Ottawa Valley.
- The first women's hockey championship for the province of Ontario was held in 1914.
- In 1916, the United States hosted an international hockey tournament in Cleveland, which featured both American and Canadian players.
- The Great Depression and World War II knocked the wind out of the gaining popularity of the sport; women did not start getting back into ice hockey until the 1960s.
- In 1967, the Dominion Ladies Hockey Tournament was held in Brampton, Ohio.
- The Dominion Ladies Hockey Tournament featured 22 teams, with players from ages nine to 50 competing.
- By the 1970s, several Canadian provinces moved to establish associations to govern female hockey teams.
- At the same time, American colleges and high schools started to form varsity and club teams for women.
- Canada held its first national championship for women's hockey in 1982.
- Eight years later, it hosted the first Women's World Ice Hockey Championships.
- Two years later, after the second world championships were held in Finland, the International Olympic Committee voted to include women's hockey in future Olympics.
- Women's ice hockey made its Olympic debut in 1998, at Nagano, Japan.
- With the World Ice Hockey Championships, and the introduction of the sport at the Olympics, women's ice hockey grew in popularity across the world.
- Canada and the United States still have the most female ice hockey players, and typically the most talented ones.
- In 1990-1991 season, there were 6,036 registered female hockey players in the United States; by 2001, there were 39,693—a 580 percent increase.

"These Bears on the Cutting Edge; State's Top Girls' Hockey Program Is Making Its Mark Nationally," Matt Eagan, *Hartford Courant*, December 1996:

When Maurice FitzMaurice started the Connecticut Polar Bears girls' ice hockey team, the prevailing wisdom was there were no female hockey players in the state. At least as far as colleges were concerned. A girl from Connecticut who wanted to play hockey ended up on a boys' team, limiting her playing time and her exposure to college scouts.

That has changed.

The Polar Bears have played in 10 national championship games, winning five, since FitzMaurice started the club 12 years ago. And the holiday tournament, which started in the first year, has grown from a one-day, four-team event at Loomis Chaffee School in Windsor into a tournament with seven divisions and 63 teams. Major college scouts have flocked to seven rinks in Connecticut since Thursday to see the nation's top talent.

The tournament will end today with semifinals and finals in each division. The Polar Bears Midget 1 team (under-19) will play Team California in a semifinal at Tri-Town Sports Center (12:50 p.m.). The other semifinal has Massachusetts teams Assabet Valley and Chelmsford at Loomis (1:15). The final is at Tri-Town (6:10 p.m.).

The Polar Bears Squirt 1 (under-12) also qualified for the semifinals and will play Team Michigan at Tri-Town (9:20 a.m.). The winner advances to the 3:10 p.m. final at Tri-Town against Assabet Valley 84 or Assabet Valley 85, who play at Loomis (9:30 a.m.).

"It's come a long way since 1985," said FitzMaurice, an attorney who lives in Wethersfield. "Every major college has been here. We've been getting the attention for the last seven or eight years and that also is attracting teams because your West Coast girls don't get as much exposure because it's a long way to go for coaches to find them."

Teams from California started appearing three years ago. This year, the tournament features three California teams, one from Seattle, and teams from Michigan, Washington, DC, and the Northeast.

The level of play also attracts the scouts.

"I've been to a lot of these tournaments," said Roy Holinges of Needles, California. "We go to Canada and around the [U.S.], I follow the California teams a lot, and this is as good as the competition gets."

Connecticut has 12 members of the U.S. National Junior group, which is the top 50 in the country. Another, Angela Ruggiero of Choate-Rosemary Hall School in Wallingford, is on the U.S. National Team which is going to China next week and is a forerunner to the 1998 U.S. Olympic team.

The idea for the tournament came shortly after the Polar Bears started their first season. Said FitzMaurice: "The idea was to start to bring in some other girls because all we did is play boys back in those days. There were no girls' teams close by and we wanted to see how we would match up in the nationals."

The Polar Bears wound up winning the national championship. Since then, they have become one of the country's elite programs against heady competition such as Minnesota, which has just one select team.

The sport has changed since that first national championship in the spring of 1986. FitzMaurice said most players on his team also play other sports and all lift weights, something that wasn't common in the 1980s.

Some of the state's top players in other sports play for the Polar Bears. Jen Wiehn is an all-state soccer player at Tolland. Meaghan Cahill was a top soccer player at Kingswood-Oxford in West Hartford.

Also, more girls are becoming interested and college-level women's hockey programs are becoming more common, a trend FitzMaurice hopes will continue after the sport makes its debut in the 1998 Olympics.

"I think people will be shocked once they see the game," FitzMaurice said. "Once that happens, some parents will start to say 'I've got a good athlete, why don't I get her started on hockey?'"

There are plenty of opportunities. Polar Bears Wiehn and Liz Macri will be attending Dartmouth; Jordan Rettig will attend Princeton. Two others are being considered by Cornell, another by Yale.

"The whole reason we started this team was to get kids exposure and educational opportunities," FitzMaurice said. "At this point, it's an emerging sport, even though the competition is getting better every year, in this state there may be 10,000 female soccer players and fewer than 100 female hockey players.

"Plus it's a team sport with high endurance and kids, as part of the tournament process, get to travel and bond with their teammates who they learn as much from as coaches and teachers or anyone else."

"Women's Hockey Semifinal; Sweden 3, USA 2 (Shootout); Progress Stings," Rachel Blount, *Star-Tribune* (Minneapolis, Minnesota), February 2006:

They had seen the movie *Miracle* so many times that some of them could recite the lines. In the hours before Friday's Olympic semifinal against the United States, Swedish forward Maria Rooth and some of her teammates decided the time had come to give women's hockey its own version of that legend.

Sweden's 3-2 shootout victory will go down as a landmark in the women's game. While Rooth and her teammates hurled themselves into a blue-and-yellow pile on the Palasport Olimpico ice, the U.S. women bit their lips and felt the sting of a day they knew would come. As far back as September, coach Ben Smith warned that Finland and Sweden were at the doorstep of a historic upset. The Finns came close, and the Swedes made it happen, finally widening the women's hockey world beyond the U.S.-Canada axis.

The Americans had gone 73-0-2 against the six Olympic participants other than Canada. That included a 25-0 record against Sweden. In the past, Rooth said, her team never quite believed it could crack the icy wall that separated the North American powers from everyone else—until they arrived at the place where miracles are born.

"We said [Thursday] we were going to make a new miracle," said Rooth, a former Minnesota Duluth player who scored the shootout winner and both of Sweden's goals in regulation. "If we just believed we could beat them, we thought it could happen. Everyone was so committed. Everyone believed."

Except on the American side. The U.S. players felt only disbelief at losing their first Olympic semifinal. As Sweden's players got high-fives from NHL stars and countrymen Peter Forsberg and Mats Sundin, goalie Chanda Gunn fought a losing battle with tears, and Angela Ruggiero couldn't grasp the reality of playing for a bronze medal.

That will happen Monday against Finland, 6-0 losers Friday to Canada.

"I'm in shock right now," Ruggiero said. "It's a huge day for Sweden. It hurts, but we have to stay positive, because we can still win a medal.

"Everybody talks about the USA and Canada, but this may just open the world's eyes to the fact that there are other teams out there. We're back on our heels right now. But if you can take something positive away from this, maybe that's it."

Swedes' confidence grew.

Four years ago, Sweden's Olympic committee considered keeping its women's hockey team home for fear it would not be competitive in the Winter Games. The Swedes had finished fifth in the 1998 Olympics, the first to include women's hockey, and surprised with bronze in 2002.

Goalie Kim Martin was only 15 when she played in the Salt Lake City Games. Friday, her brilliance in the net provided the foundation for Sweden's greatest victory. Martin made 37 saves and thoroughly frustrated the Americans with her nimble, assured play.

continued

"Women's Hockey Semifinal; Sweden 3, USA 2 (Shootout); Progress Stings," ... *(continued)*

The United States outshot Sweden 39-18, but the players' faces reflected the anxiety created by frequent miscues and breakdowns—and by Martin's impenetrability. Former UMD forward Erika Holst stripped the puck from Gophers' defenseman Lyndsay Wall behind the U.S. net and fired it to the charging Rooth for the tying shorthanded goal. The Swedes intercepted several passes deep in the American zone, and countless U.S. scoring chances sailed wide, struck the goal cage or banged off of sticks.

The United States also went 2-for-11 on power plays, including a two-player advantage that lasted more than three minutes in the second period.

"We had a lot of good opportunities on the power plays," forward Katie King said.

"We didn't put them home, and that's what hurts. We were maybe too pretty on plays and lost it a few times, and they capitalized."

A distinctly Swedish vibe began to take over the arena as Rooth's goals, little more than three minutes apart, negated a 2-0 U.S. lead. ABBA played on the sound system. Fans with horns and Tre Kroner jerseys outblared their American counterparts. The tension swelled through the scoreless third period, the overtime and the shootout.

The first five shooters missed or were stopped. Pernilla Winberg beat Gunn with a wrist shot to the stick side, and Rooth followed in similar fashion to cement one of the defining moments of these Olympics.

"When it was over, I had to ask people what happened," Holst said. "Tonight, we said, 'This is our night. We're going to win. No one can take this away from us.'"

"A breakthrough"

As Canada and the United States buried their opponents in pool play, their coaches were forced to answer questions about whether their sport belonged in the Olympics. A paucity of competitive teams recently got women's softball bounced from the Summer Olympics program.

The North American rivals had faced off in every world championship and Olympic final in history. It seemed a foregone conclusion that they would do so again, but even through their tears the U.S. players were able to acknowledge the impact their upset will have on the sport.

"It's a breakthrough for them and their program," said U.S. forward Natalie Darwitz of Eagan. "I wish it wasn't us, but it's great for women's hockey. It shows there's a lot more than the U.S. and Canada."

Sweden's coach, Peter Elander, said he took a cue from the late Herb Brooks in preparing his team. Like Brooks, who famously kept his players on the ice after a tie and made them skate to exhaustion, Elander drove his team relentlessly for the past three months.

Which goes to show that even American hockey movies have influenced the women's game abroad. Elander thanked the United States and Canada for playing the Swedes so often, allowing them to learn and develop. Many European players also are refining their games with U.S. college teams, including nine Olympians who have played for or been signed by Minnesota Duluth.

Sweden's victory resulted from its fearless and aggressive defense, a smart game plan, improved speed and conditioning, and a new attitude. Years of losses to the North Americans have affected the psyches of some opponents; the Finns, after seizing a 3-1 lead on the United States in pool play, tightened up and lost. By getting over that hurdle, the Swedes have opened a window of possibility for others.

Elander and his players speculated that Friday's upset will stimulate the growth of the game in Sweden. At the very least, it promises to give hope to hockey's have-nots.

"We said at the beginning that people were going to be surprised at how competitive this tournament was," said forward Jenny Potter of Edina. "This is disappointing, and it's hard. It's all you dream about. But they beat us. What else can you say?"

"Today's Players See Brighter Tomorrow; Growing Coaching Sorority Part of Long-term Hockey Plan," Jill Lieber, *USA TODAY*, February 2006:

TORINO—Sometimes, Jamie Hagerman, a defenseman on the U.S. women's ice hockey team, feels like a stranger in a strange land.

When she's not devoting energy to winning a gold medal, she's committed to her job as an assistant women's ice hockey coach at Harvard.

The Crimson are one of six NCAA Division I women's ice hockey programs with female head coaches—and the only Division I school with an all-female coaching staff.

"At Harvard, we talk about it a lot: 'We are the only all-women staff. Why?'" Hagerman says.

The rest of the time, Hagerman feels like one of the crowd, playing one of the fastest-growing women's sports, with participation up 400 percent in the USA in the last decade, according to USA Hockey. She is one of seven women on the Olympic team who are, or have been, coaches of women's or girls' teams.

They include Katie King, an assistant at Boston College; Courtney Kennedy, head coach at Buckingham Browne and Nichols School in Cambridge, Mass.; and Jenny Potter, who coached at a Minnesota high school.

Also: Kathleen Kauth, a former volunteer assistant coach at Brown; Tricia Dunn-Luoma, a former assistant coach at New Hampshire; and Chanda Gunn, a former Massachusetts youth league coach.

"For a while, it was a male-dominated sport," Hagerman says. "It used to be women playing a men's sport. Now it's women playing hockey. A couple of years ago you couldn't make ends meet coaching. As a part-time first assistant at Harvard, I made $20,000 my first year. Now women can make a living."

Dave Ogrean, the executive director of USA Hockey, says increasing the pool of experienced female head coaches, especially at the national and international level, is a priority.

"We need to do a better job immediately," he says. In fact, Ogrean says his goal is to generate a list of women capable of coaching the 2010 or 2014 U.S. Olympic team. (The Canadian Olympic women's team is coached by Melody Davidson, on leave as head coach at Cornell.)

Ben Smith, in his third Olympics, became the first full-time head coach of the U.S. women's national and Olympic teams in 1996. He coached the USA to the Olympic gold medal in 1998 and silver in 2002. His contract is up after Torino.

Ogrean says he understands why none of the players from those first two U.S. Olympic teams are coaching at an elite level: "They're a collection of highly educated, high-achieving, exceptional women, not just women hockey players." But he hopes, over time, some team alumni will pursue coaching.

"When we sit down to talk about the next four years and the four years after that, I want there to be a lot of women whose names legitimately jump to mind as coaching candidates," Ogrean says.

2010: Homeschooling Mother

Annie Rosewood left a good job at a San Diego hospital to become a full-time parent and home school her three children, which required planning and discipline.

Life at Home

- Annie Rosewood was born August 23, 1964, in Wilmington, Delaware.
- Her mother suffered from manic depression and divorced soon after Annie was born.
- She couldn't keep a job, had three more children from another failed marriage, and moved the family from apartment to apartment.
- When Annie was five years old, she started watching a new television show called *The Brady Bunch*, which portrayed an upper-middle-class family comprising a mother with three daughters and a father with three sons.
- It was the first time Annie had seen a blended family on television, though their problems were far tamer than those in Annie's family.
- "That's what I want," she recalled thinking. "I want to have money, a car, nice things. The path I was on wouldn't bring me nice things."
- Her own family moved every year until Annie was in the sixth grade.
- In 1974, her mother married Frank Youngblood, who then owned a bakery.
- "He was a terrible businessman, but a good stepdad," Annie said.
- They moved into his home in a white, working-class neighborhood, and stayed there.
- On her first day of class, a boy came up to her and said, "Hey, Annie! I'm Jeff. Remember me?"

Annie Rosewood's hard work in school laid the ground work to home schooling her children.

- She looked at him blankly, and saw on Jeff's face a look of hurt, which surprised her.
- When she later thought about it, she realized that she had never really bothered to remember people because faces flowed so quickly through her life—and until that moment, she hadn't realized that this wasn't normal.
- Annie worked from the time she was 10 years old.
- Her first job was as a babysitter, which usually allowed her to do her homework.
- Annie knew she would have to work hard to have a nice life, but for now, the most important thing was to keep her grades up.
- She had gone to public schools all her life, and often spent 45 minutes on the bus to school.
- The public high school she entered in the fall of 1978 was in disrepair; the toilets often clogged up and sometimes there was a roof leak.
- "But the teachers had a lot of heart, and that helped," Annie recalled.
- She didn't get much support in her school years.
- Her mother wouldn't take her to after-school activities, and her stepfather was too busy running his businesses.
- Annie became a cheerleader in high school, but had to beg rides from friends to get home.
- While her friends' parents were always in the stands during games, hers never were; "It was so depressing," Annie said. "They didn't care."
- Needing to work anyway, she quit cheerleading after only a few months.
- When her stepfather's bakery went bankrupt, he bought a pizza parlor in town, where Annie waited tables and ran the cash register.
- Sometimes she worked in the kitchen, but usually only men worked "behind the counter."
- She was very social, too, often riding around in cars with friends until 11 p.m. or later.
- She continued to make A's and B's, and was kept on a college preparatory track in high school.
- One of her favorite teachers was John Johnson, who taught biology.
- While they chatted after class one day, he asked her what she wanted to do after high school.
- "I don't know," she replied.
- She liked science, and knew she wanted to go to college, but didn't know what she wanted to study.
- John showed her a brochure about a new program that was designed to train nurses in radiation therapy at the local junior college, and that classes would run continuously for 27 months until graduation.
- Annie contacted the school, set up an interview, and filled out her application.
- She was one of six students admitted to the program.
- "They took pride in the fact that they had a high dropout rate," Annie said.
- Even so, she was one of three in her class to graduate in 1985, despite delivering pizzas for her stepfather's business in the evenings.
- She could have gone on and earned a bachelor's degree, but decided to go to work.
- "I was so desperate to get my life started, become independent, and live my life on my own," she said.
- The timing was excellent; hospitals were seeking nurses, especially those in specialties like radiology.
- She wanted to go to California, but her younger siblings needed her at home and the family needed some of her income, so she went to work at a local hospital.
- Two years later, she and a friend obtained jobs at a hospital in San Diego.
- They delayed their starting time by four months so they could drive across the country, stay in youth hostels, or camp at national parks along the way.
- They arrived in California in 1989.
- Annie met Sam Jones in early 1990, and a few years later they were married.
- Sam had been in the Navy and was inspired by Annie's job to enlist in the Army in 1994 to train as an X-ray technician.

- After his two-year stint ended, he joined the Army Reserve.
- When Annie became pregnant with their first child, they decided to move to Salem, Oregon, where a couple they knew had moved.
- Sam got a job at a local hospital, and Annie left paychecks and regular employment to be a stay-at-home mom for their new baby, Amanda.
- Their son, Lowell, was born in 1998, and Caleb arrived in 2000.
- Annie's plan had been to be a stay-at-home mom while the children were young, but as Amanda neared preschool age, Annie began talking with some of the home-schooling parents at the playground.
- Besides wanting to be an active parent, she knew a normal school schedule would make it difficult for Sam to spend much time with the children.
- His deployments with the Army Reserve had become longer, more frequent, and more unpredictable; by home-schooling, she and Sam could make their own schedule.
- Annie started home-schooling four-year-old Amanda, and followed suit with her other children.
- Under the standardized tests required in Oregon, her children performed well.
- When friends asked her how long she would continue home-schooling, she joked that her commitment was as deep as it was to natural childbirth: "We'll do it as long as it's comfortable and good for everybody. When it's not, we'll explore other options."
- Caleb had announced: "Mom, I'd like to go to public school for high school."
- That would be fine, she told him, but reminded him of his habit of hanging upside-down over a couch to read.

Life at Work

- Annie didn't start out planning to home-school her children, but by 2010 she had become a nine-year veteran teacher of her three children: Amanda, 13, Lowell, 12, and Caleb, 10.
- At 7:30 a.m., the kids stumbled out of bed and were expected to finish breakfast by 8 a.m.
- The kitchen, dining area, and den were part of one large room.
- The dining table was by sliding glass doors that overlooked their backyard, and a computer was on a small table by the wall.
- On the floor under the TV were three plastic crates filled with books, markers, pens, scissors and folders; a blue parakeet occasionally flitted across the room.
- After breakfast, Caleb would walk into the den toward his crate, pull out a well-worn spelling notebook, and settle into the recliner.
- Amanda would retreat to her bedroom.
- Lowell and his mother would sit on the couch to go over some math lessons.
- Social studies often involved maps and projects, such as building a fort out of craft sticks.
- After five or eight lessons there would be a quiz.
- When they would break at noon, Annie might suggest they watch something during lunch related to weather.

Successful home schooling took planning and discipline.

The children enjoyed educational trips throughout the year.

- Lunch ended around 1 p.m. and the school day was usually over by 3 p.m.
- Amid the routine, there were games like Scrabble, chess, and a trivia game designed around the curriculum.
- Science lessons were often the byproduct of discoveries made on excursions.
- Physical education often included trips to a pool, a tennis court or a park; they also played team soccer.
- Music education took the form of instrument lessons; all the children took violin, and Lowell was also taking guitar and considering the mandolin.
- They took art lessons at a museum in town.
- History was studied together.
- And then, there was the public library.
- Annie scheduled trips every Tuesday and tried to avoid overdue fines.
- "We usually had about 60 books out at a time," she explained.
- Annie didn't indoctrinate her children with any particular religion, but she did teach morality.
- One important aspect of home-schooling for Annie was to allow her children to become more aware of politics and the affairs of the world.
- They listened to National Public Radio and watched public television news, and then discussed what they had heard or seen.
- "I want my kids to have their eyes wide open," Annie remarked.

The Demographics of Home-Schooling
- Home-schooled students are still a small minority, but their numbers have grown rapidly since the 1990s.
- Being taught at home was most common among white, middle-income households with two parents.
- In 2010, about two million school-age children were being home-schooled, or about 4 percent of the K-12 population.
- More than 90 percent of the families were two-parent, one-salary homes, and the mother continued to be the most likely parent to stay home, according to the National Home Education Research Institute in Salem, Oregon.

- Joseph Murphy, associate dean at the Peabody College of Education of Vanderbilt University, said the advocacy group's estimate of home-schoolers might not be precise, but the number is huge compared with 1970, when only 10,000 to 15,000 children were home-schooled.
- As in previous surveys, most home-schooling parents in 2010 were conservative religious parents, predominately Protestants, but more moderate and liberal families have chosen to teach at home, Murphy told *Education Week*.
- Religious concerns were once the top reason for home-schooling, but by 2010 those concerns (30 percent) had been slightly outnumbered by those who cited the social environment of schools—from bullying to teaching practices (31 percent), Murphy said.
- Another change was the increasing variety of ways parents home-schooled, including home-school co-ops, online courses, and even taking some courses from public schools, according to *Education Week*.
- Since compulsory education laws were first passed in the early 1800s, "home school was home school, and school was school," Mr. Murphy said. "Now … it's this rich portfolio of options for kids."
- About half of state legislatures now require school districts to allow home-schooled students to enroll part-time if they want to, allowing these hybrid approaches to become "very, very typical, particularly at the middle and high school level," said Yvonne Bunn, director of home-school support for the Richmond-based Home Educators Association of Virginia.
- "It used to be it was very difficult to get materials; now we have people all over the place who want to sell to home-schoolers because they are such a good market," Bunn told *Education Week*.
- In 2007, the U.S. Department of Education found that 1.7 percent of children ages five to 17 (1.5 million) were being schooled at home, up from about 850,000 in 1999.
- By 2007, nearly 3 percent of school-age children were being taught in the home.
- "Parents give many different reasons for home-schooling their children," according to a 2009 report by the Department of Education's National Center for Education Statistics.
- "In 2007, the most common reason parents gave as the most important was a desire to provide religious or moral instruction (36 percent of students). This reason was followed by a concern about the school environment (such as safety, drugs, or negative peer pressure) (21 percent), dissatisfaction with academic instruction (17 percent), and 'other reasons,' including family time, finances, travel, and distance (14 percent).
- "Parents of about 7 percent of home-schooled students cited the desire to provide their child with a nontraditional approach to education as the most important reason for home-schooling, and the parents of another 6 percent of students cited a child's health problems or special needs," according to the report.
- The report found that white children were nearly five times more likely to be home-schooled than African-Americans.
- The home-schooling rate was 3.9 percent for whites, compared with 0.8 percent for blacks.
- About 60 percent of home-schooled students lived in households with three or more children.
- About 42 percent of regular school students had that many siblings.
- Among home-schoolers, 54 percent had one parent in the workforce and one at home.
- Among in-school students, only 20 percent had two parents with one at home.
- By income groups, the home-schooling rate was highest among students living in households with yearly incomes of $50,001 to $75,000 (3.9 percent), followed by those in the $25,001-to-$50,000 bracket (3.4 percent).
- The home-schooling rate was lower than the national 2.9 percent average for students in households with yearly incomes under $25,000 (2.1 percent) or more than $75,000 (2.7 percent).

HISTORICAL SNAPSHOT
2010

- The sculpture *L'Homme qui marche I* by Alberto Giacometti sold in London for $103.7 million, setting a new world record for a work of art sold at auction

- The Deepwater Horizon oil platform exploded in the Gulf of Mexico, killing 11 workers and resulting in one of the largest spills in history

- *Nude, Green Leaves and Bust* by Pablo Picasso sold in New York for $106.5 million, setting another new world record for a work of art sold at auction

- Scientists conducting the Neanderthal genome project announced that they had sequenced enough of the Neanderthal genome to suggest that Neanderthals and humans may have interbred

- Scientists announced that they had created a functional synthetic genome

- The first 24-hour flight by a solar-powered plane was completed by the Solar Impulse Project

- WikiLeaks, an online publisher of anonymous, covert, and classified material, leaked to the public over 90,000 internal reports about the United States-led involvement in the War in Afghanistan from 2004 to 2010

- The International Space Station surpassed the record for the longest continuous human occupation of space, having been inhabited since November 2, 2000

- President Barack Obama signed into law a landmark financial regulatory reform bill, touted as one of the greatest overhauls of the financial system since the Great Depression

- *Time* magazine named the protester as its Person of the Year to underscore the impact protesters had on dictators and world affairs

- The airline industry continued its process of consolidation when United and Continental announced a $3.2 billion hookup to create the world's largest airline

- The fast-food business got a whopper deal when the Brazilian private equity firm 3G paid $3.3 billion to acquire Burger King

- Researchers at CERN trapped anti-hydrogen atoms for a sixth of a second, marking the first time in history that humans have trapped antimatter

- WikiLeaks released a collection of more than 250,000 American diplomatic cables, including 100,000 marked "secret" or "confidential"

- Scientists announced that antiretroviral drugs have turned the AIDS epidemic around by thwarting the virus in HIV-positive patients and serving as a weapon against infection in healthy individuals

Selected Prices

Bathroom Scale, Digital	$49.99
BlackBerry Phone	$649.99
Bluetooth Headset	$99.99
Computer, Toshiba Laptop	$499.99
GPS Navigator, Garmin	$219.99
La-Z-Boy Recliner	$499.99
Pampers, 176 Count	$48.99
Refrigerator/Freezer, Whirlpool	$471.72
Sole F80 Treadmill	$1,999.99
Vacuum, Hoover WindTunnel	$129.99

"'Hybrid' Home Schools Gaining Traction," *Education Week*, Published Online August 7, 2012:

Emmy Elkin's school day starts with a cooking show.

The 10-year-old and her mom, Jill Elkin of Peachtree City, Ga., are up at 8 a.m., making breakfast along with "Iron Chef America" and chatting about algebra. Last week, Emmy left home after breakfast to meet a new Japanese tutor, around the time her sister Kayla, 14, dragged herself awake to get her independent mathematics study done before a friend came over for a joint British literature course. The sisters spent the afternoon working through a chemistry course online, with Jill Elkin giving more individual coaching to her younger daughter.

Kayla and Emmy are part of the modern generation of home-schooled students, piecing together their education from their mother, a former Fayette County math teacher, other district and university teachers, parent co-ops, and online providers.

Education policymakers and researchers have largely ignored the tremendous growth in home-schooling, particularly among these sorts of "hybrid" home-schoolers willing to blur the pedagogical and legal lines of public and private education, said Joseph Murphy, an associate dean at Peabody College of Education at Vanderbilt University and the author of *Home Schooling in America: Capturing and Assessing the Movement*. The book, an analysis of research on the topic, is being published this month by Corwin of Thousand Oaks, California.

"Historically, home school was home school, and school was school," Mr. Murphy said. "Now … it's this rich portfolio of options for kids."

Baywood Learning Center in Oakland, California, a private school for gifted students, has offered hybrid home-schooling programs for the past three years. The school has á la carte classes on individual subjects once a week, as well as a multi-age class that meets on Tuesdays and Thursdays to cover core academics. Director Grace Neufeld said demand for the latter has grown 50 percent in the last year, to about 40 students ages four to 17.

"Parents usually design a patchwork quilt of different classes and activities for their children," she said. "What I see is they sign up for various classes being held in various locations like science centers or museums or different places. They also add things like music lessons, art lessons, sports, or martial arts."

Continued

"'Hybrid' Home Schools Gaining Traction," ... *(Continued)*

Similarly, more home-schooling parents are developing formal co-ops, like the Inman Hybrid Home School Program in Inman, Georgia. Founder Holly Longino, a former health teacher at Carver Middle School in Inman, left public teaching to home-school her four children, but last year started the group classes a few times a week with five students and a handful of retired public school teachers. The teachers provide video lectures for students to use as well as in-class projects. Ms. Longino said some parents also take their children to courses at the local college and science museum, but would never consider forming a charter school.

"There's a lot of freedom in home-schooling," she said. "I don't ever want to be a school, because I don't want to lose the parental control we have."

"The Unfinished Business of Mission," *Virginia Seminary Journal*, Spring 2009:

In 1969, the year that Rich Jones entered *Virginia Theological Seminary (VTS)*, interest in overseas mission was at a low ebb in the national Church and at the Seminary. The focus of the Episcopal Church was on the turmoil in the inner cities, and funding for the overseas work of the Church was greatly reduced.

By that time, the course at VTS in World Mission, once a requirement of all students, had not been taught for several years. Nevertheless, a small but dedicated band continued to uphold and promote the historical vision of the Seminary represented by the words above the chapel altar, "Go Ye Into All the World and Preach the Gospel." Their focus was on two areas of concern:

Virginia graduates had gone overseas in the past; now, descendents of their converts were coming back to Virginia for education. But little was being done formally to help them adjust to life in a strange culture. In the early '70s, special orientation and an International Students' Forum were instituted to help them with the ongoing challenges of life in a foreign land, and to foster theological reflection on how they would take what they had learned in this culture and translate it into the terms of their own home culture when they went back.

The need was also felt to find ways for American students to experience life in the Church outside their own boundaries. This gave birth to a Committee on International Programs, which began organizing internships for seminarians to find out firsthand what it meant to be a Christian and an Anglican in another land.

Meanwhile, concern about the neglect of world mission and the need to find a new formulation for the theology of mission was troubling many minds. An exploratory meeting was held at Berkeley Divinity School at Yale, followed by the formation of a Seminarians' Consultation on Mission, an organization in which *Virginia Theological Seminary* representatives played an active role in the coming years.

Continued

"The Unfinished Business of Mission," ... *(Continued)*

At VTS, consciousness was growing that there was a need for a full-time faculty member to embody these concerns. Someone was needed to not only teach courses in the history and theology of mission, but also oversee the various organizations, programs, and activities related to that discipline—the Seminary's Missionary Society, the programs with international students, the internships for American students overseas, and the Seminary's participation in councils of the national Church concerned with the mission of the Church. Furthermore, in an ecumenical age in which dialogue between Christianity and other world religions was a growing concern, it was felt that the person who occupied such a faculty position should have expertise in at least one other world religion, and be prepared to teach courses introducing VTS students to that religion and to principles involved in interfaith dialogue.

Rich Jones was the ideal candidate for such a position. Prior to seminary, he'd worked in Vietnam teaching English as a second language. After graduation in 1972, he and his wife Jody went to Ecuador to organize and administer the theological education programs for that diocese. Back in the United States, after a period of parish ministry in the diocese in the Central Gulf Coast, Rich and his family went off to Toronto, where he enrolled in a program of doctoral studies. His Ph.D. completed, he and Jodi and their children, Kate and Sam, returned to Virginia and Rich became the Seminary's first Professor of Mission and World Religion.

2012: Nursery School Founder

Thirty-eight year-old mother of four Anne Mandeville-Long founded Moss Garden Nursery School in Chapel Hill, North Carolina, whose motto was "no child left inside."

Life at Home

- Born in New Haven, Connecticut, in July of 1959, Anne Mandeville-Long was the third daughter and fourth child of Walter and Joan Robbins.
- With two more brothers arriving after her, Anne grew up in the middle of the pack.
- Life outside the Robbins' house in Fairfield included frequent trips to the beach on Long Island Sound, winter ski trips to southern Vermont, visits to the grandparents on the coast of Virginia, and regular New York Ranger hockey games at Madison Square Garden in New York City.
- Anne started her education at the local public elementary school, and later enrolled in a private day school in a nearby town.
- Following the tradition of her family, she spent her sophomore year in high school at a boarding school in north-central Massachusetts, and returned to finish high school at the local academy.
- Between her junior and senior years, she enrolled in a summer program at the Rhode Island School of Design, where she pursued her passion for design and ceramics.
- Intent on making her own statement in life and choosing her college, she enrolled at Hampshire College in Massachusetts, a school known for its creative approach to higher education.

Anne Mandeville-Long founded Moss Garden Nursery School.

- At Hampshire, Anne focused on cultural history, and spent a semester abroad studying in Aix-en-Provence in the south of France.
- Following her graduation from Hampshire, she followed the normal trajectory of many Connecticut young people and moved to New York City; there, she found entry-level positions in advertising and sales.
- Her next move brought her back to her Connecticut hometown, where she married and had her first two sons.
- With toddlers to attend to, Anne juggled child-rearing with several years of designing, constructing and selling unique children's clothing.
- She found the apparel market a difficult and challenging industry in which to succeed.
- In her mid-thirties, Anne and her small family decided to move away from the comfortable and familiar Northeast and settled in Chapel Hill, North Carolina, with almost as much thought as throwing a dart at a map.
- With a degree of serendipity, she and her husband decided to build a house on property located only a short walk from a small private school nestled in the woods on the northern boundary of Chapel Hill.
- Now the mother of three boys, Anne enrolled her two older sons at the nearby Emerson Waldorf School.
- At the age of 38, she delivered her fourth child, a daughter named Stella.
- "I knew that I needed to find something to do beyond volunteer work at the school. My 'a-ha' moment came when I saw an ad in the school newspaper from another mother asking for someone who could provide several hours of childcare each week," Anne recalls.
- Following a meeting with the mother Lauren and her son Andrew, who was the same age as Stella, Lauren set it all in motion when she said, "I want my children to come to you."
- For the rest of the school year, Anne provided childcare for a growing number of children, including Stella.

"No Child Left Inside" was Moss Garden's philosophy.

- A typical morning would involved walks in the woods, healthy snacks and other simple activities.
- While Anne and the children were having fun, the parent group approached her with a request for more structure and a more organized program.
- "It was at this point that Moss Garden Nursery School came into being," Anne explained.
- Knowing that she needed to learn more about early-childhood education, Anne enrolled in a series of workshops and conferences at Sunbridge College in Spring Valley, New York.
- "It was at Sunbridge College that I learned about the developmental phases of children from zero to seven years old. We discussed the basics such as how children move and how they benefit from certain sensory experiences. Jumping and climbing trees are excellent activities for young children as they form their sensory awareness of the world."
- All along, Anne's knowledge of the world of young children was being reinforced by her experiences with her older sons.

Life at Work

- Moss Garden Nursery School, now in its twelfth year, admitted 12 students ranging from two and a half to five years old.
- Anne Mandeville-Long was continuously conscious of balancing her enrollment with a mix of ages, genders, and capabilities.
- "I am amazed at how the right child comes to my program when I need that child. And, of course, with 12 children, I tend to have roughly 24 parents. Sometimes I feel that I am teaching far more than 12 students.
- "Moss Garden's program is based on one goal, which is to protect childhood. Too often in our modern world, children are being robbed of their opportunity to be children. We want our children to be open, not to be fearful, and not to feel undue anxiety. It is based on this that I have a nature-based, play-based program.

Annes's background helped her provide creative, stimulating childcare.

- "We like to use the phrase, 'No Child Left Inside'," Anne said.
- "With a program which depends so much on the out-of-doors, it is essential that the children understand that we have very clear boundaries, in spite of the fact that we have no fences. If children feel safe and loved, they can relax and engage in the important work of play."
- A typical day at Moss Garden Nursery School includes the following.
- "The children arrive at 9 a.m. The parents are encouraged to bring the children to the play area and then leave as soon as possible.
- "At around 9:15, with all the children wearing their boots, we walk through the woods, rain or shine, snow or ice. The older kids run ahead, but they know where to stop. Each day we visit the same places.

- "The walk in the woods and the 15 to 20 minutes in and around the garden help the children to connect with a sense of place.
- "Some children have started out being terrified of the woods, or scared of the dogs, or afraid to get their feet or hands muddy. It is a pure delight to see how quickly this changes.
- "After our initial time outside, we go into the house. The rhythm for this next part of the morning is always 'Circle Time.'
- "They don't know it, but it is also the time in which I do my most traditional teaching.
- "As part of Circle Time, we often sing, dance and act out stories. We work with language, diction, counting, rhythm and rhymes, all in the context of a movement journey so they can create an inner picture or an imagining of the experience."
- Along with the daily rhythm of Moss Garden Nursery School, "Miss Anne," as she is affectionately known by children and parents alike, creates seasonal festivals and regular parent meetings.

A typical morning at Moss Garden included a walk in the woods.

- Parent meetings happen on three or four occasions during the school year and are helpful with creating a forum for young and new parents to discuss issues relative to child-rearing and early childhood education.
- Anne says that she tells the parents, "I want the children to be in love with learning and with the stories that go with education."
- She then related the story of Kate, who came to Moss Garden with a large dose of skepticism.
- "She would say, 'Are you telling me the truth, Miss Anne?' This questioning turned into a sense of fear, then transformed beautifully into a sense of confidence."
- With a perspective of over 12 years of teaching and nearly 25 years of parenting, Anne ponders the question, "Why do I do this?"
- The answer is, "For selfish reasons. I love it. It fits with my view of the world, of what we need to do to create the next generation of young minds who will solve the problems that we need to confront."

Nature was Anne's classroom.

Life in the Community: Research Triangle Park, North Carolina

- The Research Triangle Park (RTP) area of North Carolina includes Raleigh, Durham, and Chapel Hill.
- Moss Garden Nursery School is one of a half-dozen preschools in this area that embraces the educational philosophy of Rudolf Steiner.
- Born in Austria, Rudolf Steiner created the philosophy upon which Waldorf education was based.
- This type of education focuses on the developmental milestones and temperaments of the individual child, and emphasizes and utilizes the arts and individual thinking as the narratives through which education is achieved.
- During the economic recession that began in 2008, there was concern that enrollment in these preschool programs would drop, since families had less expendable income, but preschool enrollment has been sustained, in some cases, by the need for both parents to seek employment outside the home.
- An increasing number of studies point to the positive effects of early childhood education and the impact it has on achievement throughout the educational experience of young people.
- The RTP was created over 50 years ago by North Carolina educators and politicians who had observed that the local universities were educating North Carolina's youth for jobs that did not exist in the state.
- Drawing on the strengths among North Carolina's academic, government and industry bases, RTP is a place to attract research and development companies, and helped the state transition from an agricultural economy to one based on business.
- The RTP area is recognized as having the highest concentration of Ph.D. graduates in the country.

HISTORICAL SNAPSHOT
2012

- Hawaii's and Delaware's civil union laws went into effect
- San Francisco raised the minimum wage within its jurisdiction to over $10 per hour, making it the highest minimum wage in the country
- Kansas, Texas, Rhode Island, and Tennessee began requiring photo identification for voters as a measure to combat voter fraud
- Classified documents were leaked detailing a range of advanced non-lethal weapons proposed or in development by the U.S. Armed Forces
- The Supreme Court made a unanimous decision that telephone consumers can gain standing in federal courts to sue abusive telemarketers
- Kodak, known for its camera film for more than 100 years, filed for bankruptcy protection
- The Supreme Court unanimously ruled that the government must obtain a search warrant permitting them to install a Global Positioning System (GPS) on citizens' private property
- Super Bowl XLVI was the most watched program in the history of U.S. television, with 111.3 million viewers who witnessed the New York Giants defeat the New England Patriots 21-17
- Umar Farouk Abdulmutallab, the so-called "underwear bomber," was sentenced to life imprisonment for attempting to detonate a bomb on Northwest Airlines Flight 253 in Detroit
- The Dow Jones Industrial Average closed above 13,000 points for the first time since May 2008
- *The Artist* won five Academy Awards including Best Picture
- Maryland became the eighth state to legalize gay marriage
- BP and plaintiffs reached an agreement over compensation for the Deepwater Horizon oil spill in the Gulf of Mexico
- A study suggested that donor stem cells may prevent organ rejection in imperfectly matched transplant cases
- Chicago, Illinois-based *Encyclopaedia Britannica,* the oldest encyclopedia still in print in English, announced that it will only offer its product online.
- A jury found Virginia Tech guilty of negligence for delaying a campus warning about the Virginia Tech Massacre of 33 students in 2007
- Former Illinois Governor Rod Blagojevich reported to Federal Correctional Institution, Englewood in Littleton, Colorado, to begin serving 14 years for attempting to sell his appointment to Barack Obama's vacated senate seat
- The movie *John Carter* recorded one of the biggest losses in cinema history, forcing Disney to take a $200 million write-down and chairman Rich Ross to resign
- MIT researchers Ramesh Raskar and Andreas Velten demonstrated an augmented reality apparatus which can allow observation of a non-line-of-sight object by means of a non-mirror, reflective surface
- Guggenheim Partners, LLC purchased the Los Angeles Dodgers for $2.1 billion, the most ever paid for a professional sports franchise

Selected Prices

Bookcase $119.00

Bottled Water $1.50

Coffee Grinder $60.53

Concert Ticket, The Gregg Allman Band $159.00

Digital Cordless Phone $119.99

Kindle, 3G + Wi-Fi $189.00

Phone, Camera Flip Phone $99.00

Printer, HP All-in-One $548.88

Sofa $899.00

Toolset, 137 Pieces $99.99

My stories and puppet plays are usually about the animals, insects, trees and flowers that the children might observe around them. Storytelling can be a very effective teaching tool. It can be used to resolve conflict within the group or to address a challenging behavior. The use of metaphor is vitally important. Children will respond to Truth. Also, storytelling is used to inspire the imagination. Stories can be nourishing to young people on many levels, equivalent to a healthy meal. I observe how the children will reenact these stories with their own interpretations and make them their own. Children will take from these stories what they need and will use them to develop their own lives. One of the most important elements of storytelling for this age group is that, in the end, the children feel love and protection.

—Anne Mandeville-Long, 2012

"Bracing for $40,000 at City Private Schools," Jenny Anderson and Rachel Ohm, *The New York Times*, January 29, 2012:

There are certain mathematical realities associated with New York City private schools: There are more students than seats at the top-tier schools, at least three sets of twins will be vying head to head for spots in any class, and already-expensive tuition can only go up.

Way up.

Over the past 10 years, the median price of first grade in the city has gone up by 48 percent, adjusted for inflation, compared with a 35 percent increase at private schools nationally—and just 24 percent at an Ivy League college—according to tuition data provided by 41 New York City K-12 private schools to the National Association of Independent Schools.

Indeed, this year's tuition at Columbia Grammar and Preparatory ($38,340 for twelfth grade) and Horace Mann ($37,275 for the upper school) is higher than Harvard's ($36,305). Those 41 schools (out of 61 New York City private schools in the National Association) provided enough data to enable a 10-year analysis. (Overall, inflation caused prices in general to rise 27 percent over the past decade.)

The median twelfth-grade tuition for the current school year was $36,970, up from $21,100 in 2001-2, according to the National Association's survey. Nationally, that figure rose to $24,240 from $14,583 a decade ago.

With schools already setting tuition rates for the 2012-13 school year—The Brearley School is $38,200—parents at Horace Mann, Columbia Grammar, and Trinity are braced to find out whether they will join families at Riverdale Country School in the $40,000-a-year club. (Riverdale actually charges $40,450 for twelfth grade.) In fact, it appears to be a question not of "if," but "when."

"Within one to two years, every independent school will cost more than $40,000," said one board member at a top school, who spoke on the condition of anonymity because the school had not yet set tuition.

And that is before requests for the annual fund, tickets to the yearly auction gala and capital campaigns to build a(nother) gym.

Parents are reluctant to complain, at least with their names attached, for fear of hurting students' standing (or siblings' admissions chances). But privately, many questioned paying more for the same. "The school's always had an amazing teacher-to-student ratio, learning

Continued

"Bracing for \$40,000 at City Private Schools," ... *(Continued)*

specialists and art programs with great music and theater," said one mother whose children attend the Dalton School (\$36,970 a year). "It was great a decade ago and great now."

"They are outrageous," said Dana Haddad, a private admissions consultant, referring to tuitions. "People don't want to put a price tag on their children's future, so they are willing to pay more than many of them can afford."

Administrators at several of New York's top schools attributed the tuition inflation to rising teacher salaries, ever-expanding programs and renovations to aging buildings. They noted that tuition still covered only about 80 percent of the cost of educating each child (that is what all the fund-raising is about). As at most companies, a majority of the costs—and the fastest-growing increases—come from salaries and benefits, especially as notoriously low-paying private schools try to compete with public school compensation.

"Some New York schools have had a 5, 10, or as high as 30 percent increase in the cost of their medical plans," said Mark Lauria, the executive director of the New York State Association of Independent Schools.

And paying teachers is only a piece of the puzzle. Léman Manhattan Preparatory School has a gym whose floor is cleaned twice a day. The Trinity School has three theaters, six art studios, two tennis courts, a pool and a diving pool. Poly Prep Country Day School raised \$2 million to open a learning center this year that has six full-time employees offering one-on-one help with subjects as varied as note-taking and test-taking....

Unlike public schools, which have faced severe cutbacks in the face of dwindling state and local revenues, private schools seem only to add courses. Take foreign languages. Schools used to offer French and Spanish. Then came German and Russian. Japanese was introduced when that country looked poised to dominate the global economy. A few years ago, Mandarin was a must-have, and now many schools offer Arabic.

"Offering Mandarin is a way to prepare students for the twenty-first-century world we live in," said John Allman, Trinity's headmaster.

"Beyond SATs, Finding Success in Numbers," Tina Rosenberg, *The New York Times*, February 15, 2012:

In 1988, Deborah Bial was working in a New York City after-school program when she ran into a former student, Lamont. He was a smart kid, a successful student who had won a scholarship to an elite college. But it hadn't worked out, and now he was back home in the Bronx. "I never would have dropped out of college if I had my posse with me," he told her.

The next year Bial started the Posse Foundation. From her work with students around the city, she chose five New York City high school students who were clearly leaders—dynamic,

Continued

"Beyond SATs, Finding Success in Numbers," ... *(Continued)*

intelligent, creative, resilient—but who might not have had the SAT scores to get into good schools. Vanderbilt University was willing to admit them all, tuition-free. The students met regularly in their senior year of high school, through the summer, and at college. Surrounded by their posse, they all thrived.

Today the Posse Foundation selects about 600 students a year, from eight different cities. They are grouped into posses of 10 students from the same city and go together to an elite college; about 40 colleges now participate in the program.

Most Posse Scholars would not have qualified for their colleges by the normal criteria. Posse Scholars' combined median reading and math SAT score is only 1050, while the median combined score at the colleges Posse students attend varies from 1210 to 1475. Nevertheless, they succeed. Ninety percent of Posse Scholars graduate—half of them on the dean's list and a quarter with academic honors. A <u>survey</u> of 20 years of alumni found that nearly 80 percent of the respondents said they had founded or led groups or clubs. There are only 40 Posse Scholars among Bryn Mawr's 1,300 students, but a Posse student has won the school's best all-around student award three times in the past seven years. Posse is changing the way universities look at qualifications for college, and what makes for college success.

Sheyenne Brown went to Adlai E. Stevenson High School in the Bronx, which before its closure in 2009 was one of the worst schools in New York City. Her parents had always worked—her mother as an administrative assistant, her father in sales. But in her junior year, her family was evicted from their home—by marshals—the same day her father lost his job. They moved into a series of homeless shelters, some of them decent, some like prison cells. "We were people who do the right thing and follow the path, and you still end up in a situation you believe only happens to you if you do the wrong thing," she said. Brown went to work at McDonald's, putting in between 20 and 48 hours a week for $5.15 per hour. Her combined SAT score was 1080. She did not seem destined to attend an elite college.

Continued

"Beyond SATs, Finding Success in Numbers," ... *(Continued)*

But in her senior year, at least one of her teachers nominated her to be a Posse Scholar. She competed against thousands of other New York City students (with 14,000 nominations nationwide for 600 slots, the program is more competitive than Harvard) and won a place with 10 other students at Middlebury, a tiny liberal arts college in Vermont. She had never heard of it.

Starting in January, Brown and the 10 others in her posse began to meet weekly with a Posse staff member. The purpose of the sessions was to solidify the group and teach them what they needed to succeed at Middlebury: how to write at a college level, but just as important, how to negotiate the social world: how to deal with a diversity of race and socioeconomic status, how to communicate with people who were very different—"finding ways to express what you want to say so that people get your point and don't feel disrespected," she said. She was living in the shelter at the time.

"In a way, Middlebury was exactly what I needed," she said. "It was a convenient bubble where everything was safe and okay, and you don't have to tell everybody your business."

The posse was key. "It's so easy to get lost. I couldn't imagine going to college without a group of people I already knew. I don't think I would have made it." They were all studying different things, she said. They didn't do homework together, but they held each other accountable for doing it. "If you needed somebody to get you out of bed and get you to the library, Antoinette [a Posse member] would get you to the library." The Posse members, she said, held each other up to the standard they had set: "How you are doing in class, how you behaved socially, and whether you were supporting people you agreed to support."

Brown graduated in 2009, cum laude. Conscious of her good fortune and eager to give back, she joined Teach for America and taught sixth-grade social studies at a KIPP charter school in Newark. Now she is in graduate school at Columbia, studying theater.

2015: Artist

Born in 1960 in Boston, Elaine Alibrandi grew up dreaming of becoming an artist, despite parents and teachers who discouraged her from continuing her education and following her dream.

Life at Home

- Elaine Alibrandi had very few prospects growing up in Dorchester, a rough inner city section of Boston, Massachusetts.
- Her family lived in a small apartment in a three-decker building and had very little money.
- The insular society in which she grew up was extremely backward; the Women's Movement did not touch people's lives there.
- Her life at home was narrow, stifling, and abusive; Elaine and her sister were considered only good for cooking, cleaning, and picking up after the rest of the family.
- She was taught by nuns in Catholic elementary and high schools, where she was "the kid who could draw and write poems."
- In grammar school, girls were required to walk in line behind the boys; only the boys were allowed gym; and during roll call, all the boys' names were called first.
- Every aspect of her existence reinforced her inferior status.
- The conditions weren't any better in high school, where Elaine was offered a biased, outdated view of the world, and the choices for her career, she was told, were only four: nurse, secretary, nun, or wife and mother.

Elaine followed her creative path to become a successful mixed-media artist.

- Even though Elaine was an honor student, her guidance counselor urged her, in 1977, not to go on to college because there were openings in Dorchester for file clerks and other office help.
- Her father was against her going to college because it would take time away from her housework.
- Elaine was adamant: She knew a college education would open doors that would otherwise be closed to her forever.
- Fortunately, she lived within subway distance of Massachusetts College of Art-a four-year public college that happened to be one of the best art colleges in the United States.
- She was accepted and got a job selling women's shoes to pay for her tuition.
- When she arrived at MassArt in September 1977, she breathed a sigh of relief.
- She was finally in a place where her talent, curiosity, and love of learning were assets rather than liabilities.
- Elaine welcomed and contemplated the myriad of ideas she encountered at MassArt from students who hailed from various backgrounds and ranged in age from late teens to early fifties.

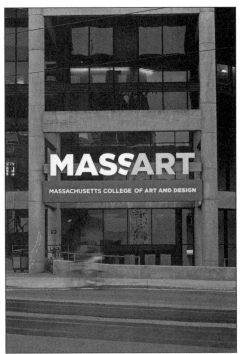

Elaine's education at MassArt refined her talent and stimulated her curiosity.

- Her art and poetry writing were honed during those years, when she was introduced to the history of art as well as being taught to work and write in various styles.
- After graduation, she continued to paint, though she didn't know how she was going to fulfill her dream of becoming a working artist.

Life at Work

- By the time Elaine earned her college degree, she had her own apartment but needed to be extremely frugal.
- She got a job in a bank and worked her way up to accountant within a few years.
- However, financial necessity conflicted with her artistic plans; even though she still painted, she did not feel like an artist.

Elaine found the balance between creating "salable" art that paid the bills, and experimenting with her own creative style.

- Her dream was to do something at home to earn money so she could be as experimental in her work as she liked and not worry about selling her paintings to pay her rent; she felt that the latter might cause her to create "salable" art instead of allowing her to follow her true creative path.
- She had already sold several paintings to co-workers and others who knew she painted.
- In the meantime, she had had many of her poems published and taken a proofreading course in Cambridge, Massachusetts, so that she could work part-time and devote more of her time to her art.
- This turned out to be a good start, and with that, she walked out of the corporate world in 1994.

Passion, Oil, cold wax, San Andreas fault gouge on wood panel, 8" x 8" x 3". Courtesy of Elaine Alibrandi.

- At first, Elaine worked through temp agencies as a proofreader, mostly at design companies, which also allowed her to take some writing and design jobs.
- Then came the Internet.
- In 1996, she bought a computer and a printer, and voila! She had an office and a studio in her home.
- Elaine had enough clients to begin her own business, progressing from proofreading to copy editing, writing, Web production, and design.
- Most importantly, she could paint every day, causing her to mature as an artist more quickly than she could ever have done painting only on the weekends.
- In 1997, Elaine got into her first group exhibition, where she sold a very large painting.
- The show's reception was crowded and a lot of fun; all she could think was that she wanted more.
- Elaine got her wish; that exhibition led to more and more shows in and around Boston, in New York City, and many other cities in the U.S.
- It also led to sales of her work and brought her to the attention of influential people in the art world.
- One day, Elaine received an email from a woman in Italy who wanted to represent her in Europe.
- Initially apprehensive, Elaine decided to ask a couple of artist friends from Italy whom she knew from having exhibited with them.

- With a resounding "Yes!" from her friends to her question of whether the representative was legitimate, she took up the offer, and in 2011 began exhibiting her work internationally, attending the shows whenever she could and even going to one of her group exhibitions in South Korea.
- At two separate artist residencies, where artists live and create together, Elaine was able to work with European and Australian artists for several weeks on Italy's Adriatic coast, on a pristine beach located in a nature reserve.
- She finally felt like an artist.

Life in the Community: Boston and Somerville, Massachusetts

- Boston is the small, historic capital of Massachusetts and is only now beginning to emerge from the doldrums of conservatism.
- Even so, galleries still very much cater to patrons of traditional art.
- Newbury Street is where the most famous and most frequented galleries are located, along with high-end boutiques and expensive restaurants.
- Some of the more interesting venues are artist-run galleries, in which exhibiting artists pay an initiation fee (about $500) plus monthly dues ($100 or more), and 40 percent of any sales they make go to the gallery.
- Members are often required to hang shows, gallery sit at exhibitions, transact sales, etc.
- The artists receive a solo show at the gallery every two years and participate in an annual group show.
- This arrangement is too expensive and burdensome for many artists.
- Since there is a dearth of non-artist-run places showing cutting-edge contemporary art in Boston, few opportunities exist in the city for artists who create daring or thought-provoking work.
- Most of the galleries that exhibit challenging work are outside the city, in places such as Somerville, which is about four miles from Boston and comprises lively squares and neighborhoods whose galleries focus more on showing leading-edge, inventive art rather than work that is most likely to sell.
- The Somerville Arts Council and the Brickbottom Artists Association are extremely active in getting provocative or unusual art seen by viewers.
- Moreover, art venues in Somerville are generally in areas where live-music halls, vibrant pubs, and eclectic cafés are located.
- Many artists participate in "Open Studios," annual events during which the public is invited into artists' studios or workspaces to view the work; these happen in nearly every city and town, including Boston and Somerville.

Boston City Hall, constructed in 1968, is still controversial in its design.

The tallest building in New England, the award-winning John Hancock Tower was built in 1976.

HISTORICAL SNAPSHOT
2015

- The United States, Iran, and five European Union powers announced an agreement on Iran's nuclear program
- In Waco Texas, biker gangs waged war against each other with chains, knives, clubs, and guns, resulting in eight deaths and 18 injuries
- The economist Jeffrey Sachs said 2015 is the last year for action on climate change
- In a 5-4 decision, the Supreme Court ruled that the Constitution guarantees a right to same-sex marriage in the United States
- President Obama announced the full re-establishment of diplomatic ties with Cuba, with the countries planning to reopen embassies in each other's capital cities
- The U.S. Food and Drug Administration approves the drug flibanserin, sometimes called the "pink pill" or the "female Viagra," designed to boost women's sexual desire
- Historic flash flooding occurred in Texas and Oklahoma in a prolonged outbreak of floods and tornadoes, leaving 17 people dead and 40 others missing
- In one week alone, two unarmed African American women died while in police custody: 28-year-old Sandra Black from Illinois and 18-year-old Kindra Chapman from Alabama
- Art auction house Christie's sold over $1 billion of art over three days-a record for the art world
- A teenage girl in Crook County, Oregon, contracted bubonic plague, possibly from an infected flea, during a hunting trip
- Flavia Pennetta defeated her childhood friend and fellow Italian Roberta Vinci to win her first Grand Slam title
- John Boehner resigned as Speaker of the House
- The New England Patriots defeated the Seattle Seahawks, 28-24, and won their fourth Super Bowl
- The Federal Communications Commission voted to regulate internet service as a telecommunications service, and thus subject broadband providers such as Comcast, Verizon, and AT&T to strict government regulation
- In Ferguson, Missouri, a state of emergency was declared after gunfire was exchanged near protests being held on the first anniversary of Michael Brown's death
- Dzhokhar Tsarnaev was sentenced to death for the 2013 Boston Marathon bombing
- African American Freddie Gray, dragged into a police van while screaming in pain, later died from multiple injuries, including his spinal cord being severed
- The Golden State Warriors defeated the Cleveland Cavaliers in six games, 4-2, for their first NBA championship in 40 years
- The Boy Scouts of America ended its ban on gay adult leaders
- The House voted to ban the display of Confederate flags at historic federal cemeteries in the Deep South
- Capt. Kristen Griest and 1st Lt. Shaye Haver made history by becoming the first two women to graduate from the Army Ranger School in the first year that the Army has opened the course to women

Selected Prices

Nikon DSLR Camera $446.95

Set of Six Travel Bottles..$7.99

Alpine Stainless Steel Tea Kettle.....................................$40.59

CD, Charity Ball by Fanny $13.99

Go Girl, Enables Women to Urinate While Standing $9.95

Unprimed, Cotton Canvas, 120" x 360"...........................$93.85

Oil Paint, Cadmium Red, 150-Milliliter Tube.................$55.99

Oil Paint Brush, Hog Bristle, Round $28.79

Stainless Steel Measuring Cups/Spoons Set $7.95

Two-Pack All-Natural Toothpaste, Trader Joe's $12.29

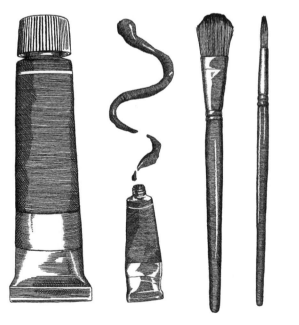

"Elaine Alibrandi Interview,"
Sam Pitcher, *TextileArtist.org*, 2014

TextileArtist.org: What initially captured your imagination about textile art?
My very first gallery show included three textile artists whose work shattered my idea of what mixed media and textile art could be. One of the pieces on display was a fabric shoe completely covered with sea glass. I loved that combination of media.

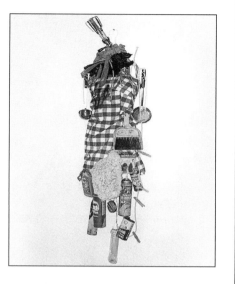

What or who were your early influences and how has your life/upbringing influenced your work?
My influences were Remedios Varo, Käthe Kollwitz, Paula Modersohn-Becker. German Expressionism as a whole had a great impact on me. Being a docent at Judy Chicago's *The Dinner Party* when it came to Boston in 1980 really opened my eyes to the possibilities of various media. Not only did the exhibit show me what could be done in an installation, but it also educated me in women's history. There were facts and bios up on the walls around the triangular dinner table about women whose accomplishments had been systematically ignored in history. That made me realize how much I had to learn on my own.

What was your route to becoming an artist?
Massachusetts College of Art. The school in the late 1970s exposed me to ideas I had never encountered, and I absorbed everything like a thirsty sponge. When I first began my studies there as a kid of 17, it was as though my psyche let out one huge sigh of relief and then shouted, "Finally!"

What is your chosen medium and what are your techniques?
I started out as a painter, but I was fascinated by the canvas itself: its weave, the way it felt on my hands, its magnification under a drop of water, the fraying of its fibers when it was cut or

ripped. That was when I began to slice canvas. I learned how to manipulate which way it would curve when primed in different ways with gesso. After that, I began adding mixed media such as wood, stones, cloth, soil, sawdust, sea sponges, hair, you name it. Gesso holds anything in place, and I often use it by itself to add texture to a piece.

My clothing pieces are either wall-hung works or freestanding ones with other media attached. There is something very evocative about clothing when it's not being worn. It has a presence that, when it is worn, fuses with the wearer, but when unworn, suggests creative possibilities to me. Just putting paint in a strategic place or adding certain media or props to clothing allows it to tell a story or depict a situation.

Continued

How would you describe your work and where do you think it fits within the sphere of contemporary art?
I would describe my work as expressive of myself. It's very unsettling, sometimes, to see that a piece I just finished is simply a disguised self-portrait.

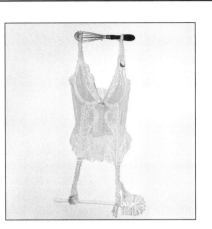

Some of my work is overtly feminist, if by "feminist" one means human rights for women. Much of my art reveals details about my personal history that some would prefer I kept hidden. However, silence perpetuates and exacerbates most problems. If some people are uncomfortable seeing or hearing about them, imagine how it felt to experience them.

I want to show people stories, because I'm not as adept at telling stories in words as I am with using images. For example, my piece titled *An Afternoon in Somalia...or Kenya...or Sudan...or....* is upsetting to many people, but it's the truth. This happens every day, and it is cruel and ugly. But it wouldn't be as powerful if I talked about the cruelty and ugliness in words.

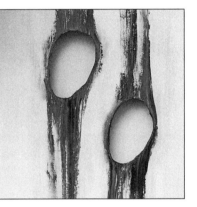

Rarely do I ever think about where my work fits in the realm of contemporary art. I suppose that's for others to decide. If anyone out there knows, please tell me!

TextileArtist.org: Tell us a bit about your process and what environment you like to work in?
Elaine Alibrandi: If I am moved by something, especially in nature, I automatically envision in my mind the art piece it will become, complete with the media I'll use to create it. I like to work alone in my studio, often in silence but mostly with music playing. I feel about music the way I do about art: If it grabs my soul, it's mine forever. It's the hand in which my heart beats.

I love working in my studio, which is in my home, although the former is taking over the latter, which is fine with me. Having my art in various stages all around the place inspires me. The great thing about my studio is that I can see my friends and neighbors, who often look up at my window to see if I'm working when they pass by. Their smiles and waves remind me that, although I'm alone in my own sacred place, I have good people around me.

Being in my studio feeds my soul. In addition to creating art, I greet the morning there; it's where I go to think and feel calm. I often sleep there if I'm working on a piece late into the night.

Continued

Do you use a sketchbook?
I always have a firm idea of what a piece will look like well before I start, so I rarely use a sketchbook unless I'm designing the composition of a work within a particular size or shape. Instead, I use a leather-bound book given to me by some very dear friends and which I've designated an "art diary" for jotting down ideas for pieces, their progress at certain intervals, how I solved problems with the media (for future reference), and finally, my feelings about the pieces when they're finished. I also fasten a small image of each piece to the diary page(s) I used.

What currently inspires you and which other artists do you admire and why?
Nature is a huge inspiration to me. Women's issues drive much of my work as well. Art that grabs my soul inspires me, as does conceptual art that is also visually interesting to me, and art that sparks an idea in my mind or some spirit of kinship with the artist. The genre doesn't matter as long as I feel a pull to look at a piece and think about it.

As for artists I admire, Cornelia Parker is a great one. Her *Hanging Fire (Suspected Arson)*, which I first saw at the Institute of Contemporary Art in Boston, totally blew me away, as does her *Subconscious of a Monument*. I admire Dawn Ng and Giuseppe Licari for their brilliant installations that dynamically employ objects, shadow, and perspective.

Tell us about a piece of work you have fond memories of and why?
That would be the very first clothing piece I ever did: *Cast Off.* I had turned 50 years old and was rethinking just about everything that was or had been important to me at certain times in my life. Looking in my closet, I examined all the dresses and accessories I didn't wear anymore and remembered how my appearance had, at one period, taken up a lot of my time and defined my feelings about myself. It had been great fun to wear those things, but they now seemed utterly irrelevant to my life as an artist.

On an impulse, I grabbed a white, beaded dress, took it into my studio, and began cutting the material with scissors. At first, I cringed a bit at ruining a piece of clothing on purpose, but I quickly became excited. The idea lunged at me: Put the shreds on stretcher bars to depict my true nature overpowering the superficial trappings of fashion that, for me, had dictated my self-esteem. It was like the Incredible Hulk splitting open his shirt! (The thought occurs to me that I should do something creative with all that unused makeup as well.)

Anyway, I removed all the beads that had been sewn on in a deliberate pattern and put them back on the dress in a scattered way that suggested they were falling down the dress.

But it needed something. Well, what's a dress without the shoes and bag to match? So I added those and it was done: In that piece, I saw myself and my priorities emerging and dominating. Another self-portrait. It's also become a very popular piece with viewers.

Another piece in which a dress, shoes, and bag are the main characters is *I Have the Fee in Here Somewhere,* which I was fortunate enough to have juried into shows in South Korea and in California. Because U.S. legislators are passing bills limiting abortion access and trying to make abortion illegal even in cases of rape and incest, I decided to create a piece with clothing that had been violently torn as if from a rape. As the title suggests, victims and other women will simply have abortions performed illegally in filthy conditions by dubious "abortionists."

Continued

How has your work developed since you began and how do you see it evolving in the future?

My work has become much more daring and diverse than when I began. I had subconscious limits as to what to use in my art and how to use it, and fears about whether a piece would turn out successfully. Now I'm completely unbound by those limitations and fears.

In the future, I want to do larger, more complex pieces and would love to create large-scale installations, particularly with cloth or clothing. I'm also planning a performance piece with another artist; I'd like to do more of that.

What advice would you give to an aspiring textile artist?

Don't be afraid to explore all avenues that interest you, even if they lead you far away from your comfort media. There is so much to experience, and I've discovered that I frequently return to a previous style with a fresh perspective once I've tried other things in my work and in

"The Guerrilla Girls, After 3 Decades, Still Rattling Art World Cages," Melena Ryzik, *The New York Times,* August 5, 2015

When you've spent 30 years wearing a gorilla mask, as the women known by the aliases Frida Kahlo and Käthe Kollwitz have, certain behavior becomes second nature. So there were Kahlo and Kollwitz, two of the pseudonymous founding members of the Guerrilla Girls, the activist, feminist art collective, preening and posing at their 30th anniversary party and retrospective in May. They sipped prosecco through straws (their gorilla lips wouldn't allow much more) at the Abrons Arts Center on the Lower East Side, while guests gazed at walls lined with the posters protesting elitism and bias that first shook the art world in the 1980s. "Do

Women Have to Be Naked to Get Into the Met Museum?" one provocatively asked. The Guerrillas' name tags identified them as pioneering dead female artists (like Alice Neel, the portraitist, or Zubeida Agha, the Pakistani modernist) whose legacies they hope to continue.

After three decades as masked crusaders for gender and racial equality in the art world-and increasingly, everywhere else-the Guerrilla Girls have lately been enjoying a victory lap. Last year, the Whitney Museum of American Art acquired the group's portfolio of 88 posters and ephemera from 1985 to 2012, documenting the number of women and minorities represented in galleries and institutions, including the Whitney itself.

"To me, they are art world royalty," said David Kiehl, the Whitney's curator for prints, who helped persuade the museum to acquire their work.

The Walker Art Center in Minneapolis also bought the Guerrilla Girls' entire collection of posters, in numbered prints, which were originally plastered on walls, phone booths and galleries in SoHo. And the posters still pop up in gallery districts, calling attention to dispropor-

Thirty years after the feminist activists began, the Guerrilla Girls are still going. Their identities remain a secret but their fight for equality in the art world still attracts legions of fans. Photo by Channon Hodge, Melena Ryzik and Erica Berenstein, August 5, 2015

tionate representation in the art world and wage inequality. The Walker is planning a Guerrilla Girls exhibition for January.

Olga Viso, the Walker's director, discovered the group as an art history student in the 1980s. "I remember feeling such pride that there were female artists out there giving voice to these concerns that we were sensing and feeling," she said, adding that coming of age with the Guerrilla Girls "totally shaped who I am and the artists I worked with."

Gloria Steinem, too, is a longtime fan. "I think they're the perfect protest group," she said, "because they have humor." One poster cataloged the advantages to being a woman artist: "Working without the pressure of success; knowing your career might pick up after you're 80; getting your picture in the art magazines wearing a gorilla suit."

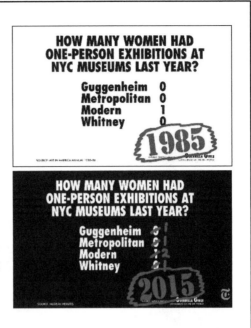

Membership has fluctuated over the years, from a high of about 30 art-world women to a few handfuls of active members now. Some women left the suit behind, seeking recognition under their own names. Others became professors or real estate agents. But most have remained committed to anonymity, filtering in and out of the crew and fretting about what it meant to be part of the world they were lampooning. "Some of us wanted a piece of the pie, and some of us wanted to blow the whole pie up," Kahlo said. "We agreed to disagree."

They still exhibit and share work in places like Reykjavik, Iceland, London and Sarajevo-their next appearance will be in September at the Printed Matter's N.Y. Art Book Fair at MoMA PS1-and lecture at colleges, where their campaigns are part of women's studies and art history classes.

A Guerrilla Girl poses in front of a billboard in 2002 that criticizes the Academy Awards not far from where they are presented in Hollywood.
guerillagirls

Today they seem prescient: They long ago took aim at issues that are flash points now, like gender bias in Hollywood, and racism in the gallery world ("Guerrilla Girls' definition of a hypocrite?" read one poster. "An art collector who buys white male art at benefits for liberal causes, but never buys art by women or artists of color.") Co-opting the look and feel of advertising, they were social media-friendly and selfie-ready before those terms existed. Though other activist groups, like the newly formed anonymous collective Pussy Galore, have taken up the cause, the Guerrilla Girls say their mission is far from over. "They're as valid today, and needed today, as they were 30 years ago," Mr. Kiehl said, "because what they're talking about is still going on." The June issue of *ArtNews*, edited by Maura Reilly, founding curator at the Elizabeth A. Sackler Center for Feminist Art at the Brooklyn Museum and current chief curator at National Academy Museum, took stock of the state of women in the art world. It found that, despite some gains, the majority of celebrated artists are still white and male, and that discrimination exists from the top down in cultural institutions.

"A Few of My Favorite Things,"
Mixed Media Art Magazine, Issue 17

A Few of My Favorite Things

Elaine Alibrandi opened up her love of mixed media about the same time she realized her closet was full of inspiration.

Awakening: *Oil, muscovite mica, milky quartz, basalt, greenschist, aluminum foil on canvas; 18" x 32" x 3"*

Plotting out with black marker where I wanted the rocks and minerals positioned on the canvas, I applied gesso generously to the canvas surface to hold these heavy rocks in place and set them in the wells of gesso I'd made for them. After letting the gesso dry and ensuring the rocks were securely fastened, I applied more gesso and partially buried crumpled aluminum foil into it so the foil would be visible only in certain places. The final step was painting the piece with oils.

My use of mixed media emerged from a need to express myself beyond paint and canvas. At first, I began using aluminum foil on canvas to create texture above and below the painted surface. After about a year of gradually using more and more foil in different ways, I ventured into other non-traditional media. Once the possibilities for my work revealed themselves, a door burst open for me—initially, my closet door. I chose a dress, shoes, and a handbag, and created my first clothing piece. I have since used clothing in many works as a way to tell a story, or to use as the basis for one.

Barricade: *Antique window frame, silk yarn, nails, oil, gesso, 46" x 34" x 3"*

After varnishing an old window frame, I drove nails partway into the inside of the right-hand opening. I then strung silk yarn, which I had coated with cold wax to stiffen it a bit, around each nail and across the opening, while leaving some slack, until I'd made a delicate web across the rough, heavy frame. When that was done, I hammered the nails fully into the frame to secure and tighten the yarn. I then painted the nails and the yarn around them with oils and applied white gesso to parts of the yarn to emphasize the web's pattern.

The immediacy and reality of using actual objects rather than representing them with paint excites and inspires me. The media I use depends on what I want to express: If I want to call attention to an interesting wedge of wood, I use the actual wood, as in "Chameleon". I've progressed to using rocks, hair, bubble wrap, interesting objects found in the street, blood (mine), and on and on, ad infinitum. My experimentation with this myriad of media makes my creations come alive.

As a result, my work has become much more conceptual. I've expressed the idea of captivity with a bloody burqa, a fence, a dress form wrapped in a tablecloth and hung with cooking utensils and cleaning supplies. I couldn't think of a better way for me, personally, as an artist, to express the sacredness of Earth than by using wood, stones, gravel, and soil in my piece Tabernacle.

Broken Image: *Broken mirror, acrylics, cold wax on wood panel, 26" x 18"*

I removed the panel from the back of a mirror and broke the mirror into approximately the pattern I hoped would result. When the mirror was in pieces, I arranged the shards on a wood panel, which I had coated with a combination of white, black, and metallic silver acrylic paint, and adhered them to the panel with gesso. After applying cold wax to the space around the mirror pieces and letting it dry, I used a palette knife and steel wool to score the wax and provide texture.

Chameleon: *Oil, cold wax, bark on wood panel, 8" x 8" x 3"*

Using gesso, I secured a wedge of cut wood onto a primed wood panel. When that was dry, I used oils thickened with cold wax to paint around the piece of wood. After allowing this layer to dry completely, I scored it and cut into it with various woodcutting tools to extend the patterns of the wood wedge outward.

Rendering an object with paint is not as difficult for me as finding ways to integrate actual objects into a piece. How do I affix thick, heavy portions of tree trunks or delicate flakes of mica onto a textured surface? How do I combine radically different types of media seamlessly? Because some of the problems I encounter are quite challenging, I often need to do a lot of initial planning before I can begin working with the media. Nevertheless, such challenges are exciting to me, especially the solving of them. Often, I'm as proud of resolving the dilemmas as I am of a finished piece that turned out well. Every piece is a puzzle that forces me to think in a different way and is, therefore, a learning experience.

MIXEDMEDIA**ART**

Drop of Water, Grain of Sand: *Oil, aluminum foil on hollowed-out canvas; 24" x 24" x 3"*

I cut a hole in this canvas roughly the shape of that in the finished piece and filled it with heavy duty aluminum foil to form a shallow well, leaving a raised brim around the well about two inches higher than the surrounding canvas. After sculpting the foil into the patterns I wanted, I adhered the edges of the foil to the canvas surrounding the hole with gesso. Covering the rest of the canvas with gessoed foil created the overall texture of the piece. I painted it to match what had inspired it: a fossil of a drop of seawater from the Altai Mountains bordering the Gobi Desert.

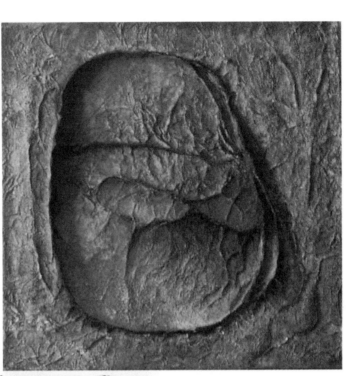

Goodbye: *Oil, sea sponges, aluminum foil on hollowed-out canvas, 28" x 24" x 6"*

This piece depicts a dying coral reef. Following the same procedure as with "Drop of Water, Grain of Sand", I plotted out with black marker and cut holes in the canvas, filling them in with gessoed aluminum foil to create shallow wells. For the dying coral, I dipped sea sponges into gesso, wrung them out, adhered them to the canvas all around the holes I'd cut out, and allowed them to dry, after which I painted them and the entire surface with oils.

In addition to objects my friends give me, eBay is a mixed-media artist's dream for just about anything at great prices. I needed empty cleaning-product cans from the 1970s and found them there. An 80-pound role of heavily rusted barbed wire. Rock and mineral specimens. An antique meat hook. I also discovered early on that heavy-bodied gesso is the best glue ever. The thinner kind comes in different colors, which I find very handy if the final piece will have a particular overall hue. Hot glue is great, along with a needle and thread, for fabric pieces.

My inspiration can come from anywhere. For example, my piece "Goodbye" resulted from my watching a documentary about endangered coral reefs. After researching how a dying reef's appearance changes over time, I printed out the most appropriate photos I'd found and lived with them in my studio for about a month. Sea sponges seemed the obvious choice to use for this piece.

Tabernacle: *Wood, canvas, oil, stones, gravel, potting soil, hair, aluminum foil, popcorn kernels, 20" x 26" x 26"*

This work was made in two separate steps. First, on the canvas on top of the box, I alternately layered the gesso and the media—stones, gravel, potting soil, hair, aluminum foil, popcorn kernels—until I had created the surfaces you see on the piece. I asked a friend to build a wooden box on which the canvas on top would fit, and once the box was finished, I adhered all the media to its surface with gesso. This took over a year to complete. I consider nature sacred (hence, the title) and wanted the box to be this height so that when viewers were obliged to lean down to examine the piece, they would unconsciously be bowing to Earth.

MIXEDMEDIA**ART**

> " Every piece is a puzzle that forces me to think in a different way and is, therefore, a learning experience. "

With a black marker on a primed, stretched canvas, I plotted out the locations and shapes of the holes I would create, cut them out, and covered them loosely with heavy duty aluminum foil, which I sculpted into my desired patterns and covered with gesso. I prepared the sponges by cutting them into the shapes I needed, dipping them into gesso thinned with water, and gently wringing them out. I had to apply them with gesso to the canvas while they were still wet; otherwise, they would not adhere as well. Also, this allowed them to expand into and against each other to provide a more dense look to the piece.

When the entire surface was ready to be painted, I used oils for the intensely resonant colors of the healthier coral in the photos; however, once I had done this, I found it very difficult to resist the temptation to leave it that way. But my plan had been to address pollution and climate change, so I painted over the beautiful greens and blues with hoary hues, as in the photos I'd used as references. Had I coated the sponges and the canvas with dark-colored gesso in the beginning, I wouldn't have had to use a tiny funnel to pour thinned oil paint into the white gessoed holes of each sponge. That's where the learning experience comes in: hopefully in the beginning, but often during the process or even after the piece is finished.

Working in mixed media has made me think differently as an artist. Whereas I used to consider how I could render something I saw, now my mind is attuned to how I can use objects as actual components in a piece. I experience a constant receptiveness when I am doing everything from walking down the street to looking at a fire in a hearth. Media are everywhere, and their possibilities are endless.

My short list of must-haves

- Latex gloves
- Heavy-bodied professional gesso
- Stretched canvas
- Wood panels
- Oils and medium

Nice-to-haves

- Cold wax
- Wood
- Rocks/minerals
- Other sundry media such as found objects
- Clothing as media

MIXEDMEDIA**ART**

Further Reading

Adams, John, Deming Family, Perkins Family, and Quincy Family. *Deming, Perkins, and Quincy Families Papers.* N.p.: n.p., n.d. Print.

Babcock, Barbara Allen. *Sex Discrimination and the Law: History, Practice, and Theory.* Boston, MA: Little, Brown, 1996. Print.

Browne, Lois. *Girls of Summer: The Real Story of the All-American Girls Professional Baseball League.* Toronto: HarperCollins, 1993. Print.

Chen, Aric. *Campbell Kids: A Souper Century.* New York: Harry N. Abrams, 2004. Print.

Cooney, Joan Ganz. *The First Year of Sesame Street: A History and Overview-final Report.* New York: Childrens Television Workshop, 1970. Print.

Cott, Nancy F. *History of Women in the United States: Historical Articles on Women's Lives and Activities.* Munich: K.G. Saur, 1992. Print.

Dahl, Linda. *Morning Glory: A Biography of Mary Lou Williams.* Berkeley: U of California, 2001. Print.

Derks, Scott, and Tony Smith. *Working Americans, 1770-1869.* Millerton, NY: Grey House, 2008. Print.

Dolezalek, Holly, and Robyn Lea. Sayre. *Standardized Testing in Schools.* Edina, MN: ABDO Pub., 2009. Print.

Dreher, Rod. *Crunchy Cons: How Birkenstocked Burkeans, Gun-loving Organic Gardeners, Evangelical Free-range Farmers, Hip Homeschooling Mamas, Right-wing Nature Lovers, and Their Diverse Tribe of Countercultural Conservatives Plan to save America (or at Least the Republican Party).* New York: Crown Forum, 2006. Print.

Egan, Bill. *Florence Mills: Harlem Jazz Queen.* Lanham, MD: Scarecrow, 2004. Print.

Foner, Philip Sheldon. *History of the Labor Movement in the United States.* New York: International, 1991. Print.

Freeman, John W. *The Metropolitan Opera Stories of the Great Operas.* New York: Metropolitan Opera Guild, 1997. Print.

Gordon, Robert. *Respect Yourself: Stax Records and the Soul Explosion.* N.p.: n.p., n.d. Print.

Graham, Bette Nesmith, Ruth I. Anderson, and Floyd Jenkins. *Oral History Interview with Bette Graham, 1977 August 3 and 1980 April 2.* N.p.: n.p., n.d. Print.

Griffin, Orwin Bradford. *The Evolution of the Connecticut State School System: With Special Reference to the Emergence of the High School,* Issue 293 Teachers college, Columbia University, 1928

Haley, Margaret A., and Robert L. Reid. *Battleground: The Autobiography of Margaret A. Haley.* Urbana: U of Illinois, 1982. Print.

Harrison, Hank. *The Grateful Dead.* London: Star International, 1975. Print.

Holtzman-Conston, Jordan. *Countercultural Sports in America: The History and Meaning of Ultimate Frisbee.* Saarbru¨cken: Lambert Academic, 2010. Print.

Jezic, Diane, and Elizabeth Wood. "Amy Marcy Cheney Beach." *Women Composers: The Lost Tradition Found.* New York: Feminist at the City U of New York, 1994. 147-55. Print.

Jones, Plummer Alston. *Libraries, Immigrants, and the American Experience.* Westport, CT: Greenwood, 1999. Print.

Kaplan, E. Ann. *Women and Film: Both Sides of the Camera.* New York: Methuen, 1983. Print.

Kempton, Arthur. *Boogaloo: The Quintessence of American Popular Music.* New York: Pantheon, 2003. Print.

Kerber, Linda K., and De Hart Jane Sherron. *Women's America: Refocusing the past.* New York: Oxford UP, 2000. Print.

Kik, J. Marcellus. *The Supreme Court and Prayer in the Public School*. Philadelphia: Presbyterian and Reformed Pub., 1963. Print.

King, Anna Matilda, and Melanie Pavich-Lindsay. *Anna: The Letters of a St. Simons Island Plantation Mistress, 1817-1859*. Athens: U of Georgia, 2002. Print.

Koca, Selim. *Transition to Hydrogen Fuel Cell Vehicles*. New York: Nova Science, 2010. Print.

Lamb, Annette. "Contemporary Libraries: 1930s." *History of Libraries*. Eduscapes, n.d. Web. 04 Nov. 2015.

LeClercq, Anne Sinkler Whaley, and Emily Wharton LeClerq. *Antebellum Plantation Household: Including the South Carolina Low Country Receipts and Remedies of Emily Wharton Sinkler*. Columbia: U of South Carolina, 1996. Print.

McDonagh, Eileen L., and Laura Pappano. *Playing with the Boys: Why Separate Is Not Equal in Sports*. Oxford: Oxford UP, 2008. Print.

Mompoullan, Chantal. *Voice of America Interviews with Eight American Women of Achievement: Grace Hopper, Betty Friedan, Nancy Landon Kassebaum, Mary Calderone, Helen Thomas, Julia Montgomery Walsh, Maya Angelou, Nancy Clark Reynolds*. Washington, D.C.?: Voice of America, United States Information Agency, 1985. Print.

Muir, William Ker. *Prayer in the Public Schools: Law and Attitude Change*. Chicago, IL: U of Chicago, 1967. Print.

Murphy, Joseph. *Homeschooling in America: Capturing and Assessing the Movement*. Thousand Oaks, CA: Corwin, 2012. Print.

Ngai, Mae M., and Jon Gjerde. *Major Problems in American Immigration History: Documents and Essays*. Boston, MA: Wadsworth, Cengage Learning, 2013. Print.

Padilla, Felix M., Nicola´s Kanellos, and Claudio Esteva. *Handbook of Hispanic Cultures in the United States*. Houston (Tex.): Arte Pu´blico, 1994. Print.

Papachristou, Judith. *Women Together: A History in Documents of the Women's Movement in the United States*. New York: Knopf, 1976. Print.

Parker, Alison M. *Purifying America: Women, Cultural Reform, and Pro-censorship Activism, 1873-1933*. Urbana: U of Illinois, 1997. Print.

Phelps, Frank V. "Rawls, Katherine Louise." *American National Biography Online*. Oxford Oxford University Press, n.d. Web.

Polsky, Richard M. *Getting to Sesame Street: Origins of the Children's Television Workshop*. New York: Praeger, 1974. Print.

Provenzo, Eugene F., John Renaud, and Asterie Baker. Provenzo. *Encyclopedia of the Social and Cultural Foundations of Education*. Thousand Oaks, CA: Sage Publications, 2009. Print.

Ronda, Bruce A. *Elizabeth Palmer Peabody: A Reformer on Her Own Terms*. Cambridge, MA: Harvard UP, 1999. Print.

Rooney, Kathleen. *Live Nude Girl: My Life as an Object*. Fayetteville: U of Arkansas, 2008. Print.

Roszak, Theodore. *The Making of a Counter Culture: Reflections on the Technocratic Society and Its Youthful Opposition*. Berkeley: U of California, 1995. Print.

Rousmaniere, Kate. *Citizen Teacher: The Life and Leadership of Margaret Haley*. Albany: State U of New York, 2005. Print.

Rowe, Susan, and Susan Humphries. *The Coombes Approach: Learning through an Experiential and Outdoor Curriculum*. London: Continuum, 2012. Print.

Ruggiero, Angela. *Breaking the Ice: My Journey to Olympic Hockey, the Ivy League, and beyond*. East Bridgewater, MA: Drummond Pub., 2006. Print.

Rui´z, Vicki, and Virginia Sa´nchez Korrol. *Latinas in the United States: A Historical Encyclopedia*. Bloomington: Indiana UP, 2006. Print.

Schroeder, Alan, Cornelius Van Wright, and Ying-Hwa Hu. *Baby Flo: Florence Mills Lights up the Stage*. N.p.: n.p., n.d. Print.

Steele, Valerie. *The Corset : A Cultural History*. New York: Yale UP, 2001. Print.

Southern Historical Collection. The Wilson Library, University of North Carolina at Chapel Hill. *Susan Davis Nye Hutchison Journals, 1815; 1826-1841*. Southern Historical Collection, The Wilson Library, University of North Carolina at Chapel Hill. Web. 30 Oct. 2015.

Thelwell, Norman. *Wrestling with a Pencil: The Life of a Freelance Artist*. London: Methuen, 1986. Print.

Thimmesh, Catherine, and Melissa Sweet. *Girls Think of Everything: Stories of Ingenious Inventions by Women*. Boston: Houghton Mifflin, 2000. Print.

Thomas, Joseph J. *Leadership Embodied: The Secrets to Success of the Most Effective Navy and Marine Corps Leaders*. Annapolis, MD: Naval Institute, 2013. Print.

Vare, Ethlie Ann., and Greg Ptacek. *Women Inventors & Their Discoveries*. Minneapolis: Oliver, 1993. Print.

Vision of Beauty The Story of Sarah Breedlove Walker. N.p.: Paw Prints, 2012. Print.

Wertheimer, Barbara M. *We Were There: The Story of Working Women in America*. New York: Pantheon, 1977. Print.

Zigler, Edward, and Sally J. Styfco. *The Hidden History of Head Start*. New York: Oxford UP, 2010. Print.

INDEX

2016 Title List

Visit www.GreyHouse.com for Product Information, Table of Contents, and Sample Pages.

General Reference

An African Biographical Dictionary
America's College Museums
American Environmental Leaders: From Colonial Times to the Present
Encyclopedia of African-American Writing
Encyclopedia of Constitutional Amendments
Encyclopedia of Gun Control & Gun Rights
An Encyclopedia of Human Rights in the United States
Encyclopedia of Invasions & Conquests
Encyclopedia of Prisoners of War & Internment
Encyclopedia of Religion & Law in America
Encyclopedia of Rural America
Encyclopedia of the Continental Congress
Encyclopedia of the United States Cabinet, 1789-2010
Encyclopedia of War Journalism
Encyclopedia of Warrior Peoples & Fighting Groups
The Environmental Debate: A Documentary History
The Evolution Wars: A Guide to the Debates
From Suffrage to the Senate: America's Political Women
Global Terror & Political Risk Assessment
Nations of the World
Political Corruption in America
Privacy Rights in the Digital Era
The Religious Right: A Reference Handbook
Speakers of the House of Representatives, 1789-2009
This is Who We Were: 1880-1900
This is Who We Were: A Companion to the 1940 Census
This is Who We Were: In the 1910s
This is Who We Were: In the 1920s
This is Who We Were: In the 1940s
This is Who We Were: In the 1950s
This is Who We Were: In the 1960s
This is Who We Were: In the 1970s
U.S. Land & Natural Resource Policy
The Value of a Dollar 1600-1865: Colonial Era to the Civil War
The Value of a Dollar: 1860-2014
Working Americans 1770-1869 Vol. IX: Revolutionary War to the Civil War
Working Americans 1880-1999 Vol. I: The Working Class
Working Americans 1880-1999 Vol. II: The Middle Class
Working Americans 1880-1999 Vol. III: The Upper Class
Working Americans 1880-1999 Vol. IV: Their Children
Working Americans 1880-2015 Vol. V: Americans At War
Working Americans 1880-2005 Vol. VI: Women at Work
Working Americans 1880-2006 Vol. VII: Social Movements
Working Americans 1880-2007 Vol. VIII: Immigrants
Working Americans 1880-2009 Vol. X: Sports & Recreation
Working Americans 1880-2010 Vol. XI: Inventors & Entrepreneurs
Working Americans 1880-2011 Vol. XII: Our History through Music
Working Americans 1880-2012 Vol. XIII: Education & Educators
World Cultural Leaders of the 20th & 21st Centuries

Education Information

Charter School Movement
Comparative Guide to American Elementary & Secondary Schools
Complete Learning Disabilities Directory
Educators Resource Directory
Special Education: A Reference Book for Policy and Curriculum Development

Health Information

Comparative Guide to American Hospitals
Complete Directory for Pediatric Disorders
Complete Directory for People with Chronic Illness
Complete Directory for People with Disabilities
Complete Mental Health Directory
Diabetes in America: Analysis of an Epidemic
Directory of Drug & Alcohol Residential Rehab Facilities
Directory of Health Care Group Purchasing Organizations
Directory of Hospital Personnel
HMO/PPO Directory
Medical Device Register
Older Americans Information Directory

Business Information

Complete Television, Radio & Cable Industry Directory
Directory of Business Information Resources
Directory of Mail Order Catalogs
Directory of Venture Capital & Private Equity Firms
Environmental Resource Handbook
Food & Beverage Market Place
Grey House Homeland Security Directory
Grey House Performing Arts Directory
Grey House Safety & Security Directory
Grey House Transportation Security Directory
Hudson's Washington News Media Contacts Directory
New York State Directory
Rauch Market Research Guides
Sports Market Place Directory

Statistics & Demographics

American Tally
America's Top-Rated Cities
America's Top-Rated Smaller Cities
America's Top-Rated Small Towns & Cities
Ancestry & Ethnicity in America
The Asian Databook
Comparative Guide to American Suburbs
The Hispanic Databook
Profiles of America
"Profiles of" Series – State Handbooks
Weather America

Financial Ratings Series

TheStreet Ratings' Guide to Bond & Money Market Mutual Funds
TheStreet Ratings' Guide to Common Stocks
TheStreet Ratings' Guide to Exchange-Traded Funds
TheStreet Ratings' Guide to Stock Mutual Funds
TheStreet Ratings' Ultimate Guided Tour of Stock Investing
Weiss Ratings' Consumer Guides
Weiss Ratings' Guide to Banks
Weiss Ratings' Guide to Credit Unions
Weiss Ratings' Guide to Health Insurers
Weiss Ratings' Guide to Life & Annuity Insurers
Weiss Ratings' Guide to Property & Casualty Insurers

Bowker's Books In Print® Titles

American Book Publishing Record® Annual
American Book Publishing Record® Monthly
Books In Print®
Books In Print® Supplement
Books Out Loud™
Bowker's Complete Video Directory™
Children's Books In Print®
El-Hi Textbooks & Serials In Print®
Forthcoming Books®
Large Print Books & Serials™
Law Books & Serials In Print™
Medical & Health Care Books In Print™
Publishers, Distributors & Wholesalers of the US™
Subject Guide to Books In Print®
Subject Guide to Children's Books In Print®

Canadian General Reference

Associations Canada
Canadian Almanac & Directory
Canadian Environmental Resource Guide
Canadian Parliamentary Guide
Canadian Venture Capital & Private Equity Firms
Financial Post Directory of Directors
Financial Services Canada
Governments Canada
Health Guide Canada
The History of Canada
Libraries Canada
Major Canadian Cities

2016 Title List

Visit www.SalemPress.com for Product Information, Table of Contents, and Sample Pages.

Science, Careers & Mathematics

Ancient Creatures
Applied Science
Applied Science: Engineering & Mathematics
Applied Science: Science & Medicine
Applied Science: Technology
Biomes and Ecosystems
Careers in Building Construction
Careers in Business
Careers in Chemistry
Careers in Communications & Media
Careers in Environment & Conservation
Careers in Healthcare
Careers in Hospitality & Tourism
Careers in Human Services
Careers in Law, Criminal Justice & Emergency Services
Careers in Manufacturing
Careers in Physics
Careers in Sales, Insurance & Real Estate
Careers in Science & Engineering
Careers in Technology Services & Repair
Computer Technology Innovators
Contemporary Biographies in Business
Contemporary Biographies in Chemistry
Contemporary Biographies in Communications & Media
Contemporary Biographies in Environment & Conservation
Contemporary Biographies in Healthcare
Contemporary Biographies in Hospitality & Tourism
Contemporary Biographies in Law & Criminal Justice
Contemporary Biographies in Physics
Earth Science
Earth Science: Earth Materials & Resources
Earth Science: Earth's Surface and History
Earth Science: Physics & Chemistry of the Earth
Earth Science: Weather, Water & Atmosphere
Encyclopedia of Energy
Encyclopedia of Environmental Issues
Encyclopedia of Environmental Issues: Atmosphere and Air Pollution
Encyclopedia of Environmental Issues: Ecology and Ecosystems
Encyclopedia of Environmental Issues: Energy and Energy Use
Encyclopedia of Environmental Issues: Policy and Activism
Encyclopedia of Environmental Issues: Preservation/Wilderness Issues
Encyclopedia of Environmental Issues: Water and Water Pollution
Encyclopedia of Global Resources
Encyclopedia of Global Warming
Encyclopedia of Mathematics & Society
Encyclopedia of Mathematics & Society: Engineering, Tech, Medicine
Encyclopedia of Mathematics & Society: Great Mathematicians
Encyclopedia of Mathematics & Society: Math & Social Sciences
Encyclopedia of Mathematics & Society: Math Development/Concepts
Encyclopedia of Mathematics & Society: Math in Culture & Society
Encyclopedia of Mathematics & Society: Space, Science, Environment
Encyclopedia of the Ancient World
Forensic Science
Geography Basics
Internet Innovators
Inventions and Inventors
Magill's Encyclopedia of Science: Animal Life
Magill's Encyclopedia of Science: Plant life
Notable Natural Disasters
Principles of Astronomy
Principles of Chemistry
Principles of Physics
Science and Scientists
Solar System
Solar System: Great Astronomers
Solar System: Study of the Universe
Solar System: The Inner Planets
Solar System: The Moon and Other Small Bodies
Solar System: The Outer Planets
Solar System: The Sun and Other Stars
World Geography

Literature

American Ethnic Writers
Classics of Science Fiction & Fantasy Literature
Critical Insights: Authors
Critical Insights: Film
Critical Insights: Literary Collection Bundles
Critical Insights: Themes
Critical Insights: Works
Critical Survey of Drama
Critical Survey of Graphic Novels: Heroes & Super Heroes
Critical Survey of Graphic Novels: History, Theme & Technique
Critical Survey of Graphic Novels: Independents/Underground Classics
Critical Survey of Graphic Novels: Manga
Critical Survey of Long Fiction
Critical Survey of Mystery & Detective Fiction
Critical Survey of Mythology and Folklore: Heroes and Heroines
Critical Survey of Mythology and Folklore: Love, Sexuality & Desire
Critical Survey of Mythology and Folklore: World Mythology
Critical Survey of Poetry
Critical Survey of Poetry: American Poets
Critical Survey of Poetry: British, Irish & Commonwealth Poets
Critical Survey of Poetry: Cumulative Index
Critical Survey of Poetry: European Poets
Critical Survey of Poetry: Topical Essays
Critical Survey of Poetry: World Poets
Critical Survey of Shakespeare's Plays
Critical Survey of Shakespeare's Sonnets
Critical Survey of Short Fiction
Critical Survey of Short Fiction: American Writers
Critical Survey of Short Fiction: British, Irish, Commonwealth Writers
Critical Survey of Short Fiction: Cumulative Index
Critical Survey of Short Fiction: European Writers
Critical Survey of Short Fiction: Topical Essays
Critical Survey of Short Fiction: World Writers
Critical Survey of Young Adult Literature
Cyclopedia of Literary Characters
Cyclopedia of Literary Places
Holocaust Literature
Introduction to Literary Context: American Poetry of the 20th Century
Introduction to Literary Context: American Post-Modernist Novels
Introduction to Literary Context: American Short Fiction
Introduction to Literary Context: English Literature
Introduction to Literary Context: Plays
Introduction to Literary Context: World Literature
Magill's Literary Annual 2015
Magill's Survey of American Literature
Magill's Survey of World Literature
Masterplots
Masterplots II: African American Literature
Masterplots II: American Fiction Series
Masterplots II: British & Commonwealth Fiction Series
Masterplots II: Christian Literature
Masterplots II: Drama Series
Masterplots II: Juvenile & Young Adult Literature, Supplement
Masterplots II: Nonfiction Series
Masterplots II: Poetry Series
Masterplots II: Short Story Series
Masterplots II: Women's Literature Series
Notable African American Writers
Notable American Novelists
Notable Playwrights
Notable Poets
Recommended Reading: 600 Classics Reviewed
Short Story Writers

2016 Title List

Visit www.SalemPress.com for Product Information, Table of Contents, and Sample Pages.

History and Social Science

The 2000s in America
50 States
African American History
Agriculture in History
American First Ladies
American Heroes
American Indian Culture
American Indian History
American Indian Tribes
American Presidents
American Villains
America's Historic Sites
Ancient Greece
The Bill of Rights
The Civil Rights Movement
The Cold War
Countries, Peoples & Cultures
Countries, Peoples & Cultures: Central & South America
Countries, Peoples & Cultures: Central, South & Southeast Asia
Countries, Peoples & Cultures: East & South Africa
Countries, Peoples & Cultures: East Asia & the Pacific
Countries, Peoples & Cultures: Eastern Europe
Countries, Peoples & Cultures: Middle East & North Africa
Countries, Peoples & Cultures: North America & the Caribbean
Countries, Peoples & Cultures: West & Central Africa
Countries, Peoples & Cultures: Western Europe
Defining Documents: American Revolution
Defining Documents: Civil Rights
Defining Documents: Civil War
Defining Documents: Emergence of Modern America
Defining Documents: Exploration & Colonial America
Defining Documents: Manifest Destiny
Defining Documents: Postwar 1940s
Defining Documents: Reconstruction
Defining Documents: 1920s
Defining Documents: 1930s
Defining Documents: 1950s
Defining Documents: 1960s
Defining Documents: 1970s
Defining Documents: American West
Defining Documents: Ancient World
Defining Documents: Middle Ages
Defining Documents: Vietnam War
Defining Documents: World War I
Defining Documents: World War II
The Eighties in America
Encyclopedia of American Immigration
Encyclopedia of Flight
Encyclopedia of the Ancient World
Fashion Innovators
The Fifties in America
The Forties in America
Great Athletes
Great Athletes: Baseball
Great Athletes: Basketball
Great Athletes: Boxing & Soccer
Great Athletes: Cumulative Index
Great Athletes: Football
Great Athletes: Golf & Tennis
Great Athletes: Olympics
Great Athletes: Racing & Individual Sports
Great Events from History: 17th Century
Great Events from History: 18th Century
Great Events from History: 19th Century
Great Events from History: 20th Century (1901-1940)
Great Events from History: 20th Century (1941-1970)
Great Events from History: 20th Century (1971-2000)
Great Events from History: Ancient World
Great Events from History: Cumulative Indexes
Great Events from History: Gay, Lesbian, Bisexual, Transgender Events

Great Events from History: Middle Ages
Great Events from History: Modern Scandals
Great Events from History: Renaissance & Early Modern Era
Great Lives from History: 17th Century
Great Lives from History: 18th Century
Great Lives from History: 19th Century
Great Lives from History: 20th Century
Great Lives from History: African Americans
Great Lives from History: American Women
Great Lives from History: Ancient World
Great Lives from History: Asian & Pacific Islander Americans
Great Lives from History: Cumulative Indexes
Great Lives from History: Incredibly Wealthy
Great Lives from History: Inventors & Inventions
Great Lives from History: Jewish Americans
Great Lives from History: Latinos
Great Lives from History: Middle Ages
Great Lives from History: Notorious Lives
Great Lives from History: Renaissance & Early Modern Era
Great Lives from History: Scientists & Science
Historical Encyclopedia of American Business
Issues in U.S. Immigration
Magill's Guide to Military History
Milestone Documents in African American History
Milestone Documents in American History
Milestone Documents in World History
Milestone Documents of American Leaders
Milestone Documents of World Religions
Music Innovators
Musicians & Composers 20th Century
The Nineties in America
The Seventies in America
The Sixties in America
Survey of American Industry and Careers
The Thirties in America
The Twenties in America
United States at War
U.S.A. in Space
U.S. Court Cases
U.S. Government Leaders
U.S. Laws, Acts, and Treaties
U.S. Legal System
U.S. Supreme Court
Weapons and Warfare
World Conflicts: Asia and the Middle East
World Political Yearbook

Health

Addictions & Substance Abuse
Adolescent Health & Wellness
Cancer
Complementary & Alternative Medicine
Genetics & Inherited Conditions
Health Issues
Infectious Diseases & Conditions
Magill's Medical Guide
Psychology & Behavioral Health
Psychology Basics

2016 Title List
Visit www.HWWilsonInPrint.com for Product Information, Table of Contents and Sample Pages

Current Biography
Current Biography Cumulative Index 1946-2013
Current Biography Monthly Magazine
Current Biography Yearbook: 2003
Current Biography Yearbook: 2004
Current Biography Yearbook: 2005
Current Biography Yearbook: 2006
Current Biography Yearbook: 2007
Current Biography Yearbook: 2008
Current Biography Yearbook: 2009
Current Biography Yearbook: 2010
Current Biography Yearbook: 2011
Current Biography Yearbook: 2012
Current Biography Yearbook: 2013
Current Biography Yearbook: 2014
Current Biography Yearbook: 2015

Core Collections
Children's Core Collection
Fiction Core Collection
Graphic Novels Core Collection
Middle & Junior High School Core
Public Library Core Collection: Nonfiction
Senior High Core Collection
Young Adult Fiction Core Collection

The Reference Shelf
Aging in America
American Military Presence Overseas
The Arab Spring
The Brain
The Business of Food
Campaign Trends & Election Law
Conspiracy Theories
The Digital Age
Dinosaurs
Embracing New Paradigms in Education
Faith & Science
Families: Traditional and New Structures
The Future of U.S. Economic Relations: Mexico, Cuba, and Venezuela
Global Climate Change
Graphic Novels and Comic Books
Immigration
Immigration in the U.S.
Internet Safety
Marijuana Reform
The News and its Future
The Paranormal
Politics of the Ocean
Racial Tension in a "Postracial" Age
Reality Television
Representative American Speeches: 2008-2009
Representative American Speeches: 2009-2010
Representative American Speeches: 2010-2011
Representative American Speeches: 2011-2012
Representative American Speeches: 2012-2013
Representative American Speeches: 2013-2014
Representative American Speeches: 2014-2015
Representative American Speeches: 2015-2016
Rethinking Work
Revisiting Gender
Robotics
Russia
Social Networking
Social Services for the Poor
Space Exploration & Development
Sports in America
The Supreme Court
The Transformation of American Cities

U.S. Infrastructure
U.S. National Debate Topic: Surveillance
U.S. National Debate Topic: The Ocean
U.S. National Debate Topic: Transportation Infrastructure
Whistleblowers

Readers' Guide
Abridged Readers' Guide to Periodical Literature
Readers' Guide to Periodical Literature

Indexes
Index to Legal Periodicals & Books
Short Story Index
Book Review Digest

Sears List
Sears List of Subject Headings
Sears: Lista de Encabezamientos de Materia

Facts About Series
Facts About American Immigration
Facts About China
Facts About the 20th Century
Facts About the Presidents
Facts About the World's Languages

Nobel Prize Winners
Nobel Prize Winners: 1901-1986
Nobel Prize Winners: 1987-1991
Nobel Prize Winners: 1992-1996
Nobel Prize Winners: 1997-2001

World Authors
World Authors: 1995-2000
World Authors: 2000-2005

Famous First Facts
Famous First Facts
Famous First Facts About American Politics
Famous First Facts About Sports
Famous First Facts About the Environment
Famous First Facts: International Edition

American Book of Days
The American Book of Days
The International Book of Days

Junior Authors & Illustrators
Eleventh Book of Junior Authors & Illustrations

Monographs
The Barnhart Dictionary of Etymology
Celebrate the World
Guide to the Ancient World
Indexing from A to Z
The Poetry Break
Radical Change: Books for Youth in a Digital Age

Wilson Chronology
Wilson Chronology of Asia and the Pacific
Wilson Chronology of Human Rights
Wilson Chronology of Ideas
Wilson Chronology of the Arts
Wilson Chronology of the World's Religions
Wilson Chronology of Women's Achievements

Grey House Publishing | Salem Press | H.W. Wilson | 4919 Route, 22 PO Box 56, Amenia NY 12501-0056